TRACEY LORD

with

LUCY ADAM

KATIE CLAMMER

LINDSAY OBERMEYER

PAULINE RICHARDS

DEBORAH SMETHURST

LINDEY TYDEMAN

A SQUARE A DAY

365 CROCHET SQUARES
one for each day of the year

Ivy Press

For Sheila, my mum, whose unfailing love
and faith in my abilities gave me wings.

First published in the UK in 2014 by

Ivy Press
210 High Street
Lewes
East Sussex BN7 2NS
United Kingdom
www.ivypress.co.uk

British Library Cataloguing-in-Publication Data
A catalogue record for this book is available from the
British Library

ISBN: 978-1-78240-141-4

This book was conceived, designed and produced by

Ivy Press
Creative Director Peter Bridgewater
Publisher Susan Kelly
Editorial Director Tom Kitch
Art Director James Lawrence
Commissioning Editor Sophie Collins
Editor Marie Clayton
Designer Ginny Zeal
Photographer Andrew Perris
Illustrators Peters & Zabransky

Printed in China

Colour origination by Ivy Press Reprographics

10 9 8 7 6 5 4 3 2 1

Distributed worldwide (except North America) by
Thames & Hudson Ltd, 181A High Holborn,
London WC1V 7QX, United Kingdom

contents

introduction

Crochet squares have a long and well-documented history within the field of hand-made textiles. All around the world different cultures have a tradition of working in motifs to create beautiful linens and exquisite shawls. Because of its versatility, crochet has enjoyed many revivals over the years, but in modern times it has seen an increase in popularity because it is so fast, economical and portable; what could be better than working on your gorgeous new blanket while travelling to work on the train? Or perhaps the prospect of relaxing after a long day by making a square each evening, and using up pieces of your yarn stash at the same time, is irresistible? Either way, this book contains a wealth of potential for the creation of future heirlooms, thoughtful gifts and stylish home furnishings.

This book is intended to be a comprehensive collection of crochet square designs that can be combined into a range of pieces, from throws and afghans to handbags and curtains. We have included squares to suit all levels of ability, from the novice to the more experienced crocheter. The squares are a mix of traditional in-the-round and linear grannies, and sometimes a combination of the two. Besides the classic designs there are lace, textural, three-dimensional and colourwork squares as well as flowers, composite blocks, cables and baubles. In short, something to tempt every crocheter's taste. The collection includes both classic and historical motif designs updated in modern colours, as well as a huge range of original blocks created specially for this book. Whether your taste is for floral or lacy, textural or modern, there is plenty to capture your imagination and get you hooked. We have arranged the designs in a delicious rainbow of colours that are bound to have you itching to get started. However, be warned that making motifs is an addictive pastime; even though this is an immense collection of designs, all the contributors and the author found they still had even more designs in their sketchbooks after this book was completed, and found it hard to stop creating.

Crochet is so much fun to play with, so do play. Crochet squares are the perfect medium for creating stunningly colourful pieces that you will treasure for ever. We hope this book will start you off on a lifelong love affair with granny squares.

Using the squares

The squares in this book are designed to work up to about the same size, allowing you to intermix them at will. You might choose to alternate different designs to create a pillow, or you could use several colour variations of a single square to make a blanket. Suggestions for use are given with many of the squares, but these are far from exhaustive. The beauty of working in motifs is that they lend themselves to such a wide range of possibilities, so you are positively encouraged to make your own choices and to devise your own colour combinations.

Each square has a symbol denoting the skill level required to complete it (see page 8). Basic stitch knowledge is all that is needed for the beginner squares, while the most complex-rated ones involve a series of different techniques and require the ability to follow a detailed pattern. Initially, choose designs that match your current level of skill and, when you are comfortable, challenge yourself with some blocks from the next level up.

There is a stitch reference section to guide you through creating less familiar stitches, and when a square uses an unusual technique or stitch this is explained at the start of the instructions. We have also included advice on how to choose colours, materials and equipment, as well as covering techniques for joining squares into a finished piece. What is not included are any prescriptive designs for completed pieces. We hope that you will use this book

as inspiration to create your own unique pieces that are entirely personal to you.

When choosing squares for your project bear in mind the end use of the piece: heavier, densely textured blocks will produce a warm fabric whereas lacy, open-textured ones will offer an airy lightness. Light or heavy blocks can be successfully mixed with medium-weight squares without greatly affecting the balance of the resulting piece, but you can also choose to blend light and heavy blocks deliberately to create a contrasting effect.

There are several ways you can approach creating your own design for a larger piece. If you are confident at drawing, simply drawing out your design idea is the most straightforward option. You could trace the design from the book to speed the process up, or use large-scale graph paper and make a design plan using coloured pencils or pens.

Another very simple method is to make up one square from each of the designs you've chosen and then make colour copies or scans of each one. Create a few more copies than you think you need of each particular square. Cut out the copied squares and arrange them until you are happy with the overall design, then secure it on a larger piece of paper as a guide while working. For a larger project you could work out part of the design in this way, then repeat it over again to your chosen size.

If you feel confident with technology, a digital program is particularly helpful when working out larger, more complex arrangements for bigger items such as blankets. Make a sample square of each type you plan to use, photograph it and save the photographs on to a computer – it's a good idea to reduce the size of each file at the same time to avoid an enormous, unworkable document. Open a new document in a word-processing or image-manipulation program and paste the photographs beside each other in repeat, moving them about until you are happy with the arrangement. This method also allows you to change colours, which is useful if you have a complicated design. Save the file when you are happy with the finished result.

choosing a hook

Crochet hooks come in many sizes and types, and it can be a little confusing to choose the right one. Check the ball band of the yarn you have chosen for the suggested hook or knitting needle size.

It is recommended that you use the suggested size, but first make up a test square and check whether the finished fabric feels acceptable to you: if it is too tight, then use a larger hook size; if it feels too loose or open, then go down a hook size. It's a good idea to start building a collection of hooks in various sizes in any case, and it is likely that you'll find that you use them all. Store them in a hook roll so that you can easily select the size you need.

Hooks are made from metal, plastic, wood or bamboo, and some have a rubber or plastic grip handle. Some hooks have a more sharply angled hook head than others. Every crocheter has their own preference – I have a beloved basic metal 4 mm (US size F/5) hook that I have been using for years – but try a few types to work out what is most comfortable for you. However, if you have any form of muscular or arthritic difficulty, it is strongly recommended that you use a hook with a comfort handle as these are designed to reduce the strain on wrists and hands.

Hook size UK	Hook size US	Suitable yarn gauge
2.0 mm	B/1	2-ply (laceweight) yarns
2.5 mm	C/2	3-ply (baby) yarns
3.0 mm	D/3	3–4-ply (fingering) yarns
3.5 mm	E/4	4-ply (sport) yarns
4.0 mm	F/5	Double knitting/DK (light worsted) yarns
4.5 mm	G/6	Double knitting/DK (thicker worsted) yarns
5.0 mm	H/8	Aran (worsted) weight yarns
5.5 mm	I/9	Aran (thicker worsted) weight yarns
6.0 mm	J/10	Chunky yarns
7.0 mm	K/10½	Super chunky yarns

The finest crochet hooks (thread hooks) are made in steel, and are used for intricate work. Larger hooks come in bamboo, plastic or aluminium, and are available in a wide range of sizes.

choosing & buying yarns

The type of yarn you choose will depend on the end use of your piece. In general, you should always use the correct hook size for the thickness of your yarn – you might occasionally be directed otherwise, but this is unusual. See page 5 for a hook size guide. Whatever the fibre type, yarn that is relatively tightly spun, with a smooth finish, is best for crochet work – particularly for the less experienced. More loosely spun yarns will easily split when being worked, and yarns with a hairy or frilly surface texture will be harder to work with. Stitch definition is also lost when yarns are less smooth.

115 mm/4.5 inches

150 mm/6 inches

The size of your square varies depending on the hook and yarn you use. These squares were made using a 3 mm (D/3) hook and 4-ply (sport) yarn, a 4 mm (F/5) hook and DK (light-worsted) yarn, and a 5 mm (F/5) hook and Aran (worsted) yarn.

Choosing yarn

There are many types of yarn fibre available and as technology develops our choice is widening. You could select fibres for their properties because of allergies, or because of ethics, or perhaps a combination of factors. In this book we have used pure wool or pure cotton for most of the squares; a few are made with acrylic, and some with bamboo. Below is an introduction to some of the more common yarn fibres you might encounter.

Wool is the most common type of knitting and crochet fibre; it is often blended with synthetic or other fibres to create an easy-care yarn. There are many breeds of sheep, each with its own characteristics, dependent on the type of terrain it inhabits. Common types of wool used in crochet and knitting include the coarse but strong Shetland and the soft, popular Merino. The latter is a good choice for most projects because it is a versatile yarn with a nice drape. Some wool can be prone to pilling and may felt or 'full' (mat together and shrink) when washed incorrectly, so check the ball label and never wash in more than lukewarm water unless you intend to felt your work. Using wool that is labelled 'superwash' eliminates the need for this precaution, because it is treated to avoid felting. Other animal-based fibres include alpaca, llama, angora, cashmere and mohair. For the motifs in this book, fibres with a less hairy texture work best; treat them with the same care as pure wool.

165 mm/6.5 inches

Cotton is a common choice for crochet work. The fibre comes from the seed pod – the 'boll' – when it bursts open. Cotton with long fibres is prized as the best quality because it produces a smooth, strong yarn when spun. Cotton washes well but may stretch if hung out when wet, so beware of hanging a heavy piece vertically; dry it flat. Cotton is a good choice for baby or children's pieces because it is not itchy and remains soft.

Acrylic is the best known of the synthetic fibres. It takes dye very well, so it is available in a wide range of bright colours. Acrylic is also economical and easy to care for, so it is a popular choice for children's wear. Other popular synthetic fibres you might see include microfibre and rayon.

Bamboo is a newer fibre to the market, with the softness of cotton but a greater drape. It also sometimes has a slight sheen to it and is a good choice for babies and children. Milk protein fibre and corn fibre are two other fairly new fibres that are soft and sustainable choices.

Silk has an incredibly long history as a textile fibre, but its slippery handle makes it unsuitable except for the more experienced. Peace silk, or tussah silk, is produced without causing any harm to the silk moths.

Blends are often a good choice as they combine the best of several fibres, often creating a more durable, easier-care yarn.

Within this book we have used yarn that is classified as 'double knit' (DK), worked on a 4 mm (US size F/5) hook. This is a medium-tension, commonly available type of yarn and is a good thickness to use if you are new to crochet because it is quite easy to see your stitches as you work them. The completed squares in this book all worked up to a size of about 15 cm (6 inches) square. However, as long as you choose the correct hook size for the yarn you are using, the squares in this book can be made in any yarn – although the completed square will vary in size; finer yarn will produce a smaller square, and thicker yarn a larger one.

You might use finer yarns to create a delicate lace throw, a curtain panel or some special table linens. Conversely, using thicker yarns would produce cosy afghans, warm pillows or even floor rugs.

Buying yarn

If you are making a large project such as a bedspread, make sure you buy plenty of yarn before you begin. It is better to have too much than to need an extra ball months later and find an obviously different dye batch, or worse still, that the colour has been discontinued. However, many of the squares in this book are perfect for using up odds and ends within your stash.

To calculate how much yarn you will need for a larger project, work up one test square in the yarn(s) you intend to use, then unravel it by pulling out the stitches and measure how much yarn was used for each colour within the square, plus extra for yarn tails at each end. This is how many metres you will need per square, per colour. Now multiply the metres for each colour by the number of squares you need to make. This gives you a total of metres for each colour. Check the ball label for the metres on each ball, and then divide the total metres for each colour by this figure. Round up to the nearest whole number: this is the number of balls of each colour you need to buy.

Example

You use 60 metres of blue and 120 metres of cream in a square.

You need to make 20 squares altogether for a lap blanket.

Multiplying 60 x 20 gives 1,200 metres, and 120 x 20 gives 2,400 metres.

The ball label says there are 240 metres to the ball so you will need 1,200 ÷ 240 = 5 balls of blue, and 2,400 ÷ 240 = 10 balls of cream for your project.

Local yarn shops are a fantastic source of advice and support, and the staff working there are likely to be as enthusiastic as you are about crochet. There are also some excellent online yarn suppliers, who often offer large discounts. The online knit and crochet communities, such as UK Hand Knitting Association, are wonderful places to seek inspiration, yarn advice and meet other like-minded crocheters; you can even start your own group.

Blended yarns are easy to work with and more durable than single-fibre yarns. They take dyes well, so a good colour range is available.

getting started

Part of the charm of crochet is that all you really need to get started is yarn and a hook of the appropriate size, but you might find it helpful to have some other small items to hand. Here are some of the accessories that you may find particularly useful.

For stitching in yarn tails a blunt darning needle is a must because it will not split the fibres when you sew. A tape measure is always useful, and a measuring gauge or rigid straight ruler will help you check your tension and the size of completed squares. Good sharp scissors are essential – never cut paper with them or they will quickly become blunt. If you intend to make any squares in the book with a spiral construction, then stitch markers are a great help. Finally, some good rust-proof pins are a vital resource for blocking your completed squares. T-head pins, which are perfect for blocking, are recommended but you can also use glass-head dress maker's pins.

Stitch markers (right) help you to identify key points in a complex pattern. A tape measure, measuring gauge, T-head or glass-head pins, and sharp scissors are other tools you are likely to find useful for crochet.

Difficulty rating

★   ★★   ★★★   ★★★★

All the patterns in this book have been given a difficulty rating that ranges from one to four stars. Patterns with one star are the simplest while those with four stars are the most challenging.

choosing colours

For some people choosing colours is almost instinctive; for others it can be challenging and confusing. The secret is that it's entirely personal: we all react to colours emotionally and for different reasons and associations. So if you have a strong feeling about using a particular set of colours, go right ahead. If you are less sure, here is some advice on how to choose great colour combinations to show off your stitching skills.

First think about the setting you have in mind for the item you are making: for instance, a throw for a conservatory or a dining room. Try and match the colours for your throw to the environment it will be used in — even if you want a statement piece you should still keep in mind the background room colours. A small supply of paint cards from your local home-improvement store can be invaluable in matching up colours and playing around with combinations and proportion before you start. Cut them up and arrange them in stripes of varying sizes until you like the effect of the proportions, then match them to the yarn colours.

The colour wheel is a great aid when selecting your colour combinations. Using hues that are next to each other gives a subtle effect, while choosing near-opposites brings strong contrasts to your work.

Within this book we have already grouped the squares into colour groups, so you can simply decide to make all your squares from one group because you know they will work well together. Or alternate squares from two completely different groups, such as red/orange mixed with blue/green.

Another easy way you can learn to combine colours effectively is by getting to know the colour wheel, which will help you put together colours. Red, yellow and blue are known as the primary colours. Orange, green and purple are the secondary colours because each is made of two primary colours mixed together. The remaining colours are termed tertiary colours.

Looking at the colour wheel, colours that sit directly opposite each other such as red and green do not seem to go together. However, the two colours that sit immediately adjacent to green (yellow-green and green-blue) work well with bright red as a three-colour combination. Equally, the pure green placed with red-orange and purple-red works just as effectively.

Another tried-and-tested formula is to use three or four colours that sit equidistant from each other on the colour wheel — for example, bright red, orange-yellow, bright green and blue-violet; or red-orange, yellow-green and purple. Such groups are known as 'triads' or 'tetrads'. You can also mix any two colours that appear to clash — such as bright blue and bright yellow — then add a neutral such as grey, cream, black or white: this will harmonise the combination and tone down the two other colours.

Another option is to use all 'warm' colours — those that run from yellow-orange right through to reddish-purple — or all 'cold' colours — those running from yellow-green to blue-violet — which will both work well. And if you add a tiny highlight of one warm colour to an all-cold colour combination (or vice versa) it will pop out and pep up the combination. For example, blue/green, turquoise and royal blue enhanced with a tiny amount of bright red is a beautiful combination that works every time.

Remember that you can find inspiration for colour choices absolutely anywhere so keep your eyes open and your camera or sketchbook to hand. Sometimes humble things can suggest lovely colours — see how a holiday became one of my most frequently used colour combinations.

This pleasing snapshot from a holiday provided the inspiration for a striking and effective colour combination.

crochet basics

Getting used to the feel of the hook and tension of the yarn through your fingers are the first skills to master. Take as long as you need for this, as tension, or gauge, is important for an even fabric.

Holding the hook

There are two most common ways to hold your hook, and most people find they are easily able to use one of them. Both work equally well, so practise moving the hook about in each of these positions and choose whichever feels the most comfortable.

1 Hold the hook as if you were holding a pencil, with the tips of your thumb and your forefinger positioned over the flat part of the hook, which helps you to turn and manoeuvre it.

2 Alternatively, hold the hook as if you were holding a knife, with the flat part of the hook again positioned between the thumb and forefinger as you grip it.

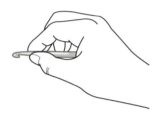

Holding the yarn

There are a few variations on the most efficient way to hold your yarn; practise a few of them until you find the one that feels most natural for you. The yarn is wrapped around your non-dominant hand to add tension, while your dominant hand holds the hook.

1 Start by wrapping the yarn once around your little finger, then carry it under your ring finger and over your middle finger and forefinger.

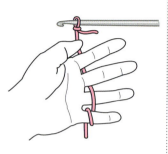

2 An alternative way to hold the yarn is to carry it over the entire back of your hand after wrapping it around your little finger – but make sure that you are able to create enough tension.

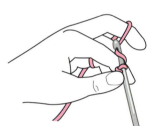

Tension

As in knitting, the tension, or gauge, of your work is especially important to obtain work of the same size and proportion to that intended by the pattern. Tension is controlled by several factors: the thickness of the yarn you use, the size of the hook, the ratio of the former to the latter and also how tightly you hold the yarn while you are working and how it flows through your fingers. Too tight work can be crisp and without any drape; too loose work can be unstable and distort the structures of the pattern. Every individual's tension is slightly different.

The squares in this book are designed to work up to 15-cm (6-inch) square after blocking, using a 4 mm (US size F/5) hook and standard double knit, or DK (light worsted), yarn. Work a test square using these materials to see if your tension matches this, and make adjustments as suggested below if it does not.

If your test square is too small, change your hook to a larger size. If your test square is too large, change your hook to a smaller size.

As you become more experienced, you will also be able to slightly adjust the tension of your yarn as you work, which will give you more control over the overall tension. It is normal for beginners to work either too tightly or too loosely, so practise will help you to arrive at a more natural tension.

starting out

Once you feel comfortable holding your hook and yarn, it is time to learn some basic moves. The section below shows how to make the starting row or round suitable for use in any crochet pattern, and for any square in this book.

Making a slip knot

To start off your crochet, you will need to make a slip knot; from this one base stitch you will be able to make further stitches.

1 Make a loop with the yarn as shown. Insert the hook into the loop, hook the yarn and pull it through.

2 This makes a loop that is now sitting on the hook itself. Pull the yarn to tighten the loop up on the hook. One slip knot made.

Yarn over hook (yoh)

This is also known as 'yarn round hook' (yrh) and many stitches call for it as part of their construction. Wrapping the yarn over the hook allows for the subsequent creation of more loops (so the stitch is taller or fuller). It is a fundamental move of crochet construction and may be repeated several times before a stitch begins to be created (as in bullion stitch, see page 20) or repeated within the steps of a stitch (as in a double treble, see page 14).

Move the hook under the tensioned yarn, then turn the hook slightly to catch the yarn so that it wraps over the hook. One yarn over hook created.

Foundation chain (ch)

The foundation chain is the starting 'row' or 'round' in crochet. Each V-shaped chain loop made is one stitch; your pattern will tell you how many chains to make. For a foundation chain row, make the number of chains specified in your pattern; for a round, join the chain into a chain ring as described right.

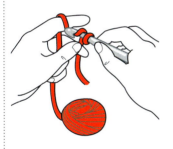 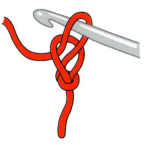

1 Hold the hook containing the slip knot in your dominant hand, and tension your yarn around your non-dominant hand. Insert the hook under the yarn and turn the hook slightly to catch the yarn.

2 Pull the hook (with the yarn) through the slip knot on your hook to make a new loop. One chain made.

3 Continue in this way, adjusting your non-dominant hand as you make more chains so you always hold the work close to the last stitch made to maintain tension. Create the number of chains specified by your pattern. To count them, you should count every V-shaped chain apart from the one that is currently on your hook.

Foundation chain ring

Squares that are worked 'in-the-round' may call for a foundation ring, or a chain ring. This is a group of chain stitches that are joined together with a slip stitch to form a ring. Before you work the chain ring you will need to work the specified number of chain stitches as directed in the pattern.

1 Insert the hook into the first chain stitch made (not the slip knot), so there are two loops on the hook, one at the top and one at the bottom. Catch the tensioned yarn with the hook.

2 Pull the yarn through both loops that are on the hook, leaving one loop on the hook and thereby joining the chains into a ring. Chain ring created.

Magic ring

A magic ring or loop, also known as a sliding loop or ring, is used when you are making a block in the round and do not want a hole in the centre, or if you want the size of the centre hole to be adjustable.

1 Make a small loop of yarn around your finger, leaving a long tail of yarn on the left; insert the hook into the centre of the loop and draw the working yarn through the loop and the tail strand.

2 Chain one stitch to secure the magic ring. Now begin to work the number of chains specified to begin your pattern (minus the one you just made).

3 Work your stitches into the ring as directed. When you have completed the round, pull the trailing tail of yarn that you left at the start to close the ring and tighten the work. Magic ring created.

basic stitches

In this section you can learn how to work the most common crochet stitches, which build on the basic moves above to form stitches and fabric.

Slip stitch (sl st)

Slip stitch is a very simple stitch, most commonly used to join pieces of crochet together, to join a new colour or to move the hook and yarn from one place to another within a piece without growing the fabric. Slip stitch is the shortest crochet stitch of all.

1 Insert the hook into the stitch to be worked, from front to back.

2 Wrap the yarn over the hook and draw through the stitch and the loop already on the hook. One loop left on the hook, one slip stitch created.

Double crochet (dc)

Double crochet is the shortest of the common crochet stitches. It makes a dense and neat fabric and grows relatively slowly as it is worked.

When starting a new fabric with dc, after working the initial foundation chain you usually miss the first stitch and start to work your first dc stitch into the second chain from the hook.

When working a new row of dc into an established piece, you will start the row with one chain (ch 1), which – unlike on other basic stitches – does not count as a stitch; it is simply there to bring the work up to the correct height to continue a new row (see Working in rows, page 16). You will usually work the first dc stitch of the row into the same space as the chain stitch; similarly, do not work a dc into the turning chain at the end of the row.

1 Insert the hook into the second chain from the hook (or the next stitch to be worked), from front to back, yarn over hook, then draw the yarn back through the stitch (2 loops on hook).

2 Wrap the yarn over the hook again and draw through two loops, leaving one loop on the hook. One double crochet made.

Half-treble crochet (htr)

Half-treble crochet is a common stitch that sits between double and treble crochet in terms of the height of the stitch it creates. It results in a fairly firm fabric.

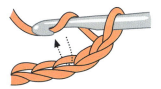

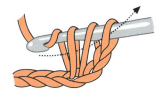

1 Wrap the yarn over the hook, then insert the hook into the third chain from the hook (or the next stitch to be worked), from front to back.

2 Yarn over hook one more time, draw the yarn back through the stitch (3 loops on hook), yarn over hook and draw through all three loops.

3 This leaves one loop on the hook. One half-treble crochet made.

tip When starting a new fabric with htr, after working the initial foundation chain you usually miss the first two stitches (which are equivalent to the height of 1 htr) and start to work your first htr stitch into the third chain from the hook.

When working a new row of htc into an established piece, you will start the row with two chain stitches (ch 2), which count as 1 htr – you will usually see this in instructions in ( ) brackets or mentioned as a turning chain (tch). This chain is to bring the work up to the correct height to continue a new row (see page 18). You work the first htr of the row into the next stitch and the last htr of the row into the top of the turning chain at the end of the row.

Treble crochet (tr)

Treble crochet is higher than half-treble crochet and is probably the most common crochet stitch. It is quite fast to work and produces a softer fabric than double crochet.

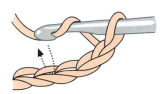

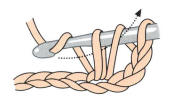

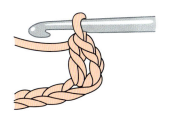

1 Wrap the yarn over the hook, then insert the hook into the fourth chain from the hook (or the next stitch to be worked), from front to back.

2 Yarn over hook one more time, then draw the yarn back through the stitch (3 loops on hook). Yarn over hook and draw through two loops (2 loops on hook).

3 Yarn over hook one more time and draw through two loops, leaving one loop on the hook. One treble crochet made.

tip When starting a new fabric with tc, after working the initial foundation chain you will usually miss the first three stitches (which are equivalent to the height of 1 tr) and start to work your first tr stitch into the fourth chain from the hook.

When working a new row of tr into an established piece, you will start the row with three chain stitches (ch 3), which count as 1 tr – you will usually see this in instructions in ( ) brackets or mentioned as a turning chain (tch). This chain is to bring the work up to the correct height to continue a new row. You then miss the first three chains and work the first treble crochet of the row into the fourth chain from the hook; work the last tr of the row into the top of the turning chain st at the end of the row.

Half-double treble crochet (hdtr)

Half-double treble crochet is a relatively uncommon stitch that sits between treble and double treble crochet in terms of the height of the stitch. The fabric it creates is a little looser and thicker than a treble-crochet fabric, but more stable than an all-double treble crochet fabric, so it can be useful in the crocheter's stitch library.

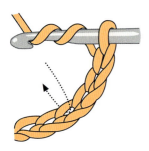 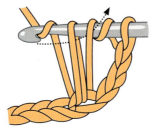 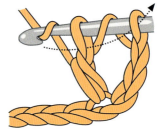

1 Wrap the yarn twice over the hook, then insert the hook into the fourth chain from the hook (or the next stitch to be worked), from front to back.

2 Yarn over hook one more time, then draw the yarn back through the stitch (4 loops on hook). Yarn over again and draw through two loops (3 loops on hook).

3 Yarn over the hook one more time and draw through all three loops, leaving one loop on the hook. One half-double treble made.

tip When starting a new fabric with hdtr, after working the initial foundation chain you will usually miss the first three stitches (equivalent to the height of 1 hdtr) and work your first hdtr stitch into the fourth chain from the hook.

When working a new row of hdtr into an established piece, you will start the row with three chain stitches (ch 3), which count as 1 hdtr. Work the first hdtr of the row into the next stitch and the last hdtr of the row into the top of the turning chain at the end of the row.

Double treble crochet (dtr)

Double treble crochet is taller than treble crochet, having an extra yarn over and draw through of the yarn. It creates an open fabric.

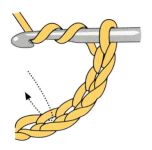  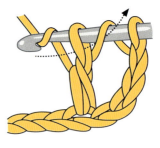 

1 Wrap the yarn twice over the hook, then insert the hook into the fifth chain from the hook (or the next stitch to be worked), from front to back.

2 Yarn over hook one more time, then draw the yarn back through the stitch (4 loops on hook). Yarn over again and draw through two loops (3 loops on hook).

3 Yarn over hook again and draw through two loops (2 loops on hook).

4 Wrap the yarn over the hook one more time and draw through two loops, leaving one loop on the hook. One double treble crochet made.

tip When starting a new fabric with dtr, after working the initial foundation chain you will usually miss the first four stitches (equivalent to the height of 1 tr) and work your first dtr stitch into the fifth chain from the hook.

When working a new row of dtr into an established piece, you will start the row with four chain stitches (ch 4), which count as 1 dtr. You work the first dtr of the row into the next stitch and the last dtr of the row into the top of the turning chain at the end of the row.

Triple treble crochet (ttr)

Triple treble crochet is a tall crochet stitch that may be used to add extra height at corners, or within front- or back-post stitch patterns (see page 21).

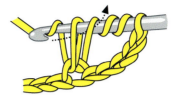

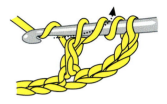

1 Wrap the yarn over the hook three times, then insert the hook into the sixth chain from the hook (or the next stitch to be worked), from front to back.

2 Yarn over hook one more time, draw the yarn back through the stitch (5 loops on hook). Yarn over hook again and then draw through two loops (4 loops on hook).

3 Yarn over hook one more time and draw through two loops (3 loops on hook).

4 Yarn over hook one more time and draw through two loops (2 loops on hook).

5 Wrap the yarn over one last time and draw through, leaving one loop on the hook. One triple treble made.

Quadruple treble crochet (quad tr)

Quadriple treble crochet is the next tallest stitch after triple treble. It is worked as triple treble, but involves wrapping the yarn over one more time at the beginning, and making one more 'yarn over, draw through 2 loops' manoeuvre at step 2. The equivalent turning chain for quadruple treble is ch 6.

Quintruple treble (quin tr)

This stitch and so on involve yet another yarn over at the beginning of the stitch, and another 'yarn over, draw through 2 loops' at step 2. As the stitches become taller, they are less stable and more open, so are more rarely used. The equivalent turning chain for quintruple treble is ch 7; add one more chain stitch each time for taller stitches.

tip When starting a new fabric with ttr, after working the initial foundation chain you will usually miss the first five stitches (equivalent to the height of 1 ttr) and work your first ttr stitch into the sixth chain from the hook.

When working a new row of ttr into an established piece, start the row with five chain stitches (ch 5), which count as 1 ttr. Work the first ttr of the row into the next stitch and the last ttr of the row into the top of the turning chain at the end of the row.

making a square

The squares in this book are made by working in rounds or rows, or sometimes a combination of the two. This section tells you how to work each method.

Beginning/turning chains

When working in rounds or rows, you will need to work a number of chain stitches at the start of each row to bring the work up the same height as the stitches to be worked in the row. These are known as 'beginning chains' when working in the round and 'turning chains' when working in rows. The table on the right shows how many chain stitches to work to bring your yarn up to the same height as the most common stitches.

When you are reading a pattern, you might see an instruction such as 'ch 3 (counts as 1 tr)', which means that the 3 chains are the equivalent height of 1 tr, and that together they are going to count as the first stitch. Sometimes, you may see 'ch 5 (counts as 1 tr, ch 2)', which means that the 5 chains are the equivalent of 1 tr plus 2 ch – the final 2 chains are usually a spacing device within the pattern, which is particularly common in filet crochet designs.

Equivalent number of chains for each stitch:

Double crochet (dc):	ch 1
Half-triple crochet (htr):	ch 2
Treble crochet (tr):	ch 3
Half-double treble crochet (hdtr):	ch 3
Double treble crochet (dtr):	ch 4
Triple treble crochet (ttr):	ch 5
Quadruple treble crochet (quad tr):	ch 6

Working in rows

Blocks worked in rows are known as 'linear' crochet and are worked by going backwards and forwards turning the work at the end of each row unless you are directed otherwise.

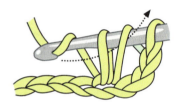

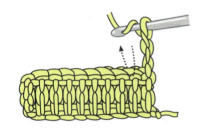

Working the first row

Begin by making a foundation chain, as directed on page 11, with the number of chains specified in your pattern. Often the pattern will state '(equals X sts plus Y ch)', which means that the extra chain stitches required for you to bring your yarn up to the right height to work the row have been included in the number given for the foundation chain. These extra chain stitches are usually counted together as the first stitch of the row. The exception to this is when working double crochet, where the ch 1 that is needed to turn the row is ignored.

To start the first row, insert your hook into the specified chain stitch (the example is shown using treble crochet, so you are working into the fourth chain from hook). This means you must count down the number of stitches from the hook – not including the one on the hook itself – to locate the correct chain stitch. You should find that the missed chains then stand up beside the subsequent stitches at the same height and resemble the first stitch. Work every subsequent stitch in the row into the next chain stitch along.

Working the next row

When you have reached the end of the foundation chain row and have worked a stitch into the last chain, you must turn the work round so that the new row can be worked across the top of the last one. Then work a turning chain of the required number of chains for the stitch you are using (see table).

Starting with the next stitch along, work each following stitch into the top of the stitch directly below. Always insert the hook into the two top loops of each stitch instead of just one, unless directed otherwise. Occasionally you may be asked to work the first stitch into the same space as the turning chain.

At the end of the row, unless directed otherwise, work the last stitch into the top chain stitch of the turning chain at the end of the last row. This is often referred to as the 'top of beg ch' in the patterns in this book. You may occasionally be directed not to work a stitch into the turning chain, or you may be directed to work into a different chain within the turning chain instead of the top one (for example 'in 3rd ch of the beg ch-5') – this is to maintain the spacing of the pattern.

Working in rounds

Blocks that are worked 'in-the-round' are worked in rounds instead of rows. This means that you work around and around the centre, and do not turn the work over unless you are directed to. When working in rounds, you will usually need to work some chain stitches at the start of each round as a beginning chain, see page 11. Before working a round you will need to make a foundation chain ring (see page 11) with the number of chains specified in your pattern. If you are just practising, try making a ring with six chains.

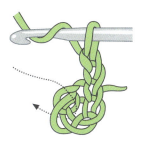 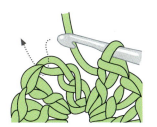

1 To start working the first round, work the beginning chain, then insert your hook into the centre of the chain ring rather than into a particular stitch to work each stitch for the first round – the example is shown in tr. Yarn over, insert the hook into the centre of the ring, yarn over and complete the tr stitch as normal. Repeat for the remaining tr.

2 When you have made the required number of stitches for your first round, join the first and last stitches together to seal the round by working a slip stitch into the top chain stitch of the beginning chain. You are now ready to start the next round.

Joining yarn

Most of the motifs in this book will require you to change yarn at some point. Often there will be a specific instruction for where to join the new yarn – which will not always be at the same point you fastened off the last yarn used. If you are not given a specific place to join in the new yarn, join where the last yarn finished. The intarsia method is shown here in step 2.

1 To join into a specific stitch or chain space, insert the hook into the specified stitch or space, catch the new yarn, leaving a tail at least 10 cm (4 inches) long, and work one chain stitch to secure. You can now continue with the new yarn.

2 There are various ways to join a new yarn where the last yarn ended, or to change colour. When working the last stitch in the old yarn, do not work the last step of the stitch and leave the last two loops on the hook. Drop the old yarn and pick up the new yarn, then work the last step of the stitch in the new yarn, drawing it through both loops. It will form the top of the stitch and you can now continue with the new yarn.

> **tip** When working multicoloured patterns from a chart, generally it is a good idea to pre-wind some small balls of each colour to be used before you begin. You can then use the method above to change colour and join in a new small ball for each area of colour. See page 18 for more guidance on how to work from charts.

Fastening off

When you have finished using a particular yarn – and do not need to change to a new yarn into the same space – or when you have finished a piece of work completely, you will need to fasten off your yarn securely so the work does not unravel.

Cut the working yarn, leaving a tail of at least 10 cm (4 inches) or longer if you need to sew the work to another piece. Wrap it over your hook and pull it right through the last stitch on the hook.

Working into front or back loops

Usually crochet stitches are worked into the two top loops of a stitch in the previous row, but sometimes instructions will call for working into only the front or back loops of a stitch. All this means is that you should insert your hook into either the loop that is closest to you at the front, or the one at the back furthest away, not into both of them at the same time. The effect created is to push the work slightly forwards or towards the back. It is also often employed to allow you to work two rounds or rows into the same stitch – one row worked into the front loops, then another into the back loops – which is useful for creating flower motifs.

Working colour patterns from a chart

Some of the blocks in this book have a chart for you to follow to achieve the design instead of written instructions for every colour change. It is often easier to track detailed colourful patterns this way. When using a chart, it is a good idea to photocopy the page and cross off each row as you work it.

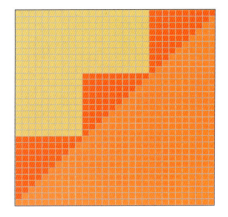

Start reading the chart at the bottom right-hand corner. Each square represents one stitch. Read the odd-numbered (right side) rows from right to left, and even-numbered (wrong side) rows from left to right. The chart does not include the turning ch-1 stitch for each row.

When changing colours, use the method described on page 17 and wind separate balls or lengths of yarn for each colour area before you begin. In the chart above, there would be a maximum of three colours employed in any one row; other designs may have many more. If you only have to work one or two stitches in a contrast colour, you can carry the main yarn across the back of the work loosely – this is called stranding but is not suitable for larger areas of colour.

tip When you work with multiple colours, ensure you keep all the yarn ends at the wrong side of the work, otherwise you may find the yarn is inaccessible when you need to change colour and you would have to unravel the work.

decorative stitches

These stitches use variations on the basic moves to create texture, shapes or surface pattern. Some are made by creating a series of incomplete stitches, then joining them all in one final move; others require you to insert the hook in a different position than usual. This is where the fun begins!

Clusters (cl)

A cluster is the term used for a group of stitches that are joined together at the top. They may be of any stitch size, or of varying stitch sizes (for example '1 tr, 1 dtr, 1 tr'). The term cluster is also sometimes loosely used to refer to a group of stitches that occur in the same space but are not necessarily joined at the top.

When a 'beginning cluster' is specified, the turning chain is counted as the first stitch, then the cluster is completed as described right, missing the first stitch. A cluster is worked by leaving the last loop of each stitch on the hook, then joining all the stitches together with one last yarn over – the example shows a cluster made with three treble crochet stitches.

1 Wrap the yarn over the hook, then insert into the stitch or space to be worked; yarn over hook again, draw through work; yarn over and draw through two loops (2 loops on hook). Repeat this step for the other two treble crochet stitches, always leaving the last loop on the hook (4 loops on hook). Wrap the yarn again and draw it through all four loops.

2 This leaves one loop on hook. One cluster made.

Note: Sometimes, particularly in the early rounds of some squares, groups of two or three stitches are worked into one space (or the foundation ring) then joined at the top. These may be referred to as clusters.

Make bobble (MB)

A bobble stitch is created from a cluster of stitches worked into the same place and joined together tightly at the top. Bobbles are most commonly made from between three and five stitches, often using treble crochet. They are a highly textured stitch and work best when worked with the wrong side of the fabric facing you, and when placed next to shorter stitches to emphasise their texture. However, bobbles also occur in other background fabrics and can be made from other stitches such as double treble.

Bobbles made from four or more stitches benefit from working a chain stitch to secure them after completion; this also aligns the bobble better within the fabric. However, take care not to count this extra chain as a stitch when you are working the next round or row. The example shows a bobble made with three treble crochet stitches.

Work three treble crochet stitches into the same space or stitch, leaving the last loop of each stitch still on the hook (4 loops on the hook). Wrap the yarn over the hook one more time and then draw through all four loops, leaving one loop on the hook. One bobble made.

Popcorn (pc)

A popcorn is a group of (usually) treble crochet stitches that are worked into the same stitch at their base, then joined at the top as described right, to create a pleasing raised texture. Popcorns commonly consist of between three and five stitches – the instructions will specify how many stitches to make.

When a 'beginning popcorn' stitch is specified, the turning chain is counted as the first stitch, then the popcorn is completed as described right, missing the first stitch. The example shows a popcorn made with four treble crochet stitches.

1 Work the required number of treble crochet stitches into the specified space or stitch. At the end of the last treble crochet stitch, remove the hook from the working loop and insert it into the top (both loops) of the first treble crochet of the group. Pick up the dropped loop again.

2 Now draw the dropped loop through the first treble crochet loop to close the popcorn. You may find it helpful to work a chain stitch to secure the popcorn.

Puff stitch

A puff stitch is a group of half-treble crochet stitches, commonly between three and five, worked into the same space or stitch and joined at the top. Puff stitch creates a soft and squidgy fabric that feels wonderful. It can be tricky to master because the half-treble crochet should be worked relatively loosely – you may find it helpful to pull down on the fabric below the stitch with your left hand as you complete step 2, to help the hook pass through all the loops.

When a 'beginning puff stitch' is specified, the turning chain counts as the first half-treble crochet, then the stitch is created as detailed below. The example shows a puff stitch made with three half-treble crochets.

1 Wrap the yarn over the hook, then insert the hook into the next stitch to be worked, from front to back. Yarn over hook again and draw through to the front, but not through the wrapped loops (3 loops on hook).

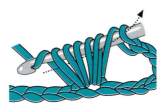

2 Repeat step 1 two more times, inserting the hook into the same stitch and leaving the loops on the hook as you go (7 loops on hook). Yarn over hook and draw through all the loops, leaving one loop on the hook.

3 Work a chain stitch to secure. One puff stitch created. Puff stitches created with more than three half-treble crochets have step 1 repeated one more time for each stitch; they also feel more 'padded'.

Bullion stitch

Bullion stitch, also known as roll stitch, is relatively unusual – it is a little like working a French knot embroidery stitch and creates a rounded, textured oval. It is used for decorative purposes to add texture and is commonly created by wrapping the yarn between seven and ten times over the hook.

Wrap the yarn over the hook as many times as specified in the pattern, then insert the hook into the stitch or space to be worked. Yarn over hook again and draw a loop through to the front. Yarn over hook one more time and pull through all the loops on the hook. You might find you have to pick the loops off the hook one by one, by hand, depending on the type of yarn you are using. Work a chain stitch to secure and bring the working yarn back up to the height of the row. One bullion stitch created.

Crocodile stitch

Crocodile stitch is a relatively new stitch; it is named for its resemblance to crocodile scales, because it forms layers of petal or scale shapes as it is worked. It is a complex stitch but one that is methodical in construction, so it is easy to work once it is mastered. The resulting fabric is stunning and idiosyncratic.

Crocodile stitch is constructed by creating a framework of pairs of stitches with chains between, so each pair forms the rung of a 'ladder', then working each scale around a rung. The technique of working into the side, or around the post of the stitches forming the rung is the most important part of working the stitch. It is also usually necessary to manoeuvre the work while you create this stitch, rotating it or turning it from front to back to access the rungs, to allow the scales to lay in a given direction. There are many variations on this stitch – some employing a chain space in the scales, some using an extra single treble crochet to space out the scales, some employing a picot at the tip – and varying numbers and types of stitch can be employed to create the scales. In the example here each scale is worked with ten treble crochet stitches.

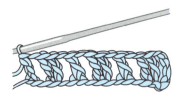

1 First work the ladder row as directed in the pattern. The one shown here is constructed of repeats of [one treble crochet, make one chain, miss two chains, two treble crochets into next chain, make one chain, miss two chains]. Do not turn the work.

2 To make the first scale, rotate the work so that the ladder hangs, allowing you to work into the side post of the treble crochet stitches in the rung. With RS facing, work five treble crochet stitches around the side post of the first of the two treble crochet stitches, forming the rung.

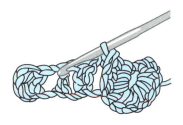

3 Rotate the work 180 degrees and fold the ladder down in front so that you can access the second treble crochet stitch in the rung. Work five treble crochet stitches around the side post of this. One crocodile scale completed.

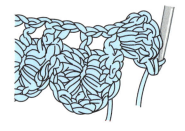

4 To move along the row, work one slip stitch into the top of the next stitch along the row. Now flip the work back over so that the 'ladder' hangs behind, allowing you to access the next pair of treble crochet stitches. Repeat steps 2 and 3 for the next scale. Build up the fabric by alternating rows of ladders and scales.

Working around stitch posts

Sometimes known as 'raised' or 'relief' stitches, working around stitch posts is a technique that involves inserting the hook around the vertical stem (post) of a stitch – either at the front or at the back – instead of into the top to create a stitch. Consequently, the stitch produced is either pushed forwards to stand slightly raised from the background, or lies behind the top of the stitch from the last row exposing it as a horizontal ridge, depending on whether you have worked into the front or the back of the last stitch.

Post stitches can be created with any stitch size and can be positioned anywhere within the fabric – for example, diagonally to the stitch being worked. The position of the post stitch will be specified in the pattern. Post stitches are a highly effective way to add pattern but do increase the thickness of the fabric quite substantially if they are worked in any quantity.

Front-post treble crochet (FPtr)

To begin working into the front post, first bring the hook to the front of the work.

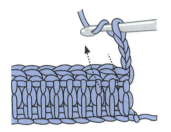 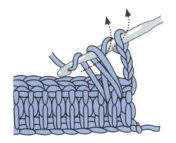 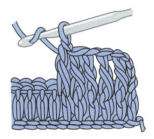

1 Wrap the yarn over the hook and insert the hook from right to left into the front of the vertical stem (post) of the stitch being worked, bringing the hook out on the front of the fabric.

2 Yarn over hook, draw through the work and yarn over hook again. Draw through only the first two loops.

3 Yarn over hook again and draw through the last two loops on the hook. One front-post treble crochet made. When working the next stitch take care not to accidentally work into the stitch behind the post stitch; ensure you move one stitch along the row to continue.

Back-post treble crochet (BPtr)

To begin working into the back post, first take the hook to the back of the work.

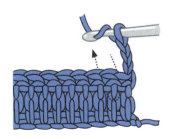 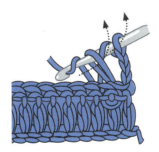 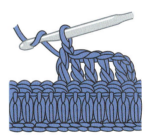

1 Wrap the yarn over the hook and insert the hook from right to left into the back of the vertical stem (post) of the stitch being worked, bringing the hook out again at the back of the fabric.

2 Yarn over hook, draw through the work and yarn over hook again. Draw through only the first two loops.

3 Yarn over hook again and draw through the last two loops on the hook. One back-post treble crochet made. When working the next stitch, take care not to accidentally work into the stitch in front of the post stitch; ensure you move one stitch along the row to continue.

Spike stitches

Spike stitches are created by inserting the hook into a lower part of the fabric than usual instead of directly into the next stitch due to be worked. It is possible to work spike stitches one or more stitches to the left or right of the position of the next stitch, and one or more rows below the last row. Spike stitches are usually made from double crochet stitches.

The most important thing you need to remember when working a spike stitch is to draw the spiked loop up to the same height as the row you are currently working before proceeding with the rest of the stitch. The work will pucker if you do not do this. The example pictured above right shows a spike stitch made with one double crochet stitch.

Locate the stitch that the pattern instructions specify you need to work into next for the spike. Insert the hook into this stitch, wrap the yarn over the hook and then draw through to the front. Pull this loop up to the same height as the row you are working on. Complete the stitch as normal. One spike double crochet made. Take care not to accidentally work into the stitch under the spike as your next working stitch; make sure you move one stitch along the row to continue.

tip Sometimes instructions will call for you to work a group of spike stitches together, into a range of positions within the last rows, and then to join them all together into a cluster. Pay careful attention to the exact positioning, because it will skew the pattern if you work into the wrong row or stitch. Counting the rows down and stitches along with your fingers is helpful to locate positions.

Crab stitch

Crab stitch, sometimes called reverse double crochet, is used as a decorative feature in a design. It produces a ridged edge as it is worked in the opposite direction to the usual – from left to right for the right-handed. The stitches twist in response to the counter-intuitive move, creating the textural effect. It is also possible to work other stitches in this way, for example reverse treble crochet will create a deeper level of ridge and twist.

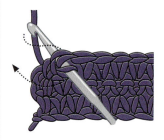 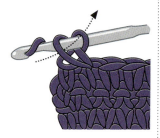

1 After completing the last row, do not turn the work if you would usually do so at that point. Position the hook below the work and insert it back into the next stitch to the right; this will feel somewhat counter-intuitive. Catch the yarn and pull through, and twist the hook so that it is positioned upwards as normal.

2 Yarn over hook and complete as a regular double crochet stitch (see page 12). One crab stitch made. Insert the hook into the next stitch along to the right and continue as steps 1 and 2 along the row to the end.

Surface crochet

This is a simple stitch that is most commonly used to embellish designs, usually once the work is complete. It is a little like the chain stitch made in embroidery. Once you master the technique, you can use it to 'draw' designs freely onto the fabric.

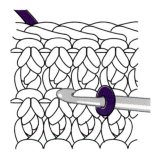 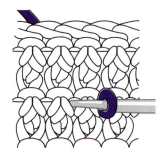 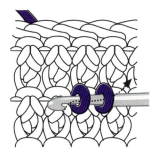 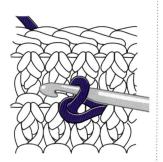

1 Keeping the working yarn at the back of the work throughout, insert the hook at the point you want to begin, from front to back. Catch the working yarn with the hook and pull a loop through to the front.

2 Now insert the hook, from front to back, at the next point you want to make a stitch – this is usually one stitch or space along a row or column of stitches.

3 Catch the working yarn with the hook again and pull through a second loop. Draw the second loop through the first one.

4 This creates a chain stitch on the surface. Repeat steps 2 and 3 to form a line of chain stitches, creating your pattern as directed, or as you want. When you reach the end, pull the tail through the last chain stitch to secure.

finishing off

These final techniques explain how to finish off your masterpiece professionally, to show it off to full effect and to ensure it lasts a long time.

Blocking your work

Many knitters and crocheters baulk at the prospect of blocking work after it is finished; after many hours spent creating your labour of love, it can seem tedious and unnecessary to go through the process of blocking when all you want to is wear or use your item immediately. However, it cannot be overstated what a difference blocking makes to the quality of the finished work and it is particularly crucial when working with squares because, by pinning them out, you can create perfect squares with defined corners. It is not difficult and can be strangely satisfying – and it helps greatly with the task of joining squares together.

There are two methods to choose from, depending on the yarn fibre you have used. Acrylic and wool/acrylic blends should be blocked with the cold-water method; the faster steam method can be used for wool, silk, linen and cotton. Check the ball label of your yarn for fibre information and iron temperature guidance.

For each method you will need somewhere to block on to, and plenty of pins. Special T-shape blocking pins are available, or you can use glass-head pins. You can make a surface by covering a flat board with two layers of wadding and a piece of cotton fabric – the board should measure at least 61 x 91.5 cm (24 x 36 inches) so the cotton fabric will need to be a little bigger to allow for it to overlap on to the back. Or you can use an ironing board, but this will only allow you to block one or two squares at a time.

In both cases you will need to mark out a 15-cm (6-inch) square area (or several, spaced at least 2.5 cm/1 inch apart) using a pencil. Pin out your finished block, using the marked square as a template. Start at the corners, then pin the sides. Ease the block down with your hands as you go, gently persuading it into a perfect square.

Cold-water method Spray the block with cold water from a spray bottle until it is damp throughout but not saturated. Pat the block to distribute the water through all the fibres, then put the board somewhere flat and let the block dry completely before removing the pins.

Steam blocking Set a steam iron at the correct temperature for the yarn, and hold it above the block at a height of approximately 2–2.5 cm (¾–1 inch) for 1 to 2 minutes, steaming continuously over the block. Lay the board flat and leave the block to dry completely before removing the pins.

Darning in ends

When you have completed the final row or round of your work, you will need to neaten it up before use. This should be completed at the end of every block, although in some cases it is recommended in the pattern that yarn tails are sewn in at interim stages of the work. To sew in ends neatly, turn the work so the wrong side is facing you and thread a yarn tail into a blunt knitter's or chenille needle. Weave the yarn tail over and under adjacent stitches, trying not to follow one row or round but going backwards and forwards, which will make the yarn less likely to work itself free. When you have woven into about ten stitches, cut the tail. Repeat for every yarn tail in the block.

It is possible to deal with yarn tails while you are working so that there are less to stitch in at the end. This is achieved by carrying the old yarn tail along the top of the stitches being worked, so that it is hidden by the new yarn and stitches that cover it. This is not a secure method for loose fabrics or taller stitches such as double treble, but it works well with denser fabrics and short stitches such as double crochet.

Joining completed squares

When making a composite piece with your squares, first lay them all out in your chosen arrangement so you can make any final adjustments to the positioning if necessary. For a larger piece it is helpful to take a photograph as a reference for when you start to join them up. There are various methods for joining squares together into a larger piece, but before you begin it is strongly recommended that you block all your squares (see left). Whichever method you choose you should first work the horizontal seams; join each square in the top row to the square beneath in the second row, then join the bottom edge of each square in the second row to the top edge of the corresponding square in the third row. Continue until all the horizontal edges are joined so the squares are in columns, then work along the vertical edges to join the columns to complete the piece.

Always darn in the ends of the yarn and block your work – the more practised you become at this, the neater the result.

Sewing squares together

If you choose to sew your squares together, use a blunt knitter's needle or chenille needle to avoid splitting the fibres. There are several stitches you may use.

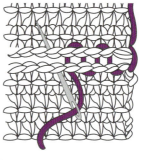

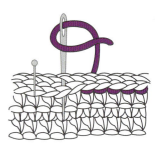

1 To sew with overcast stitch, place the motifs next to each other with their right sides facing upwards. Use a length of contrast or matching yarn and make overcast stitches as shown to join the squares together.

2 To sew with woven stitch, place the squares next to each other with the wrong side facing upwards. Use a length of matching yarn and work in and out of the stitches as shown, similar to a Kitchener or mattress stitch construction. Work firmly but not too tightly.

3 To sew with backstitch, place the squares together, with right sides facing, and work a row of backstitch along the edge, under the top of the last stitches, using a length of matching yarn. It can be helpful to pin the squares together.

Abbreviations

The following abbreviations have been used in this book.

beg	begin(s)/beginning
blo	back loop only
BPtr	Back-post treble crochet (see page 21)
ch	chain (see page 11)
cl	cluster (see page 18)
cont	continue/continuing
dc	double crochet (see page 12)
dec	decrease(s); decreasing; decreased
dtr	double treble crochet (see page 14)
flo	front loop only
foll	follows/following
FPtr	front-post treble crochet (see page 21)
htr	half-treble crochet (see page 13)
hdtr	half-double treble crochet (see page 14)
inc	increase(s); increasing; increased
JAYGo	join-as-you-go method (see page 25)
lp(s)	loop(s)
m	marker
MB	make bobble (see page 19)
pc	popcorn (see page 19)
quad tr	quadruple crochet (see page 15)
quin tr	quintuple treble (see page 15)
rem	remain(s)/remaining
rep	repeat/repeating
RH	righthand
RS	right side
rnd(s)	round(s)
rev dc	reverse double crochet
sl st	slip(ped) stitch (see page 12)
sp	spaces
st(s)	stitches
tch	turning chain
tog	together
tr	treble crochet (see page 13)
ttr	triple treble crochet (see page 15)
WS	wrong side
yoh	yarn over hook (see page 11)
*	starting point
**	ending point

Crocheting squares together

With each of these methods you can choose whether to seam the squares with wrong sides together (for a prominent seam) or right sides together (for a more subtle seam). In each case, using a contrast yarn offers the opportunity for adding a decorative effect by highlighting the seams, although you can use a matching yarn instead if you want the seams to blend in.

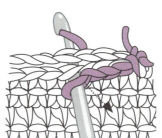

1 A slipstitch seam creates a ridge if the squares are joined with wrong sides together. If you prefer a subtler 'stitched' look, join the squares with right sides together. Using a contrast or matching yarn, insert the hook into both top loops of each square and work a slipstitch (see above) to join them together; repeat all along the edge, pulling the work gently to stop it becoming too tight.

2 A single crochet seam again allows for use of contrast yarn to highlight the joins. Choose whether you want to have a prominent seam or a subtler one and place your squares accordingly. Work in the same way as for the slipstitch method above, but work single crochet stitches (see page 12) instead.

Join-as-you-go (JAYGo)

For certain types of square, particularly traditional granny squares, it is possible to join your squares together while working the final round of the following square, a method known as 'join-as-you-go' or 'JAYGo'. A few of the squares in this book employ this method within their construction; crocheters with some experience will also find that there are various other squares that could be adapted to the JAYGo method.

Although the JAYGo method is appealing because it is quick and allows you to grow your project as you complete individual squares, you must plan ahead for the finished result and complete the squares in a logical order. There are various seaming stitches that are used for the JAYGo method, but the example here shows how to join traditional chain and double crochet granny squares by this method.

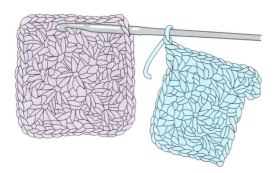

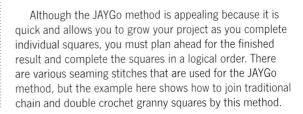

1 Complete your first square in the usual way. Work the second square, but on the final round only work the first edge, including the first part of the corner group (here the 3 tr of a [3 tr, ch 2, 3 tr] group). Insert the hook into the corner space of the first square as shown, and work 1 dc INSTEAD of working the first ch of the ch 2 for the usual corner spacing. Now work ch 1, 3 tr into the corner space of the second square as usual.

2 Now, instead of working the usual ch 1 on the second square, work 1 sc into the next space along the edge of the first square. *Work the next 3 tr group into the next ch-1 space on the second square as normal, then work another 1 dc into the next space along the edge of the first square instead of the usual ch 1. Repeat from * for the length of the edge, as far as the next corner space.

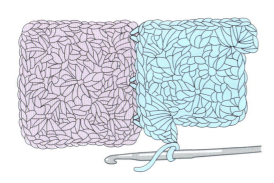

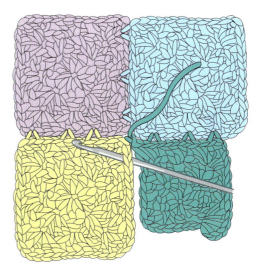

3 When you reach the next corner space, work the first 3 tr of the corner group as usual, then work 1 dc into the next corner space of the first square. Ch 1, 3 tr as usual to complete the corner group of the second square. Continue with the final round of the second square as normal and fasten off.

4 To join subsequent squares, simply follow the formula of replacing the ch 1 spaces along the edges of the square you are working with 1 dc into the ch-1 space on the square you are attaching to. When you reach a corner group where you must join to two other squares, work 1 dc into the corner space of each adjoining square in lieu of the usual ch 2 between your 3-tr corner groups on the square you are working.

***

romany

A detailed popcorn square that is redolent of the intricate wood carvings and wheels of Romany caravans. Perfect for pretty table linens and lacy blankets.

A
B
C

Special stitches used:

Beg popcorn (beg pc): Ch 3, make popcorn with 3 tr (*see page 19*).

Popcorn (pc): Make popcorn with 4 tr.

Dtr popcorn (dtr pc): 4 dtr in st, slip last loop off hook, insert hook in first dtr made, pick up dropped loop and draw though st just made, creating popcorn.

Foundation ring: Using yarn A, ch 5, join with sl st to form ring, or use magic ring method.

Round 1: Ch 1, 11 dc in ring, sl st in first dc to join – 12 sts.

Round 2: Ch 5 (counts as 1 tr, ch 2), 1 tr in next dc, *ch 2, 1 tr in next dc; rep from * 9 times, ch 2, sl st in top of beg ch-3 to join.

Round 3: Sl st in next ch-2 sp, beg pc in same sp, *ch 4, pc in next ch-2 sp; rep from * 10 times, ch 4, sl st in top of beg pc to join. Fasten off yarn A.

Round 4: Join yarn B to any ch-4 sp, 4 dc in same sp, *ch 3, 4 dc in next ch-4 sp; rep from * 10 times, ch 3, sl st in top of beg ch-3 to join.

Round 5: Sl st in next 3 sts to ch-3 sp, beg pc in same sp, ch 3, pc in same sp, ch 3, *[pc, ch 3, pc] in next ch-3 sp, ch 3; rep from * 10 times, sl st in top of beg pc to join. Fasten off yarn B.

Round 6: Join yarn C to any ch-3 sp between two pc, ch 1, *3 dc in same sp, ch 1, 3 htr in next ch-3 sp, ch 2, pc in next ch-3 sp, ch 2, [tr pc, ch 4, dtr pc] in next ch-3 sp, ch 2, pc in next ch-3 sp, ch 1; rep from * 3 times, sl st in beg dc to join.

Round 7: Ch 1, 1 dc in each of next 2 sc, *1 dc in next ch-1 sp, 1 dc in each of next 3 htr, 2 dc in next ch-2 sp, 1 dc in top of pc, 2 dc in next ch-2 sp, 1 dc in top of dtr pc, 5 dc in next ch-4 sp, 1 sc in top of dtr pc, 2 dc in next ch-2 sp, 1 dc in top of pc, 2 dc in next ch-2 sp, 1 dc in each of next 3 htr, 1 dc in next ch-1 sp**, 1 dc in each of next 3 dc***; rep from * to *** 2 times, then from *to ** 1 time, sl st in first dc to join.

Round 8: Ch 1, 1 dc in each st and 3 dc in centre st of each corner; rep to end of rnd, sl st in first dc to join.

Fasten off and darn in ends neatly.

★★★★
barnacles

A very distinctive block, this organic square is challenging to work but the results are stunning. A chain of circles is created, then joined into a grid, before being stabilized with a border. Each piece will be unique and a certain amount of your own judgement is necessary for this block, according to the yarn used.

Note: When working sl sts to right, turn work to WS, then turn back after sl sts are completed. Positioning guidelines are given based on combination of yarn and hook used here; use your own judgement when working out how many sl sts to work before beginning next circle by continually laying work out flat to check how it looks. Thicker or thinner yarn may require more or fewer sl sts for circles to be spaced evenly apart. Aim to line circles up in a square – it does not matter if they are misaligned or at various angles; that is the intended effect.

A

B

C

CIRCLES

Circle 1: Ch 6, sl st in first ch to form ring, ch 3 (counts as 1 tr), 15 tr in ring, sl st in top of beg ch-3 to join. Do not fasten off.

Circle 2: Ch 6, sl st in first ch to form ring*, [ch 3, 3 tr] in ring, adjust position of your hold so you can access rem sts of ring, 12 tr in ring (you may need to bend last circle back to access sts). Do not fasten off.

Circle 3: Sl st in next 3 tr to left of where you ended circle 2; make circle as for Circle 2.

Circle 4: Sl st in next 3 tr to left of where you ended Circle 3, complete as Circle 2.

Lay 4 circles out to form a square, with Circle 4 slightly overlapping Circle 1.

Circle 5: Sl st 4 tr anti-clockwise around Circle 1, complete as Circle 2.

Circle 6: Sl st 3 sts to left of where you ended Circle 5, complete as Circle 2.

Circle 7: Sl st 2 sts to right of where you ended Circle 6, complete as Circle 2.

Circle 8: As Circle 7.

Circle 9: Sl st 2 sts to left of where you ended Circle 8, complete as Circle 2.

Circle 10: Complete as Circle 2, in same st as you ended Circle 9.

Circle 11: Complete as Circle 2, in same st as you ended Circle 10.

Circle 12: Complete as Circle 2, in same st as you ended Circle 11.

Circle 13: Sl st 1 st to left of where you ended Circle 12, complete as Circle 2.

Circle 14: sl st 4 sts to right of where you ended Circle 13, complete as Circle 2.

Circle 15: Sl st 2 sts to right of where you ended Circle 14, complete as Circle 2.

Circle 16: Sl st 2 sts to left of where you ended Circle 15, complete as Circle 2.

You should now have a mesh of 16 circles, joined at various angles.

BACK JOIN

Using a darning needle, work a couple of stitches to secure each motif tog at centre of each side, where they touch. Alternatively make a criss-cross ch grid on WS of work as follows: join yarn A in any back-post tr of an outer circle, ch 3, join to next circle, ch 3, join to back-post tr on outer edge of same circle, cont to connect circles tog in this way, working one horizontal grid line and one vertical. Turn work back to RS.

BORDER

Round 1: Join yarn B to any corner circle, at corner ch 3, miss 1 st, 1 dc in next tr (forms corner), *ch 6, 1 dc in centre tr of next circle; rep from * 2 times **, ch 2, 1 dc in next tr (forms corner), rep from * 2 times and from * to ** 1 time, sl st in first ch to join. Fasten off yarn B.

Round 2: Join yarn C in any ch-6 sp, *[1 dc, 1 htr, 4 tr, 1 htr, 1 sc] in each ch-6 sp and [1 dc, 1 htr, 2 tr, 1 dtr, 2 tr, 1 htr, 1 dc] in each corner ch-3 sp; rep from * to end, sl st in first dc to join.

Fasten off and darn in all ends.

3

***

poppy

A dimensional flower with a velvety frilly centre, this square is particularly effective when worked with a highly contrasting background. Perfect as the centrepiece of a pillow or as part of a flower-garden blanket. The flower also makes a great brooch or hairpin in its own right.

A
B
C
D
E

Foundation ring: Using yarn A, begin with magic ring method, ch 10, sl st in first ch to join.

POPPY

Round 1: Join yarn B to any st, ch 8, 1 dc in same st, ch 8, [1 dc, ch 8, 1 dc, ch 8] in each st to end of round, sl st in first st to join – 20 ch-8 loops.

Round 2: Working behind ch-lps of Round 1, [ch 5, miss 4 lps, sl st in dc on Round 1]; rep 4 times, sl st in first ch of ch-5 to join. Fasten off yarn B.

Round 3: Join yarn C and on RS, [ch 3 (counts as 1 tr), 5 tr in first ch-5 (behind petals), sl st across to next ch-5 loop]; rep 4 times, sl st in ch-1 sp to join.

Petal 1: Ch 3 (counts as first tr), 1 tr in each of next 5 sts, turn work to WS, ch 1 (counts as 1 dc), 1 dc in each of next 4 sts and 1 dc in last sp, turn back to RS, sl st in next dc, 2 htr, 1 dc, sl st in last sp, sl st all down side of petal and up in 3rd ch of ch-3 of next petal.

Petals 2 to 5: As Petal 1. On Petal 5, sl st in base of Petal 1 to join. Fasten off yarn C.

SQUARE

Round 1: (WS) Sl st yarn D to any secure st between petals, [ch 4, 1 dc in any secure st of Round 3] 5 times, sl st in first sl st to join.

Round 2: Ch 4 (counts as 1 dtr), 7 dtr in same ch-4 loop, *[8 dtr in next ch-4 loop] 4 times, sl st in top of beg ch-4 to join – 40 dtr in total.

Round 3: With WS facing, sl st in top of next dtr, ch 3 (counts as 1 tr), [1 tr, ch 2, 2 tr] in same st, 1 tr in each of next 9 dtr, *[2 tr, ch 2, 2 tr] in next st (forms next corner sp), 1 tr in each of next 9 dtr; rep from * 2 times, 1 tr in each of 9 dtr to end, sl st in top of beg ch-3 to join. Fasten off yarn D.

Round 4: Join yarn E to any ch-2 corner sp, ch 3 (counts as 1 tr), 2 tr in same ch-2 sp, ch 3, 3 tr in the same sp, *[miss next 2 sts, 3 tr in sp between sts] 4 times across side of square**, [3 tr, ch 3, 3 tr] in next corner ch-2 sp; rep from * 2 times, then from * to ** 1 time, join with sl st in top of beg ch-3 to form a square.

Round 5: Sl st in next two sts along to corner sp, ch 3 (counts as 1 tr), 2 tr in same ch-2 sp, ch 3, 3 tr in the same sp, *[3 tr in sp between sts] 6 times across side of square**, [3 tr, ch 3, 3 tr] in next corner ch-2 sp; rep from * 2 times, then from * to ** 1 time, join with sl st in top of beg ch-3.

Round 6: Sl st in next two sts along to corner sp, ch 3 (counts as 1 tr), 2 tr in same ch-2 sp, ch 3, 3 tr in the same sp, [3 tr in sp between sts] 7 times across side of square, [3 tr, ch 3, 3 tr] in next corner ch-2 sp; rep to end of rnd, join with sl st in top of beg ch-3.

Round 7: Sl st in next two sts along to corner sp, ch 1 (counts as 1 dc), *[1 dc in each st along side and 5 dc in each corner ch-3 sp]; rep from * 3 times, sl st in beg ch-1 to join.

Round 8: Sl st in next two sts along to corner sp, ch 1 (counts as 1 dc), 1 dc in same sp, 2 dc in next dc, *1 dc in each st along to next dc-5 corner group, [2 dc**, 2 dc in same dc, 2 dc in corner dc-5; rep from * 2 times, then from * to ** 1 time, sl st in beg ch-1 to join.

Fasten off and darn in ends neatly.

***

cross my heart

An intricately textured square that employs interesting techniques to create its heart-and-cross pattern. This pattern is a little challenging but the effect is sweet and worth the concentration. Mix this block with other heart blocks for a cute blanket or bedspread for a girl.

Special stitch used:

Crab stitch (crab st): Double crochet worked in reverse (*see page 22*).

Foundation chain: Using yarn A, ch 20.

Row 1: 1 sc in 2nd ch from hook, 1 dc in every ch to end, turn – 19 dc.

Row 2: Ch 1, 1 tr in first dc, *ch 1, miss 2 dc, [1 hdtr, 1 dtr, 1 dc, 1 dtr, 1 hdtr] in next dc, ch 1, miss 1 dc, 1 sl st in next dc; rep from * 2 times, finishing with 1 tr in final dc. Do not fasten off. Turn.

Row 3: Join yarn B, ch 1, 2 tr in first tr, *ch 2, 1 sl st in dc in centre of heart from Row 2, ch 2**, 1 tr to left of next sl st, ch 1, 1 tr to right of same sl st (makes 'cross'); rep from * 1 time and from * to ** 1 time, 2 tr in final tr, turn.

Row 4: Ch 1, 2 tr in first tr, *ch 1, 1 sl st in next sl st, ch 1, [1 hdtr, 1 dtr, 1 dc, 1 dtr, 1 hdtr] in next ch-1 sp (above 'cross'); rep from * 1 time, ch 1, 1 sl st in next sl st, ch 1, 2 tr in final tr, turn.

Row 5: Using yarn A, ch 1, 2 tr in first tr, ch 1, *1 tr to left of next sl st ch 1, 1 tr to right of same sl st (makes 'cross')**, ch 2, 1 sl st in dc in centre of heart from Row 4, ch 2; rep from * 1 time, and from * to ** 1 time, ch 1, 2 tr in final tr, turn.

Row 6: Ch 1, 2 tr in first tr, *ch 1, [1 hdtr, 1 dtr, 1 dc, 1 dtr, 1 hdtr] in next ch-1 sp (above 'cross'), ch 1, 1 sl st in sl st in centre of heart; rep from * 1 time, ch 1, [1 hdtr, 1 dtr, 1 dc, 1 dtr, 1 hdtr] in next ch-1 sp, ch 1, 2 tr in final tr, turn.

Row 7: Using yarn B, ch 1, 2 tr in first tr, ch 1, *1 sl st in dc in centre of heart from Row 6, ch 2, 1 tr to left of next sl st, ch 1, 1 tr to right of same sl st (makes 'cross'), ch 1; rep from * 1 time, ch 1, 1 sl st in centre of next heart from Row 6, ch 2, 2 tr in final tr, turn.

Rows 8 to 11: Rep Rows 4 to 7.

Row 12: Rep Row 4.

Row 13: Rep Row 5.

Row 14: Rep Row 6.

Row 15: Ch 1, 1 dc in every tr, hdtr and dtr to end of row – 19 dc.

Fasten off.

BORDER (WORKED IN ROUNDS)

Round 1: Join yarn A in any corner, ch 1, [2 dc, ch 2, 2 dc] in corner sp, *1 dc in every st to next corner, [2 dc, ch 2, 2 dc] in corner sp; rep from * 2 times, 1 dc in every st to end, sl st in first dc to join.

Round 2: Ch 3 (counts as 1 tr), [1 tr, ch 2, 2 tr] in same sp (forms corner), *[miss 1 dc, 2 tr in next dc, ch 1] to next corner sp, [2 tr, ch 2, 2 tr] in corner ch-2 sp; rep from * 2 times, [miss 1 dc, 2 tr in next dc, ch 1] to end, sl st in top of beg ch-3 to join.

Round 3: Ch 2 (counts as 1 htr), [1 htr, ch 2, 2 htr] in same corner sp, *[miss 1 tr, 1 htr in next tr, 1 htr in next ch-1 sp] to next corner sp, [2 htr, ch 2, 2 htr] in corner ch-2 sp; rep from * 2 times, [miss 1 tr, 1 htr in next tr, 1 htr in next ch-1 sp] to end, sl st in top of beg ch-2 to join. Fasten off yarn A.

Round 4: Join yarn B in any corner ch-2 sp, 1 crab st in every htr around, working 2 crab sts in each corner sp, sl st in first crab st to join.

Fasten off and darn in ends neatly.

A

B

★★★★
fairy grotto

A fascinating square that uses the unusual bullion stitch, and clusters of treble crochets and half-double trebles to form seashell scallops. This block was inspired by the ancient seashell grottoes that can be found on the UK coastline and has oodles of textural interest.

A
B
C
D

Special stitches used:

Bullion stitch (bullion st): Yoh 7 times, insert hook in st or sp to be worked, yoh, pull through all loops on hook, ch 1 to secure (*see page 20*).

Treble-crochet cluster (tr cl): Make cluster scallop with 5 tr (*see page 18*).

Half-double treble cluster (hdtr cl): Make cluster scallop with 9 hdtr.

Foundation ring: Using yarn A, make a magic ring.

Round 1: Ch1, 24 sc in ring, sl st in first dc to join.

Round 2: Ch 1, 1 dc in each dc around, sl st to first dc to join.

Round 3: Ch 3, 1 bullion st in next dc, [1 tr in next dc, 1 bullion st in next dc] 11 times; sl st in top of beg ch-3 to join. Fasten off yarn A.

Round 4: Join yarn B, ch 1, *1 dc in top of next bullion st, 1 dc in ch-st that secures same bullion st, 1 dc in next tr; rep from * all around motif, sl st in first dc to join – 36 sts. Fasten off yarn B.

Round 5: Join yarn A, ch 3 (counts as 1 htr, ch 1), miss 1 dc, [3 htr, ch 3, 3 htr] in next dc (forms 1st corner), *ch 1, miss 1 dc, 1 htr in next dc, ch 1, 1 dc in each of next 2 dc, miss 1 dc, ch 1, 1 sc in each of next 2 dc, ch 1**, 1 htr in next dc, ch 1, [3 htr, ch 3, 3 htr] in next dc (forms 2nd corner); rep from * 2 times and from * to ** 1 time, sl st in 2nd ch of beg ch-3 to join. Fasten off yarn A.

Round 6: Join yarn C in centre st of first corner 3-htr group, ch 3 (counts as 1 tr), 4 tr in same st (counts as 1 tr cl), ch 5, miss [1 htr, ch 3, 1 htr], 1 tr cl in centre htr of next 3-htr group, *miss [1 htr, ch 1, 1 htr, ch 1, 2 dc], work 1 tr cl in next ch-1 sp; miss [2 dc, ch 1, 1 htr, ch 1, 1 htr]**,

1 tr cl in next htr (centre of 3-htr group), ch 5, miss [1 htr, ch 3, 1 htr], 1 tr cl in next htr (centre of 3-htr group); rep from * 2 times, and from * to ** 1 time, sl st in top of beg ch-3 to join. Fasten off yarn C.

Round 7: Join yarn A in same st, ch 5, *working over ch-5 from Round 6, [1 tr, ch 3, 1 tr] in missed ch-3 sp from Round 5 (forms corner), [ch 5, 1 tr in next missed ch-1 sp from Round 5] 2 times, **ch 5; rep from * 3 times, ending last rep at **.

Round 8: Ch 1, 6 dc in next ch-5 sp, *1 tr in next tr, [1 tr, 1 bullion st, ch 3, 1 bullion st, 1 dc] in next ch-3 corner sp, 1 tr in next tr, [6 dc in next ch-5 sp, 1 dc in next tr] 2 times**, 6 dc in next ch-5 sp; rep from * 3 times, ending last rep at **, sl st in first ch-1 to join, sl st along to 3rd dc of next 6-dc group. Fasten off yarn A.

Round 9: Join yarn D in same st, ch 4 (counts as 1 hdtr), 8 hdtr in same st (counts as 1 hdtr cl), ch 7, *miss all corner bullion sts, ch-3 sp and trs, and first 2 dc of next 6-dc group, 1 hdtr cl in next (3rd) dc**, [miss rem 3 dc of same group, next dc, and first 2 dc of next 6-dc group, 1 hdtr cl in next dc] 2 times, ch 7; rep

from * 2 times and from * to ** 1 time, miss rem 3 dc of same group, next dc and first 2 dc of next 6-dc group, 1 hdtr cl in next dc, sl st in top of beg ch-3 to join. Fasten off yarn D.

Round 10: Join yarn A, ch 6, 1 sc in 5th (centre) hdtr of next scallop, ch 3, *3 tr in next ch-7 sp, [1 tr, 1 bullion st, ch 3, 1 bullion st, 1 tr] in missed ch-3 from Round 8, 3 tr in same ch-7 sp from Round 9, [ch 3, 1 dc in 5th tr (centre) of next scallop, ch 3, 1 dtr in dc between scallops (sc above tr of Round 7)] 2 times**, ch 3, 1 dc in 5th tr of next scallop, ch 3; rep from * 3 times, but ending last rep at **, sl st in 3rd ch of beg ch-6 to join.

Fasten off and darn in ends neatly. Block square to straighten corners.

★★★★

vintage lace

Inspired by antique doily patterns, this delicate, feminine block is intricate to work and offers a challenge to the more experienced crocheter. Tiny details are peppered throughout, which build to produce a complex design.

A
B
C
D

Special stitches used:

Beg cluster (beg cl): Ch 3, make cluster with 2 tr (*see page 18*).

Cluster (cl): Make cluster with 3 tr.

Popcorn (pc): Make popcorn with 4 tr (*see page 19*).

Foundation ring: Using yarn A, ch 8, sl st in first ch to form ring, or use magic ring method.

Round 1: Ch 2, beg cl in ring, ch 3, [cl in ring, ch 3] 7 times, sl st in top of beg cl – 8 ch-3 sps.

Round 2: Sl st in first ch-3 sp, ch 1, *[1 sc, ch 3, 1 dc] in same ch-3 sp; rep from * in each ch-3 sp to end of rnd, sl st in first dc to join. Fasten off yarn A.

Round 3: Join yarn B in next dc st, ch 3, pc in next ch-3 sp, ch 3, *1 dc in each of next 2 dc, ch 3, pc in next ch-3 sp, ch 3; rep from * to last dc, 1 dc in last dc, sl st in first dc to join.

Round 4: Sl st in next ch-3 sp, ch 1, 3 dc in same ch-3 sp, ch 3, *3 dc in each of next 2 ch-3 sps, ch 3; rep from * to last ch-3 sp, 3 dc in last ch-3 sp, sl st in first dc to join. Fasten off yarn B.

Round 5: Join yarn C in ch-3 sp, ch 3 (counts as first tr), 4 tr in same ch-3 sp, ch 3, miss 1 dc, 1 dc in next dc, miss next 2 dc, *1 dc in next dc, ch 3, 5 tr in next ch-3 sp, ch 3, miss 1 dc, 1 dc in next dc, miss next 2 dc; rep from * to end of rnd, ending ch 3, sl st in top of beg ch-3 to join.

Round 6: Ch 2, [miss next st, yoh, insert hook in next st, yoh, draw through a loop, yoh, draw through 2 lps] 2 times, yoh, draw through all 3 lps on hook, *ch 4, 2 dc in next ch-3 sp, ch 2, 2 dc in next ch-3 sp, ch 4, [yoh, insert hook in first tr st of 5 tr in last rnd, yoh, draw through lp, yoh, draw through 2 lps, miss next st] 2 times, yoh, insert hook in last tr st of 5 tr in last rnd, yoh, draw through a lp, yoh, draw through all 4 lps on hook (counts as a dec cl); rep from * to last dec cl, ch 4, 2 dc in next ch-3 sp, ch 2, 2 dc in next ch-3 sp, ch 4, sl st in top of beg dec cl to join.

Round 7: Sl st in next ch-4 sp, ch 1, 2 dc in same ch-4 sp, *ch 2, 1 dc in next ch-2 sp, ch 2, 2 dc in next ch-4 sp, ch 3 across top of dec cl, 2 dc in next ch-4 sp; rep from * 7 times, ch 2, 1 dc in next ch-2 sp, ch 2, 2 dc in next ch-4 sp, ch 3 across top of dec cl, sl st in first sc to join. Fasten off yarn C.

Round 8: Join yarn D in any ch-3 sp that goes across top of dec cl, ch 2 (counts as first htr); 2 htr in same ch-3 sp, *ch 1, 2 tr in 2nd dc, ch 1, 1 dtr in next dc, ch 1, 2 tr in next dc, ch 1, [2 dtr, ch 3, 2 dtr] in next ch-3 sp (forms corner), ch 1, miss 1 dc, 2 tr in next dc, ch 1, 2 dtr in next dc, ch 1, 2 tr in next dc, ch 1, miss 1 dc**, 3 htr in ch-3 sp that goes across top of dec cl; rep from * 2 times, then from * to ** 1 time, sl st in top of beg ch-2 to join.

Round 9: Ch 1, 1 dc in each st and each ch-1 sp, and 3 dc in each corner sp to end of rnd, sl st in first dc to join.

Round 10: Ch 1, 1 dc in each st and 3 dc in centre st of each corner 3-dc group to end of rnd, sl st in first dc to join.

Fasten off and darn in ends neatly.

7

*

winchmore

A
B
C

This easy block is another modern take on filet, here combining contemporary brights and pastels together for a surprising colour pop. Perfect for use in picnic blankets, throws or window treatments, this blends beautifully with our other modern filets.

Foundation chain: Using yarn A, ch 7.

Row 1: 1 tr in 4th ch from hook, 1 tr in each of rem 3 ch, turn.

Row 2: Ch 3 (counts as 1 tr), 1 tr in every tr to end, turn. Fasten off yarn A.

Round 3: Using yarn B, ch 4 (counts as 1 tr, ch 1) *miss 1 tr, ch 1, 1 tr in next tr; rep from * to last tr, [1 tr, ch 3, 1 tr] in last tr, work down side of square, *[ch 1, miss 1 st, 1 tr in next tr] to last st, [1 tr, ch 3, 1 tr] in last st** working along base of square, rep from * to **, work up side of square to last corner, [ch 1, miss 1 tr, 1 tr in next tr] to last corner, ch 3, sl st in 3rd ch of beg ch-4 to join.

Round 4: Ch 4 (counts as 1 tr, ch 1), *[miss 1 tr, ch 1, 1 tr in next tr] to corner ch-3 sp, [1 tr, ch 3, 1 tr] in 2nd ch of ch-3 at corner; rep from * 3 times, [miss 1 tr, ch 1, 1 tr in next tr] to end. Ch 1, miss 1 tr, sl st in 3rd ch of beg ch-4 to join. Fasten off yarn B.

Round 5: Using yarn C, rep Round 4. Fasten off yarn C.

Round 6: Using yarn A, ch 1, *1 dc in every st and every ch-sp to corner, [1 dc, ch 1, 1 dc] in 2nd ch of corner ch-3; rep from * 3 times, 1 dc in every st and every ch-sp to end, sl st in first sc to join. Fasten off yarn A.

Round 7: Using yarn B, rep Round 4. Fasten off yarn B.

Rounds 8 to 9: Using yarn C, rep Round 4.

Fasten off and darn in ends.

8

***

geisha

A
B
C
D

This block uses unusually tall stitches to create its Japanese-themed pattern. Mix with other flower blocks for a light summer throw.

Special stitches used:

Beginning 3-treble-crochet cluster (beg 3-tr cl): Ch 2, make cluster with 2 tr (*see page 18*).

3-treble-crochet cluster (3-tr cl): Make cluster with 3 tr.

Picot-3: Ch 3 (at point to add picot), sl st in first ch of ch-3, creating picot loop.

Foundation ring: Using yarn A, ch 4, sl st in first ch to form ring.

Round 1: Ch 1, 16 dc in ring, sl st in first dc to join. Fasten off yarn A.

Round 2: Join yarn B in any dc, beg 3-tr cl, ch 3, miss 1 dc, *3-tr cl in next dc, ch 3; rep from * 7 times, sl st in top of beg cl to join. Fasten off yarn B.

Round 3: Join yarn C in any ch-3 sp, ch 3 (counts as 1 tr), [1 tr, ch 2, 2 tr] in next ch-3 sp, *ch 6, [2 tr, ch 3, 2 tr] in next ch-3 sp; rep from * 6 times, ch 3, 1 tr in 3rd ch of beg ch-3 to join.

Round 4: Ch 3, *[2 tr, ch 2, 2 tr] in next ch-2 sp, ch 6; rep from * 6 times, [2 tr, ch 2, 2 tr] in next ch-2 sp, ch 3, sl st in first ch of beg ch-3 to join. Fasten off yarn C.

Round 5: Join yarn D in any ch- 2 sp, ch 3 (counts as 1 tr), picot-3, [1 tr, picot-3] 4 times in next ch-2 sp, ch 6, *[1 tr, picot-3] 5 times in next ch-2 sp, ch 6; rep from * 6 times, sl st in 3rd ch of beg ch-3 to join. Fasten off.

Round 6: Join yarn D in middle picot, ch 3 (counts as 1 tr), ch 9, 1 dc over next ch-6 sp of Rounds 5, 4 and 3 tog, ch 9, *1 tr in next middle picot, ch 9, 1 dc over next ch-6 sp of Rounds 5, 4 and 3 tog, ch 9; rep from * 6 times, sl st in 3rd ch of beg ch-3 to join.

Round 7: *[1 quad tr, 1 ttr, 3 dtr, 1 ttr, 1 quad tr] in next dc, 1 dc in next tr; rep from * 7 times, sl st in first st to join. Fasten off yarn D.

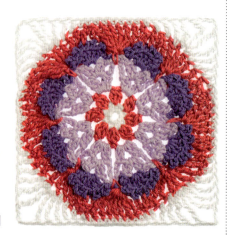

Round 8: Join yarn A in any middle dtr from Round 7, *1 dc in same st, 1 dc in each of next 3 sts, 1 htr in next st, 1 tr in next st, 1 dtr in next st, 1 ttr in next st, [2 quad tr, ch 4, 2 quad tr] in next st (middle tr Round 7), 1 ttr in next st, 1 dtr in next st, 1 tr in next st, 1 htr in next st, 1 dc in each of next 3 sts; rep from * 3 times, sl st in first st to join.

Fasten off and darn in ends.

dragonfly lace

A delicate filigree lace reminiscent of dragonfly wings, this would work well in a summer throw or scarf; repeat in a series of pastels for a pretty gift.

Foundation chain: Ch 35.

Row 1: 1 dc in 2nd ch from hook, 1 dc in every ch to end, turn.

Row 2: ch 3 (counts as 1 tr), 3 tr in first dc, miss 4 dc, 4 tr in next dc, *ch 5, miss 3 dc, 1 dc in next dc, ch 5, miss 3 dc, 4 tr in next dc, miss 4 dc, 4 tr in next dc; rep from * to end, turn.

Row 3: Ch 3 (counts as 1 tr), 3 tr in first tr, miss 6 tr, 4 tr in next tr, *ch 3, 1 dc in next dc, ch 3, 4 tr in next tr, miss 6 tr, 4 tr in next tr; rep from * to end, working last group of 4 tr in top of ch-3 from last row, turn.

Row 4: Ch 3, (counts as 1 tr), 3 tr in next tr, miss 6 tr, 4 tr in next tr, *ch 5, 1 dc in next dc, ch 5, 4 tr in next tr, miss 6 tr, 4 tr in next tr; rep from * to end, working last group of 4 tr in top of beg ch-3 from last row, turn.

Row 5: Ch 8 (counts as 1 tr, ch 5), 1 dc between next 2 group of 4 tr, *ch 5, miss 3 tr, 4 tr in each of next 2 tr, ch 5, 1 dc between next 2 groups of 4 tr; rep from * to last 4-tr group, ch 5, 1 tr in top of beg ch-3 of last row, turn.

Row 6: Ch 6 (counts as 1 tr, ch 3), 1 dc in next dc, ch 3, *4 tr in next tr, miss 6 tr, 4 tr in next tr, ch 3, 1 dc in next dc, ch 3; rep from * to last ch-sp, 1 tr in 3rd ch of beg ch-8 of last row, turn.

Row 7: Ch 8 (counts as 1 tr, ch 5), 1 dc in next dc, ch 5, *4 tr in next tr, miss 6 tr, 4 tr in next tr, ch 5, 1 dc in next dc, ch 5; rep from * to last ch-sp, 1 tr in 3rd ch of ch-6 at beg of last row, turn.

Row 8: Ch 3 (counts as 1 tr), 3 tr in first tr, 4 tr in next tr, *ch 5, 1 dc between next 2 groups of 4 tr, ch 5, miss 3 tr, 4 tr in each of next 2 tr; rep from * to end, working last group of 4 tr in 3rd of ch-8 at beg of last row.

Row 9: Rep Row 3.

Row 10: Rep Row 4.

Row 11: Rep Row 5.

Row 12: Rep Row 6.

Row 13: Rep Row 7.

Row 14: *Ch 4, 1 dc in each of next 2 tr, ch 3, miss 4 tr, 1 dc in each of next 3 tr, ch 4, 1 dc in each of next 3 dc, ch 3, 1 dc in each of next 2 dc, ch 4, 1 dc in 3rd ch of ch-8 of last row, turn.

Row 15: Ch 1, 4 dc in ch-4 sp, 1 dc in each of next 2 dc, 3 dc in next ch-3 sp, 1 dc in each of next 3 dc, 4 dc in next ch-4 sp, 1 dc in each of next 3 dc, 3 dc in next ch-3 sp, 1 dc in each of last 2 dc, 4 dc in last ch-4 sp.

Fasten off and darn in ends.

10 **

sea anemone

An organic, central fan motif with ribbed detail from front-post stitches, this block is lightweight and fun to work up, a perfect summer evening project for throws or stylish pillows. Mix with other lace blocks, or try it with bold florals.

Special stitch used:

Front-post treble crochet (FPtr): Bring hook to front, work in front vertical post of next st, inserting hook from right to left, draw yarn through and work st as usual (*see page 27*).

Foundation ring: Ch 4, sl st in first ch to form ring.

Round 1: Ch 2 (counts as 1 htr), 15 htr in ring, sl st in top of beg ch-2 to join.

Round 2: Ch 3 (counts as 1 tr), *1 FPtr in next htr, 3 tr in next htr; rep from * 7 times, 1 FPtr in next htr, 2 htr in last st (at base of beg ch-3), sl st in top of beg ch-3 to join.

Round 3: Ch 3 (counts as 1 tr), *1 FPtr in next FPtr, 2 tr in next tr, 1 tr in next tr, 2 tr in next tr; rep from * 7 times, 1 FPtr in next FPtr, 2 tr in next tr, 1 tr in next tr, 1 tr in base of beg ch-3, sl st in top of beg ch-3 to join.

Round 4: Sl st along to 3rd dc, ch 3 (counts as 1 tr), 8 tr in same st, * miss 2 tr, sl st in next FPtr, miss 2 tr, 9 tr in next tr; rep from * 7 times, sl st in last FPtr, sl st in top of beg ch-3 to join.

Round 5: Ch 7 (counts as 1 tr, ch 4), *1 dc in 5th tr of next shell, ch 4, [1 tr, ch 3, 1 tr] in next sl st, ch 4; rep from * 7 times, 1 dc in 5th tr of next shell, ch 4, [1 tr, ch 3] in base of beg ch-7, sl st in 3rd ch of beg ch-7 to join.

Round 6: Sl st in next ch-4 lp, *4 dc in ch-4 lp, [2 htr, 2 tr] in next ch-4 lp, [3 tr, ch 3, 3 tr] in next ch-3 corner sp, [2 tr, 2 htr] in next ch-4 lp, 4 dc in next ch-4 lp, 2 dc in next ch-3 lp; rep from * 4 times, sl st in first sc to join.

Round 7: Ch 1, *1 dc in every st to corner ch-3 sp, [2 dc, ch 1, 2 dc] in corner ch-3 sp; rep from * 3 times, 1 dc in every st to end, sl st in first dc to join.

Fasten off and darn in ends.

---

11 ****

klee

Inspired by the artist of the same name, this complex, bright block is based on a painting of a hill town. Work with a separate ball or length of yarn for each area of colour over the pattern and remember to keep the yarn tails on the wrong side. The pleasing embroidery details are completed at the end, in simple chain stitch.

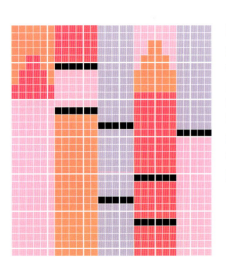

Foundation chain: Using yarn A, ch 29.

Row 1: 1 dc in 2nd ch from hook, 1 dc in every ch to end, turn.

Begin chart, changing colour where indicated and using separate ball of yarn for each colour area.

Rows 2 to 31: Ch 1, 1 dc in every dc to end, turn.

Row 32: Rep Row 2 using only yarn A.

EMBROIDERY

Using lengths of yarn A and a blunt darning needle, stitch arches and trees on to motif as shown in the photograph, using embroidered chain stitch.

Fasten off and darn in ends neatly. Block work to shape.

****

tulip

A very dimensional flower with curled petals, this block would make a great centrepiece for a flower pillow or throw – and as part of a larger flower-garden blanket it would be stunning.

Special stitches used:

2-half-treble-crochet cluster (2-htr cl): Make cluster with 2 htr in same st or sp.

5-triple-treble cluster (5-ttr cl): Make cluster with 5 ttr in same st or sp (*see page 18*).

Foundation ring: Using yarn A, ch 4, sl st in first ch to form ring.

Round 1: Ch 2 (counts as 1 htr), 11 htr in ring, sl st in top of beg ch-2 to join.

Round 2: *Ch 2 (counts as 1 htr), 2-htr cl in same st, ch 2, sl st in same st, sl st in each of next 2 sts; rep from * 5 times, ending with sl st in first ch of beg ch-2 to join. Fasten off yarn A.

Round 3: Join yarn B in any sl st at base of petal from Round 2, *ch 4, miss 1 sl st of next petal, sl st in next sl st (of next petal, this is every alternate petal); rep from * 2 times, ending with sl st in first sl st.

Round 4: *5 dc in next ch-4 sp, 1 dc in next sl st; rep from * 2 times.

Round 5: *Ch 3 (counts as 1 tr), 1 tr in same st, [1 tr in next st, 2 tr in next st] 2 times, 1 tr in next st, turn, ch 1, 1 dc in every tr to end of petal, turn, ch 2 (counts as 1 htr), 2-htr cl in each of next 2 dc, 1 htr in each of next 3 dc, miss 1 dc, 1 htr in next dc, ch 2, sl st in last dc, sl st down side of petal to base, sl st in next 2 dc; rep from * 2 times – 3 petals made.

Round 6: Sl st in back lp of next dc from Round 4, sl st in next 4 sc, rep Round-5 method of making petals, creating 3 petals within back lps of Round 4. Fasten off yarn B – 6-petal tulip made.

Round 7: Join yarn C between any 2 petals of Round 6, 1 dc in same sp, [ch 10, 1 dc in sp between next 2 petals] 2 times, sl st in first dc to join.

Round 8: Ch 3 (counts as 1 tr), *11 tr in next ch-10 sp, 1 tr in next dc; rep from * 2 times, 11 tr in last ch-10 sp, sl st in top of beg ch-3 to join.

Round 9: Ch 5, *5-ttr cl in next tr, ch 2, miss 3 tr, 1 tr in next tr, miss 3 tr, ch 2**, 5-ttr cl in next tr, ch 5, rep from * 2 times and from * to ** 1 time, sl st in top of beg ch-5 to join. Fasten off yarn C.

Round 10: Join yarn A in any corner ch-5 sp, *[4 dc, ch 2, 4 dc] in same sp, 1 dc in top of 5-ttr cl, 4 dc in next ch-2 sp, 1 dc in next tr, 4 dc in next ch-2 sp, 1 dc in next 5-ttr cl; rep from * 3 times, sl st in first dc to join. Fasten off yarn A.

Round 11: Join yarn D in any ch-2 corner sp, *[2 dc, ch 1, 2 dc] in ch-2 sp, 1 dc in every dc to next corner; rep from * 3 times, sl st in first sc to join.

Round 12: Ch 3 (counts as 1 tr), ch 1, *[1 tr, ch 3, 1 tr] in corner ch-1 sp, ch 1, 1 tr in next dc, [ch 1, miss 1 st, 1 tr in next dc] 10 times; rep from * 3 times, omitting last tr from last rep. Fasten off yarn D.

Round 13: Join yarn B, ch 1, 1 dc in back lp only of every tr and every ch-st to corner, 3 dc in back lp of centre ch-st of corner ch-3; rep from * 3 times, sl st in first dc to join.

Fasten off and darn in all ends.

13

**

four suns

A twist on an old pattern, this lace square sizes up the stitches from a vintage design and adds frilly edges to bring it up to date. Makes delicate coasters as it is, or group several together for a table linen set to bring out for those special occasions.

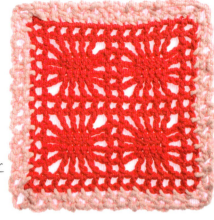

Foundation chain: Using yarn A, ch 29 (counts as 26 sts, 3 tch).

Row 1: 1 tr in 5th ch from hook, *ch 1, miss 1 ch, 1 tr in next ch; rep from * to end of row.

Row 2: Ch 3 (counts as 1 tr, ch 1), miss 1 st, 1 tr in next st, *ch 3, 1 dtr in each of next 4 tr, ch 3, miss 1 st, 1 tr in next st, ch 1, miss 1 st, 1 tr in next st; rep from * 1 time, completing row.

Row 3: Ch 3 (counts as 1 tr, ch 1), miss 1 st, 1 tr in next st, *ch 3, 1 dc in each of next 4 dtr, ch 3, 1 tr in next tr, ch 1, miss 1 st, 1 tr in next st; rep from * 1 time, completing row.

Rows 4 to 5: Ch 3 (counts as 1 tr, ch 1), miss 1 st, 1 tr in next st, *ch 3, 1 dc in each of next 4 dc, ch 3, 1 tr in next tr, ch 1, miss 1 st, 1 tr in next st; rep from * 1 time, completing row.

Row 6: Ch 3 (counts as 1 tr, ch 1) miss 1 st, 1 tr in next st, *ch 1, [1 dtr in next tr, dc ch 1] 4 times, 1 tr in next tr, ch 1, miss 1 st, 1 tr in next st; rep from * 1 time, completing row.

Rows 7 to 12: Rep Rows 1 to 6. Fasten off yarn A.

Row 13: Ch 3 (counts as 1 tr, ch 1), miss 1 st, 1 tr in next st, [ch 1, miss 1 st, 1 tr in next st] to end of row.

Round 14: Using yarn B, insert hook in corner of work, ch 3, miss 1 st, 1 htr in next st, *ch 3, miss 1 st, 1 htr in next st; rep from * around all 4 edges of work, sl st in 2nd ch of beg ch-3 to join.

Round 15: Rep Round 14 from * around all 4 edges of work, but this time working htr in 2nd ch of each ch-3 loop, sl st in first st to join.

Fasten off and darn in ends neatly.

14

*

gentle waves

This lovely, delicately textured square has a simple repeated pattern throughout. Perfect for baby blankets or afghans, it also complements more complex squares.

Foundation chain: Ch 27.

Row 1: Ch 1, 1 dc in 2nd ch from hook and in every ch to end, turn.

Row 2: Ch 2, miss first dc, 1 tr in next dc, *1 dc in next dc, 1 tr in next dc; rep from * to end of row, ending with last tr in top of tch, turn.

Rows 3 to 23: Ch 2, miss first tr, *1 tr in next dc, 1 dc in next tr; rep from * to end, ending with last dc in top of tch, turn.

Row 24: Ch 1, 1 dc in every st to end.

Fasten off and darn in ends neatly.

★★
aspen

A simple star motif in a lacy block, this square would also look great worked in festive colours or in midnight blue and white – a good, medium-weight block for mixing with others or for use in throws and blankets.

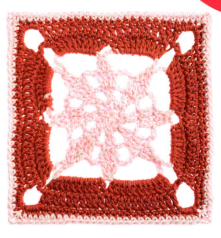

A
B

Special stitches used:

Beginning cluster (beg cl): Ch 2, make cluster with 2 tr (*see page 18*).

Cluster (cl): Make cluster with 3 tr.

Foundation ring: Using yarn A, ch 4, sl st in first ch to form ring.

Round 1: Ch 1, *1 dc in ring, ch 3; rep from * 7 times, 1 dc in ring, ch 1, sl st in first dc to join. Fasten off.

Round 2: Sl st in next ch-3 sp, ch 3 (counts as 1 tr), 1 tr in same ch-3 sp, *ch 2, 2 tr in next ch-3 sp; rep from * 6 times, ch 2, sl st top of beg ch-3 to join.

Round 3: Ch 3 (counts as 1 tr), 1 tr in same st, 2 tr in next st, ch 3 *[2 tr in next st] 2 times, ch 3; rep from * 6 times, sl st in top of beg ch-3 to join.

Round 4: Miss next st, beg cl in next 2 sts, *ch 10, miss next st, cl in next 3 sts; rep from * 6 times, ch 10, sl st in first ch of beg cl to join. Fasten off.

Round 5: Join yarn B in any ch-10 sp, ch 3 (counts as 1 tr), 9 tr in same ch-10 sp, 10 tr in next ch-10 sp, ch 3, *[10 tr in next ch-10 sp] 2 times, ch 3; rep from * 2 times, sl st in top of beg ch-3 to join.

Round 6: Ch 3 (counts as 1 tr), 1 tr in each of next 19 sts, ch 5, *1 tr in each of next 20 sts, ch 5; rep from * 2 times, sl st in top of beg ch-3 to join.

Round 7: Ch 1, 1 dc in each of next 19 sts, *[3 dc, ch 2, 3 dc] in next ch-5 sp, 1 dc in

each of next 20 sts; rep from * 2 times, [3 dc, ch 2, 3 dc] in next ch-5 sp, sl st in first dc to join. Fasten off.

Round 8: Join yarn A in any ch-2 sp, ch 1, *[1 dc, ch 2, 1 dc] in corner ch-2 sp, 1 dc in each st to next corner ch-2 sp; rep from * 3 times, sl st in first dc to join.

Fasten off and darn in ends.

★★
serendipity

Clusters offer this granny-type square a different texture, making it ideal for beginners to increase their skill levels and practise working stitches together.

A
B
C
D

Special stitches used:

Beginning 3-treble-crochet cluster (beg 3-tr cl): Ch 3, make cluster with 2 tr (*see page 20*).

3-treble-crochet cluster (3-tr cl): Make cluster with 3 tr.

Beginning 3-double treble cluster (beg 3-dtr cl): Ch 4, make cluster with 3 dtr.

3-double treble cluster (3-dtr cl): Make cluster with 3 dtr.

Foundation ring: Using yarn A, make a magic ring.

Round 1: Beg 3-tr cl in ring, ch 3, *3-tr cl in ring, ch 3; rep from * 4 times, sl st in top of beg ch-3 to join. Fasten off yarn A.

Round 2: Join yarn B in any ch-3 sp, [beg 3-tr cl, ch 2, 3-tr cl] in same sp, ch 2, *3-tr cl, ch 2, 3-tr cl] in next sp, ch 2; rep from *

4 times, sl st in top of beg ch-3 to join. Fasten off.

Round 3: Join yarn C in any ch-2 sp, [beg 3-dtr cl, ch 4, 3-dtr cl] in same sp (forms corner), ch 2, [3-dtr cl in next sp, ch 2] twice, *[3-dtr cl, ch 4, 3-dtr cl] in next sp (forms corner), ch 2, [3-dtr cl in next sp, ch 2] twice; rep from * 2 times, sl st in top of beg ch-4 to join. Fasten off yarn C.

Round 4: Join yarn D in any ch-2 sp, beg 3-dtr cl, ch 4, 3-dtr cl] in same sp (forms corner), ch 2, [3-dtr cl in next sp, ch 2] 3 times, *[3-dtr cl, ch 4, 3-dtr cl] in next sp (forms corner), ch 2, [3-dtr cl in next sp, ch 2] 3 times; rep from * 2 times, sl st in top of beg ch-4 to join. Fasten off yarn D.

Round 5: Join yarn B in any ch-4 sp, [beg 3-dtr cl, ch 6, 3-dtr cl] in same sp (forms corner), ch 2, [3-dtr cl in next sp, ch 2] 4 times, *[3-dtr cl, ch 6, 3-dtr cl] in next sp (forms corner), ch 2, [3-dtr cl in next sp,

ch 2] 4 times; rep from * 2 times, sl st in top of beg ch-4 to join. Fasten off yarn B.

Round 6: Join yarn C in any ch-6 sp, [beg 3-dtr cl, ch 2, 3-dtr cl, ch 4, 3-dtr cl, ch 2, 3-dtr cl] in same sp (forms corner), ch 2, [3-dtr cl, ch 2, 3-dtr cl, ch 2] in same space 5 times, *[3-dtr cl, ch 2, 3-dtr cl, ch 4, 3-dtr cl, ch 2, 3-dtr cl] in same sp (forms corner), ch 2 [3-dtr cl, ch 2, 3-dtr cl, ch 2, 3-dtr cl] in same sp 5 times; rep from * 2 times, sl st in top of beg ch-4 to join.

Fasten off and darn in ends.

*

bridget

A
B

This bold block was inspired by Op artist Bridget Riley, and its optical effect would work well in a bright, graphic blanket, pillow or throw for a modern interior setting. Using black and white would give a really striking effect: whatever colours you decide to opt for, keep them starkly contrasting.

Note: Carry yarn not currently in use along top of row being worked, so it is hidden in sts and is carried along until you next need it; this eliminates the need to sew in ends and avoids messy joinings.

Foundation ring: Using yarn A, ch 4, sl st in first ch to form ring.

Round 1: Ch 3 (counts as 1 tr), 7 tr in ring, join yarn B, 8 tr in ring, sl st in top of beg ch-3 to join.

Round 2: Ch 3 (counts as 1 tr), 1 tr in same st, 2 tr in each of next 7 tr, join yarn B, 2 tr in each of next 8 tr, sl st in top of beg ch-3 to join.

Round 3: Using yarn A, ch 3 (counts as 1 tr), [2 tr in next tr, 1 tr in next tr] 7 times, 2 tr in next tr, change to yarn B, [1 tr in next tr, 2 tr in next tr] 8 times, sl st in top of beg ch-3 to join.

Round 4: Using yarn A, ch 3 (counts as 1 tr), [2 tr in next tr, 1 tr in each of next 2 tr] 7 times, 2 tr in next tr, 1 tr in next tr, switch to yarn B, [1 tr in next tr, 2 tr in next tr, 1 tr in next tr] 8 times, sl st in top of beg ch-3 to join.

Round 5: Continuing with yarn B, ch 1, 1 dc in same st, 1 dc in each of next 3 tr, *1 htr in each of next 2 tr, 1 tr in each of next 2 tr, [3 tr, ch 2, 3 tr] in next tr (forms corner), 1 tr in next 2 tr, 1 htr in next 2 tr, 1 dc in next 7 tr, 1 htr in each of next 2 tr, 1 tr in each of next 2 tr, [3 tr, ch 2, 3 tr] in next tr (forms corner), 1 tr in each of next 2 tr, 1 htr in each of next 2 tr, 1 dc in each of next 3 tr**, change to yarn A, 1 dc in each of next 4 tr; rep from * to ** 1 time, sl st in first sc to join.

Round 6: Ch 3 (counts as 1 tr), 1 tr in each of next 10 sts, [3 tr, ch 2, 3 tr] in next ch-2 corner sp, 1 tr in each of next 21 sts, [3 tr, ch 2, 3 tr] in next ch-2 corner sp, 1 tr in each of next 10 sts**, switch to yarn A, 1 tr in each of next 11 sts; rep from * to ** 1 time, sl st in top of beg ch-3 to join.

Round 7: Continuing in yarn A, ch 1, 1 dc in each of next 13 tr, [2 dc, ch 1, 2 dc] in next corner ch-2 sp, 1 dc in each of next 27 tr, [2 dc, ch 1, 2 dc] in next corner ch-2 sp, 1 dc in each of next 14 tr**, change to yarn B, rep from * to ** 1 time, sl st in first dc to join.

Fasten off and darn in ends.

**
ruby

A ridged, textural square that is made by alternating front- and back-post stitches, this block is warm and cosy, perfect for winter blankets, especially when worked in jewel tones for extra richness.

A
B
C
D
E

Special stitches used:

Front-post treble crochet (FPtr): Bring hook to front, work in front vertical post of next st, inserting hook from right to left, draw yarn through and work st as usual (*see page 21*).

Back-post treble crochet (BPtr): Bring hook to back, work in back vertical post of next st, inserting hook from left to right, draw yarn through and work st as usual.

Front-post double treble (FPdtr): Yoh 2 times, insert hook through front of st post from right to left, yoh, draw yarn through, [yoh, draw through 2 loops] 3 times.

Back-post half treble crochet (BPhtr): Yoh, insert hook in vertical post of next st at back from right to left, complete htr st as normal.

Foundation ring: Using yarn A, make ring, ch 1.

Round 1: 6 dc in ring, sl st in first dc to join.

Round 2: Ch 1, 2 dc in every dc to end, sl st in first ch to join. Fasten off yarn A.

Round 3: Using yarn B, ch 1, *3 dc in next dc, 1 dc in each of next 2 dc; rep from * 3 times, sl st in top of first ch to join.

Round 4: Ch 1, 1 dc in each dc to end, sl st in first ch to join – 20 dc.

Round 5: Ch 1, 1 dc in next dc, *3 dc in next dc, 1 dc in each of next 4 dc; rep from * 3 times, 1 dc in last 3 dc, sl st in first ch to join.

Round 6: Ch 1, 1 dc in each of next 2 dc, *3 dc in next dc, 1 dc in each of next 6 dc; rep from * 2 times, 3 dc in next dc, 1 dc in each of next 4 dc, sl st in first ch to join. Fasten off yarn B.

Round 7: Join yarn C in 2nd dc of any corner 3 dc group, ch 3 (counts as 1 tr), [1 tr, ch 3, 2 tr] in same sp (forms corner), 1 tr in each of next 8 dc, *[2 tr, ch 3, 2 tr] in 2nd dc of next corner 3 dc group (forms corner), 1 tr in each of next 8 dc; rep from * 3 times, sl st in top of beg ch-3 to join. Fasten off yarn C.

Round 8: Join yarn D in any ch-3 corner sp, ch 3 (counts as 1 tr), [1 tr, ch 3, 2 tr] in same sp (forms corner), 1 BPtr in each of next 12 tr, *[2 tr, ch 3, 2 tr] in next sp (forms corner), 1 BPtr in each of next 12 tr; rep from * 2 times, sl st in top of beg ch-3 to join. Fasten off yarn D.

Round 9: Join yarn E in any ch-3 corner sp, ch 3 (counts as 1 tr), [1 tr, ch 3, 2 tr] in same sp (forms corner), 1 FPtr in each of next 16 tr, *[2 tr, ch 3, 2 tr] in next sp (forms corner), 1 FPtr in each of next 16 tr; rep from * 2 times, sl st in top of beg ch-3 to join. Fasten off yarn E.

Round 10: Join yarn B in any ch-3 corner sp, ch 3 (counts as 1 tr), [1 tr, ch 3, 2 tr] in same sp (forms corner), 1 BPtr in each of next 20 tr, *[2 tr, ch 3, 2 tr] in next sp (forms corner), 1 BPtr in each of next 20 tr; rep from * 2 times, sl st in top of beg ch-3 to join. Fasten off yarn B.

Round 11: Join yarn C in any ch-3 corner sp, ch 3 (counts as 1 tr), [1 tr, ch 3, 2 tr] in same sp (forms corner), 1 FPtr in each of next 4 tr, 1 FPdtr in each of next 16 tr, 1 FPtr in each of next 4 tr, *[2 tr, ch 3, 2 tr] in next sp (forms corner), 1 FPtr in each of next 4 tr, 1 FPdtr in each of next 16 tr, 1 FPtr in each of next 4 tr; rep from * 2 times, sl st in top of beg ch-3 to join. Fasten off yarn C.

Round 12: Join yarn D in any ch-3 corner sp, ch 2 (counts as 1 htr), [1 htr, ch 3, 2 htr] in same sp (forms corner), 1 BPhtr in each of next 28 sts, *[2 htr, ch 3, 2 htr] in next ch-3 sp (forms corner), 1 BPhtr in each of next 28 sts; rep from * 2 times, sl st in top of beg ch-3 to join. Fasten off yarn D.

Round 13: Join yarn C in any ch-3 corner sp, ch 1, 6 dc in same sp (forms corner), 1 BPhtr in each of next 32 sts, *6 dc in next ch-3 sp (forms corner), 1 BPhfr in each of next 32 sts; rep from * 2 times, sl st in top of beg ch-3 to join.

Fasten off and darn in ends.

**

fiesta

A highly textured square that uses the traditional 'blackberry salad' stitch pattern of bobbles and treble crochet. It is effective worked in a single colour but we have changed colour every two rows to accentuate the stitch pattern.

A
B
C
D
E
F

Special stitch used:

Make bobble (MB): Make bobble with 5 tr (*see page 19*).

Foundation chain: Using yarn A, ch 30 (counts as 27 sts, 3 tch), turn.

Row 1: (RS) miss 3 ch (counts as 1 tr), 1 tr in 4th ch from hook and in each ch to end, turn.

Row 2: (WS) Ch 1, 1 dc in next 3 tr, *make bobble (MB), 1 dc in next 3 tr; rep from * to end, 1 dc in top of tch, turn. Change to yarn B.

Row 3: Ch 3 (counts as 1 tr), 1 tr in each st across row to end (do not work in tch), turn.

Row 4: Ch 1, 1 dc in first tr, *MB, 1 dc in next 3 tr; rep from * to last 3 sts, MB, 1 dc in next tr, 1 dc in top of tch, turn. Change to yarn C.

Row 5: Rep Row 3.

Row 6: Rep Row 2.

Row 7: Change to yarn D, rep Row 3.

Row 8: Rep Row 4.

Row 9: Change to yarn B, rep Row 3.

Row 10: Rep Row 2.

Row 11: Change to yarn E, rep Row 3.

Row 12: Rep Row 4.

Row 13: Change to yarn C, rep Row 3.

Row 14: Rep Row 2.

Row 15: Change to yarn A, rep Row 3.

Row 16: Rep Row 4.

Row 17: Change to yarn B, rep Row 3.

Row 18: Rep Row 2.

Row 19: Change to yarn F, rep Row 3.

Fasten off and darn all ends in neatly.

*

juliette

A simple but effective design using pairs of clusters throughout. Worked up in a light, soft wool, this makes a warm, delicate block useful for throws, shawls and baby blankets.

A

Special stitches used:

Beginning cluster (beg cl): Ch 3, make cluster with 2 tr (*see page 18*).

Cluster (cl): Make cluster with 3 tr.

Foundation ring: Ch, sl st in first ch to form ring.

Round 1: Ch 3 (counts as 1 tr), beg cl in ring, ch 5, *cl in ring, ch 2 **, cl in ring, ch 5; rep from * 2 times, and from * to ** 1 time, sl st in 3rd of beg ch-3 to join.

Round 2: Sl st in corner ch-sp, ch 3 (counts as 1 tr), [beg cl, ch 2, cl] in same sp, *ch 2, 3 tr in next ch-2 sp, ch 2**, [cl, ch 2, cl] in next ch-5 sp; rep from * 2 times, then from * to ** 1 time, sl st in top of beg ch-3 to join.

Round 3: Sl st in next ch-2 corner sp, ch 3 (counts as 1 tr), [beg cl, ch 2, cl] in same sp, ch 2, 2 tr in next ch-2 sp,1 tr in each of next 3 tr, 2 tr in next ch-2 sp, ch 2**, [cl, ch 2, cl] in next ch-2 sp; rep from * 2 times, then from * to ** 1 time, sl st in top of beg ch-3 to join.

Round 4: Sl st in corner ch-sp, ch 3 (counts as 1 tr), [beg cl, ch 2, cl] in same sp, *ch 2, 2 tr in next ch-2 sp, 1 tr in each of next 7 tr, 2 tr in next ch-2 sp, ch 2**, [cl, ch 2, cl] in next ch-2 sp; rep from * 2 times, then from * to ** 1 time, sl st in top of beg ch-3 to join.

Round 5: Sl st in corner ch-sp, ch 3 (counts as 1 tr), [beg cl, ch 2, cl] in same sp, *ch 2, 2 tr in next ch-2 sp, 1 tr in each of next 11 tr, 2 tr in next ch-2 sp, ch 2**, [cl, ch 2, cl] in next ch-2 sp; rep from * 2 times, then from * to ** 1 time, sl st in top of beg ch-3 to join.

Round 6: Sl st in corner ch-sp, ch 3 (counts as 1 tr), [beg cl, ch 2, cl] in same sp, *ch 2, 2 tr in next ch-2 sp, 1 tr in each of next 15 tr, 2 tr in next ch-2 sp, ch 2**, [cl, ch 2, cl] in next ch-2 sp; rep from * 2 times, then from * to ** 1 time, sl st in top of beg ch-3 to join.

Round 7: Ch 1, 1 dc in same st, *1 dc in top of cl, 5 dc in corner sp, 1 dc in top of cl, 1 dc in ch-1 sp, 1 dc in each tr st, 1 dc in ch-1 sp; rep from * 3 times, sl st in first sc to join. Fasten off and darn in ends.

*
coconut ice

A delicate texture that is deceptively easy to work. Works really well in children's or babies' blankets, because of its soft drape and warmth.

A
B
C

Foundation chain: Using yarn A, ch 36.

Row 1: *[1 dc, 1 ch, 1 tr] in 3rd ch from hook, miss 2 ch; rep from * to last st, 1 dc in last ch, turn.

Row 2: Ch 1 (counts as 1 dc), miss first dc and next tr, *[1 dc, 1 ch, 1 tr] in next ch 1 sp, miss 1 dc and 1 tr; rep from * to last dc and tch, 1 dc in tch, turn.

Rows 3 to 8: Rep Row 2. Fasten off yarn A.

Rows 9 to 10: Rep Row 2, using yarn B.

Row 11: Rep Row 2, using yarn C.

Rows 12 to 13: Rep Row 2, using yarn B.

Rows 14 to 21: Rep Row 2, using yarn A.

Optional border: Using yarn A, with RS facing, 21 dc around each side of square, 3 dc in each corner sp.

Fasten off and darn in ends neatly.

*
filet stripe

A good introduction to working in filet crochet, this is a very lightweight square that benefits from being worked in a slightly smaller hook size to add firmness to the delicate mesh.

A
B
C

Foundation chain: Using yarn A, ch 31.

Row 1: 1 dc in 2nd ch from hook, 1 dc in every ch to end, turn.

Row 2: Ch 4 (counts as 1 tr, 1 ch), miss 1 dc, 1 tr in next dc, *ch 1, miss 1 dc, 1 tr; rep from * to end of row.

Row 3: Ch 4 (counts as 1 tr, 1 ch), miss 1 tr, [1 tr in next tr, ch 1] to end, 1 tr in 3rd ch of beg ch 4.

Row 4: Rep Row 2. Fasten off yarn A and change to yarn B.

Rows 5 to 7: Rep Row 2. Fasten off yarn B and change to yarn C.

Rows 8 to 10: Rep Row 2. Fasten off yarn C and change to yarn B.

Rows 11 to 13: Rep Row 2. Fasten off yarn B and change to yarn A.

Rows 14 to 16: Rep Row 2.

Row 17: Ch 1, 1 dc in next and every tr and 1 dc in every ch-1 sp to end of row.

Fasten off and darn all ends in neatly.

23

****

vineyard

A gloriously textured block that uses popcorn and lace techniques to evoke delicate wood carvings of traditional caravans or chalets.

A
B
C

Special stitches used:

Beginning popcorn (beg pc): Ch 3, make popcorn with 4 tr (*see page 19*).

Popcorn (pc): Make popcorn with 5 tr.

Foundation ring: Using yarn A, ch 8, sl st in first ch to form ring.

Round 1: Ch 4, 27 dtr in centre ring, sl st in top of beg ch-4 to join. Fasten off, cut yarn and weave in ends.

Round 2: Join yarn B in top of any dtr st, ch 5 (counts as 1 dtr, ch 1), *1 dtr in next st, ch 1; rep from * all around (26 times), sl st in 4th ch of beg ch-5 to join.

Round 3: Sl st in next ch-1 sp, 1 dc in same sp, *[ch 3, 1 dc in next sp] 6 times, ch 7, 1 dc in next ch-1 sp; rep from * all around, ch 3, sl st in first dc to join. Fasten off, cut yarn and weave in ends.

Round 4: Join in yarn C in ch-3 lp just made, beg pc in same loop, ch 2, [pc in next lp, ch 2] 5 times, join in yarn B at top of last pc made, ch 3, [2 tr, ch 3] 2 times in next ch-7 lp, *[join yarn C, pc in next lp, ch 2] 6 times, join yarn B at top of last pc made, ch 3, [2 tr, ch 3] 2 times in next lp; rep from * 2 times, sl st in top of first pc made.

Round 5: Join yarn C in next ch-2 sp along, beg pc in same lp, ch 2, [pc in next lp, ch 2] 4 times, join in yarn B at top of last pc made, ch 5, [2 tr, ch 5] 2 times in next corner lp, *[join yarn C, pc in next lp, ch 2] 5 times, join yarn B at top of last pc made, ch 5, [2 tr, ch 5] 2 times in next corner lp; rep from * 2 times, sl st in top of first pc. Fasten off, cut yarn and weave in ends from Rounds 4 and 5.

Round 6: Join yarn A in any corner sp, *5 dc in corner sp, 1 dc in each of next 2 tr, 5 dc in next ch-5 sp, 1 dc in top of

pc, [1 dc in next ch-2 sp, 1 dc in top of pc] 4 times, 5 dc in next ch-5 sp, 1 dc in each of next 2 tr; rep from * 3 times, sl st in first dc to join.

Round 7: *1 dc in each dc to corner, (1 dc in each of next 2 dc, 3 dc in next st, 1 dc in each of next 2 dc); rep from * 3 times, sl st in first dc to join.

Fasten off and darn in ends. Block work.

24

*

✓

tiny star

This traditional granny square has a tiny central star shape that could be picked out in a contrasting colour to add sparkle to your colour combination. Quick to work up and easy to mix and match.

A
B
C

Foundation ring: Using yarn A, ch 4, sl st in first ch form ring.

Round 1: Ch 3 (counts as 1 tr), *1 tr in ring, ch 1; rep from * 6 times (8 tr and 8 sps), sl st in top of 3rd of 3-ch. Fasten off yarn A.

Round 2: Join yarn B in any ch-1 sp, ch 3, 2 tr in same sp, *ch 1, 3 tr in next ch-1 sp; rep from *6 times, ch 1, sl st in top of 3-ch to join.

Round 3: 2 sl st along to next ch-1 sp, ch 3 (counts as 1 tr), 2 tr in same sp, ch 1 [3 tr, ch 3, 3 tr] in next sp (forms corner), *ch 1, 3 tr in next ch-1 sp, ch 1, [3 tr, ch 3, 3 tr]** in next sp (forms next corner); rep from * to ** 2 times, sl st in top of 3-ch to join. Fasten off yarn B.

Round 4: Join yarn C to any 3-ch corner sp, ch 3 (counts as 1 tr), [2 tr, ch 3, 3 tr] in same sp, *[ch 1, 3 tr] in each ch-1 sp along side of square, ch 1, **[3 tr, ch 3,

3 tr] in next corner sp; rep from * 2 times, then from * to ** 1 time, sl st in top of 3-ch to join.

Round 5: 2 sl st along to next ch-3 sp, ch 3 (counts as 1 tr), [2 tr, ch 3, 3 tr] in same corner sp, *[ch 1, 3 tr] in each ch-1 sp along side of square, ch 1**, [3 tr, ch 3, 3 tr] in next 3-ch corner sp; rep from * 2 times, then from * to ** 1 time, sl st in top of 3-ch to join.

Round 6: 2 sl st along to next ch-3 sp, ch 3 (counts as 1 tr), [2 tr, ch 3, 3 tr] in same corner sp, *[ch 1, 3 tr] in each ch-1 sp along side of square, ch 1, **[3 tr, ch 3, 3 tr] in next 3-ch corner sp; rep from * 2 times and from * to ** 1 time, sl st in top of 3-ch to join.

Round 7: 2 sl st along to next ch-3 sp, ch 3 (counts as 1 tr), [2 tr, ch 3, 3 tr] in same corner sp, *[ch 1, 3 tr] in each ch-1 sp along side of square, ch 1, **[3 tr, ch 3,

3 tr] in next 3-ch corner sp; rep from * 2 times, then from * to ** 1 time, sl st in top of 3-ch to join. Fasten off yarn C.

Round 8: Join yarn A in any 3-ch corner sp, ch 3 (counts as 1 tr), [1 tr, ch 3, 2 tr] in same corner sp, *1 tr in every st each ch-1 sp along side of square, and [2 tr, ch 3, 2 tr] in every corner sp, sl st in top of 2-ch to join.

Fasten off yarn A and darn all ends in neatly.

* * * *

peony

A complex flower with sculpted petals and a tufted centre, inspired by the huge pale pink blooms of spring. This pretty block would work well as a central motif, or make four or nine for a pillow cover.

A
B
C

Foundation ring: Using yarn A, ch 4, sl st in first ch to form ring.

Round 1: Ch 2 (counts as 1 htr), 11 htr in ring, sl st in front lp of top of beg ch-2 to join.

Round 2: [Ch 7, sl st in front lp of next htr] 11 times, ch 7, sl st in back lp of tch from Round 1 to join.

Round 3: [Ch 7, sl st in back lp of next hdc] 11 times, ch 7, sl st in tch from Round 1 to join.

Round 4: Ch 2 (counts as 1 htr), 1 htr in same sp, 2 htr in every htr from Round 1, sl st in front lp of top of beg ch-2 to join.

Round 5: [Ch 7, sl st in front lp of next htr] 23 times, ch 7, sl st in back lp of tch-3 from Round 4 to join.

Round 6: Turn work to back (WS facing), [ch 6, miss 2 sts, 1 htr in back lp of next htr] 8 times, sl st in first ch-6 lp.

Round 7: Still with WS facing, [1 dc, 1 htr, 4 tr, 1 htr, 1 dc] in every ch-6 lp to end of rnd, sl st in back lp of first dc to join, turn work to RS.

Round 8: Working in front lps only of each petal, [1 dc, 1 htr, 4 tr, 1 htr, 1 dc] to end of rnd, sl st in first sc to join. Fasten off yarn A.

Round 9: Join yarn B between petal just completed and next one along, 1 dc in same sp, [ch 6, 1 dc in next sp between petals] 7 times, ch 6, sl st in first dc to join.

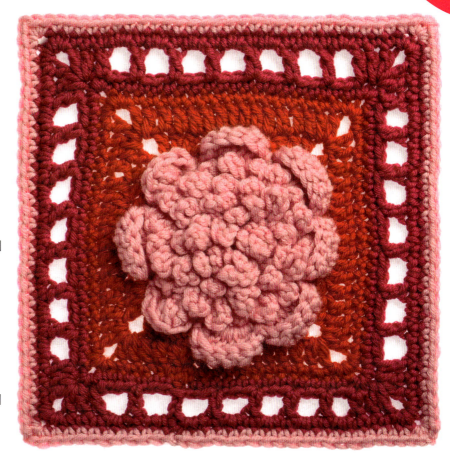

Round 10: Sl st in ch-6 sp, *6 dc in same ch-6 sp, [3 tr, ch 3, 3 tr] in next ch-6 sp; rep from * 3 times, sl st in first sc to join.

Round 11: Ch 3 (counts as 1 tr),1 tr in each of next 8 sts, *[2 tr, ch 3, 2 tr] in corner ch-3 sp**, 1 tr in each of next 12 sts; rep from * 2 times, then from * to ** 1 time, 1 tr in each of next 3 sts, sl st in top of beg ch-3 to join.

Round 12: Ch 1, 1 dc in every st and [2 dc, ch 1, 2 dc] in every corner ch-3 sp all around square, sl st in ch-1 to join. Fasten off yarn B.

Round 13: Join yarn C, rep Round 12, using yarn C.

Round 14: Ch 3 (counts as 1 tr), [ch 2, miss 2 sts, 1 tr in next st] 5 times, *[2 tr, ch 3, 2 tr] in corner ch-1 sp, 1 tr in next st **, [ch 2, miss 2 sts, 1 tr in next st] 7 times; rep from * 2 times and from * to ** 1 time, ch 2, miss 2 sts, 1 tr in next st, ch 2, sl st in top of beg ch-3 to join. Fasten off yarn C.

Round 15: Join yarn D, rep Round 12 using yarn D.

Fasten off and darn in ends neatly.

*

glitter

A simple basic block is embellished with cross stitches to create a more complex-looking square. This is an easy block that would enhance any winter blanket or throw, and is perfect for use in baby blankets.

A
B
B

Foundation chain: Using yarn A, ch 29.

Row 1: 1 dc in 2nd ch from hook, 1 dc in every ch to end, turn.

Rows 2 to 31: Ch 1, 1 dc in every dc to end, turn. Fasten off at the end of Row 31.

BORDER

Round 1: Join yarn C, ch 1, 1 dc in same st, *1 dc in every dc to next corner, [1 dc, ch 1, 1 dc] in corner st, 27 dc along side of square to next corner, [1 dc, ch 1, 1 dc] in next corner; rep from * 1 time, sl st in first dc to join. Fasten off yarn C.

EMBROIDERY

Using a length of yarn B and a darning needle, beginning at bottom RH corner of square RS facing, insert needle in sp 1 st and 1 row in from corner. Work cross stitch over 2 sts and 2 rows. Miss 1 row, bring needle up in row above (to correspond vertically with cross st just made), work another cross st, rep up square until you are 1 row from top of square, rotate work 180 degrees, miss 1 st, and make next row of cross stitches to align with last, down to bottom. Repeat until you have covered square, leaving a sp of 1 row at top and bottom, and 1 st at each side.

Fasten off and darn in ends.

***

flourish

This block features a doily pattern centre and a billowy, frilly flower, making it a bold design suitable for use in a range of blankets, throws and pillows. It's quick to work up, so it's good if you need to create a last-minute gift that belies the time spent on it.

A
B
C
D

Foundation ring: Using yarn A, ch 4, sl st in first ch to form ring.

Round 1: Ch 5 (counts as 1 tr, ch 2), [1 tr, ch 2] 7 times in ring, sl st in 3rd ch of beg ch-5 to join.

Round 2: Ch 3 (counts as 1 tr), 2 tr in same tr, ch 2, *3 tr in next tr, ch 2; rep from * 6 times, sl st in top of beg ch-3.

Round 3: Ch 3 (counts as 1 tr), 1 tr in same st, *1 tr in next tr, 2 tr in next tr, ch 2, 2 tr in next tr; rep from * 6 times, 1 tr in next tr, 2 tr in next tr, ch 2, sl st in top of beg ch-3 to join.

Round 4: Ch 3 (counts as 1 tr), 1 tr in same tr, *1 tr in each of next 3 tr, 2 tr in next tr, ch 2, 1 tr in next tr; rep from * 6 times, 1 tr in each of next 3 tr, 2 tr in next tr, ch 2, sl st in top of beg ch-3 to join. Fasten off yarn A.

Round 5: Join yarn B, ch 1, 1 dc in same st, *ch 6, miss 5 tr, 1 dc in next tr, ch 2, miss 2 ch, 1 dc in next tr; rep from * 6 times, ch 6, miss 5 tr, 1 dc in next tr, ch 2, miss 2 ch, sl st in first dc to join. Fasten off yarn B.

Round 6: Join yarn C into any ch-2 sp, ch 3 (counts as 1 tr), 3 tr in same ch-2 sp, *10 dtr in next ch-6 sp**, 4 tr in next ch-2 sp; rep from * 7 times and from * to ** 1 time, sl st in top of beg ch-3 to join. Fasten off yarn C.

Round 7: (WS) Join yarn D around post of dc from Round 5, ch 3, *1 dc around post of next dc, ch 8, 1 dc around post of next dc, ch 3, 1 dc around post of next dc, ch 6**, 1 dc around post of next dc; rep from * 6 times, and from * to ** 1 time, sl st in first dc to join.

Round 8: (RS) Ch 1, *8 dc in next ch-6 sp, 4 htr in next ch-3 sp, [5 tr, 1 dtr, ch 2, 1 dtr, 5 tr] in next ch-8 sp, 4 htr in next ch-3 sp; rep from * 3 times, sl st in first dc to join. Fasten off yarn D.

Round 9: Join yarn B, *sl st in back lp of next st, ch 1, miss 1 st; rep from * to end, sl st in first sl st to join.

Fasten off and darn in ends.

berry farm

With its little berries and lattices, this block has all the charm of a summer day's fruit picking. The berries are made with the old pineapple stitch techniques and the lattices with crossed double treble stitches. This is an interesting block to make, and it has loads of uses.

A
B
C

Special stitches used:

Pineapple (pn): Insert hook in next st to be worked, yoh, draw through, *yoh, insert hook in same place 2 rows below, yoh, draw through and pull through 2 lps; rep from * 5 times (6 tr with last lp of each unfinished, plus first yoh – 8 lps on hook), yoh, draw through all lps.

Crossed double trebles (crossed dtr): Insert hook behind dtr just worked and work in specified st, complete dtr st as normal.

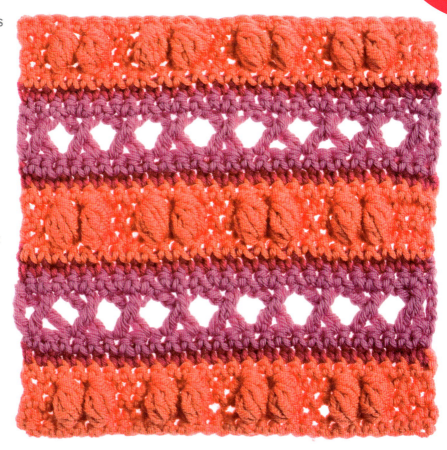

Foundation row: Using yarn A, ch 28.

Row 1: 1 dc in 2nd ch from hook, 1 dc in every ch to end, turn.

Row 2: Ch 1, 1 dc in every dc to end, turn.

Row 3: Rep Row 2.

Row 4: Ch 1, *1 dc in each of next 3 dc, pn in next dc, 1 dc in next dc, pn in next dc; rep from * 3 times, 1 dc in each of last 3 dc, turn.

Row 5: Rep Row 2. Fasten off yarn A.

Row 6: Join yarn B, rep Row 2. Fasten off yarn B.

Row 7: Join yarn C, rep Row 2.

Row 8: Ch 4, miss 2 dc, 1 dtr in next dc, ch 1, 1 crossed dtr behind base of ch-4 in 2nd st to right of last dtr, *ch 1, miss 3 sts, 1 dtr in next st, ch 1, 1 crossed dtr behind last dtr worked, in 2nd st to right of last dtr; rep from * 7 times, 1 dtr in same st as last st, turn.

Row 9: Ch 1, miss 1 st, 1 dc in every st to last 2 sts, miss 1 st, 1 dc in top of ch-4 at beg of row 8, turn. Fasten off yarn C.

Row 10: Rep Row 6.

Rows 11 to 13: Join yarn A, rep Row 2.

Row 14: Rep Row 4.

Row 15: Rep Row 2.

Row 16: Rep Row 6.

Rows 17 to 19: Rep Rows 7 to 9.

Row 20: Rep Row 6.

Rows 21 to 25: Rep Rows 11 to 15.

Fasten off and darn in ends.

29

***

aloha

Full of scallops and popcorns, this square has a flavour of the tropics and feels wonderfully textured to work up. Use bright, vibrant colours to enhance the exotic feel even more.

A
B

Special stitches used:

Beginning popcorn (beg pc): Ch 3, make popcorn with 4 tr (*see page 19*).

Popcorn (pc): Make popcorn with 5 tr.

Foundation ring: Using yarn A, begin with magic ring method.

Round 1: Beg pc in ring, ch 2, *pc in ring, ch 1; rep from * 6 times, sl st in top of beg pc to join.

Round 2: Sl st in first ch-2, beg pc in ch-2, ch 4, *pc in next ch-2, ch 4; rep from * 6 times, sl st in top of beg pc to join.

Round 3: Ch 1, 1 dc in same st, *[1 dc, 1 htr, 3 tr, 1 htr, 1 dc] in ch-4**, 1 dc in top of next pc; rep from * 7 times ending last rep at **, sl st in first dc to join. Fasten off yarn A.

Round 4: With yarn B, sl st in centre of first scallop (2nd tr), ch 1, 1 dc in same st, ch 1, *[1 dtr, ch 3, 1 dtr] in same dc between scallops (first corner), ch 1, 1 dc in 2nd tr of next scallop, ch 1, 1 dtr in dc between scallops, ch 1, **1 dc in 2nd st of next scallop, ch 1; rep from * 3 times ending at **, sl st in first dc to join.

Round 5: Ch 2 (counts as 1 dc), 2 dc in ch-1 sp, *1 dc in dtr, [1 dc, 1 htr, 1 tr, 1 hdtr, 1 dtr, 1 hdtr, 1 tr, 1 htr, 1 dc] in ch-3 sp, 1 dc in dtr, 2 dc in ch-1 sp, 1 dc in dc , 2 dc in ch-1 sp, 1 dc in htr, 2 dc in ch-1 sp, **1 dc in dc , 2 dc in ch-1 sp; rep from * 3 times ending at **, sl st in first ch-2 to join. Fasten off yarn B.

Round 6: Using yarn A, sl st in dc above first dtr at first corner, ch 1, 1 dc in same st, *ch 7, 1 dc to dc above next htr, [ch 3, miss 2 dc, 1 dc in next st] 4 times; rep

from * 3 times but omit last 1 dc in next st of rep, sl st in first dc to join.

Round 7: Ch 1, *[1 dc, 1 htr, 1 tr, 2 hdtr, 2 dtr, 2 hdtr, 1 tr, 1 htr, 1 dc] in ch-7 sp, [5 dc in ch-3 space] 4 times; rep from * 3 times, sl st in beg ch-1 to join.

Fasten off and darn in all ends neatly.

30

**

fandango

This versatile and striking square builds like a jigsaw as it is worked; the interlocking fan shapes create an interesting triangulated pattern that is so much fun to make.

A
B
C
D
E

Foundation ring: Using yarn A, ch 5, join with sl st to form ring, or use magic ring method.

Round 1: Ch 3, (counts as first tr), 15 tr in ring, sl st in top of beg ch-3 to join.

Round 2: Ch 3, 1 tr in sp immediately next to ch-3 (will be tight, which is correct), *ch 2, miss 2 tr, 2 tr in sp between next 2 sts; rep from * 6 times, ch 2, sl st in top of beg ch-3 to join. Fasten off yarn A.

Round 3: Join yarn B in any ch-2 sp, ch 3 (counts as 1 tr), [1 tr, ch 2, 2 tr] in same ch 2 sp, *[2 tr, ch 2, 2 tr] in next ch-2 sp, rep from * 6 times, sl st in top of beg ch-3 to join. Fasten off yarn B.

Round 4: Join yarn C in any ch-2 sp, 3 ch (counts as 1 tr), [2 tr, ch 2, 3 tr] in same ch-2 sp, *1 dc in next sp (not a ch-2 sp, found between cluster groups), [3 tr, ch 2, 3 tr] in next ch-2 sp; rep from * 6 times, sl st in top of beg ch-3 to join.

Round 5: Sl st in next 2 tr along to next ch-2 sp, ch 3 (counts as 1 tr), [2 tr, ch 2, 3 tr] in same ch-2 sp, *ch 3, [3 tr, ch 2, 3 tr] in next ch-2 sp; rep from * 6 times, sl st in top of beg ch-3 to join. Fasten off yarn C.

Round 6: Join yarn D in any ch-2 sp, ch 3 (counts as 1 tr), [3 tr, ch 2, 4 tr] in same ch-2 sp, *[ch 1, 1 dc, ch 1] in next ch-3 sp, [4 tr, ch 2, 4 tr] in next ch-2 sp; rep from * 6 times, sl st in top of beg ch-3 to join. Fasten off yarn D.

Round 7: Join yarn E in any ch-2 sp, ch 3 (counts as 1 tr), [3 tr, ch 2, 4 tr] in same ch-2 sp (forms corner), *[2 dtr, 1 tr, 2 dtr] in top of next dc st, 1 dc in next ch-2 sp, [2 dtr, 1 tr, 2 dtr] in top of next dc, [4 tr, ch 2, 4 tr] in next ch-2 sp (forms 2nd corner); rep from * 2 times, [2 dtr, 1 tr, 2 dtr] in top of next dc, 1 dc in next ch-2 sp, [2 dtr, 1 tr, 2 dtr] in top of last dc, sl st in top of beg ch-3 to join.

Round 8: Ch 1, 1 dc in top of each st and 3 dc in each corner sp to end of rnd, sl st in first dc to join.

Round 9: Ch 1, 1 dc in each dc and 3 dc in centre st in each corner sp to end of rnd, sl st in first dc to join.

Fasten off and darn ends in neatly.

★ ★ ★
confetti

Layers and layers of crocodile stitch petals make this an intriguing and complex square to work, but the results are stunning. Mix with lighter or medium-weight blocks, because this is quite a heavy square.

Special stitches used:

Picot-3: Ch 3 (at point to add picot), sl st in first ch of ch-3, creating picot loop.

10-st crocodile (10-st croc): 5 tr in side post of tr st, picot-3, 5 tr in side post of next tr st (*see page 20*).

6-st crocodile (6-st croc): 3 tr in side post of tr st, picot-3, 3 tr in side post of next tr st.

Bubble stitch (bubble st): With WS facing, [1 dc, 1 dtr, 1 sl st, completing sl st from WS to push bubble to right side of work] in next st.

A
B
C

Foundation chain: Using yarn A, ch 34.

Row 1: Miss 3 ch (counts as first tr), 1 tr in next st, ch 1, 2 tr in next st, *miss next 2 sts, 1 tr in next st, ch 1, miss next 2 sts, 2 tr in next st, ch 1; rep from * 3 times, miss next 2 sts, 2 tr in next st, ch 1.

Row 2: Ch 1, *10-st croc in first 2 tr of last row, sl st in single tr st of last row; rep from * 4 times, 10-st croc in last 2 tr sts of last row, sl st 3rd ch of beg ch-3 of last row.

Row 3: Ch 4 (counts as 1 tr, ch 1), *2 tr in st between two 10-st crocs, ch 1, tr in middle of 10-st croc, ch 1; rep from * to the end of the row.

Row 4: Ch 1, *6-st croc in 2 tr sts of last row, sl st in single tr st of last row; rep from * to end of row, sl st in 3rd ch of beg ch-4 of last row. Fasten off, cut yarn and weave in ends.

Row 5: Join yarn B in st just made, ch 3, 1 tr in same st as ch-3, ch 1, *1 tr in st in middle of 6-st croc, ch 1, 2 tr in st between two 6-st crocs, ch 1; rep from * to end of row ending with 2 tr in top of ch from 2 rows below (Row 3), ch 1.

Row 6: Rep Row 2.

Row 7: Rep Row 3.

Row 8: Rep Row 4. Fasten off, cut yarn and weave in ends.

Row 9: Join yarn C in st just made, rep Row 5.

Row 10: Rep Row 2.

Row 11: (Bubble Row) *Bubble st in same st just finished (middle of 10-st croc), bubble st in st between two 10-st croc sts; rep from * to end of row.

Row 12: Turn to WS, with WS facing, ch 3, 1 tr in same st as ch-3 (in lps behind bubble st in middle of 10-st croc), *ch 1, 1 tr in back lps of next bubble st, ch 1, 2 tr in back lps of next bubble st, ch 1; rep from * to end of last bubble st, sl st in base of tr st just worked.

Row 13: Turn work to RS and rep Row 2 but working sl st in base of single tr, then sl st in base of first tr of 2 tr pairs, so that petals fall in opposite direction. Turn work 180 degrees to access first tr of pair of 2 trs when beg to work croc st. Fasten off, cut yarn and weave in ends.

Row 14: Turn work to WS and join yarn B in top of ch from two rows below (Row 12) in middle of a 10-st croc, ch 4 (counts as 1 tr, ch 1), *2 tr in top of single tr from two rows below (Row 12), ch 1, 1 tr in st in middle of 10-st croc, ch 1; rep from * to end of row, sl st in base of tr st just worked.

Row 15: Turn work to RS, work as Row 4 but again adjusting position of sl sts as given for Row 2, and turning work where necessary. Do not fasten off but cont in same colour.

Row 16: Turn work to WS, ch 3, 1 tr in same st as ch-3, *ch 1, 1 tr in st in middle of 6-st croc, ch 1, 2 tr in single tr, ch 1; rep from * to end of row, sl st in base of tr st just worked.

Row 17: Turn work to RS, rep Row 13. Fasten off, cut yarn and weave in ends.

Rows 18 to 21: Rep Rows 14 to 17 using yarn A. Fasten off, cut yarn and weave in ends.

Block work to make the crocodile stitches lie straight and flatter.

***

squiggle

An unusual, diagonally worked block with an extravagant frill along the centre, this square works well in a group of four to create a frilly diamond effect; rotate the colours for even more impact. Feels as good as it looks!

A
B
C

Foundation chain: Using yarn A, ch 2, 3 dc in 2nd ch from hook, turn – 3 sts.

Row 1: (RS) Ch 1, 2 dc in first dc, 1 dc in next dc, 2 dc in last dc, turn – 5 sts.

Row 2: (WS) Ch 1, 2 dc in first dc, 1 dc in each dc to last dc, 2 dc in last dc – 7 sts.

Rows 3 to 4: Rep Row 2.

Row 5: Ch 1, 1 dc in every dc to end, turn.

Rows 6 to 9: Rep Rows 2 to 5.

Rows 10 to 13: Rep Rows 2 to 5.

Rows 14 to 17: Rep Rows 2 to 5.

Rows 18 to 22: Rep Rows 2 to 5.

Rows 23 to 24: Rep Row 2 – 41 sts by end of Row 24.

MAKE FRILL

Row 1: Using yarn A, and working in Front lp only of each dc, 2 dc in every dc along row, turn.

Row 2: 2 tr in every dc along row. Fasten off yarn A.

Trim: Join yarn C to first tr, sl st in every tr along row. Fasten off yarn C.

Return to completing main block.

Row 27: Join yarn B, working in back lps only of last row of main block made (before frill was constructed), rep Row 5.

Row 28: Ch 1, miss 1 dc, 1 dc in each dc along to last 2 dc; miss 1 dc, 1 dc in last dc, turn.

Rows 29 to 30: Rep Row 28.

Row 31: Rep Row 5.

Rows 32 to 35: Rep Rows 28 to 31.

Rows 36 to 39: Rep Rows 28 to 31

Rows 40 to 43: Rep Rows 28 to 31.

Rows 44 to 47: Rep Rows 28 to 31.

Rows 48 to 51: Rep Rows 28 to 31.

Row 52: Ch 1, miss 1 dc, 1 dc in next 2 dc, miss next dc, 1 dc in next dc.

Row 53: Ch 1, tr3tog. Fasten off yarn B.

Darn in all ends neatly. Block lightly to avoid squashing the frill.

*

traditional granny square

The most recognisable and best-loved of all the traditional crochet squares, the granny square consists of treble crochets and chains and is simple to master. This one-colour version grows quickly and can be easily extended to any size you prefer.

A

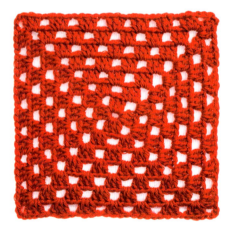

Foundation ring: Ch 6, sl st in first ch to form ring.

Round 1: Ch 3 (counts as 1 tr), 2 tr in centre of ring, [2 ch, 3 tr in ring] 3 times, 2 ch, sl st in 3rd ch of 3-ch to join.

Round 2: Sl st along to centre of next corner, ch-3 sp, ch 6, (counts as 1 tr, 3 ch), 3 tr in same sp, *ch 1, [3 tr, ch 3, 3 tr] in next ch-3 sp (forms corner); rep from * 2 times, ch 1, 2 tr in same sp as you began 6-ch, sl st in 3rd ch of 6-ch to join.

Round 3: Sl st along to centre of next corner ch-3 sp, ch 6 (counts as 1 tr, 3 ch), 3 tr in same sp, *ch 1, 3 tr in next ch-1 sp, ch 1, **[3 tr, ch 3, 3 tr] in next corner ch-3 sp; rep from * 2 times and from * to ** 1 time, 2 tr in same sp as you began 6-ch, sl st in 3rd of 6-ch to join.

Round 4: Sl st along to centre of next corner ch-3 sp, ch 6 (counts as 1 tr, 3 ch), 3 tr in same sp, *ch 1, [3 tr in next ch-1 sp, ch 1] 2 times, **[3 tr, ch 3, 3 tr] in next corner ch-3 sp; rep from * 2 times and from * to ** 1 time, 2 tr in same sp as you began 6-ch, sl st in 3rd ch of 6-ch to join.

Round 5: Sl st along to centre of next corner ch-3 sp, ch 6 (counts as 1 tr, 3 ch), 3 tr in same sp, *ch 1, [3 tr in next ch-1 sp, ch 1] 3 times, **[3 tr, ch 3, 3 tr] in next corner ch-3 sp; rep from * 2 times and from * to ** 1 time, 2 tr in same sp as you began 6-ch, sl st in 3rd of 6-ch to join.

Round 6: Sl st along to centre of next corner ch-3 sp, ch 6 (counts as 1 tr, 3 ch), 3 tr in same sp, *ch 1, [3 tr in next ch-1 sp, ch 1] 4 times, **[3 tr, ch 3, 3 tr] in next corner ch-3 sp; rep from * 2 times and from * to ** 1 time, 2 tr in same sp as you began 6-ch, sl st in 3rd of 6-ch to join.

Round 7: Sl st along to centre of next corner ch-3 sp, ch 6 (counts as 1 tr, 3 ch), 3 tr in same sp, *ch 1, [3 tr in next ch-1 sp, ch 1] 5 times, **[3 tr, ch 3, 3 tr] in next corner ch-3 sp; rep from * 2 times and from * to ** 1 time, 2 tr in same sp as you began 6-ch, sl st in 3rd of 6-ch to join.

Fasten off yarn and darn in ends neatly.

* spanish lace

A pretty pattern based on a vintage lace design, this would be lovely repeated in groups of six as place mats, or as a length of ten joined to create a runner.

A
B

Foundation ring: Using yarn A, ch 8, join with sl st to form ring.

Round 1: Ch 2 (counts as 1 dc), 15 dc in ring, sl st in 2nd ch of beg ch-2 to join.

Round 2: Ch 5 (counts as 1 htr, ch 3), *miss 1 dc, 1 htr in next dc, ch 3; rep from * 6 times, sl st in 2nd chain of beg ch-5 to join.

Round 3: [1 dc, 1 htr, 3 tr, 1 htr, 1 dc] in each ch-sp, sl st in first sc; rep to end of rnd – 8 petals.

Round 4: Ch 2, *ch 3, 1 dc in 2nd tr of next petal, ch 6, 1 dc in 2nd tr of next petal, ch 3, 1 htr in sp before next dc at beg of next petal, ch 3, 1 htr in same sp; rep from * 2 times, ch 3, 1 dc in 2nd tr of next petal, ch 6, 1 dc in 2nd tr of next petal, ch 3, 1 htr in sp before tr at beg of next petal, ch 3, sl st in first ch of beg ch-3 to join.

Round 5: *Ch 4, [3 tr, ch 3, 3 tr] in next ch-6 sp, ch 4, 1 tr in next htr, ch 3, 1 tr in

next htr; rep from * until end of rnd, sl st in first ch of beg ch-4 to join.

Round 6: *Ch 5, 1 tr in each of next 3 tr, ch 5, insert hook in 3rd ch from hook and 1 dc (picot formed), ch 2, 1 tr in each of next 3 tr, ch 5, sl st in next tr, ch 4, insert hook in 3rd ch from hook and 1 dc (picot formed), ch 1, sl st in next tr; rep from * to end of rnd, sl st in first ch of beg ch-5. Fasten off yarn.

Round 7: Using yarn B, *insert hook in any corner picot of the work, 1 dc, ch 6, sl st in first ch after next group of 3 tr (first ch of next ch-4 loop), ch 3, sl st in picot in the middle of work, ch 3, sl st in last ch of next ch-4 lp, (last ch before next group of 3 tr), ch 6, sc in corner picot, ch 1; rep from * around other 3 corners of work.

Round 8: Working around square, 2 dc in corner sp, *6 sc in ch-6 sp, 1 dc in next dc, 3 dc in next ch-3 sp, 1 dc in next dc, 6 dc

in next ch-6 sp**, 3 dc in next corner sp; rep from * 3 times, ending last rep at **; 1 dc in last corner sp, sl st in first dc to join.

Rounds 9 to 10: Working around square, 1 dc in every dc along side and 3 dc in middle dc of corner group of 3 dc, sl st in first dc to join.

Fasten off and darn in ends neatly. Block square.

***

spike clusters

A fun-to-work stitch pattern that produces striking spiky clusters that dip in the rows below. You could vary the number of plain rows between each spike cluster row to add even more interest, but do not work fewer than three rows of plain, or you could try alternating more colours to add even more depth.

A
B

Special stitch used:

Cluster spike stitch (spike cl): Insert hook down one row and two sts to right, draw through to height of current row (2 lps on hook), insert hook down two rows and one st to right, draw through to height of current row (3 lps on hook), insert hook directly below, down three rows, draw through to height of current row (4 lps on hook), insert hook down two rows and one st to left, draw through to height of current row (5 lps on hook), insert hook down one row and two sts to left, draw through to height of current row (6 lps on hook), insert hook in next sc on current row (st due to be worked next if spike cl not worked), draw through lp (7 lps on hook), yoh and draw through all lps on hook.

Foundation chain: Using yarn A, ch 30.

Row 1: 1 dc in 2nd ch from hook, 1 dc in every ch to the end, turn.

Rows 2 to 6: Ch 1, 1 dc in every dc to the end, turn – 29 sts. Fasten off yarn A.

Row 7: Join yarn B, ch 1, 1 dc in each of first 2 dc, *1 spike cl in next dc, 1 dc in next 5 sc; rep from * 4 times; 1 spike cl in next sc, 1 dc in rem 2 dc, turn.

Rows 8 to 12: Ch 1, 1 dc in every dc to end. Fasten off yarn B.

Row 13: Join yarn A, ch 1, 1 dc in each of first 5 dc, *1 spike cl in next dc, 1 dc in next 5 dc; rep from * 4 times, turn.

Rows 14 to 18: Ch 1, 1 dc in every dc to end. Fasten off yarn A.

Row 19: Rep Row 7.

Rows 20 to 24: Ch 1, 1 dc in every dc to end. Fasten off yarn B.

Row 25: Rep Row 13.

Rows 26 to 30: Ch 1, 1 dc in every dc to end. Fasten off yarn A.

Row 31: Rep Row 7.

Rows 32 to 35: Ch 1, 1 dc in every dc to end.

Fasten off and darn in ends neatly.

★★★
filet dot

This circular filet lace motif would look stylish repeated over a curtain in a strong primary hue, as we have done here: perfect for a modern interior with a vintage twist. Alternatively, try repeating it for a lightweight bedspread or throw.

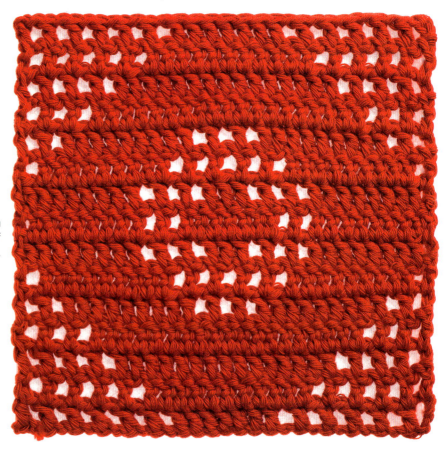

Foundation chain: Ch 31.

Row 1: Ch 3 (counts as 1 tr, ch 1), miss 1 ch, 1 tr in next ch, *ch 1, miss 1 ch, 1 tr in next ch**; rep from * to ** 4 times, 1 tr in each of next 6 ch; rep from * to ** to end of row, turn – 15 filet squares, with squares 7, 8 and 9 filled.

Row 2: Ch 3 (counts as 1 tr, ch 1), miss 1 st, 1 tr in next st, *ch 1, miss 1 st, 1 tr in next st **; rep from * to ** 3 times, 1 tr in each of next 10 sts, rep from * to ** to end of row, turn.

Row 3: Ch 3 (counts as 1 tr, ch 1), miss 1 st, 1 tr in next st, *ch 1, miss 1 st, 1 tr in next st **; rep from * to ** 2 times, 1 tr in each of next 14 sts; rep from * to ** to end of row, turn.

Row 4: Ch 3 (counts as 1 tr, ch 1), miss 1 st, 1 tr in next st, *ch 1, miss 1 st, 1 tr in next st, ch 1, miss 1 st, 1 tr in each of next 19 sts, [ch 1, miss 1 st, 1 tr in next st] 2 times, ch 1, miss 1 st, 1 tr in last st, turn.

Row 5: Ch 3 (counts as 1 tr, ch 1), miss 1 st, 1 tr in next st, ch 1, miss 1 st, 1 tr in next st, 1 tr in each of next 8 sts, [ch 1, miss 1 st, 1 tr in next st] 2 times, ch 1, miss 1 st, 1 tr in each of next 9 sts, ch 1, miss 1 st, 1 tr in next st, ch 1, miss 1 st, 1 dc in last st, turn.

Row 6: Ch 3 (counts as 1 tr), 1 tr in each of next 10 sts, *ch 1, miss 1 st, 1 tr in next st; rep from * 4 times, 1 tr in each of next 10 sts, ch 1, miss 1 st, 1 tr in last st, turn.

Row 7: Ch 3 (counts as 1 tr), 1 tr in each of next 8 tr, [ch 1, miss 1 st, 1 tr in next st] 2 times, ch 1, miss 1 st, 1 tr in each of next 3 sts, [ch 1, miss 1 st, 1 tr in next st] 2 times, ch 1, miss 1 st, 1 tr in each of next 9 sts, turn.

Row 8: Ch 3 (counts as 1 tr), 1 tr in each of next 8 sts, ch 1, miss 1 st, 1 tr in next st, ch 1, miss 1 st, 1 tr in each of next 7 tr, ch 1, miss 1 st, 1 tr in next st, ch 1, miss 1 st, 1 tr in each of next 9 sts, turn.

Row 9: Rep Row 7.

Row 10: Rep Row 6.

Row 11: Rep Row 5.

Row 12: Rep Row 4.

Row 13: Rep Row 3.

Row 14: Rep Row 2.

Row 15: Rep Row 1.

Fasten off and darn in ends neatly.

★★★★
fluted flower

A complex but beautifully textured square, this is an update on a classic floral motif that flutes in gentle pleats as it is made.

Foundation ring: Using yarn A, ch 6, join with sl st to form ring.

Round 1: Ch 3 (counts as 1 tr), 17 tr in ring, sl st in top of ch-3 to join. Fasten off yarn A.

Round 2: Join yarn B, ch 8 (counts as 1 tr, ch 5), [1 tr in next tr, ch 5] 17 times, sl st in 3rd of 8-ch to join. Fasten off yarn B.

Round 3: Join yarn C, *1 dc in each of next ch 2, [1 dc, ch 1, 1 dc] in next ch, 1 dc in each of next ch 2, miss 1 tr; rep from * 17 times.

Round 4: 1 dc in next 3 dc, *[1 sc, ch 1, 1 dc] in next ch-1 sp, 1 dc in next 5 dc; rep from * 16 times, [1 dc, ch 1, 1 dc] in next ch-1 sp, 1 dc in next 2 dc.

Round 5: 1 dc in next 4 dc, *[1 dc, ch 1, 1 dc] in next ch-1 sp, 1 dc in next 6 dc; rep from * 16 times, [1 dc, ch 1, 1 dc] in next ch-1 sp, 1 dc in next 2 dc.

Round 6: 1 dc in next 5 dc, *[1 dc, ch 1, 1 dc] in next ch-1 sp, 1 dc in next 7 dc; rep from * 16 times, [1 dc, ch 1, 1 dc] in next ch-1 sp, 1 dc in next 2 dc.

Round 7: *Ch 5, 1 dc in 4th dc of next 7-dc group (above tr missed in Round 3); rep from * 16 times, ch 5, sl st in base of first ch-5. Fasten off yarn C.

Round 8: Join yarn D in any ch-5 lp, 2 dc in same ch-5 lp, 2 htr in same lp, ch 1, 3 tr in next ch-5 lp, ch 1, [3 tr, ch 2, 3 tr] in next ch-5 lp (forms corner), ch 1, [3 tr, 1 htr] in next ch-5 lp, ch 1, [1 htr, 4 dc, 1 htr] in next ch-5 lp, ch 1, [1 htr, 3 tr] in next ch-5 lp, ch 1, [3 tr, ch 2, 3 tr] in next ch-5 lp (forms 2nd corner), ch 1, 3 tr in next ch-5 lp, ch 1, [2 htr, 2 dc] in next ch-5 lp, ch 1, [2 dc, 2 htr] in next ch-5 lp, ch 1, 3 tr in next ch-5 lp, ch 1, [3 tr, ch 2, 3 tr] in next ch-5 lp (forms 3rd corner), ch 1, [3 tr, 1 htr] in next ch-5 lp, ch 1, [1 htr, 4 dc, 1 htr] in next ch-5 lp, ch 1, [1 htr, 3 tr] in next ch-5 lp, ch 1, [3 tr, ch 2, 3 tr] in next ch-5 lp (forms last corner), ch 1, 3 tr in next ch-5 lp, ch 1, [2 htr, 2 dc] in last ch-5 lp, ch 1, sl st in first dc to join.

Round 9: Ch 1, working one st in top of each st below and one st in each ch-1 sp, work as foll: 4 dc, 2 htr, 6 tr, [3 tr, ch 2, 3 tr] in ch-2 corner sp (first corner), 4 tr, 3 htr, 8 dc, 3 htr, 5 tr (first side), [3 tr, ch 2, 3 tr] in next ch-2 corner sp (2nd corner), 5 tr, 2 htr, 8 dc, 2 htr, 6 tr (2nd side), [3 tr, ch 2, 3 tr] in ch-2 corner sp (3rd corner), 4 tr, 3 htr, 8 dc, 3 htr, 5 tr (3rd side), [3 tr, ch 2, 3 tr] in ch-2 corner sp (4th corner), 5 tr, 2 htr, 4 dc (4th side), sl st in first dc to join.

Round 10: 1 dc in every st along side of motif, [2 dc, ch 2, 2 dc] in every ch-2 corner sp, sl st in first dc to join. Fasten off.

38 * hearth rug

This super-chunky textured square imitates the knitted rib fabrics of cosy winter jumpers, evoking thoughts of toasting marshmallows by the fireside. Easy to work, it's thick and heavy, useful for floor coverings and table mats, or as a highlight square with medium-weight squares around it.

A
B
C

Special stitches used:

Front-post treble crochet (FPtr): Bring hook to front, work in front vertical post of next st, inserting hook from right to left, draw yarn through and work st as usual (*see page 21*).

Back-post treble crochet (BPtr): Bring hook to back, work in back vertical post of next st, inserting hook from left to right, draw yarn through and work st as usual (*see page 21*).

Foundation chain: Ch 40, turn.

Row 1: Miss 3 ch, 1 tr in next ch and every ch to end, turn.

Row 2: Ch 2, (counts as 1 tr), *1 FPtr in next tr, 1 BPtr in next tr; rep from * to end, ending with 1 tr in tch, turn.

Row 3: Ch 2 (counts as 1 tr), *1 BPtr in next tr, 1 FPtr in next tr; rep from * to end, ending with 1 tr in tch, turn.

Row 4 and all even-numbered rows: Rep Row 2, foll colour sequence as below:

Row 5 and all odd-numbered rows: Rep Row 3, foll colour sequence as below:

Rows 6 to 7: Use yarn B.

Row 8: Use yarn C.

Rows 9 to 10: Use yarn B.

Row 11: Use yarn A.

Rows 12 to 13: Use yarn B.

Row 14: Use yarn C.

Rows 15 to 16: Use yarn B.

Rows 17 to 21: Use yarn A.

Fasten off and darn all ends in neatly. When blocking, maintain the rib texture; do not stretch out the fabric so much that it loses elasticity. The block should be square.

39 ★★★★ kilim

A colourwork square with a complex design, worked entirely in double crochet, using the intarsia method of changing colour (see page 17 in Techniques section for details). Rich colours maintain the vivid tones of the Middle Eastern carpets which inspired this design.

A
B
C
D
E

Notes: Beg at bottom RH corner of chart, work 32 rows of chart in dc. When foll chart, read odd-numbered rows (RS rows) from right to left, and even-numbered rows (WS rows) from left to right. Use a separate ball or length of yarn for each area of colour; change colours where indicated. Keep all yarn ends at back (WS) of work.

When changing colours, if gap between where yarn is located in last row and where it is needed on current row is more than two stitches apart, fasten off yarn and join in a new ball or length to avoid long floats on back of work.

Foundation chain: Using yarn A, ch 32 (counts as 31 sts, 1 tch), turn.

Begin chart as follows:

Row 1: (RS) 1 dc in 2nd ch from hook and in each ch to end, turn – 31 sts.

Rows 2 to 32: Ch1, 1 dc in every dc, turn.

At the end of the chart, fasten off yarns and darn in all ends neatly.

**

little knop

Little chain loops make tiny bobbly rings on this square; ensure the yarn that you choose for the knop rings contrasts strongly with the background stripes to show the texture off to full advantage.

A
B
C
D

Special stitch used:

Knop: Ch 5, sl st in sc just worked to form ring. Cont along row as usual. On foll row, when working over knops, ensure you work in dc/sl st instead of in first ch of ch-5 lp.

Foundation chain: Using yarn A, ch 31.

Row 1: 1 htr in 3rd ch from hook, 1 htr in every ch to end of row, turn.

Row 2: Ch 2 (counts as 1 htr), 1 htr in every htr along row, ending with last htr in top of turning chain from Row 1. Fasten off yarn A.

Row 3: Join yarn B, ch 1, 1 dc in each of next 4 htr, *[ch 5, sl st in same dc, 1 dc in each of next 5 htr]; rep from * to end, ending with last dc in tch-2. Fasten off yarn B.

Row 4: Join yarn C, rep Row 2, being careful to work htr in dc sts and not in first ch of ch-5 lps. Bend knops over to back of work to help you access dc to left of knop.

Rows 5 to 6: Rep Row 2. Fasten off yarn C.

Row 7: Join yarn B, rep Row 3. Fasten off yarn B.

Row 8: Join yarn D, rep row 4.

Rows 9 to 10: Rep Row 2. Fasten off yarn D.

Row 11: Join yarn B, rep Row 3. Fasten off yarn B.

Row 12: Join yarn A, rep Row 4.

Rows 13 to 14: Rep Row 2. Fasten off yarn A.

Row 15: Join yarn B, rep Row 3. Fasten off yarn B.

Row 16: Join yarn C, rep Row 4.

Rows 17 to 18: Rep Row 2. Fasten off yarn C.

Row 19: Join yarn B, rep Row 3. Fasten off yarn B.

Row 20: Join yarn D, rep Row 4.

Row 21: Rep Row 2.

Fasten off and darn all ends in neatly.

**

home fires

Four smaller mitred squares are arranged together to form a larger square featuring a central cross through their striped tones. Using a pair of darker colours, then a pair of lighter ones accentuates the shadow effect.

A
B
C
D

Special stitch used:

Double crochet 3 stitches together (dc3tog): Insert hook, yoh, insert hook in next st, yoh, insert hook in next st, yoh, draw through all loops on hook, decreasing 2 sts.

Foundation chain: Using yarn A, ch 28.

Row 1: 1 dc in 2nd ch from hook, 1 dc in each ch to end, turn.

Row 2: Ch 1, 1 dc in each of next 12 dc, dc3tog, 1 dc in each of next 12 dc, turn. Fasten off yarn A, join yarn B.

Row 3: Ch 1, 1 dc in each of next 11 dc, dc3tog, 1 dc in each of next 11 dc, turn.

Row 4: Ch 1, 1 dc in each of next 10 dc, dc3tog, 1 dc in each of next 10 dc, turn. Fasten off. Join yarn C.

Row 5: Ch 1, 1 dc in each of next 9 dc, dc3tog, 1 dc in each of next 9 dc, turn. Fasten off yarn B, join yarn C.

Row 6: Ch 1, 1 dc in each of next 8 dc, dc3tog, 1 dc in each of next 8 dc, turn.

Row 7: Ch 1, 1 dc in each of next 7 dc, dc3tog, 1 dc in each of next 7 dc, turn.

Row 8: Ch 1, 1 dc in each of next 6 dc, dc3tog, 1 dc in each of next 6 dc, turn. Fasten off. Join yarn D.

Row 9: Ch 1, 1 dc in each of next 5 dc, dc3tog, 1 dc in each of next 5 dc, turn. Fasten off yarn C, join yarn D.

Row 10: Ch 1, 1 dc in each of next 4 dc, dc3tog, 1 dc in each of next 4 dc, turn.

Row 11: Ch 1, 1 dc in each of next 3 dc, dc3tog, 1 dc in each of next 3 dc, turn.

Row 12: Ch1, 1 dc in each of next 2 dc, dc3tog, 1 dc in each of next 2 dc, turn.

Row 13: Ch1, 1 dc in next dc, dc3tog, 1 dc in next dc, turn.

Row 14: Dc3tog.

Fasten off yarn and darn in all ends neatly.

Make 3 more squares in exactly the same way. Arrange them in a cross formation as shown, or as you prefer, and join them using either 1 dc worked in every st along, worked in appropriately coloured yarn, or by slip stitching with a darning needle.

*
thermal

Worked almost entirely in half treble crochets, this beginner block has plenty of rounds, allowing scope for creative colour play. Here, we have contrasted warm and cold colours, but you could also have fun with lights and darks.

A
B
C
D
E
F
G
H
I
J

Foundation ring: Using yarn A, make a magic circle, ch 1 to join.

Round 1: 12 dc in ring, sl st in first dc to join.

Round 2: Ch 3 (counts as 1 tr), 1 tr in same st, 2 tr in each dc, sl st in first tr to join. Fasten off.

Round 3: Join yarn B, ch 7 (counts as 1 tr, ch 4), 1 tr in same sp (forms corner), 1 tr in each of next 5 tr, *[1 tr, ch 4, 1 tr] in next st (forms corner), 1 tr in each of next 5 sts; rep from * 2 times, sl st in 3rd ch of beg ch-7 to join. Fasten off.

Round 4: Join yarn C in any ch-4 sp, ch 2 (counts as 1 htr), [1 htr, ch 2, 2 htr] in same st (forms corner), 1 htr in each of next 7 tr, *[2 htr, ch 2, 2 htr] in same sp (forms corner), 1 htr in each of next 7 tr; rep from * 2 times, sl st in top of beg ch-2 to join. Fasten off.

Round 5: Join yarn D in any ch-2 sp, ch 2 (counts as 1 htr), [1 htr, ch 2, 2 htr] in same sp (forms corner), miss 1 htr, 1 htr in each of next 10 htr, *[2 htr, ch 2, 2 htr] in same sp (forms corner), miss 1 htr, 1 htr in each of next 10 htr; rep from * 2 times, sl st in top of beg ch-2 to join. Fasten off.

Round 6: Join yarn E in any ch-2 sp, ch 2 (counts as 1 htr), [1 htr, ch 2, 2 htr] in same sp (forms corner), miss 1 htr, 1 htr in each of next 13 htr, *[2 htr, ch 2, 2 htr] in same sp (forms corner), miss 1 htr, 1 htr in each of next 13 htr; rep from * 2 times, sl st in top of beg ch-2 to join. Fasten off.

Round 7: Join yarn F in any ch-2 sp, ch 2 (counts as 1 htr), [1 htr, ch 2, 2 htr] in same sp (forms corner), miss 1 htr, 1 htr in each of next 16 htr, *[2 htr, ch 2, 2 htr] in same sp (forms corner), miss 1 htr, 1 htr in each of next 16 htr; rep from * 2 times, sl st in top of beg ch-2 to join. Fasten off.

Round 8: Join yarn G join in any ch-2 sp, ch 2 (counts as 1 htr), [1 htr, ch 2, 2 htr] in same sp (forms corner), miss 1 htr, 1 htr in each of next 19 htr, *[2 htr, ch 2, 2 htr] in same sp (forms corner), miss 1 htr, 1 htr in each of next 19 htr; rep from * 2 times, sl st in top of beg ch-2 to join. Fasten off.

Round 9: Join yarn H in any ch-2 sp, ch 2 (counts as 1 htr), [1 htr, ch 2, 2 htr] in same sp (forms corner), miss 1 htr, 1 htr in each of next 22 htr, *[2 htr, ch 2, 2 htr] in same sp (forms corner), miss 1 htr, 1 htr in each of next 22 htr; rep from * 2 times, sl st in top of beg ch-2 to join. Fasten off.

Round 10: Join yarn I in any ch-2 sp, ch 2 (counts as 1 htr), [1 htr, ch 2, 2 htr] in same sp (forms corner), miss 1 htr, 1 htr in each of next 25 htr, *[2 htr, ch 2, 2 htr] in same sp (forms corner), miss 1 htr, 1 htr in each of next 25 htr; rep from * 2 times, sl st in top of beg ch-2 to join. Fasten off.

Round 11: Join yarn J in any ch-2 sp, ch 1, *[2 dc, ch 2, 2 dc] in same sp (forms corner), miss 1 htr, 1 dc in each of next 28 htr; rep from * 3 times, sl st in first dc to join.

Fasten off and darn in ends neatly.

*
double granny

A bolder version of the striped granny block, this simple square is fast to work up and is equally effective in toning shades or bright primaries. Multiple blocks can be rotated and pieced together to form an intricate striped design.

A
B
C
D

Foundation chain: Using yarn A, ch 28.

Row 1: 1 tr in 3rd ch from hook, 1 tr in every ch to end, turn.

Row 2: Ch 3 (counts as 1 tr), 1 tr in same sp, [miss 2 ch, 3 tr in next ch] 8 times, 1 tr in last ch, turn.

Row 3: Ch 3 (counts as 1 tr), 1 tr in same sp, [3 tr in each ch sp] 8 times, 1 tr in last ch, turn. Fasten off yarn A.

Rounds 4 to 5: Join yarn B. Rep Row 3, turn. Fasten off yarn B.

Rounds 6 to 7: Join yarn C, rep Row 3. Fasten off yarn C.

Rounds 8 to 9: Join yarn D, rep Row 3. Fasten off yarn D.

Rounds 10 to 11: Join yarn C, rep Row 3. Fasten off yarn C.

Rounds 12 to 13: Join yarn B, rep Row 3. Fasten off yarn B.

Rounds 14 to 15: Join yarn A, rep Row 3. Turn.

Round 16: Ch 3 (counts as 1 tr), 1 tr in each dc to the end.

Fasten off and darn all ends in neatly.

***
flag

An advanced level square of solid colours, worked entirely in double crochet, using a separate ball of yarn for each colour area. Use similar tones, as we have here, to create depth or starkly contrasting colours for a patchwork effect.

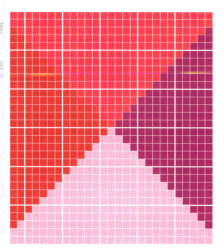

A
B
C
D

Note: Beg at bottom RH corner of chart, work 30 rows of chart in dc. When foll chart, read odd-numbered (RS) rows from right to left, and even-numbered (WS) from left to right. Use a separate ball or length of yarn for each area of colour; change colours where indicated. Keep all yarn ends at back (WS) of work.

Foundation chain: Using yarn A, ch 28 (counts as 27 sts, 1 tch), turn.

Begin chart as follows:

Row 1: (RS) 1 dc in 2nd ch from hook and in each ch to end, turn – 27 sts.

Rows 2 to 30: Ch 1, 1 dc in every dc, turn.

Border: With RS facing, join C to top RH corner, [1 dc, ch 1, 1 dc] in corner, 1 dc in every st along top of square, [1 dc, ch 1, 1 dc] in next corner, 28 dc evenly along side of square, [1 dc, ch 1, 1 dc] in next corner, 1 dc in every ch st along bottom of square, [1 dc, ch 1, 1 dc] in last corner, 28 dc evenly along last side of square, sl st in first dc to join.

Fasten off yarns and darn in all ends neatly.

45

**

diagonal stripe

A basic diagonally constructed square that increases and decreases to form its shape. Using tonal colours as we have here gives a subtle effect; you could use contrasting brights for a starker feel.

Foundation chain: Using yarn A, ch 2, 3 dc in 2nd ch from hook, turn.

Row 1: Ch 1, 2 dc in first dc, 1 dc in next dc, 2 dc in last dc, turn – 5 sts.

Row 2: Ch 1, 2 dc in first dc, 1 dc in each dc to last dc, 2 dc in last dc – 7 sts.

Rows 3 to 4: Rep Row 2.

Row 5: Ch 1, 1 dc in every dc to end, turn.

Rows 6 to 9: Rep Rows 2 to 5. Fasten off yarn A.

Rows 10 to 13: Using yarn B, rep Rows 2 to 5.

Rows 14 to 17: Rep Rows 2 to 5. Fasten off yarn B.

Rows 18 to 22: Using yarn C, rep Rows 2 to 5.

Rows 23 to 24: Rep Row 2 to 41 sts by end of Row 24. Fasten off yarn C.

Row 25: Join yarn D, rep Row 5.

Row 26: Ch 1, miss 1 dc, 1 dc in each dc along to last 2 dc, miss 1 dc, 1 dc in last dc, turn.

Rows 27 to 28: Rep Row 26.

Row 29: Rep Row 5.

Rows 30 to 32: Rep Rows 26 to 28. Fasten off yarn D, join yarn E.

Row 33: Rep Row 29.

Rows 34 to 37: Rep Rows 26 to 29.

Rows 38 to 41: Rep Rows 26 to 29.

Row 42: Rep Row 26. Fasten off yarn E, join yarn F.

Rows 43 to 45: Rep Rows 27 to 29.

Rows 46 to 49: Rep Rows 26 to 29.

Row 50: Ch 1, miss 1 dc, 1 dc in next 2 dc, miss next dc, 1 dc in next dc.

Row 51: Ch 1, tr3tog.

Fasten off and darn in all ends. Block square to straighten edges, if necessary.

46

**

dog rose

Named after the pretty shrub, this medium-weight lacy square works up fast and lends itself to a variety of potential colour combinations and a wide range of uses. Pale roses, vivid roses – they would all work well in this pattern. You could create a whole rose garden!

Foundation ring: Using yarn A, ch 6, join with sl st to form ring.

Round 1: Ch 1, 16 dc in ring, sl st in first dc to join.

Round 2: Ch 6 (counts as 1 tr, ch 3), miss 2 dc, [1 tr in next dc, ch 3, miss 1 dc] 7 times, sl st to join. Fasten off yarn A, join yarn B.

Round 3: Ch 1, [1 dc, 1 htr, 3 tr, 1 htr, 1 dc] in same sp, *[1 dc, 1 htr, 3 tr, 1 htr, 1 dc] in next ch-3 sp; rep from * 6 times, sl st in first dc to join.

Round 4: Ch 1, 1 dc in same sp, ch 6, [1 dc between next 2 dc, ch 6] 7 times, sl st in first dc to join.

Round 5: Ch 1, [1 dc, 1 htr, 5 tr, 1 htr, 1 dc] in same sp, *[1 dc, 1 htr, 5 tr, 1 htr, 1 dc] in next ch-6 sp; rep from * 6 times, sl st in first dc to join. Fasten off yarn B.

Round 6: Join yarn C to 2nd tr of any petal, ch 1, 1 dc in same sp, ch 6, miss 2 tr, 1 dc in next tr, [ch 6, 1 dc in 2nd tr of next petal, ch 6, miss 2 tr, 1 tr in next tr] 7 times, sl st in first dc to join.

Round 7: Sl st in next ch-6 sp, ch 3 (counts as 1 tr), [3 tr, ch 4, 4 tr] in same sp, *ch 4, 1 dc in next ch-6 sp, [ch 6, 1 dc in next ch-6 sp] 2 times, ch 4**, [4 tr, ch 4, 4 tr] in next ch-6 sp; rep from * 2 times, then from * to ** 1 time, sl st in top of beg ch-3 to join.

Round 8: Ch 3 (counts as 1 tr), 1 tr in each of next 3 tr, *[3 tr, ch 3, 3 tr] in corner sp, 1 tr in each of next 4 tr, (ch 1, 3 tr in next ch-6 sp) 4 times, ch 1**, 1 tr in each of next 4 tr; rep from * 2 times and from * to ** 1 time, sl st to top of beg ch-3 to join.

Fasten off and darn ends in neatly.

* * *

ammonite

Four individual patches make up this block, each with a spiral shell within. This square takes a little concentration but the results are worth it. A great block for use in ocean-themed afghans or baby blankets.

A
B
C
D
E

Foundation ring: Using yarn A, begin with magic ring method.

Round 1: Ch 1, [3 dc, 4 htr, 5 tr] in ring. Pull tail to close.

Round 2: Working in top of every st of rnd below, 1 tr, [2 tr in next st] 3 times, [2 hdtr in next st] 3 times, [2 dtr in next st] 3 times, [3 ttr in next stitch] 2 times (spiral shell made). Fasten off yarn A and join yarn B.

Round 3: 1 ttr in same sp as last ttr made, 1 dtr in same sp, [1 tr in next st] 4 times, [3 tr, ch 1, 3 tr] in next st (forms corner), [1 tr in next st, 2 tr in next st] 2 times, 1 hdtr in next st, [3 hdtr, ch 1, 3 hdtr] in next st (forms 2nd corner), 1 hdtr in next st, 2 tr in next st, 1 tr in next st, 2 tr in next

st, 1 hdtr in next st, [3 hdtr, ch 1, 3 hdtr] in next st (forms 3rd corner), 1 hdtr in next st, 1 tr in each of next 2 sts, 2 htr in next st, 1 htr in each of next 2 sts, [3 htr, ch 1, 3 htr] in next st (forms last corner), 1 dc in last rem st, sl st in first ttr to join.

Fasten off and darn in ends.

Make one more patch exactly the same, using yarns A and B, and another two using yarn C (for A) and yarn D (for B).

Block all patches before joining.

Arrange patches as you prefer; we have placed ours in a spiral arrangement. Using yarn E, place two patches tog, RS tog, and work along one join in dc, working through all four lps at a time (in foll st of each

patch). Once you reach the end of the join, place a third patch RS tog and cont along adjoining join to end (L-shaped join completed). Now attach other patch using another L-shaped join in same way.

Fasten off and darn in ends. Re-block square if necessary.

* *

bobble frame

Bobbles frame a plain centre, creating a bold pattern that works well when used in repeat over a larger piece such as a bedspread or an afghan.

A

Special stitch used:

Make bobble (MB): Make bobble with 5 tr (see page 19).

Foundation chain: Ch 30 (counts as 29 ch, 1 tch).

Row 1: 1 dc in 2nd ch from hook,1 dc in every ch along row, turn – 29 sts.

Row 2: Ch 1, 1 dc in every dc to end.

Row 3: 1 dc in each of next 2 dc, MB in next st, [1 dc in each of next 3 dc, MB] 5 times, 1 dc in each of rem 2 dc, turn.

Rows 4 to 6: Rep Row 2.

Row 7: Rep Row 3.

Rows 8 to 10: Rep Row 2.

Row 11: 1 dc in each of next 2 dc, MB in next st, 1 dc in each of next 3 dc, MB, 1 dc in each of next 15 dc, MB, 1 dc in each of next 3 dc, MB, 1 dc in each of last 2 dc, turn.

Rows 12 to 14: Rep Row 2.

Row 15: Rep Row 11.

Rows 16 to 18: Rep Row 2.

Row 19: Rep Row 11.

Rows 20 to 22: Rep Row 2.

Row 23: Rep Row 11.

Rows 24 to 26: Rep Row 2.

Row 27: Rep Row 3.

Rows 28 to 30: Rep Row 2.

Row 31: Rep Row 3.

Rows 32 to 33: Rep Row 2.

Fasten off, darn in all ends neatly and block square.

★★★

sevilla

A complex block with a lace fan pattern at its heart, this square has all the flourish of the flamenco. Created in warm tones to echo its inspiration, it would work well in a variety of uses, including pretty throws and scarves, lighter blankets and table linens.

A
B
C
D
E

Foundation ring: Using yarn A, ch 4, sl st in first ch to form ring.

Round 1: Ch 1, 12 dc in ring, sl st in first dc to join.

Round 2: Join yarn B in any dc st, ch 3 (counts as 1 tr), [ch 1, 1 tr] in same st, [1 tr, ch 1, 1 tr] in next st, ch 4, miss 2 sts, *[1 tr, ch 1, 1 tr] in next st, ch 1, [1 tr, ch 1, 1 tr] in next st, ch 4, rep from * 1 time, sl st in top of beg ch-3 to join. Do not fasten off.

Round 3: Cut 3 lengths of yarn C. Join one length in front lp of same st just worked, *[ch 3, miss 1 st, sl st in next st] 3 times, fasten off ** (end of first fan), join next length of yarn C after ch-4 sp, in front lp of first tr of next group; rep from * to ** (end of 2nd fan), join last length of yarn C in front lp of first tr of next fan; rep from * to ** (end of 3rd fan).

Round 4: Pick up yarn B again, ch 3 (counts as 1 tr), ch 1, 1 tr in same sp, *[1 tr, ch 1, 1 tr] in next tr (working in back lps where front lp is occupied by yarn C), ch 1; rep from * 2 times, ch 2**; rep from * to ** 2 times, sl st in top of beg ch-3 to join.

Round 5: Ch 3 (counts as 1 tr), [ch 1, 1 tr in next tr] 7 times, ch 4**, 1 tr in next tr; rep from * 1 time, and from * to ** 1 time, sl st in top of beg ch-3 to join. Do not fasten off.

Round 6: Cut 3 lengths of yarn D, join one length in front lp of same st just worked, *[ch 3, miss 1 ch, sl st in next tr] 7 times, fasten off ** (end of first fan), join next length of yarn D after ch-4 sp, in front lp of first tr of next group; rep from * to ** (end of 2nd fan), join last length of yarn D in front lp of first tr of next fan; rep from * to ** (end of 3rd fan).

Round 7: Ch 3 (counts as 1 tr), 1 tr in same st, 2 tr in bck lps of next 7 tr, ch 5, *2 tr in back lps of next 8 tr, ch 5; rep from * 1 time, sl st in top of beg ch-3 to join.

Round 8: Ch 4 (counts as 1 tr, ch 1), [miss 1 st, 1 tr in next tr, ch 1] 15 times, *ch 6, [1 tr in next tr, ch 1, miss 1 st] 15 times, 1 tr in last tr; rep from * 1 time, ch 6, sl st in top of beg ch-3 to join. Fasten off.

Round 9: Cut 3 lengths of yarn C, join one length in front lp of same st just worked, *[ch 3, miss 1 ch, sl st in next tr] 15 times, fasten off ** (end of first fan), join next length of yarn C after ch-6 sp, in front lp of first tr of next group; rep from * to ** (end of 2nd fan), join last length of yarn C in front lp of first tr of next fan; rep from * to ** (end of 3rd fan).

Round 10: Join yarn E in ch-1 sp after st just finished, 1 dc in same ch-1 sp, [1 dc in next ch-1 sp) 14 times, *ch 2, 1 dc in next ch-6 sp, ch 2, [1 dc in next ch-1 sp] 15 times; rep from * 1 time, sl st in first dc to join.

Round 11: Ch 1, 1 dc in same st, 1 dc in next st, 1 htr in next 2 sts, 1 tr in next 2 sts, [3 tr, ch 2, 3 tr] in next st, 1 tr in next 2 sts, 1 htr in next 2 sts, 1 dc in next 3 sts, 3 dc in next ch-2 sp, 2 htr in next ch-2 sp, 1 tr in next 2 sts [3 tr, ch 2, 3 tr] in next st, 1 tr in next 2 sts, 1 htr in next 2 sts, 1 dc in next 6 sts, 1 htr in next 2 sts, 2 tr in next ch-2 sp, [3 tr, ch-2, 3 tr] in next st, [2 tr, 1 htr] in next ch-2 sp, 1 htr in next st, 1 dc in next 6 sts, 1 htr in next 2 sts, 1 tr in next 2 sts, [3 tr, ch 2, 3 tr] in next st, 2 tr in next 2 sts, 1 htr in next st, [1 htr, 1 dc] in next ch-2 sp, 1 dc in next st, 2 dc in next ch-2 sp, sl st in first dc to join. Fasten off.

Round 12: Join yarn A in same st, 1 dc in same st, 1 dc in each st to corner, *3 dc in ch-2 corner sp, 1 dc in every st to next ch-2 corner sp; rep from * 2 times, 3 dc in ch-2 corner sp, 1 dc in every st to end, sl st in first dc to join. Fasten off.

Round 13: Join yarn B in any middle dc in corner, [ch 3, miss 1 dc, sl st in next dc] all the way around square to end, sl st in first ch to join.

Fasten off and darn in ends.

★★★
moulin rouge

With all the extravagance of a frilly can-can skirt, this block makes a bold statement and is irresistible to play with. Although it's especially dimensional, it's not too dense so can still be used in a variety of blankets, pillows and bedspreads.

Note: When working rows immediately after frills, ensure you work in sts that contrast yarns are also worked in; count sts during row if you are not sure.

A
B
C
D

Foundation ring: Using yarn A, ch 4, sl st in first ch to form ring.

Round 1: Ch 2 (counts as 1 tr), 1 htr in ring, [3 tr, 2 htr] in ring 3 times, 3 tr in ring, sl st in top of beg ch-2 to join.

Round 2: Ch 2 (counts as 1 htr), 1 htr in each of next 2 sts, [5 htr in next st, 1 htr in each of next 4 sts] 3 times, 5 htr in next st, 1 htr in last st, sl st in top of beg ch-2 to join. Do not fasten off.

Frill 1: Sl st yarn B in next st to left of last working st, [ch 6, miss 3 sts, sl st in next st] 8 times, ch 6, sl st in beg sl st to join, *[2 dc, 5 htr, 2 dc] in next ch-6 loop, sl st in sl st at base; rep from * 7 times. Fasten off.

Round 3: Bend frill forwards, pick up lp of yarn A and tighten, keeping frill bent forwards to access sts that yarn B is worked in, ch 3 (counts as 1 tr), 1 tr in each of next 4 sts, [5 tr in next st, 1 tr in each of next 8 sts] 3 times, 5 tr in next st, 1 tr in each of next 3 sts, sl st in top of beg ch-3 to join.

Round 4: Ch 2 (counts as 1 htr), 1 htr in each of next 6 sts, [5 htr in next st, 1 htr in each of next 12 sts] 3 times, 5 htr in next st, 1 htr in each of last 5 sts, sl st in top of beg ch-2 to join. Do not fasten off.

Frill 2: Sl st yarn C in next st to left of last working st, [ch 6, miss 3 sts, sl st in next st] 16 times, ch 6, sl st in beg sl st to join, *[2 dc, 5 htr, 2 dc] in next ch-6 loop, sl st in sl st at base; rep from * 16 times. Fasten off.

Round 5: Bend frill forwards to access sts that yarn C is worked in, pick up yarn A, ch 3 (counts as 1 tr), 1 tr in each of next 8 sts, [3 tr in next st, 1 tr in each of next 16 sts] 3 times, 3 tr in next st, 1 tr in each of next 7 sts, sl st in top of beg ch-3 to join.

Round 6: Ch 2 (counts as 1 htr), 1 htr in each of next 10 sts, [5 htr in next st, 1 htr in each of next 20 sts] 3 times, 5 htr in next st, 1 htr in each of next 9 sts, sl st in top of beg ch-3 to join. Do not fasten off.

Frill 3: Sl st yarn D in next st to left of last working st, [ch 6, miss 3 sts, sl st in next st] 20 times, ch 6, sl st in beg sl st to join, *[2 dc, 5 htr, 2 dc] in next ch-6 loop, sl st in sl st at base; rep from * 20 times. Fasten off.

Round 7: Bend frill forwards to access all sts, pick up yarn A, ch 1, 1 dc in each of next 12 htr, [2 dc, ch 1, 2 dc] in next htr, 1 dc in each of next 24 htr] 3 times, [2 dc, ch 1, 2 dc] in next htr, 1 dc in each of next 11 htr, sl st in beg ch-1 to join.

Fasten off and darn in ends.

★★★★

abstract granny

A
B
C
D
E

Inspired by the striking artwork of Piet Mondrian, this block is another all-double crochet, solid-colour square, which would look really unique repeated over a coverlet or pillow. The black lines are surface crocheted in after the block is completed.

Special stitch used:

Surface crochet: 1 sl st over vertical post of each st around motif, creating a chain-stitch effect (*see page 22*).

Notes: When working this pattern prepare 3 separate small balls of colour C before you begin. Work each separate area of colour using a different ball of yarn, joining on last lp of each st of last area of colour. Keep all yarn ends at WS of work throughout: otherwise, when you need to change colour, yarn may be on RS and inaccessible.

Read chart from left to right on RS rows, and from right to left on WS rows.

SQUARE

Foundation chain: Using yarn A, ch 29.

Row 1: (WS) 1 dc in 2nd ch from hook, 1 dc in every ch to end, turn.

Row 2: (RS, first row of chart) Ch 1, 1 dc in every ch to end, turn.

Rows 3 to 37: Rep Row 2, working rem 34 rows of chart, keeping yarn ends on WS.

Fasten off and darn in ends neatly. Block work before adding trim.

SURFACE CROCHET TRIM

Using A, with RS facing, insert hook at join between yellow and white areas, where they meet black border at Row 2. Surface crochet up in a straight vertical line to edge of large red block. Fasten off.

Insert hook at RH edge of block where yellow and white areas meet. Using yarn A, surface crochet horizontally along top edge of yellow area to first surface crocheted vertical line. Fasten off.

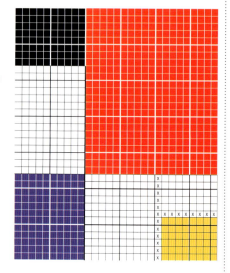

***
pyracantha

Inspired by the beautifully bright shrub of the same name, this block combines bobbles and spikes to create the effect of spiny branches. Both thick and textural, work it up in cosy wools for a warm winter afghan.

A
B
C
D
E

Special stitches used:

Make bobble (MB): Make bobble with 5 tr (*see page 19*). Carry yarn not in use along WS of work on bobble rows (*see page 18*).

Spike stitch (spike st): Insert hook in sp in row below next st to be worked (here 2 or 3 rows below), yoh, pull yarn through to height of row being worked, complete stitch as normal (*see page 22*).

Foundation chain: Using yarn A, ch 30.

Row 1: 1 dc in 2nd ch from hook, 1 dc in every ch to end, turn.

Row 2: Ch 1, 1 dc in every sc to end, turn.

Rows 3 to 4: Rep Row 2. Fasten off yarn A.

Row 5: Join yarn B, ch 1, 1 dc in first dc, *spike st in 2 rows down, spike st in 3 rows down; rep from * to last dc, 1 dc in last dc, turn. Fasten off.

Row 6: Join yarn A, ch 1, 1 dc in each of next 2 dc, *using yarn C, MB in next dc, using yarn A, 1 dc in each of next 2 dc; rep from * to end of row, turn. Fasten off yarn C but not yarn A.

Rows 7 to 10: Rep Row 2.

Row 11: Rep Row 5.

Row 12: Rep Row 6 using yarn D to make bobbles instead of yarn C.

Rows 13 to 16: Rep Row 2.

Row 17: Rep Row 5.

Row 18: Rep Row 6 using yarn E to make bobbles instead of yarn C.

Rows 19 to 22: Rep Row 2.

Row 23: Rep Row 5.

Row 24: Rep Row 12.

Rows 25 to 28: Rep Row 2.

Row 29: Rep Row 5.

Row 30: Rep Row 6.

Rows 31 to 32: Rep row 2.

Fasten off and darn in ends. Block work.

**
tahoe

A cosy mitre square pattern that reminds us of toasting marshmallows over a bonfire, this is simple to work but is constructed in a different way than the usual mitre corner blocks. Mix it up with other offset squares, or other geometric filets for a modern afghan.

A
B

Foundation chain: Using yarn A, ch 9.

Row 1: 1 tr in 4th ch from hook, 1 tr in each ch to end, turn.

Row 2: Ch 3 (counts as 1 tr), 1 tr in each of next 6 tr, turn.

Row 3: Rep Row 2, turn. Fasten off.

Row 4: Join yarn B, ch 3 (counts as 1 tr) *ch 1, miss 1 tr, 1 tr in next tr; rep from * 2 times, ch 3, 1 tr in same sp, working down side of square, rep from * to end. Fasten off.

Row 5: Join yarn A, ch 3 (counts as 1 tr), 1 tr in every tr and in every ch-1 sp to corner ch-3 sp, [1 tr, ch 3, 1 tr] in corner sp, 1 tr in every tr down side of square to end, turn.

Rows 6 to 7: Rep Row 5. Fasten off.

Row 8: Join yarn B, ch 3 (counts as 1 tr) *ch 1, miss 1 tr, 1 tr in next tr; rep from * to corner ch-3 sp, [1 tr, ch 3, 1 tr] in same corner sp, rep from * to end of row, turn.

Row 9: Rep Row 5.

Row 10: Rep Row 8 using yarn A (do not fasten off).

Row 11: Rep Row 5. Fasten off.

Row 12: Rep Row 8.

Rows 13 to 14: Rep Row 5.

Row 15: 1 dc in every tr to corner ch-3 sp, [1 dc, ch 2, 1 dc] in corner sp, 1 dc in every tr down side of square to end of row, turn.

Row 16: Rep Row 15.

Fasten off and darn in ends neatly. Block work if necessary.

54 **

loopy

A soft textural pile fabric that works well for rugs, throws, cushions or accessories. Reminiscent of fake fur, this is a wonderfully tactile square that matches well with busier, thicker squares.

Special stitch used:

Loop stitch (lp st): Insert hook in st, wrap yarn over forefinger. Catch both strands of lp with hook and pull through st (3 lps on hook), yoh and pull through all three lps.

Foundation chain: Ch 30.

Row 1: Miss 2 ch, 1 dc in each ch to end, turn.

Row 2: Ch 1 (counts as 1 dc), miss 1 dc, 1 dc in each dc to end, turn.

Row 3: Ch 1 (counts as 1 dc), miss 1 dc, 1 dc, 1 lp st in each dc to last 2 sts, 2 dc, turn.

Rows 4 to 35: Rep Rows 2 and 3 in order.

Rows 36 to 37: Rep Row 2.

Fasten off yarn and darn in ends.

55 ***

marigold

A statement flower block with big bright petals, worked individually before being joined in a square. The flower centre would make a gorgeous pin or corsage on its own, while the block works well for table runners, light throws, cushion covers or curtains.

Foundation ring: Using yarn A, ch 4, sl st in first ch to form ring.

Round 1: Ch 3 (counts as 1 tr), 11 dtr in ring, sl st in top of ch-3 to join. Fasten off yarn A.

Round 2: Join yarn B, *ch 9, sl st in 7th ch, 1 tr in each of next 6 ch, sl st in next dtr; rep from * to end of rnd. Fasten off yarn B – 12 petals formed.

Round 3: Join yarn C, sl st in top of first petal, 1 dc in the same st, *ch 5, 1 dc in top of next petal; rep from * to end of rnd omitting final dc, sl st in first dc to join.

Round 4: Ch 4 (counts as 1 dtr), [2 dtr, ch 2, 3 dtr] in same sp, *[1 hdtr, 1 tr, 2 htr, 1 tr, 1 hdtr] in next ch-5 sp, 1 dtr in dc, [1 hdtr, 1 tr, 2 htr, 1 tr, 1 hdtr] in next ch-5 sp**, [3 dtr, ch 2, 3 dtr] in next dc; rep from * 3 times ending at **, sl st in top of beg ch-4 to join.

Fasten off and darn all ends in neatly.

*hundertwasser

A beginner's square that packs a visual punch, inspired by the designer's favourite artist. Great for pillows, afghans and baby blankets, or try it in making a handbag. This pattern is best worked in a flat, smooth yarn for maximum effect.

Foundation ring: Using A, begin with magic ring method.

Round 1: Ch 3 (counts as 1 tr), 15 tr in ring, sl st in top of beg ch-3 to join. Fasten off yarn A.

Round 2: Join yarn B, ch 1, 1 dc in same st, 1 dc in each of next 2 tr, 3 dc in next tr, *1 dc in each of next 3 tr, 3 dc in next tr; rep from * 2 times, sl st in first dc to join. Fasten off yarn B.

Round 3: Join yarn C, ch 3 (counts as 1 tr), 1 tr in each of next 3 dc, *3 tr in next dc, 1 tr in each of next 5 dc; rep from * 3 times, ending last rep with 1 tr in last dc, sl st in top of beg ch-3 to join. Fasten off yarn C.

Round 4: Join yarn D, ch 1, 1 dc in same st, 1 dc in each of next 4 tr, *3 dc in next tr, 1 dc in each of next 7 tr; rep from * 3 times, ending last rep with 1 dc in each of last 2 tr, sl st in first dc to join. Fasten off yarn D.

Round 5: Join yarn A, ch 3 (counts as 1 tr), 1 tr in each of next 5 dc, *3 tr in next dc, 1 tr in each of next 9 dc; rep from * 3 times, ending last rep with 1 tr in each of the last 3 tr, sl st in top of beg ch-3 to join. Fasten off yarn A.

Round 6: Join yarn B, ch 3 (counts as 1 tr), 1 tr in each of next 6 tr, *3 tr in next tr, 1 tr in each of next 11 tr; rep from * 3 times, end last rep with 1 tr in each of last 4 tr, sl st in top of beg ch-3 to join. Fasten off yarn B.

A
B
C
D

Round 7: Join yarn C, ch 1, 1 dc in same st, 1 dc in each of next 7 tr, *5 dc in next tr, 1 dc in each of next 13 tr; rep from * 3 times, ending last rep with 1 dc in each of last 5 tr, sl st in first dc to join. Fasten off yarn C.

Round 8: Join yarn D, ch 3 (counts as 1 tr), 1 tr in each of next 9 dc, *5 tr in next dc, 1 tr in each of next 17 dc; rep from * 3 times, ending last rep with 1 tr in final 7 dc, sl st in top of beg ch-3 to join.

Round 9: Join yarn D, ch 3 (counts as 1 tr), 1 tr in each of next 9 tr, * 7 tr in next tr, 1 tr in each of next 21 tr; rep from * 3 times, ending last rep with 1 tr in each of final 11 tr, sl st in top of beg ch-3 to join.

Fasten off and darn in ends neatly.

57

**

popcorn circle

With its central ring of popcorns, this block has a wonderful texture and works up relatively quickly. Mixes well with plainer squares and stripes.

Special stitches used:

Beginning popcorn (beg pc): Ch 3, make popcorn with 4 tr (*see page 19*).

Popcorn (pc): Make popcorn with 5 tr.

Foundation ring: Using yarn A, begin with magic ring method.

Round 1: Ch 3 (counts as 1 tr), 15 tr more in ring, sl st in top of ch-3 to join – 16 sts.

Round 2: Beg pc in next tr, *2 tr in next st, pc in next st; rep from * 7 times ending with 2 tr in last st, sl st in top of beg pc to join – 24 sts.

Round 3: Ch 3 (counts as 1 tr), *2 tr in next st, 1 tr in next st; rep from * to end of rnd omitting final 1 tr, sl st in top of ch-3 (top of pc equals 1 st).

Round 4: Ch 1, 1 dc in same st, *ch 4, miss 2 sts, 1 dc in next st, ch 2, miss 2 sts, 1 dc in next st, ch 2, miss 2 sts, **1 dc in next st; rep from * to end of rnd ending at **, sl st in beg ch-1 to join.

Round 5: Ch 3 (counts as 1 tr), *[5 tr, ch 2, 5 tr] in next ch-4 sp, 1 tr in next dc, 3 tr in next ch-2 sp, 2 tr in next dc, 3 tr in next ch-2 sp, 1 tr in next dc; rep from * 3 times omitting last 1 tr, sl st in top of beg ch-3 to join.

Round 6: Ch 4 (counts as 1 tr, ch 1), miss 1 tr, 1 tr in next tr, ch 1, miss 1 tr, 1 tr in next tr, ch 1, *[1 tr, ch 2, 1 tr] in ch-2 sp (first corner), **[ch 1, miss 1 tr, tr in next tr] 10 times, ch 1; rep from * 2 times and from * to ** 1 time, [ch 1, miss 1 tr, tr in next tr] 7 times, ch 1, sl st in 3rd ch of beg ch-4 to join.

Round 7: Ch 3, [1 tr in next ch-1 sp, 1 tr in next tr] 3 times, *[1 tr, ch 2, 1 tr] in next ch-2 sp, ** [1 tr in next tr, 1 tr in next ch-1 sp] 11 times, 1 tr; rep from * 2 times and from * to ** 1 time, [1 tr in next tr, 1 tr in next ch-1 sp] 7 times; sl st in top of beg ch-3 to join.

Fasten off and darn in all ends neatly.

58

**

heartland

A solid square, worked entirely in double crochet, it carries along the yarn not being worked behind the central motif area. This is a great square for baby afghans or bedspreads.

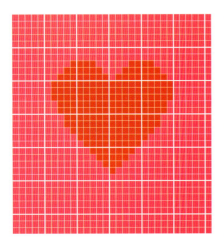

Notes: When working the central motif, carry the main yarn A along the top of the stitches of the last row and work over it (along with the stitch itself) when creating a stitch using yarn B, concealing it as you go along. This eliminates the need to use a separate ball of yarn for each colour.

Beginning at bottom RH corner of chart, work 33 rows of chart in dc. When foll the chart, read odd-numbered (RS) rows from right to left, and even-numbered (WS) rows from left to right.

Foundation chain: Using yarn A, ch 32 (counts as 31 sts, 1 tch), turn.

Begin chart as follows:

Row 1 (RS): 1 dc in 2nd ch from hook and in each ch to end, turn – 31 sts.

Rows 2 to 33: Ch 1, 1 dc in every dc, turn.

Fasten off yarns and darn in all ends neatly.

***
cherry pie

With a little 'pastry' and bobbly cherries, this fun square is a firm and warm addition to any blanket or afghan; pieced together in lengths, these blocks would also make fantastic festive table runners.

Special stitch used:

Make bobble (MB): Make bobble with 5 tr (*see page 19*).

Foundation ring: Using yarn A, ch 6, join with sl st to form ring.

Round 1: Ch 1, 12 dc in ring, sl st in first dc to join.

Round 2: Ch 1, [1 dc in next dc, 2 dc in next dc] 6 times, sl st in first dc to join – 18 dc.

Round 3: Ch 1, [1 dc in each of next 2 dc, 2 dc in next dc] 6 times, sl st in first dc to join – 24 dc.

Round 4: Ch 1, [1 dc in each of next 3 dc, 2 dc in next dc] 6 times, sl st in first dc to join – 30 dc.

Round 5: Ch 1, 1 dc in same sp, [1 dc in each of next 2 dc, MB] 10 times (10 bobbles made), sl st in first dc to join.

Round 6: Ch 1, 1 dc in same sp, [1 dc in each of next 2 dc, 2 dc in next dc] 10 times, sl st in first dc to join – 42 sts.

Round 7: Ch1, 1 dc in same sp, [1 dc in each of next 6 dc, 2 dc in next dc] 6 times, sl st in first dc to join – 48 sc.

Round 8: Ch 1, 1 dc in same sp [1 dc in each of next 7 dc, 2 dc in next dc] 6 times, sl st in first dc to join – 54 dc.

Round 9: Rep Round 5 – 18 bobbles.

Round 10: Ch 1, 1 dc in same sp, [1 dc in each of next 3 dc, 2 dc in next dc] 13 times, 2 dc in last dc, sl st in first dc to join – 68 sts. Change to yarn B, do not fasten off yarn A.

Round 11: Using yarn B, 1 dc in front loop of every st around, sl st in first dc to join. Fasten off yarn B.

Round 12: Using yarn A, ch 1, 1 dc in next 4 dc, *1 htr in each of next 2 dc, 1 tr in next tr, [3 tr, ch 3] in next dc, 3 tr in next dc, 1 tr in next dc, 1 htr in each of next 2 dc**, 1 dc in next 9 dc; rep from * 2 times and from * to ** 1 time, 1 dc in each of next 5 dc, sl st to first dc to join.

Round 13: Ch 3 (counts as 1 tr), 1 tr in each of next 10 sts, *[3 tr, ch 3, 3 tr] in ch-3 corner sp**, 1 tr in each of next 21 sts to corner; rep from * 2 times and from * to ** 1 time, 1 tr in each of next 11 sts, sl st in top of beg ch-3 to join. Fasten off yarn A.

Round 14: Using yarn C, 1 dc in every st around square and [2 dc, ch 2, 2 dc] in every ch-3 corner sp to end, sl st in first dc to join.

Round 15: [Ch 3, miss 2 dc, 1 dc in next dc] all around square.

Fasten off and darn in ends neatly.

***

ladybird

This cute block is bound to be loved by children and adults alike, and would be fantastic in a blanket or pillow for the nursery. Bobbles are set into the ladybird's body to make her spots; add more or fewer according to your own ideal ladybird.

A
B
C
D

Special stitch used:

Make bobble (MB): Make bobble with 5 tr (*see page 19*).

Foundation ring: Using yarn A, make magic ring, ch 1 to secure.

Round 1: 8 dc in ring, sl st in first dc to join.

Round 2: Ch 1, 2 dc in every dc around to end, sl st in first sc to join – 16 sts.

Round 3: Ch 1, *2 dc in next dc, 1 dc in next dc; rep from * to end, sl st in first dc to join.

Round 4: Ch 1, *2 dc in next dc, using yarn B, MB in next dc, using yarn A, 2 dc in next dc; rep from * 5 times, sl st in first dc to join. Fasten off yarn B but not yarn A.

Round 5: Ch 1, 1 dc in every dc around including ch-1 sts securing each bobble, sl st in first htr to join.

Round 6: Ch 1, *1 dc in each of next 2 dc, 2 dc in next dc; rep from * to end, sl st in first dc to join. Fasten off yarn A.

Round 7: Join yarn B in same st; sl st 1 st back along edge, ch 4 (counts as 1 dtr), [1 dtr, 2 tr, 1 htr] in same dc, ch 1, [1 htr, 2 tr, 2 dtr] in next dc, ch 2, miss 3 dc, 1 ttr in next dc, ch 6, miss 4 dc, 1 dc in next dc, ch 6, miss 4 dc, 1 ttr in next dc, ch 3, miss 3 dc, 1 dc in each of next 3 dc, ch 4, miss 3 dc, 1 ttr in next dc, ch 6, miss 4 dc, 1 dc in next dc, ch 6, miss 4 dc, 1 ttr in next dc, ch 2, miss 3 dc, sl st in top of beg ch-4 to join. Fasten off yarn B.

Round 8: Join yarn C in next ttr along, ch 3 (counts as 1 tr), [2 tr, ch 2, 3 tr] in same st (forms corner), 6 tr in next ch-6 lp, 1 tr in next dc, 6 tr in next ch-6 lp, [3 tr, ch 2, 3 tr] in next ttr, 5 tr in next ch-4 lp, 1 tr in each of next 3 dc, 5 tr in next ch-4 lp, [3 tr, ch 2, 3 tr] in next ttr, 6 tr in next ch-6 lp, 1 tr in next dc, 6 tr in next ch-6 lp, [3 tr, ch 2, 3 tr] in next ttr, 2 tr in next ch-2 sp, 1 dc in each of next 4 sts, 1 tr in ch-1 sp between clusters, 1 dc in each of next 4 sts, 2 tr in next ch-2 sp, sl st in top of beg ch-3 to join. Fasten off yarn C.

Round 9: Join yarn D in any ch-2 corner sp, ch 2 (counts as 1 htr), [1 htr, ch 2, 2 htr] in same sp (forms corner), *1 htr in each of next 19 sts, **[2 htr, ch 2, 2 htr] in next ch-2 corner sp; rep from * 2 times and from * to ** 1 time, sl st in top of beg ch-2 to join. Fasten off yarn D.

Round 10: Join yarn A in any ch-2 corner sp, ch 1, *1 dc in every htr along edge to corner ch-2 sp, 3 dc in corner ch-2 sp; rep from * to end, sl st in first dc to join.

Round 11: Ch 1, 1 dc in same sp, *using yarn B, MB in next dc, using yarn A, 1 dc in each of next 21 dc, MB in next dc, **[using yarn A, 2 dc, ch 2, 2 dc] in next ch-2 corner sp; rep from * 2 times and from * to ** 1 time, sl st in top of beg ch-2 to join.

Fasten off and darn in ends neatly.

** carnaby

Ridges are formed from front- and back-post treble crochet in this block, giving it a detailed, textured feel and making it appear more complex than it is to make. A firm, solid block, beautiful for warm blankets and afghans.

Special stitches used:

Front-post treble crochet (FPtr): Bring hook to front, work in front vertical post of next st, inserting hook from right to left, draw yarn through and work st as usual (*see page 21*).

Back-post treble crochet (BPtr): Bring hook to back, work in back vertical post of next st, inserting hook from left to right, draw yarn through and work st as usual (*see page 21*).

Foundation ring: Using yarn A, ch 4, join with sl st to form ring.

Round 1: Ch 3 (counts as 1 tr); [2 tr, ch 2, 3 tr] in ring, [ch 2, 3 tr] 2 times, sl st in top of ch-3 to join. Fasten off yarn A.

A
B
C
D
E

Round 2: Join yarn B in any ch-2 sp, ch 3 (counts as 1 tr), [2 tr, ch 2, 3 tr] in same sp, *1 tr in next 3 sts, [3 tr, ch 2, 3 tr] in next ch-2 sp; rep from * 2 times, 1 tr in next 3 sts, sl st in top of ch-3 to join. Fasten off yarn B.

Round 3: Join yarn C in any ch-2 sp, ch 3, 1 tr in same sp, *1 FPtr in each tr along to corner ch-sp, **[2 tr, ch 2, 2 tr] in corner ch-sp; rep from * 2 times, then from * to ** 1 time, [2 tr, ch 2] in last corner ch-sp, sl st in top of ch-3 to join. Fasten off yarn C.

Round 4: Join yarn D in any ch-2 sp, ch 3, 1 tr in same sp, *1 tr in every tr along side to corner ch-sp, **[2 tr, ch 2, 2 tr] in corner ch-sp; rep from * 2 times and from * to ** 1 time, [2 tr, ch 2] in last corner ch-sp, sl st in top of ch-3 to join. Fasten off yarn D.

Round 5: Join yarn E in any ch-2 sp, ch 3, 1 tr in same sp, 1 BPtr in every tr along side to corner ch-sp, **[2 tr, ch 2, 2 tr] in corner ch-sp; rep from * 2 times and from * to ** 1 time, [2 tr, ch 2] in last corner ch-sp, sl st in top of ch-3 to join. Fasten off yarn E.

Round 6: Rep Round 5 using yarn C. Fasten off yarn C.

Round 7: Rep Round 3 using yarn B. Fasten off yarn B.

Round 8: Join yarn A in any corner ch-sp, ch 1, 1 dc in same sp, 1 dc in every tr along to corner ch-sp, [2 dc, ch 1, 2 dc] in corner ch-sp; rep from * 2 times, then from * to ** 1 time, [2 tr, ch 1] in last corner ch-sp, sl st in first ch-1 to join.

Fasten off and darn in ends neatly.

**
toadstool

A
B

Essentially a traditional granny square construction, with puff stitches instead of straight treble crochet. The contrast yarn is carried across the rounds, inside the stitches of the main colour, eliminating the need for darning in ends. This block has a wonderful texture and would make a great table linen set.

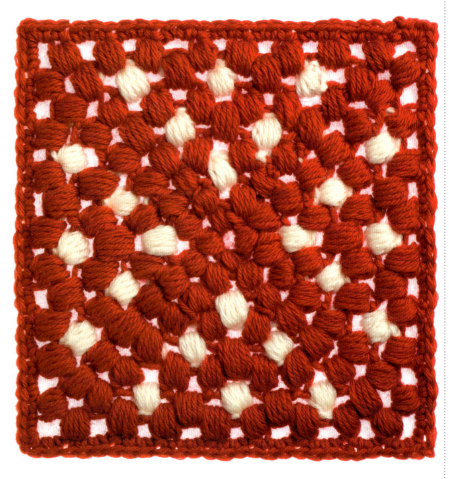

Special stitches used:

3-treble-crochet puff stitch (3-trpf):
Make puff stitch with 3 tr, ch 1 to seal pf (see page 19).

4-treble-crochet puff stitch (4-trpf):
Make puff stitch with 3 tr, ch 1 to seal pf.

5-treble-crochet puff stitch (5-trpf):
Make puff stitch with 5 tr, ch 1 to seal pf.

Notes: In this design, the rounds where two colours occur are worked as two separate rounds; on the first round, two chain gaps are left to be worked in second colour. The round is then worked in the second colour, working in the gaps left and chaining where the main colour occurs. On the following round, the stitches are worked over both sets of chains.

Take care to work over stitches only from the round immediately before – it is easy to work over more rounds accidentally.

Foundation ring: Using yarn A, ch 6, sl st in first ch to form ring.

Round 1: *Ch 2, 3-trpf; rep from * 3 times, sl st in top of ch-2 to join.

Round 2: Ch 2, [4-trpf, ch 3, 5-trpf] in same ch-2 sp, ch 3, *[5-trpf, ch 3, 5-trpf] in next ch-2 sp, ch 3; rep from * to end of rnd, sl st in top of beg ch-2 to join.

Round 3: Ch 2, [4-trpf, ch 3, 5-trpf] in same ch-3 sp, ch 5, miss 1 ch-sp, [5-trpf, ch 3, 5-trpf] in next ch-3 sp; rep from * to end of rnd, sl st in top of beg ch-2 to join. Do not fasten off yarn A.

Round 4: Join yarn B with sl st in any ch-5 sp, ch 2, 4-trpf, *ch 3, sl st in centre ch of ch-3 made in corner sp (this helps anchor yarn B down), ch 3, 5-trpf in next empty ch-sp from last rnd; rep from * 2 times, ch 3, sl st in centre ch of ch-3 made in corner sp, ch 3, sl st in top of beg ch-2 to join (4 contrast puffs made). Fasten off yarn B.

Round 5: Pick up yarn B again, working over both sets of chains from Rounds 3 and 4, ch 2, [4-trpf, ch 3, 5-trpf] in corner sp, *ch 3, [5-trpf in next ch-sp, ch 3] 2 times**, [5-trpf, ch 3, 5-trpf] in next ch-3 corner sp; rep from * 2 times, then from * to ** 1 time, sl st in top of beg ch-2 to join.

Round 6: Ch 2, [4-trpf, ch 3, 5-trpf] in same corner ch-sp, *ch 5, miss next ch-3 sp, 5-trpf, ch 5**, [5-trpf, ch 3, 5-trpf] in ch-3 corner sp; rep from * 2 times, then from * to ** 1 time, sl st in top of beg ch-2 to join. Do not fasten off yarn A.

Round 7: Join yarn B with *sl st in centre ch of ch-3 corner sp (this helps anchor yarn B down), ch 5, [5-grpf in next empty ch-sp from last rnd, ch 5] 2 times; rep from * 3 times, sl st in first sl st to join – 8 contrast puffs made. Fasten off yarn B.

Round 8: Using yarn A again, working over both sets of chains as in Round 5, ch 2, [4-trpf, ch 3, 5-trpf] in same corner ch-sp, *ch 3, [5-trpf in next ch-sp, ch 3] 4 times**, [5-trpf, ch 3, 5-trpf] in next ch-3 corner sp; rep from * 2 times, then from * to ** 1 time, sl st in top of beg ch-2 to join.

Round 9: Ch 2, [4-trpf, ch 3, 5-trpf] in same corner ch-sp, *ch 5, miss next ch-3 sp, [5-trpf, ch 5] 2 times**, [5-trpf, ch 3, 5-trpf] in ch-3 corner sp; rep from * 2 times, then from * to ** 1 time, sl st in top of beg ch-2 to join. Do not fasten off yarn A.

Round 10: Using yarn B, join with *sl st in centre ch of ch-3 corner sp, ch 5, [5-trpf in next empty ch-sp from last rnd, ch 5] 3 times; rep from * 3 times, sl st in first sl st to join – 8 contrast puffs made. Fasten off yarn B.

Round 11: Using yarn A again, working over both sets of chains as in Round 8, ch 2, [4-trpf, ch 3, 5-trpf] in same corner ch-sp, *ch 3, [5-trpf in next ch-sp, ch 3] 6 times**, [5-trpf, ch 3, 5-trpf] in next ch-3 corner sp; rep from * 2 times, then from * to ** 1 time, sl st in top of beg ch-2 to join.

Round 12: 1 dc in every st and 2 dc in every ch-3 sp around square, [2 dc, ch 1, 2 dc] in every corner ch-sp.

Fasten off and darn in ends neatly. It is essential to block this square; it will lie beautifully flat once this is done.

★★

bobble heart

A mass of pink bobbles creates a fabulously plush texture for this block. Try to choose a slightly thinner yarn for the contrast (B), otherwise the volume of bobbles may distort the square shape. Lovely for the centre of a baby blanket.

A

B

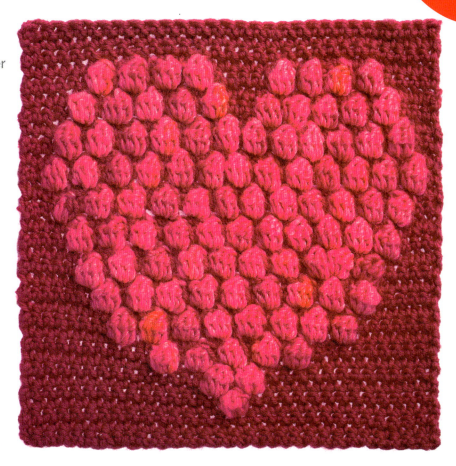

Special stitch used:

Make bobble (MB): Make bobble with 5 tr (*see page 19*).

Special stitch note: Carry yarn not in use along back of work when creating bobble pattern.

Foundation chain: Using yarn A, ch 32 (counts as 31 ch, 1 tch).

Row 1: 1 dc in 2nd ch from hook, 1 dc in every ch along row, turn – 31 sts.

Rows 2, 3, 4 and every alt row: Ch 1, 1 dc in every dc along, turn.

Row 5: Ch 1, 1 dc in each of next 15 dc, using yarn B, MB in next dc, using yarn A, 1 dc in each of rem 15 dc, turn.

Row 7: Ch 1, 1 dc in each of next 14 dc, using yarn B, MB in next dc, using yarn A, 1 dc in next sc, using yarn B, MB in next dc, using yarn A, 1 dc in each of rem 14 dc, turn.

Row 9: Ch 1, 1 dc in each of next 11 dc, [using yarn B, MB in next dc, using yarn A, 1 dc in next sc] 5 times, 1 dc in each of rem 10 sc, turn.

Row 11: Ch 1, 1 dc in each of next 8 dc, [using yarn B, MB in next dc, using yarn A, 1 dc in next dc] 8 times, 1 dc in each of rem 7 dc, turn.

Row 13: Ch 1, 1 dc in each of next 7 dc, [using yarn B, MB in next dc, using yarn A, 1 dc in next dc] 9 times, 1 dc in each of rem 6 dc, turn.

Row 15: Ch 1, 1 dc in each of next 6 dc, [using yarn B, MB in next dc, using yarn A, 1 dc in next dc] 10 times, 1 dc in each of rem 5 dc, turn.

Row 17: Ch 1, 1 dc in each of next 5 dc, [using yarn B, MB in next dc, using yarn A, 1 dc in next dc] 11 times, 1 dc in each of rem 4 dc, turn.

Row 19: Ch 1, 1 dc in each of next 4 dc, [using yarn B, MB in next dc, using yarn A, 1 dc in next dc] 12 times, 1 dc in each of rem 3 dc, turn.

Row 21: Ch 1, 1 dc in each of next 3 dc, [using yarn B, MB in next dc, using yarn A, 1 dc in next dc] 13 times, 2 dc in each of rem 1 dc, turn.

Row 23: Rep Row 19.

Row 25: Ch 1, 1 dc in each of next 5 dc, *[using yarn B, MB in next dc, using yarn A, 1 dc in next dc] 5 times, 1 dc in each of next 2 dc; rep from * 1 time, 1 dc in each of last 2 dc, turn.

Row 27: Ch 1, 1 dc in each of next 6 dc, *[using yarn B, MB in next dc, using yarn A, 1 dc in next dc] 4 times, 1 dc in each of next 5 dc; rep from * 1 time, omitting last dc, turn.

Rows 29 to 34: Rep Row 2.

Fasten off and darn in ends neatly.

* *

basket

An attractive textured block that uses front- and back-post stitch to create a cosy, woven-effect fabric. Our square here has been worked in relatively thick yarn, giving a dense, warm fabric; for a more draped, open fabric, use a regular yarn to hook size.

A

Special stitches used:

Front-post treble crochet (FPtr): Bring hook to front, work in front vertical post of next st, inserting hook from right to left, draw yarn through and work st as usual (*see page 21*).

Back-post treble crochet (BPtr): Bring hook to back, work in back vertical post of next st, inserting hook from left to right, draw yarn through and work st as usual (*see page 21*).

Foundation chain: Ch 25.

Row 1: 1 tr in 3rd chain from hook, 1 tr in each ch to last ch, 1 htr in last ch, turn.

Row 2: Ch 2, miss first htr from last rnd, 1 FPtr around the post of each of next 3 tr, [1 BPtr around post of each foll 3 tr, 1 FPtr around post of each of next 3 tr] 4 times, 1 htr in top of ch-3, turn.

Row 3: Ch 2, miss first htr from last rnd, 1 BPtr around post of each of next 3 tr, [1 FPtr around post of each foll 3 tr, 1 BPtr around post of each of foll 3 tr] 4 times, 1 htr in top of ch-2, turn.

Row 4: Rep Row 3.

Rows 5 to 6: Rep Row 2.

Rows 7 to 8: Rep Row 3.

Rows 9 to 10: Rep Row 2.

Rows 11 to 12: Rep Row 3.

Rows 13 to 14: Rep Row 2.

Rows 15 to 16: Rep Row 3.

Fasten off and darn in ends neatly.

*

bobble ridge

An unusual construction for bobbles that uses double treble stitches on a background of double crochet, giving extra height. Worked in a cotton yarn, this produces a twisty effect; worked in soft wool, it creates a larger, squidgy bobble, offering you a choice of textures.

A

Special stitch used:

Make double treble bobble (MDTB): Leaving last loop of each st on hook, 3 dtr in next st, yoh and draw through all 4 loops, bend 3 dtr over to form a bobble (*see page 19*).

Foundation chain: Ch 30, turn.

Row 1: (RS) Miss 1 ch, 1 dc in each ch to end, turn.

Row 2: Ch 1 (counts as 1 dc), 1 dc in each dc to end, turn.

Row 3: Rep Row 2.

Row 4: Ch 1 (counts as 1 dc), 1 dc in first dc, 1 dc in each of next 3 dc, *MDTB in next dc, 1 dc in each of next 9 dc; rep from * 2 times, MDTB in next dc, 1 dc in each of last 4 dc.

Row 5: Rep Row 2.

Rows 6 to 31: Rep Rows 4 and 5.

Rows 32 to 33: Rep Row 2 two times. Fasten off.

* lazy daisy

A light, lacy square with a central flower motif that is composed of chain stitches. Easy and quick to work up, this square would make adorable curtain panels or table runners.

A

Special stitch used:

Cluster (cl): Make cluster with 3 tr (*see page 18*).

Foundation ring: Ch 5, sl st in first ch to form ring.

Round 1: Ch 1, 11 dc in ring, sl st in first ch.

Round 2: *Ch 15, sl st in next dc; rep from * 11 times, working last sl st in sl st at end of Round 1.

Round 3: Sl st along to centre of first lp, *ch 4, 1 dc in next lp, ch 4, cl in next lp, ch 4, cl in same lp, ch 4, 1 dc in next lp; rep from * 3 times, working last dc in sl st at beg of rnd.

Round 4: Sl st along to centre of first ch-4 sp, ch 3, [yoh, insert hook in same sp, yoh, draw through 2 lps] 2 times, yoh, draw through all lps on hook (counts as cluster), *ch 4, 1 dc in next sp, ch 4, [cl, ch 4, cl] in next ch-4 sp (forms corner), ch 4, 1 dc in new ch-4 sp, ch 4, cl in next sp; rep from * 3 times omitting last cl, and sl st in top of beg ch-3 to join.

Round 5: Sl st in next sp, ch 6 (counts as 1 htr, ch 4), 1 tr in next sp, ch 4, [cl, ch 4, cl] in next ch-4 sp (forms corner), ch 4, 1 tr in next sp, ch 4, 1 htr in next sp, ch 4, *1 htr in next sp, ch 4, 1 tr in next sp, ch 4, [cl, ch 4, cl] in next ch-4 sp (forms corner), ch 4, 1 tr in next sp, ch 4, 1 htr in next sp, ch 4; rep from * 2 times, sl st in first ch to join.

Round 6: Sl st in next sp, ch 3, [yoh, insert hook in same sp, yoh, draw through 2 lps] 2 times, yoh, draw through all lps on hook (counts as cluster), ch 4, cl in next sp, ch 4, *[cl, ch 4, cl] in corner cl sp, ch 4, [cl in next sp, ch 4] 5 times; rep from * 2 times, [cl, ch 4, cl] in corner cl sp, ch 4, [cl in next sp, ch 4] 3 times, sl st in top of beg ch-3 to join.

Fasten off yarn and darn in ends neatly.

** prairie rose

Large scallops frame a nubbly popcorn rose, making this block a perfect centrepiece for a throw or pillow cover. Work up in a flat, smooth yarn to emphasize the patterning.

A

B

Special stitches used:

Beginning popcorn (beg pc): Ch 3, make popcorn with 4 tr (*see page 19*).

Popcorn (pc): Make popcorn with 5 tr.

Foundation ring: Using yarn A, begin with magic ring method.

Round 1: Beg pc in ring, ch 3, *pc in ring, ch 3; rep from * 6 times, sl st in top of beg pc to join.

Round 2: Ch 1 *[1 dc, 1 htr, 3 tr, 1 htr, 1 dc] in ch-3 lps to end of rnd, sl st in first dc to join.

Round 3: Ch 1, *[1 tr in back of top of pc from Round 1 (go behind work to locate this), ch 6]; rep from * to end of rnd, sl st in first tr to join.

Round 4: Ch 1, sl st along to first ch-6, *[1 dc, 1 htr, 1 tr, 1 hdtr, 4 dtr, 1 hdtr, 1 tr, 1 htr, 1 dc] in ch-6 sp, 1 dc in next tr; rep from * to end of rnd omitting last dc, sl st in ch-1 to join. Fasten off yarn A.

Round 5: Using yarn B, sl st in 2nd dtr of Round 4, [ch 3, 2 tr, ch 3, 3 tr] in same st (first corner), *ch 2, 1 dtr in dc between two petals, ch 2, 1 dc in 2nd dtr of next petal, ch 2, 1 dtr in dc between two petals, ch 2**, [3 tr, ch 3, 3 tr] in 2nd dtr of next petal; rep from * to end of rnd ending at **, sl st in beg ch-3 to join.

Round 6: Ch 4 (counts as 1 tr, ch 1), *[3 tr, ch 2, 3 tr] in ch-3 sp, ch 1, 1 tr in 6th tr of Round 5 corner, 2 tr in ch-2 sp, 1 tr in dtr, 2 tr in ch-2 sp, 1 tr in dc, 2 tr in ch-2 sp, 1 tr in dtr, 2 tr in ch-2 sp**, 1 tr in first tr of Round 5 corner, ch 1; rep from * to end of rnd ending at **, sl st in ch-4 to join.

Fasten off and darn in ends neatly.

68

*
tiny lace

A useful, plainer block that is easy and quick to work up and mixes well with many other blocks. Use with more decorative grannies or flower blocks, or mix with other textural squares to make a plainer composite piece. It is an excellent beginner block.

Special stitch used:

Make bobble (MB): Make bobble with 3 tr (*see page 19*).

Foundation chain: Ch 33.

Row 1: [1 tr, ch 1, 1 tr] in 5th ch from hook, *miss 2 ch, [1 tr, ch 1, 1 tr] in next ch; rep from * to end of row, turn.

Row 2: Ch 3 (counts as 1 tr), *MB in next ch-1 sp, ch 2; rep from * to end of row, 1 tr in last st, turn.

Row 3: Ch 1, 1 dc in first tr, *1 dc in top of next bobble, 2 dc in next ch-2 sp; rep from * to end of row, 1 dc in last st, turn.

Row 4: Ch 4 (counts as 1 tr, ch 1), *miss 1 dc, 1 tr in next dc, ch 1; rep from * to end of row, 1 tr in last st, turn.

Row 5: Ch 1, 1 dc in each tr and every ch-1 sp to end of row, turn.

Row 6: Ch 3 (counts as 1 tr), miss 1 dc, *[1 tr, ch 1, 1 tr] in next dc, miss 2 dc; rep from * to end of row, 1 tr in last st, turn.

Rows 7 to 11: Rep Rows 2 to 6.

Rows 12 to 16: Rep Rows 2 to 6.

Fasten off and darn in ends neatly.

69

*
sheila

This lacy flower was found in a vintage doily and would look equally good in pastel colours. This block is great for beginners to practise basic stitches.

Special stitches used:

3-double treble cluster (3-dtr cl): Make cluster with 3 dtr (*see page 18*)

4-double treble cluster (4-dtr cl): Make cluster with 4 dtr.

Foundation ring: Using yarn A, ch 4, sl st in first ch to form ring.

Round 1: Ch 5 (counts as 1 tr, ch 2), *1 tr in ring, ch 2; rep from * 6 times, sl st in 3rd ch of beg ch-5 to join.

Round 2: Sl st in first ch-2 sp, ch 3 (counts as 1 tr), 3 tr in same sp, ch 1, *4 tr in next ch-2 sp, ch 1; rep from * 6 times, sl st in top of beg ch-3 to join. Fasten off.

Round 3: Join yarn B, ch 4 (counts as 1 dtr), 3d-tr cl, *ch 2, 1 dtr in next ch-1 sp, ch 2, 4-dtr cl; rep from * 6 times, ch 2, 1 dtr in next ch-1 sp, ch 2, sl st in top of first 3-dtr cl to join.

Round 4: Sl st in next ch-2 sp, 1 dc in same sp, *ch 5, 1 dc in next ch-2 sp: rep from * 14 times, ch 5, sl st in first dc to join.

Round 5: Sl st in next ch-5 sp, 1 dc in same sp, *ch 6, 1 dc in next ch-5 sp; rep from * 14 times, ch 6, sl st in first dc to join.

Round 6: Ch 7 (counts as 1 dtr, ch 3), 1 dtr in same st, *ch 2, 1 dc in next ch-6 sp, [ch 3, 1 sc in next ch-6 sp] 3 times, ch 2**, [1 dtr, ch 3, 1 dtr] in next dc; rep from * 2 times and from * to ** 1 time, sl st in 4th ch of beg ch-7 to join.

Round 7: Ch 2 (counts as 1 htr), *5 htr in next ch-3 sp (forms corner), 1 htr in next dtr, 2 htr in next ch-2 sp, 1 htr in next dc, 3 htr in next ch-3 sp, 1 htr in next dc, 3 dc in next ch-3 sp, 1 htr in next dc, 3 htr in next ch-3 sp, 1 htr in next dc, 2 htr in next ch-2 sp**, 1 htr in next dtr; rep from * 2 times, and from * to ** 1 time, sl st in top of beg ch-2 to join. Fasten off.

Round 8: Join yarn C, ch 1, 1 dc in same st, 1 dc in each of next 3 htr, 3 dc in next htr (3rd htr of corner 5-htr group), *1 dc in every st to next corner htr, 3 dc in next htr; rep from * 2 times, 1 dc in every st to beg of rnd, sl st in first dc to join.

Fasten off and darn in ends.

***
pomegranate

Little puff stitches reminiscent of pomegranate seeds pepper this sweet block, giving it a subtle but pleasing texture. Here we have used harmonious colours, but it would look equally effective worked in a range of contrasts or even one colour.

A
B
C
D

Special stitch used:

Puff stitch (pf): Make puff stitch with 3 tr, ch-1 to seal pf (see page 19).

Foundation ring: Using yarn A, make a magic ring.

Round 1: Ch 3 (counts as 1 tr), [1 pf in ring, 1 tr in ring] 5 times, 1 pf in ring, sl st in top of beg ch-3 to join. Fasten off yarn A.

Round 2: Join yarn B in any st, ch 1, 1 dc in every st including ch-1 to secure pf to end, sl st in first dc to join – 18 sts. Fasten off yarn B.

Round 3: Join yarn C, ch 4 (counts as 1 tr, ch 1), *1 pf in next dc, ch 1, 1 tr in next dc; rep from * 7 times, 1 pf in last dc, ch 1, sl st in 3rd ch of beg ch-4 to join. Fasten off yarn C.

Round 4: Join yarn D in any st, ch 1, 1 dc in every st around to end, sl st in first dc to join. Fasten off yarn D.

Round 5: Join yarn A in any dc, ch 3 (counts as 1 tr), 1 pf in same st, *ch 2, miss 1 dc, 1 pf in next dc; rep from * 16 times, ch 2, sl st in top of beg ch-3 to join. Fasten off yarn A.

Round 6: Join yarn B in any ch-2 sp, ch 1, *2 dc in ch-2 sp, ch 1; rep from * to end, sl st in first dc to join. Fasten off yarn B.

Round 7: Join yarn C in any dc, ch 1, 1 dc in every dc and in every ch-1 sp to end, sl st in first dc to join.

Round 8: Ch 3 (counts as 1 tr), [2 tr, ch 3, 3 tr] in same sp (forms corner), *1 tr in next dc, 1 htr in each of next 2 dc, 1 dc in each of next 8 dc, 1 htr in each of next 2 dc, 1 tr in next dc**, [3 tr, ch 3, 3 tr] in next dc; rep from * 2 times, and from * to ** 1 time, sl st in top of beg ch-3 to join. Fasten off yarn C.

Round 9: Join yarn D in any ch-3 corner sp, ch 1, *[1 dc, ch 2, 1 dc] in corner sp, 1 dc in every st to next ch-3 corner sp; rep from * 3 times, sl st in first dc to join. Fasten off yarn D.

Round 10: Join yarn A in any ch-2 corner sp, ch 3 (counts as 1 tr), *[1 pf, ch 3, 1 pf] in corner sp, [ch 2, miss 1 dc, 1 pf in next dc] 10 times to corner, miss 1 sc, ch 2; rep from * 3 times, sl st in top of beg ch-3 to join. Fasten off yarn A.

Round 11: Join yarn C in any ch-3 corner sp, ch 1, 5 dc in corner sp, 2 dc in every ch-2 sp to next corner; rep from * 3 times, sl st in first sc to join.

Fasten off and darn in ends.

*

roots

A beginner-level textured block, it works up quickly to create a bold stripe pattern. Great for mixing and matching – rotate the blocks before joining for a patchwork effect.

A
B
C

Foundation chain: Using yarn A, ch 35.

Row 1: 1 dc in 2nd ch from hook; *ch 2, miss 2 ch, 1 dc in next ch; rep from * , ending row with 1 dc in last ch, ch 3, turn.

Row 2: 1 htr in first dc, *miss 2 sts , 3 tr in next dc; rep from * , ending row with 1 tr in last st, ch 3, turn.

Row 3: 1 htr in first st, *miss 2 sts, 3 tr in next st; rep from * , ending row with 2 tr in last st, ch 3, turn.

Row 4: 1 htr in first st, *3 tr in middle tr of the 3-tr cluster below, miss 2 sts; rep from * , ending row with 1 tr in last htr, ch 3, turn.

Rows 5 to 6: Rep Row 2.

Row 7: Rep Row 2, fasten off yarn A.

Row 8: Join yarn B, rep Row 2.

Rows 9 to 11: Rep Row 2.

Row 12: Rep Row 2, fasten off yarn B.

Row 13: Join yarn C, rep Row 2.

Rows 14 to 17: Rep Row 2.

Rows 18 to 19: Rep Row 1.

Fasten off and darn in ends neatly.

★★★

poinsettia

A familiar festive flower, this block has layered petals created by working up and down chains. This could also be made in other colours to resemble lilies or aloe vera, or used in repeat for special table decorations, pillows or throws.

A
B
C
D
E

Foundation ring: Using yarn A, ch 4, sl st in first ch to form ring.

Round 1: Ch 3 (counts as 1 htr, ch 1), [1 htr, ch 1] 7 times in ring, sl st in 2nd ch of beg ch-3 to join. Fasten off.

Round 2: Join yarn B in any ch-1 sp, ch 1, 1 dc in every ch-1 sp and every htr to end, sl st in first dc to join.

Round 3: *Ch 8, 1 dc in 2nd ch from hook, 1 htr in each of next 2 ch, 1 tr in each of next 2 ch, 1 dtr in each of last 2 ch, miss 1 bc at base of petal, sl st in next dc, ch 1, turn, 1 sl st in every st along petal to tip, ch 1, turn, 1 dc in first sl st, 1 htr in each of next 2 sl sts, 1 tr in each of next 2 sl sts, 1 dtr in each of last 2 sl sts, miss 1 dc, sl st in next dc at base; rep from * 3 times, sl st in first petal base to join – 4 petals made. Fasten off.

Round 4: Join yarn C to any sl st in centre of any petal at back of base (where centred ridge meets base). Working behind petals of Round 3, repeat Round 3 from * to create 4 petals that sit behind, and alternate to, Round 3 petals. Sl st in first petal of Round 4 to join. Fasten off.

Round 5: Join yarn D at tip of any petal, 2 dc in same st, *ch 7, 2 dc in tip of next petal; rep from * 6 times, ch 7, sl st in first dc to join.

Round 6: Ch 2 (counts as 1 htr), *7 dc in next ch-7 loop, 1 htr in each of next 2 dc, [4 tr, ch 2, 4 tr] in next ch-7 loop (forms corner), 1 htr in each of next 2 dc; rep from * 3 times, omitting last htr, sl st in top of beg ch-2 to join. Fasten off.

Round 7: Join yarn E in same st, sl st in next st along, ch 3 (counts as 1 htr, ch 1), *[1 htr, ch 1] to next corner ch-2 sp, [1 htr, ch 1, 1 htr, ch 1] in corner ch-sp; rep from * 3 times, [1 htr, ch 1] to end, sl st in 2nd ch of beg ch-3 to join.

Round 8: Ch 1, 1 dc in every htr and in every ch-1 sp to corner, 3 dc in corner ch-1 sp; rep from * to end, sl st in first dc to join.

Fasten off and darn in ends neatly.

*
st george's cross

This striking square is deceptively simple to make and has a Maltese cross motif at its heart. It would look equally stunning created in especially strong primary colours, or black, white and one bright hue.

A
B
C

Foundation ring: Using yarn A, ch 4, join with sl st to form ring.

Round 1: Ch 3 (counts as 1 tr), 2 tr in ring, ch 4, *3 tr in ring, ch 4; rep from * 2 times, sl st in top of beg 3-ch to join. Fasten off yarn A.

Round 2: Join yarn B, ch 3 (counts as 1 tr), 1 tr in each of next 2 tr, [3 tr, ch 4, 3 tr] in next ch-4 sp, *1 tr in each of next 3 tr, [3 tr, ch 4, 3 tr] in next ch-4 sp; rep from * 2 times, sl st in top of 3-ch to join. Fasten off yarn B.

Round 3: Join yarn C, ch 3 (counts as 1 tr), 1 tr in next 2 tr, *ch 2, miss next 3 tr, [3 tr, ch 4, 3 tr, ch 2] in next ch-4 sp, miss next 3 tr**, 1 tr in next 3 tr; rep from * 2 times, then from * to ** 1 time, sl st in top of 3-ch to join.

Round 4: Ch 3 (counts as 1 tr), 1 tr in next 2 tr, *3 tr in every ch-2 sp and 1 tr in every tr along side of square to corner**, [3 tr, 4 ch, 3 tr] in next corner ch-4 sp; rep from * 2 times and from * to ** 1 time, 3 tr in last ch-2 sp, sl st in top of 3-ch to join. Fasten off yarn C.

Round 5: Join yarn A, rep Round 4. Fasten off yarn A.

Round 6: Join yarn B, rep Round 4.

Fasten off and darn in ends neatly.

**
deck chairs

This fun square is composed of nine small squares that are worked in simple stripes of double crochet. They are then rotated to form a simple pattern and sewn together. Careful arrangement of each square of colour forms a larger diagonal colour repeat.

A
B
C
D

Foundation chain: Using yarn A, ch 11 (counts as 10 sts, 1 tch).

Row 1: 1 dc in 2nd ch from hook, 1 dc in each ch to end, turn.

Row 2: Ch 1, 1 dc in every st, turn.

Row 3: Rep Row 2.

Rows 4 to 7: Rep Row 2, using yarn B.

Rows 8 to 11: Rep Row 2, using yarn A.

Fasten off and darn in ends.

Create 2 more squares in the same way in the same colours, 3 squares using yarn C instead of A, and 3 using yarn D instead of A. You should now have 9 squares.

Completing the square: Arrange the squares as shown in the photograph here. Take care that they are all RS facing. Stitch them together using either overcast stitch or backstitch, or, if you prefer, you could crochet the squares together using slip stitch or double crochet and a length of yarn B.

75

***

wonderfully woolly

Inspired by elaborate and heavily textured Victorian crochet, this block combines both popcorns and post stitches to produce a dense, warm square that is ideal for using in a winter afghan.

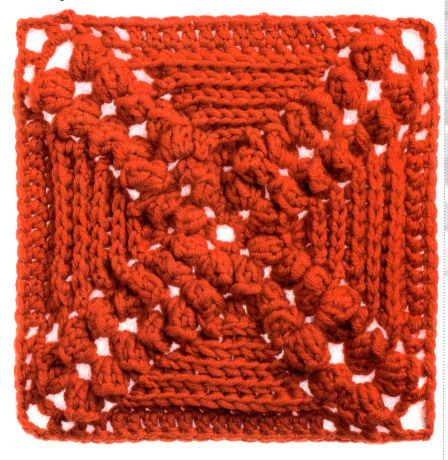

Special stitches used:

Beginning popcorn (beg pc): Ch 3, make popcorn with 4 tr (*see page 19*).

Popcorn (pc): Make popcorn with 5 tr.

Back-post treble crochet (BPtr): Bring hook to back, work in back vertical post of next st, inserting hook from left to right, draw yarn through and work st as usual (*see page 21*).

Foundation ring: Begin with magic ring method.

Round 1: Ch 1, 1 dc in ring [ch 4, 2 dc in ring] 3 times, ch 4, 1 dc in ring, sl st in ch-1 to join.

Round 2: Sl st in first ch-4 sp, *ch 1, 1 dc in same sp, ch 2, [beg pc, ch 5, pc] in same sp**, ch 2 [pc, ch 5, pc] in next ch-4 sp; rep from * 2 times, ch 2, sl st in top of first pc to join.

Round 3: Sl st in first pc, ch 1, [beg pc, ch 5, pc] in same sp, *ch 2, 3 tr in next sp, ch 2, pc in next ch-5 sp, ch 5, pc in same sp; rep from * 2 times, ch 2, 3 tr in next sp, ch 2, sl st in top of first pc to join.

Round 4: Sl st in first ch-5 sp, [beg pc, ch 5, pc] in same sp, *ch 2, 2 BPtr in dc of last rnd, 1 BPtr in middle dc of last rnd, 2 BPtr in last tr of last rnd, ch 2**, pc in next sp, ch 5, pc in same sp; rep from * 2 times, on final side, rep from * to **, sl st in top of beg pc to join.

Round 5: Sl st in first ch-5 sp, [beg pc, ch 5, pc] in same sp, *ch 2, 2 BPtr in first BPtr of last rnd, 1 BPtr in each of next 3 BPtr of last rnd, 2 BPtr in last BPtr of last rnd, ch 2**, pc in next sp, ch 5, pc in same sp; rep from * 2 times, on final side rep from * to **, sl st in top of beg pc to join.

Round 6: Sl st in first ch-5 sp; [beg pc, ch 5, pc] in same sp, *ch 2, 2 BPtr in first BPtr of last rnd, 1 BPtr in each of next 5 BPtr of last rnd, 2 BPtr in last BPtr of last rnd, ch 2**, pc in next sp, ch 5, pc in same sp; rep from * 2 times, on final side rep from * to **, sl st in top of beg pc to join.

Round 7: Sl st in first ch-5 sp, beg pc, ch 5, pc in same sp, *ch 2, 2 BPtr in first BPtr of last rnd, 1 BPtr in each of next 7 BPtr of last rnd, 2 BPtr in last BPtr of last rnd, ch 2**, pc in next sp, ch 5, pc in same sp; rep from * 2 times, on final side rep from * to **, sl st in top of beg pc to join.

Round 8: Sl st in first ch-5 sp, beg pc, ch 5, pc in same sp, *ch 2, 2 BPtr in first BPtr of last rnd, 1 BPtr in each of next 9 BPtr of last rnd, 2 BPtr in last BPtr of last rnd, ch 2**, pc in next sp, ch 5, pc in same sp; rep from * 2 times, on final side rep from * to **, sl st in top of beg pc to join.

Round 9: Ch 1, 1 dc in same sp, ch 3 (counts as 1 tr, 1 ch), 1 tr in corner sp, *ch 5, 1 tr in same sp, ch 1, 1 tr in top of pc, ch 1, 1 tr in next ch-2 sp, ch 1, 1 tr in each of next 13 sts, ch 1, 1 tr in next sp, ch 1, 1 tr in top of pc, ch 1**, 1 tr in corner sp, rep from * 2 times, then on final side from * to **, sl st in top of first dc to join.

Fasten off and darn in ends neatly.

*

sundae

A cheery design to brighten up any interior; make multiples for a sunny cushion or a welcoming throw. Use sunshine colours to add to the vibrancy.

A
B

Special stitches used:

Make 2-double treble bobble (2-dtr MB): Make bobble with 2 dtr (see page 19).

Make 3-double treble bobble (3-dtr MB): Make bobble with 3 dtr.

Foundation ring: Using yarn A, ch 4, join with sl st to form ring.

Round 1: Ch 3 (counts as 1 dtr), 2-dtr MB in ring, ch 3, *3-dtr MB, ch 3; rep from * 4 times, sl st in top of first bobble to join. Fasten off yarn A.

Round 2: Join yarn B, ch 5 (counts as 1 dtr, ch 2), 1 dtr in ch-2 sp, *ch 2, 1 dtr in top of next bobble, ch 2, 1 dtr in next ch-2 sp; rep from * to end of rnd ending with ch 2, sl st in 3rd ch of beg ch-5 to join.

Round 3: Ch 5 (counts as 1 dtr and ch 1), *1 dtr in ch-2 sp, ch 1, 1 dtr in next st,

ch 1; rep from * to end of rnd, sl st in 4th ch of beg ch-5 to join. Fasten off yarn B.

Round 4: Sl st yarn A in first ch-1 sp, ch 3 (counts as 1 tr), [2 tr, ch 3, 3 tr] in same sp (first corner), *[ch 1, miss next ch-1 sp, 3 tr in next ch-1 sp] 1 time **, ch 1, [3 tr, ch 3, 3 tr] in next ch-1 sp; rep 2 times, then from * to ** 1 time, sl st in top of beg ch-3 to join.

Round 5: Sl st in next 2 tr, sl st in next ch-3 sp, ch 3 (counts as 1 tr), [2 tr, ch 3, 3 tr] in ch-3 sp (first corner), *ch 1, 3 tr in next ch-1 sp, miss next ch-1 sp, ch 1, [3 tr in next ch-1 sp, ch 1] 2 times**, [3 tr, ch 3, 3 tr] in next ch-3 sp; rep from * to end of rnd ending last rep at **, sl st in top of beg ch-3 to join.

Round 6: Sl st in next 2 tr, sl st in next ch-3 sp, ch 3 (counts as 1 tr), [2 tr, ch 3, 3 tr] in same ch-3 sp (first corner), *ch 1, 3 tr in next ch-1 sp, miss next ch-1 sp,

ch 1, [3 tr in next ch-1 sp, ch 1] 3 times**, [3 tr, ch 3, 3 tr] in next ch-3 sp; rep from * to end of rnd, ending last rep at **, sl st in top of beg ch-3 to join. Fasten off yarn A.

Round 7: Sl st yarn B in first ch-3 sp, ch 1, *5 dc in next ch-3 sp, 1 dc in each tr and ch-1 sp across; rep from * to end of rnd, sl st in beg dc to join.

Fasten off and darn ends in neatly.

***

filet heart

As with all filet work, the charm of this square is truly revealed when it is used in a context that allows the light to stream through: create multiples and use them in a border for a plainer filet curtain panel. Even repeated around a lampshade would set this block off to advantage.

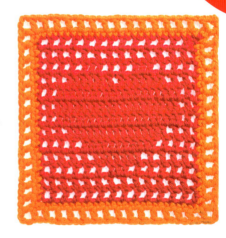

A
B

Note: To 'fill' a square, work 1 tr instead of [ch 1, miss 1 ch].

Foundation chain: Using yarn A, ch 27.

Row 1: Ch 3 (counts as 1 tr, ch 1), 1 tr in 6th ch from hook, *ch 1, miss 1 ch, 1 tr in next ch; rep from * to end of row, turn – 13 squares in total.

Row 2: Rep Row 1.

Row 3: Rep Row 1, but fill square 7.

Row 4: Rep Row 1, but fill squares 6 to 8.

Row 5: Rep Row 1, but fill squares 5 to 9.

Row 6: Rep Row 1, but fill squares 4 to 10.

Row 7: Rep Row 1, but fill squares 3 to 11.

Rows 8 to 9: Rep Row 7.

Row 10: Rep Row 1, but fill squares 4 to 6 and 8 to 10.

Row 11: Rep Row 1, but fill squares 5 and 9.

Rows 12 to 13: Rep Row 1. Fasten off yarn A.

Round 14: Using yarn B, 1 dc in every tr, and 1 dc in every ch-1 sp, [1 dc, ch 1, 1 dc] in every corner st (27 sts along each edge, not inc ch 1), sl st in first dc to join.

Round 15: Ch 4 (counts as 1 tr, ch 1), miss 1 tr, 1 tr in next st, *ch 1, miss 1 st, 1 tr in next st; rep from * to corner, ch 3, 1 tr in next dc, miss 1 dc; rep from * to end of square, sl st in 3rd ch of beg ch-4 to join.

Fasten off and darn in ends neatly.

78

*
simple stripe

A useful, simple square that can be mixed and matched with almost anything. Perfect for beginners, this square is worked entirely in double crochet and has a firm texture, making it hard-wearing and practical.

A
B
C

Foundation chain: Using yarn A, ch 30.

Row 1: 1 dc in 2nd chain from hook, 1 dc in every ch to end, turn.

Row 2: Ch 1, 1 dc in every dc to end, turn.

Rows 3 to 12: Rep Row 2. Fasten off yarn A.

Row 13: Join yarn B, ch 1, 1 dc in every dc to end.

Rows 14 to 16: Rep Row 13. Fasten off yarn B.

Row 17: Join yarn C, ch 1, 1 dc in every dc to end.

Row 18: Ch 1, 1 dc in every dc to end. Fasten off yarn C.

Row 19: Join yarn B, ch 1, 1 dc in every dc to end.

Row 20: Ch 1, 1 dc in every dc to end. Fasten off yarn B.

Row 21: Join yarn A, ch 1, 1 dc in every dc to end.

Rows 22 to 37: Ch 1, 1 dc in every dc to end.

Fasten off and darn in ends neatly.

79

★★★
dogwood

Full of delicious picots and interesting shaping, this square was inspired by the Missouri gardens of the designer. Working in the picot loops can be fiddly, but is easy once you get used to it.

A
B

Special stitch used:

Picot-3: Ch 3 (at point to add picot), sl st in first ch of ch-3, creating picot loop.

Foundation ring: Begin with magic ring method.

Round 1: Using yarn A, ch 3 (counts as 1 tr), 11 tr in ring, sl st in top of ch-3 to join. Fasten off yarn A.

Round 2: Join yarn B, *ch 3, 2 dtr in same st, picot-3 at top of dtr, [2 dtr, ch 3, sl st] in next tr, ch 1, miss next st, sl st in next st; rep from * 3 times (Note: no need to do join, as final st of rep is sl st). Fasten off yarn B.

Round 3: Join yarn A, [1 dc, ch 1, 1 dc] (referred to as '3-lp' in picot-3 of first petal), *ch 5, 1 dtr in next ch-1 sp between two petals, ch 5**, [1 dc, ch 1, 1 dc] in next picot-3; rep from * 3 times, ending last rep at **, sl st in first dc to join.

Round 4: *Ch 4 over 3-lp, 1 dc in 2nd dc of 3-lp, 5 dc in next ch-5 sp, 1 dc in next dtr, 5 dc in next ch-5 sp, 1 dc in first dc of 3-lp; rep from *, sl st in top of beg of ch-4 to join.

Round 5: Ch 3 (counts as 1 tr), *[5 tr, ch 2, 5 tr] in next ch-4 sp, [1 tr in next dc, ch 1, miss 1 dc] 6 times**, 1 tr in next dc; rep from *, ending last rep at **, sl st in top of beg ch-3 to join.

Round 6: Ch 3 (counts as 1 tr), 1 tr in each of next 5 tr, *[2 tr, ch 2, 2 tr] in next ch-2 sp (forms first corner), 1 tr in each of next 5 tr, 1 tr in each of next 18 tr along side; rep from * to end of rnd omitting final 6 tr, sl st in top of beg ch-3 to join. Fasten off yarn A.

Round 7: Join yarn B; ch 1, 1 dc in same st, 1 dc in each of next 6 tr, *[1 dc, picot-3, 1 dc] in next ch-2 sp, 1 dc in each of next 27 dc; rep from * to end of rnd omitting last 7 dc, sl st in first dc to join.

Fasten off and darn all ends in neatly.

picot square

A familiar traditional pattern often found in vintage afghans or cot blankets, this is a highly adaptable block that can be used effectively in multiples or mixed with other squares.

A

B

C

Special stitch used:

Picot-3: Ch 3 (at point to add picot), sl st in first ch of ch-3, creating picot loop.

Foundation ring: Using yarn A, ch 6, join with sl st to form ring, or use magic ring method.

Round 1: Ch 3, (counts as 1 tr), 15 tr in ring, sl st in top of beg ch-3 to join.

Round 2: Ch 5, (counts as 1 tr, ch 2), *1 tr in next tr, ch 2; rep from * 14 times, sl st in 3rd ch of beg ch-4 to join.

Round 3: Sl st in next ch-2 sp, ch 3 (counts as 1 tr), 2 tr in same sp, *ch 1, 3 tr in next ch-2 sp, ch 1; rep from * 14 times, sl st in top of beg ch-3 to join. Fasten off yarn A.

Round 4: Join yarn B in any ch-1 sp with dc st, ch 3, 1 dc in next ch-1 sp, ch 6, *1 dc in next ch-1 sp, [ch 3, 1 dc in next ch-1 sp] 3 times, ch 6; rep from * 2 times, [ch 3, 1 dc in next ch-1 sp] 2 times, sl st in first dc to join.

Round 5: Sl st in next ch-3 sp, ch 3 (counts as 1 tr), 2 tr in same sp, [5 tr, ch 2, 5 tr] in next ch-6 lp, *3 tr in each of next 3 ch-3 sps, [5 tr, ch 2, 5 tr] in next ch-6 lp; rep from * 2 times, 3 tr in each of last 2 ch-3 sps, sl st in top of beg ch-3 to join.

Round 6: Ch 4 (counts as 1 tr, ch 1), [miss next tr, 1 tr in next st, ch 1] 3 times, *[2 tr, ch 2, 2 tr] in next corner sp, ch 1**, [miss next tr, 1 tr in next st, ch 1] 9 times; rep from * 2 times; then from * to ** 1 time, ch 1, [miss next tr, 1 tr in next st, ch 1] 5 times, sl st in top of beg ch-3 to join. Fasten off yarn B.

Round 7: Join yarn C to any corner sp, ch 3 (counts as 1 tr), *1 tr in each st and in each ch-1 sp to corner, [2 tr, ch 2, 2 tr] in each corner sp; rep from * all the way around, ending 1 tr in same sp as beg ch-3, sl st in top of beg ch-3 to join.

Round 8: Ch 1, 1 dc in each of next 8 tr, [*2 dc, picot-3, 1 dc] in corner sp, 1 dc in each of next 10 sts, picot-3 in next st, [1 dc in next 2 sts, picot-3] 4 times, 1 dc in each st to the corner sp; rep from * 2 times, 1 dc in each of next 9 tr, picot-3 in next st, [1 dc in next 2 sts, picot-3] 4 times, 1 dc in each st to beg dc, sl st in first dc to join.

Fasten off and darn in ends neatly.

**

cactus flower

This large-scale flower block mixes perfectly with plainer, denser blocks, including textural squares and four-patch grannies, to enhance its shell structures and give it centre stage. Although it looks complex, it works up quickly.

A
B
C

Foundation ring: Using yarn A, ch 4, sl st in first ch to form ring.

Round 1: *Ch 3 (counts as 1 tr), 17 tr, sl st in top of beg ch-3 to join. Fasten off.

Round 2: Join B in any st, *ch 3 (counts as 1 tr), 2 tr in same st, *ch 3, miss 2 sts, 3 tr in next st; rep from * 4 times, ch 3, sl st in top of beg ch 3 to join.

Round 3: Ch 3 (counts as 1 tr), 3 tr in next st, 1 tr in next st, ch 4, *1 tr in next st, 3 tr in next st, 1 tr in next st, ch 4; rep from * 4 times, sl st in top of beg ch-3 to join.

Round 4: Ch 3 (counts as 1 tr), 1 tr in same st, 1 tr in next st, ch 1, miss next st, 1 tr in next st, 2 tr in next st, ch 3, 1 dc in ch-4 sp, ch 3, *2 tr in next st, 1 tr in next st, ch 1, miss next st, 1 tr in next st, 2 tr in next st, ch 3, 1 dc in ch-4 sp, ch 3; rep from * 4 times, sl st in top of beg ch-3 to join. Fasten off.

Round 5: Join yarn C in same st where Round 4 ended, *1 dc in next tr, ch 2, miss 2 sts, [1 dc, ch 5, 1 dc] in next ch-1 sp, ch 2, miss 2 sts, 1 dc in next tr, ch 5; rep from * 5 times, sl st in first dc to join.

Round 6: *[7 tr, ch 1, 7 tr] in ch-5 loop, 1 dc in next dc, ch 2, [1 dc, ch 5, 1 dc] in next ch-5 loop, ch 2, 1 dc in next dc; rep from * 5 times, sl st in first dc to join. Fasten off.

Round 7: Join yarn A in same st where Round 6 ended, *1 dc in next dc, 1 dc in each of next 7 tr, ch 2, 1 dc in each of next 7 tr, 1 dc in next dc, [3 tr, ch 3, 3 tr] in next ch-5 loop; rep from * 5 times, sl st in first dc to join.

Round 8: Sl st in next 7 dc to next ch-2 sp, *1 dc in ch-2 sp, ch 6, 2 tr in next ch-3 sp, ch 3, miss 3 sts, [2 quad tr, ch 3, 2 ttr] in next dc, ch 3, 1 dc in next ch-2 sp, ch 6, 1 dc in next ch-3 sp, ch 6, 1 dc in next ch-2 sp, miss next 7 sts, [2 ttr, ch 3, 2 quad tr] in next dc, ch 3, 2 tr in next ch-3 sp, ch 6; rep from * 1 time, sl st in first dc to join.

Round 9: Ch 1, *7 dc in next ch-6 sp, 4 dc in next ch-3 sp, 1 dc in each of next 2 sts, [2 dc, ch 2, 2 dc] in next ch-3 sp, 1 dc in each of next 2 sts, 4 dc in next ch-3 sp, 1 dc in each of next 2 sts, [7 dc in next ch-6 sp] 2 times, 1 dc in each of next 2 sts, 4 dc in next ch-3 sp, 1 dc in each of next 2 sts, [2 dc, ch 2, 2 dc] in next ch-3 sp, 1 dc in each of next 2 sts, 4 dc in next ch-3 sp, 7 dc in next ch-6 sp; rep from * 1 time, sl st in first dc to join.

Fasten off and darn in ends.

★★★★

asymmetrical poppy

An interesting design that plays with offsetting a central motif. Different-sized stitches are used for the petals and centre, so take care when following the instructions. This floral block would be stunning worked in repeat to make a flower-garden throw.

A
B
C
D

Foundation ring: Using yarn A, begin with magic ring method.

Round 1: Ch 1, [2 dc, 2 htr, 5 tr, 2 htr, 2 dc] in ring, sl st in first ch-1 to join – 13 sts. Fasten off.

Round 2: Join yarn B, ch 1, 1 dc in same st, [1 dc, 1 htr] in next st, [1 htr, 1 tr] in next st, 2 tr in next st, [1 tr, 1 hdtr] in next st, 3 dtr in next st, [1 hdtr, 1 tr] in next st, 2 tr in next st, [1 tr, 1 htr] in next st, [1 htr, 1 dc] in next st, 1 dc in each rem st, sl st in beg ch-1 to join – 23 sts. Fasten off.

Round 3: Join yarn C, ch 1, 1 dc in same st, [2 dc in next st, 1 dc in each of next 2 sts] 7 times, 2 dc in next st, 1 dc in next st, sl st in first dc to join – 32 sts. Fasten off.

Round 4: Join yarn A, ch 1, 1 dc in same st, ch 4, miss 3 sts, 1 dc in next st, ch 4, miss 3 sts, 1 dc in next st, [ch 5, miss 3 sts, 1 dc in next st] 5 times, ch 4, sl st in first dc to join.

Round 5: Ch 1, 1 dc in same st, [1 htr, 3 tr, 1 htr] in ch-4 sp, 1 dc in next dc, [1 htr, 3 tr, 1 htr] in next ch-4 sp, 1 dc in next dc, *[1 htr, 2 tr, 3 hdtr, 2 tr, 1 htr] in next ch-5 sp, 1 dc in next sc; rep from * 4 times, [1 htr, 3 tr, 1 htr] in next ch-4 sp, sl st in first dc to join.

Round 6: Ch 2, 1 htr in same sp, ch 6, 1 htr in next dc (sp between petals), ch 6, 1 htr in next dc, [ch 8, 1 htr in next dc] 5 times, ch 6, sl st in first htr to join.

Round 7: Ch 1, 1 dc in same sp, *[1 htr, 7 tr, 1 htr] in ch-6 sp, 1 dc in next htr; rep from * 1 time, **[1 htr, 2 tr, 2 hdtr, 3 dtr, 2 hdtr, 2 tr, 1 htr] in next ch-8 sp, 1 dc in next htr; rep from ** 4 times, [1 htr, 7 tr, 1 htr] in last ch-6 sp, sl st in first dc to join. Fasten off.

Round 8: Join yarn D in centre (2nd) dtr of 2nd larger shell along (4th petal along from where yarn C ended), ch 1, 1 dc in same st, ch 4, 1 dtr in next dc, ch 4, [1 tr, ch 3, 1 tr] in 2nd dtr of next shell, ch 4, 1d tr in next dc, ch 3, 1 dc in 2nd dtr of new shell, ch 3, 1 dtr in next dc, ch 4, [1 tr, ch 3, 1 tr] in 2nd dtr of next shell, ch 5, 1 dtr in next dc, ch 3, 1 dc in 4th tr of next shell, ch 3, 1 dtr in next dc, ch 3, [1 tr, ch 3, 1 tr] in 4th tr of next shell, ch 3, 1 dtr in next sc, ch 2, 1 dc in 4th tr of next shell, ch 3, 1 dtr in next dc, ch 4, 1 dc in 2nd dtr of next shell, ch 2, miss 1 dtr, [1 tr, ch 3, 1 tr] in next st, ch 3, 1 dtr in next dc, ch 3, sl st in first dc to join.

Round 9: Join yarn B in last st, 5 dc in next ch-4 lp, 1 dc in next dtr, 5 dc in next ch-4 lp, 1 dc in next tr, [2 htr, 1 tr, ch 3, 1 tr, 2 htr] in next ch-3 lp, 1 dc in next tr, 5 dc in next ch-4 lp, 1 dc in next dtr, 4 dc in next ch-3 lp, 1 dc in next dc, 4 dc in next ch-3 lp, 1 dc in next dtr, 5 dc in next ch-4 lp, 1 dc in next tr, [2 htr, 1 tr, ch 3, 1 tr, 2 htr] in next ch-3 lp, 1 dc in next tr, 6 dc in next ch-5 lp, 1 dc in next dtr, 4 dc in next ch-3 lp, 1 dc in next dc, 4 dc in next ch-3 lp, 1 dc in next dtr, 4 dc in next ch-3 lp, 1 dc in next tr, [2 htr, 1 tr, ch 3, 1 tr, 2 htr] in next ch-3 lp, 1 dc in next tr, 4 dc in next ch-3 lp, 1 dc in next dtr, 3 dc in next ch-2 lp, 1 dc in next dc, 4 dc in next ch-3 lp, 1 dc in next dtr, 5 dc in next ch-4 lp, 1 dc in next dc, 2 dc in next ch-2 lp, 1 dc in next tr, [2 htr, 1 tr, ch 3, 1 tr, 2 htr] in next ch-3 lp, 1 dc in next tr, 4 dc in next ch-3 lp, 1 dc in next dtr, 4 dc in next ch-3 lp, sl st in first dc to join.

Round 10: Ch 1, *1 dc in every st to ch-3 corner sp, [2 dc, ch 1, 2 dc] in ch-3 corner sp; rep from * 3 times, sl st in first dc to join.

Fasten off and darn in ends neatly.

*

arcade square

A familiar pattern that is a lattice version of the traditional granny square structure. This block is a good beginner square and mixes particularly well with other designs.

A
B
C
D

Foundation ring: Using yarn A, ch 5, join with sl st to form ring, or use magic ring method.

Round 1: Ch 1, (counts as 1 tr), 15 tr in ring, sl st in top of beg ch-3 to join.

Round 2: Ch 4, (counts as 1 tr, ch 1), *1 tr in next tr, ch 1; rep from * 15 times, sl st in 3rd ch of beg ch-4 to join. Fasten off yarn A.

Round 3: Join yarn B in any ch-1 sp, ch 3 (counts as 1 tr), 1 tr, ch 3, 2 tr in same sp, *[ch 1, 1 dc in next ch-1 sp] 3 times, ch 1**, [2 tr, ch 3, 2 tr] in next ch-1 sp; rep from * 2 times, then from * to ** 1 time, sl st in top of beg ch-3 to join. Fasten off yarn B.

Round 4: Join yarn C in any corner ch-3 sp, ch 3 (counts as 1 tr), [1 tr, ch 3, 2 tr] in same corner sp, *ch 2, [1 dc, ch 1 in next ch-1 sp] 3 times, 1 dc, ch 2**, [2 tr, ch 3, 2 tr] in next ch-3 corner sp; rep from * 2 times and from * to ** 1 time, sl st in top of beg ch-3 to join.

Round 5: Sl st in next tr, sl st in in ch-3 corner sp; ch 3 (counts as first tr), [2 tr, ch 3, 3 tr] in same corner sp, ch 2, *[1 tr, ch 1 in next ch-sp] 4 times, 1 tr, ch 2**, [3 tr, ch 3, 3 tr] in next ch-3 corner sp; rep from * 2 times and from * to **1 time, sl st in top of beg ch-3 to join. Fasten off yarn C.

Round 6: Join yarn D in any corner ch-3 sp, ch 3 (counts as 1 tr), [2 tr, ch 3, 3 tr] in same corner sp, ch 2, *[1 tr, ch 1 in next ch-sp] 5 times, 1 tr, ch 2**, [3 tr, ch 3, 3 tr] in next ch-3 corner sp; rep from * 2 times, then from * to ** 1 time, sl st in top of beg ch-3 to join.

Round 7: Sl st in next 2 tr, sl st in ch-3 corner sp, ch 3 (counts as 1 tr), [2 tr, ch 3, 3 tr] in same corner sp, ch 2, *[1 tr, ch 1 in next ch-sp] 6 times, 1 tr, ch 2**, [3 tr, ch 3, 3 tr] in next ch-3 corner sp; rep from * 2 times and from * to ** 1 time, sl st in top of beg ch-3 to join. Fasten off yarn D.

Round 8: Join yarn A in any ch-3 corner sp, ch 3 (counts as 1 tr), [2 tr, ch 3, 3 tr] in same corner sp, 1 tr in each of next 3 tr, 2 tr in next ch-2 sp, *1 tr in next tr, 1 tr in next ch-1 sp; rep from * 6 times, 2 tr in next ch-2 sp, 1 tr in each of next 3 tr**, [3 tr, ch 3, 3 tr] in ch-3 corner sp; rep from * 2 times and from * to ** 1 time, sl st in top of beg ch-3 to join.

Round 9: Ch 1, *1 dc in each tr, 3 dc in each ch-3 corner sp; rep from * to end of rnd, sl st in first dc to join.

Fasten off and darn in ends neatly.

fans

A simple scalloped pattern that mixes well with other textural blocks or with more complex floral squares. This block has a wide range of potential uses and is a good beginner square to extend skills beyond a granny square.

A

Foundation chain: Ch 32.

Row 1: 1 dc in 2nd ch from hook, 1 dc in next ch, *ch 3, miss 3 ch, 1 dc in each of next 3 ch; rep from * to last 5 ch, ch 3, miss 3 ch, 1 dc in each of last 2 ch, turn.

Row 2: Ch 1, 1 dc in first dc, *5 tr in next ch-3 sp, miss 1 dc, 1 dc in next dc; rep from * to end of row, turn.

Row 3: Ch 3, *1 dc in 2nd, 3rd and 4th sts of next 5 tr group, ch 3; rep from * to end of row, ending last rep with 1 dc worked in 2nd, 3rd and 4th sts of last 5 tr group; ch 2, 1 dc in last st, turn.

Row 4: Ch 3, 2 tr in next ch-2 sp, miss 1 dc, 1 dc in next dc, *5 tr in next ch-3 sp, miss 1 dc, 1 dc in next dc; rep from * to end, 3 tr in last ch-3 sp, turn.

Row 5: Ch 1, 1 dc in each of first 2 tr, *ch 3, 1 dc in 2nd, 3rd and 4th sts of next 5-tr group; rep from * to end, with last rep ending at ch 3, 1 dc in each of 2nd tr and 3rd ch of beg ch-3, turn.

Rows 6, 10, 14 and 18: Rep Row 2.

Rows 7, 11, 15 and 19: Rep Row 3.

Rows 8, 12, 16 and 20: Rep Row 4.

Rows 9, 13, 17 and 21: Rep Row 5.

Fasten off and darn in ends neatly.

tequila sunrise

A subtly textured square that is gently ridged, with tiny spike stitches throughout. This design works well in a shiny yarn, which will catch the light and highlight this delicate pattern.

A

Special stitch used:

Spike stitch (spike st): Insert hook in top of dc one rnd below, yoh, pull yarn through to height of rnd being worked, complete stitch as normal (see *page 22*).

Foundation chain: Ch 31, turn.

Row 1: 1 dc in 2nd ch from hook, 1 dc in every ch to end, turn.

Row 2: Ch 1, 1 dc in back lp of every dc from Row 1, turn.

Row 3: Ch 1, miss first dc, 1 dc in back lp of each of next 2 dc, *spike st below next dc, 1 dc in back lp of each of next 3 dc; rep from * along row, ending 1 dc in back lp of last dc, sl st in ch-1 of last row (this gives straight edge), turn.

Row 4: Ch 1, miss first dc, 1 dc in back lp of every dc from last row to end, sl st in ch-1 of last row, turn.

Row 5: Ch 1, miss first dc, *1 dc in row below next dc, 1 dc in back lp of each of next 3 dc; rep from * to end, sl st in ch-1 of last row, turn.

Row 6: Ch 1, miss first dc, 1 dc in back lp of every dc from last row to end, sl st in ch-1 of last row, turn.

Rows 7 to 37: Rep Rows 3, 4, 5 and 6 in correct order.

Fasten off and darn in ends neatly.

★★★
folksy

This highly patterned block resembles a homespun sampler, full of texture and stitch changes. It is a dense fabric, so mix it with medium-weight blocks in afghans or blankets. Good for use in pillow covers or table mats, too.

A
B
C

Foundation chain: Using yarn A, ch 30 (counts as 29 sts, 1 tch).

Row 1: 1 dc in 2nd ch from hook, 1 dc in every ch to end, turn.

Row 2: Ch 1, 1 dc, *1 tr, 1 dtr, 1 tr, 1 dc; rep from * to end, turn. Fasten off yarn A.

Row 3: Join yarn B, ch 3 (counts as 1 dtr), 1 tr, 1 dc, *1 tr, 1 dtr**, 1 tr, 1 dc; rep from * to end, ending last rep at **, turn.

Row 4: Rep Row 3. Fasten off yarn B.

Row 5: Join yarn A, ch 1, 1 dc, *1 tr, 1 dtr, 1 tr, 1 dc; rep from * to end, turn.

Row 6: Ch 1, 1 dc in every st to end, turn. Fasten off yarn A.

Row 7: Join yarn B, rep Row 6. Fasten off yarn B.

Row 8: Join yarn C, rep Row 6. Fasten off yarn C.

Row 9: Join yarn A, ch 3 (counts as 1 tr, 1 ch), miss 1 st, 1 tr, *ch 1, miss 1 st, 1 tr; rep from * to end, turn. Fasten off yarn A.

Row 10: Join yarn C, rep Row 6. Fasten off yarn C.

Row 11: Join yarn B, rep Row 6. Fasten off yarn B.

Row 12: Join yarn A, rep Row 6.

Row 13: Rep Row 2. Fasten off yarn A.

Rows 14 to 15: Join yarn B, rep Row 3. Fasten off yarn B.

Row 16: Join yarn A, rep Row 5.

Row 17: Rep Row 6. Fasten off yarn A.

Rows 18 to 19: Join yarn C, ch 2 (counts as 1 tr), 1 tr in every st to end, turn.

Row 20: Rep Row 6. Fasten off yarn C.

Row 21: Join yarn A, rep Row 18.

Row 22: Rep Row 6. Fasten off yarn A.

Row 23: Join yarn B, rep Row 6.

Fasten off and darn in ends neatly.

★
granny stripes

A twist on the traditional granny pattern, this square is at its most effective when eye-popping contrast colours are used. No chain spaces are made between the groups of treble crochet, so a dense, warm fabric is produced.

A
B
C
D
E
F

Foundation chain: Using yarn A, ch 32 (counts as 31 ch, 1 tch).

Row 1: 1 dc in 2nd ch from hook and 1 dc in each ch to end, turn.

Row 2: Ch 3, (counts as 1 tr), 1 tr in same place, [miss 2 dc, 3 tr in next dc] 9 times, miss 2 dc, 2 tr in next dc, turn. Join yarn B.

Row 3: Ch 3, (counts as 1 tr), [3 tr in next sp between tr groups] 9 times, 1 tr in 3rd of 3-ch, turn. Join in yarn C.

Row 4: Ch 3, (counts as 1 tr), 1 tr in same place, [3 tr in next sp between tr groups] 8 times, 2 tr in 3rd of 3-ch, turn. Change to yarn B.

Row 5: Ch 3, (counts as 1 tr), [3 tr in next sp between tr groups] 9 times, 1 tr in 3rd of 3-ch, turn. Change to yarn A.

Rows 6 to 15: Rep Rows 4 and 5 five times, changing colours as directed below:

Row 6: Use yarn A.

Row 7: Use yarn D.

Row 8: Use yarn A.

Row 9: Use yarn B.

Row 10: Use yarn E.

Row 11: Use yarn B.

Row 12: Use yarn A.

Row 13: Use yarn F.

Row 14: Use yarn A.

Row 15: Use yarn B.

Row 16: Ch 1, 1 dc in each tr.

Fasten off yarn and darn in all ends neatly.

**

granada

A traditional block with a tiny God's eye motif at its centre, this works up quickly and mixes well with other grannies. Equally effective worked in a single colour or tonal colours as in our sample here.

A
B
C
D

Foundation ring: Using yarn A, ch 8, join with sl st to form ring, or use magic ring method.

Round 1: Ch 1, 16 dc in ring, join with sl st in first dc.

Round 2: *Ch 7, miss 3 dc, 1 dc in next dc; rep from * 3 times, sl st in first dc to join.

Round 3: Sl st in next ch-3 sp, ch 3 (counts as 1 tr), 1 tr in same sp, *ch 3, 2 tr in same sp, ch 3, tr2tog (inserting hook in same sp for first draw through lps and in next ch-7 sp for second draw through lps), ch 2, 2 tr in same ch-7 sp; rep from * 3 times omitting last 2 tr at end of last rep, sl st in top of beg ch-3 to join. Fasten off yarn A.

Round 4: Join yarn B to any ch-3 corner sp, ch 3 (counts as first tr), [1 tr, ch 3, 2 tr] in same corner sp, *ch 2, miss next 2 tr, 3 tr in next ch-2 sp, 1 tr in top of tr2tog cluster from rnd below, 3 tr in next ch-2 sp, ch 2**, miss next 2 tr, [2 tr, ch 3, 2 tr] in next corner ch-sp; rep from * 2 times, then from * to ** 1 time, sl st in top of beg ch-3 to join. Fasten off yarn B.

Round 5: Join yarn C to any corner ch-3 sp, ch 3 (counts as 1 tr), [2 tr, *ch 3, 3 tr] in same corner sp, ch 2, miss next 2 tr, 2 tr in next ch-2 sp, ch 1, miss next 1 tr, 1 tr in each of next 5 tr, ch 1, miss next 1 tr, 2 tr in next ch-2 sp, ch 2**, 3 tr in next ch-3 corner sp; rep from * 2 times and from * to ** 1 time, sl st in top of beg ch-3 to join. Fasten off yarn C.

Round 6: Join yarn D to any ch-3 corner sp, ch 3 (counts as 1 tr), [2 tr, *ch 3, 3 tr] in same corner sp, 1 tr in each of next 3 tr, ch 2, 1 tr in each of next 2 tr, ch 1, miss next tr, 1 tr in each of next 3 tr, ch 1, miss next tr, 1 tr in each of next 2 tr, ch 2, 1 tr in each of next 3 tr**, 3 tr in corner ch-3 sp; rep from * 2 times and then from * to ** 1 time, sl st in top of beg ch-3 to join.

Round 7: Ch 3, (counts as 1 tr), 1 tr in each of next 2 tr, *[3 tr, ch 3, 3 tr] in next ch-3 corner sp, 1 tr in each of next 6 tr, 2 tr in ch-2 sp, 1 tr in each of next 2 tr, 1 tr in next ch-1 sp, 1 tr in each of next 3 tr, 1 tr in next ch-1 sp, 1 tr in each of next 2 tr, 2 tr in next ch-2 sp, 1 tr in each of next 6 tr; rep from * 3 times omitting last 3 tr at end of last rep, sl st in top of beg ch-3 to join.

Round 8: Ch 1, *1 dc in each tr and 3 dc in each ch-3 corner sp; rep from * to end of rnd, sl st in first dc to join.

Fasten off and darn in ends neatly.

*

lotus

Multiple rounds of crocodile stitches create layers of petals with a hidden centre. This really unusual square is fun to work and creates a dense block that is sure to become a talking point in any interior design.

A
B
C

Special stitch used:

Crocodile stitch (croc st): 5 tr in side post of tr st, 5 tr in side post of next tr st, sl st in top of next tr (*see page 20*).

Foundation ring: Using yarn A, ch 5, sl st in first ch to form ring.

Round 1: Ch 1, 16 dc in ring, sl st in first dc to join.

Round 2: Ch 3 (counts as first tr), 1 tr in each of next 3 sts, *4 ch (forms corner), 1 tr in each of next 4 sts; rep from * 2 times, 4 ch, sl st in top of beg ch-3 to join. Fasten off, cut yarn and weave in ends.

Round 3: Join yarn B in any corner sp, ch 3 (counts as 1 tr), 2 tr in same sp, *1 tr in each of next 4 sts, 3 tr in next corner sp, ch 2 (forms corner), 3 tr in same corner sp; rep from * 2 times, 1 tr in each of next 4 sts, 3 tr in first corner sp, ch 2, sl st in top of beg ch-3 to join.

Round 4: Turn work to WS and work backwards, sl st in last ch-2 sp worked, sl st in next tr st, turn work to RS, *[croc st in next 3 tr] 3 times, sl st in next dc; rep from * 3 times, on the last sl st, fasten off, cut yarn and weave in ends.

Round 5: Join yarn C in any corner sp, ch 3 (counts as 1 tr), 1 tr in same sp, *[1 tr in middle of croc st, 2 tr in sp between 2 croc sts] 2 times, 1 tr in middle of croc st, 2 tr in corner sp, 4 ch (forms corner), 2 tr in same corner sp; rep from * 2 times, [1 tr in middle of croc st, 2 tr in sp between 2 croc sts] 2 times, 1 tr in middle of croc st, 2 tr in corner sp, 4 ch (forms corner), sl st in top of beg 3-ch to join.

Round 6: Ch 1, turn work to WS and work backwards, sl st in middle of corner ch sts, turn work to RS, *[croc st in next 3 tr] 3 times, croc st in next 2 tr, sl st in middle of corner ch sts; rep from * 3 times, on the last sl st fasten off, cut yarn and weave in ends.

Round 7: Join yarn B in any corner sp, ch 3 (counts as 1 tr), 1 tr in same sp, *[1 tr in middle of croc st, 2 tr in sp between 2 croc sts] 3 times; 1 tr in middle of croc st, 2 tr in corner sp, 3 ch (forms corner), 2 tr in same corner sp; rep from * 2 times, [1 tr in middle of croc st, 2 tr in sp between 2 croc sts] 3 times, 1 tr in middle of croc st, 2 tr in corner sp, ch-3 (forms corner), sl st in top of beg 3-ch to join.

Round 8: Ch 1, turn work to WS and work backwards, sl st in middle of corner ch sts, turn work to RS, *[croc st in next 3 tr] 4 times, croc st in next 2 tr, sl st in middle of corner ch sts; rep from * 3 times, on last sl st, fasten off, cut yarn and weave in ends.

Round 9: Join yarn A in any corner sp, 1 dc in the corner 1 dc in each tr and 1 dc between each tr (25 dc across one side), 3 dc in each corner, sl st in beg dc to join, ending with 2 dc in corner.

Round 10: Ch 3 (counts as first tr), 2 tr in same st (corner), *1 tr in each dc, 3 tr in middle st of corner 3 dc; rep from * to end of rnd, sl st in top of beg ch-3 to join.

Fasten off, cut yarn and weave in ends. Block work.

victoria's corner

An elegant lattice block that resembles carved woodwork patterns, this works up quickly and is easy to mix and match.

A
B
C

Foundation ring: Using yarn A, begin with magic ring method.

Round 1: Ch 3, tr2tog in ring, *ch 3, tr3tog in ring; rep from * 6 times, sl st in top of first cluster to join. Fasten off.

Round 2: Join yarn B, ch1, 5 dc in first ch-3 sp, *5 dc in next ch-3 sp; rep from * 6 times, sl st in beg ch-1 to join.

Round 3: Ch 1, 1 dc in same st, *ch 5, 1 dc in sp where last row scallops meet; rep from * 7 times, ending at ch 5, sl st in first dc to join.

Round 4: Ch 1, sl st in first ch-5 sp, *7 dc in next ch-5 sp; rep from * to end of rnd, sl st in beg ch-1 to join. Fasten off.

Round 5: With yarn C, sl st in centre dc (4th st) of first scallop, [ch 3, 2 tr, ch 3, 3 tr] in same st (first corner), *ch 3, 1 dc

in 4th st of next scallop, ch 3 **[3 tr, ch 3, 3 tr] in next scallop; rep from * 2 times and from * to ** 1 time, sl st in beg ch-3 to join.

Round 6: Sl st in next 2 tr, sl st in ch-3, ch 3 (counts as 1 tr), [2 tr, ch 3, 3 tr] in ch-3 sp (first corner)*, ch 1, 5 tr in ch-5 space, 1 tr in dc, 5 tr in next ch-5 sp, ch 1, **[3 tr, ch 3, 3 tr] in next ch-3 sp; rep from * 2 times, then from * to ** 1 time, sl st in top of beg ch-3 to join. Fasten off yarn C.

Round 7: Join yarn B, sl st in first ch-3 sp, ch 3 (counts as 1 tr), [2 tr, ch 3, 3 tr] in ch-3 sp (first corner), *ch 1, 3 tr in ch-1 sp, 1 tr in each of next 11 tr, 3 tr in next ch-1 sp, ch 1, **[3 tr, ch 3, 3 tr] in next ch-3 sp; rep from * 2 times, then from * to ** 1 time, sl st in top of beg ch-3 to join. Fasten off yarn B.

Round 8: Join yarn A, ch 2, 1 htr in same st, 1 htr in each of next 2 tr, 5 dc in ch-3 sp, *1 htr in each of next 3 tr, 1 htr in next ch-1 sp, 1 htr in each of next 17 tr, 1 htr in next ch-1 sp, 1 htr in each of next 3 tr, **5 htr in ch-3 sp; rep from * 3 times, ending last rep at **, sl st in top of beg ch-2 to join.

Fasten off and darn in ends neatly.

marsh mill

Inspired by an ancient windmill in the designer's home village, this square has a central spiral motif with a fine frame that creates an open, lacy motif. This is a challenging motif to work that pays rewards with the finished result.

A
B

Foundation ring: Using yarn A, ch 8, sl st in first ch to form ring.

Round 1: Ch1 (counts as 1 dc), 15 dc in ring, sl st in first ch to join.

FIRST SAIL OF WINDMILL

Row 1: Ch 12, 1 dc in 3rd ch from hook, 1 dc in next ch, 8 tr around ch made, 1 dc in each of last 3 ch sts, sl st in next dc along in ring, turn.

Row 2: Ch 2, 1 dc in each of next 3 dc, [ch 4, miss 1 dc, 1 dc in next dc] 4 times, 1 dc in each of next 2 dc, 1 dc in 2nd of beg ch-2, turn.

Row 3: Ch 1 (counts as 1 dc), 1 dc in each of next 3 dc, [4 dc in next ch-4 lp, 1 dc in next dc] 4 times, 1 dc in each of last 2 dc, sl st in next dc along in ring, turn.

SECOND SAIL OF WINDMILL

Row 1: Ch 11, sl st in st between 2nd and 3rd lp of first sail, turn, 1 dc in each of next 3 ch sts, 8 dc around ch made, 1 dc in each of last 3 ch, sl st in next dc along in ring, turn, complete as first sail, but on 2nd row, end with 1 dc in each of last 3 dc instead of last 2 dc and tch.

Work 6 more sails in this way. Fasten off.

Stitch tip of first spoke to sp between 2nd and 3rd lps of 8th sail.

BORDER

Round 1: Join yarn A to any sp between sails (where tip of one sail attaches to another), ch 5 (counts as 1 ttr), [ch 4, 1 ttr] in same sp (forms corner), *ch 4, 1 dc in each of sts 5 to 9 on sail edge, ch 5, 1 dc in each of sts 5 to 9 on next sail edge, ch 4**, [1 ttr, ch 4, 1 ttr] in next sp

between 2 sails; rep from * 2 times, then from * to ** 1 time, sl st in top of beg ch-5 to join. Fasten off yarn A.

Round 2: Join yarn B in any ch-4 corner sp, ch 1, [2 dc, ch 2, 3 dc] in corner ch-4 sp, *5 dc in next ch-4 sp, 1 dc in each of next 5 dc, 5 dc in next ch-5 sp**, [3 dc, ch 2, 3 dc] in next corner ch-4 sp; rep from * 2 times, then from * to ** 1 time, sl st in beg dc to join.

Fasten off and darn in ends neatly.

*

tangerine dream

A
B

This super-simple square is quick to work up and looks effective with its bold pattern. A great square to mix and match with more elaborate ones, or work up loads in varying strong colours for a bold, bright afghan.

Foundation ring: Using yarn A, ch 4, join with sl st to form ring.

Round 1: Ch 5 (counts as 1 tr, 2 ch), [3 tr in ring, ch 2] 3 times, 2 tr in ring, sl st in 3rd of beg 5-ch to join.

Round 2: Sl st along to centre of next 2-ch sp, ch 7 (counts as 1 tr, 4 ch), *2 tr in same sp, 1 tr in each of next 3 tr**, [2 tr, ch 4] in corner ch sp; rep from * 2 times, then from * to ** 1 time, 1 tr in first corner ch sp, sl st in 3rd of beg 7-ch to join.

Round 3: Sl st along to 3rd ch of next 4-ch sp, ch 7 (counts as 1 tr, 4 ch), *2 tr in same sp, 1 tr in each of next 7 tr**, [2 tr, ch 4] in corner ch sp; rep from * 2 times, then from * to ** 1 time, 1 tr in first corner ch sp, sl st in 3rd of beg 7-ch to join.

Round 4: Sl st along to 3rd ch of next 4-ch sp, ch 7 (counts as 1 tr, 4 ch), *2 tr in same sp, 1 tr in each of next 11 tr**, [2 tr, ch 4] in corner ch sp; rep from * 2 times, then from * to ** 1 time, 1 tr in first corner ch sp, sl st in 3rd of beg 7-ch to join.

Round 5: Sl st along to 3rd ch of next 4-ch sp, ch 7 (counts as 1 tr, 4 ch), *2 tr in same sp, 1 tr in each of next 15 tr**, [2 tr, ch 4] in corner ch sp; rep from * 2 times, then from * to ** 1 time, 1 tr in the first corner ch sp, sl st in 3rd of beg 7-ch to join.

Round 6: Sl st along to 3rd ch of next 4-ch sp, ch 7 (counts as 1 tr, 4 ch), *2 tr in same sp, 1 tr in each of next 19 tr**, [2 tr, ch 4] in corner ch sp; rep from * 2 times, then from * to ** 1 time, 1 tr in first corner ch sp, sl st in 3rd of beg 7-ch to join.

Round 7: Sl st along to 3rd ch of next 4-ch sp, ch 7 (counts as 1 tr, 4 ch), *2 tr in same sp, 1 tr in each of next 23 tr**, [2 tr, ch 4] in corner ch sp; rep from * 2 times, then from * to ** 1 time, 1 tr in first corner ch sp, sl st in 3rd of beg 7-ch to join. Fasten off yarn A. Join yarn B to same sp.

Round 8: Sl st along to 3rd ch of next 4-ch sp, ch 7 (counts as 1 tr, 4 ch), *2 tr in same sp, 1 tr in each of next 27 tr**, [2 tr, ch 4] in corner ch sp; rep from * 2 times, then from * to ** 1 time, 1 tr in first corner ch sp, sl st in 3rd of beg 7-ch to join.

Fasten off and darn all ends in neatly.

★★★
tiger lily

A striking and bold flower that has a flavour of the East about it; use as a defined central motif for a composite design, or individually, joined in lengths, for a table centrepiece. Equally gorgeous worked in a plain colour for an elegant bedspread.

A
B
C
D

Special stitches used:

Picot-3: Ch 3 (at point to add picot), sl st in first ch of ch-3, creating picot loop.

Spike stitch (spike st): Insert hook in space between clusters two rnds below, yoh, pull yarn through to height of rnd being worked, complete stitch as normal (*see page 22*).

Foundation ring: Using yarn A, ch 5, sl st in first ch to form ring.

Round 1: Ch 3, 1 tr in centre ring, ch 2, *2 tr, ch 2; rep from * 7 times, sl st in top of beg ch-3 to join. Fasten off, cut yarn and weave in ends.

Round 2: Join yarn B in any ch-2 sp, *1 dc in ch-2 sp, ch 4; rep from * 7 times, sl st in first dc st to join.

Round 3: Sl st in next ch-4 sp, *[1 dc, ch 1, 3 tr, picot-3, 2 tr, ch 1, 1 dc] in this sp; rep 7 times, sl st in first dc to join. Fasten off, cut yarn and weave in ends.

Round 4: Join yarn C in sp between two petals, *spike st in between two petals, ch 6; rep from * 7 times, sl st in first spike st to join.

Round 5: Sl st in next ch-6 sp, *[1 dc, ch 1, 4 tr, picot-3, 3 tr, ch 1, 1 dc] in this sp; rep 8 times in total, sl st in first dc to join. Fasten off, cut yarn and weave in ends.

Round 6: Join yarn D in sp between two petals, *spike st in between two petals, ch 8; rep from * 7 times, sl st in first spike st to join.

Round 7: Sl st in next ch-8 sp, *[1 dc, ch 1, 5 tr, picot-3, 4 tr, ch 1, 1 dc] in this sp; rep from * 7 times, sl st in first dc to join. Fasten off, cut yarn and weave in ends.

Round 8: Join yarn A in sp between two petals, *spike st in between two petals, ch 9; rep from * 7 times, sl st in first spike st to join.

Round 9: Sl st in next ch-9 sp, *[1 dc, ch 1, 4 tr, 1 dtr, ch 3, 1 tr in first ch of ch-3, 1 dtr, 4 tr, ch 1, 1 dc] in this sp; rep 7 times, sl st in first dc to join. Fasten off, cut yarn and weave in ends.

Round 10: Join yarn B in sp between two petals, *spike st in between two petals, ch 9; rep from * 7 times, sl st in first spike st to join.

Round 11: Sl st in ch-9 sp, [3 ch, 3 tr, 1 dtr, 1 ttr, 2 ch, 1 ttr, 1 dtr, 4 tr] in corner sp, *1 htr in next st (spike st from rnd below), 9 htr in next ch-9 sp, 1 htr in next st (spike st from rnd below), [4 tr, 1 dtr, 1 ttr, 2 ch, 1 ttr, 1 dtr, 4 tr] in corner sp; rep from * 2 times, 1 htr in next st (spike st from rnd below), 9 htr in next ch-9 sp, 1 htr in next st (spike st from rnd below), sl st in top of beg ch-3 to join.

Round 12: Ch 3 in same st (counts as first tr), *1 tr in each st below, [2 tr, ch 2, 2 tr] in each corner sp; rep from * to end of rnd, sl st in first tr to join.

Fasten off, cut yarn and weave in ends. Block work.

★★★★

berber

An unusual block with a carpet pile texture, this was inspired by Middle Eastern and North African rugs and has a colourful pattern that resembles weaving. Choose a harmonious palette of yarn for this thick, warm square and give it pride of place in a pillow or lap blanket.

A
B
C
D
E

Special stitch used:

Loop stitch (loop st): Insert hook in st, wrap yarn over forefinger, catch both strands of lp with hook and pull through st (3 lps on hook), yoh and pull through all three lps.

Foundation ring: Using yarn A, make a magic ring.

Round 1: Ch 3 (counts as 1 tr), *[1 dtr, 1 tr, 2 htr, 1 tr) in ring; rep from * 2 times, [1 dtr, 1 tr, 1 htr) in ring, join with sl st in top of beg ch-3.

Round 2: Ch 1, *3 dc in next dtr, 1 dc in each of next 4 sts; rep from * 3 times, sl st in first ch to join. Fasten off.

Round 3: Join yarn B, 1 dc in each of next 2 dc, *3 dc in next dc (2nd dc of 3-dc corner group)**, 1 dc in every dc to next corner; rep from * 2 times, and from * to ** 1 time, 1 dc in every dc to end, sl st in first dc to join. Fasten off.

Round 4: Join yarn C in same st, ch 1, 1 loop st in each dc around square, sl st in first ch to join. Fasten off, do not cut loops.

Round 5: Join yarn D in any corner st, ch 3 (counts as 1 tr), [2 tr, ch 2, 3 tr] in same st (forms corner), *1 tr in each of next 8 sts**, [3 tr, ch 2, 3 tr] in next st (forms corner); rep from * 2 times and from * to ** 1 time, sl st in top of beg ch-3 to join. Fasten off.

Round 6: Join yarn E in any corner ch-2 sp, ch 1, *3 dc in same corner sp, 1 dc in every tr to next corner; rep from * 3 times, sl st in first dc to join. Fasten off.

Round 7: Join yarn B in any ch-1 corner sp, ch 1, 3 dc in same corner sp, *change to yarn A, 1 dc in each of next 2 dc, change to yarn B, 1 dc in each of next 2 dc**; rep from * 3 times, change to yarn A, 3 dc in next corner dc, change to yarn B, 1 dc in each of next 2 dc; rep from * to ** 3 times, change to yarn A, 1 dc in each of next 2 dc, change to yarn B, 3 dc in corner

sc; rep from * to ** 4 times, change to yarn A, 3 dc in corner dc, change to yarn B, 1 dc in each of next 2 dc; rep from * to ** 3 times, change to yarn A, 1 dc in each of next 2 dc, sl st in first dc to join.

Round 8: Ch 1, 1 dc in next dc, 3 dc in next dc, 1 dc in next dc; rep from * to ** (of Round 7) 4 times, change to yarn A, 1 dc in next dc, 3 dc next dc, 1 dc in next dc, change to yarn B, 1 dc in each of next 2 dc; rep from * to ** (of Round 7) 3 times, change to yarn A, 1 dc in each of next 2 dc, change to yarn B, 1 dc in next dc, 3 dc in next dc, 1 dc in next dc; rep from * to ** (of Round 7) 4 times, change to yarn A, 1 dc in next dc, 3 dc in next dc, 1 dc in next dc, change to yarn B, 1 dc in each of next 2 dc; rep from * to ** (of Round 7) 3 times, change to yarn A, 1 dc in each of last 2 dc, sl st in first dc to join.

Round 9: Ch 1, 1 dc in each of next 2 dc, 3 dc in next dc, 1 dc in each of next 2 dc; rep from * to ** (of Round 7) 4 times, change to yarn A, 1 dc in each of next 2 dc, 3 dc in next dc, 1 dc in each of next 2 dc, change to yarn B, 1 dc in each of next 2 dc; rep from * to ** (of Round 7) 3 times, change to yarn A, 1 dc in each of next 2 dc, change to yarn B, 1 dc in each

of next 2 dc, 3 dc in next dc, 1 dc in each of next 2 dc; rep from * to ** (of Round 7) 4 times, change to yarn A, 1 dc in each of next 2 dc, 3 dc in next dc, 1 dc in each of next 2 dc, change to yarn B, 1 dc in each of next 2 dc; rep from * to ** (of Round 7) 3 times, change to yarn A, 1 dc in each of last 2 dc, sl st in first dc to join. Fasten off both yarns.

Round 10: Join yarn E in any centre dc of 3-dc corner group, ch 1, *3 dc in same dc, 1 dc in every dc to next corner; rep from * 3 times, sl st in first dc to join. Fasten off.

Round 11: Join yarn C in any st; ch 1, 1 loop st in every dc around square, sl st in first ch to join. Fasten off.

Round 12: Join yarn A in any corner dc, ch 3 (counts as 1 tr), [1 tr, ch 3, 2 tr] in same sp, *1 tr in every st to next corner dc, [2 tr, ch 3, 2 tr] in same st; rep from * 2 times, 1 tr in every st to end, sl st in top of beg ch-3 to join.

Fasten off and darn in ends.

Using sharp scissors, cut loops and trim pile to even size. Block work and press pile outwards to show colourful pattern. You may need to re-trim pile after blocking.

*
beach crab

A bold square worked using both linear and in-the-round methods, this has a central block of crab stitch ridges to add textural interest.

A
B

Special stitch used:

Crab stitch (crab st): Double crochet worked in reverse (*see page 22*). Work 1 crab st in front loop of st only, as specified.

Foundation chain: Using yarn A, ch 16.

Row 1: 1 dc in 2nd ch from hook, 1 dc in every ch to end, turn – 15 dc.

Row 2: Ch 2 (counts as 1 tr) 1 tr in every dc to end. DO NOT TURN WORK.

Row 3: Working from LEFT to RIGHT, ch 1, 1 crab st in front lp of every tr to end, sl st in top of beg ch-2 to join.

Row 4: Working from left to right, ch 2 (counts as 1 tr), working in back lp only, 1 tr in every st to end.

Rows 5, 7, 9 and 11: Rep Row 3.

Rows 6, 8, 10 and 12: Rep Row 4.

Now begin working in rnds.

Round 1: Ch 1, *[1 htr, ch 2, 1 htr] in same sp (forms corner), 1 htr in every st to next corner; rep from * 3 times, sl st in first ch to join – 15 sts per side. Fasten off.

Round 2: Join yarn B in any ch-2 corner sp, ch 1, *[2 htr, ch 2, 2 htr, ch 1] in same corner sp, [miss 1 htr, 1 htr in next htr, ch 1] to next corner sp; rep from * 3 times, sl st along to next corner sp.

Round 3: Ch 1, *[2 htr, ch 2, 2 htr, ch 1] in same corner sp, [1 htr, ch 1] in every ch-1 sp along side of square to next corner sp; rep from * 3 times, sl st along to next corner sp. Fasten off.

Round 4: Join yarn A in any ch-2 corner sp, *[ch 1, 2 htr, ch 2, 2 htr, ch 1] in same corner sp, [1 htr, ch 1] in every ch-1 sp

along side of square to next corner sp; rep from * 3 times, sl st in first ch to join.

Round 5: Working from LEFT to RIGHT ch 1, 1 crab st in every st and ch st and 2 crab sts in every ch-2 corner sp around square to end, sl st to first ch to join.

Fasten off and darn in ends neatly.

**
florentine

An open lacy block that is reversible, so useful for lightweight summer throws and scarves. The loopy petals are made by pulling chain loops through the central flower 'trumpet'; they would look effective worked in a dark colour against a light flower and background.

A
B
C
D

Foundation ring: Using yarn A, ch 6, sl st in first ch to form ring.

Round 1: Ch 1, 16 dc in ring, sl st in first dc to join. Fasten off yarn A.

Round 2: Join yarn B with sl st in any dc, ch 12, miss 1 dc, sl st in next dc; rep from * 7 times, sl st in first sl st to join. Fasten off yarn B.

Round 3: Join yarn C in any dc from Round 1 in the miss st between each ch-12 lp, ch 3 (counts as 1 htr, ch 1), *2 htr in sp between 2 sl sts each side of ch-12 lp, [1 htr, ch 1] in next dc**, 1 htr in next dc; rep from * 6 times and from * to ** 1 time, sl st in 2nd of beg ch-3 to join.

Round 4: Ch 1, 1 dc in same st, *ch 1, 1 dc in next st, ch 2 (over the top of the

next ch-12 lp), miss 1 st, 1 dc in next st; rep from * to end, sl st in first dc to join. Fasten off yarn C.

Round 5: Turn to WS, join yarn D in any ch-12 lp at top, 1 dc in same st, *ch 7, 1 dc in top of next ch-12 lp; rep from * 7 times, sl st in first dc to join.

Round 6: *Ch 4, sl st in same st to make lp, [4 dc, ch 4, 4 dc] in next ch-7 lp; rep from * 7 times, sl st in first ch to join.

Round 7: Sl st in top of next ch-4 lp, ch 8 (counts as 1 tr, ch 5), *1 dc in next ch-4 lp, ch 5, 1 tr in next ch-4 lp, ch 5, [1 ttr, ch 3, 1 ttr] in next ch-4 lp (forms corner), ch 5**, 1 tr in next ch-4 lp, ch 5; rep from * 2 times and from * to ** 1 time, sl st in 3rd ch of beg ch-8 to join.

Round 8: Ch 1, 1 dc in same st, *5 dc in next ch-5 lp, 1 dc in next dc, 5 dc in next ch-5 lp, 1 dc in next tr, 5 dc in next ch-5 lp, 1 dc in next ttr, [2 dc, ch 1, 2 dc] in corner ch-3 sp, 1 dc in next ttr, 5 dc in next ch-5 lp**, 1 dc in next tr; rep from * 2 times and from * to ** 1 time, sl st in first dc to join.

Fasten off and darn in ends neatly.

*

cobbles

This simple textural square creates a soft, nubbly surface that retains its drape. Perfect for snuggly blankets, this is an easily mastered pattern that can be worked to any dimensions.

Foundation chain: Ch 33 (counts as 30 sts, 3 tch), turn.

Row 1: Miss 2 ch (counts as 1 dc), [1 htr, 1 tr] in next ch, *miss 2 ch, [1 dc, 1 htr, 1 tr] in next ch; rep from * to last 3 ch, miss 2 ch, 1 dc in last ch, turn.

Row 2: Ch 1, (counts as 1 dc), [1 htr, 1 tr] in first st, *miss [1 tr, 1 htr], [1 dc, 1 htr, 1 tr] in next dc; rep from * to last 3 sts, miss [1 tr, 1 htr], 1 dc in top of tch, turn.

Rows 3 to 22: Rep Row 2.

Fasten off and darn in ends neatly.

★★★

coral

A highly textured, frilly design that is truly unusual; this block lends itself to being used in both interior and fashion pieces. It is equally stunning in an amazing handbag or a gorgeous pillow.

Foundation chain: Ch 32.

BASE 12.5 x 12.5 cm (5 x 5 inches)

Row 1: 1 tr in 8th ch from hook, *ch 2, miss next 2 ch, 1 tr in next ch; rep from * to end of row, turn.

Row 2: Ch 5 (counts as 1 tr, ch 2), 1 tr in tr, *ch 2, miss next 2 ch**, 1 tr in next tr; rep from * across row, ending last rep at **, 1 tr in 3rd ch of beg ch from last row, turn.

Rows 3 to 10: Rep Row 2.

FRILLS

Rows 10 to 9: Ch 3, 4 tr in last tr, *5 tr on to ch-2 sp of Row 9**, 5 tr on to next tr post of Row 10, 5 tr on to ch-2 sp of Row 10, 5 tr on to next tr post of Row 10; rep from * to end of row, ending last rep at **.

Rows 9 to 7: 5 tr on to end tr post of Row 9, 5 tr on to end tr post of Row 8, *5 tr on to next ch-2 of Row 7**, 5 tr on to next tr post of Row 8, 5 tr on to ch-2 sp of Row 8, 5 tr on to next tr post of Row 8; rep from * to end of row, ending last rep at **.

Rows 7 to 6: 5 tr on end tr post of Row 7, 5 tr on to end tr post of Row 6, *5 tr on next ch-2 of row 6**, 5 tr on to next dc post of row 6, 5 tr on to ch-2 sp of Row 7, 5 tr on to next tr post of Row 6; rep from * to end of row, ending last rep at **.

Rows 5 to 4: 5 tr on to end tr post of Row 5, 5 tr on to end tr post of Row 4, *5 tr on next ch-2 of Row 4**, 5 tr on to next tr post of Row 4, 5 tr on to ch-2 sp of Row 5, 5 tr on to next tr post of Row 4; rep from * to end of row, ending last rep at **.

Rows 3 to 2: 5 tr on end tr post of Row 3, 5 tr on to end tr post of Row 2, *5 tr on next ch-2 of Row 2**, 5 tr on to next tr post of Row 4, 2 tr on to ch-2 sp of Row 3, 5 tr on to next tr post of Row 2; rep from * to end of row, ending last rep at **.

Row 1: 5 tr on to end post of Row 1, *5 tr on to ch-2 of Row 1, 5 tr on tr post of Row 1**, 5 tr on ch-2 of Row 2; rep from * to end of row, ending last rep at **.

Fasten off.

samurai

Redolent of Japanese Samurai armour with its ridges and lattice, this block has an Asian flavour and is fun to work up. It would look dramatic worked in the strong tones of Asian-style lacquer work such as black and scarlet.

A
B

Special stitch used:

Back-post treble crochet (BPtr): Bring hook to back, work in back vertical post of next st, inserting hook from left to right, draw yarn through and work st as usual (*see page 21*).

Foundation ring: Using yarn A, ch 5, join with sl st to form ring.

Round 1: Ch 3 (counts as 1 tr), 2 tr in ring, [ch 2, 3 tr] 3 times in ring, ch 2, sl st in top of beg ch-3 to join – 12 sts.

Round 2: Sl st along to next ch-2 corner sp, ch 3 (counts as 1 tr), [2 tr, ch 2, 3 tr] in same sp, ch 2, *[3 tr, ch 2, 3 tr in next ch-2 sp], ch 2; rep from * 2 times, sl st in beg ch-3 to join – 24 sts.

Round 3: Ch 1, 1 dc in same st, 1 dc in each of next 2 tr, *3 dc in next ch-2 corner sp (forms corner), 1 dc in each of next 3 tr, 2 dc in next ch-2 sp, 1 dc in each of next 3 tr**; rep from * to ** 2 times, on final side 1 dc in each of next 3 tr, 2 dc in last ch-2 sp, sl st in first dc to join – 8 dc on each side, 3 dc in corner sps.

Round 4: Ch 1, 1 dc in same st, 1 dc in each of next 3 dc, 3 dc in corner dc, *1 dc in each of next 10 dc, 3 dc in corner dc; rep from * 2 times, on final side, 1 dc in each of rem 6 dc, sl st in first dc to join. Fasten off yarn A.

Round 5: Join yarn B in any corner dc, ch 1, 1 dc in same st, 2 dc in same st (forms corner) *1 dc in each of next 12 dc**, 3 dc in next dc corner st; rep from * 2 times, and from * to ** 1 time, sl st in first dc to join.

Round 6: Sl st in next corner dc, ch 3 (counts as 1 tr), [2 tr, ch 2, 3 tr] in same sp to form corner, *miss 2 sts, ch 1, [1 tr in next st, ch 1, miss 1 st] 6 times, ch 1; rep from * 3 times, sl st in top of beg ch-3 to join.

Round 7: Ch 3 (counts as 1 tr), 1 tr in each of the next 2 sts, [3 tr, ch 2, 3 tr] in next corner sp, *1 tr in each of the next 3 tr, ch 1, [1 BPtr, ch 1] in each of next 6 tr from last rnd**, 1 tr in each of next 3 tr, [3 tr, ch 2, 3 tr] in next corner sp]; rep from * 2 times, then from * to ** 1 time, sl st in top of beg ch-3 to join.

Round 8: Ch 3 (counts 1 tr), 1 tr in each of next 5 sts, [3 tr, ch 2, 3 tr] in next corner sp, *1 tr in each of next 6 tr, ch 1, [1 BPtr, ch 1], in each of next 6 BPtr**, 1 tr in each of next 6 tr, [3 tr, ch 2, 3 tr] in next corner sp; rep from * 2 times, then from * to ** 1 time, sl st in top of beg ch-3 to join.

Round 9: Ch 3 (counts 1 tr), 1 tr in each of next 8 tr, [2 tr, ch 4, 2 tr] in next corner sp, *1 tr in each of next 9 tr, ch 1, [1 dtr, ch 1] in each of next 6 BPtr**, 1 tr in each of next 9 tr, [2 tr, ch 4, 2 tr] in next corner sp; rep from * 2 times, and from * to ** 1 time, sl st in ch-4 to join.

Fasten off and darn in ends neatly.

100 *
pennants

A
B
C
D

This festive block has loads of tiny flags, just like a party banner. It's light and lacy, perfect for summer throws or for use in a curtain. An interesting structure that will grab your attention.

Note: The image of the square has been turned to show the flag effect.

Foundation chain: Using yarn A, ch 30. Fasten off yarn A.

Row 1: Join yarn B, 1 dc in 2nd ch from hook; *[ch 6, 1 dc in 3rd ch from hook, 1 tr in each of next 3 ch], miss 3 ch, 1 dc in next ch; rep from * to end, turn. Fasten off yarn B.

Row 2: Join yarn A in last st, ch 6 (counts as 1 ttr, ch 1), *1 dc in ch at tip of first 'flag', ch 3; rep from * ending with 1 dc in ch at tip of last flag, ch 1, 1 ttr in last dc (forms base of flag), turn. Fasten off yarn A.

Row 3: Join yarn C in top of last ttr in last rnd, rep Row 1. Fasten off yarn C.

Row 4: Join yarn A, rep Row 2. Fasten off yarn A.

Row 5: Join yarn D in top of last ttr in last rnd, rep Row 1. Fasten off yarn D.

Row 6: Join yarn A, rep Row 2. Fasten off yarn A.

Row 7: Join yarn B in top of last ttr in last rnd, rep Row 1. Fasten off yarn B.

Row 8: Join yarn A, rep Row 2.

Round 9: Using yarn A, [2 dc, ch 4, 2 dc] in every corner st, with 3 dc in every ch-lp between flags and 1 dc in base or tip of every flag (every st where flags are attached to ch), 5 dc in each ttr or ch-6 sp along sides of square, sl st in first dc to join.

Fasten off, darn in all ends neatly and block square.

101 ***
hawkweed

A
B

A delicate flower square with a 3D centre and picot edgings, which is plenty of fun to work up. Change colour frequently when working to enhance the intricacy of this beautiful design.

Special stitch used:

Picot-3: Ch 3 (at point to add picot), sl st in first ch of ch-3, creating picot loop.

Foundation ring: Using yarn A, begin with magic ring method.

Round 1: Ch 1, 8 dc in ring, sl st in first dc to join.

Round 2: Ch 1, *1 dc in next dc, ch 12; rep from * 7 times, sl st in first dc to join.

Round 3: Bring yarn to front of work, *ch 3, sl st in 2nd ch from hook, sl st in base of petal; rep from * 7 times, sl st in base of first ch-3 to join. Fasten off yarn A.

Round 4: Using yarn B, sl st in top of first ch-12, ch 1, 1 dc in same place, *ch 4, 1 dc in top of next ch-12 petal lp; rep from * 7 times, omit final 1 dc; sl st in beg dc to join.

Round 5: Ch 1 (counts as 1 dc), *[1 dc, 1 htr, 1 tr, 1 hdtr, 1 dtr, 1 hdtr, 1 tr, 1 htr, 1 dc] in ch-4 lp, 1 dc in dc; rep from * to end of rnd, omit final dc, sl st in ch-1 to join. Fasten off yarn B.

Round 6: With yarn A, sl st in top of first scallop (on 1 dtr), ch 1, 1 dc in same sp, *ch 3, 1 dtr in dc between scallops, ch 3, 1 dc at top of next scallop; rep from * to end of rnd ending with ch 3, sl st in first ch-1 to join.

Round 7: Ch 5 (counts as 1 dc and ch 4), 1 dc in same st (first corner), *4 dc in ch-3 sp, 1 dc in next dtr, 4 dc in next ch-3 sp, 1 dc in next dc, 4 dc in next ch-3 sp, 1 dc in next dtr, 4 dc in next ch-3 sp**, [1 dc, ch 4, 1 dc] in next dc; rep from * to end of rnd, ending last rep at **, sl st in first ch of beg ch-5 to join.

Round 8: Ch 1, *[3 tr, 1 dtr, picot-3, 1 dtr, 3 tr] in ch-4 lp, ch 3, [1 dc, picot-3,1 dc] in st above dtr of Round 6, ch 3, [1 dc, picot-3, 1 dc] in dc in centre of scallop, ch 3, [1 dc, picot-3, 1 dc] in st above dtr of Round 6, ch 3, 1 dc at base of ch-4 lp; rep from * 3 times, ch 1 to first ch-1.

Fasten off and darn in ends.

**

aztec

A graphic square of solid colour that is worked entirely in double crochet, using the intarsia method of changing colour (see page 17 in Techniques section for details). This is a good, simple square, which is useful for practising using a grid.

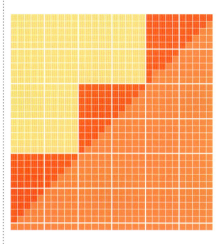

A
B
C

Note: Beg at bottom RH corner of chart, work 31 rows of chart in dc. When foll chart, read odd-numbered (RS) rows from right to left, and even-numbered (WS) rows from left to right. Use separate ball of yarn for each area of colour, change colours where indicated. Keep all yarn ends at back (WS) of work.

Foundation chain: Using yarn A, ch 31 (counts as 30 sts, 1 tch), turn.

Row 1: (RS) 1 dc in 2nd ch from hook and in each ch to end, turn – 30 sts.

Begin chart as follows:

Row 2 and all subsequent rows: Ch 1, 1 dc in every dc, turn.

At end of chart, fasten off yarns and darn in ends neatly.

***

ballina

A chunky textured cable block that suggests warm Aran knits. Double trebles are crossed to create 'cable' effects, and the stitch pattern is further emphasized through the use of front- and back-post stitches.

A

Special stitches used:

Front-post double treble (FPdtr): Yoh 2 times, insert hook through front of st post from right to left, yoh, draw yarn through, [yoh, draw through 2 loops] 3 times (see page 21).

Back-post double treble (BPdtr): Yoh 2 times, insert hook through back of st post from right to left, yoh, draw yarn through, then [yoh, draw through 2 loops] 3 times.

Foundation chain: Ch 28.

Row 1: 1 dc in 2nd ch from hook and 1 dc in every dc to end of row, turn.

Row 2: Ch 2 (counts as 1 htr), 1 htr in same st and 1 htr in every dc to end of row, turn.

Row 3: Ch 2 (counts as 1 htr), 3 htr, 4 FPdtr, 4 htr, 4 FPdtr, 4 htr, 4 FPdtr, 4 htr, turn.

Row 4: Ch 2 (counts as 1 htr), 3 htr, 4 BPdtr, 4 htr, 4 BPdtr, 4 htr, 4 BPdtr, 4 htr, turn.

Row 5: Ch 2 (counts as 1 htr), 3 htr, *miss 2 sts, 1 FPdtr in each of next 2 sts, working in front of the 2 sts just worked 1 FPdtr in each of missed 2 sts, 4 htr; rep from * 2 times, turn.

Rows 6, 8, 10, 12, 14, 16 and 18: Rep Row 4.

Rows 7, 11, 15 and 19: Rep Row 3.

Rows 9, 13 and 17: Rep Row 5.

Row 20: Rep Row 2.

Row 21: Ch 1, 1 dc in every st to end of row.

Fasten off. Darn in ends neatly.

*

granny's round

A twist on our familiar favourite. Choose either close-toned colours, as we have done here, or eye-popping contrasts to pick out the circular shape.

A
B
C
D

Foundation ring: Using yarn A, ch 5, sl st in first ch to form ring.

Round 1: Ch 3 (counts as 1 tr), 2 tr, ch 1, [3 tr, ch 1] 5 times in ring, sl st in top of 3-ch to join. Fasten off yarn A.

Round 2: Join yarn B in any ch-1 sp, ch 3 (counts as 1 tr), 2 tr in same sp, ch 1, 3 tr in same sp, *[ch 1, 3 tr, ch 1, 3 tr] in next sp; rep from * to end of rnd, ch 1, sl st in top of ch-3 to join. Fasten off yarn B.

Round 3: Join yarn C to any ch-1 sp, ch 3, 2 tr in same sp, ch 1, [3 tr, ch 1] in all 1-ch sps to beg, sl st in top of ch-3 to join. Fasten off yarn C.

Round 4: Join yarn D in any sp between 3-tr groups, ch 3, 2 tr in same sp, ch 2, 3 tr in same sp *3 htr in next sp, ch 1, 3 htr in next sp, ch 1, [3 htr, ch 3, 3 htr] in next sp to form corner; rep from * 3 times, sl st in top of ch-3 to join.

Round 5: Sl st in next 3-ch corner sp, ch 3 (counts as 1 tr), [2 tr, ch 2, 3 tr] in same corner sp, *[ch 1, 3 tr] in each 1-ch sp along**, Ch 1 [3 tr, ch 3, 3 tr] in next corner sp; rep from * 2 times, then from * to ** 1 time, sl st in top of beg ch-3 to join.

Round 6: Rep Round 5. Fasten off yarn D.

Round 7: Join yarn A to any ch-3 corner sp and rep Round 5.

Round 8: Ch 1, 1 dc in the same st, 1 dc in each 1-ch sp and in each st, and 3 dc in each ch-3 corner sp, sl st in first dc to join.

Fasten off and darn in ends neatly.

*

greek cross

A simple pattern that is at its best worked in a clean, flat yarn that will highlight the design. An easy square to size up or down due to its rhythmic structure that is quickly grasped – it is good for bedspreads or afghans.

A
B

Foundation ring: Using yarn A, ch 6, sl st in first ch to form ring.

Round 1: Ch 3 (counts as 1 tr), 15 tr in ring, sl st in 3rd of beg ch-3 to join.

Round 2: Ch 3 (counts as 1 tr), 2 tr in same st as last sl st from Round 1, ch 2, miss 1 tr, 1 tr in next tr, ch 2, miss 1 tr, *3 tr in next tr, ch 2, miss 1 tr, 1 tr in next tr, ch 2, miss 1 tr; rep from * 2 times, sl st in 3rd of ch-3 at start of rnd.

Round 3: Ch 3 (counts as 1 tr), 5 tr in next tr, *1 tr in next tr, (ch 2, 1 tr in next tr) 2 times, 5 tr in next tr; rep from * 2 times, [1 tr in next tr, ch 2] 2 times, sl st in 3rd of beg ch-3 to join.

Round 4: Ch 3 (counts as 1 tr), 1 tr in each of next 2 tr, 5 tr in next tr, *1 tr in each of next 3 tr, ch 2, 1 tr in next tr, ch 2, 1 tr in each of next 3 tr, 5 tr in next tr; rep from * 2 times, 1 tr in each of next 3 tr, ch 2, 1 tr in next tr, ch 2, sl st in 3rd of beg ch-3 to join.

Round 5: Ch 3 (counts as 1 tr), 1 tr in each of next 4 tr, 5 tr in next tr, *1 tr in each of next 5 tr, ch 2, 1 tr in next tr, ch 2, 1 tr in each of next 5 tr, 5 tr in next tr; rep from * 2 times, 1 tr in each of next 5 tr, ch 2, 1 tr in next tr, ch 2, sl st in 3rd of beg ch-3 to join.

Round 6: Ch 3 (counts as 1 tr), 1 tr in each of next 6 tr, 5 tr in next tr, *1 tr in each of next 7 tr, 2 tr in next 2-ch sp, 1 tr in next tr, 2 tr in next 2-ch sp, 1 tr in next 7 tr, 5 tr in next tr; rep from * 2 times, 1 tr in each of next 7 tr, 2 tr in next 2-ch sp, 1 tr in next tr, 2 tr in next 2-ch sp, sl st in 3rd of beg ch-3 to join. Change to yarn B.

Round 7: Ch 3 (counts as 1 tr), 1 tr in each of next 8 tr, 5 tr in next tr, *1 tr in each of next 23 tr, 5 tr in next tr; rep from * 2 times, 1 tr in each of next 14 tr, sl st in 3rd of beg ch-3 to join. Fasten off and darn in ends neatly.

gypsy wheel

A light, lacy square that mixes well with other lightweight blocks. This block is equally pretty worked in one colour to create a doily effect or you could try deeper hues for a rustic appeal.

A
B
C

Foundation ring: Using yarn A, ch 4, join with sl st to form ring.

Round 1: Ch 1 (counts as 1 dc), 11 dc in the ring, sl st in ch-1 to join.

Round 2: Ch 6 (counts as 1d tr, 2 ch), 1 dtr in next st, *ch 2, 1 dtr in next st; rep from * to end of rnd, ch 2, sl st in 4th ch of beg ch-6 to join.

Round 3: Ch 5 (counts as 1 dtr, ch 1), *1 dtr in same ch-2 sp, ch 1, 1 dtr in next st, ch 1; rep from * to end of rnd, sl st in 4th ch of beg 5-ch to join. Fasten off yarn A.

Round 4: Join yarn B, ch 3 (counts as 1 tr), 2 tr, ch 3, 3 tr in first ch-1 sp (first corner), ch 1 *[1 tr, ch 1] in each of next 5 ch-1 sps**, [3 tr, ch 3, 3 tr] in next ch-3 sp, ch 1; rep from * to end of rnd ending last rep at **, sl st in top of beg ch-3 to join.

Round 5: Sl st in next 2 tr, sl st in ch-3 sp, ch 3 (counts as 1 tr), [2 tr, ch 3, 3 tr] in same ch-3 sp (first corner), *ch 1, 3 tr in next ch-1 sp, [miss next ch-1 sp, ch 1, 3 tr in next ch-1 sp] 2 times, miss next ch-1 sp, ch 1**, [3 tr, ch 3, 3 tr] in next ch-3 sp; rep from * to end of rnd ending last rep at **, sl st in top of beg ch-3 to join.

Round 6: Sl st in next 2 tr, sl st in next ch-3 sp, ch 3 (counts as 1 tr), [2 tr, ch 3, 3 tr] in ch-3 sp (first corner), *ch 1, 3 tr in next ch-1 sp, ch 1, [3 tr in next ch-1 sp, ch 1] 3 times**, [3 tr, ch 3, 3 tr] in next ch-3 sp; rep from * to end of rnd ending last rep at **, sl st in top of beg ch-3 to join. Fasten off yarn B.

Round 7: Join yarn C, sl st in first ch-3, ch 3 (counts as 1 tr), [2 tr, ch 3, 3 tr] in ch-3 sp (first corner), *ch 1, 3 tr in next ch-1 sp, ch 1, [3 tr in next ch-1 sp, ch 1] 4 times**, [3 tr, ch 3, 3 tr] in next ch-3 sp; rep from * to end of rnd ending last rep at **, sl st in top of beg ch-3 to join.

Fasten off and darn in ends neatly.

hum

By working in only the back loop of stitches on every row, and alternating colours, a defined stripe pattern is created with a slightly ridged texture. A great block for mixing with others; here, we have used eye-popping contrasts, but you could choose softer, harmonious tones if you prefer.

A
B

Foundation chain: Using yarn A, ch 27.

Row 1: 1 htr in 2nd ch from hook, 1 htr in every ch to end, turn. Fasten off yarn A.

Row 2: Join yarn B, ch 2, 1 htr in back lp only of every htr to end, turn. Fasten off yarn B.

Row 3: Join yarn A. Ch 2, 1 htr in back lp only of every htr to end, turn. Fasten off yarn A.

Rows 4 to 18: Rep Rows 2 and 3 to create stripes.

Fasten off and darn in ends neatly.

**

celandine

This flower filet square is made in three shades of one colour – when choosing colours remember heavily contrasting colours distract from the pattern. It works well in scarves or throws where a light, drapey fabric is required.

A
B
C

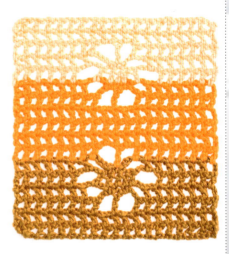

Foundation chain: Using yarn A, ch 40.

Row 1: 1 tr in 6th ch from hook, [ch 1, miss 1 ch, 1 tr in next ch] 18 times, turn.

Row 2: Ch 4 (counts as 1 tr, ch 1), miss 1 tr, [ch 1, 1 tr in next tr] 17 times, ch 1, 1 tr in last ch-sp, turn.

Row 3: Ch 4 (counts as 1 tr, ch 1), miss first tr, *ch 1, 1 tr in next tr**; rep from * 6 times, ch 4, miss 1 tr, 1 dtr in next tr, ch 4, miss 1 tr, 1 tr in next tr; rep from * to ** 6 times, ch 1, 1 tr in last st, turn.

Row 4: Ch 4 (counts as 1 tr, ch 1), miss first tr, *ch 1, 1 tr in next tr**; rep from * 5 times, ch 4, 1 dc in next ch-4 sp, 1 dc in next dtr, 1 dc in next ch-4 sp, ch 4, miss next tr, 1 tr in next tr; rep from * to ** 5 times, ch 1, 1 tr in last ch sp, turn.

Row 5: Ch 4 (counts as 1 tr, ch 1), miss first tr, * ch 1, 1 tr in next tr**; rep from * 4 times, ch 5, 1 tr in next ch sp, 1 tr in each of next 3 dc, 1 tr in next ch-4 sp, ch 5, miss next tr, 1 tr in next tr; rep from * to ** 4 times, ch 1, 1 tr in last st, turn.

Row 6: Ch 4 (counts as 1 tr, ch 1), miss first tr, *ch 1, 1 tr in next tr**; rep from * 4 times, ch 1, 1 tr in next ch-5 sp, ch 5, miss next tr, 1 dc in each of next 3 tr, ch 5, 1 tr in next ch-5 sp; rep from * to ** 5 times, ch 1, 1 tr in last ch sp, turn. Fasten off.

Row 7: Join yarn B, ch 4 (counts as 1 tr, ch 1), miss first tr, *ch 1, 1 tr in next tr**; rep from * 5 times, ch 1, 1 tr in next ch-5 sp, ch 3, 1 dtr in centre dc of next 3 dc, ch 3, 1 tr in next ch-5 sp; rep from * to ** 5 times, ch 1, 1 tr in last sp, turn.

Row 8: Ch 4 (counts as 1 tr, ch 1), miss first tr, *ch 1, 1 tr in next tr**; rep from

* 6 times, ch 1, 1 tr in next ch-3 sp, ch 1, 1 tr in next dtr, ch 1, 1 tr in next ch-3 sp; rep from * to ** 7 times, ch 1, 1 tr in last sp, turn.

Rows 9 to 10: Rep Row 2.

Rows 11 to 16: Rep Rows 3 to 8, changing to yarn C for Row 13 onwards.

Row 17: Rep Row 2.

Fasten off and darn in ends.

**

havana

A lacy flower block that uses outlines of different-coloured chains to build up its form. This square is especially easy to work up once you get into the rhythm and could be worked in a host of lively colourways: take care to keep the tropical flavour though.

A
B
C

Foundation ring: Using yarn A, ch 8, sl st in first ch to form ring.

Round 1: Ch 1, 16 dc in ring, sl st in first dc to join. Fasten off.

Round 2: Join yarn B in any dc, ch 4 (counts as 1 dtr), 2 dtr in first dc, 3 dtr in next dc, ch 5, *miss 2 dc, 3 dtr in each of next 2 dc, ch 5; rep from * 2 times, sl st in top of beg ch-4 to join.

Round 3: Ch 1, 1 dc in same st, *[1 htr, 1 tr] in next dtr, 2 dtr in each of next 2 dtr, [1 tr, 1 htr] in next dtr, 1 dc in next dtr, [3 dc, ch 1, 3 dc] in next ch-5 loop**, 1 dc in next dtr; rep from * 2 times and from * to ** 1 time, sl st in first dc to join. Fasten off.

Round 4: Join yarn C, ch 1, 1 dc in same sp, *ch 5, 1 dc in 2nd dtr of next petal, ch 2, 1 dc in 3rd dtr of petal, ch 5, 1 dc in next dc, ch 3, 1 htr in next ch-1 sp, ch 3**,

1 dc in next dc; rep from * 2 times and from * to ** 1 time, sl st in first dc to join. Fasten off.

Round 5: Join yarn B, ch 1, 1 dc in same st, *ch 6, [1 dc, ch 2, 1 dc] in next ch-2 sp, ch 6, 1 dc in next dc, ch 4, 1 htr in next htr, ch 4**, 1 dc in next sc; rep from * 2 times and from * to ** 1 time, sl st in first dc to join. Fasten off.

Round 6: Join yarn A, ch 1, 1 dc in same st, *ch 7, [1 dc, ch 2, 1 dc] in next ch-2 sp, ch 7, 1 dc in next dc, ch 5, 1 htr in next htr, ch 5**, 1 dc in next dc; rep from * 2 times and from * to ** 1 time, sl st in first dc to join.

Round 7: Join yarn B in any ch-2 sp, ch 1, 1 dc in same st, *ch 6, 1 tr in next dc, ch 5, [2 dtr, ch 3, 2 dtr] in next htr, ch 5, 1 tr in next dc, ch 6**, 1 dc in next ch-2 sp; rep from * 2 times and from * to ** 1 time, sl st in first dc to join.

Round 8: Ch 1, *5 dc in next ch-6 lp, 1 dc in next tr, 5 dc in next ch-5 lp, 1 dc in each of next 2 dtr, [2 dc, 2 htr, 2 dc] in next ch-3 sp, 1 dc in each of next 2 dtr, 5 dc in next ch-5 lp, 1 dc in next tr, 5 dc in next ch-6 lp, 1 dc in next dc; rep from * 3 times, sl st in first dc to join.

Fasten off and darn in ends neatly.

lattice

***

This trellis-type pattern is achieved by working long stitches around the front posts and down in rows below, which creates a mesh on the surface of the fabric. A dense block that is especially optical in effect, this would mix equally well with other textural blocks or graphic geometries for a modern look.

A

B

Special stitches used:

Front-post double treble (FPdtr): Yoh 2 times, insert hook through front of st post from right to left, yoh, draw yarn through, [yoh, draw through 2 loops] 3 times (*see page 21*).

Front-post double treble two stitches together (FPdtr2tog): Work 2 double treble sts joined at top and worked in front posts of sts at specified points in rows below.

Foundation chain: Using A, chain 28.

Row 1: 1 dc in 2nd ch from hook, 1 dc in every ch to end, turn.

Rows 2 to 3: Ch 1, 1 dc in every dc to end, turn. Fasten off.

Row 4: Join yarn B, ch 1, 1 dc in each of first 3 dc, 1 FPdtr2tog over next dc, working first FPdtr around 2nd dc of Row 1, miss 3 dc in Row 1, work 2nd FPdtr around next dc of Row 1, *miss 1 dc in Row 3, 1 dc in each of next 3 dc of Row 3, 1 FPdtr2tog over next dc, working first FPdtr around base of last FPdtr, miss 3 dc in Row 1, work 2nd FPdtr around next dc in Row 1; rep from * 4 times, 1 dc in each of last 3 dc of Row 3, turn. Fasten off.

Rows 5 to 7: Using yarn A, ch 1, 1 dc in every st to end, turn. Fasten off.

Row 8: Using yarn B, ch 1, 1 dc in first dc, 1 FPdtr under top posts (but above background fabric) of first FPdtr2tog from last FPdtr2tog row, *miss 1 dc in last row, 1 dc in each of next 3 dc, 1 FPdtr2tog

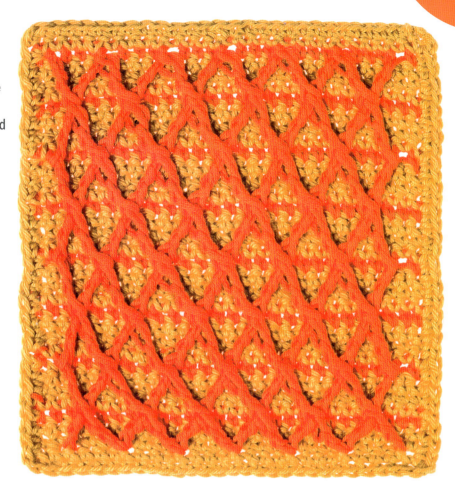

under top posts (above background fabric) of last FPdtr2tog and next FPdtr2tog; rep from * 4 times, 1 FPdtr under top posts of last FPdtr2tog, 1 dc in final dc, turn.

Rows 9 to 11: Rep Rows 5 to 7.

Row 12: Using yarn B, ch 1, 1 dc in each of first 3 dc, 1 FPdtr2tog over next st, working first FPdtr around top of first FPdtr and under top posts (but above background fabric) of next FPdtr2tog, *miss 1 dc, 1 dc in each of next 3 dc, 1 FPdtr2tog under top posts but above background fabric of last FPdtr2tog and next FPdtr2tog; rep from * 4 times, 1 dc in each of last 3 dc.

Rows 13 to 15: Rep Rows 5 to 7.

Row 16: Rep Row 8.

Rows 17 to 19: Rep Rows 5 to 7.

Row 20: Rep Row 12.

Rows 21 to 23: Rep Rows 5 to 7.

Row 24: Rep Row 8.

Rows 25 to 27: Rep Rows 5 to 7.

Row 28: Rep Row 12.

Rows 29 to 31: Rep Rows 5 to 7.

Row 32: Rep Row 8.

Row 33: Rep Row 5.

BORDER

Ch 1, 2 dc in same st (corner sp made), 1 dc in every st around square, working 2 dc in each corner, sl st in first dc to join.

Fasten off and darn in ends.

111

**

millefeuille

A

B

C

A repeating pattern of variable-height stitches creates a layered, wavy design that is especially effective when worked in three colours that are close to each other on the colour wheel, as we have done here. This block also looks great repeated and rotated to make a patchwork-effect throw.

Foundation chain: Using yarn A, ch 29.

Row 1: 1 dc in 2nd ch from hook, 1 dc in each ch to end, turn. Fasten off yarn A.

Row 2: Join yarn B, ch 4 (counts as 1 dtr), *1 ttr in each of next 2 sts, 1 dtr in next st, 1 tr in each of next 2 sts, 1 dtr in next st; rep from * 3 times, 1 ttr in next 2 sts, 1 dtr in last st, turn. Fasten off yarn B.

Row 3: Join yarn C, ch 4 (counts as 1 dtr), 1 tr in each of next 2 sts, 1 dtr in next st, 1 ttr in each of next 2 sts, 1 dtr in next st; rep from * 3 times, 1 tr in next 2 sts, 1 dtr in last st, turn. Fasten off yarn C.

Row 4: Join yarn A, ch 1, 1 dc in each st to end, turn.

Row 5: Rep Row 4. Fasten off yarn A.

Rows 2 to 5 form pattern, rep these 4 rows 3 times.

Fasten off and darn in ends neatly

112

**

peacock fans

A

A familiar pattern beloved of the Victorians, this lace has been updated in a bright colour and worked into an afghan square. Work in a flat, shiny or matt yarn to show off the pattern to best advantage.

Foundation chain: Ch 26.

Row 1: 1 dc in 2nd ch from hook, *miss 5 ch, 13 ttr in next ch, miss 5 ch, 1 dc in next ch; rep from * to end of row, turn.

Row 2: Ch 5 (counts as 1 ttr), 1 ttr in first st, *ch 4, miss 6 ttr, 1 dc in next ttr, ch 4, miss 6 ttr**, [1 ttr, ch 1, 1 ttr] in next st; rep from * to ** 1 time, 2 ttr in last dc, turn.

Row 3: Ch 1, 1 dc in first st, *miss [1 ttr, ch 4], 13 ttr in next dc, miss [ch 4, 1 ttr], 1 dc in next ch; rep from * to end of row, turn.

Rows 4 to 5: Rep Rows 2 to 3.

Rows 6 to 7: Rep Rows 2 to 3.

Rows 8 to 9: Rep Rows 2 to 3.

Row 10: Rep Row 2. Do not fasten off.

BORDER

Round 1: Ch 1, 2 dc in top of beg ch-5, 1 dc in next ttr, 4 dc in next ch-4 sp, 1 dc in next dc, 4 dc in next ch-4 sp, 1 dc in next ttr, 1 dc in next ch-1 sp, 1 dc in next ttr, 4 dc in next ch-4 sp, 1 dc in next dc, 4 dc in next ch-4 loop, 1 dc in next ttr, 4 dc in next ch-5 loop, 1 dc in next dc, 4 dc in next ch-5 sp, 1 dc in next st, 4 dc in next ch-5 sp, 1 dc in corner, 4 dc in next ch-4 sp, 1 dc in base of fan, 4 dc in next ch-4 sp, 1 dc in next ch, 4 dc in next ch-4 sp, 1 dc in base of fan, 4 dc in next ch-4 sp, 1 dc in next st (corner), [4 dc in next ch-5 sp, 1 dc in next st] 3 times, 4 dc in next ch-5 sp, sl st in first dc to join.

Round 2: Ch 3 (counts as 1 tr), 6 tr in same st, *[miss 2 sts, sl st in next dc, miss 2 dc, 7 tr in next dc] 3 times to corner; rep from * around entire motif to end, sl st in top of beg ch-3 to join.

Fasten off and darn in ends neatly.

buttercups

A variation on the usual popcorn stitch, this block has large popcorn stitches made from drouble trebles as well as regular treble-crochet popcorns. Its bold circular design makes it a great square to include in a geometric or contemporary throw or afghan.

Special stitches used:

Double treble popcorn (dtr pc): Make popcorn with 8 dtr (*see page 19*).

Popcorn (pc): Make popcorn with 8 tr.

Foundation ring: Using yarn A, ch 10, sl st in first ch to form ring.

Round 1: Ch 5 (counts as 1 tr, ch 2), *1 pc in ring, ch 2**, 1 tr in ring, ch 2; rep from * 3 times then from * to ** 1 time, sl st in 3rd ch of beg ch-5 to join. Fasten off yarn A.

Round 2: Join yarn B in any pc, ch 3 (counts as 1 tr), 2 tr in same pc, 1 tr in next ch-2 sp, 1 tr in next tr, 1 tr in next ch-2 sp, *3 tr in next pc, 1 tr in next ch-2 sp, 1 tr in next tr, 1 tr in next ch-2 sp; rep from * 3 times, sl st in top of beg ch-3 to join. Fasten off yarn B.

Round 3: Join yarn A, ch 6 (counts as 1 dtr, ch 2), 1 dtr pc in next st, ch 2, 1 dtr in next st, ch 6, miss 3 sts, *1 dtr in next st, ch 2, 1 dtr pc in next st, ch 2, 1 dtr in next st, ch 6, miss 3 sts; rep from * 3 times, sl st in 4th ch of beg ch-6 to join. Fasten off yarn A.

Round 4: Join yarn B, ch 3 (counts as 1 tr), 2 tr in next sp, 1 tr in next dtr pc, 2 tr in next sp, 1 tr in next dtr, 6 tr in next ch-6 sp, *1 tr in nexr dtr, 2 tr in next sp, 1 tr in next dtr pc, 2 tr in next sp, 1 tr in next dtr, 6 tr in next ch-6 sp; rep from * 3 times, sl st in top of beg ch-3 to join. Fasten off yarn B.

Round 5: Join yarn A, ch 4 (counts as 1 dtr), [1 dtr, ch 2, 2 dtr] in same sp (forms corner), miss 1 st, 1 dtr in each of next 15 sts *[2 dtr, ch 2, 2 dtr] in next st (forms corner), miss 1 st, 1 dtr in each of next 15 sts; rep from * 2 times, sl st in top of beg ch-4 to join. Fasten off yarn A.

Round 6: Join yarn B in any ch-2 corner sp, ch 4 (counts as 1 dtr), [1 dtr, ch 2, 2 dtr] in same sp (forms corner), 1 dtr in each of next 5 sts, 1 tr in each of next 4 sts, 1 dc in next st, 1 tr in each of next 4 sts, 1 dtr in each of next 5 sts *[2 dtr, ch 2, 2 dtr] in next st (forms corner), 1 dtr in each of next 5 sts, 1 tr in each of next 4 sts, 1 dc in next st, 1 tr in each of next 4 sts, 1 dtr in each of next 5 sts; rep from * 2 times, sl st in top of beg ch-4 to join.

Round 7: Ch 1, 2 dc in next st, *[2 dc, ch 3, 2 dc] in same sp (forms corner)**, 1 dc in each of next 23 sts; rep from * 2 times, and from * to ** 1 time, 1 dc in each of next 21 sts, sl st in beg ch-1 to join.

Fasten off.

***

rajah

A bold motif built up with unusually tall stitches, this peacock feather-like block has a myriad possibilities and is bound to attract loads of admiring glances. Repeat it around the edge of a throw or blanket for a truly stunning design.

A
B
C
D

Special stitches used:

Half-triple treble (httr): Yoh 3 times, insert hook in indicated st/sp, draw through a lp, [yoh, draw through 2 lps] 2 times, yoh, draw through 3 lps (*see page 15*).

Half-quadruple treble (hquad tr): Yoh 4 times, insert hook in indicated st/sp, draw through a lp, [yoh, draw through 2 lps] 3 times, yoh, draw through 3 lps (*see page 15*)..

Foundation ring: Using yarn A, ch 4, sl st in first ch to form ring.

Round 1: Ch 3 (counts as 1 tr), 13 tr in ring, sl st in top of beg ch-3 to join. Fasten off.

Round 2: Join yarn B in any st, 1 dc in same st, 2 dc in next st, 2 htr in next st, 2 tr in next st, 2 hdtr in next st, 2 dtr in next st, 2 httr in next st, 3 ttr in next st, 2 httr in next st, 2 dtr in next st, 2 hdtr in next st, 2 tr in next st, 2 htr in next st, 2 dc in next st, sl st in first st to join. Fasten off.

Round 3: Join yarn C in same st, 1 dc in same st, 2 htr in next st, 1 tr in next st, 2 tr in next st, 1 hdtr in next st, 2 hdtr in next st, 1 dtr in next st, 2 dtr in next st, 1 httr in next st, 2 httr in next st, 1 ttr in next st, 2 ttr in next st, 1 hquad tr in next st, 2 hquad tr in next st, 3 quad tr in next st, 2 hquad tr in next st, 1 hquad tr in next st, 2 ttr in next st, 1 ttr in next st, 2 httr in next st, 1 httr in next st, 2 dtr in next st, 1 dtr in next st, 2 hdtr in next st, 1 hdtr in next st, 2 tr in next st, 1 tr in next st, 2 tr in next st, 1 htr in next st, sl st in first st to join. Fasten off.

Round 4: Join yarn D in same st, 1 dc in same st, 1 dc in each of next 4 sts, 1 htr in each of next 3 sts, 1 tr in each of next 2 sts, 2 tr in next st, 1 tr in next st, 1 hdtr in next st, 2 hdtr in next st, 1 hdtr in next st, 1 dtr in next st, 2 dtr in next st, 1 httr in next st, 2 httr in next st, 1 ttr in next st, 2 ttr in next st, 1 hquad tr in next st, 2 hquad tr in next st, 2 quad tr in next st, 3 quad tr in next st, 2 quad tr in next st, 2 hquad tr in next st, 1 hquad tr in next st, 2 ttr in next st, 1 ttr in next st, 2 httr in next st, 1 httr in next st, 1 dtr in next st, 2 dtr in next st, 1 hdtr in next st, 1 tr in next st, 2 tr in next st, 1 tr in next st, 1 htr in each of next 4 sts, 1 dc in each of next 2 sts, sl st in first st to join. Fasten off.

Round 5: Join yarn B in last st, *1 htr in next st, 2 htr in each of next 2 sts, 2 tr in each of next 2 sts, 2 dtr in each of next 2 sts, [3 ttr, ch 3, 3 ttr] in next st, 2 dtr in each of next 2 sts, 2 tr in each of next 2 sts, 2 htr in each of next 2 sts; rep from * 3 times, sl st in first htr to join. Fasten off.

Round 6: Join yarn C in same st, *1 dc in every st to corner, 3 dc in corner ch-3 sp; rep from * 3 times, 1 dc in every st to end, sl st in first dc to join. Fasten off.

Round 7: Join A in same st, *1 dc in every st to centre dc of corner 3-dc group, [1 dc, ch 2, 1 dc] in corner dc; rep from * 3 times, 1 dc in every dc to end, sl st in first st to join.

Fasten off, darn in ends and block work.

cistus

A square with a 3D rose at the centre, lovely for a bedspread or cushions and equally effective when worked in wool or cotton yarn. You could try edging the petals with a line of surface crochet to add another colour.

Foundation ring: Ch 8, sl st in first ch to form ring.

Round 1: Ch 3 (counts as 1 tr), 1 tr in ring, *ch 3, 2 tr in ring; rep from * 6 times, ch 3, sl st in top of beg ch-3 to join.

Round 2: Sl st in centre of next ch-3 lp, 1 dc in same place as sl st, *ch 4, 1 dc in next ch-3 lp; rep from * 7 times, ch 4, sl st in first dc to join.

Round 3: [1 dc, 1 htr, 5 tr, 1 htr, 1 dc] in each ch-4 lp, sl st in first dc to join.

Round 4: *Ch 6, inserting hook from back of work, 1 dc around next dc of Round 2; rep from * to end.

Round 5: [1 dc, 1 htr, 7 tr, 1 htr, 1 dc] in each ch-6 lp, sl st in first dc to join.

Round 6: Ch 8, inserting hook from back of work, 1 dc around next dc of Round 2; rep from * to end.

Round 7: [1 dc, 1 htr, 9 tr, 1 htr, 1 dc] in each ch-8 lp, sl st in first dc to join.

Round 8: Ch 10, inserting hook from back of work, 1 dc around next dc of Round 2; rep from * to end.

Round 9: Ch 9 (counts as 1 ttr, ch 3), 1 ttr in st at base of ch-9 lp, *[ch 1, 1 tr in next ch-10 lp] 3 times in same lp, [ch 1, 1 tr in next ch-10 lp] 3 times in next lp, ch 1**, [1 ttr, ch 3, 1 ttr] in dc between next 2 lps; rep from * 2 times, and from * to ** 1 time, sl st in 6th ch of beg ch-9 to join.

Round 10: Sl st in first ch-3 lp, ch 3 (counts as 1 tr), [1 tr, ch 3, 1 tr] in same lp, *1 tr in next ttr, [1 tr in next ch-1 sp, 1 tr in next tr] 6 times, 1 tr in next ch-1 sp, 1 tr in next ttr**, [2 tr, ch 2, 2 tr] in next ch-3 sp; rep from * 2 times and from * to ** 1 time, sl st in top of beg ch-3 to join.

Round 11: Ch 3 (counts as 1 tr), *1 tr in next tr, [2 tr, ch 3, 2 tr] in next ch-3 sp**, 1 tr in each of next 18 sts; rep from * 2 times and from * to ** 1 time, 1 tr in each of last 16 sts, sl st in top of beg ch-3 to join.

Round 12: Ch 3 (counts as 1 tr), *1 tr in each of next 3 tr, [2 tr, ch 3, 2 tr] in next ch-3 sp**, 1 tr in each of next 20 tr; rep from * 2 times and from * to ** 1 time, 1 tr in each of last 16 tr, sl st in top of beg ch-3 to join.

Round 13: Ch 3 (counts as 1 tr), *1 tr in each of next 5 tr [2 tr, ch 3, 2 tr] in next ch-3 sp**, 1 tr in each of next 22 tr; rep from * 2 times and from * to ** 1 time, 1 tr in each of last 16 sts , sl st in top of beg to join.

Fasten off.

116

**

retro deco

A familiar four-patch block given a twist by the addition of popcorns, this square has a pleasing texture and is easy to work up. You could choose to vary the colours in each patch, or make them all the same; whichever option you pick, this is a versatile block with many uses.

A

B

C

Special stitches used:

Beginning popcorn (beg pc): Ch 3, make popcorn with 4 tr.

Popcorn (pc): Make popcorn with 5 tr (*see page 19*).

Foundation ring: Using yarn A, ch 4, sl st to first ch to form ring.

Round 1: Beg pc in ring, ch 3, *1 pc, ch 3; rep from * 2 times, sl st in centre of beg pc to join. Fasten off.

Round 2: Join yarn B in any ch-3 sp, [beg pc, ch 3, 1 pc] in same sp, ch 6, *[1 pc, ch 3, 1 pc] in next ch-3 sp, ch 6; rep from * 2 times, sl st in centre of beg pc to join. Fasten off.

Round 3: Join yarn C in any ch-6 sp, ch 3 (counts as 1 tr), [2 tr, ch 3, 3 tr] in same sp (forms corner), 1 tr in next pc, 2 tr in next ch-6 sp, 1 tr in next pc, *[3 tr, ch 3, 3 tr] in next sp (forms corner), 1 tr in next pc, 2 tr in next ch-6 sp, 1 tr in next pc; rep from * 2 times, sl st in top of beg ch-3 to join. Fasten off.

Create 1 more square in the same way in the same colours; make 2 more squares using yarn B instead of A and yarn A instead of yarn B. You should now have 4 squares.

Place all four squares WS and join tog using yarn C and sc sts.

BORDER

Round 1: (WS) Join yarn C, ch 1, *1 dc in every st and 3 dc in every ch-3 sp around

outside of composite square to corner, 5 dc in each corner ch-3 sp; rep from * to end, sl st in first dc to join.

Round 2: Ch 1, *1 dc in each dc around square to corner, 3 dc in 3rd dc of each corner 5-dc group; rep from * to end, sl st to beg ch-1 to join.

Fasten off and darn in ends.

117

***

st clements

This lacy block has little, raised-up insert hoops, giving extra interest to a pretty design. This square is wonderful to work up and its lightness makes it ideal for use in a special table set or summer blanket.

A

B

C

Special stitch used:

Make bobble (MB): Make bobble with 2 dtr (*see page 19*).

Foundation chain: Using yarn A, ch 24, sl st in first ch to form ring.

Round 1: Ch 5, *miss 1 ch, 1 tr in next ch, ch 2; rep from * 10 times, sl st in 3rd ch of beg ch-5, sl st in next ch-2 sp.

Round 2: Ch 3 (counts as 1 tr), 1 tr in same ch-2 sp, ch 2, *2 tr in next ch-2 sp, ch 2; rep from * 10 times, sl st in top of beg ch-3 to join.

Round 3: *Ch 4, MB in next tr, ch 4, 1 dc in next ch-2 sp; rep from * 11 times, sl st in first ch of beg ch-4 to join. Fasten off.

Round 4: Join yarn B in top of any bobble, *ch 6, sl st in top of next bobble; rep from * 11 times, sl st in first ch of beg ch-6 to join.

Round 5: *Ch 8, sl st in next sl st; rep from * 11 times. Fasten off.

Round 6: Join yarn C in any sl st from Round 4, sl st in next ch-6 sp, *9 dc in same ch-6 sp, sl st in first dc of 9-dc group, pull lps through to WS and fasten off; rep from * 11 times, 1 time in each ch-6 sp.

Round 7: Join yarn B in 4th ch of any ch-8 lp from Round 5, *ch 7, sl st in 4th ch of next ch-8; rep from * 10 times, ch 7, sl st in first sl st (where yarn was joined).

Round 8: Ch 6, 1 sc in sl st from Round 7, [1 tr, ch 2, 1 tr] in same sp (forms corner), *ch 6, 1 dc in sl st from Round 7 (in ch-8 group) 3 times, [1 tr, ch 2, 1 tr] in same sl st; rep from * 2 times, [ch 6, 1 dc in

next sl st from Round 7] 2 times, sl st in first ch of beg ch-6 to join.

Round 9: Sl st in next ch-2 corner sp, *5 dc in corner sp, 9 dc in each of next 3 ch-6 sps; rep from * 3 times, sl st in first dc to join.

Fasten off and darn in ends.

god's eye

Inspired by the South American wool weavings of the same name, this block has a pleasing bobble pattern and looks best worked in pale to mid-tones to show off the texture. Mix with other bobble blocks or grannies for a warm throw.

Special stitch used:

Make bobble (MB): Make bobble with 5 tr (*see page 19*).

Foundation chain: Ch 30.

Row 1: 1 dc in 2nd ch from hook, 1 dc in each ch to end, turn.

Row 2 and every alt row: Ch 1, 1 dc in each dc to end, turn.

Row 3: Ch 1, 1 dc in each of next 14 dc, MB in next dc, 1 dc in each of next 14 dc, turn.

Row 5: Rep Row 3.

Row 7: Ch 1, 1 dc in each of next 12 dc, MB in next dc, 1 dc in each of next 3 dc, MB in next dc, 1 dc in each of next 12 dc, turn.

Row 9: Ch 1, 1 dc in each of next 10 dc, MB in next dc, 1 dc in each of next 7 dc, MB in next dc, 1 dc in each of next 10 dc, turn.

Row 11: Ch 1, 1 dc in each of next 8 dc, MB in next dc, [1 dc in each of next 5 dc, MB in next dc] 2 times, 1 dc in each of next 8 dc, turn.

Row 13: Ch 1, 1 dc in each of next 6 dc, MB in next dc, [1 dc in each of next 7 dc, MB in next dc] 2 times, 1 dc in each of next 6 dc, turn.

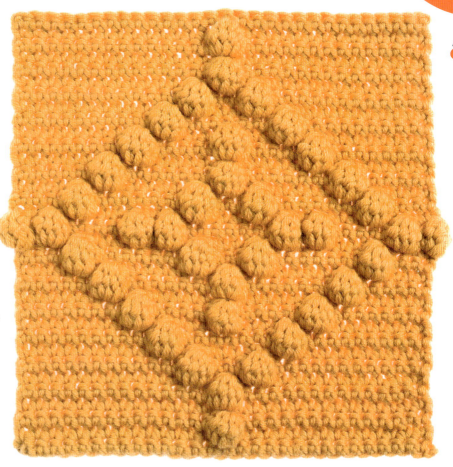

A

Row 15: Ch 1, 1 dc in each of next 4 dc, MB in next dc, * 1 dc in each of next 7 dc, MB in next dc**, 1 dc in each of next 3 dc, MB in next dc; rep from * to **, 1 dc in each of last 4 dc, turn.

Row 17: Ch 1, MB in first dc, *1 dc in next dc, MB in next dc, **1 dc in each of next 5 dc, MB in next dc; rep from * to **, 1 dc in each of next 7 dc, MB in next dc; rep from * to **, 1 dc in each of next 5 dc, MB in next dc; rep from * to **, ending MB in last dc, turn.

Row 19: Rep Row 15.

Row 21: Rep Row 13.

Row 23: Rep Row 11.

Row 25: Rep Row 9.

Row 27: Rep Row 7.

Row 29: Rep Row 5.

Row 31: Rep Row 3.

Row 33: Rep Row 2.

Fasten off and darn in ends. Block if necessary.

119

*

red aster

With its bold, spiky flower centre, this square would make a fantastic addition to a composite flower blanket piece, or it can be used in multiples for lovely, contemporary table linen.

A

B

C

Foundation ring: Using yarn A, ch 8, join with sl st to form ring.

Round 1: Ch 1, *1 dc in ring, ch 6, working down ch-6, [1 dc in 3rd ch from hook, miss 1 ch, 1 dc in next ch, 1 htr in next ch, 1 htr in side of base st]; rep from * 7 times. Fasten off yarn A.

Round 2: Join yarn B in top of any 6-ch petal, ch 4, *[1 tr in next ch-6 petal, ch 2, 1 tr in same st, ch 4, 1 tr in top of next ch-6 petal, ch 4]; rep from * 3 times, omitting last tr and ch-4, sl st in first petal to join.

Round 3: Ch 1, 1 dc in same st, *[4 dc in next ch-4 sp, 1 dc in next tr, 3 dc in the next ch-2 sp, 1 dc in the next tr, 4 dc in next ch-4 sp, 2 dc in next tr]; rep from * 3 times, omitting last dc in last rep, sl st in first dc to join. Fasten off yarn B.

Round 4: Join yarn C in top above 1-tr petal, ch 3 (counts as 1 tr), 1 tr in each of next 8 dc [ch 5, miss 3 sts, 1 tr in each of next 12 tr, ch 5, miss 3 tr, 1 tr in next st]; rep 2 times, 1 tr in each of last 4 tr, sl st in top of beg ch-3 to join.

Round 5: Ch 3 (counts as 1 tr), 1 tr in each of next 8 tr along *[3 tr, ch 3, 3 tr] in corner sp**, 1 tr in each of next 12 tr in next 12 tr; rep from * 2 times, then from * to ** 1 time, 1 tr in each of next 3 tr, sl st in top of ch-3 to join.

Round 6: Ch 3 (counts as 1 tr), 1 tr in each of next 11 tr along, *[3 tr, ch 2, 3 tr] in corner sp, 1 tr in each of next 18 tr; rep from * 2 times ending 6 tr on final side, join with sl st in top of ch-3.

Fasten off and darn in ends neatly.

120

**

mandarin lace

A filigree background frames a bright clustered centre in this quick-to-work block. Use a fairly tight tension or size down a hook to avoid a floppy square, because the double treble stitches make for an especially open fabric.

A

B

C

D

Special stitch used:

Beginning treble crochet cluster (beg tr cl): Ch 3, 1 tr in same st, make cluster with 3 tr (*see page 18*).

Treble crochet cluster (tr cl): Make cluster with 4 tr.

Foundation ring: Using yarn A, ch 6, join with sl st to form ring.

Round 1: Ch 1, 12 htr in ring, sl st in beg ch-1 to join. Fasten off yarn A.

Round 2: Join yarn B, ch 1, 2 dc in each htr, sl st in beg ch-1 to join. Fasten off yarn B.

Round 3: Join yarn C, ch 3, 3 tr in same sp, *[ch 4, miss 3 dc, 4 tr] in next st; rep from * 4 times, ch 4, sl st in top of beg ch-3 to join. Fasten off yarn C.

Round 4: Join yarn D, *beg tr cl, [ch 4, 1 dc in next ch-4 lp, ch 4**, tr cl in next 4-tr group]; rep from * 4 times, then from * to ** 1 time, sl st in top of first beg tr cl to join. Fasten off yarn D.

Round 5: Join yarn A in beg of next ch-4 sp, ch 3, [2 tr, ch 3, 3 tr] in same sp (corner), *[ch 2, 3 dc in next sp] 2 times, ch 2**, [3 tr, ch 3, 3 tr] in next sp (corner); rep from * 2 times, then from * to ** 1 time, sl st in top of beg ch-3 to join.

Round 6: Sl st in next corner sp, ch 4, [2 dtr, ch 3, 3 dtr] in same sp (corner), *ch 2, [1 dtr, ch 2, 1 dtr] in next ch-2 sp, ch 2, 1 dtr in next ch-2 sp, ch 2, [1 dtr, ch 2, 1 dtr] in next ch-2 sp, ch 2**, [3 dtr, ch 3, 3 dtr] in next sp (corner); rep from * 2 times, then from * to ** 1 time, sl st in top of beg ch-4 to join.

Round 7: Sl st in next corner sp, ch 4, [2 dtr, ch 3, 3 dtr] in same sp (corner), *ch 2, [1 dtr, ch 2, 1 dtr] in next ch-2 sp, ch 2, [1 dtr, ch 2] in each of the next 4 sps, [1 dtr, ch 2, 1 dtr] in next ch-2 sp, ch 2**, [3 dtr, ch 3, 3 dtr] in same sp (corner); rep from * 2 times, then from * to ** 1 time, sl st in top of beg ch-4 to join.

Round 8: Ch 1, [1 dc in each dtr, 3 dc in each corner sp and 2 dc in each ch-2 sp] to end of rnd, sl sl in first dc to join.

Fasten off and darn in ends neatly.

★★★★
salsa

With its large fruity slices, this block is reminiscent of a tropical carnival. It is highly textural and the segments are worked individually before being joined together. This gives scope for mixing up colours to your heart's content: create your own cocktail!

A
B
C

Special stitches used:

Popcorn (pc): Make popcorn with 7 htr (*see page 19*).

Beginning popcorn (beg pc): Ch 3, make popcorn with 6 tr.

Note: This square does not start in the centre but in the centre of each segment. The segments are worked individually and then placed in circle.

Foundation ring: Leaving a long tail of yarn, ch 10, sl st in first ch to join.

Round 1: Ch 3, (counts as 1 tr), 14 tr in ring, turn.

Round 2: Ch 5 (counts as 1 tr, ch 2), miss next 2 tr, 1 tr in next tr, [ch 2, miss 1 tr, 1 tr in next tr] 6 times, turn.

Round 3: Beg pc in first tr, *[ch 3, 1 pc] in next ch-2 sp; rep from * 6 times. Fasten off, leaving a long tail of yarn.

Make 3 segments using yarn A and 3 using yarn B.

Arrange segments RS facing, so that first pc of each overlaps next – this forms circle. Pin work to secure, turn to WS and stitch segments tog at centre using yarn tails and darning needle. Using outer yarn tails, sl st down each segment on inside (flat) edge to where it sits behind 3rd pc (from centre) of next segment. Stitch to secure. Rep with other segments.

BORDER

Round 1: Join yarn C around 4th (middle) pc of any segment (at base and back of pc) 1 dc in same st, ch 12, 1 dc in same place in next segment; rep from * 4 times, ch 12, sl st in first dc to join.

Round 2: Ch 2 (counts as 1 htr), 11 htr in next ch-12 lp, [12 htr in next ch-12 lp] 5 times, sl st in top of beg ch-2 to join.

Round 3: Ch 2 (counts as 1 htr), *1 dc in each of next 5 sts, 1 htr in each of next 3 sts, 1 tr in each of next 3 sts, [3 tr, ch 2, 3 tr] in next st (forms corner), 1 tr in each of next 3 sts, 1 htr in each of next 3 sts; rep from * 3 times omitting last htr on last rep; sl st in top of beg ch-2 to join.

Round 4: Ch 4 (counts as 1 tr, ch 1), miss 1 st, 1 tr in next st, *ch 1, miss 1 st, 1 tr in next st**; rep from * to ch-2 corner sp, [1 tr, ch 3, 1 tr] in ch-2 corner sp; rep from * 3 times, and from * to ** to end, sl st in 3rd ch of beg ch-3 to join.

Round 5: Ch 1, *1 dc in each tr and in each ch-1 sp to corner, [2 dc, ch 1, 2 dc] in corner ch-3 sp; rep from * 3 times, 1 dc in each tr and every ch-1 sp to end, sl st in first dc to join.

Fasten off and darn in ends.

***

glastonbury

A | B | C | D

An intricate construction that appears to be a double mitre corner, but is made as one mitre, changing colour to achieve the double effect. Count squares as you go to ensure you have increased in the right place, and this square works up quickly.

Note: When switching colours, always bring last yarn to front of work.

Foundation chain: Using yarn A, ch 7.

Row 1: 1 tr in 5th ch from hook, ch 1, miss 1 ch, 1 tr in last ch, turn.

Row 2: Ch 4 (counts as 1 tr, ch 1), miss 1 ch, 1 tr in next tr, ch 1, miss 1 ch, 1 tr in last tr, turn. Fasten off.

Row 3: Join yarn B, ch 4 (counts as 1 tr, *ch 1), miss 1 ch, 1 tr in next tr; rep from * to end of row, working down side of square, ch 4, 1 tr in same st as last tr, [ch 1, miss 1 ch, 1 tr in next tr] 3 times, turn. Fasten off.

Row 4: Join yarn C, ch 4 (counts as 1 tr, ch 1), [miss 1 ch, 1 tr in next tr, ch 1] 2 times, miss 1 ch, [1 tr, ch 4, 1 tr] in next ch st (in ch-4 sp), [ch 1, miss 1 ch, 1 tr in next tr] 2 times, ch 1, miss 1 ch, 1 tr in 3rd ch of ch-4 at end, turn.

Row 5: Ch 4 (counts as 1 tr, ch 1), [miss 1 ch, 1 tr in next tr, ch 1] 3 times, miss 1 ch, [1 tr, ch 4, 1 tr] in next ch st (in ch-4 sp), [ch 1, miss 1 ch, 1 tr in next tr] 3 times, ch 1, miss 1 ch, 1 tr in 3rd ch of ch-4 at end, turn. Fasten off.

Row 6: Join yarn A, ch 4 (counts as 1 tr, ch 1), [miss 1 ch, 1 tr in next tr, ch 1] 4 times, miss 1 ch, [1 tr, ch 4, 1 tr] in next ch st (in ch-4 sp), [ch 1, miss 1 ch, 1 tr in next tr] 4 times, ch 1, miss 1 ch, 1 tr in 3rd ch of ch-4 at end, turn.

Row 7: Ch 4 (counts as 1 tr, ch 1), [miss 1 ch, 1 tr in next tr, ch 1] 5 times, miss 1 ch, [1 tr, ch 4, 1 tr] in next ch st (in ch-4 sp), [ch 1, miss 1 ch, 1 tr in next tr] 5 times, ch 1, miss 1 ch, 1 tr in 3rd ch of ch-4 at end, turn. Fasten off.

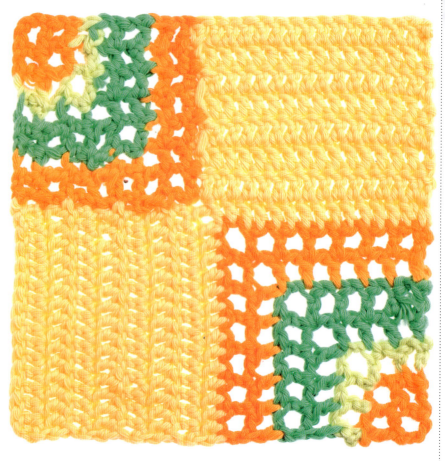

Row 8: Join yarn D ch 3 (counts as 1 tr), 1 tr in every st and ch-1 sp to corner, 1 tr in first 2 ch of ch-4, ch 3, 1 tr in each of last 2 ch sts, 1 tr in every st and every ch-sp to end, turn.

Row 9: Ch 3 (counts as 1 tr), 1 tr in each of next 15 tr, change to yarn A, 1 tr in next tr, ch 4 (counts as 1 tr, ch 1), miss 1 ch, 1 tr, change to yarn D, 1 tr in each of next 16 tr, turn.

Row 10: Ch 3 (counts as 1 tr), 1 tr in each of next 15 tr, change to yarn A, 1 tr in next tr, ch 1, miss 1 ch, 1 tr, ch 4 (counts as 1 tr, ch 1), miss 1 ch, 1 tr in next tr, ch 1, miss 1 ch, 1 tr in next tr, change to yarn D, 1 tr in each of next 16 tr, turn.

Row 11: Ch 3 (counts as 1 tr), 1 tr in each of next 15 tr, change to yarn, 1 tr in next tr, ch 1, miss 1 ch, 1 tr in next tr, change to yarn C, ch 1, miss 1 ch, 1 tr in next tr, ch 4 (counts as 1 tr, ch 1), miss 1 ch, 1 tr in next tr, change to yarn A, [ch 1, miss 1 ch, 1 tr in next tr] 2 times, change to yarn D, 1 tr in each of next 16 tr, turn.

Row 12: Ch 3 (counts as 1 tr), 1 tr in each of next 15 tr, change to yarn A, 1 tr in next tr, ch 1, miss 1 ch, 1 tr in next tr, change to yarn C, [ch 1, miss 1 ch, 1 tr in next tr] 2 times, ch 4 (counts as 1 tr, ch 1), miss 1 ch, 1 tr in next tr, ch 1, miss 1 ch, 1 tr in next tr, change to yarn A, [ch 1, miss 1 ch, 1 tr in next tr] 2 times, change to yarn D, 1 tr in each of next 16 tr, turn.

Row 13: Ch 3 (counts as 1 tr), 1 tr in each of next 15 tr, change to yarn A, 1 tr in next tr, ch 1, miss 1 ch, 1 tr in next tr, change to yarn C, [ch 1, miss 1 ch, 1 tr in next tr] 2 times, change to yarn B, ch 1, miss 1 ch, 1 tr in next tr, ch 4 (counts as 1 tr, ch 1), miss 1 ch, 1 tr in next trc, change to yarn C, [ch 1, miss 1 ch, 1 tr in next tr] 2 times, change to yarn A, [ch 1, miss 1 ch, 1 tr in next tr] 2 times, change to yarn D, 1 tr in each of next 16 tr, turn.

Continued on page 109

Row 14: Ch 3 (counts as 1 tr), 1 tr in each of next 15 tr, change to yarn A, 1 tr in next tr, ch 1, miss 1 ch, 1 tr in next tr, change to yarn C, [ch 1, miss 1 ch, 1 tr in next tr] 2 times, change to yarn B, ch 1, miss 1 ch, 1 tr in next tr, change to yarn A, ch 1, miss 1 ch, 1 tr in next tr, ch 4 (counts as 1 tr, ch 1), miss 1 ch, 1 tr in next tr, change to yarn B, ch 1, miss 1 ch, 1 tr in next tr, change to yarn C, [ch 1, miss 1 ch, 1 tr in next tr] 2 times, change to yarn A, [ch 1, miss 1 ch, 1 tr in next tr] 2 times, change to yarn D, 1 tr in each of next 16 tr, turn.

Row 15: Ch 3 (counts as 1 tr), 1 tr in each of next 15 tr, change to yarn A, 1 tr in next tr, ch 1, miss 1 ch, 1 tr in next tr, change to yarn C, [ch 1, miss 1 ch, 1 tr in next tr] 2 times, change to yarn B, ch 1, miss 1 ch, 1 tr in next tr, change to yarn A, [ch 1, miss 1 ch, 1 tr in next tr] 2 times, ch 4 (counts as 1 tr, ch 1), miss 1 ch, 1 tr in next tr, ch 1, miss 1 ch, 1 tr in next tr, change to yarn B, ch 1, miss 1 ch, 1 tr in next tr, change to yarn C, [ch 1, miss 1 ch, 1 tr in next tr] 2 times, change to yarn A [ch 1, miss 1 ch, 1 tr in next tr] 2 times, change to yarn D, 1 tr in each of last 16 tr.

Fasten off and darn in all ends.

** **

adobe

An openwork lace with bold simple shapes, this block works up quickly and is great for summer throws as it has good drape and is wonderfully cool. Mix with other lightweight lace blocks for a pretty picnic blanket.

Special stitch used:

Picot-3: Ch 3 (at point to add picot), sl st in first ch st.

Foundation ring: Using yarn A, ch 4, sl st in first ch to form ring.

Round 1: Ch 5 (counts as 1 tr, ch 2), *1 tr, ch 2 in ring; rep from * 6 times, sl st in 3rd ch of beg ch-5 to join.

Round 2: Ch 3 (counts as 1 tr), * 3 tr in next ch-2 sp, 1 tr in next st; rep from * 6 times, 3 tr in next ch-2 sp, sl st in top of beg ch-3 to join. Fasten off.

Round 3: Join yarn B in top of any st, ch 3 (counts as tr), 1 tr in same st, ch 7, *miss 3 sts, 2 tr in next st, ch 7; rep from * 6 times, sl st in top of beg ch-3 to join.

Round 4: Ch 3 (counts as 1 tr), 2 tr in next st, ch 7, *1 tr in next st, 2 tr in next st, ch 7; rep from * 6 times, sl st in top of beg ch-3 to join.

Round 5: Ch 3 (counts as 1 tr), 1 tr in next st, picot-3, 2 tr in next st, ch 5, 1 dc in ch-7 sps from Rounds 3 and 4, picot-3, 1 dc in same ch-7 sps, ch 5, *1 tr in each of next 2 sts, picot-3, 2 tr in next st, ch 5, 1 dc in ch-7 sps from Rounds 3 and 4, picot-3, 1 dc in same ch-7 sp, ch 5; rep from * 6 times, sl st in top of beg ch-3 to join. Fasten off.

Round 6: Join yarn A in any picot-3 between 4 tr in rnd below, *1 dc in same st, ch 10, [3 tr, picot-3, 3 tr] in next picot-3 between 4 tr in rnd below, ch 10; rep from * 3 times, sl st in first dc to join.

Round 7: Ch 1, *12 dc in next ch-10 sp, 1 dc in each of next 3 sts, [1 dc, picot-3, 1 dc] in corner sp, 1 dc in each of next 3 sts, 12 dc in next ch-10 sp; rep from * 3 times, sl st in first dc to join. Fasten off.

Round 8: Join yarn B in any st, 1 dc in each st all around, [1 dc, picot-3, 1 dc] in each corner sp, sl st in first dc to join.

Fasten off and darn in ends.

123

A

B

109

124 ✷✷ chequers

A reversible square with a pleasing bridge pattern on the other side, this plays with simple solid stitches to create a complex-looking fabric with a chequered texture. Great for mixing with plainer blocks, this is warm and soft to handle.

A
B
C

Foundation chain: Using yarn A, ch 32.

Row 1: 1 tr in 4th ch from hook, *ch 2, miss 2 ch, 1 tr in each of next 2 ch; rep from * to end, joining in yarn B on last tr, turn.

Row 2: Using yarn B, ch 2, *1 tr in each of 2 miss chs on Row 1, ch 2; rep from * to end, ending with ch 1 instead of ch 2, sl st in top of beg ch-3 of Row 1, join yarn C, turn.

Row 3: Using yarn C, ch 3, 1 tr in miss tr on last row, *ch 2, 1 tr in each of 2 miss tr on last row; rep from * to end, pulling yarn A through on last tr, turn.

Row 4: Using yarn A; rep Row 2.

Row 5: Using yarn B, rep Row 3.

Row 6: Using yarn C, rep Row 2.

Row 7: Using yarn A, rep Row 3.

Row 8: Using yarn B, rep Row 2.

Row 9: Using yarn C, rep Row 3.

Work another 16 rows, alt Rows 2 and 3, and yarns A, B and C.

Round 26: Using yarn A, work a rnd of dc around entire square (26 dc on each side, distributed evenly), and [2 dc, ch 1, 2 dc] in each corner, sl st in first dc to join.

Fasten off, turn square over to see reverse pattern, then select which side you would like to use as RS before you darn in ends.

125 ✷ filet block

A bold central block creates the focus for this simple, graphic square. Good for repeating to form modern table linens with a retro flavour, this square works up quickly and is easy to grasp.

A

Foundation chain: Ch 29.

Row 1: 1 dc in 2nd ch from hook, 1 dc in every ch to end of row, turn.

Row 2: Ch 2 (counts as 1 tr), 1 tr in every dc to end of row, turn.

Row 3: Ch 2, miss 1 tr, 1 tr in each of next 2 tr, *ch 3, miss 3 tr, 1 tr in next tr; rep from * 5 times, 1 tr in each of next 2 tr, turn.

Rows 4 to 5: Rep Row 3.

Row 6: Ch 2 (counts as 1 tr), 1 tr in each of next 2 sts, ch 3, miss 3 sts, [1 tr in next tr, 3 tr, in next ch-3 sp] 4 times, 1 tr in next tr, ch 3, miss 3 sts, 1 tr in each of next 3 sts, turn.

Rows 7 to 11: Rep Row 6.

Rows 12 to 15: Rep Row 3.

Row 16: Rep Row 2.

Row 17: Ch 1, 1 dc in every st to end of row.

Fasten off and darn in ends neatly.

**

daisy chain

Reminiscent of 1960s' Flower Power, this lively pattern is fun to work and creates a beautifully wavy stripe when it is worked in alternating colours.

A
B
C

Special stitch used:

Cluster (cl): Make cluster from 6 tr (*see page 18*), then ch 1 to form an 'eye'.

Foundation chain: Ch 30.

Row 1: 1 dc in 2nd chain from hook, 1 dc in each st to end.

Row 2: Ch 1, 1 dc in first dc, *miss 2 dc, 7 tr in next dc, miss 2 dc, 1 dc in next dc; rep from * 4 times, miss 2 dc, 4 tr in next dc, turn. Fasten off yarn A.

Row 3: (RS) Join yarn B in first tr with dc, ch 2, *1 cl over next 6 tr, drawing lps through 3 of current shell group, miss 1 dc, and 3 sts of next shell group, ch 1 (eye), ch 2, 1 dc in next tr, ch 2; rep from * 4 times, 1 cl over last 3 tr in row, ch 1, turn.

Row 4: Ch 3, 3 tr in eye of first cl in row, 1 dc in next dc, *7 tr in next eye, dc in next dc; rep from * 4 times, 1 dc in top of ch-2. Fasten off yarn B, turn.

Row 5: Join yarn C in first dc with dc, 1 cl over first 3 tr of shell, ch 1 (eye), ch 2, 1 dc in next tr, *1 cl over next 6 tr (3 sts of current shell group), miss 1 dc, and 3 sts of next shell group), ch 1 (eye), ch 2, 1 dc in next tr; rep from * 4 times, 1 dc in ch-3.

Row 6: Ch 1, *7 tr in next eye, 1 dc in dc; rep from * 4 times, 4 tr in last eye. Fasten off yarn C.

Row 7: Using yarn A, rep Row 3.

Row 8: Rep Row 4. Fasten off yarn A.

Row 9: Using yarn B, rep Row 5.

Row 10: Rep row 6. Fasten off yarn B.

Row 11: Using yarn C, rep Row 3.

Row 12: Rep row 4. Fasten off yarn C.

Row 13: Using yarn A, rep Row 5.

Row 14: Rep row 6. Fasten off yarn A.

Row 15: Using yarn B, 1 dc in first tr, ch 1, ch 2, *1 cl over next 6 tr (3 sts of current shell group, miss 1 dc and 3 sts of next shell group), ch 1 (eye), ch 2, 1 dc in next tr, ch 2; rep from * 4 times, 1 cl worked over last 3 tr.

Fasten off and darn in ends neatly.

**

citrus

An unusual four-patch square that has raised-up segments made by working around the posts of stitches, and behind the central layer. This versatile and pretty block mixes well with many other squares and would look equally good in lilacs and pinks.

A
B
C
D
E

Special stitch used:

Crab stitch (crab st): Double crochet worked in reverse (*see page 22*).

Foundation ring: Using yarn A, ch 4, sl st in first ch to join ring.

Round 1: *Ch 3 (counts as 1 tr), 1 tr in same sp, 3 dc around post of last tr made, sl st in base ring to join; rep from * 3 times. Fasten off.

Round 2: Turn work to WS, join yarn B to any ch-3 sp, *ch 3 (counts as 1 tr), 1 tr in same sp, 3 dc around post of last tr made, sl st in same sp, ch 3 to sit behind next segment, sl st in top of next segment; rep from * 3 times, sl st in first ch of beg ch-3 to join. Fasten off.

Round 3: Join yarn C in any corner sp, *ch 3 (counts as 1 tr), 1 dc in next dc, 1 tr in next dc, 1 dtr in next dc, 1 dtr in sp that joins to Round 1, ch 2, sl st in ch-3 sp on next segment to join; rep from * 3 times, sl st in first ch of beg ch-3 to join.

Round 4: Ch 3 (counts as 1 tr), 1 tr in same sp, [ch 3, 2 tr] in same sp (forms corner), 1 tr in each of next 3 sps, 2 tr in next sp, *[2 tr, ch 3, 2 tr] in next sp (forms corner), 1 tr in each of next 2 sps, 2 trc in the next sp; rep from * 2 times, sl st in top of beg ch-3 to join. Fasten off.

Create 2 squares in the same way in the same colours; make 2 more squares using yarn D instead of A and yarn E instead of B. You should now have 4 squares.

Place squares WS tog, join with dc in arrangement shown.

BORDER

Round 1: With RS facing, join yarn C to any ch-3 corner sp, ch 2 (counts as 1 htr), [1 htr, ch 1, 2 htr] in same corner sp, *1 htr in each tr to next corner, **[2 htr, ch 1, 2 htr] in corner sp; rep from * 2 times and from * to ** 1 times, sl st in top of beg ch-2 to join.

Round 2: Ch 1, 1 crab st in each htr all around square, sl st in beg ch-1 to join.

Fasten off and darn in ends.

128

*

log cabin

A B C

A simple four-patch block that uses a clever working-round-the-side of stitch posts technique to turn corners. This versatile square has endless scope for working in your own colour combinations, and mixes extremely well with many other blocks in the book.

Foundation ring: Using yarn A, make a magic loop, ch 3 (counts as 1 tr), 11 tr in loop, tighten.

Round 1: Ch 3 (counts as 1 tr), 1 tr in each of next tr, 6 tr in next tr (forms corner), *1 tr in each of next 2 tr, 6 tr in next tr (forms corner); rep from * 2 times, sl st in top of beg ch-3 to join.

Round 2: Ch 3 (counts as 1 tr), 1 trc in each of next 5 tr, *ch 3 (counts as 1 tr), 2 tr in side post of last tr made**, 1 tr in same tr, 1 tr in each of next 8 tr; rep from * 2 times then from * to ** 1 time, 1 tr in each of next 3 tr, sl st in top of beg ch-3 to join.

Fasten off.

SQUARE 1 ONLY

Round 3: Join yarn B, ch 1, 1 dc in each tr and [2 dc, ch 1, 2 dc] in every ch-3 corner sp to end, sl st in first dc to join. Fasten off.

Make Squares 2 and 4 as Square 1 but using C instead of A and omitting Round 3; Make Square 3 as Square 1 omitting Round 3.

With RS of Square 1 facing you, work along edge of Round 3 of Square 1 and Round 2 of Square 2, then at centre refold work and attach Square 4, again with RS of Square 1 facing you. Using yarn B, substitute ch-1 at corner with sl st in corner of square being joined, then insert hook in 2 sts closest tog on each dc along (front st of square behind with back st of square in front), 1 dc in each st. When joining Square 4 to corners

of Squares 3 and 2, work 1 dc in each corner to secure in place.

Using yarn B, ch 1, 1 dc in each dc around square, working ch-2 in each corner sp.

Fasten off and darn in ends.

129

**

inca gold

A

A spider's web of bullion stitches makes up this filigree square, lovely for use in window treatments or summery throws and wraps. Use a pale colour to enhance the subtlety of the bullion stitch texture.

Special stitch used:

Bullion stitch (bullion st): Yoh 7 times, insert hook in st or sp to be worked, yoh, draw lp through to front, yoh, pull through all lps on hook, ch 1 to secure (see page 20).

Foundation ring: Ch 6, sl st in first ch to form ring.

Round 1: Ch 3 (counts as 1 tr), 15 tr in ring, sl st in top of beg ch-3 to join.

Round 2: Ch 3 (counts as 1 tr), 1 bullion st in same st, *[1 bullion, 1 tr] in next tr, [1 tr, 1 bullion] in next tr; rep from * 6 times, [1 bullion, 1 tr] in next tr, sl st in top of beg ch-3 to join.

Round 3: Ch 3 (counts as 1 tr), *1 bullion st in each of next 2 bullion sts, 1 tr in next tr, ch 2, 1 tr in next tr; rep from * 6 times,

1 bullion in each of next 2 bullion, 1 tr in next tr, ch 2, sl st in top of beg ch-3 to join.

Round 4: Ch 2 (counts as 1 htr), *1 dc in each of next 2 bullion, 1 htr in next tr, ch 4, 1 tr in next tr, 1 bullion in each of next 2 bullion, 1 tr in next tr, ch 4**, 1 htr in next tr; rep from * 2 times and from * to ** 1 time, sl st in first ch to join.

Round 5: Ch 3 (counts as 1 tr), *1 bullion in each of next 2 dc, 1 tr in next htr, ch 6, 1 tr in next tr, 1 bullion in each of next 2 bullion, 1 tr in next tr, ch 6**, 1 tr in next htr; rep from * 2 times, and from * to ** 1 time, sl st in top of beg ch-3 to join.

Round 6: Ch 2 (counts as 1 htr), *1 dc in each of next 2 bullion, 1 htr in next tr, ch 8, 1 tr in next tr, 1 bullion in each of next 2 bullion, 1 tr in next tr, ch 8**, 1 htr in next tr; rep from * 2 times and from * to ** 1 time, sl st in first ch to join.

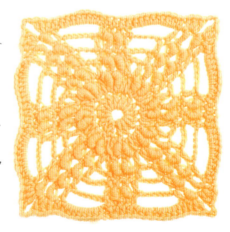

Round 7: Ch 2 (counts as 1 htr), 1 htr in each of next 3 sts, *8 htr in next ch-8 lp, 1 htr in next tr, [2 htr 1 tr] in top of next bullion, ch 3, [1 tr, 2 htr] in top of next bullion, 1 htr in next tr, 8 htr in next ch-8 lp**, 1 htr in each of next 4 sts; rep from * 2 times, and from * to ** 1 time, sl st in top of beg ch-2 to join.

Fasten off and darn in ends.

★★★
solaris

An interestingly textured square with contrasting flat, dense double-crochet border and dimensional lacy insert, this is a great block for mixing with other intensely patterned squares. It would also look great repeated in alternating colours, using yarn A for yarn B and vice versa.

Foundation ring: Using yarn A, make a magic ring.

Round 1: Ch 3 (counts as 1 tr), 11 tr in ring, sl st in top of beg ch-3 to join.

Round 2: Ch 3 (counts as 1 tr) 2 tr in same st, 3 tr in each st to end, sl st in top of beg ch-3 to join. Fasten off.

Round 3: Join yarn B, *ch 9, miss 2 sts, 1 dc in next st, ch 6, miss 2 sts, 1 dc in next st, ch 6, miss 2 sts**, 1 dc in next st; rep from * 2 times then from * to ** 1 time, sl st in first ch of beg ch-9 to join.

Round 4: *[1 tr in ch-9 sp, 1 dc around post of same tr] 6 times in next ch-9 sp, [5 dc in next ch-6 sp] 2 times; rep from * 3 times, sl st in first tr to join.

Round 5: Sl st in sp between 3rd and 4th dc of 6-tr group, ch 6 (counts as 1 tr, ch 3), 1 tr in same sp (forms corner), 1 tr in each of next 2 sps between dc, miss 2 sts, 1 dc in each of next 10 dc, miss 2 sts, 1 tr in each of next 3 sps between dc, *ch 3, 1 tr in the same sp (forms corner), 1 tr in each of next 2 sps, miss 2 sts, 1 dc in each of next 10 dc, miss 2 sts, 1 tr in each of next 3 sps; rep from * 2 times, sl st in 3rd ch of beg ch-6 to join. Fasten off.

Round 6: Join yarn A in any corner ch-3 sp, [1 dc, ch 3, 1 dc] in same sp (forms corner), 1 dc in each of next 16 sts, *[1 dc, ch 3, 1 dc] in next st (forms corner), 1 dc in each of next 16 sts; rep from * 2 times, sl st to first dc to join.

Round 7: [1 dc, ch 3, 1 dc] in same sp (forms corner), 1 dc in each of next 18 sts, *[1 dc, ch 3, 1 dc] in same sp (forms corner), 1 dc in each of next 18 sts; rep from * 2 times, sl st in first dc to join.

Round 8: [1 dc, ch 3, 1 dc] in same sp (forms corner), 1 dc in each of next 20 sts, *[1 dc, ch 3, 1 dc] in same sp (forms corner), 1 dc in each of next 20 sts; rep from * 2 times, sl st in first dc to join.

Round 9: [1 dc, ch 3, 1 dc] in same sp (forms corner), 1 dc in each of next 22 sts, *[1 dc, ch 3, 1 dc] in same sp (forms corner), 1 dc in each of next 22 sts; rep from * 2 times, sl st in first dc to join.

Round 10: [1 dc, ch 3, 1 dc] in same sp (forms corner), 1 dc in each of next 24 sts, *[1 dc, ch 3, 1 dc] in same sp (forms corner), 1 dc in each of next 24 sts; rep from * 2 times, sl st in first dc to join.

Round 11: [1 dc, ch 3, 1 dc] in same sp (forms corner), 1 dc in each of next 26 sts, *[1 dc, ch 3, 1 dc] in same sp (forms corner), 1 dc in each of next 26 sts; rep from * 2 times, sl st in first dc to join.

Round 12: [1 dc, ch 3, 1 dc] in same sp (forms corner), 1 dc in each of next 28 sts, *[1 dc, ch 3, 1 dc] in same sp (forms corner), 1 dc in each of next 28 sts; rep from * 2 times, sl st in first dc to join.

Round 13: Ch 6 (counts as 1 tr, ch 3), 1 tr in same corner sp, 1 tr in each of next 30 sts, *[1 tr, ch 3, 1 tr] in next corner sp (forms corner), 1 tr in each of next 30 sts; rep from * 2 times, sl st in 3rd ch of beg ch-6 to join.

Fasten off and darn in ends.

* bumblebee

Worked initially in linear form to create the little bees, this block is then completed in the round to form its stripy border. Slightly larger popcorns are used to add extra texture. This fun square would work well in a child's blanket or pillow cover. Team with the ladybird block for more impact!

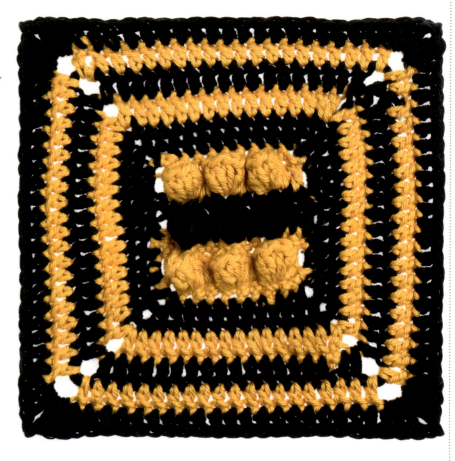

Special stitch used:

Popcorn (pc): Make popcorn with 6 tr (*see page 19*).

Foundation chain: Using yarn A, ch 12.

Row 1: 1 dc in 2nd ch from hook, 1 dc in each ch to end, turn – 11 dc.

Row 2: (WS) Ch 3 (counts as 1 tr), 1 tr in next st, *1 pc in next st, 1 tr in next 2 sts; rep from * 2 times, turn.

Row 3: Ch 1, *1 dc in each of next 2 sts, 1 dc in top of next pc; rep from * 2 times, 1 dc in each of last 2 sts, turn. Fasten off yarn A.

Row 4: Join yarn B, rep Row 2.

Row 5: Rep Row 3. Fasten off yarn B.

Row 6: Join yarn A, rep Row 2. Fasten off yarn A.

Round 7: Join yarn B in any corner sp, ch 4 (counts as 1 dc, ch 3), 1 dc in same sp (forms corner), *1 dc in each of next 8 dc, miss last dc, [1 dc, ch 3, 1 dc] in next sp (forms corner), 1 dc along side of square 8 times**, [1 dc, ch 3, 1 dc] in next corner sp (forms corner); rep from * to ** 1 time, sl st in corner sp to join.

Round 8: Ch 4 (counts as 1 dc, ch 3), 1 dc in same sp (forms corner), *1 dc in each of next 10 dc, [1 dc, ch 3, 1 dc] in next corner ch-2 sp (forms corner), 1 dc in each of next 10 dc**, [1 dc, ch 3, 1 dc] in next corner ch-2 sp (forms corner); rep from * to ** 1 time, sl st in corner ch-2 sp to join.

Round 9: Ch 4 (counts as 1 dc, ch 3), 1 dc in same sp (forms corner), *1 dc in each of next 12 dc, [1 dc, ch 3, 1 dc] in next corner ch-3 sp, 1 dc in each of next 12 dc**, [1 dc, ch 3, 1 dc] in next ch-3 sp; rep from * to ** 1 time, sl st in corner ch-3 sp to join. Fasten off yarn B.

Round 10: Join yarn A in any corner sp, ch 6 (counts as 1 tr, ch 3), 1 tr in same sp (forms corner), 1 tr in each of next 14 dc, *[1 tr, ch 3, 1 tr] in next ch-3 sp, 1 tr in each of next 14 dc; rep from * 2 times, sl st in 3rd ch of beg ch-6 to join. Fasten off yarn A.

Round 11: Join yarn B in any corner sp, ch 6 (counts as 1 tr, ch 3), 1 tr in same sp (forms corner), 1 tr in each of next 16 tr, *[1 tr, ch 3, 1 tr] in next corner sp, 1 tr in each of next 16 tr; rep from * 2 times, sl st in 3rd ch of beg ch-6 to join. Fasten off yarn B.

Round 12: Join yarn A in any corner sp, ch 6 (counts as 1 tr, ch 3), 1 tr in same sp (forms corner), 1 tr in each of next 18 tr, *[1 tr, ch 3, 1 tr] in next corner sp, 1 tr in each of next 18 tr; rep from * 2 times, sl st in 3rd ch of beg ch-6 to join. Fasten off.

Round 13: Join yarn B in any corner sp, ch 3 (counts as 1 tr), [2 tr, ch 2, 3 tr] in same corner sp (forms corner), 1 tr in each of next 20 tr, *[3 tr, ch 2, 3 tr] in next corner sp, 1 tr in each of next 20 tr; rep from * 2 times, sl st in top of beg ch-3 to join.

Fasten off and darn in ends neatly.

van gogh

Named for the artist because of the texture's resemblance to his thick paint and the colours in *Sunflowers*, this block showcases the fascinating 'block diagonal' stitch technique and is the sister block to Teatime. Mix with plain blocks or grannies, this is adaptable and enjoyable to work.

A
B
C
D
E

Foundation chain: Using yarn A, ch 5, 1 dc in 3rd, 4th and 5th ch from hook, turn.

Row 1: Ch 5, 1 dc in 3rd, 4th and 5th ch from hook, flip work upwards to access base, sl st in ch-2 sp of foundation ch, ch 2, 3 dc in same sp, turn.

Row 2: Ch 5, 1 dc in 3rd, 4th and 5th ch from hook, flip work up, *sl st in ch-2 sp of Row 1, ch 2, 3 dc in same sp; rep from * 1 time, turn. Fasten off.

Row 3: Join yarn B, ch 5, 1 dc in 3rd, 4th and 5th ch from hook, flip work up, *sl st in ch-2 sp of Row 2, ch 2, 3 dc in same sp; rep from * 2 times, turn.

Row 4: Ch 5, 1 dc in 3rd, 4th and 5th ch from hook, flip work up, *sl st in ch-2 sp of Row 3, ch 2, 3 dc in same sp; rep from * 3 times, turn.

Rows 5 to 11: Rep Row 4, but rep from * 4, 5, 6, 7, 8, 9 and 10 times accordingly, using yarn colours as below, turn.

Rows 5 to 6: Yarn B.

Row 7: Yarn C.

Rows 8 to 9: Yarn D. Rows 10–11: Yarn E.

Row 12: (Start dec) sl st in each of first 3 dc, *sl st in next ch-2 sp, ch 2, 3 sc in same sp; rep from * 10 times, sl st in last ch-2 sp, turn.

Row 13: Sl st in first 3 dc, *sl st in next ch-2 sp, ch 2, 3 dc in same sp; rep from * 9 times, sl st in last ch-2 sp, turn.

Rows 14 to 21: Rep Row 13, but rep from * 8, 7, 6, 5, 4, 3 and 2 times accordingly, using yarns as below, turn.

Rows 14 to 15: Yarn D.

Row 16: Yarn C.

Rows 17 to 20: Yarn B.

Row 21: Yarn A.

Row 22: Sl st in first 3 dc, sl st in next ch-2 sp, ch 2, 3 dc in same sp, sl st in last ch-2 sp, turn.

Row 23: Ch 1, 1 dc in each of last 3 dc.

Fasten off.

BORDER

Round 1: Join yarn C in any corner sp, ch 1, *[1 htr, ch 1, 1 htr] in corner sp, 1 htr in every st to next corner sp; rep from * 3 times, sl st in first ch to join.

Round 2: Rep Round 1.

Round 3: Sl st in ch-1 corner sp, *[2 htr, ch 2, 2 htr] in corner sp, miss 2 htr, [1 dc, 1 tr, 1 dc] in next htr 8 times; rep from * 3 times, sl st in first htr to join.

Fasten off and darn in ends.

*

maui

A cheerful bloom that evokes the tropics, designed to brighten up gloomy days. This square is fast to work up and has a slightly raised, clustered centre.

A
B
C

Special stitches used:

Make bobble (MB): Make bobble with 2 tr.

Spike stitch (spike): Insert hook in top of dc two rnds below, yoh, pull yarn through to height of rnd being worked, complete stitch as normal (see page 22).

Foundation ring: Using yarn A, ch 4, sl st in first ch to form ring.

Round 1: Ch 1, [MB, ch 4] 6 times, sl st in top of first cl to join.

Round 2: Ch 1, 1 tr in same st (top of first bobble), ch 3, 2 tr in same st, *[1 dc, ch 3, 1 dc) in next ch-4 sp, [2 tr, ch 3, 2 tr] in top of next bobble; rep from * 4 times, 1 dc, ch 4, 1 dc in last ch-4 sp, sl st in first ch to join. Fasten off.

Round 3: Join yarn B in any ch-3 sp, ch 1, 1 tr in same sp, ch 4, 1 tr in next ch-3 sp, *ch 4, 1 tr in next ch-3 sp; rep from * 9 times, ch 4, sl st in first tr to join.

Round 4: Sl st in first ch-4 sp, [ch 2, 2 tr in same ch-4 sp, ch 2, 3 tr in same sp], *sl st in next ch-4 sp, ch 1, [3 tr, ch 2, 3 tr] in same ch-4 sp; rep from * 10 times, sl st in top of beg ch-2 to join. Fasten off.

Round 5: Join yarn C in any ch-2 sp, ch 3, [2 tr, ch 2, 3 tr] in same ch-2 sp, *[ch 5, 1 dc in ch-2 sp of next shell] 2 times, ch 5, [3 tr, ch 2, 3 tr] in ch-2 sp of next shell; rep from * 2 times, [ch 5, 1 dc in ch-2 sp of next shell] 2 times, sl st in top of beg ch-2 to join.

Round 6: Sl st in first ch-2 corner sp, [ch 3, 2 tr, ch 1, 3 tr] in same corner sp, *[1 dc, 1 htr, 2 tr, 1 htr, 1 dc] in each of next 3 ch-5 sps, [3 tr, ch 1, 3 tr in next ch-2 corner sp]; rep from * 2 times, [1 dc,

1 htr, 2 tr, 1 htr, 1 dc] in each of next 3 ch-5 sps, sl st in first ch of beg ch-3 to join.

Round 7: Sl st in first ch-1 corner sp, [2 dc, ch 1, 2 dc] in same corner sp, *1 dc in each of next 3 tr, [1 dc in each of next 6 sts, 1 spike dc in row 5 in next st] 2 times, 1 dc in each of next 9 sts [2 dc, ch 1, 2 dc] in next corner sp; rep from * 3 times, sl st in first dc to join.

Fasten off and darn in ends neatly.

★★★★

zinnia

A dimensional flower with an imaginative construction, Zinnia has a delicately lacy background, producing a pretty flower block that is interesting to work up and offers a wide range of potential uses, from scarves to throws, summer blankets to linens.

A
B
C

Foundation ring: Using yarn A, ch 10, sl st in first ch to form ring.

Round 1: Ch 3 (counts as 1 tr), 1 tr in ring, *ch 5, 2 tr in ring; rep from * 8 times, sl st in top of beg ch-3 to join.

Round 2: Sl st in top of next ch-5 lp, 1 dc in same st, *ch 4, 1 dc in top of next ch-5 lp; rep from * 8 times, ch 4, sl st in first dc to join.

Round 3: Ch 1, *5 tr in 2nd part of ch-5 lp from Round 1, miss 2 tr, 5 tr in first part of next ch-5 lp from Round 1; rep from * 9 times, sl st in top of first tr to join. Fasten off.

Round 4: Turn to WS, join yarn B, ch 1, *6 dc in next ch-4 lp; rep from * 9 times, sl st in top of first dc to join.

Round 5: Turn to RS, *ch 6, miss 2 dc, 1 dc in next dc; rep from * 19 times, sl st in beg ch-1 to join.

Round 6: 3 sl st along to 3rd ch of next ch-6 lp, 1 dc in same st, *ch 8, 1 dc in centre of next ch-6 lp, [ch 5, 1 dc in centre of next ch-6 lp] 4 times; rep from * 3 times, sl st in first dc to join. Fasten off.

Round 7: Join yarn C to any ch-8 lp, ch 3 (counts as 1 tr), 4 tr in same sp, [ch 3, 5 tr] in same sp (forms corner), 5 tr in each of next 4 ch-5 lps, *[5 tr, ch 3, 5 tr] in next ch-5 lp (forms corner), 5 tr in each of next 4 ch-5 lps; rep from * 2 times, sl st in top of beg ch-3 to join.

Round 8: Sl st along to next ch-3 sp, ch 2 (counts as 1 htr), 1 htr in same sp, [ch 3, 2 htr] in same sp (forms corner), miss 1 tr, [1 htr in each of next 4 tr, miss 1 tr] 6 times, *[2 htr, ch 3, 2 htr] in next sp (forms corner), miss 1 tr, [1 htr in each of next 4 tr, miss 1 tr] 6 times; rep from * 2 times, sl st in top of beg ch-2 to join.

Fasten off and darn in ends.

**
calendula

A nubbly popcorn flower offers the focus for this granny-type square. Easy and fast to work, this offers lots of possibilities for colour variations and playful application – think funky throws, shawls, handbags or scarves.

A
B
C
D
E

Special stitches used:

Beginning popcorn (beg pc): Ch 3, make popcorn with 3 tr (*see page 19*).

Popcorn (pc): Make popcorn with 4 tr.

Spike stitch (spike st): Insert hook in top of clusters two rnds below, yoh, pull yarn through to height of rnd being worked, complete stitch as normal (*see page 22*).

Foundation ring: Using yarn A, ch 8, sl st in first ch form ring.

Round 1: Ch 4, (counts as 1 tr, ch 1), *[1 tr, ch 1] in ring 15 times, sl st in 3rd ch of beg ch-4 to join. Fasten off yarn A.

Round 2: Join yarn B, beg pc in any ch-1 sp; *[ch 1, 1 pc] in next ch-1 sp; rep from * 14 times, ch 1, sl st in top of first pc to join. Fasten off yarn B.

Round 3: Join yarn C in any ch-1 sp, ch 4 (counts as 1 dc, ch 3), *[1 dc in next ch-1 sp, ch 3] 3 times, [2 tr, ch 2, 2 tr] in next ch-1 sp (to form corner), ch 3; rep from * 2 times, [1 dc in next ch-1 sp, ch 3] 3 times, [2 tr ch 3, 1 tr] in last corner ch-sp, sl st in 3rd ch of beg ch-4 to join. Fasten off yarn C.

Round 4: Join yarn D in any ch-3 corner sp; ch 5, (counts as 1 tr, 2 ch), miss [2 tr, ch 3, 1 dc], *[4 tr in next ch-3 sp, ch 2] 2 times, miss [1 dc, ch 3, 2 tr], [4 tr, ch 2, 4 tr] in next ch-3 sp, ch 2, miss [2 tr, ch 3, 1 dc]; rep from * 2 times, [4 tr, ch 2, 3 tr in last ch-2 corner sp, sl st in 3rd ch of beg ch-5 to join.

Round 5: Sl st in next ch-2 sp, ch 3 (counts as 1 tr), 3 tr in same sp, *[4 tr in next ch-2 sp] 3 times, [4 tr, ch 3, 4 tr] in next corner ch-sp**; rep from * 2 times, then from * to ** 1 time, sl st in top of beg ch-3 to join.

Round 6: Ch 3 (counts as 1 tr), 3 tr in same sp, *[4 tr in next ch-2 sp] 4 times along side of square, [4 tr, ch 3, 4 tr] in next corner ch-sp**; rep from * 2 times, then from * to ** 1 time, sl st in top of ch-3 to join.

Round 7: Ch 3 (counts as 1 tr), 3 tr in same sp, *[4 tr in next ch-2 sp] 5 times along side of square, [4 tr, ch 3, 4 tr] in next corner ch-sp**; rep from * 2 times, then from * to ** 1 time, sl st in top of beg ch-3 to join. Fasten off yarn D.

Round 8: Join yarn E in any ch-3 sp, ch 1, *1 dc in same sp, 1 dc in every tr around, working spike st in centre of each 4-tr group of Round 6, 4 dc in each ch-3 corner sp; rep from * all around square, 3 dc in last corner sp, sl st in first dc to join.

Round 9: Ch 1, 1 dc in same st, 1 dc in every st and 2 dc in middle st of each corner group around square, sl st in first sc to join.

Fasten off and darn in ends neatly.

kandinsky

✳✳✳

This complex and colourful block is made up from four small squares. They can be worked individually and joined using the JAYGo method, or worked separately and stitched together afterwards.

Special technique:

Join-as-you-go (JAYGo): On final round of Squares 2 to 4, insert hook in corner ch-3 sp of first, fully completed square, yoh, pull through, 3 htr as usual; rep along joining side, working in both edges and making sure that working yarn remains under the hook. Keep tension tight (*see page 25*).

Note: This block has been worked in a tight stitch using a 3 mm (US D/3) hook to create a firm fabric. Size down your hook to achieve the same size square.

A
B
C
D
E
F
G
H
I
J
K

SQUARE 1

Foundation ring: Using yarn A, begin with magic ring method.

Round 1: Ch 3 (counts as 1 tr), 11 tr in ring, sl st in top of beg ch-3 to join. Fasten off yarn A.

Round 2: Join yarn B in any tr st, ch 3 (counts as 1 tr), 1 tr in same st, 2 tr in each of next 11 tr, sl st in top of beg ch-3 to join.

Round 3: Ch 3 (counts as 1 tr), 1 tr in same st, [1 tr in next st, 2 tr in next st] 11 times, sl st in top of beg ch-3 to join. Fasten off yarn B.

Round 4: Join yarn C, ch 1, 1 dc in each st to end of rnd, sl st in beg ch-1 to join. Fasten off yarn C.

Round 5: Join yarn D, ch 5 (counts as 1 tr, ch 2), 1 tr in same st, *1 dc in each of the next 2 sts, sl st in next 4 sts, 1 dc in each of the next 2 sts**, 1 tr in next st, [ch 3, 1 tr] in same st (corner); rep from * 2 times, on final side rep from * to **, sl st in 3rd ch of beg ch-5 to join.

Round 6: Sl st along to next ch-3 corner sp, ch 3 (counts as 1 htr, ch 1), [1 htr, ch 3, 2 htr] in same sp, *3 htr in every st along side of sq, ending 3 htr in last st before next corner sp**, [2 htr, ch 3, 2 htr] in next ch-3 corner sp; rep from * to ** 2 times, and from * to ** 1 time, sl st in top of beg ch-3 to join. Fasten off yarn D.

SQUARE 2

Rep Square 1 for Rounds 1 to 5, in colours as below:

Foundation ring: Use yarn E.

Round 1: Use yarn E.

Round 2: Use yarn C.

Round 3: Use yarn F.

Round 4: Use yarn B.

Round 5: Use yarn G.

Round 6: Sl st along to centre of ch-3 corner sp, ch 3 (counts as 1 htr, ch 1), 1 htr, *3 htr in every st along side of sq**, [2 htr, ch 3, 2 htr] in next ch-3 corner sp; rep from * to ** 2 times, on final side 2 htr in last corner ch-3 sp and INSTEAD of ch-3, JAYGo to Square 1: 2 htr in same corner sp, rep from *, inserting hook using JAYGo method in each sp along between 3 htr of Round 6 of Square 1, 3 htr in every other st, ending with JAYGo in corner sp of Square 1, sl st in top of beg ch-3 to join. Fasten off yarn E.

SQUARE 3

Rep Square 1 for Rounds 1 to 5, in colours as below:

Foundation ring: Use yarn D.

Round 1: Use yarn D.

Round 2: Use yarn H.

Round 3: Use yarn H.

Round 4: Use yarn E.

Round 5: Use yarn A.

Round 6: Sl st along to other side of ch-3 corner sp, ch 3 (counts as 1 htr), 1 htr in same sp, *3 htr in every st along side of sq**, [2 htr, ch 3, 2 htr] in next ch-3 corner sp; rep from * to ** 2 times, on final side 2 htr in last corner ch-3 sp and INSTEAD of the ch-3, JAYGo to Square 2 in bottom RH corner: 2 htr in same corner sp; rep from *, inserting hook using JAYGo method in each sp along between 3 htr of Round 6 of Square 2, 3 htr in every other st, ending 2 htr in final corner sp of round, and final JAYGo in corner sp of Square 2, sl st in top of beg ch-3 to join. Fasten off yarn D.

Continued on page 119

SQUARE 4

Rep Square 1 for Rounds 1 to 5, in colours as below:

Foundation ring: Use yarn C.

Round 1: Use yarn C.

Round 2: Use yarn I.

Round 3: Use yarn J.

Round 4: Use yarn B.

Round 5: Use yarn E.

Round 6: Sl st along to centre of ch-3 corner sp, ch 3 (counts as 1 htr, ch 1), 1 htr, *3 htr in every st along side of sq**, [2 htr, ch 3, 2 htr] in next ch-3 corner sp, 2 htr in last corner ch-3 sp and INSTEAD of ch-3, JAYGo to bottom RH corner of Square 1: 2 htr in same corner sp; rep from * to ** 1 time, inserting hook using JAYGo method in each sp along between 3 htr of Round 6 of Square 1, 2 htr in corner sp, JAYGo in bottom LH corner sp of Square 1, insert hook in corner sp of Square 3 to attach, 2 htr in same corner sp; rep from * to ** 1 time to next corner, 2 htr in corner sp, JAYGo to bottom LH corner sp of Square 2, [2 htr, ch 1, 2 hdc] in same corner sp (of Square 4); rep from * to **, sl st in top of beg ch-3 to join. Fasten off yarn E.

EDGING

Join yarn K in any ch-3 corner sp, ch1, 1 dc in same st, 1 dc in each st around composite square, 4 dc in each corner ch-3 sp, sl st in first ch-1 join.

Fasten off and darn in all ends neatly.

★★★

patchwork

Although this block looks complex, it takes patience rather than skill as each little patch is created separately, then joined into the quilt pattern. Have fun designing your own layouts of patches – the possibilities are endless.

PATCHES

Foundation ring: Using yarn A, ch 4, sl st in first chain to form ring.

Round 1: Ch 2 (counts as 1 htr), 2 htr in ring, *ch 1, 3 htr in ring; rep from * 2 times, ch 1, sl st in top of beg ch-2 to join.

Fasten off.

Create 25 patches in total; 9 patches using yarn A; 8 using yarn B; 8 using yarn C.

Using a tapestry needle, stitch the patches tog through the back lps only, to make a patchwork design.

BORDER

Round 1: Join yarn D in any corner sp, ch 1, *[2 dc, ch 2, 2 dc] in corner sp, 1 dc in every dc or ch-1 sp to next corner sp; rep from * 3 times, sl st in first ch to join.

Round 2: Sl st in next ch-2 corner sp, ch 1,* [2 htr, ch 1, 2 htr] in corner sp, 1 htr in every dc to next corner sp; rep from * 3 times, sl st in first ch to join.

Round 3: Sl st in next ch-1 corner sp, *[1 dc, ch 1, 1 dc] in corner sp, 1 dc in every htr to next corner sp; rep from * 3 times, sl st in first ch to join.

Fasten off and darn in ends.

137

A
B
C
D

**

puffy circle

With a plethora of puff stitches, this block feels fabulously soft and squidgy. The central motif makes a great coaster in its own right without the border, and the square is challenging enough for the more experienced crocheter to enjoy.

A
B
C
D

Special stitches used:

3-treble-crochet puff stitch (3-trpf):
Make puff stitch with 3 tr, ch 1 to seal pf (*see page 19*).

5-treble-crochet puff stitch (5-trpf):
Make puff stitch with 5 tr, ch 1 to seal pf.

Foundation ring: Using yarn A, ch 6, sl st in to first ch to form ring.

Round 1: *Ch 2, 3-trpf; rep from * 5 times, sl st in top of beg ch-2 to join.

Round 2: Ch 2, *[5-trpf, ch 1, 5-trpf] in next 2-ch sp, ch 1; rep from * 5 times, sl st in top of beg ch-2 to join.

Round 3: Ch 2, *[5-trpf, ch 1, 5-trpf] in same ch-1 sp, ch 1, 5-trpf in next ch-1 sp, ch 1; rep from * to end of rnd, sl st in top of beg ch-2 to join.

Round 4: Ch 2, *[5-trpf, ch 1, 5-trpf] in same ch-1 sp, ch 1 [5-trpf in next ch-1 sp, ch 1] 2 times; rep from * to end of rnd, sl st in top of beg ch-2 to join.

Round 5: Ch 2, *[5-trpf, ch 1, 5-trpf] in same ch-1 sp, ch 1, [5-trpf in next ch-1 sp, ch 1] 3 times; rep from * to end of rnd, sl st in top of beg ch-2 to join. Fasten off yarn A.

Round 6: Join yarn B in any ch-1 sp, ch 1, 1 dc in every ch-1 sp and in every st to end of rnd, sl st in first dc to join. Fasten off yarn B.

Round 7: Join yarn C, ch 1, 1 dc in each of next 5 dc, *ch 7, miss 3 dc, 1 dc in next dc, ch 3, miss 1 dc, 1 dc in next dc, [ch 3, miss 3 dc, 1 dc in next dc] 2 times, ch 3, miss 1 dc, 1 dc in next dc, ch 7, miss 3 dc**, 1 dc in each of next 11 dc; rep from * to **, 1 dc in each of next 6 dc, sl st in first dc to join.

Round 8: Ch 2, (counts as 1 htr), 1 htr in each of next 4 dc, *[2 htr, 2 tr, ch 3, 2 tr, 2 htr] in next ch-7 sp, [3 htr in next ch-3 sp] 4 times, [2 htr, 2 tr, ch 3, 2 tr, 2 htr] in next ch-7 sp**, 1 htr in each of next 11 dc; rep from * to **, 1 htr in each of next 6 dc, sl st in top of ch-2 to join. Fasten off yarn C.

Round 9: Join yarn D in any ch-3 corner sp, ch 3 (counts as 1 tr); [2 tr, ch 3, 3 tr] in same corner sp, *1 tr in each htr st to next corner, [3 tr, ch 3, 3 tr] in next corner sp; rep from * 3 times, 1 tr in each hole along final side, sl st in top of beg ch-3 to join.

Round 10: 1 dc in every st and [2 dc, ch 1, 2 dc] in every corner ch-2 sp.

Fasten off and darn in ends neatly.

*

rose garden

Bright and bold, especially when worked in complementary colours, as in our sample here. Create a simple and quick flower-garden afghan by working the rosy centres in different colours.

A
B

Foundation ring: Using yarn A, ch 5, join with sl st to form ring.

Round 1: Ch 2 (counts as 1 htr), 11 htr in ring, sl st in top of ch-2 – 12 sts.

Round 2: Ch 2 (counts as 1 htr), *2 htr in next st, 1 htr in next st; rep from * to end of rnd, ending with 2 htr in last st, sl st in top of beg ch-2 to join – 24 sts.

Round 3: Ch 2 (counts as 1 htr), *2 htr in next st, 1 htr in next st; rep from * to end of rnd, sl st in top of beg ch-2 to join – 36 sts.

Round 4: Ch 2 (counts as 1 htr), *2 htr in next st, 1 htr in each of next 2 sts; rep from * to end of rnd, sl st in top of beg ch-2 to join – 48 sts. Fasten off yarn A.

Round 5: Join yarn B, ch 3 (counts as 1 tr), [2 tr, ch 2, 3 tr] in the same st (first corner), *[ch 1, miss 2 sts, 2 tr in next st] 2 times, ch 1, miss 2 sts, [3 tr, ch 2, 3 tr] in same st; rep from * 2 times, ending with [ch 1, miss 2 sts, 2 tr in next st] 2 times, ch 1, sl st in top of beg ch-3 to join.

Round 6: Sl st along to corner ch-sp, ch 3 (counts as 1 tr), [2 tr, ch 2, 3 tr] in same st (first corner), *(ch 1, miss 2 sts, 2 tr in ch-1 sp) 3 times, ch 1, miss 2 sts [3 tr, ch 2, 3 tr] in same st; rep from * 2 times, ending with [ch 1, miss 2 sts, 2 tr in next ch-sp] 3 times, ch 1; sl st in top of beg ch-3 to join.

Round 7: Sl st in corner ch-sp, ch 3 (counts as 1 tr), [2 dc, ch 2, 3 tr] in same st (first corner), *[ch 1, miss 2 sts, 2 tr in next ch-sp] 4 times, ch 1, miss 2 sts, [3 tr, ch 2, 3 tr] in same st; rep from * 2 times, ending with [ch 1, miss 2 sts, 2 tr in next ch-sp] 4 times, ch 1, join to top of beg ch-3. Fasten off yarn B.

Round 8: Join yarn A, ch 2 (counts as 1 htr), 1 htr in next 2 tr, *5 htr in ch-2 space, 1 htr in every tr and 1 htr in every ch-1 sp along side (19 htr); rep from * 3 times, end with 16 htr, sl st in top of ch-3 to join. Fasten off.

· ·

****

rosebuds

A striking floral block that uses a clever curling technique to create little flower buds. This square would be pretty at the heart of a larger piece.

A
B
C
D

Special stitch used:

Rosebud: Ch 12, 5 tr in 5th ch from hook, 5 tr in each of next 6 ch, curling shape as you go, sl st in base of first ch of beg 12-ch to join.

Foundation ring: Using yarn A, ch 6, sl st in first ch to form ring.

Round 1: Ch 1, 10 dc in ring, sl st in first dc to join.

Round 2: *1 rosebud, sl st in each of next 2 dc; rep from * 4 times – 5 rosebuds. Fasten off.

Round 3: (WS) Join yarn B in same st, working behind rosebuds, *ch 6, sl st in st between rosebuds; rep from * 4 times, sl st in first ch to join.

Round 4: Ch 1, *8 tr in next ch-6 sp; rep from * 4 times, sl st in beg ch-1 to join.

Round 5: * 1 rosebud in same st, sl st in next 3 dc, *1 rosebud in next st, sl st in next 3 dc; rep from * 8 times – 10 rosebuds. Fasten off.

Round 6: (WS) Using yarns C and D tog, join in any st from Round 4, ch 3 (counts as 1 tr) 1 tr in each of next 39 sts, sl st in top of beg ch-3 to join, turn.

Round 7: (RS) Ch 3 (counts as 1 tr), [2 tr, ch 3, 3 tr] in same st (forms corner), 1 tr in each of next 9 tr, *[3 tr, ch 3, 3 tr] in next st (forms corner), 1 tr in each of next 9 tr; rep from * 2 times, sl st in top of beg ch-3 to join.

Round 8: Sl st in next corner ch-3 sp, ch 3 (counts as 1 tr), [2 tr, ch 3, 3 tr] in same sp (forms corner), 1 tr in each of next 15 tr, *[3 tr, ch 3, 3 tr] in next ch-3 sp, 1 tr in each of next 15 tr; rep from * 2 times, sl st in top of beg ch-3 to join. Fasten off yarn C.

Round 9: Using yarn D only, sl st in next corner ch-3 sp, ch 3 (counts as 1 tr), [2 tr, ch 3, 3 tr] in same sp (forms corner), 1 tr in each of next 21 tr, *[3 tr, ch 3, 3 tr] in next ch-3 sp, 1 tr in each of next 21 tr; rep from * 2 times, sl st in top of beg ch-3 to join.

Fasten off and darn in ends neatly.

141

*
hove

A
B
C

A simple hexagon motif helps teach how to turn hexagons into square shapes. This block mixes equally well with other traditional squares or with more modern geometrics.

Foundation ring: Using yarn A, ch 6, sl st in first ch to form ring.

Round 1: Ch 4 (counts as 1 tr, ch 1), *1 tr in ring, ch 1; rep from * 10 times, sl st in 3rd ch of beg ch-4 to join.

Round 2: Ch 3 (counts as 1 tr), 2 tr in next ch-1 sp, 1 tr in next tr, ch 2, [1 tr in next tr, 2 tr in next ch-sp, 1 tr in next tr, ch 2] 5 times, sl st in 3rd top of beg ch-3 to join. Fasten off yarn A.

Round 3: Join yarn B, ch 3 (counts as 1 tr) 1 tr in same st, 1 tr in each of next tr, 2 tr in next tr, ch 2, miss 2 ch, [2 tr in next tr, 1 tr in each of next 2 tr, 2 tr in next tr, ch 2, miss 2 ch] 5 times, sl st in top of beg ch-3 to join. Fasten off yarn B.

Round 4: Join yarn C, ch 3 (counts as 1 tr), 1 tr in same tr, 1 tr in each of next 4 tr, 2 tr in next tr, ch 2, miss 2 ch, [2 tr in next tr, 1 tr in each of next 4 tr, 2 tr in next tr, ch 2, miss 2 ch] 5 times, sl st in top of beg ch-3 to join.

Round 5: Ch 3 (counts as 1 tr), 1 tr in same tr, 1 tr in each of next 6 tr, 2 tr in next tr, ch 2, miss 2 ch, [2 tr in next tr, 1 tr in each of next 6 tr, 2 tr in next tr, ch 2, miss 2 ch] 5 times, sl st in top of beg ch-3 to join. Fasten off yarn C.

Round 6: Using yarn D, ch 5 (counts as 1 tr, *ch 2), miss 1 tr, 1 tr in each of next 4 tr, ch 2, miss 1 tr, 1 tr in next tr, ch 2, miss 2 tr, 1 tr in next tr; rep from * 5 times, sl st in 3rd ch of beg ch-5 to join.

Round 7: Ch 3 (counts as 1 tr), 1 tr in same tr, *2 tr in next ch-2 sp, 1 tr in each of next 4 tr, 2 tr in next ch-2 sp, 2 tr in next tr, ch 2, 1 tr in next tr; rep from * 5 times, sl st in top of beg ch-3 to join. Fasten off yarn D.

Round 8: Join yarn C, 1 dc in same st, *1 dc in each of next 12 tr, 1 dc in next ch-2 sp, ch 19, 2 dc in next ch-2 sp, ch 19, 1 dc in next ch-2 sp; rep from * 3 times, omitting last dc in last rep, sl st in first dc to join.

Round 9: Ch 1, working in ch sts instead of ch-sp, 1 dc in each of next 25 sts, *[1 dc, ch 2, 1 dc] in next ch st (forms corner)**, 1 dc in each of next 28 sts; rep from * 2 times and from * to ** 1 time, 1 dc in each of last 3 sts, sl st in first dc to join.

Fasten off and darn in ends.

****

twisted lily

The petals of this lily flower are twisted around before being anchored into the outer frame, giving extra dimension to this square. Mix it with other dimensional flowers in an extravagant flower-garden piece or use it as a centrepiece for a pillow or table setting.

A
B
C

Foundation ring: Using yarn A, make a magic ring.

Round 1: Ch 2 (counts as 1 htr), 11 htr in ring, sl st in top of beg ch-2 to join.

Round 2: *Ch 6, 2 htr in 4th ch from hook, ch 2, sl st in same ch, sl st in next 2 ch to base, sl st in front lp of same st, sl st in front lp of each of next 3 sts at base; rep from * 2 times, sl st in first ch to join.

Round 3: Ch 2 (counts as 1 htr), 2 htr in back lp of each of next 11 dc, 1 htr in back lp of last hdc, sl st in top of beg ch-2 to join. Fasten off.

Round 4: Join yarn B in any htr, *ch 10, 1 dc in 2nd ch from hook, 1 htr in each of next 2 ch, 1 tr in each of next 2 ch, 1 dtr in each of last 4 ch to base (forms petal), miss 2 htr (from Round 3), sl st in next htr, ch 1, turn, sl st in every st to tip of petal, ch 4, turn, sl st in same st, 1 dc in next sl st, 1 htr in each of next 2 sl sts, 1 tr in each of next 2 sl sts, 1 dtr in each of last 4 sl sts, miss 2 htr, sl st in each of next 3 htr; rep from * 2 times, sl st in first ch to join.

Round 5: Sl st in each of next 3 htr, behind petals of Round 4 into sts from Round 3; rep Round 4 from *, working behind petals so Round 5 petals fall alternately in terms of spacing. Fasten off yarn B – 6 petals made.

Round 6: (WS) Join yarn B in 4th dtr of any petal (counting from the base of the petal), 1 dc in same st, *ch 5, 1 dc in same place on next petal of Round 4, ch 5, 1 dc in same place on next petal of Round 5; rep 1 time, ch 5, 1 dc in same place on next petal of Round 4, ch 5, sl st in first dc to join. Fasten off yarn B.

Round 7: (RS) Rejoin yarn B to tip of any petal, *ch 5, 1 ttr in next ch-5 sp of Round 6, ch 5, twisting next petal clockwise 180 degrees (it will naturally tend towards this), 1 dc in ch-4 lp at tip of next petal; rep from * 5 times, ending with 1 dc in first dc to join. Fasten off yarn B.

Round 8: Join yarn C in any ch-5 sp, ch 3 (counts as 1 tr), 5 tr in same ch-5 sp, [6 tr in next ch-5 sp] 11 times, sl st in top of beg ch-3 to join.

Round 9: Ch 2 (counts as 1 htr), 1 htr in next 11 tr, *[3 tr, ch 2, 3 tr] in next tr (forms corner), 1 htr in next 17 tr; rep from * 3 times, 1 htr in next 5 tr, sl st in top of beg ch-2 to join. Fasten off yarn C.

Round 10: Join yarn D in any ch-2 corner sp, *[1 dc, ch 2, 1 dc] in ch-2 corner sp, 1 dc in every st to next corner; rep from * 4 times, sl st in first dc to join.

Fasten off and darn in ends.

*

babushka

This delightfully playful square uses unconventional methods of colour changing to create a colourful centre. Best worked with a dark background to accentuate the bright inner motif, as this adds to the overall 'Russian' feel of the pattern.

A
B
C
D
E
F
G
H

Special stitch used:

Make bobble (MB): Make bobble with 2 tr in designated st or sp.

Note: Depending on your chosen joining method, you may switch from ch-2 to ch-1 on colour changeovers on Round 3. For example, if you opt to tie yarn on and off, then use ch-2, but if you are pulling new yarn though loop of last colour, then use ch-1.

Foundation ring: Using yarn A, ch 5, join with sl st to form ring.

Round 1: Ch 3 (counts as 1 tr), 1 tr, ch 2, MB, ch 2, MB, ch 2, MB, drop yarn A, join yarn B, ch 2, MB, ch 2, MB, ch 2, MB, ch 2, MB, ch2, sl st in top of ch-3 to join. Drop yarn B.

Round 2: Join yarn C to ch-2 sp between colours A and B, [ch 3 (counts as 1 tr), 1 tr, ch 2, MB] in same sp, ch 2, *[MB, ch 2, MB], drop yarn C, join yarn D and rep from * 2 times, join yarn E and rep from * 2 times, join yarn F and rep from * 2 times, sl st in top of beg ch-3 to join. Fasten off yarn C, D, E and F.

Round 3: Join yarn G to ch-2 sp between colours F and B, [ch 3 (counts as 1 tr), 1 tr, ch 2, MB] in same st, *ch 2, [MB, ch 2, MB] in same st, join yarn D and rep from * 2 times, join yarn A and rep from * 2 times, join yarn E and rep from * 2 times, join yarn G and rep from * 2 times, join yarn F and rep from * 2 times, join yarn B and rep from * 2 times, sl st in top of beg ch-3 to join. Fasten off yarn G, D, A, E, F and B.

Round 4: Join yarn H to any ch-2 sp, [ch 3 (counts as 1 tr), 2 tr, ch 3, 3 tr] in same sp (forms corner), *ch 2, 1 htr in next ch-2 sp, ch 2, miss 1 sp, 1 htr in next ch-2 sp, ch 2,

miss 1 sp, 1 htr in next ch-2 sp, ch 2, miss 1 sp, [3 tr, ch 3, 3 tr]** in next sp (forms corner); rep from * to ** 2 times, then ch 2, miss 1 sp, 1 htr in next ch-2 sp, ch 2, miss 1 sp, 1 htr in next ch-2 sp, ch 2, miss 1 sp, 1 htr in next ch-2 sp, ch 2, sl st in top of ch-3 to join.

Round 5: Sl st in next ch-3 corner sp, [ch 3 (counts as 1 tr), 2 tr, ch 2, 3 tr] in same sp (to form corner), *1 tr in each of next 3 sts, [ch 1, 2 tr in next ch-2 sp]; rep in next 3 ch-2 sps, 1 tr in each of next 3 tr, [3 tr, ch 2, 3 tr] in next ch-3 corner sp**; rep from * to ** 2 times, then on final side 1 tr in each of the next 3 tr, [ch 1, 2 tr in next ch-2 sp]; rep in next 3 ch-2 sps, 1 tr in each of the next 3 tr, sl st in top of ch-3 to join.

Round 6: Sl st in next ch-3 corner sp, [ch 3 (counts as 1 tr), ch 2, 3 tr] in same sp (first corner), *[ch 2, miss 2 sts, 1 tr in next st, ch 2, miss 2 sts, 1 tr in next st] rep to corner, [3 tr, ch 3, 3 tr] in same sp (forms

corner); rep from * 2 times, then on final side **ch 2, miss 2 sts, 1 tr in next st, ch 2, miss 2 sts, 1 tr in next st; rep from ** to corner, sl st in top of ch-3 to join. Fasten off yarn H. Note: On this rnd ensure you count first slightly hidden st after last 3 tr of corner, otherwise sps between ch-2 sts will not add up.

Round 7: Join yarn C to any ch-3 corner sp, [ch 2 (counts as 1 htr), 2 htr, ch 2, 3 htr] in same sp (forms corner), *[ch 2, miss 2 sts, 1 htr in next st, ch 2, miss 2 sts, 1 htr in next st] rep to corner, [3 htr, ch 2, 3 htr] in same sp (forms corner); rep from * 2 times, then on final side of square **ch 2, miss 2 sts, 1 htr in next st, ch 2, miss 2 sts, 1 htr in next st; rep from ** to corner, sl st in top of ch-2 to join.

Round 8: Ch 1, 1 dc in each st and 2 dc in each 2-st sp, 1 dc in each htr and 3 dc in each corner sp, sl st in top of ch-1 to join.

Fasten off and darn in ends neatly.

dahlia

***

A bright and cheery bloom worked in increasing groups of treble crochet, this block works fantastically well as a central motif in a pillow, or try multiples in a flower-garden throw. Guaranteed to bring a smile to your face!

A
B
C

Foundation ring: Using yarn A, begin with magic ring method.

Round 1: Ch 3 (counts as 1 tr), 11 tr in ring, sl st in top of beg ch-3 to join – 12 sts.

Round 2: Ch 3 (counts as 1 tr), 1 tr in same st, *2 tr in next st; rep from * to end of rnd, sl st in top of beg ch-3 to join. Fasten off yarn A – 24 sts.

Round 3: Join yarn B, ch 4 (counts as 1 tr, ch 1), 1 tr in same st, *miss 2 sts, [1 tr, ch 1, 1 tr] in next st; rep from * to end of rnd, sl st in top of beg ch-3 to join.

Round 4: Ch 3 (counts as 1 tr), [1 tr, ch 1, 2 tr] in same ch-1 sp, *[2 tr, ch 1, 2 tr] in next ch-1 sp; rep from * to end of rnd, sl st in top of beg ch-3 to join.

Round 5: Ch 3 (counts as 1 tr); [2 tr, ch 1, 3 tr] in same ch-1 sp, *[3 tr, ch 1, 3 tr] in next ch-1 sp; rep from * to end of rnd, sl st in top of beg ch-3 to join.

Round 6: Ch 1, 1 sc in same st, *9 tr in same ch-1 sp, 1 dc in sp between petals; rep from * to end of rnd, omitting last dc, sl st in first dc to join. Fasten off yarn B.

Round 7: Join yarn C with sl st in 5th tr of first petal (scallop), [ch 3, dc2tog, ch 3 dc3tog] in same sp (first corner), *ch 3, dc3tog in sp between 2 petals, ch 3, 1 sc in 5th dc of next petal, ch 3, dc3tog in space between next 2 petals, ch 3**, [dc3tog, ch 3, dc3tog] in 5th tr of next petal; rep from * 3 times, ending at **, sl st in top of dc2tog to join.

Round 8: Ch 2, 1 htr in same sp, *5 htr in ch-3 corner sp, 1 htr in next dc3tog, 4 htr in next ch-3 sp, 1 htr in next dc3tog, 4 htr in ch-3 sp, 1 htr in sc, 4 htr in ch-3 sp, 1 htr in dc3tog, 4 htr in ch-3 sp**, 1 htr in dc3tog; rep from * 3 times, ending last rep at **, sl st in first htr to join.

Fasten off and darn in ends neatly.

rosa

*

Breezy and bold, this is a great beginner motif to develop skills beyond the regular granny square. Rosa mixes well with other granny blocks and with plain texture squares.

A
B

Special stitches used:

Make 2-treble crochet bobble (2-tr MB): Make bobble with 2 tr (see page 19).

Make 3-treble crochet bobble (3-tr MB): Make bobble with 3 tr.

Foundation ring: Using yarn A, begin with magic ring method.

Round 1: Ch 3, 2-tr MB in ring, *ch 3, 3-tr MB in ring; rep from * 6 times, ch 3, sl st in top of first bobble to join.

Round 2: Sl st in ch-3 sp, ch 3, 2 tr in same ch-3 sp, *ch 2, 3 tr in next ch-3 sp; rep from * 6 times, ch 2, sl st in top of beg ch-3 to join.

Round 3: Ch 1, *1 dc in top of middle st of 3-tr cluster from last rnd, 5 tr in ch-2 sp; rep from * 7 times, sl st in first dc to join. Fasten off A.

Round 4: Join yarn B in 3rd tr (middle tr) of first scallop, [ch 3 (counts as 1 tr), 2 tr, ch 3, 3 tr] in same st (first corner), *ch 3, 1 dc in 3rd tr of next scallop, ch 3, 3 tr, ch 3, 3 tr in 3rd tr of next scallop; rep from * 3 times, omitting final 3 tr, ch 3, 3 tr, sl st in top of beg ch-3 to join.

Round 5: Sl st in first 2 tr of first corner, sl st in ch-3 sp, [ch 3, 2 tr, ch 3, 3 tr] (first corner), *ch 1, 3 tr in next ch-3 sp, 1 tr in next dc, 3 tr in next ch-3 sp, ch 1**, [3 tr, ch 3, 3 ch] in next corner ch-3; rep from * 2 times, then from * to ** 1 time, sl st in beg ch-3 to join.

Round 6: Sl st in first 2 tr of first corner, sl st in ch-3 sp, [ch 3, 2 tr, ch 3, 3 tr] (first corner), *ch 1, 1 tr in every tr and 3 tr in each ch-1 sp (13 tr)**, ch 1, [3 tr, ch 3, 3 ch] in next corner ch-3; rep from * 2 times, then from * to ** 1 time, sl st in beg ch-3 to join.

Round 7: Sl st in first 2 tr of first corner, sl st in ch-3 space, ch 3, 2 tr, ch 3, 3 tr (first corner), *ch 1, 1 tr in every tr and 3 tr in each ch-1 sp (19 tr)**, ch 1, (3 tr, ch 3, 3 ch) in next corner ch-3; rep from * 2 times, and from * to ** 1 time, sl st in beg ch-3 to join.

Fasten off.

***
japonica

A highly dimensional flower sits amidst a stretchy mesh in this super-fun square. The mesh pattern has a rhythmic structure that is easy to adapt to other sizes; used in repeat, this square would make a brilliant handbag – or a lovely shawl or light throw.

A
B
C
D

Foundation ring: Using yarn A, ch 12, join with sl st to form ring.

Round 1: Ch 1 (counts as 1 dc), 1 dc in ring, ch 6, sl st over side of last dc, *2 dc in ring, ch 6, sl st over side of 2nd dc; rep from * 6 times, sl st in first dc to join. Fasten off yarn A.

Round 2: Using yarn B, ch 3 (counts as 1 tr), *11 tr in same ch-6 loop, sl st in first dc between petals, sl st in next ch-6 lp, ch 3**; rep from * to ** on all lps to end of rnd, sl st in base of beg ch-3 to join. Fastem off yarn B.

Round 3: Using yarn C and working behind petals of last rnd, ch 1 in any sl st between petals, 1 dc in same st, *ch 4, 1 dc in st between petals**; rep from * to ** 6 times, ch 3, sl st in base of beg ch-1 to join.

Round 4: Sl st in next ch-4 corner sp, *ch 4, sl st in same sp, [ch 3, sl st in next ch-3 sp] 2 times; rep from * 3 times, making last sl st in base of beg ch-4 to join.

Round 5: Sl st in next ch-4 corner sp, *ch 4, sl st in same sp, [ch 3, sl st in next ch-3 sp] 3 times; rep from * 3 times, making last sl st in base of beg ch-4 to join.

Round 6: Sl st in next ch-4 corner sp, *ch 4, sl st in same sp, [ch 3, sl st in next ch-3 sp] 4 times; rep from * 3 times, making last sl st in base of beg ch-4 to join.

Round 7: Sl st in next ch-4 corner sp, *ch 4, sl st in same sp, [ch 3, sl st in next ch-3 sp] 5 times; rep from * 3 times, making last sl st in base of beg ch-4 to join.

Round 8: Sl st in next ch-4 corner sp; *ch 4, sl st in same sp [ch 3, sl st in next ch-3 sp] 6 times; rep from * 3 times, making last sl st in base of beg ch-4 to join.

Round 9: Sl st in next ch-4 corner sp, *ch 4, sl st in same sp [ch 3, sl st in next ch-3 sp] 7 times; rep from * 3 times, making last sl st in base of beg ch-4 to join.

Round 10: Sl st in next ch-4 corner sp, *ch 4, sl st in same sp [ch 3, sl st in next ch-3 sp] 8 times; rep from * 3 times, making last sl st in base of beg ch-4 to join.

Round 11: Sl st in next ch-4 corner sp, *ch 4, sl st in same sp [ch 3, sl st in next ch-3 sp] 9 times; rep from * 3 times, making last sl st in base of beg ch-4 to join.

Round 12: Sl st in next ch-4 corner sp, *ch 4, sl st in same sp [ch 3, sl st in next ch-3 sp] 10 times; rep from * 3 times, making last sl st in base of beg ch-4 to join.

Round 13: Sl st in next ch-4 corner sp, *ch 4, sl st in same sp [ch 3, sl st in next ch-3 sp] 11 times; rep from * 3 times, making last sl st in base of beg ch-4 to join. Fasten off yarn C.

Round 14: Using yarn D, join to any ch-4 corner sp, ch 3 (counts as 1 tr), *[1 tr, ch 2, 2 tr] in same corner sp, [ch 2, 1 tr in next ch-3 sp] 11 times, ch 2 **, 1 tr in next corner ch-sp; rep from * 3 times, ending last rep at **, sl st in top of beg ch-3 to join.

Round 15: Sl st in next corner sp, ch 1 (counts as 1 dc), 2 dc in corner ch-2 sp (first corner), 1 dc in each tr, 2 dc in each ch-2 sp, 3 dc in each corner ch-sp; rep all around square, 1 dc in tr, sl st in top of beg ch-1 to join.

Fasten off and darn in ends neatly.

**
meadow

A filet grid base with dimensional wild flowers worked in it, this is a fantasy flower garden that you can really go to town with. Use the filet mesh as if each square was a ring for an in-the-round square, and build your flowers from there. Once you get to grips with the method, you can add flowers wherever you choose.

Special stitch used:

Make bobble (MB): Make bobble with 2 tr (*see page 19*).

Note: Treat square sps as if they were centred rings when working flowers; when working centres, remember to work with WS facing, then push centres through to the RS once completed.

Foundation chain: Using yarn A, ch 32 (counts as 27 sts, 5 tch).

Row 1: 1 tr in 6th ch from hook, [ch 1, miss 1 ch, 1 tr in next ch] 13 times to end, turn.

Row 2: Ch 4 (counts as 1 tr, ch 1), miss ch-1 sp, 1 tr in next and every tr and in each ch-1 sp to last 2 sts, ch 1, miss next ch-1 sp, 1 tr in top of beg ch-3 (from Round 1).

Row 3: Ch 4 (counts as 1 tr, ch 1), miss next ch-1 sp, 1 tr in first tr, 1 tr in each of next 2 tr, [ch 1, miss 1 tr, 1 tr in next tr] 10 times, 1 tr in each of next 2 tr, ch 1, miss ch-1 sp, 1 tr in top of beg ch-3 (from Round 2).

Rows 4 to 12: Rep Row 3.

Row 13: Rep Row 2.

Row 14: Ch 4 (counts as 1 tr, ch 1), [1 tr in next tr, ch 1] 13 times, 1 tr in 3rd ch of beg ch-4. Fasten off.

A
B
C
D
E

FLOWERS

Select where you would like to place your flower – we have placed flowers in each corner, 1 square in from the side and from the bottom, and in the centre.

Round 1: Treating a square sp as if it were a ring, join yarn B to any ch-sp or bar of square, 3 dc in each side bar or horizontal bar of square, 1 dc in each corner st (you may need to poke hook in st with some vigour to access) – 16 sts.

Round 2: Working around motif, sl st in next st, *ch 2, MB, sl st down side of bobble in base of tr, sl st in next dc in ring; rep from * 8 times – 8 petals. Fasten off.

Create another 4 flowers in same way – or more or less, according to your preference. We have made 3 more flowers using yarn B and one using yarn C.

FLOWER CENTRE

Turn work so WS is facing, attach yarn D to any corner bar (of yarn A) around flower base (4 pairs of corner bars at back of flower motif), *ch 6, sl st in same sp, ch 6, sl st in next corner bar; rep from * around base of flower. Fasten off, leaving a long tail.

Push flower centres through to RS, making sure all frills have gone through. Use yarn tail to secure in place from behind, sewing stitches to corner bars to prevent frills slipping back to WS.

Fasten off and darn in all ends neatly.

***

niamh

A B C

A multilayered dimensional flower that is constructed over a series of chain loops, this lovely block is designed to take centre stage in a floral piece, or for repetition in a gorgeous pillow.

Special stitch used:

Picot-3: Ch 3 (at point to add picot), sl st in first ch of 3-ch to create picot lp.

Foundation ring: Using yarn A, ch 4, sl st in first ch to form ring.

Round 1: Ch 3 (counts as 1 tr), 23 tr in ring, sl st in top of beg ch-3 to join.

Round 2: Ch 6 (counts as 1 tr, ch 3), *miss 1 tr, 1 tr in next tr, ch 3; rep from * 10 times, sl st in 3rd ch of beg ch-6 to join.

Round 3: *Ch 9, miss 1 ch, 1 dc in next ch st, 1 htr in next st, 1 tr in each of next 2 sts, 1 dtr in each of next 4 sts, miss ch-3 sp, 1 dc in next tr from round below; rep from * 11 times.

Round 4: Working first up one side of each petal, then down the other, ch 1, *1 dc in each ch st (of ch-9 from last rnd), [1 dc, picot-3, 1 dc] in ch st at top of petal, 1 dc in each st down other side of petal, 1 dc in st between each petal; rep from * 11 times. Fasten off yarn A.

Round 5: Join yarn B in any unworked tr from Round 1, working behind petals of Round 4, ch 5 (counts as 1 htr, ch 3), *miss 1 st, 1 htr in next (unworked) st, ch 3; rep from * 10 times, sl st in 2nd ch of beg ch-5 to join.

Round 6: *Ch 8, miss 1 ch, 1 dc in next ch st, 1 htr in next ch, 1 tr in each of next 2 ch sts, 1 dtr in each of next 3 sts, miss ch-3 sp, 1 dc in next htr from rnd below; rep from * 11 times.

Round 7: Working first up one side of each petal then down the other, ch 1, *1 dc in each ch st (of ch-8 from last rnd), [1 dc, picot-3, 1 dc] in ch st at top of petal, 1 dc in each st down other side of petal, 1 dc in st between each petal; rep from * 11 times. Fasten off yarn B.

Round 8: Join yarn C in any worked tr st from Round 1, working behind petals of Rounds 4 and 7, ch 4 (counts as 1 dc, ch 3), *miss 1 st, 1 dc in next (worked) st,

ch 3; rep from * 10 times, sl st in first dc to join.

Round 9: *Ch 7, miss 1 ch, 1 dc in next ch st, 1 htr in next st, 1 tr in each of next 2 sts, 1 dtr in each of next 2 sts, miss ch-3 sp, 1 dc in next dc from rnd below; rep from * 11 times.

Round 10: Working first up one side of each petal then down the other, ch 1, *1 dc in each ch st (of ch-7 from last rnd), [1 dc, picot-3, 1 dc] in ch st at top of petal, 1 dc in each st down other side of petal, 1 dc in st between each petal; rep from * 11 times. Fasten off yarn C.

Round 11: Turn work to WS and work from back, join yarn B in any tr post from Round 2, 1 dc around this tr post, *ch 5, 1 dc around next tr post, ch 8, miss 1 tr post, 1 dc around next tr post; rep from * 2 times, ch 5, 1 dc around next tr post, ch 8, miss 1 tr post, sl st in first dc to join.

Round 12: Turn work to RS, fold petals down and work in ch lps created in last round, sl st in nearest ch-8 sp, [ch 3, 2 tr, 1 dtr, 1 ttr, ch 2, 1 ttr, 1 dtr, 3 tr] in this ch-8 sp, *1 tr in next st, 7 tr in next

ch-5 sp, 1 tr in next st, [3 tr, 1 dtr, 1 ttr, ch 2, 1 ttr, 1 dtr, 3 tr] in next ch-8 sp; rep from * 2 times, 1 tr in next st, 7 tr in next ch-5 sp, 1 tr in next st, sl st in top of beg ch-3 to join.

Round 13: Ch 3, *1 tr in each st to corner, [2 tr, ch 2, 2 tr] in corner sp; rep from * 3 times, sl st in 3rd ch of beg ch-3 to join. Fasten off yarn B.

Round 14: Join yarn C, rep Round 13.

Round 15: Ch 1, *1 dc in each st to corner ch-2 sp, [1 dc, picot-3, 1 dc] in ch-2 corner sp; rep from * 3 times, sl st in first dc to join. Fasten off yarn C.

Round 16: Join yarn A in any st, ch 1, *1 dc in each st to corner picot-3, [1 dc, picot-3, 1 dc] in ch-3 corner picot; rep from * 3 times sl st in first sc to join. Fasten off yarn A.

Round 17: Join yarn B in any st, ch 1, *1 dc in each st to corner, [1 dc, picot-3, 1 dc] in corner picot-3; rep from * 3 times, sl st in first dc to join.

Fasten off and darn in ends.

amaryllis

**

An extravagant, multilayered flower that stands tall from its base, this block is deceptively straightforward to work. It lends itself to making a bold statement in many ways such as on pillows, as a table centrepiece, an elaborate bedspread or as a feminine scarf.

A
B
C
D

Foundation ring: Using yarn A, ch 4, sl st in first ch to form ring.

Round 1: *Ch 10, sl st in next ch, ch 10, sl st in same ch; rep from * 3 times, fasten off — 8 ch-10 lps.

Round 2: *[1 dc, 1 htr, 8 tr, ch 2, 8 tr, 1 htr, 1 dc] in next ch-10 sp; rep from * 7 times, sl st in first dc to join. Fasten off yarn A.

Round 3: Turn work to WS, join yarn B in any sl st from Round 1, *ch 14, sl st in next sl st from Round 1; rep from * 7 times, on last rep sl st in first sl st — 8 ch-14 lps.

Round 4: Turn work to RS, fold down first round of petals to access ch-14 lps, *[1 dc, 1 htr, 12 tr, ch 2, 12 tr, 1 htr, 1 dc] in next ch-14 sp; rep from * 7 times, sl st in first dc to join. Fasten off yarn B.

Round 5: Turn work to WS, join yarn C in any sl st from Round 3, *ch 18, sl st in next sl st from Round 3; rep from * 7 times, on last rep sl st in first sl st to join — 8 ch-18 lps.

Round 6: Turn work to RS, fold down petals from Rounds 2 and 4 to access ch-18 lps, *[1 dc 1 htr, 2 tr, 14 dtr, ch 3, 14 dtr, 2 tr, 1 htr, 1 dc] in next ch-18 sp; rep from * 7 times, sl st in first dc to join. Fasten off yarn C.

Round 7: Turn work to RS, join yarn D in any sl st from Round 5, *ch 20, sl st in next sl st from Round 5; rep from * 6 times, ch 15, 1 ttr in first sl st to join.

Round 8: [Ch 5 (counts as 1 ttr), 5 ttr, 4 ch, 6 ttr] in next ch-20 sp, *ch 1, 4 dtr in next ch-20 sp, ch 1, [6 ttr, ch 4, 6 ttr] in next ch-20 sp; rep from * 2 times, ch 1, 4 dtr in next ch-20 sp, ch 1, sl st in top of beg ch-5 to join.

Round 9: Ch 1, *1 dc in each st and in each ch-1 sp to corner, 5 dc in corner ch-4 sp; rep from * 3 times, sl st in first dc to join. Fasten off.

Round 10: Join yarn B in any st, *1 dc in every st to centre dc of corner 5-dc group, 3 dc in corner dc; rep from * 3 times, sl st in first dc to join. Fasten off.

Round 11: Join yarn A in any st, *1 dc in every st to centre dc of corner 3-dc group, 3 sd in corner dc; rep from * 3 times, sl st in first st to join.

Fasten off and darn in ends.

150

**

sunflower

This lively dimensional flower square is fun to work and would look effective used in multiples over a bedspread, or as the central focus of a plainer piece.

Special stitch used:

Double treble 5 stitches together (dtr5tog): [Yoh 2 times, pull through 2 sts] 5 times, yoh and draw through all rem lps on hook.

Foundation ring: Using yarn A, make magic ring, ch 1, 6 dc in ring, pull tail to tighten ring.

Round 1: 2 dc in each dc to end of rnd, sl st in top of first dc to join – 12 sts.

Round 2: Ch 1, 2 dc in same st, 2 dc in each dc to end of rnd, sl st in top of first dc to join – 24 sts. Fasten off yarn A.

Round 3: Join yarn B, ch 4 (counts as first dtr), 4 dtr in same st [for each dtr when 4 sts are on hook pull through 2 sts 2 times, leaving 2 sts on hook, yoh 2 times, insert hook, pull through 2 sts on hook

3 times, leaving 2 sts on hook; rep 2 times, in final dtr, yoh 2 times, pull through 2 sts 4 times joining all sts in one st on hook], [ch 3, miss 1 dc, dtr5tog in each st] 10 times, sl st in 3rd of beg ch-4 to join – 12 sunflower petals of 5 dtrs each made. Fasten off yarn B.

Round 4: Join yarn C in any ch-3 sp, 3 ch (counts as 1 tr), [2 tr, ch 3, 3 tr] in same ch-3 sp (forms corner), *[ch 2, 2 htr] in next sp, [ch 2, 2 htr] in next sp**, ch 2, [3 tr, ch 3, 3 tr] in next sp (forms corner); rep from * 2 times, then from * to ** 1 time, sl st in top of ch-3 to join. Fasten off yarn C.

Round 5: Join yarn D in any ch-3 corner sp, ch 4 (counts as 1 dtr), [2 dtr, ch 3, 3 dtr] in same corner sp, *ch 3, 2 dtr in next sp, ch 3, 2 dtr in next sp, ch 3, 2 dtr in next sp, ch 3**, [3 dtr, ch 3, 3 dtr] in next corner sp; rep from * 2 times, then from * to ** 1 time, sl st in top of ch-4 to join.

Round 6: Sl st in beg of ch-3 corner sp, ch 4 (counts as 1 dtr), [2 dtr, ch 3, 3 dtr] in same corner sp, *[1 dtr in each of next 3 sts, 3 dtr in next ch-3 sp, 1 dtr in each of next 2 dtr, 2 dtr in next ch-3 sp] 3 times, 1 dtr in each of next 3 sts**, [3 dtr, ch 3, 3 dtr] in next corner sp; rep from * 2 times, then from * to ** 1 time, sl st in top of ch-4 to join.

Fasten off and darn in ends neatly.

....

151

***

dream catcher

A light and lacy block for a summer throw, or to add pretty styling to a dinner table. This block uses a range of stitches and techniques and is fun to work up. Cut lengths of yarn D before you begin, for use in the contrast bobbles.

Special stitches used:

Beginning double treble cluster (beg dtr cl): Ch 4, *yoh 2 times, insert hook in ring, yoh and pull through a lp, yoh and draw through 2 lps 2 times; rep from * 3 times, yoh and draw through all lps (see page 18).

Double treble cluster (dtr cl): Yoh 2 times, insert hook in ring; yoh and pull through a lp, yoh and draw through 2 lps 2 times; rep from * 4 times, yoh, draw through all lps.

Beginning popcorn (beg pc): Ch 3, make popcorn with 4 tr (see page 19).

Popcorn (pc): Make popcorn with 5 tr.

Foundation ring: Using yarn A, ch 5, sl st in first ch to form ring.

Round 1: Beg dtr cl in ring, ch 5, *1 dtr cl in ring; ch 5; rep from * 6 times; sl st in top of beg dtr cl to join. Fasten off.

Round 2: Join yarn B in any ch-5 sp, *1 dc, ch 2, sl st in first dc, ch 6 to next ch-5 sp; rep from * 6 times, 1 dc, ch 2, sl st in first dc, ch 3, 1 tr in first dc to join.

Round 3: Ch 3 (counts as 1 tr), 3 tr in first ch-6 sp, *[4 tr, ch 2, 4 tr] in next ch-6 sp; rep from * 6 times, 4 tr in first ch-6 sp, ch 2, sl st in top of beg ch-3 to join. Fasten off.

Round 4: Join yarn C in any ch-2 sp, *[1 dc, ch 3, 1 dc] in ch-2 sp, ch 9; rep from * 7 times, sl st in first dc to join.

Round 5: Join yarn D in any ch-3 sp, beg pc in ch-3 sp, join yarn C, ch 3, [4 dc, ch 3, 4 dc] in next ch-9 sp, *ch 3; join yarn D, pc in next ch-3 sp, join yarn C, ch 3, [4 dc, ch 3, 4 dc] in next ch-9 sp; rep from * 6 times, ch 3, sl st in top of beg pc to join. Fasten off.

Round 6: Join yarn A in any ch-3 sp between two 4-dc groups, *1 dc in this ch-3 sp, ch 4, 1 tr in top/back of next pc,

ch 4, [1 dtr, ch 3, 1 ttr, ch 3, 1 dtr] in next ch-3 sp (forms corner), ch 4, 1 tr in top of next pc, ch 4, 1 dc in next ch-3 sp; rep from * 3 times, sl st in first dc to join.

Round 7: *5 dc in next 2 ch-4 sps, 4 dc in next ch-3 sp, ch 3 (forms corner tip), 4 dc in next ch-3 sp, 5 dc in next 2 ch-4 sps, 1 dc in next 2 dc sts; rep from * 3 times, sl st in first st to join.

Fasten off and darn in ends.

★★★
tricolour

A traditional square that uses pairs of clusters to create its fan-like pattern, this block is lots of fun to work and creates a solid piece that is good for mixing in with more open lacy structures.

A
B
C
D

Special stitches used:

Beginning cluster (beg cl): Make cluster with 5 dtr (*see page 18*).

Cluster (cl): Make cluster with 6 dtr.

Foundation ring: Using A, ch 5, join with sl st to form ring, or use magic ring method.

Round 1: Ch 4, (counts as first dtr), 5 dtr in ring, [ch 3, 6 dtr in ring] 3 times, ch 3, sl st in top of beg ch-4 to join.

Round 2: Ch 3, work beg cl in each of next 5 dtr, *ch 5, sl st in 2nd ch-3 (from Round 1), ch 5**, cl in next 6 dtr; rep from * 2 times, then from * to ** 1 time, sl st in top of beg ch-3 to join. Fasten off yarn A.

Round 3: Join yarn B in top of any cl, *[3 dtr, ch 1, 3 dtr, ch 1, 3 dtr] in next ch-3 sp from Round 1, splitting grouping in half between join (3 dtr, ch 1, 3 dtr, ch 2 in first half, then 3 dtr, ch 1 3 dtr in second half), sl st in top of next cl; rep from * 3 times, sl st in top of first cl to join. Fasten off yarn B.

Round 4: Join yarn C in top of any cl from Round 2, ch 4 (counts as first dtr), 5 dtr in same sp, *[6 dtr, ch 2, 6 dtr] in next ch-2 sp**, 6 dtr in sl st at top of next cl; rep from * 2 times, then from * to ** 1 time, sl st in top of beg ch-4 to join. Fasten off yarn C.

Round 5: Join yarn D with sl st in last st made, ch 1, 1 dc in each of next 6 dtr, 1 tr in each sp between groups of dtr worked in Round 3, *1 dc in each of next 6 dtr, 3 dc in ch-2 corner sp**, [1 dc in each of next 6 dtr, 1 tr in sp between groups of dtr worked in Round 3] 2 times; rep from * 2 times, then from * to ** 1 time, 1 dc in each of next 6 dtr, 1 tr in sp between groups of dtr worked on Round 3, sl st in first dc to join. Fasten off yarn D.

Round 6: Join yarn C to any dc from last rnd, ch 3, 1 tr in each dc and tr worked in rnd below, working 3 tr in centre st of each 3-dc corner combination, sl st in top of beg ch-3 to join. Fasten off yarn C.

Round 7: Join yarn B to any tr from last rnd, rep Round 6.

Round 8: Ch 1, 1 dc in same sp, 1 dc in each tr of last rnd, 3 dc in each middle st of corner combination, sl st in first dc to join.

Fasten off and darn in ends neatly.

153

**

charlie

Inspired by 1970s' knitwear designs, this bright block lends itself to being worked in a host of retro colour combinations or bright graphic tones. Work with a separate ball or length of yarn for each area of colour over the zigzag pattern and remember to keep the yarn tails on the wrong side.

A
B
C

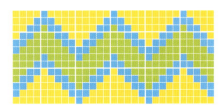

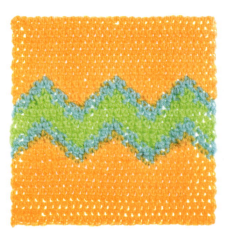

Foundation chain: Using yarn A, ch 30.

Row 1: 1 dc in 2nd ch from hook, 1 dc in every ch to end, turn.

Row 2 and every foll row: Ch 1, 1 dc in every dc to end, turn.

Rows 3 to 9: Rep Row 2.

Rows 10 to 22: Rep Row 2 and work 13 rows of chart, keeping yarn tails at WS of work.

Rows 23 to 31: Rep Row 2, using only yarn A.

Fasten off and darn in ends neatly. Block work to size.

154

***

iona

This block suggests all the comfort of a cosy cable-knit jumper and is named after the beautiful Scottish isle. Cables are created here by using front- and back-post stitches and crossing the central stitches at intervals. Mix this block with other snuggly textural blocks for a comforting winter afghan.

A
B

Special stitches used:

Front-post treble crochet (FPtr): Bring hook to front, work in front vertical post of next st, inserting hook from right to left, draw yarn through and work st as usual (*see page 21*).

Back-post treble crochet (BPtr): Bring hook to back, work in back vertical post of next st, inserting hook from left to right, draw yarn through and work st as usual.

Foundation chain: Using yarn A, ch 28.

Row 1: Ch 2 (counts as 1 htr), 1 htr in each ch to end of row.

Row 2: Ch 2 (counts as 1 htr), 1 htr, 3 FPtr, 2 htr, 1 FPtr, 1 htr, ch 1, miss 1 st, 2 htr, 4 FPtr, 2 htr, ch 1, miss 1 st, 1 htr, 1 FPtr, 2 htr, 3 FPtr, 2 htr, turn.

Row 3: Ch 2 (counts as 1 htr), 1 htr, 3 BPtr, 2 htr, 1 BPtr, 1 htr, ch 1, miss 1 st, 2 htr, 4 BPtr, 2 htr, ch 1, miss 1 st, 1 htr, 1 BPtr, 2 htr, 3 BPtr, 2 htr, turn.

Row 4: Ch 2 (counts as 1 htr), 1 htr, 3 FPtr, 2 htr, 1 FPtr, 1 htr, ch 1, miss 1 st, 2 htr, miss 2 sts, 1 FPtr in each of next 2 sts, working in front of 2 sts just worked 1 FPtr in each of 2 miss sts, 2 htr, ch 1, miss 1 st, 1 htr, 1 FPtr, 2 htr, 3 FPtr, 2 htr, turn.

Rows 5 to 16: Rep Rows 3 to 4.

Row 17: Rep Row 3, turn.

Row 18: Ch 1, 1 dc in every st to end of row, fasten off yarn A.

Rows 19 to 20: Using yarn B, ch 1, 1 dc in every st to end of row. Fasten off yarn B.

Row 21: Join yarn B to bottom of square with RS facing, ch 1, 1 dc in every st of foundation ch to end of row.

Fasten off yarn B and darn in ends neatly.

* nine square granny

Creating smaller granny squares and joining them in this way adds a contrast of scale when using this square alongside regular grannies. Easy to work, mix it up with a myriad of colours for even more pop!

A
B
C
D
E

SQUARE 1

Foundation ring: Using yarn A, ch 6, join with sl st to form ring.

Round 1: Ch 3 (counts as 1 tr), 2 tr in ring, ch 3, *3 tr in ring, ch 3; rep from * 2 times, sl st in top of beg ch-3 to join. Fasten off yarn A.

Round 2: Join yarn B in any ch-3 sp, ch 3 (counts as 1 tr), [2 tr, ch 3, 3 tr] in same sp (forms corner), *ch 1, [3 tr, ch 3, 3 tr] in next ch-3 sp (forms next corner); rep from * 2 times, ch 1, sl st in top of beg ch-3 to join. Fasten off yarn B.

SQUARES 2 and 3

Rep Rounds 1 and 2 using yarn C for Round 1 and Yarn B for Round 2.

SQUARES 4 and 5

Rep Rounds 1 and 2 using yarn D for Round 1 and Yarn B for Round 2.

SQUARES 6, 7, 8 and 9

Rep Rounds 1 and 2 using yarn E for Round 1 and Yarn B for Round 2.

Join nine small grannies tog using dc joining method: with RS facing and using yarn B, work a row of dc in both sets of tr sts (both lps on each sq, a total of 4 lps).

Edging Round 1: Join yarn B in any tr, ch 1, work around composite square as follows: 1 dc in each tr along side of composite square, 1 dc in every ch-1 sp, 3 dc in every external corner of composite square, and 2 dc in ch-3 sps of internal corners of grannies where they join each other, sl st in first ch-1 to join.

Edging Round 2: Ch 1, 1 dc in each dc to end of rnd.

Fasten off and darn all ends in neatly.

** windows

A super-sized play on filet crochet, this simple grid makes an effective contemporary lace panel, suitable for mixing with our other filet blocks, or using with plainer textural squares.

A
B
C

Foundation chain: Using yarn A, ch 23.

Row 1: Ch 5 (counts as 1 quad tr), 1 quad tr in 6th ch from hook, 1 quad tr in each of next 4 ch, ch 3, [miss 3 ch, 1 quad tr in next ch, ch 3] 3 times, miss 3 ch, 1 quad tr in each of next 5 ch to end, turn.

Row 2: Ch 8 (counts as 1 quad tr, ch 3), miss 3 sts, 1 quad tr in next quad tr, 1 quad tr in each of next 3 ch sts, 1 quad tr in next quad tr, ch 3, miss 3 sts, 1 quad tr in next quad tr, ch 3, miss 3 sts, 1 quad tr in next quad tr, 1 quad tr in each of next 3 ch sts, 1 quad tr in first quad tr of next quad tr group, ch 3, miss 3 sts, 1 quad tr in last quad tr of quad tr group, turn.

Row 3: Ch 8 (counts as 1 quad tr and 3 ch), miss 3 ch, 1 quad tr in first st of quad tr group of prev row, ch 3, miss 3 sts, 1 quad tr in last st of quad tr group of last row, 1 quad tr in each of next 3 ch sps, 1 quad tr in next quad tr, 1 quad tr in each of next 3 ch sps, 1 quad tr in first st of next qud tr group, ch 3, 1 qud tr in next qud tr, ch 3, 1 quad tr in last quad tr, turn.

Row 4: Rep Row 3.

Row 5: Rep Row 2.

Row 6: Rep Row 1. Fasten off yarn A.

Row 7: Using yarn B, 1 dc in each st and in each ch-st all around square (when working up and down vertical sides of block work in side posts of sts, working 3 dc in each side post and 1 dc in top of st), at each corner, [1 dc, ch 1, 1 dc] in same st. Fasten off yarn B.

Rows 8 to 9: Join yarn C, rep Round 7, but working 1 dc in every st all around square, and [1 dc, ch 1, 1 dc] in every corner.

Fasten off and darn in ends. Block square to 15 cm (6 inches).

* yellowstone

A simple but effective four-patch square that would work in a host of colour combinations, this block is useful for mixing with many other grannies, and is a good square for beginners to practise joining skills.

A
B

Special stitches used:

Beginning treble-crochet cluster (beg tr cl): Ch 2, 1 tr in same st (*see page 18*).

Cluster (cl): Make cluster with 2 tr.

Foundation ring: Using yarn A, ch 4, sl st in first ch to form ring.

Round 1: Beg tr cl in ring, *[ch 1, 2-tr cl in ring] 11 times, ch 1, sl st in top of first tr cl to join. Fasten off yarn A.

Round 2: Join yarn B in any ch-1 sp, ch 2 (counts as 1 htr), 1 htr in same ch-1 sp, *2 hdc in next ch-1 sp, [2 tr, ch 2, 2 tr] in next ch-1 sp, 2 htr in next ch-1 sp; rep from * 2 times, 2 htr in next ch-1 sp, [2 tr, ch 2, 2 tr] in next ch-1 sp, sl st in top of beg ch-2 to join.

Round 3: Ch 1, 1 dc in each of next 5 sts, *3 dc in next ch-2 sp, 1 dc in each of next 8 sts; rep from * 2 times, 3 dc in in next ch-2 sp, 1 dc in each of next 3 sts, sl st in first dc to join. Fasten off yarn B.

Make another 3 small squares in the same way.

Join 2 squares tog by placing RS together, sl st across one edge through front lps only. Join another 2 squares tog in the same way. Join these 2 strips of squares tog along one long edge with RS tog.

Round 4: Join yarn B in any corner sp, ch 2 (counts as 1 htr), *1 htr in each of next 22 sts to centre st in next corner [1 htr, ch 2, 1 htr] in centre corner st; rep from * 2 times, 1 htr in each of next 22 sts to centre corner st, [1 htr, ch 2] in centre corner st, sl st in top of beg ch-2 to join. Fasten off.

Round 5: Join yarn A in any corner sp, ch 2 (counts as 1 htr), *1 htr in each of next 24 sts to next corner ch-2 sp, [1 htr, ch 2, 1 htr] in ch-2 corner sp; rep from * 2 times, 1 htr in each of next 24 sts to last ch-2 corner sp, [1 htr, ch 2] in ch-2 sp, sl st in top of beg ch-2 to join. Fasten off yarn A.

Round 6: Join yarn B in any ch-2 corner sp, ch 2 (counts as 1 htr), *1 htr in each of next 26 sts to next ch-2 corner sp, [1 htr, ch 2, 1 htr] in ch-2 sp; rep from * 2 times, 1 htr in each of next 26 sts to last ch-2 corner sp, [1 htr, ch 2] in ch-2 sp, sl st in top of beg ch-2 to join. Fasten off yarn B.

Round 7: Join yarn A in any ch-2 corner sp, *3 dc in corner sp, 1 dc in each of next 28 sts; rep from * 3 times, sl st in first dc to join.

Fasten off and darn in ends neatly.

**

buzz

Best worked in eye-popping contrasting colours, this pattern has retro charm and would make a fabulously funky throw or afghan, perfect for the modern interior.

A
B

Special stitch used:

Spike stitch (spike st): Insert hook in sp in row below next st to be worked (here 1, 2 or 3 rows below), yoh, pull yarn through to height of row being worked, complete stitch as normal (see page 22).

Foundation chain: Using yarn A, ch 28.

Row 1: 1 dc in 2nd ch from hook, 1 dc in every dc to end of row, turn.

Rows 2 to 4: Ch 1, 1 dc in every dc to end, turn. Fasten off yarn A.

Row 5: Join yarn B, ch 1, 1 dc in first 2 dc, *spike sts: 1 dc in row below next dc, 1 dc in 2 rows below next dc, 1 dc in 3 rows below next dc, 1 dc in 2 rows below next dc, 1 sc in row below next dc, 1 dc in next sc; rep from * 3 times, 1 dc in last dc.

Rows 6 to 8: Ch 1, 1 dc in every dc to end. Fasten off yarn B.

Row 9: Join yarn A, ch 1, 1 dc in 2 rows below first dc, 1 dc in 3 rows below next dc, 1 dc in 2 rows below next dc, 1 dc in row below next dc, 1 dc in next dc, *spike sts: 1 dc in row below, 1 dc in 2 rows below next dc, 1 dc in 3 rows below next dc, 1 dc in 2 rows below next dc, 1 dc in row below next dc, 1 dc in next dc; rep from * 3 times, 1 dc in row below next dc, 1 dc in 2 rows below next dc, 1 dc in 3 rows below next dc, 1 dc in last dc.

Rows 10 to 12: Ch 1, 1 dc in every dc to end.

Row 13: Rep Row 5.

Rows 14 to 16: Ch 1, 1 dc in every dc to end.

Row 17: Rep Row 9.

Rows 18 to 20: Ch 1, 1 dc in every dc to end.

Row 21: Rep Row 5.

Rows 22 to 24: Ch 1, 1 dc in every dc to end.

Row 25: Rep Row 9.

Rows 26 to 28: Ch 1, 1 dc in every dc to end.

Row 29: Rep Row 5.

Rows 30 to 32: Ch 1, 1 dc in every dc to end.

Row 33: Rep Row 9.

Rows 34 to 36: Ch 1, 1 dc in every dc to end.

Row 37: Rep Row 5.

Rows 38 to 40: Ch 1, 1 dc in every dc to end.

Fasten off and darn in ends neatly.

**

african flower

A well-known and well-loved design that creates beautiful scalloped petals separated by spike stitches, and outlined in contrast double crochet, this block works well in multiples for a pillow or bedspread.

A

B

C

D

Special stitch used:

Spike stitch (spike st): Insert hook in sp between clusters of two rnds below, yoh, pull yarn through to height of rnd being worked, yoh, pull through two lps on hook (*see page 22*).

Foundation ring: Ch 5, join with sl st to form ring, or use magic ring method.

Round 1: Ch 3 (counts as first tr), 1 tr, ch 1, [2 tr, ch 1] 7 times, sl st in top of beg ch-3 to join – 8 groups of 2 tr. Fasten off yarn A.

Round 2: Join yarn B in any ch-1 sp, ch 3, 2 tr in same ch-1 sp, ch 1, [3 tr in next ch-1 sp, ch 1] 7 times, sl st in top of beg ch-3 to join – 8 ch-3 clusters. Fasten off yarn B.

Round 3: Join yarn C in any ch-1 sp from round below, [ch 3, 1 tr, ch 2, 2 tr] all in same ch-1 sp, [2 tr, ch 2, 2 tr] in next ch-1 sp], 7 times, sl st in top of beg ch-3 to join.

Round 4: Sl st in next tr, sl st in next ch-2 sp, ch 3, 6 tr in same ch-2 sp, [7 tr in next ch-2 sp] 7 times, sl st in top of beg ch-3 to join. Fasten off yarn C.

Round 5: Join yarn A in any tr from last rnd, ch 1, 1 dc in each tr, spike st between shell clusters created in rnd below, sl st in first dc to join. Fasten off yarn D.

Round 6: Join yarn B in any spike st from last rnd, ch 2 (counts as 1 htr) in spike st, *1 dc in next 4 dc from rnd below, 1 htr in next st, 1 tr in each of next 2 sts, [1 dtr, ch 3, 1 dtr] in spike st (forms corner), 1 tr in each of next 2 sts, 1 htr in next st, 1 dc in each of next 4 sts, 1 htr in next 2 sts; rep from * 3 times, omitting last 1 htr on last rep, sl st in top of beg ch-2 to join. Fasten off yarn B.

Round 7: Join yarn D in ch-3 sp of any corner, ch 3 (counts as first tr), [1 tr, ch 3, 2 tr] in same sp, *1 tr in each tr, [2 tr, ch 3, 2 tr] in next corner ch-sp; rep from * 2 times, 1 tr in each tr, sl st in top of beg ch-3 to join. Fasten off yarn D.

Round 8: Join yarn B in any ch-3 sp of any corner, ch 1, *3 dc in same corner sp, 1 dc in each st to next corner; rep from * 3 times, sl st in first dc to join. Fasten off yarn B.

Round 9: Join yarn C in any ch-3 sp of any corner, rep Round 7.

Round 10: Rep Round 8.

Fasten off and darn in ends neatly.

★★★
pistachio shell

This is a delicately patterned block with textural appeal in its central popcorn ring. Multiple rounds of petals are joined with connecting contrasting rows, giving a complex appearance that is easier to work that it looks! Gorgeous for inclusion in a special blanket or throw.

A
B
C
D

Special stitches used:

Beginning popcorn (beg pc): Ch 3, make popcorn with 4 tr (*see page 19*).

Popcorn (pc): Make popcorn with 5 tr.

Foundation ring: Using yarn A, ch 6, sl st in first ch to form ring.

Round 1: Ch 3 (counts as 1 tr), 15 tr in ring. Fasten off yarn A.

Round 2: Join yarn B in any tr, beg pc in same st, ch 3, miss 1 tr, change to yarn C (secure new yarn with 1 dc and carry yarn not in use at back of work), pc in next tr, ch 3, miss 1 tr, *change to yarn B, pc in next tr, ch 3, miss 1 tr, change to yarn A; rep from * 2 times, sl st in top of beg pc to join. Fasten off yarn B.

Round 3: Join yarn D in any ch-3 sp, ch 1, [1 dc, 1 htr, 2 tr, 1 htr, 1 dc] in same ch-3 sp, ch 1, *[1 dc, 1 htr, 2 tr, 1 htr, 1 dc] in next ch-3 sp, ch 1; rep from * 6 times, sl st in first ch to join.

Round 4: Join yarn A in any ch-1 sp between two petals, ch 6 (counts as 1 dc, ch 5), 1 dc in next ch-1 sp between 2 petals, *ch 5, 1 dc in next ch-1 sp between petals; rep from * 5 times, ch 5, sl st in first ch to join. Fasten off yarn A.

Round 5: Join yarn C in any ch-5 lp, ch 1, *[1 dc, 1 htr, 3 tr, 1 htr, 1 dc] in same ch-5 lp, ch 1; rep from * 7 times, sl st in first ch to join. Fasten off yarn C.

Round 6: Join yarn B in any ch-1 sp between 2 petals, ch 7 (counts as 1 dc, ch 6), 1 dc in next ch-1 sp between next 2 petals, *ch 6, 1 dc in next ch-1 sp between petals; rep from * 5 times, ch 6, sl st in first ch to join. Fasten off yarn B.

Round 7: Join yarn D in any ch-6 lp, ch 1, *[1 dc, 1 htr, 3 tr, 1 dtr, 3 tr, 1 htr, 1 dc] in same lp, ch 1; rep from * 7 times, sl st to first ch to join. Fasten off yarn D.

Round 8: Join yarn A in any ch-1 sp between 2 petals, ch 9 (counts as 1 dc, ch 8), 1 dc in next ch-1 sp between next 2 petals, *ch 8, 1 dc in next ch-1 between petals; rep from * 5 times, ch 8, sl st in first ch to join. Fasten off yarn A.

Round 9: Join yarn C in any ch-8 lp, ch 1, *[1 dc, 1 htr, 6 tr, 1 htr, 1 dc] in same lp, ch 1; rep from * 7 times, sl st in first ch to join.

Round 10: Sl st along to 3rd tr of next petal, ch 3 (counts as 1 tr), [1 tr, ch 3, 2 tr] in same st (forms corner), ch 8, miss 10 sts, 1 dc in next tr, ch 8, miss 10 sts, *[2 tr, ch 3, 2 tr] in next st (forms corner), ch 8, miss 10 sts, 1 dc in next tr, ch 8, miss 10 sts; rep from * 2 times, sl st in top of beg ch-3 to join. Fasten off yarn C.

Round 11: Join yarn D in any ch-3 corner sp, ch 3 (counts as 1 tr), [1 tr, ch 3, 2 tr] in same sp (forms corner), 1 tr in each of next 2 tr, 12 tr in next ch-8 sp, 1 tr in next dc, 12 tr in next ch-8 sp, 1 tr in each of next 2 tr, *[2 tr, ch 3, 2 tr] in next corner sp, 1 tr in each of next 2 tr, 12 tr in next ch-8 sp, 1 tr in next dc, 12 tr in next ch-8 sp, 1 tr in each of next 2 tr; rep from * 2 times, sl st in top of beg ch-3 to join.

Fasten off and darn in ends neatly.

161 ★★★

saguaro

Inspired by a cactus owned by the author, this square is a bonanza of spike stitches, which combine to produce a complex colour pattern. Small auxiliary circles are created in the corners allowing for more spikes. This square is fun to work but do ensure you block it once it's complete as the spike stitches tend to distort the fabric a little.

A
B
C
D
E

Special stitch used:

Spike stitch (spike st): Insert hook in top of st 2 rnds below next st to be worked, yoh, pull yarn through to height of rnd being worked, complete st as normal (*see page 22*).

Foundation ring: Using yarn A, make a magic ring, ch 1 to secure.

Round 1: 8 dc in ring, sl st in first dc to join.

Round 2: Ch 2, 2 htr in every dc to end, 1 htr in last st, sl st in top of beg ch-2 to join – 16 htr. Fasten off yarn A.

Round 3: Join yarn B, ch 1, *1 dc in next st, 1 spike st in next st 2 rows below; rep from * to end, sl st in first dc to join. Fasten off yarn B.

Round 4: Join yarn C, ch 3 (counts as 1 tr), 2 tr in every st to last st, 1 tr in last st (at base of ch-3), sl st in top of beg ch-3 to join – 32 tr. Fasten off yarn C.

Round 5: Join yarn D, ch 1, *1 dc in next st, 1 spike st in next st 2 rows below; rep from * to end, sl st in first dc to join. Fasten off yarn D.

Round 6: Join yarn E, ch 3 (counts as 1 tr), 2 tr in every st to last st, 1 tr in last st (at base of ch-3), sl st in top of beg ch-3 to join – 64 tr. Fasten off yarn E.

Round 7: Join yarn A, ch 1, *1 dc in next st, 1 spike st in next st 2 rows below; rep from * to end, sl st in first dc to join.

Round 8: (Baby Cactus Round) Ch 4, sl st in st at base of ch-4, *ch 2, sl st in 2nd st to the left, turn, 8 tr in ch-4 ring, sl st in 2nd ch to left to lie baby cactus flat. Fasten off yarn A**. Turn to RS again, miss 14 dc, join A in next st, ch 4, sl st in same st; rep from * to ** to complete 2nd cactus. Turn to RS again, miss 14 dc, join A in next st, ch 4, sl st in same st; rep from * to ** complete 3rd cactus. Turn to RS, miss 14 dc, join A in next st, ch 4, sl st in same st; rep from * to ** to complete last cactus. Fasten off yarn A.

Round 9: (RS) Join yarn D in first st of cactus, ch 2, 1 htr in same st, 2 htr in every st around first baby cactus section, *ch 1, miss 1 dc, 1 dc in each of next 9 sts, miss 1 dc, ch 1**, 2 htr in every st of next baby cactus section; rep from * 2 times and from * to ** 1 time, sl st in top of beg ch-2 to join. Fasten off.

Round 10: Join yarn C in first st of cactus, ch 1, *[1 dc in same htr, 1 spike dc in next st 2 rows below] 4 times, 3 htr in next htr, [1 dc in next htr, 1 spike dc in next st 2 rows below] 4 times, 1 dc in next ch-1 sp, [ch 3, miss 2 dc, 1 tr in next dc] 2 times, ch 3, 1 dc in next ch-1 sp; rep from * 3 times, sl st in first dc to join. Fasten off yarn C.

Round 11: Join yarn E in first st of cactus, ch 3 (counts as 1 tr), 1 tr in each of next 3 dc, *1 htr in each of next 2 dc, 1 dc in each of next 2 dc, 1 htr in each of next 2 sts, 3 htr in next st (corner), 1 htr in each of next 2 sts, 1 dc in each of next 2 dc, 1 htr in each of next 2 dc, 1 tr in each of next 4 sts [2 htr in next ch-3 sp, 1 tr in next tr] 2 times, 2 htr in next ch-3 sp**, 1 tr in each of next 3 dc; rep from * 2 times and from * to ** 1 time, sl st in top of beg ch-3 to join.

Fasten off and darn in ends. Block work to flatten it out.

*

crocus patch

Full of spring colour and cheer, this granny square variant uses chain stitches to separate clusters into buds and blossoms. Using a darker colour for the single-crochet rows between 'flower' rows adds to the overall effect.

A
B
C
D
E

Special stitches used:

2-half-treble crochet cluster (2-htr cl): Make cluster with 2 htr in same st or sp (*see page 18*).

3-half-treble crochet cluster (3-htr cl): Make cluster with 3 htr in same st or sp.

Foundation ring: Using yarn A, ch 4, sl st in first ch to join.

Round 1: Ch 2 (counts as 1 htr), 2 htr in ring, ch 2, [3 htr in ring, ch 2] 2 times, sl st in top of beg ch-2 to join. Fasten off yarn A.

Round 2: Join yarn B in any ch-2 sp, ch 1, *[2 dc, ch 1, 2 dc] in same sp, ch 1; rep from * 3 times, sl st in first ch to join. Fasten off yarn B.

Round 3: Join yarn C in any corner ch-1 sp, ch 3 (counts as 1 htr, ch 1), 1 htr in same sp, *ch 1, [1 htr, ch 1, 1 htr, ch 1, 1 htr] in next ch-1 sp, ch 1**, [1 htr, ch 1, 1 htr, ch 1, 1 htr, ch 1, 1 htr] all in next ch-1 sp; rep from * 2 times and from * to ** 1 time, [1 htr, ch 1, 1 htr, ch 1] in last corner ch-1 sp, sl st in 2nd ch of beg ch-3 to join. Fasten off yarn C.

Round 4: Join yarn B in any corner ch-1 sp, ch 1, [2 dc, ch 1, 2 dc] in same sp, *1 dc in next ch-1 sp, 2 dc in next ch-1 sp, [1 dc in next ch-1 sp] 2 times, 2 dc in next ch-1 sp, 1 dc in next ch-1 sp **, [2 dc, ch 1, 2 dc] in next ch-1 sp; rep from * 2 times and from * to ** 1 time, sl st in first ch to join. Fasten off yarn B.

Round 5: Join yarn D in any corner ch-1 sp, ch 2 (counts as 1 htr), 2-htr cl in same sp, *[ch 2, miss 2 sts, 3-htr cl in next st] 3 times, ch 2, miss 2 sts**, [3-htr cl, ch 2, 3-htr cl] in next ch-1 sp; rep from * 2 times and from * to ** 1 time, [3-htr cl, ch 2] in last ch-1 corner sp, sl st in top of beg ch-2 to join. Fasten off yarn D.

Round 6: Join yarn A in any ch-2 corner sp, ch 1, *[2 dc, ch 1, 2 dc] in same sp, [3 dc, ch 1 in next ch-2 sp] 4 times; rep from * 3 times, sl st in first ch to join. Fasten off yarn A.

Round 7: Join yarn B in any corner ch-1 sp, *[2 dc, ch 1, 2 dc] in same sp, [3 dc, ch 1 in next sp between groups of 3 dc] 5 times; rep from * 3 times, sl st in first ch to join. Fasten off yarn B.

Round 8: Join yarn E in any ch-1 corner sp, ch 4 (counts as 1 tr, ch 1), 1 tr in same sp, *[1 tr, ch 1, 1 tr, ch 1, 1 tr] in next sp between 3-dc groups] 6 times**, [1 tr, ch 1, 1 tr, ch 1, 1 tr, ch 1, 1 tr] all in next corner ch-1 sp; rep from * 2 times and from * to ** 1 time, [1 tr, ch 1, 1 tr, ch 1] in last corner ch-1 sp, sl st in 3rd ch of beg ch-4 to join. Fasten off yarn D.

Round 9: Join yarn B in any corner ch-1 sp, ch 1, [2 dc, ch 1, 2 dc] in same sp, *1 dc in every ch-1 sp and between each group of tr clusters to corner**, [2 dc, ch 1, 2 dc] in corner ch-1 sp; rep from * 2 times and from * to ** 1 time, sl st in first ch to join.

Fasten off and darn in ends.

163 ** turtle

A B C D

With its hexagon structure this block resembles a turtle's shell, and the mid-row colour changes add interest as it is worked. This design can look either contemporary or traditional. On Round 3, carry the yarn not in use along the row, working stitches over it as you go.

Foundation ring: Using yarn A, ch 6, sl st in first ch to form ring.

Round 1: Ch 4 (counts as 1 dtr) 2 dtr in ring, ch 1 [3 dtr in ring, ch 1] 5 times, sl st in top of beg ch-4 to join.

Round 2: [1 tr in ch-1 sp, ch 7] 6 times, sl st in first dc to join. Fasten off yarn A.

Round 3: Join yarn B, *[1 htr, 2 tr, 3 dtr, 2 tr, 1 htr] in first ch-7 sp**, change to yarn C; rep from * to **, change to yarn B; rep from * to **, change to yarn C; rep from * to **, change to yarn B; rep from * to **, change to yarn A; rep from * to **, sl st in first htr to join. Fasten off.

Round 4: Join yarn D, ch 4 (counts as 1 dtr) 1 dtr in every htr, 1 tr in every tr and 1 htr in every dtr to end, sl st in top of beg ch-4 to join. Fasten off yarn D.

Round 5: Join yarn B, ch 3 (counts as 1 tr) ch 2 [1 tr in each of next 8 sts, ch 2] 5 times, 1 tr in each of next 7 sts, sl st in top of beg ch-3 to join. Fasten off yarn B.

Round 6: Join yarn C in first tr of 8, 1 dc in each of next 8 dc, ch 18, miss 10 ch, 1 dc in each of next 2 tr, ch 18, miss 10 ch, 1 dc in each of next 8 dc, ch 18, miss 10 ch, 1 dc in each of next 2 tr, ch 18, sl st in first dc to join.

Round 7: Ch 1, 1 dc in each of next 16 dc, ch 3, [1 dc in each of next 22 dc, ch 3], 3 times, 1 dc in each of last 7 dc, sl st in first dc to join. Fasten off yarn C.

Round 8: Join yarn B, ch 3 (counts as 1 tr) *1 tr in every st to corner, ch 3; rep from * 3 times, 1 tr in every st to end, sl st in top of beg ch-3 to join.

Fasten off and darn in ends.

164 ** maya

A B C D E F G H I J K L M

A lively linear block created in simple colourful patterns. You might find it helpful to photocopy the chart, then cross off each row as you go as there are many colour changes, but the resulting square is worth the effort.

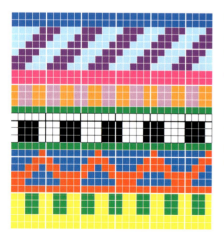

Foundation chain: Using yarn A, ch 30.

Row 1: (First row of chart) 1 dc in 2nd ch from hook, 1 dc in every ch to end, turn.

Work the rem 29 rows of chart, keeping yarn ends on WS of work.

Row 2 and every foll row: Ch 1, 1 dc in every dc to end, turn.

Fasten off and darn in ends neatly. Block work.

****

double daisy

A double layer of petals frames a textured bobbly centre in this flower block; picot stitches are used to define the leaves. This is challenging but is fun to work up and creates an especially dimensional block, which is perfect for a focus in a flower-garden afghan or blanket.

Special stitches used:

Make bobble (MB): Make bobble with 4 tr (*see page 19*).

Picot-3: Ch 3 (at point to add picot), sl st in first ch of 3-ch, creating picot lp.

2-treble crochet cluster (2-tr cl): Make cluster with 2 tr in same st or sp (*see page 18*).

2-double treble cluster (2-dtr cl): Make cluster with 2 dtr in same st or sp.

Foundation ring: Using yarn A, ch 6, sl st to first ch to form ring.

Round 1: Ch 1, 16 dc in ring, join with sl st in first sc.

Round 2: Ch 1, 1 dc in every st around, join with sl st in first dc.

Round 3: Ch 1, 2 dc in every st to end, join with sl st in first dc.

Round 4: Ch 1, [2 dc in next dc, 1 dc in next dc] to end, join with sl st in first dc.

Round 5: Ch 1, 1 dc in each of next 2 dc; *MB in next dc, 1 dc in each of next 3 dc; rep from * to end, omitting last 2 dc from last rep, join with sl st in first dc.

Round 6: Rep Round 2, fasten off yarn A.

Round 7: Join yarn B in the front lp of same st, cont working in front lps only, ch 2, [1 tr, 1 dtr] in next dc, [1 dtr, 1 tr, 1 htr] in next dc (first petal made), *1 dc in each of next 2 dc, [ch 2, 1 tr, 1 dtr] in next dc, [1 dtr, 1 tr, 1 htr] in next dc (2nd petal made); rep from * 10 times, 1 dc in each of last 2 dc, join with sl st in base of beg ch-2.

Round 8: Sl st in back lp of last st from Round 6, turn work over, working with WS facing, 1 dc in back lp of every st from Round 6 around, join with sl st in first dc. turn work back to RS facing.

Round 9: Ch 1, working in front lps only of Round 8, *1 dc in each of next 2 dc, [ch 2, 1 tr, 1 dtr] in next dc, [1d tr, 1 tr, 1 htr] in next dc; rep from * 11 times; join with sl st in first dc. Fasten off yarn B.

Round 10: Join yarn C in back lp of last st of Round 8, cont working in back lps only, *ch 3, picot-3, 2-tr cl in same sp, 2-tr cl in next dc, 2-dtr cl in next dc, picot-3, ch 4, sl st in same st as 2-dtr cl, sl st in next dc, ch 4, picot-3, 2-tr cl in same dc, 2-tr cl in each of next 2 dc, picot-3, ch 3, sl st in same st as last 2-tr cl, sl st in each of next 6 dc; rep from * 3 times, join with sl st to first ch of beg ch-3. Fasten off yarn C.

Round 11: Rejoin yarn C in picot-3 lp at top of RH (first) 2-dtr cl at any corner, 1 dc in same st, ch 4, 1 ttr between 2 leaves at corner (at base of leaves, at bottom of Round 10), *ch 4, 1 dc in picot-3 lp at top of next 2-dtr cl, ch 4, 1 dc in picot-3 lp at top of next 2-tr cl, ch 6, 1 dc in picot-3 lp at top of next 2-tr cl (at start of next 2 leaves), ch 4**, 1 dc in next picot-3 lp, ch 4, 1 ttr in sp between leaves; rep from * 2 times, and from * to ** 1 time, join with sl st in first dc. Fasten off yarn C.

Round 12: Join yarn D in any ttr st at corner, ch 3, [1 tr, ch 2, 2 tr] in same st (forms corner), *[4 tr in next ch-4 sp, ch 1] 2 times, 6 tr in next ch-6 sp, [ch 1, 4 tr in next ch-4 sp] 2 times**, [2 tr, ch 2, 2 tr] in next ttr; rep from * 2 times, and from * to ** 1 time, join with sl st in first tr.

Fasten off and darn in all ends neatly.

* * * *

suspension

A

B

A highly unusual block that builds a diamond-shaped filet motif through increases and decreases, then attaches it to the border via an ingenious use of chain loops. Although it is complex, it has a rhythmic structure. Use with other modern filets for a unique throw.

Foundation chain: Using yarn A, ch 3.

Row 1: Ch 4 (counts as 1 tr, ch 1), miss 2 ch, 1 tr in each of last 2 ch, turn.

Row 2: Ch 5, 1 tr in 6th st from hook, ch 1, miss 1 ch, 1 tr in next ch, ch 1, 1 dtr in last ch, turn.

Row 3: Ch 5, 1 tr in 6th st from hook, [ch 1, miss 1 ch, 1 tr in next tr] 3 times, ch 1, 1 dtr in last ch, turn.

Row 4: Ch 5, 1 tr in 6th st from hook, [ch 1, miss 1 ch, 1 tr in next tr] 5 times, ch 1, 1 dtr in last ch, turn.

Row 5: Ch 5, 1 tr in 6th st from hook, [ch 1, miss 1 ch, 1 tr in next tr] 7 times, ch 1, 1 dtr in last ch, turn.

Row 6: Ch 5, 1 tr in 6th st from hook, [ch 1, miss 1 ch, 1 tr in next tr] 9 times, ch 1, 1 dtr in last ch, turn

Row 7: Ch 5, 1 tr in 6th st from hook, [ch 1, miss 1 ch, 1 tr in next tr] 11 times, ch 1, 1 dtr in last ch, turn.

Row 8: Miss 2 ch, insert hook in next tr, ch 3 (counts as 1 tr, ch 1), miss 1 ch, 1 tr in next tr, [ch 1, miss 1 ch, 1 tr in next tr] 9 times, miss 1 ch, 1 dtr in last st, turn.

Row 9: Ch 3 (counts as 1 tr, ch 1), miss 1 tr, 1 tr in next tr, [ch 1, miss 1 ch, 1 tr in next tr] 7 times, miss 1 ch, 1 dtr in last st, turn.

Row 10: Ch 3 (counts as 1 tr, ch 1), miss 1 tr, 1 tr in next tr, [ch 1, miss 1 ch, 1 tr] 5 times, miss 1 ch, 1 dtr in last st, turn.

Row 11: Ch 3 (counts as 1 tr, ch 1), miss 1 tr, 1 tr in next tr, [ch 1, miss 1 ch, 1 tr] 3 times, miss 1 ch, 1 dtr in last st, turn.

Row 12: Ch 3 (counts as 1 tr, ch 1), miss 1 tr, 1 tr in next tr, ch 1, miss 1 ch, 1 tr in next tr, miss 1 ch, 1 dtr in last st, turn.

Row 13: Ch 3 (counts as 1 tr, ch 1), miss 1 tr, 1 tr in next tr, turn.

Row 14: Ch 1, *3 dc in next ch-sp, ch 5, 1 dtr in last square of Row 11, ch 16, sl st in last square of Row 10, ch 10, sl st in 8th ch of ch 16, ch 5, 1 dtr in last square of Row 9, ch 5; rep from * 3 times (keeping the position of each dtr symmetrical to above instruction), fasten off yarn A.

Row 15: Join yarn B, ch 1, 1 dc in same st, 1 dc in each of next 2 dc, *5 dc in next ch-5 sp, 1 dc in next dtr, 5 dc in next ch-5 sp, [2 dc, ch 1, 2 dc] in centre of ch-16 lp, 5 dc in next ch-5 sp, 1 dc in next dtr, 5 dc in next ch-5 lp**, 1 dc in each of next 3 dc; rep from * 2 times and from * to ** 1 time, sl st in first dc to join.

Row 16: Ch 1, *1 dc in every dc to corner, [2 dc, ch 2, 2 dc] in corner ch-1 sp; rep from * to end, sl st in first dc to join.

Fasten off and darn in all ends.

junction

This simple construction creates a really unusual block. It is a lightweight square that works best when combined with other, denser blocks in a composite piece. A modern twist on traditional filet, this has loads of possibilities for the modern home.

Foundation chain: Using yarn A, ch 31.

Row 1: Ch 4 (counts as 1 tr, ch 1), miss 1 ch, 1 tr in next ch, ch 25, miss 25 ch, 1 tr in next ch, ch 1, miss 1 ch, 1 tr in last ch, turn.

Row 2: Ch 4 (counts as 1 tr, ch 1), miss 1 ch, 1 tr in next tr, ch 1, miss 1 ch, 1 tr in next ch, ch 21, miss 21 ch, 1 tr in next ch, ch 1, miss 1 ch, 1 tr in next tr, ch 1, miss 1 ch, 1 tr in last tr, turn.

Row 3: Ch 4 (counts as 1 tr, ch 1), miss 1 ch, [1 tr in next tr, ch 1, miss 1 ch] 2 times, 1 tr in next ch, ch 17, miss 17 ch, 1 tr in next ch, [ch 1, miss 1 ch, 1 tr in next tr] 3 times, turn.

Row 4: Ch 4 (counts as 1 tr, ch 1), miss 1 ch, [1 tr in next tr, ch 1, miss 1 ch] 3 times, 1 tr in next ch, ch 13, miss 13 ch, 1 tr in next ch [ch 1, miss 1 ch, 1 tr in next tr] 4 times, turn.

Row 5: Ch 4 (counts as 1 tr, ch 1), miss 1 ch, [1 tr in next tr, ch 1, miss 1 ch] 4 times, 1 tr in next ch, ch 9, miss 9 ch, 1 tr in next ch, [ch 1, miss 1 ch, 1 tr in next tr] 5 times, turn.

Row 6: ch 4 (counts as 1 tr, ch 1), miss 1 ch, [1 tr in next tr, ch 1, miss 1 ch] 5 times, 1 tr in next ch, ch 5, miss 5 ch, 1 tr in next ch [ch 1, miss 1 ch, 1 tr in next tr] 6 times, turn. Fasten off yarn A.

Row 7: Join yarn B, ch 4 (counts as 1 tr, *ch 1), miss 1 ch, 1 tr in next tr or ch; rep from * to end of row, turn.

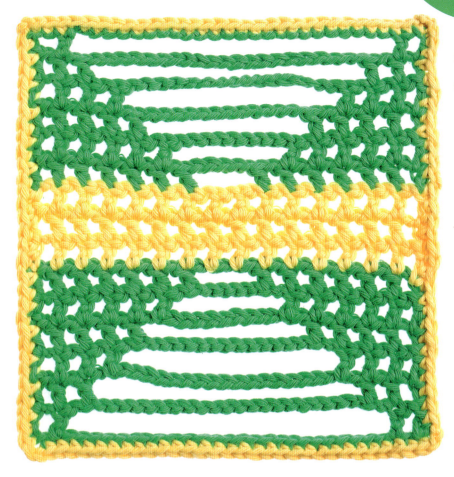

Rows 8 to 9: Rep Row 7, fasten off after Row 9.

Row 10: Join yarn A, rep Row 6 (do not fasten off).

Row 11: Rep Row 5.

Row 12: Rep Row 4.

Row 13: Rep Row 3.

Row 14: Rep Row 2.

Row 15: Rep Row 1.

Fasten off.

BORDER

Using yarn B, ch 1, *1 dc in every ch and every tr to corner, ch 2 at corner, 1 dc in every ch-sp and base of every row to next corner, ch 2; rep from * 1 time, sl st in ch-1 at beg to join.

Fasten off and darn in ends.

A
B

167

143

168 *
roulade

This large-scale round motif has interesting corners adding an unusual element to a familiar pattern. A good beginner square, it has rustic appeal and would work well with all the other wheel motifs in this book.

A
B

Foundation ring: Using yarn A, ch 5, sl st in first ch to form ring.

Round 1: Ch 4 (counts as 1 tr, ch 1), [1 tr, ch 1] 7 times in ring, sl st in 3rd ch of beg ch-4 to join.

Round 2: Ch 4 (counts as 1 tr, ch 1), [1 tr in next tr, ch 1, 1 tr in next ch-1 sp, ch 1] 7 times, 1 tr in last tr, ch 1, sl st in 3rd ch of beg ch-4 to join.

Round 3: Ch 7 (counts as 1 ttr, ch 2) miss 1 tr, *1 ttr in ch-1 sp, ch 2, miss 1 tr; rep from * 15 times to end, sl st in 5th ch of beg ch-7 to join.

Round 4: Ch 3 (counts as 1 tr) *1 tr in next ttr, 2 tr in next ch-2 sp; rep from * to end, sl st in top of beg ch-3 to join.

Round 5: Ch 4 (counts as 1 tr, ch 1) [1 tr, ch 1] in every st to end, sl st in 3rd ch of beg ch-4 to join. Fasten off yarn A.

Round 6: Join yarn B, ch 4 (counts as 1 dtr) 1 dtr in next st, 1 dtr in next ch-1 sp, 1 dtr in next st, miss 9 sts, 1 dc in each of next 2 sts, ch 9, miss 9 sts, [1 dtr in next ch-1 sp, 1 dtr in next tr] 2 times, ch 9, miss 9 sts, 1 dc in each of next 2 sts, ch 9, sl st in top of beg ch-3.

Round 7: Ch 6, miss 4 dtr, *9 dc in next ch-9 sp, 1 dc in each of the next 2 dc, 9 dc in next ch-9 sp**, ch 6, miss 4 dtr; rep from * 2 times and from * to ** 1 time, sl st in first ch of beg ch-6 to join.

Round 8: Ch 1, *1 dc in each of next 3 ch sts, ch 3, 1 dc in each of next 3 ch sts, 1 dc in each of next 20 dc; rep from * 3 times, sl st in first ch to join.

Fasten off and darn in ends.

169 **
tethered

Two rings of chain stitches are trapped between treble crochet stitches in this unusual block. Enjoyable to work, this square works equally well made in bright colours or pastels – but make sure you create the chain in a contrast colour to show off its interesting placement.

A
B

Foundation ring: Using yarn A, ch 14, sl st in first ch to form ring.

Round 1: Ch 3 (counts as 1 tr) 5 tr in ring, ch 2, [6 tr in ring, ch 2] 4 times, sl st in top of beg ch-3 to join.

Round 2: [Ch 6, miss 3 tr, 1 dc in next tr] 10 times, sl st in first ch to join. Fasten off yarn A.

Round 3: Using yarn B ch 4, 1 dc in 3rd ch of next ch-6, [ch 8, 1 dc in 3rd ch of next ch-6] 9 times, ch 4, sl st in first ch to join.

Round 4: Ch 7, 1 dc in 4th ch of next ch-8, [ch 7, 1 dc in 4th ch of next ch-8] 9 times, sl st in first ch join.

Round 5: Ch 8 (counts as 1 tr, ch 5) miss 4 ch, [1 tr in next ch, ch 5, miss 4 ch] 15 times, sl st in 3rd ch of beg ch-8 to join.

Round 6: Ch 1, 1 dc in every st to ends, sl st in first sc to join.

Round 7: Ch 1, [1 dc in each of next 6 dc, ch 7, miss 7 dc, 1 dtr in each of next 4 dc, ch 7, miss 7 dc] 4 times, sl st in first dc to join.

Round 8: Ch 1, 1 dc in each of next 12 sts (including ch), [ch 10, miss 4 sts, 1 dc in each of next 20 sts], 3 times, ch 10, miss 4 sts, 1 dc in each of 8 sts, sl st to first dc to join.

Fasten off and darn in ends.

CHAIN DECORATIONS

Using yarn A, ch 145, weave through Round 5 two times as shown, working under and over tr sts, sl st in first ch join in a lp.

Fasten off and darn in ends.

bamboo

A repeating pattern of front- and back-post stitches creates the stems of the bamboo, and spike cluster stitches form the leaves. This is a subtle pattern that benefits best from being worked in a flat, smooth yarn to add definition.

Special stitches used:

Back-post treble crochet (BPtr): Bring hook to back, work in back vertical post of next st, inserting hook from left to right, draw yarn through and work st as usual.

Front-post treble crochet (FPtr): Bring hook to front, work in front vertical post of next st, inserting hook from right to left, draw yarn through and work st as usual (*see page 21*).

Cluster spike stitch (spike cl): Instead of in next st to be worked insert hook down one row and two sts to right, draw through to height of current row (2 lps on hook), insert hook down two rows and one st to right, draw through to height of current row (3 lps on hook), insert hook directly below, down three rows, draw through to height of current row (4 lps on hook), insert hook down two rows and one st to left, draw through to height of current row (5 lps on hook), insert hook down one row and two sts to left, draw through to height of current row (6 lps on hook), insert hook in next dc on current row (st that would have been worked next if spike not worked), draw through lp (7 lps on hook), yoh and draw through all lps on hook to create cluster (*see pages 18 and 22*).

Note: Spike clusters can cover other sts on current row that need to be worked; ensure you do not miss any sts when cont to work row after completing spike cluster to avoid pattern becoming inaccurate.

Foundation chain: Ch 31 (counts as 29 ch, 2 tch).

Row 1: 1 tr in 2nd ch from hook, 1 tr in every ch along row, turn – 29 sts.

Row 2: Ch 2, [1 tr in each of next 4 tr, 1 BPtr in next tr] 5 times, 1 tr in each of last 4 tr, turn.

Row 3: Ch 2, [1 tr in each of next 4 tr, 1 FPtr in next tr] 5 times, 1 tr in each of last 4 tr, turn.

Row 4: Rep Row 2.

Row 5: Rep Row 3.

Row 6: Ch 1, 1 dc in every st to end, turn.

Row 7: Rep Row 6.

Row 8: Rep Row 6.

Row 9: Ch 1, [1 tr in each of next 4 dc, 1 spike cl] 5 times, 1 dc in each of next 4 dc, turn.

Row 10: Rep Row 1.

Row 11: Rep Row 3.

Row 12: Rep Row 6.

Row 13: Rep Row 6.

Row 14: Rep Row 6.

Row 15: Rep Row 9.

Rows 16 to 21: Rep Rows 10 to 15.

Row 22: Rep Row 1.

Row 23: Rep Row 6.

Fasten off and darn in ends neatly.

**
lichen

A B

A delicate open lace pattern that is relatively quick and easy to work up, this lends itself to table linens and window treatments for the summer. Use toning yarns for a subtle effect.

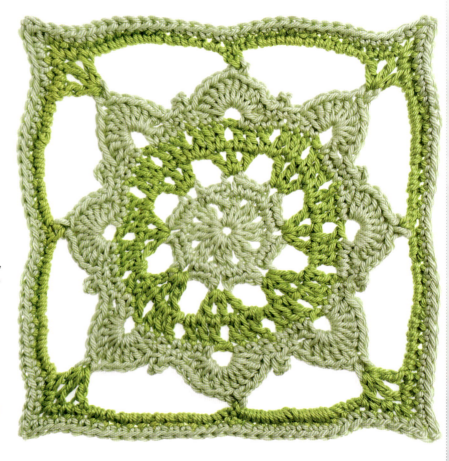

Special stitch used:

Picot-3: Ch 3 (at point to add picot), sl st in first ch of ch-3, creating picot lp.

Foundation ring: Using yarn A, ch 4, sl st in first ch to form ring.

Round 1: Ch 3 (counts as 1 tr), 1 tr in ring, ch 1, *2 tr in ring, ch 1; rep from * 6 times, sl st in 3rd ch of beg ch-3 to join.

Round 2: 1 dc in same st, ch 3, 1 dc in next st, 2 dc in next ch-1 sp, *1 dc in next st, ch 3, 1 dc in next st, 2 dc in next ch-1 sp; rep from * 6 times, sl st in first dc to join. Fasten off yarn A.

Round 3: Join yarn B in any ch-3 sp, ch 4 (counts as 1 tr, ch 1), [1 tr, ch 1, 1 tr, ch 1] in same ch-3 sp, ch 1, *[1 tr, ch 1] 3 times in next ch-3 sp, ch 1; rep from * 6 times, sl st in top of beg ch-3 to join.

Round 4: Ch 3 (counts as 1 tr), *1 tr in next ch-1 sp, ch 1, miss next st, 1 tr in next ch-1 sp, 1 tr in next st, [1 tr, ch 1, 1 tr] in next ch-2 sp, 1 tr in next st; rep from * 6 times, 1 tr in next ch-1 sp, ch 1, miss next st, 1 tr in next ch-1 sp, 1 tr in next st, [1 tr, ch 1, 1 tr] in next ch-2 sp, sl st in top of beg ch-3 to join. Fasten off yarn B.

Round 5: Join yarn A in any ch-1 sp, *1 dc in ch-1 sp, 1 dc in each of next 3 sts, ch 3, miss next ch-1 sp, 1 dc in each of next 3 sts; rep from * 7 times, sl st in first dc to join.

Round 6: *Picot-3, 1 dc in each of next 2 sts, [5 tr, picot-3, 5 tr] in next ch-3 sp, miss 2 sts, 1 dc in next st; rep from * 7 times, sl st in base of first picot-3 to join. Fasten off.

Round 7: Join yarn B in any picot-3 at top of 5 tr petals, *1 dc in picot-3, ch 10, [1 tr, ch 1, 1 tr, ch 1, 1 tr] in next picot-3 (at top of 5 tr petals), ch 10; rep from * 3 times, sl st in first dc to join.

Round 8: *1 dc in dc, 12 dc in next ch-10 sp, 1 dc in next st, 1 dc in next ch-1 sp, [1 dc, ch 2, 1 dc] in next st, 1 dc in next ch-1 sp, 1 dc in next st, 12 dc in next ch-10 sp; rep from * 3 times, sl st in first dc to join. Fasten off.

Round 9: Join yarn A in any ch-2 corner sp, [1 dc, ch 2, 1 dc] in corner sp, *1 dc in each st to next corner**, [1 dc, ch 2, 1 dc] in corner sp; rep from * 2 times and from * to ** 1 time, sl st in first dc to join.

Fasten off and darn in ends.

**
lime juice

A delightfully textured square that is fun to work as it employs an unusual side puff stitch worked over the post of stitches to make a horizontal bobble.

A

Special stitch used:

Side puff stitch (side puff): 1 tr in specified st or sp, *yoh, insert hook around post of same tr, yoh and pull through 1 lp; rep from * 2 times (7 lps on hook), yoh, pull through all lps on hook, ch 1 to close side puff stitch (*see page 19*).

Foundation chain: Ch 28.

Row 1: 1 dc in 2nd ch from hook, 1 dc in every ch to end, turn.

Row 2: Ch 1, 1 dc in every dc to end, turn.

Row 3: Ch 2, miss first dc, *1 side puff in next dc, miss 1 dc; rep from * to last st, 1 tr in last st, turn.

Row 4: Ch 1, 1 dc in every side puff st and every tr (do not work in closing ch sts), 1 dc in top of beg ch-2 to finish row.

Rows 5 to 20: Rep Rows 3 and 4 alternately.

Rows 21 to 22: Rep Row 2.

Fasten off and darn in ends neatly.

---

*
filet diamond

Best worked in a fairly sturdy yarn, this is an open-textured square that grows really quickly in a contemporary lacy pattern. Perfect for use in curtain panels or to mix with more closely textured, denser blocks in a throw.

A

Foundation chain: Ch 27.

Row 1: Ch 3 (counts as 1 dtr) 1 dtr in each of next 12 ch, ch 2, miss 2 ch, 1 dtr in each of next 13 ch to end, turn.

Row 2: Ch 3 (counts as 1 dtr), 9 dtr, ch 2, miss 2 sts, 1 dtr, ch 2, miss 2 sts, 1 dtr, ch 2, miss 2 sts, 10 dtr, turn.

Row 3: Ch 3 (counts as 1 dtr), 6 dtr, *ch 2, miss 2 sts, 1 dtr; rep from * 4 times, 6 dtr, turn.

Row 4: Ch 3 (counts as 1 dtr), 3 dtr, *ch 2, miss 2 sts, 1 dtr; rep from * 6 times, 3 dtr, turn.

Row 5: Ch 3 (counts as 1 dtr) *ch 2, miss 2 sts, 1 tr; rep from * 8 times, turn.

Row 6: Rep Row 4.

Row 7: Rep Row 3.

Row 8: Rep Row 2

Row 9: Rep Row 1.

Fasten off and darn in ends neatly.

killarney

A complex cable and post stitch block creates a knit-like appearance; it is challenging but fascinating to work. Best made in a flat, thicker yarn to emphasize the cables.

Special stitches used:

Front-post double treble (FPdtr): Yoh hook 2 times, insert hook through front of st post from right to left, yoh, draw yarn through, [yoh, draw through 2 lps] 3 times (*see page 21*).

Back-post double treble (BPdtr): Yoh 2 times, insert hook through back of st post from right to left, yoh, draw yarn through, [yoh, draw through 2 lps] 3 times.

Foundation row: Ch 28.

Row 1: 1 dc in 2nd ch from hook, 1 dc in every ch to end, turn.

Row 2: Ch 2 (counts as 1 htr), 1 htr in every dc to end of row, turn.

Row 3: Ch 2 (counts as 1 htr), 1 htr in each of next 5 htr, 1 FPdtr in next htr, 1 htr in each of next 14 htr, 1 FPdtr in next htr, 1 htr in each of next 6 htr, turn.

Row 4: Ch 2 (counts as 1 htr), 1 htr in each of next 4 htr, 1 BPdtr in next FPdtr, 1 htr in next htr, 1 BPdtr in next FPdtr, 1 htr in each of next 12 htr, 1 BPdtr in next FPdtr, 1 htr in next htr, 1 BPdtr in next FPdtr, 1 htr in each of last 5 htr, turn.

Row 5: Ch 2 (counts as 1 htr), 1 htr in each of next 3 htr, 1 FPdtr in next BPdtr, 1 htr in each of next 3 htr, 1 FPdtr in next BPdtr, 1 htr in each of next 10 htr, 1 FPdtr in next BPdtr, 1 htr in each of next 3 htr, 1 FPdtr in next BPdtr, 1 htr in each of next 4 htr, turn.

Row 6: Ch 2 (counts as 1 htr), 1 htr in each of next 2 htr, 1 BPdtr in next FPdtr, 1 htr in each of next 2 htr, ch 4, 1 htr in each of next 3 htr, 1 BPdtr in next FPdtr, 1 htr in each of next 2 htr, 1 BPdtr in each of next 4 htr, 1 htr in each of next 2 htr, 1 BPdtr in next FPdtr, 1 htr in each of next 2 htr, ch 4, 1 htr in each of next 3 htr, 1 BPdtr in next FPdtr, 1 htr in each of next 3 htr, turn.

Row 7: Ch 2 (counts as 1 htr), 1 htr in each of next 2 htr, 1 FPdtr in next BPdtr, 1 htr in each of next 2 htr, ch 4, 1 htr in each of next 3 htr, 1 FPdtr in next BPdtr, 1 htr in each of next 2 htr, 1 FPdtr in each of next 4 BPdtr, 1 htr in each of next 2 htr, 1 FPdtr in next BPdtr, 1 htr in each of next 2 htr, ch 4, 1 htr in each of next 3 htr, 1 FPdtr in last BPdtr, 1 htr in each of last 3 htr, turn.

Row 8: Ch 2 (counts as 1 htr), 1 htr in each of next 2 htr, 1 BPdtr in next FPdtr, 1 htr in each of next 3 htr, ch 4, 1 htr in each of next 2 htr, 1 BPdtr in next FPdtr, 1 htr in each of next 2 htr, miss 2 FPdtr, 1 BPdtr in each of next 2 FPdtr, 1 FPdtr in each of 2 miss FPdtr, 1 htr in each of next 2 htr, 1 BPdtr in next FPdtr, 1 htr in each of next 3 htr, ch 4, 1 htr in each of next 2 htr, 1 BPdtr in next FPdtr, 1 htr in each of last 3 htr, turn.

Row 9: Ch 2 (counts as 1 htr), 1 htr in each of next 3 htr, 1 FPdtr in next BPdtr, 1 htr in each of next 3 htr, 1 FPdtr in next BPdtr, 1 htr in each of next 3 htr, 1 FPdtr in each of next 4 FP/BPdtr, 1 htr in each of next 3 htr, 1 FPdtr in next BPdtr, 1 htr in each of next 3 htr, 1 FPdtr in next BPdtr, 1 htr in each of next 4 htr, turn.

Row 10: Ch 2 (counts as 1 htr), 1 htr in each of next 4 htr, 1 BPdtr in next FPdtr, 1 htr in next hdtr, 1 BPdtr in next FPdtr, 1 htr in each of next 4 htr, 1 BPdtr in each of next 4 FPdtr, 1 htr in each of next 4 htr, 1 BPdtr in next FPdtr, 1 htr in next htr, 1 BPdtr in next FPdtr, 1 htr in each of next 5 htr, turn.

Row 11: Ch 2 (counts as 1 htr), 1 htr in each of next 5 htr, miss [1 BPdtr, 1 htr], 1 FPdtr in next BPdtr, 1 htr in each of next 5 sts, miss 2 BPdtr, 1 FPdtr in each of next 2 BPdtr, 1 BPdtr in each of 2 miss BPdtr, 1 htr in each of next 5 htr, miss [1 BPdtr, 1 htr], 1 FPdtr next BPdtr, 1 htr in each of last 6 sts.

Row 12: Rep Row 10.

Row 13: Rep Row 9.

Row 14: Rep Row 8.

Row 15: Rep Row 7.

Row 16: Rep Row 6.

Row 17: Rep Row 5.

Row 18: Rep Row 4.

Row 19: Ch 2 (counts as 1 htr), 1 htr in each of next 4 htr, miss [1 BPdtr, 1 htr], 1 FPdtr in next BPdtr, 1 FPdtr in miss BPdtr (work over last FPdtr), 1 htr in each of next 13 htr, miss [1 BPdtr, 1 htr], 1 FPdtr in next BPdtr, 1 FPdtr in miss BPdtr (over last FPdtr), 1 htr in each of last 6 htr, turn.

Row 20: ch 2 (counts as 1 htr), 1 htr in every st to end.

Fasten off and darn in ends.

bobble cross

Working bobbles on alternate rows gives this square a defined pattern. Repeating this square to make a throw or blanket would be effective as it would create a pattern of bobble crosses and squares. Lighter colours of yarn show off the texture best.

A

Special stitch used:

Make bobble (MB): Make bobble with 5 tr (*see page 19*).

Foundation chain: Ch 30 (counts as 29 ch, 1 tch).

Row 1: 1 dc in 2nd ch from hook, 1 dc in every ch along row, turn – 29 sts.

Row 2: Ch 1, 1 dc in next 13 dc, MB in next dc, 1 dc in next dc, MB in next dc, 1 dc in each of rem 13 dc of row, turn.

Row 3 and every alt row: Ch 1, 1 dc in every dc along row, turn.

Row 4: Rep Row 2.

Row 6: Rep Row 2.

Row 8: Rep Row 2.

Row 10: Rep Row 2.

Row 12: Rep Row 2.

Row 14: Rep Row 2.

Row 16: Ch 1, 1 dc in next dc, [MB in next dc, 1 dc in next dc] 6 times, 1 dc in next 4 dc, [MB in next dc, 1 dc in next dc] 6 times, turn.

Row 18: Rep Row 16.

Row 20: Rep Row 2.

Row 22: Rep Row 2.

Row 24: Rep Row 2.

Row 26: Rep Row 2.

Row 28: Rep Row 2.

Row 30: Rep Row 2.

Row 32: Rep Row 2.

Row 33: Rep Row 3, omitting last turn.

Fasten off and darn in ends neatly.

parsley

A linear square, this has a textural motif in the centre created using chain loops. This is a simple way to add interest to a plain one-colour square, and it feels irresistible to play with.

A

Foundation chain: Ch 32.

Row 1: 1 dc in 2nd ch from hook and in every ch to end, turn.

Row 2: Ch 1 (counts as 1 dc), 1 dc in every dc to end, turn.

Rows 3 to 12: Rep Row 2.

Row 13: Ch 1 (counts as 1 dc), 1 dc in each of next 14 dc, 1 dc in back lp of next dc, *ch 10, 1 dc in back lp of next dc; rep from * 1 time, 1 dc in each of next 14 dc, turn.

Row 14: Ch1 (counts as 1 dc), 1 dc in every dc to end, working in back (empty) lp of each dc at base of ch-10 lps, turn.

Row 15: Ch1 (counts as 1 dc), 1 dc in each of next 13 dc, 1 dc in back lp of next dc, *ch 10, 1 dc in back lp of next dc; rep from * 3 times, 1 dc in each of next 13 dc, turn.

Row 16: Rep Row 14.

Row 17: Ch 1 (counts as 1 dc), 1 dc in each of next 11 dc, 1 dc in back lp of next dc, *ch 10, 1 dc in back lp of next dc; rep from * 7 times, 1 dc in each of next 11 dc, turn.

Row 18: Rep Row 14.

Row 19: Ch 1 (counts as 1 dc), 1 dc in each of next 9 dc, 1 dc in back lp of next dc, *ch 10, 1 dc in back lp of next dc; rep from * 9 times, 1 dc in each of next 9 dc, turn.

Rows 20, 22, 24 and 26: Rep Row 14.

Row 21: Rep Row 17.

Row 23: Rep Row 15.

Row 25: Rep Row 13.

Rows 27 to 37: Rep Row 2.

Fasten off and darn in ends.

177

*

puzzle

A great beginner square that plays with positioning of motifs to create a bold geometric pattern. Take care to insert the hook into the chain stitches when directed, not into the chain loops; this is the only fiddly part of this square.

A
B
C
D
E

Foundation ring: Using yarn A, make a magic ring.

Round 1: Ch 4 (counts as 1 dtr), [3 tr, 1 dtr] 3 times in ring, 3 tr, sl st in top of beg ch-4 to join. Fasten off yarn A.

Round 2: Join yarn B in any dtr st, *ch 7, sl st in next dtr; rep from * 3 times.

Round 3: Ch 3 (counts as 1 tr), *1 tr in each of next 3 ch sts (not ch-7 lp, in each ch st), [2 tr, ch 3, 2 tr] in next ch, 1 tr in each of next 3 ch, **1 tr in next sl st; rep from * 2 times and from * to ** 1 time, sl st in top of beg ch-3 to join. Fasten off yarn B.

Round 4: Join yarn C in 2nd ch of any ch-3 corner sp, *ch 5, miss 5 sts, 1 tr in next tr (above corner of Round 1), ch 5, miss 5 sts, **sl st in 2nd ch of next ch-3 corner group; rep from * 2 times and from * to ** 1 time, sl st in first sl st to join.

Round 5: Ch 3, *1 tr in each of next 5 ch sts, [2 tr, ch 3, 2 tr] in next tr, (corner), 1 tr in each of next 5 ch sts**, 1 tr in next sl st; rep from * 2 times and from * to ** 1 time, sl st in top of beg ch-3 to join. Fasten off yarn C.

Round 6: Join yarn D in 2nd ch of any corner ch-3 sp, *ch 8, miss 8 sts, 1 dtr in next tr (above corner of Round 2), ch 8, miss 8 sts**, sl st in 2nd ch of next ch-3 corner group; rep from * 2 times and from * to ** 1 time, sl st in first sl st to join.

Round 7: Ch 3 (counts as 1 tr), *1 tr in each of next 8 ch sts, [2 tr, ch 3, 2 tr] in next dtr, 1 tr in each of next 8 ch sts**, 1 tr in next sl st; rep from * 2 times and from * to ** 1 time, sl st in top of beg ch-3 to join. Fasten off yarn D.

Round 8: Join yarn E in any corner ch-3 sp, ch 1, *[2 dc, ch 1, 2 dc] in same sp, 1 dc in every st along to next corner ch-3 sp; rep from * 3 times, sl st in first dc to join. Fasten off.

Round 9: Join yarn D in any corner ch-3 sp, rep Round 8.

Fasten off and darn in ends neatly.

178

*

greenwood

An update on a classic doily pattern, this block is composed of simple stitches that combine to produce a lightweight lace pattern. A great beginner block for those ready to progress beyond the granny.

A
B
C
D

Special stitches used:

2-treble-crochet cluster (2-tr cl): Make cluster with 2 tr in same st or sp (see page 18).

3-treble-crochet cluster (3-tr cl): Make cluster with 3 tr in same st or sp.

Foundation ring: Using yarn A, ch 4, sl st in first ch to form ring.

Round 1: Ch 4 (counts as 1 tr, ch 1), *1 tr in ring, ch 1; rep from * 10 times, sl st in 3rd of beg ch-4 to join. Fasten off yarn A.

Round 2: Join yarn B, ch 3 (counts as 1 tr), 2-tr cl in same sp (counts as 3-tr cl), *ch 3, 3-tr cl in next ch-2 sp; rep from * 10 times, ch 3, sl st in top of beg ch-3 to join. Fasten off yarn B.

Round 3: Join yarn C in next ch-3 sp, ch 1, 1 dc in same sp, *ch 5, 1 dc in next ch-3 sp; rep from * 10 times, ch 2, 1 tr in first dc to join. Fasten off yarn C.

Round 4: Join yarn D in any ch-5 sp, ch 1, 1 dc in same sp, *ch 5, 1 dc in next ch-5 sp, ch 1, [5 tr, ch 3, 5 tr] in next ch-5 sp, ch 1**, 1 dc in next ch-5 sp; rep from * 2 times and from * to ** 1 time, sl st in first dc to join. Fasten off yarn D.

Round 5: Join yarn A in any corner ch-3 sp, ch 3 (counts as 1 tr), [2-tr cl, ch 3, 3-tr cl] in same sp (forms corner), *miss 2 sts, ch 2, 1 dc in next st, miss 2 sts, ch 4, 1 dc in next ch-1 sp, ch 6, 1 dc in next ch-1 sp, ch 4, miss 2 sts, 1 dc in next st, ch 2**, [3-tr cl, ch 3, 3-tr cl] in next ch-3 corner sp; rep from * 2 times and from * to ** 1 time, sl st in top of beg ch-3 to join. Fasten off yarn A.

Round 6: Join yarn B in any ch-3 corner sp, ch 2 (counts as 1 htr), [2 htr, ch 3, 3 htr] in same sp, *ch 1, 1 dc in next ch-2 sp, ch 2, 1 dc in next ch-4 sp, ch 3, 1 dc in next ch-6 sp, ch 3, 1 dc in next ch-4 sp, ch 2, 1 dc in next ch-2 sp, ch 1, **[3 htr, ch 3, 3 htr] in next ch-3 corner sp; rep from * 2 times and from * to ** 1 time, sl st in top of beg ch-2 to join.

Round 7: Ch 1, sl st to next corner sp, *5 dc in next ch-3 corner sp, 1 dc in each of next 3 htr, 1 dc in next ch-1 sp, 1 dc in next dc, [3 dc in next ch-3 sp, 1 dc in next dc] 2 times, 2 dc in next ch-2 sp, 1 dc in next dc, 1 dc in each of next 3 htr; rep from * 3 times, sl st in first dc to join.

Fasten off and darn in ends neatly.

★★★
lily of the valley

This delicate block has a central raised circle of popcorn 'bells' atop a bed of leaves, making it an ideal block for use in a lightweight blanket. It would be stunning repeated on a bedspread for a fresh spring theme.

A
B
C
D

Special stitches used:

Beginning popcorn (beg pc): Ch 3, make popcorn with 6 tr (*see page 19*)

Popcorn (pc): Make popcorn with 7 tr.

4-treble crochet cluster (4-tr cl): Make cluster with 4 tr (*see page 18*)

2-half-treble crochet cluster (2-htr cl): Make cluster with 2 htr (*see page 18*)

Foundation ring: Using yarn A, ch 4, sl st in first ch to form ring.

Round 1: Ch 1, 12 dc in ring, sl st in first dc to join.

Round 2: Ch 5 (counts as 1 tr, ch 2), [1 tr in next dc, ch 2] 11 times to end, sl st in 3rd ch of beg ch-5 to join. Fasten off yarn A.

Round 3: Join yarn B in any tr, 1 dc in same st, *ch 3, 1 dc in next tr; rep from * to end, sl st in first dc to join. Fasten off yarn B.

Round 4: Join yarn A, beg pc in next ch-3 sp, *ch 3, pc in next ch-3 sp; rep from * to end, sl st in top of beg ch-3 to join. Fasten off yarn A.

Round 5: Join yarn C in any ch-3 sp, ch 3 (counts as 1 tr), [2 tr, 1 dtr, ch 2, 1 dtr, 3 tr] in same ch-3 sp, *1 dc in next ch-3 sp, sl st in next ch-3 sp, [3 tr, 1 dtr, ch 2, 1 dtr, 3 tr] in same ch-3 sp; rep from * 4 times, 1 dc in last ch-3 sp, sl st in top of beg ch-3 to join. Fasten off yarn C.

Round 6: Join yarn B in any ch-2 sp between leaves, *1 dc in same sp, ch 4, 1 ttr in next ch-3 sp of Round 4 below, working over the dc of Round 5, ch 4, 1 dc in next ch-2 sp; rep from * 4 times, ch 4, 1 ttr in next ch-3 sp of Round 4 below, ch 4, sl st in first dc to join. Fasten off yarn B.

Round 7: Join yarn A in any dc st, ch 5 (counts as 1 htr, ch 3), *1 htr in ch-4 sp, ch 3, 1 htr in next ttr, ch 3, 1 htr in next ch-4 sp, 1 htr in next dc; rep from * 5 times omitting last htr on last rep, sl st in 2nd ch of beg ch-5 to join. Fasten off yarn A.

Round 8: Join yarn D in any ch-3 sp, ch 2 (counts as 1 htr), [1 htr, ch 2, 1 2-htr cl] in same ch-3 sp, [2-htr cl, ch 2, 2-htr cl] in next ch-3 sp] 3 times, *[4-tr cl, ch 2, 4-tr cl] in next ch-3 sp, (forms corner)**, [2-htr cl, ch 2, 2-htr cl] in next ch-3 sp] 5 times; rep from * 2 times and from * to ** 1 time, [2-htr cl, ch 2, 2-htr cl] in last ch-3 sp, sl st in top of beg ch-2 to join. Fasten off yarn D.

Round 9: Join yarn B in any corner ch-2 sp, *3 dc in corner ch-2 sp, 1 dc in next tr4tog, 1 dc between next tr4tog and 2-htr cl, [1 dc in next 2-htr cl, 1 dc in next ch-2 sp, 1 dc in next 2-htr cl, 1 dc in sp between sts] 4 times, 1 dc in next tr4tog; rep from * 3 times, sl st in first dc to join.

Fasten off and darn in ends.

*

ripple

A classic pattern composed of stitches of varying heights that combine to create a rippled effect, this block is easy to make and would be effective used in a winter blanket, throw or afghan.

A

B

Foundation: Using yarn A, Ch 34.

Row 1: 1 dc in 2nd ch from hook and in every ch to end, turn.

Row 2: Ch 1, 1 dc in each dc to end of row. Fasten off, turn.

Row 3: Join yarn B, ch 4 (counts as 1 dtr), 1 dtr in next st, ch 1, miss 1 st, 1 tr in next st, ch 1, miss 1 st, 1 htr in next st, ch 1, miss 1 st, [1 dc in next st, ch 1, miss 1 st] 2 times, 1 htr in next st, ch 1, miss 1 st, 1 tr in next st, ch 1, miss 1 st, [1 dtr in next st, ch 1, miss 1 st] 2 times, 1 tr in next st, ch 1, miss 1 st, 1 htr in next st, ch 1, miss 1 st, [1 dc in next st, ch 1, miss 1 st] 2 times, 1 htr in next st, ch 1, miss 1 st, 1 tr in next st, ch 1, miss 1 st, 1 dtr in each of next 2 sts, turn.

Row 4: Ch 4 (counts as 1 dtr), 1 dtr in next st, ch 1, miss next ch-1 sp, 1 tr in next st, ch 1, miss next ch-1 sp, 1 htr in next st, ch 1, miss next ch-1 sp, [1 dc in next st, ch 1, miss next ch-1 sp] 2 times, 1 htr in next st, ch 1, miss next ch-1 sp, 1 tr in next st, ch 1, miss next ch-1 sp, [1 dtr in next st, ch 1, miss next ch-1 sp] 2 times, 1 tr in next st, ch 1, miss next ch-1 sp, 1 htr in next st, ch 1, miss next ch-1 sp, [1 dc in next st, ch 1, miss next ch-1 sp] 2 times, 1 htr in next st, ch 1, miss next ch-1 sp, 1 tr in next st, ch 1, miss next ch-1 sp, 1 dtr in each of next 2 sts. Fasten off yarn B, turn.

Row 5: Join yarn A, 1 dc in each st and each ch-1 sp to end, turn.

Row 6: Ch 1, 1 dc in each st to end. Fasten off yarn A, turn.

Row 7: Join yarn B in last st, ch 1, 1 dc in each of next 2 sts, ch 1, miss 1 st, 1 htr in next st, ch 1, miss 1 st, 1 tr in next st, ch 1, miss 1 st, [1 dtr in next st, ch 1, miss 1 st] 2 times, 1 tr in next st, ch 1, miss 1 st, 1 htr in next st, ch 1, miss 1 st, [1 dc in next st, ch 1, miss 1 st] 2 times, 1 htr in next st, ch 1, miss 1 st, 1 tr in next st, ch 1, miss 1 st, [1 dtr in next st, ch 1, miss 1 st] 2 times, 1 tr in next st, ch 1, miss 1 st, 1 htr in next st, ch 1, miss 1 st, 1 dc in each of next 2 sts, turn.

Row 8: Ch 1, 1 dc in each of next 2 sts, ch 1, miss next ch-1 sp, 1 htr in next st, ch 1, miss next ch-1 sp, 1 tr in next st, ch 1, miss next ch-1 sp, [1 dtr in next st, ch 1, miss next ch-1 sp] 2 times, 1 tr in next st, ch 1, miss next ch-1 sp, 1 htr in next st, ch 1, miss next ch-1 sp, [1 dc in next st, ch 1, miss next ch-1 sp] 2 times, 1 trc in next st, ch 1, miss next ch-1 sp, 1 tr in next st, ch 1, miss next ch-1 sp, [1 dtr in next st, ch 1, miss next ch-1 sp] 2 times, 1 tr in next st, ch 1, miss next ch-1 sp, 1 htr in next st, ch 1, miss next ch-1 sp, 1 dc in next 2 sts. Fasten off yarn B, turn.

Row 9: Join yarn A, 1 dc in each st and each ch-1 sp to end, turn.

Row 10: Ch 1, 1 dc in each dc to end of row. Fasten off yarn A, turn.

Repeat Rows 3 to 10 one time and then Rows 3 to 6 one time after that. Do not fasten off, but continue around square working 3 dc in each corner st, and 32 sc along each side, 2 times around.

Fasten off and darn in ends.

*
vivid

This simple block demonstrates how easy it is to produce a show-stopping piece by using colour effectively. Redolent of the deep ocean floor, this is a perfect block to create a dazzling bedspread or pillow cover in no time.

A
B
C
D
E
F

Foundation ring: Using yarn A, begin with magic ring method, 12 tr in ring. Fasten off yarn A.

Round 1: Join yarn B in any tr, [ch 3, 4 tr] in same st, *1 tr in each of next 2 tr, 5 tr in foll tr; rep from * 2 time, 1 tr in each of final 2 tr, sl st in ch-3 to join. Fasten off yarn B.

Round 2: Join yarn C in any centre tr of 5-tr corner group, [ch 3, 4 tr] in same st, *1 tr in every st to next centre st of 5-tr corner, 5 tr in centre st of 5-tr corner; rep from * 2 times, 1 tr in each rem st, sl st in ch-3 to join. Fasten off yarn C.

Round 3: Join yarn D in any centre tr of 5-tr corner group, [ch 3, 4 tr] in same st, *1 tr in every st to next centre st of 5-tr corner, 5 tr in centre st of 5-tr corner; rep from * 2 times, 1 tr in each rem tr, sl st in ch-3 to join. Fasten off yarn D.

Round 4: Join yarn A in any centre tr of 5-tr corner group, [ch 3, 4 tr] in same st, *1 tr in every st to next centre st of 5-tr corner, 5 tr in centre st of 5-tr corner; rep from * 2 times, 1 tr in each rem tr, sl st in ch-3 to join. Fasten off yarn A.

Round 5: Join yarn E in any centre tr of 5-tr corner group, [ch 3, 4 tr] in same st, *1 tr in every st to next centre st of 5-tr corner, 5 tr in centre st of 5-tr corner; rep from * 2 times, 1 tr in each rem tr, sl st in ch-3 to join. Fasten off yarn E.

Round 6: Join yarn F in any centre tr of 5-tr corner group, [ch 3, 4 tr] in same st, *1 tr in every st to next centre st of 5-tr corner, 5 tr in centre st of 5-tr corner; rep from * 2 times then 1 tr in each rem tr, sl st in ch-3 to join.

Fasten off and darn all ends in neatly.

**
mojito

A sister block to the Tequila Sunrise block in the red/orange section, this uses spike stitches on alternate rows to create a subtle texture. Useful to combine with more highly patterned blocks, this works best in a flat, shiny or matt yarn to highlight its spiky texture.

A

Special stitch used:

Spike stitch (spike): Insert hook in top of st 1 row below next st to be worked, yoh, pull yarn through to height of rnd being worked, complete specified st as normal (see page 22).

Foundation chain: Ch 29.

Row 1: 1 dc in 2nd ch from hook, 1 dc in every ch to end, turn.

Row 2: Ch 1, 1 dc in every dc to end, turn.

Row 3: Ch 1, 1 dc in first dc, *1 dc spike in row below next dc, 1 dc in next dc; rep from * to end, ending 1 dc in last dc, turn.

Row 4: Rep Row 2.

Row 5: Rep Row 3.

Row 6: Rep Row 2.

Row 7: Ch 1, 1 dc in first 2 dc, *1 dc in next dc, 1 dc spike in row below next dc; rep from * to end, turn.

Row 8: Rep Row 2.

Row 9: Rep Row 7.

Rows 10 to 36: Rep rows in sequence as foll: Row 2, Row 3, Row 2, Row 3, Row 2, Row 7, Row 2, Row 7.

Fasten off, darn in ends and block if necessary.

183 **

crosspatch

An unusual combination of intarsia solid colours and filet, this modern mesh square would lend itself to being used in contemporary window treatments, table linens or in any type of throw or blanket.

A
B
C

Foundation chain: Using yarn A, ch 10, change to yarn B, ch 21.

Row 1: Ch 3 (counts as 1 tr, ch 1) miss 1 ch, 1 tr in next ch, [ch 1, miss 1 ch, 1 tr in next ch] 7 times, ch 1, miss 1 ch, 1 tr in each of next 3 ch, change to yarn A, 1 tr in each of next 10 ch, turn.

Row 2: Ch 3 (counts as 1 tr), 1 tr in each of next 9 tr, change to yarn B, 1 tr in each of next 3 tr, [ch 1, miss 1 ch, 1 tr in next tr] 9 times, turn.

Row 3: Rep Row 1.

Row 4: Rep Row 2.

Row 5: Rep Row 1, fasten off yarn A.

Row 6: Join yarn C, ch 3 (counts as 1 tr), 1 tr in each of next 9 tr, change to yarn B, 1 tr in each of next 3 tr, [ch 1, miss 1 ch, 1 tr in next tr] 9 times, turn.

Row 7: Ch 4 (counts as 1 tr, ch 1), miss 1 ch, 1 tr in next tr, [ch 1, miss 1 ch, 1 tr in next tr] 7 times, ch 1, 1 tr in each of next 3 tr, change to yarn C, [ch 1, miss 1 ch, 1 tr in next tr] 5 times, turn.

Row 8: Ch 4 (counts as 1 tr, ch 1), miss 1 ch, 1 tr in next dc, [ch 1, miss 1 ch, 1 tr in next tr] 3 times, change to yarn B, ch 1, 1 tr in each of next 3 tr, [ch 1, miss 1 ch, 1 tr in next tr] 9 times, turn.

Row 9: Rep Row 7.

Row 10: Ch 4 (counts as 1 tr, ch 1), miss 1 ch, 1 tr in next tr, [ch 1, miss 1 ch, 1 tr in next tr] 3 times, change to yarn B, ch 1, 1 tr in each of next 21 tr, fasten off yarn B, turn.

Row 11: Join yarn A, ch 3 (counts as 1 tr) 1 tr in each of last 9 tr, change to yarn C, 1 tr in each of next 3 tr, [ch 1, miss 1 ch, 1 tr in next tr] 9 times, turn.

Row 12: Ch 4 (counts as 1 tr, ch 1) miss 1 tr, 1 tr in next tr, [ch 1, miss 1 ch, 1 tr in next tr] 8 times, 1 tr in each of next 2 tr, change to yarn A, 1 tr in each of next 10 tr, turn.

Row 13: Rep Row 11.

Row 14: Rep Row 12.

Row 15: Rep Row 11.

Fasten off and darn in ends.

184 **

dandelion

A frilly centre is achieved through the use of picot loops in this cheery block. Quick to work up, this bold design would work well on a child's blanket, mixed with other bright flowers or grannies.

A
B
C
D

Special stitch used:

Picot-4: Ch 4 (at point to add picot), sl st in first ch of ch-4, creating picot lp.

Foundation ring: Using yarn A, make a magic ring.

Round 1: Ch 2 (counts as 1 htr), 11 htr in ring, sl st in top of beg ch-2 to join.

Round 2: Ch 2 (counts as 1 htr), 1 htr in next htr, 2 htr in each rem htr around, join with sl st in top of front lp only of beg ch-2.

Round 3: *Ch 4, sl st in 4th ch from hook (picot-4 formed), sl st in front lp only of next htr; rep from * around, ending with sl st in back lp of last st of Round 2.

Round 4: Bending picots over so you can access back lps of Round 2, *ch 8, sl st in back lp of next htr from Round 2; rep from * around, ending with sl st in first st – 24 ch-8 lps made. Fasten off yarn A.

Round 5: Join yarn B in 5th ch of any ch-8 lp, 1 dc in same st, *ch 2, 1 dc in 5th ch of next ch-8 lp; rep from * 22 times, ch 2, sl st in first dc to join.

Round 6: Ch 1, [2 dc in next ch-2 sp, ch 1] all around motif, sl st in beg ch-1 to join. Fasten off yarn B.

Round 7: Join yarn C, ch 2 (counts as 1 htr), *[1 tr, 1 dtr] in next dc, miss 1 dc, ch 3, [1 dtr, 1 tr] in next dc (first corner), 1 htr in next dc, [ch 1, miss 1 dc, 1 dc in next st] 6 times**, 1 htr in next dc; rep from * around, ending last rep at **, sl st in top of beg ch-2 to join.

Round 8: Ch 3 (counts as 1 tr), 1 tr in every st and every ch-1 sp around and [3 tr, ch 2, 3 tr] in each corner ch-3 sp, sl st in top of beg ch-3 to join. Fasten off yarn C.

Round 9: Join yarn D, ch 2 (counts as 1 htr), 1 htr in next st and every st around and 3 htr in every corner ch-2 sp.

Fasten off and darn in ends neatly.

*

full moon

Worked up in bright analogous shades of yarn, this bold, simple block resembles the moon surrounded by a foggy halo. A good beginner square and easy to mix.

A
B
C

Foundation ring: Using yarn A, ch 5, join with sl st to form ring.

Round 1: Ch 3 (counts as 1 tr), 11 tr in ring, sl st in top of ch-2 to join – 12 sts.

Round 2: Ch 3 (counts as 1 tr), *2 tr in next st; rep from * to end of rnd ending 1 tr in first st, sl st in top of ch-3 to join – 24 sts.

Round 3: Ch 3 (counts as 1 tr), *2 tr in next st, 1 tr in next st; rep from * to end of rnd, sl st in top of ch-3 to join – 36 sts. Finish off yarn A.

Round 4: Join yarn B, ch 3 (counts as 1 tr), 1 tr in each of next 8 tr, ch 3, *1 tr in each of next 9 tr, ch 3; rep from * 2 times, sl st in top of beg ch-3 to join.

Round 5: Ch 3 (counts as 1 tr), 1 tr in each of next 8 tr, [1 tr, ch 4, 1 tr] in ch-3 sp, *1 tr in next 9 tr, [1 tr, ch 4, 1 tr] in ch-3 sp; rep from * 2 times, sl st in top of beg ch-3 to join. Fasten off yarn B.

Round 6: Join yarn C, ch 3 (counts as 1 tr), 1 tr in each of next 9 tr, [1 tr, ch 5, 1 tr] in ch-3 sp, *1 tr in each of next 11 tr, [1 tr, ch 5, 1 tr] in ch-3 sp; rep from * 2 times, 1 tr in final tr, sl st in top of beg ch-3 to join.

Round 7: Ch 3 (counts as 1 tr), 1 tr in each of next 10 tr, [1 tr, ch 5, 1 tr] in ch-3 sp, *1 tr in each of next 13 tr, [1 tr, ch 5, 1 tr] in ch-3 sp; rep from * 2 times, 1 tr in final 2 tr, sl st in top of beg ch-3 to join.

Fasten off and darn in ends neatly.

**

rio

As cheerful as the Brazilian sunshine, this block combines bright colours and bullion stitch to fantastic textural effect. The regular pattern is easy to master and this square works well with plainer squares as well as graphic blocks and grannies.

A
B
C
D
E
F

Special stitch used:

Bullion stitch (bullion): Yoh 10 times, insert hook in st or sp to be worked, yoh, draw loop through to front, yoh, pull through all loops on hook, ch 1 to secure (*see page 20*).

Foundation chain: Using yarn A, ch 26.

Row 1: 1 dc in 2nd ch from hook, 1 dc in every ch to end – 25 sts. Fasten off.

Row 2: Join yarn B, ch 2, 1 st in first dc, *1 bullion in next dc, miss 1 dc, 1 tr in next dc; rep from * 7 times, turn. Fasten off yarn B.

Row 3: Join yarn C, ch 2, 1 tr in first tr, *1 bullion in next tr, miss 1 tr, 1 tr in next tr; rep from * 7 times, turn. Fasten off yarn C.

Row 4: Rep Row 3, using yarn D.

Rows 5 to 6: Rep Row 3, using yarn E.

Rows 7 to 8: Rep Row 3, using yarn A.

Rows 9 to 10: Rep Row 3, using yarn B.

Row 11: Rep Row 3, using yarn C.

BORDER

Round 1: Join yarn F in any corner sp, *[2 dc, ch 2, 2 dc] in corner sp, 1 dc in every dc to next corner, [2 dc, ch 2, 2 dc] in corner sp, work 25 dc evenly along side of square to corner; rep from * 1 time, sl st in first dc to join.

Round 2: Ch 2 (counts as 1 htr), [1 htr, ch 2, 2 htr] in corner ch-2 sp, ch 1, [miss 1 dc, 1 htr in next dc, ch 1] to next corner ch-2 sp, [2 htr, ch 2, 2 htr] in corner ch-2 sp; rep from * 2 times and from * to ** 1 time, sl st in top of beg ch-2 to join.

Fasten off and darn in ends neatly.

★★★★

spring basket

A posy of rosebud stitches forms the theme of this block, which is also full of back-post stitches, giving it a layered appearance. This is a firm block, so mix with other lighter blocks or use in repeat for stunning table linens.

A
B
C
D

BUDS

Special stitch used:

Back-post treble crochet (BPtr): Bring hook to back, work in back vertical post of next st, inserting hook from left to right, draw yarn through and work st as usual (see page 21).

Foundation ring: Using yarn A, ch 6, sl st in first ch to form ring.

Round 1: Ch 1 (counts as 1 dc), 15 dc in ring. Fasten off.

Round 2: Working each bud using a different colour, join new colour, *ch 5, 1 dc in 2nd ch from hook, 5 htr in each of next 3 ch, sl st in beg of ch, sl st in next 2 dc at base, fasten off and change to next bud colour; rep from * 7 times, sl st in first ch at base to join. Fasten off.

Round 3: Turn work to WS, join yarn B in last htr of first bud, 1 dc in same st, *ch 4, sl st in last htr of next bud; rep from * 7 times, sl st in first ch of beg ch-3 to join.

Round 4: Turn work to RS, sl st in next ch-4 sp, ch 3 (counts as 1 tr), 3 tr in same sp, *4 tr in next ch-4 sp; rep from * 6 times, sl st in top of beg ch-3 to join. Fasten off yarn B.

Round 5: Turn work to WS, join yarn B between any 4-tr group from Round 4 and sl st from Round 3, ch 3 (counts as 1 tr), [1 tr, ch 4, 2 tr] in same sp (forms corner), ch 2, 2 tr in next sp between next 4 tr from Round 4 and sl st from Round 3, 2 tr between next sl st and 4-tr group, ch 2, *[2 tr, ch 4, 2 tr] in next sp between sl st and 4 tr group (forms corner), ch 2, 2 tr in next sp between 4-tr group and sl st, 2 tr in next sp between sl st and 4-tr group, ch 2; rep from * 2 times, sl st in top of beg ch-3 to join. Fasten off yarn B.

Round 6: Turn work to RS, join yarn C in any ch-4 corner sp, ch 3 (counts as 1 tr), [1 tr, ch 3, 2 tr] in same sp (forms corner), 1 BPtr in each of next 2 tr, 2 tr in next ch-2 sp, 1 BPtr in each of next 4 tr, 2 tr in next ch-2 sp, 1 BPtr in each of next 2 tr, *[2 tr, ch 3, 2 tr] in next sp (forms corner), 1 BPtr in each of next 2 tr, 2 tr in next ch-2 sp, 1 BPtr in each of next 4 tr, 2 tr in next ch-2 sp, 1 BPtr in each of next 2 tr; rep from * 2 times, sl st in top of beg ch-3 to join. Fasten off yarn C.

Round 7: Join yarn D join in any ch-3 corner sp, ch 3 (counts as 1 tr), [1 tr, ch 3, 2 tr] in same sp (forms corner), 1 BPtr in each of next 16 sts, *[2 tr, ch 3, 2 tr] in next ch-3 sp (forms corner), 1 BPtr in each of next 16 sts; rep from * 2 times, sl st in top of beg ch-3 to join. Fasten off yarn D.

Round 8: Join yarn B in any ch-3 corner sp, ch 3 (counts as 1 tr), [1 tr, ch 3, 2 tr] in same sp (forms corner), 1 BPtr in each of next 20 sts, *[2 tr, ch 3, 2 tr] in next ch-3 sp (forms corner), 1 BPtr in each of next 20 sts; rep from * 2 times, sl st in top of beg ch-3 to join.

Round 9: Sl st in next ch-3 corner sp, ch 1 (counts as 1 dc), [1 dc, ch 2, 2 dc] in same sp (forms corner), 1 dc in each of next 24 sts, *[2 dc, ch 2, 2 dc] in next ch-3 sp (forms corner), 1 dc in each of next 24 sts; rep from * 2 times, sl st in beg ch-1 to join.

Round 10: Sl st in next ch-2 corner sp, ch 1 (counts as 1 dc), [1 dc, ch 2, 2 dc] in same sp (forms corner), 1 dc in each of next 28 sts, *[2 dc, ch 2, 2 dc] in next ch-2 sp (forms corner), 1 dc in each of next 28 sts; rep from * 2 times, sl st in beg ch-1 to join.

Fasten off and darn in all ends.

**

curly kale

Inspired by the tasty leafy vegetable, this block has 3D appeal with its tufts and curls, created by relatively simple methods. A tactile square, it would work well for children's pillows or blankets – the curls cannot become detached.

Special stitches used:

Half-treble 3 stitches together (htr3tog): 3 htr, leaving last lp of each on hook, yoh and draw through all lps.

Back-post treble crochet (BPtr): 1 tr worked in the back post of the stitch (*see page 21*).

Foundation ring: Using yarn A, ch 4, sl st in first dc to form ring.

Round 1: Ch 6 (counts as 1 dtr, ch 2), [1 dtr, ch 4] 7 times in ring, sl st in 4th ch of beg ch-6 to join. Fasten off yarn A.

Round 2: Join yarn B in any ch-2 sp, ch 3, (counts as 1 tr), 2 tr in same ch-2 sp, 1 tr in next dtr, [3 tr in next ch-2 sp, 1 tr in next dtr] 7 times, sl st in top of beg ch-3 to join.

Round 3: Ch 1, 1 dc in same st, 1 dc in each of next 2 tr, *1 htr in each of next 2 tr, 5 tr in next tr, 1 htr in each of next 2 tr**, 1 dc in each of next 3 tr; rep from *2 times and from * to ** 1 time, sl st in first dc to join. Fasten off yarn B.

Round 4: Join yarn A in 4th tr of any 5-tr corner group (counting R to L), *ch 2 (counts as 1 htr), 1 htr in each of next 10 tr, ch 2, (counts as 1 htr), 2 htr around side post of last htr worked, turn, ch 2, 1 htr in each of next 2 htr, turn, htr3tog, fasten off. Join yarn A in next (4th) tr of 5-tr group; rep from * 3 times. **Join yarn B around post of any beg ch-2 from Round 4, ch 2 (counts as 1 htr), 2 htr in same sp,

turn, ch 2 (counts as 1 htr), 1 htr in each of next 2 htr, turn, htr3tog, fasten off; rep from ** for rem 3 sides, so that there is a tuft at each edge. Fasten off yarn A.

Round 5: Join yarn B in any empty tr from Round 3 (between tufts), ch 4 (counts as 1 dtr), [1 dtr, ch 3, 2 dtr) in same st, *1 BPtr in first row of tuft, 1 tr in each of next 9 htr, 1 BPtr in first row of next tuft**, [2 dtr, ch 3, 2 dtr)`in next tr from Round 3; rep from * 2 times and from * to **1 time, sl st in top of beg ch-4 to join. Fasten off yarn B.

Round 6: Join yarn A in last st, ch 2 (counts as 1 htr), 1 htr in next dtr, *3 htr in next ch-3 sp, to make curlicue ch 8,

2 dc in 2nd ch from hook, 4 dc in each of next 6 ch, 2 htr in same ch-3 sp**, 1 htr in each of next 15 sts; rep from * 2 times and from * to ** 1 time, sl st in top of beg ch-2 to join. Fasten off.

Round 7: Join yarn B, ch 3 (counts as 1 tr), 1 tr in each of next 4 htr, *[2 tr, ch 1, 2 tr] in back of curlicue at base**, 1 tr in each of next 18 htr; rep from * 2 times and from * to ** 1 time, 1 tr in each of last 13 htr, sl st in top of beg ch-3 to join.

Fasten off and darn in all ends.

A
B

189

**

corner filet

A
B

A bold and simple design that mixes filet with plain treble crochet stitches. This block repeats well to create a contemporary throw, or mix it with other filet blocks for a comforting but modern blanket.

Foundation row: Using yarn A, ch 33.

Row 1: 1 tr in 4th ch from hook, 1 tr in every ch to end, turn.

Row 2: Ch 3 (counts as 1 tr), 1 tr in every tr to end, turn.

Rows 3 to 4: Rep Row 2.

Row 5: Ch 3 (counts as 1 tr), 1 tr in each of next 10 tr; on 10th tr, when pulling through final lp, drop yarn A to front of work and pull through yarn B, using yarn B, *ch 1, miss 1 tr, 1 tr in next tr; rep from * to end, turn.

Row 6: Ch 4 (counts as 1 tr), *ch 1, miss 1 ch, 1 tr in next tr; rep from * 8 times, ensuring yarn B is hanging at front of work, ch 1 by bringing through yarn A, 1 tr in each of next 11 tr (with yarn A), turn.

Rows 7, 9, 11, 13 and 15: Rep Row 5.

Rows 8, 10, 12 and 14: Rep Row 6.

At end of Row 15, fasten off and darn in ends.

190

*

all-seeing

A
B
C

A bold filet circle motif that works well mixed with other filets, or with other circle-in-a-square blocks. Work directly into each chain stitch instead of the chain-space itself when directed, to give the structure to the outer frame.

Foundation ring: Using yarn A, ch 4, sl st in first ch to form ring.

Round 1: Ch 1, 10 dc in ring, sl st in first dc to join.

Round 2: Ch 4 (counts as 1 tr, ch 1), [1 tr, ch 1] in every tr to end, sl st in 3rd ch of beg ch-4 to join.

Round 3: Ch 5 (counts as 1 tr, ch 2), [1 tr, ch 2] in every tr to end, sl st in 3rd ch of beg ch-5 to join.

Round 4: Ch 5 (counts as 1 tr, ch 2), miss 1 st, [1 tr in next st, ch 2, miss 1 st] to end, sl st in 3rd ch of beg ch-5 to join.

Round 5: Ch 4 (counts as 1 tr, ch 1), [1 tr in next tr, ch 1] to end, sl st in 3rd ch of beg ch-5 to join. Fasten off yarn A.

Round 6: Using yarn B, ch 4 (counts as 1 tr, ch 1) miss 1 tr, [1 tr in next st, ch 1, miss 1 ch] to end, sl st in 3rd ch of beg ch-4 to join.

Round 7: Rep Round 6. Fasten off yarn B.

Round 8: Join yarn C, 1 dc in same st, 1 dc in each of next 5 sts or ch-sps, *ch 7, miss 6 sts, 1 ttr in next ch-sp, ch 7, 1 ttr in next ch-sp, ch 7, miss 8 sts, 1 dc in each of next 5 sts or ch-sps; rep from * 2 times, ch 7, miss 6 sts, 1 ttr in next ch-sp, ch 7, miss 1 ch, 1 ttr in next ch-sp, ch 7, sl st in first dc to join.

Round 9: Ch 1, (working in individual ch sts and not ch-sps) 1 dc in each of next 12 sts, [1 dc, ch 1, 1 dc] in next st, *1 dc in each of next 28 sts, [1 dc, ch 1, 1 dc] in next st; rep from * 2 times, 1 dc in each of next 16 sts, sl st in first dc to join.

Fasten off and darn in ends.

*

margarita

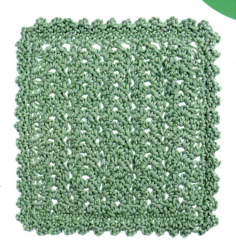

* * *

*

margarita

191

This clever stitch pattern works up quickly to produce a delicate texture, framed by a pretty border. This square looks great on its own for use as drink coasters, or stitch repeats together for a cosy, pretty bedspread.

A

Foundation row: Ch 27.

Row 1: 1 dc in 2nd ch from hook, 1 dc in every ch to end, turn – 26 sts.

Row 2: Ch 1, 1 htr in first dc, *miss 1 dc, 2 htr in next dc, ch 2, 2 htr in next dc, miss 1 dc**, 1 dc in next dc; rep from * 3 times and from * to ** 1 time, 1 htr in last dc, turn.

Row 3: Ch 1, 1 htr in first htr, *[2 htr, ch 2, 2 htr] in next ch-2 sp**, 1 dc in next dc; rep from * 3 times, then from * to ** 1 time, 1 htr in last htr, turn.

Rows 4 to 16: Rep Row 3.

Row 17: Ch 1, 1 tr in first htr, ch 1, *1 dc in next ch-2 sp, ch 1, 1 tr in next dc, ch 1; rep from * to end, turn.

Row 18: Ch 1, 1 dc in every st to end.

BORDER

Round 1: Ch 1, [2 dc, ch 1, 2 dc] in same corner sp, *1 dc in every st along edge of square to next corner**, [2 dc, ch 1, 2 dc] in next corner; rep from * 2 times, and from * to ** 1 time, sl st in first ch-1 to join.

Round 2: Ch 1, [1 dc, ch 3, 1 dc] 2 times in same corner sp, *miss 1 dc, [1 dc, ch 3, 1 dc] in next dc; rep from * to next corner **, [1 dc, ch 3, 1 sc] 2 times in next corner sp; rep from * 2 times and from * to ** 1 time, sl st to first ch-1 to join.

Fasten off and darn in ends.

*

audrey

192

Neat boxes of bobbles make this block reminiscent of lady-like crocheted jackets from the 1950s and 60s. A dense, textural block that mixes well with multicoloured or plainer squares alike.

A

Special stitch used

Make bobble (MB): Make bobble with 4 tr, ch 1 to secure (*see page 19*).

Foundation chain: Ch 28.

Row 1: 1 dc in 2nd ch from hook and in every ch to end, turn.

Row 2: Ch 1, 1 dc in every dc to end, turn.

Rows 3 to 5: Rep Row 2.

Row 6: Ch 1, 1 dc in each of next 3 dc, *[MB in next dc, 1 dc in next dc] 3 times, 1 dc in each of next 2 dc; rep from * 2 times, turn.

Rows 7 to 9: Rep Row 2.

Rows 8 to 10: Rep Row 6.

Rows 11 to 13: Rep Row 2.

Rows 14 to 18: Rep Rows 6 to 10.

Rows 19 to 21: Rep Row 2.

Rows 22 to 26: Rep Rows 6 to 10.

Rows 27 to 31: Rep Row 2.

Fasten off and darn in ends. Block square.

popcorn forest

A textured variation on the classic granny, this square feels deliciously nubbly to work and is just as adaptable as the regular granny square. It feels as if it is curling up as you work it, but the final rounds give it a straight structure and flatten it out.

A
B
C
D

Special stitches used:

Beginning popcorn (beg pc): Ch 3, make popcorn with 4 tr (*see page 19*).

Popcorn (pc): Make popcorn with 5 tr.

Foundation ring: Using yarn A, ch 4, join with sl st to form ring

Round 1: Beg pc in ring, ch 4, *pc in ring, ch 4; rep from * 2 times, sl st in ch at top of beg pc to join. Fasten off yarn A.

Round 2: Join yarn B in any ch-4 sp, [beg pc, ch 4, pc] in same ch-4 sp, *ch 2, [pc, ch 4, pc] in next ch-4 sp; rep from * 2 times, ch 2, sl st in ch at top of beg pc to join.

Round 3: Sl st in next ch-4 sp, [beg pc, ch 4, pc] in same ch-4 sp, *ch 2, pc in ch-2 sp, ch 2**, [pc, ch 4, pc] in next ch-4 sp; rep from * 2 times, then from * to ** 1 time, sl st in top of beg pc to join. Fasten off yarn B.

Round 4: Join yarn C in any ch-4 sp, [beg pc, ch 4, pc] in same ch-4 sp, *[ch 2, pc in next ch-2 sp] 2 times, ch 2**, [pc, ch 4, pc] in next ch-4 sp; rep from * 2 times, then from * to ** 1 time, sl st in ch at top of beg pc to join.

Round 5: Sl st in next ch-4 sp, [beg pc, ch 4, pc] in same ch-4 sp, *[ch 2, pc in next ch-2 sp] 3 times, ch 2**, [pc, ch 4, pc] in next ch-4 sp; rep from * 2 times, then from * to ** 1 time, join with sl st in ch at top of beg pc. Fasten off yarn C.

Round 6: Join yarn D in next ch-4 sp, ch 3 (counts as 1 tr), [2 tr, ch 2, 3 tr] in same ch-4 sp, *[ch 1, 3 tr] in each ch-2 sp along side of square to corner, ch 1**, [3 tr, ch 3, 3 tr] in next corner ch-4 sp; rep from * 2 times, then from * to ** 1 time, join with sl st in top of beg ch-3.

Round 7: Sl st in first 4-ch sp, ch 3 (counts as 1 tr), [2 tr, ch 3, 3 tr] in same ch-4 sp, *[ch 1, 3 tr] in each ch-2 sp along side of square to corner, ch 1**, [3 tr, ch 2, 3 tr] in next corner ch-4 sp; rep from * 2 times and from * to ** 1 time, sl st in top of ch-3 to join. Fasten off yarn D.

Round 8: Rep Round 7, using yarn A.

Round 9: Join yarn B to any ch-4 sp, ch 1 in same sp, 3 dc in ch-4 sp, *1 dc in each tr, and 1 dc in each ch-1 sp to corner ch-4 sp, 3 dc in each corner ch-4 sp; rep from * 3 times, sl st in first dc to join.

Fasten off and darn in ends neatly.

morning glory

A bold and intricate square that slowly increases out from the centre to create a paper cut-out effect. Playing with colours to focus in or out of the centre adds to the 3D look.

A
B
C
D

Special stitch used:

Make bobble (MB): Make bobble with 3 tr (*see page 19*).

Foundation ring: Using yarn A, begin with magic ring method.

Round 1: Ch 1 (counts as 1 dc), 7 dc in lp, sl st in ch-1 to join.

Round 2: Ch 5 (counts as 1 tr, 2 ch), *1 tr in next dc, ch 2; rep from * to end of rnd, sl st in 3rd ch of beg ch-5 to join.

Round 3: Ch 3, 3 tr in ch-2 sp, *ch 3, 4 tr in next ch-2 sp; rep from * to end of rnd, ending last rep with ch 3, sl st in top of beg ch-3 to join. Fasten off yarn A.

Round 4: Join yarn B, sl st in first ch-3 sp, ch 3 (counts as 1 tr), [1 tr, ch 4, 2 tr] in same ch-3 sp, *[2 tr, ch 4, 2 tr] in next ch-3 sp; rep from * to end of rnd, sl st in top of beg ch-3 to join.

Round 5: Sl st in next tr and ch-4 sp, ch 3 (counts as 1 tr), [1 tr, ch 5, 2 tr] in same ch-4 sp, *[2 tr, ch 5, 2 tr] in next ch-4 sp; rep from * to end of rnd, sl st in top of beg ch-3 to join. Fasten off yarn B.

Round 6: With yarn C, sl st in ch-5 sp, ch 3, 8 tr in same sp, *1 dc in sp between 2-tr clusters**, 9 tr in next ch-5 sp; rep from * to end of rnd, ending last rep at **, 1 dc in sp between final 2-tr clusters, sl st in top of beg ch-3 to join. Fasten off yarn C.

Round 7: With yarn D, sl st in 5th tr of first scallop, ch 1, 1 dc in same sp, ch 3, *MB in dc between scallops, ch 3, [MB, ch 3, MB] in 5th dc of next scallop, ch 3, MB in next dc, ch 3**, 1 dc in 5th tr of next scallop, MB in next dc, ch 3; rep from * to end of rnd ending last rep at **, sl st in beg dc to join.

Round 8: Ch1 (counts as 1 dc), 5 tr in ch-3 sp, 1 dc in top of bobble, 5 tr in next ch-3 sp, *1 dc in top of bobble, 7 tr in corner ch-3 sp, 1 dc in top of bobble, 5 tr in ch-3 sp, 1 dc in bobble, 5 tr in ch-3 sp**, 1 dc in dc, 5 tr in ch-3 sp; rep from * to end of rnd, ending last rnd at **, sl st in beg ch-1 to join.

Fasten off and darn in ends neatly.

mallorca

A classic palm leaf pattern given an update by adding an angular shape, this suggests tiled floors and hot summer days; combine it with other lacy textures for a cheery throw or use it repeated for a summery shawl.

A
B

Foundation row: Using yarn A, ch 33.

Row 1: 1 tr in 5th ch from hook, * ch 2, miss 6 ch, [1 tr, ch 3, 1 tr] in next ch; rep from * to end.

Row 2: Ch 3, 3 tr in next ch-3 sp, *[4 tr, ch 3, 4 tr] in next ch-3 sp; rep from * to end, ending with 4 tr in last ch-3 sp.

Row 3: Ch 4, 1 tr in first st, *ch 2, [1 tr, ch 3, 1 tr] in next ch-3 sp; rep from * to end, ending with [1 tr, ch 1, 1 tr] in top of ch-3.

Rows 4, 6, 8 and 10: Rep Row 2.

Rows 5, 7 and 9: Rep Row 3.

Row 11: Ch 4 (counts as 1 dc), ch 3, 1 dc in top of first cluster*, ch 3, 1 tr in sp between 2 clusters (between first and last of each group), ch 3**, 1 dc in next ch-3 sp; rep from * 2 times and from * to ** 1 time, 1 dc in last tr of last cluster.

BORDER

Round 1: Ch 1, 1 dc in same st, ch 2, *1 dc in next ch-3 sp, ch 2; rep from * to corner, 1 dc in next dc, **ch 2, 1 dc in side post of first tr of last row of clusters, ch 2, 1 dc in next ch-3 sp; rep from ** 3 times to corner, ch 2, 1 dc in base of first ch, ch 2, ***1 dc in next ch-6 sp, 1 dc in base of next fan; rep from *** 2 times, 1 dc in next ch-6 sp, ch 2, 1 dc in base of last fan, ch 2, [1 dc around post of ch-3 sp, ch 2] 7 times to end, sl st in first dc to join. Fasten off.

Round 2: Join yarn B, [3 dc, ch 1] in each ch-2 sp all around square.

Fasten off and darn in ends.

**

arbour

Although this block has a bobble texture, it is composed of chains and double crochet. Chain loops form a subtle effect best enhanced by using a thicker yarn than usual for your hook, or a smaller hook for your regular yarn.

A

Foundation chain: Ch 28.

Row 1: 1 dc in 2nd ch from hook, 1 dc in each of next 5 ch, ch 4, [1 dc in each of next 7 ch, ch 4] 2 times, 1 dc in each of next 7 dc, turn.

Row 2: Ch 1, 1 dc in each of next 6 dc, ch 4, 1 dc in each of next 2 dc, ch 4, [1 dc in each of next 5 dc, ch 4, 1 dc in each of next 2 dc, ch 4] 2 times, 1 dc in each of next 5 dc, turn.

Row 3: Ch 1, 1 dc in next dc, [ch 4, 1 dc in each of next 3 dc, ch 4, 1 dc in each of next 4 dc] 3 times, 1 dc in each of next 3 dc, ch 4, 1 dc in each of last 2 dc, turn.

Row 4: Ch 1, 1 dc in each of next 3 dc, [ch 4, 1 dc in next dc, ch 4, 1 dc in each of next 6 dc] 3 times, ch 4, 1 dc in next dc, ch 4, 1 dc in each of next 2 dc, turn.

Row 5: Ch 1, 1 dc in each of next 2 dc, [ch 4, 1 dc in next dc, ch 4, 1 dc in each of next 6 dc] 3 times, ch 4, 1 dc in next dc, ch 4, 1 dc in each of next 3 dc, turn.

Row 6: Ch 1, 1 dc in each of next 2 dc, [ch 4, 1 dc in each of next 3 dc, ch 4, 1 dc in each of next 4 dc] 3 times, ch 4, 1 dc in each of next 3 dc, ch 4, 1 dc in next dc, turn.

Row 7: Ch 1, 1 dc in each of next 5 dc, [ch 4, 1 dc in each of next 2 dc, ch 4, 1 dc in each of next 5 dc] 3 times, 1 dc in last dc, turn.

Row 8: Ch 1, [1 dc in each of next 7 dc, ch 4] 3 times, 1 dc in each of next 6 dc, turn.

Rows 9, 21 and 28: Rep Row 7.

Rows 10, 20 and 27: Rep Row 6.

Rows 11, 19 and 26: Rep Row 5.

Rows 12, 18 and 25: Rep Row 4.

Rows 13, 17 and 24: Rep Row 3.

Rows 14, 16 and 23: Rep Row 2.

Rows 15 and 22: Ch 1, 1 dc in each of next 6 dc, ch 4, [1 dc in each of next 7 dc, ch 4] 2 times, 1 dc in each of next 78 dc, turn.

Row 29: Rep row 15.

Fasten off and darn in ends neatly.

***

greek key

Inspired by ancient Greek ceramic patterns, this classic design is worked in linear repeat, in double crochet throughout. Carry the contrast yarn not in use at the back of the work and remember to always keep the yarn tails on the wrong side of the work.

A
B
C

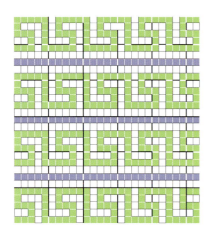

Foundation chain: Using yarn A, ch 28.

Row 1: (First row of chart) 1 dc in 2nd ch from hook, 1 dc in every ch to end, turn.

Work remaining 29 rows of chart, ensuring you keep yarn ends on WS.

Row 2 and every foll row: Ch 1, 1 dc in every dc to end, turn.

Row 31: Rep Row 2 using yarn A only.

Fasten off and darn in ends neatly.
Block work.

***

lucky clover

A distinctive central motif that makes a strong statement defines this interesting block. It's challenging but fun to work up and would look beautiful repeated over a bedspread, or used for special table linens.

A
B

Foundation ring: Using yarn A, ch 6, sl st in first ch to form ring.

Round 1: Ch 1, 16 dc in ring, sl st in first ch to join.

Round 2: Ch 1, 1 dc in each of first 3 dc, ch 9, 1 sl st in same dc, *1 dc in each of next 4 dc, ch 9, sl st in same dc; rep from * 2 times, 1 dc in last dc, sl st in first dc to join.

Round 3: Sl st along to next ch-9 sp, *[2 htr, 2 tr, 14 dtr, 2 tr, 2 htr] in ch-9 sp, miss 1 dc, 1 dc in each of next 2 dc, miss 1 dc; rep from * 3 times, 1 dc in each of last 2 dc. Fasten off.

Round 4: Join yarn B in any sp between 2 dc between petals, *ch 16, miss 12 sts, 1 dc in next dtr, [ch 16, 1 dc in next sp between 2 sd between clover petals; rep from * 3 times, sl st in first dc to join.

Round 5: Ch 1, 1 dc in same st, *sl st in each of next 2 ch, 1 dc in each of next 2 ch, 1 tr in each of next 4 ch, 1 dtr in next ch, ch 4, sl st in each of next 14 sts, ch 4, 1 dtr in next ch, 1 tr in each of next 4 ch, 1 dc in next dc, sl st in each of next 2 ch, 1 dc in dc between the petals; rep from * 3 times, sl st in beg ch-1 to join.

Round 6: Sl st up spoke to next ch-4 sp, turn work to WS, *ch 6, sl st in next ch-4 sp on next spoke, *4 dc in ch-4 sp, 1 dc in front lp only of each of next 14 sl sts, 4 dc in next ch-4 sp, sl st in next ch-4 sp; rep from * 3 times, sl st in first ch of beg ch-6 to join.

Round 7: (RS) Sl st in next st, ch 3, *1 tr in each of next 3 sts, 1 tr in each of next 15 dc, 1 tr in each of the next 3 dc, 5 tr in next ch-6 sp, ch 4, 5 tr in same sp (forms corner); rep from * 3 times, sl st in top of beg ch-3 to join.

Round 8: Ch 1, 1 dc in same sp, 1 dc in each st to corner, 3 dc in corner sp; rep from * 3 times, sl st in first sc to join.

Fasten off and block work to define shape.

···

***

irish moss

Named because it was designed on St Patrick's day, this block uses varying stitch heights to create crescent-shaped spokes that are then linked at the back by a filet band. A lightweight and unusual block that would work well in traditional or contemporary pieces alike.

A
B

Foundation ring: Using yarn A, ch 6, sl st in first ch to form ring.

Round 1: Ch 3 (counts as 1 tr), 15 tr in ring, sl st in top of beg ch-3 to join.

Round 2: *Ch 8, 2 dc in 2nd ch from hook, 2 htr in next ch, 2 tr in next ch, 2 dtr in next ch, 2 tr in next ch, 1 htr in next ch, 1 dc in last ch, sl st in same tr at base of ring, 1 dc in each of next 2 tr; rep from * 7 times, sl st in first ch of beg ch-8 to join. Fasten off.

Round 3: Join yarn B in first tr (counting up from base) of any spoke at top, 1 dc in same st, *ch 6, 1 dc in same place on next spoke; rep from * 6 times, ch 6, sl st in first dc to join, push all ch lps behind spokes.

Round 4: Ch 6 (counts as 1 tr, ch 3), *[1 tr, ch 3] 2 times in next ch-6 sp, 1 tr in next dc, ch 3; rep from * to end, sl st in 3rd ch of beg ch-6 to join.

Round 5: Ch 5 (counts as 1 htr, ch 3), *1 dc in tip of spoke from Round 3, ch 3, miss 1 htr, 1 htr in next htr, ch 3, [2 htr, 1 tr, ch 2, 1 tr, 2 htr] in next htr (forms corner), ch 3, 1 dc in tip of next spoke from Round 3, ch 3, miss 1 htr, 1 htr in next htr, ch 3**, 1 htr in next htr, ch 3; rep from * 2 times and from * to ** 1 time, sl st in 2nd ch of beg ch-5 to join.

Round 6: Ch 5 (counts as 1 htr, ch 3), [1 htr in next htr, ch 3] 3 times, *miss [1 htr, 1 tr], [1 htr, ch 3, 1 htr] in next ch-2 sp**, miss [1 tr, 1 htr], [1 htr, ch 3 in next htr] 7 times; rep from * 2 times and from * to ** 1 time, sl st in top of beg ch-2 to join.

Fasten off and darn in ends.

****
watermelon

Deliciously fruity, this block has bobble 'seeds' that are worked in a contrasting colour, and a colourwork signature striped skin. Team it with Salsa and Citrus for a real cocktail of a throw – mixed through with plainer squares it will be sure to refresh all who see it.

A
B
C
D
E
F

Special stitch used:

Make bobble (MB): with 3 tr, ch 1 to secure (*see page 19*). Use either separate lengths of yarn B for seeds (neater option), or carry yarn at back, depending on whether you plan the piece to be seen from the back or not.

Foundation ring: Using yarn A, make a magic ring.

Round 1: Ch 3 (counts as 1 tr), 17 tr in ring, sl st in top of beg ch-3 to join.

Round 2: Ch 3 (counts as 1 tr), 1 tr in same st, MB using yarn B in next tr, ch 1 to change to yarn A, *2 tr in each of next 2 tr, MB in next tr, ch 1 to change to yarn A; rep from * 4 times, 2 tr in last tr, sl st in top of beg ch-3 to join.

Round 3: Ch 3 (counts as 1 tr), 1 tr in next tr, *1 tr in top of bobble, 1 tr in next tr, 2 tr in next tr, 1 tr in each of next 2 tr; rep from * to end, sl st in top of beg ch-3 to join.

Round 4: Ch 3 (counts as 1 tr), 1 tr in next tr, *2 tr in next tr, 1 tr in each of next 2 tr, MB in next tr, ch 1 to change to yarn A, 1 tr in each of next 2 tr; rep from * 5 times, omitting last 2 tr on last rep, sl st in top of beg ch-3 to join.

Round 5: Ch 2 (counts as 1 htr), 1 htr in same st, [1 htr in each of next 2 tr, 2 htr in next tr] to end, sl st in top of beg ch-2 to join.

Round 6: Join yarn C in any st, 2 dc in same st, *1 dc in each of next 3 sts, 2 dc in next st; rep from * to end, sl st in first dc to join – 70 sts. Fasten off yarn C.

Round 7: Join yarn D, ch 1, *1 dc in each of next 2 dc, change to yarn E, 1 dc in each of next 2 dc, change to yarn D; rep from * to end, sl st in first dc to join.

Round 8: Ch 1, *1 dc in each of next 2 dc, change to yarn E, 2 dc in next dc, 1 dc in next dc, change to yarn D; rep from * to end, sl st in first dc to join. Fasten off yarn D.

Round 9: Ch 1, 1 dc in each of next 10 dc, *1 htr in each of next 3 dc, 1 tr in each of next 2 dc, [3 tr, ch 2, 3 tr] in next dc, 1 tr in each of next 2 dc, 1 htr in each of next 3 dc**, 1 dc in each of next 11 dc; rep from * 2 times and from * to ** 1 time, sl st in first sc to join. Fasten off.

Round 10: Join yarn F, ch 1, 1 dc in every st to corner, 3 dc in corner ch-2 sp; rep from * 3 times, sl st in first dc to join.

Fasten off and darn in ends.

deuce

A basic, diagonally constructed square that increases and decreases to form its shape. Using tonal colours as we have here gives a subtle effect; you could use contrasting brights for a starker feel.

Foundation chain: Using yarn A, ch 2, 3 dc in 2nd ch from hook, turn.

Row 1: Ch 1, 2 dc in first dc, 1 dc in next dc, 2 dc in last dc, turn – 5 sts.

Row 2: Ch 1, 2 dc in first dc, 1 dc in each dc to last dc, 2 dc in last dc – 7 sts.

Rows 3 to 4: Rep Row 2.

Row 5: Ch 1, 1 dc in every dc to end, turn.

Rows 6 to 9, 10 to 13, 14 to 17, 18 to 21: Rep Rows 2 to 5.

Rows 22 to 23: Rep Row 2 (41 sts by end of Row 23). Fasten off.

Row 24: Join yarn B, rep Row 5.

Row 25: Ch 1, miss 1 dc, 1 dc in each dc to last 2 dc, miss 1 dc, 1 dc in last dc, turn.

Rows 26 to 27: Rep Row 25.

Row 28: Rep Row 5.

Rows 29 to 32, 33 to 36, 37 to 40, 41 to 44, 45 to 48: Rep Rows 26 to 29.

Row 49: Ch 1, miss 1 dc, 1 dc in each of next 2 dc, miss next dc, 1 dc in next dc.

Row 50: Ch 1, tr3tog.

BORDER

Starting at corner, 3 dc in corner, 1 dc in every st around top and side of square, change to yarn A, 3 dc in corner, 1 dc in every st to end, sl st in first dc to join.

A
B
C

TRIM

Using yarn C, ch 20, 1 dc in dc 4 sts from RH edge in colour A section, 4 rows down from point where colours change in diagonal, ch 10, attach ch with 1 dc in colour B section, 4 rows down and 8 sts in from edge (working lattice zigzag as shown), ch 10, miss 7 dc, attach ch with 1 dc to dc in same row of colour A section, miss 7 sts of colour B section, ch 10, dc in next dc in colour B section; rep to edge to 4 sts from edge at opposite end, ch 8, attach at same point exactly opposite in colour B section, ch 10, miss 3 dc, 1 dc in next dc in colour A section, ch 10, miss 7 sts, 1 dc in next dc in colour B section; rep to end, being sure chs form criss-cross pattern resembling shoelaces, ch 15, fasten off.

Darn in ends, knot each end of ch 2 times.

Using yarn C, backstitch along entire row located 8 rows from point where colours change at diagonal seam, on each section, and again 2 rows further towards edge in each section (4 joins stitched).

Fasten off and darn in all ends. Block square to straighten edges if necessary.

**

italian cross

An intricate square with a beautifully puffed centre, this block has an elegant feel and would make a sophisticated throw or pillow cover when mixed with plainer blocks to show off its detail.

A
B
C

Special stitches used:

Beginning puff stitch (beg pf): Ch 2 (counts as 1 htr), make puff st with 3 htr and join together at top (*see page 19*).

Puff stitch (pf): Make puff stitch with 4 htr joined together at top.

Foundation ring: Using yarn A, ch 4, join with sl st to form ring.

Round 1: Ch 3 (counts as 1 tr), 11 tr in ring, sl st in 3rd ch of ch-3 to join. Fasten off yarn A.

Round 2: Join yarn B, ch 2 (counts as 1 htr), beg pf in same st, *[ch 1, pf in next st] 2 times, ch 5**, pf in next st; rep from * 2 times and from * to ** 1 time, join with sl st in top of beg pf.

Round 3: Sl st in next ch-1 sp, ch 2 (counts as 1 htr), beg pf in same sp, *ch 1, pf in next sp, ch 2, 5 tr in next ch-5 sp, ch 2**, pf in next ch-1 sp; rep from * 2 times, then from * to **1 time, sl st in top of beg pf to join.

Round 4: Sl st in next ch-1 sp, ch 2 (counts as 1 htr), beg pf in same sp, *ch 3, miss ch 2, [1 tr in next tr, ch 1] 2 times, [1 tr, ch 1, 1 tr, ch 1, 1 tr] in next tr (forms corner), [ch 1, 1 tr in next tr], 2 times, ch 3, miss ch-2**, pf in next ch-1 sp; rep from * 2 times, then from * to ** 1 time, join with sl st in top of beg pf. Fasten off yarn B.

Round 5: Join yarn C to first tr in corner, ch 4 (counts as 1 tr, 1 ch), *[1 tr in next tr, ch 1] 2 times, [1 tr, ch 1, 1 tr, ch 1, 1 tr] in next tr (forms corner), [ch 1, 1 tr in next tr] 3 times, 3 tr in next ch -3 sp, ch 1, 3 tr in next ch-3 sp**, 1 tr in next tr, ch 1; rep from * 2 times, then from * to ** 1 time, sl st in 3rd ch of ch-3 to join.

Round 6: Ch 4 (counts as 1 tr, ch 1), *[1 tr in the next tr, ch 1] 3 times, [1 tr, ch 1, 1 tr, ch 1, 1 tr] in next tr (forms corner), [ch 1, 1 tr in next tr] 4 times, 1 tr in each of next 3 tr, 1 tr in ch-1 sp, 1 tr in next 3 tr, ch 1**, 1 tr in next tr, ch 1; rep from * 2 times, then from * to ** 1 time, sl st in 3rd ch of beg ch-4 to join.

Round 7: Ch 4 (counts as 1 tr, ch 1), *[1 tr in next trc, ch 1) 4 times, [1 tr, ch 1, 1 tr, ch 1] in next tr (forms corner), [ch 1, 1 tr in next tr] 5 times**, 1 tr in each of next 8 tr, ch 1; rep from * 2 times, then from * to ** 1 time, 1 tr in each of next 7 tr, sl st in 3rd ch of beg ch-4 to join.

Fasten off and darn in ends neatly.

****
field of clover

A complex square that illustrates how to work a five-leaf motif in a square shape. The intricate and clever construction methods are combined with an unusual motif, to make this challenging but fun square really satisfying to work. Use as a centrepiece for a composite pillow cover or throw to show off your talents.

A
B

Special stitch used:

Make bobble (MB): Make bobble with 2 tr (*see page 19*).

Foundation ring: Using yarn A, begin with magic ring method.

Round 1: Ch 3, 14 tr in ring, sl st in top of beg ch-3 to join.

Round 2: *Ch 4, [ch 3, MB in 4th st from hook through both halves of st, ch 3, sl st in same 4th st from hook] 2 times (3-leaf shamrock), ch 3, miss 2 sts, sl st in next st; rep from * 4 times, sl st in first ch of beg ch-7 to join. Fasten off yarn A.

Round 3: Join yarn B, sl st in top of 2nd petal of first shamrock, 1 dc in same st, *ch 5, 1 dc in top of 3rd petal of same shamrock, 1 dc in top of first petal of next shamrock, ch 5**, 1 dc in top of 2nd petal of same shamrock; rep from * to end of rnd ending last rep at **, sl st in first dc to join.

Round 4: Ch 1, 1 dc in same sp, *5 dc in next ch-5 sp, 1 dc in each of next 2 dc, 5 dc in next ch-5 sp**, 1 dc in next dc; rep from * 4 times, ending last rep at **, sl st in first dc to join.

Round 5: Ch 1, 1 dc in same sp, *ch 4, miss next 6 dc, 1 tr in next dc, ch 1, 1 tr in next dc, ch 4, miss next 5 dc**, 1 dc in next dc; rep from * 4 times, ending last rep at **, sl st in first dc to join.

Round 6: Ch 2, *6 dc in next ch-4 sp, 1 dc in next tr, 2 dc in next ch-1 sp, 1 dc in next tr, 6 dc in next ch-4 sp, miss 1 st; rep from * to end of rnd, sl st in top of beg ch-2 to join – 80 sts.

Round 7: [Ch 3, 1 tr, ch 3, 2 tr] in same sp (first corner), *1 tr in each of next 19 dc**, [2 tr, ch 3, 2 tr] in next tr; rep from * 3 times ending last rep at **, sl st in top of beg ch-3 to join. Fasten off yarn B.

Round 8: Sl st yarn A to next ch-3 sp, [ch 3, 4 tr] in same sp (first corner), *1 tr in each of next 23 tr**, 5 tr in next ch-3 sp; rep from * to end of rnd ending last rep at **, sl st in top of beg ch-3 to join.

Fasten off and darn in ends neatly.

**

mint choc chip

A
B
C
D
E
F
G
H

Loads of spike stitches make this block interesting to work, and it allows plenty of scope for optical colour mixing. Use a flat, matt yarn to ensure the spike pattern shows up effectively. Fantastic for mixing with other circle-in-a-square blocks.

Special stitch used:

Spike stitch (spike): Insert hook in top of st 2 rnds below next st to be worked, yoh, pull yarn through to height of rnd being worked, complete specified st as normal (*see page 22*).

Foundation ring: Using yarn A, make a magic ring.

Round 1: Ch 1, 16 dc in ring, sl st in first dc to join. Fasten off yarn A.

Round 2: Join yarn B in any dc, 1 dc in same st, [ch 2, miss 1 dc, 1 dc in next dc] 7 times, ch 2, sl st in first dc to join. Fasten off yarn A.

Round 3: Join yarn C in any ch-2 sp, *4 dc in ch-2 sp; rep from * 7 times, sl st in first dc to join.

Round 4: Join yarn D in any dc above Round 2 dc, 1 dc in same dc, *1 dc in next dc, 1 spike dc in next ch-2 gap from Round 2, 1 dc in each of next 2 dc; rep from * 7 times, sl st in first dc to join.

Round 5: Join yarn E in any dc spike st from last rnd, *1 dc in dc spike st, ch 4; rep from * 7 times, sl st in first dc to join.

Round 6: Join yarn F in any ch-4 sp, *4 htr in ch-4 sp, [3 htr, ch 2, 3 htr] in next ch-4 sp; rep from * 3 times, sl st in first htr to join.

Round 7: Join yarn G in any ch-2 corner sp, ch 2 (counts as 1 htr), [2 htr, ch 2, 3 htr] in corner sp, *1 htr in each of next 3 htr, 1 spike htr in next ch-4 sp of Round 5, 1 htr in next htr, 1 spike htr in same ch-4 sp in Round 5, 1 htr in each of next 3 htr**, [3 htr, ch 2, 3 htr] in next ch-2 corner sp; rep from * 2 times and from * to ** 1 time, sl st in top of beg ch-2 to join.

Round 8: Sl st in next corner sp, ch 2 (counts as 1 htr), [2 htr, ch 2, 3 htr] in corner sp, *1 htr in each of next 14 htr**, [3 htr, ch 2, 3 htr] in corner ch-2 sp; rep from * 2 times and from * to ** 1 time, sl st in top of beg ch-2 to join. Fasten off.

Round 9: Join yarn H in any ch-2 sp, ch 3 (counts as 1 tr), [2 tr, ch 2, 3 tr] in corner sp, *miss 1 htr, 1 tr in each of next 2 htr, [1 spike tr in Round 8, 1 tr in next htr] 7 times, miss 1 htr, [3 tr, ch 2, 3 tr] in corner sp; rep from * 3 times, sl st in top of beg ch-3 to join.

Round 10: Sl st in ch-2 corner sp, ch 2 (counts as 1 htr), [2 htr, ch 2, 3 htr] in corner sp, ch 1, *[miss 1 tr, 1 htr in each of next 2 tr, ch 1] 7 times, ch 1, [3 htr, ch 2, 3 htr] in corner sp, ch 1; rep from * 2 times, [miss 1 tr, 1 htr in each of next 2 tr, ch 1] 7 times, ch 1, sl st top of beg ch-2 to join.

Fasten off and darn in ends.

✱✱✱

palmetto

A fan-like arrangement of bullion stitches creates this intricate pattern. A lightweight, lacy block good for use in summer throws or wraps; use a light-coloured yarn to emphasise the pretty textures.

A

Special stitch used:

Bullion stitch (bullion st): Yoh 7 times, insert hook in st or sp to be worked, yoh, draw lp through to front, yoh, pull through all lps on hook, ch 1 to secure (*see page 20*).

Foundation ring: Make a magic ring, ch 1 to secure.

Round 1: 8 dc in ring, sl st in first dc to join.

Round 2: Ch 2 (counts as 1 htr), [2 htr in next dc] 7 times, 1 htr in first dc, sl st in top of beg ch-2 to join.

Round 3: Ch 6 (counts as 1 tr, ch 3), miss 1 htr, *1 ttr in next htr, ch 3, miss 1 htr**, 1 tr in next htr, ch 3, miss 1 htr; rep from * 2 times, and from to ** 1 time, sl st in 3rd ch of beg ch-6 to join.

Round 4: Ch 1, *3 dc in next ch-3 lp, 6 bullion sts in next ttr, 3 dc in next ch-3 lp, 1 dc in next tr; rep from * 3 times, sl st in first dc to join.

Round 5: Ch 6 (counts as 1 tr, ch 3), 1 bullion st in each of next 6 bullion sts, *ch 3, miss 3 dc, 1 tr in next dc, ch 3, miss 3 dc, 1 bullion st in each of next 6 bullion sts; rep from * 2 times, ch 3, sl st in 3rd ch of beg ch-6 to join.

Round 6: Ch 7 (counts as 1 dtr, ch 3), 1 dtr in same st, *ch 4, 1 htr in top of next bullion st, 1 htr in ch beside first bullion st, [1 dc in top of next bullion st, 1 dc in ch st beside same bullion st] 3 times, 1 dc in top of next bullion st, 1 htr in ch st next to same bullion st, 1 htr in top of last bullion st of group, ch 4**, [1 dtr, ch 3, 1 dtr] in next tr; rep from * 2 times and from * to ** 1 time, sl st in 4th ch of beg ch-7 to join.

Round 7: Ch 3 (counts as 1 tr), [2 tr, ch 3, 3 tr) in next ch-3 sp, *3 tr in next ch-4 sp, 1 htr in each of next 2 sts, 1 dc in each of next 6 sts, 1 htr in each of next 2 sts, 3 tr in next ch-4 sp**, [3 tr, ch 3, 3 tr] in next ch-3 sp; rep from * 2 times, and from * to ** 1 time, sl st in top of beg ch-3 to join.

Round 8: Ch 1, 1 dc in each of next 2 tr, *[2 dc, ch 1, 2 dc] in next corner ch-3 sp, 1 dc in every st to next corner; rep from * 2 times, [2 dc, ch 1, 2 dc] in last corner ch-3 sp, 1 dc in every st to end, sl st in first dc to join.

Fasten off and darn in ends.

**

grace

An updated doily pattern is given a fresh twist by working it in vivid green. Work in cotton for summer-weight throws or table linens.

A
B

Note: On Round 7, use 4 separate small balls of yarn A, and carry yarn B over top of sts of last rnd when not in use, working it under sts being made in yarn A.

Foundation ring: Using yarn A, ch 4, sl st in first ch to form ring.

Round 1: Ch 1, 16 dc in ring, sl st in first dc to join.

Round 2: *1 dc in next st, ch 8, miss 3 sts; rep from * 3 times, sl st in first dc to join.

Round 3: *[1 dc, 1 htr, 9 tr, 1 htr, 1 dc] in next ch-8 sp; rep from * 3 times, sl st in first dc to join. Fasten off yarn A.

Round 4: Join yarn B in same st, *1 dc in next htr, ch 4, miss 1 st, 1 dc in next st, [ch 4, miss 2 sts, 1 dc in next st) 2 times, ch 4, miss 1 st, 1 dc in next st, ch 4, miss

2 sts; rep from * 3 times but replace last ch-4 with [ch 1, 1 tr] in first dc to join.

Round 5: *Ch 4, 1 dc in next ch-4 sp; rep from * 18 times, ch 1, 1 tr in first ch-4 sp to join.

Round 6: *Ch 8, *[1 dc in next ch-4 sp, ch 4] 4 times, 1 dc in next ch 4 sp; rep from * 3 times, replace last ch-4 with ch 1, 1 tr in first ch-4 sp to join.

Round 7: *Join yarn A, [6 tr, ch 5, 6 tr] in ch-8 sp, change to yarn B, [1 dc in next ch-4 sp, ch 4] 3 times, 1 dc in next ch-4 sp; rep from * 3 times, replace last [ch 4, 1 dc] with [ch 1, 1 tr in first ch-4 sp] to join. Fasten off yarn A.

Round 8: Cont with yarn B, *1 dc in same ch-4 sp, ch 8, 3 dc in next ch-5 sp, ch 8, 1 dc in next ch-4 sp, ch 8, miss next ch-4 sp; rep from * 3 times, sl st in first dc to join.

Round 9: *10 dc in next ch-8 sp, miss 1 st, [1 dc, ch 3, 1 dc] in next st, [10 dc in next ch-8 sp] 2 times; rep from * 3 times, sl st in first dc to join. Fasten off.

Round 10: Join yarn A in any st, *1 dc in each st to corner ch-3 sp, [1 dc, ch 3, 1 dc] in each corner ch-3 sp; rep from * 3 times, sl st in first dc to join. Fasten off and darn in ends.

---

*

delta

A simple but striking flower with slightly raised petals, this is a lovely beginner square that goes beyond the traditional granny. Great for mixing with other bold flower squares.

A
B
C
D

Foundation ring: Using A, make a magic ring, ch 2, 1 tr in ring, ch 2, *2 tr, ch 2 in ring; rep from * 6 times, sl st in top of beg ch-2 to form ring. Fasten off yarn A.

Round 1: Join yarn B in any ch-2 sp, [ch 1, 1 dc, 2 tr, 1 dc] in each ch-2 sp, sl st in first ch to join. Fasten off yarn B.

Round 2: Join yarn C in any ch-1 sp, *Ch 5, 1 dc in next ch-1 sp; rep from * 6 times, ch 5, sl st in first ch of beg ch-5 to join.

Round 3: Ch 1, [1 dc, 1 htr, 1 tr, ch 2, 1 tr, 1 htr, 1 dc] in every ch-5 sp, sl st in first ch to join. Fasten off yarn C.

Round 4: Join yarn D in any dc of Round 2, 1 dc in same st, *ch 5, 1 dc in next dc; rep from * 7 times, tuck ch-5 lps behind petals of Round 3.

Round 5: [Ch 2, 3 tr, ch 2, 4 tr] in first ch-5 sp, *4 tr in next ch-5 sp, [4 tr, ch 2, 4 tr] in next ch-5 sp; rep from * 3 times, 4 tr in last ch-5 sp, sl st in top of beg ch-2 to join, sl st in next ch-2 corner sp.

Round 6: [Ch 2, 3 tr, ch 2, 4 tr] in corner sp, *4 tr in next sp between 4 tr groups from Round 5, 4 tr in next sp, [4 tr, ch 2, 4 tr] in next corner sp; rep from * 2 times, sl st in top of beg ch-2 to join, sl st in next ch-2 corner sp.

Round 7: [Ch 2, 3 tr, ch 2, 4 tr] in corner sp, *[4 tr in next sp] 3 times, [4 tr, ch 2, 4 tr] in corner sp; rep from * 3 times, [4 tr in next sp] 3 times.

Round 8: Ch 1, ([2 htr, ch 1, 2 htr] in corner sp, *1 htr in every tr along side of square to corner**, [2 htr, ch 1, 2 htr] in corner sp; rep from * 2 times and from * to ** 1 time. Fasten off yarn D.

Round 9: Join yarn A in any corner sp, ch 1, [2 htr, ch 1, 2 htr] in same corner sp, *1 htr in every htr along side of square to corner**, [2 htr, ch 1, 2 htr] in next corner sp; rep from * 2 times and from * to ** 1 time.

Fasten off and darn in all ends neatly.

nelly

*

Alternating longer and shorter stitches within a traditional granny structure means it's possible to play with stitch sizes even if you are a beginner. We have used light and then dark colours in sequence to highlight the pattern.

A
B
C
D
E
F

Foundation ring: Using yarn A, ch 4, sl st in first ch to form ring.

Round 1: Ch 4 (counts as 1 dtr), 2 dtr in ring, ch 2, [3 dtr in ring, ch 2] 3 times, sl st in top of beg ch-4 to join. Fasten off yarn A.

Round 2: Join yarn B in any ch-2 corner sp, ch 1 (counts as 1 dc), [2 dc, ch 3, 2 dc] in same sp, ch 2, *[3 dc, ch 3, 3 dc] in next ch-2 sp, ch 2; rep from * 3 times, sl st in first ch to join. Fasten off yarn B.

Round 3: Join yarn C in any ch-3 corner sp, ch 4 (counts as 1 dtr), [2 dtr, ch 3, 3 dtr] in same sp, ch 2, 3 dtr in next ch-2 sp, ch 2, *[3 dtr, ch 2, 3 dtr] in next ch-3 sp, ch 2, 3 dtr in next ch-2 sp, ch 2; rep from * 2 times, sl st in top of beg ch-4 to join. Fasten off yarn C.

Round 4: Join yarn D in any ch-3 corner sp, ch 1 (counts as 1 dc), [2 dc, ch 3, 2 dc]

in same sp, [ch 2, 3 dc in next ch-2 sp] 2 times, ch 2, *[3 dc, ch 3, 3 dc] in next ch-3 sp, [ch 2, 3 dc in next ch-2 sp] 2 times, ch 2; rep from * 2 times, sl st in first ch to join. Fasten off yarn D.

Round 5: Join yarn E in any ch-3 corner sp, ch 4 (counts as 1 dtr), [2 dtr, ch 3, 3 dtr] in same sp, [ch 2, 3 dtr in next ch-2 sp] 3 times, ch 2, *[3 dtr, ch 3, 3 dtr] in next ch-3 sp, [ch 2, 3 dtr in next ch-2 sp] 3 times, ch 2; rep from * 2 times, sl st in top of beg ch-4 to join.

Round 6: Join yarn F in any ch-3 corner sp, ch 1, (counts as 1 dc) [2 dc, ch 3, 3 dc] in same sp, [ch 2, 3 dc in next ch-2 sp] 4 times, ch 2, *[3 dc, ch 3, 3 dc] in next ch-3 corner sp, [ch 2, 3 dc in next ch-2 sp] 4 times, ch 2; rep from * 2 times, sl st in first ch to join. Fasten off.

Round 7: Join yarn A in any ch-3 corner sp, ch 1 (counts as 1 dc), [1 dc, ch 1, 2 dc] in same sp, [ch 2, 3 dc in next ch-2 sp] 5 times, ch 2, *[2 dc, ch 1, 2 dc] in next corner ch-3 sp, [ch 2, 3 dc in next ch-2 sp] 5 times, ch 2; rep from * 2 times, sl st in first ch to join.

Fasten off and darn in ends neatly.

flotilla

**

Like a regatta on a sunny day, this graphic block is easy to grasp with its regular, repeating pattern. Remember to keep all the yarn tails at the back of the work. Great for mixing with some of the other nautical-themed blocks, this is equally at home in use on a boy's blanket or a modern, graphic afghan.

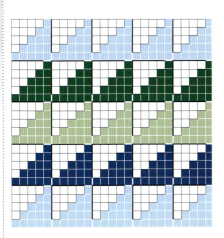

A
B
C
D
E

Foundation chain: Using yarn A, ch 26.

Row 1: (First row of chart) 1 dc in 2nd ch from hook, 1 dc in every ch to end, turn.

Work rem 24 rows of chart, ensuring you keep yarn ends on WS of work.

Rows 2 to 25: Ch 1, 1 dc in every dc to end, turn.

BORDER

Join yarn F in top RH corner st, ch 1, [2 dc, ch 1, 2 dc] in same st, 1 dc in every st along top of square to next corner, [2 dc, ch 1, 2 dc] in corner st, 1 dc in every sp between rows down side of square to next corner, [2 dc, ch 1, 2 dc] in corner st, 1 dc in every st along bottom of square

to next corner, [2 dc, ch 1, 2 dc] in next corner st, 1 dc in every sp between rows up final side of square to end, sl st in first dc to join.

Fasten off and darn in ends neatly. Block work to shape.

*

modern mesh

A
B
C

Proving that lace doesn't always have to be old-fashioned, this pleasingly graphic square is fast and easy to work up and looks really stylish repeated for a light throw. Perfect for adorning summer rooms or picnic chairs, and easily adaptable to bright or pastel colour combinations.

Foundation ring: Using yarn A, ch 6, sl st in first ch to form ring.

Round 1: Ch 1, 16 dc in ring, sl st in first dc to join. Fasten off yarn A.

Round 2: Join yarn B, ch 6 (counts as 1 tr, ch 3) *miss 1 st, 1 tr in next st, ch 3; rep from * 6 times, sl st in 3rd ch of beg ch-6 to join.

Round 3: Sl st in next sp, ch 3 (counts as 1 tr), [1 tr, ch 3, 2 tr] in same sp (forms corner), ch 1, 2 tr in next ch-3 sp, ch 1, *[2 tr, ch 3, 2 tr] in same sp (forms corner), ch 1, 2 tr in next ch-1 sp, ch 1; rep from * 2 times, sl st in top of beg ch-3 to join. Fasten off yarn B.

Round 4: Join yarn C in any corner ch-3 sp, ch 6 (counts as 1 tr, ch 3), 1 tr in same sp (forms corner), ch 1, [1 tr, ch 1] in each of next 5 ch-1 sps or sps between tr groups, *[1 tr, ch 3, 1 tr, ch 1] in next sp (forms corner), [1 tr, ch 1] in each of next 5 ch-1 sps or sps between tr groups; rep from * 2 times, sl st in 3rd ch of beg ch-6 to join.

Round 5: Sl st in next corner sp, ch 3 (counts as 1 tr), [1 tr, ch 3, 2 tr] in same sp (forms corner), ch 1, [1 tr, ch 1] in each of next ch-1 sps, *[2 tr, ch 3, 2 tr, ch 1] in next sp (forms corner), [1 tr, ch 1] in each of next 6 ch-1 sps; rep from * 2 times, sl st in top of beg ch-3 to join.

Round 6: Sl st 2 times along to next corner sp, ch 3 (counts as 1 tr), [1 tr, ch 3, 2 tr] in same sp (forms corner), ch 1, [1 tr, ch 1] in each of next 9 ch-1 sps or sps between tr groups, *[2 tr, ch 3, 2 tr, ch 1] in next sp (forms corner), [1 tr, ch 1] in each of next 9 ch-1 sps or sps between tr groups; rep from * 2 times, sl st in top of beg ch-3 to join.

Round 7: Sl st 2 times along to next corner sp, ch 3 (counts as 1 tr), [1 tr, ch 3, 2 tr] in same sp (forms corner), ch 1, [1 tr, ch 1] in each of next 12 ch-1 sps or sps between tr groups, *[2 tr, ch 3, 2 tr, ch 1] in next sp (forms corner), [1 tr, ch 1] in each of next 12 ch-1 sps or sps between tr groups; rep from * 2 times, sl st in top of beg ch-3 to join.

Round 8: Sl st 2 times along to next corner sp, ch 1, [2 dc, ch 2, 2 dc] in same sp (forms corner), 1 dc in each of next 2 tr, [1 dc in next ch-1 sp, 1 dc in next tr] 12 times along side of square, 1 dc in next sp, *1 dc in each of next 2 tr, [2 dc, ch 2, 2 dc] in next sp (forms corner), 1 dc in each of next 2 tr, [1 dc in next ch-1 sp, 1 dc in next tr] 12 times along side of square; rep from * 2 times, sl st in first ch to join.

Fasten off and darn in ends neatly.

***
bear paws

Perfect for a cot blanket or a special baby gift, this cute block uses bobbles to make the bear toes: make it in your child's favourite colour or to coordinate with the nursery.

Special stitch used:

Make bobble (MB): Make bobble with 5 tr, ch-1 to secure (*see page 19*).

SMALL SQUARES

Foundation ring: Using yarn A, make a magic ring.

Round 1: Ch 1, 8 dc in ring, sl st in first dc to join.

Round 2: Ch 1, 2 dc in each dc to end, sl st in first dc to join.

Round 3: Ch 1, 1 dc in every dc to end, sl st in first dc to join.

Round 4: Rep Round 2.

Round 5: Ch 1, 1 dc in next dc, *MB in next dc, 1 dc in each of next 2 dc; rep from * 4 times, MB in next dc, 1 dc in next dc, change to yarn B and fasten off yarn A, ch 1, 1 dc in each of next 4 dc, **2 dc in next dc, 1 dc in each of next 3 dc; rep from ** 2 times, 1 dc in last dc, sl st in first sc of yarn A to join.

Round 6: Ch 3 (counts as 1 tr), 1 htr in same st, [1 dc in each of next 2 dc, 1 htr in each of next 2 dc] 2 times, *[1 htr, 1 tr] in next dc, ch 1, [1 tr, 1 htr] in next dc (forms corner)**, [1 htr in each of next 2 dc, 1 dc in each of next 2 dc] 2 times; rep from * to ** 1 time, 1 dc in next dc, sl st in each of next 6 dc, 1 dc in next dc; rep from * to ** 1 time, 1 dc in next dc, sl st in each of next 6 dc, 1 dc in next dc, [1 htr, 1 tr] in next dc, ch 1, sl st in top of beg ch-3 to join. Fasten off.

A
B
C
D

Make 1 more square in these colours and 2 further squares using yarn A but with yarn C instead of yarn B.

Arrange squares so they are in an alternate pattern (as in photograph). Place 2 squares RS tog and, beginning at corner ch-1 sp, sl st together along vertical join using yarn D. Rep for foll 2 squares, then rep across horizontal join.

BORDER

Using yarn D, join in any corner ch-1 sp, ch 2 (counts as 1 htr), *1 htr in each st and each ch-1 sp to next corner ch-1 sp, 3 htr in corner ch-1 sp; rep from * 3 times, sl st in top of beg ch-2 to join.

Fasten off, darn in ends and block.

212 ★★

scrunch

A tactile, dense square with a soft pile, this pattern is best worked in a clean, flat yarn that shows off its appealing texture. Gorgeous for throws, blankets, rugs or cushions.

A

Foundation chain: Ch 33.

Row 1: 1 dc in 2nd ch from hook, 1 dc in every ch to end, turn.

Row 2: Ch 1, 1 dc in every dc to end, turn.

Row 3: Rep Row 2.

Row 4: Ch 1, 1 dc in each of next 2 dc, *ch 8, 1 dc in back lp of next st to create ch lp; rep from * until 2 dc remain, 1 dc in each of last 2 dc, turn.

Row 5: Ch 1, as you work fold ch lps forwards to access empty lps from Row 4, 1 dc in empty lp of each dc of Row 4 to end, turn.

Rows 6 to 29: Rep Rows 4 and 5 alternately.

Row 30: Rep Row 2.

Fasten off and darn in ends neatly.

213 ★★

ivan

A bold and striking block that gives the illusion of being worked in four separate squares – but is, in fact, only one – this is an easy block of colours. Great for use in boys' blankets or bedspreads, this mixes well with a host of other blocks in this book.

A
B
C
D
E

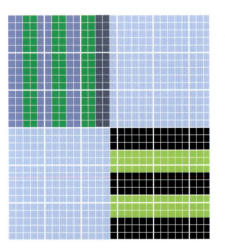

Note: Use separate balls of yarn for each area of colour.

Foundation chain: Using yarn A, ch 14, change to yarn B, ch 15.

Begin chart, changing colour where indicated.

Row 1: (First row of chart) 1 dc in 2nd ch from hook and 1 dc in every ch to end, turn.

Work rem 29 rows of chart, keeping yarn ends on WS of work.

Rows 2 to 30: Ch 1, 1 dc in every dc to end, turn.

Fasten off and darn in ends neatly. Block work to shape.

alice

Full of puffy roll stitches, this granny-type block has more going on than it appears. Lovely for mixing with flatter grannies as a textural contrast, the crab-stitch edging adds one last touch of stitch interest.

A
B
C
D

Special stitches used:

Side puff stitch (side pf): 1 tr in specified st or sp, *yoh, insert hook around post of last tr, yoh and pull through 1 lp; rep from * 2 times (7 lps on hook), yoh, pull through all lps on hook, ch 1 to close side puff st (*see page 19*).

Crab stitch (crab st): Single crochet worked in reverse (*see page 22*).

Foundation ring: Using yarn A, ch 4, sl st in first ch to form a ring.

Round 1: Ch 1, 8 dc in ring, sl st in first dc to join. Fasten off yarn A.

Round 2: Join yarn B in any dc, ch 2, [1 side pf around post of ch-2, ch 2, 1 tr, 1 side pf around post of tr] in same sp, *ch 1, miss 1 dc, [1 tr, 1 side pf around post of tr, ch 2, 1 tr, 1 side pf around post of tr] in next dc; rep from * 2 times, ch 1, sl st in top of first side pf to join. Fasten off yarn B.

Round 3: Join yarn C in any ch-2 corner sp, [ch 1, 1 dc, ch 2, 2 dc] in same corner sp, *ch 1, 2 dc in next ch-1 sp, ch 1, [2 dc, ch 2, 2 dc] in next ch-2 corner sp; rep from * 2 times, ch 1, 2 dc in next ch-1 sp, ch 1, sl st in first ch to join. Fasten off yarn C.

Round 4: Join yarn D in any ch-2 corner sp, ch 2, [1 side pf around post of ch-2, ch 2, 1 tr, 1 side pf around post of tr] in same sp, *[ch 1, 1 tr in next ch-1 sp, 1 side pf around post of tr] 2 times, ch 1, [1 tr, 1 side pf around post of tr, ch 2, 1 tr, 1 side pf around post of tr] in next ch-2 corner sp; rep from * 2 times, [ch 1, 1 tr in next ch-1 sp, 1 side pf around post of tr] 2 times, ch 1, sl st in top of first side pf to join. Fasten off yarn D.

Round 5: Join yarn A in any ch-2 corner sp, [ch 1, 1 dc, ch 2, 2 tr] in corner sp, *[ch 1, 2 dc in next ch-1 sp] 3 times, [ch 1, 2 dc, ch 2, 2 dc] in next ch-2 corner sp; rep from * 2 times, [ch 1, 2 dc in next ch-1 sp] 3 times, ch 1, sl st in first ch to join.

Round 6: [Ch 1, 1 dc, ch 2, 2 dc] in corner sp, *[ch 1, 2 dc in next ch-1 sp] 4 times, [2 dc, ch 2, 2 dc] in next corner ch-2 sp; rep from * 2 times, [ch 1, 2 dc in next ch-1 sp] 4 times, ch 1, sl st in first ch to join. Fasten off yarn A.

Round 7: Join yarn B in any ch-2 corner sp, [ch 2, 1 side pf around post of ch-2, ch 2, 1 tr, 1 side pf around post of tr] in corner ch-2 sp, *[ch 1, 1 tr, 1 side pf around post of tr] in next ch-1 sp 5 times, **[1 tr, side pf around post of tr, 1 tr, side pf around post of tr) in next ch-2 corner sp; rep from * 2 times and from * to ** 1 time, sl st in top of beg ch-2 to join. Fasten off yarn B.

Round 8: Join yarn C in any ch-2 corner sp, [ch 1, 1 dc, ch 2, 2 dc] in ch-2 corner sp, *[ch 1, 2 dc in next ch-1 sp] 6 times, [ch 1, 2 dc, ch 2, 2 dc] in corner ch-2 sp; rep from * 2 times, [ch 1, 2 dc in next ch-1 sp] 6 times, ch 1, sl st in first ch to join.

Round 9: [Ch 1, 1 dc, ch 2, 2 tr] in corner sp, *[ch 1, 2 dc in next ch-1 sp] 7 times, [ch 1, 2 dc, ch 2, 2 dc] in corner sp; rep from * 2 times, [ch 1, 2 dc in next ch-1 sp] 7 times, ch 1, sl st in first ch to join. Fasten off yarn C.

Round 10: Join yarn D in any ch-2 corner sp, [ch 3, 1 tr, ch 2, 2 tr] in same corner sp, *[ch 1, 2 tr in next ch-1 sp] 8 times, [ch 1, 2 tr, ch 2, 2 tr] in corner sp; rep from * 2 times, [ch 1, 2 tr in next ch-1 sp] 8 times, ch 1, sl st in top of beg ch-3 to join. Fasten off yarn D.

Round 11: Join yarn A in any ch-2 corner sp, *3 crab sts in corner ch-2 sp, 1 crab st in every st to next corner; rep from * 3 times, sl st in first crab st to join.

Fasten off and darn in ends.

215

*

simple cross

A basic central block of solid colours useful for mixing with more detailed squares, this has a tiny motif that is made separately and attached at the end. You could vary the type of motif you place here, or add more, according to your taste.

Note: Prepare 2 separate balls of yarn B before you begin. Use separate balls of yarn for each colour and keep yarn tails at WS of work.

Foundation chain: Using yarn A, ch 29.

Row 1: 1 dc in 2nd ch from hook, 1 dc in every ch to end, turn. Fasten off yarn A.

Row 2: Join yarn B, ch 1, 1 dc in each of next 11 dc, change to yarn A, 1 dc in each of next 6 dc, change to yarn B, 1 dc in each of next 11 dc, turn.

Row 3: Ch 1, 1 dc in each of next 11 dc, change to yarn A, 1 dc in each of next 6 dc, change to yarn B, 1 dc in each of next 11 dc, turn.

Rows 4 to 12: Rep Row 3. Fasten off.

Row 13: Join yarn A, ch 1, 1 dc in every dc to end, turn.

Rows 14 to 18: Rep Row 13.

Row 19: Rep Row 2.

Rows 20 to 30: Rep Row 3. Fasten off.

Row 31: Using yarn A, sl st in every dc along row to end. Fasten off yarn A.

TRIM

Foundation ring: Using yarn C, ch 4, sl st in first ch to form ring.

Round 1: ch 1, 12 dc in ring, sl st in first dc to join.

Round 2: Ch 3 (counts as 1 tr), ch 1, [1 tr in next dc, ch 1] 11 times, sl st in top of beg ch-3 to join.

Fasten off. Stitch in centre of cross as shown in photograph. Darn in all ends neatly and block work.

216

**

sea foam

A undulating lacy design makes up this pretty block, which would be equally effective worked in one colour, or with every lace stripe a different tone. A good block for working in cotton yarns for use in summer picnic blankets.

Foundation chain: Using yarn A, ch 32.

Row 1: 1 dc in 2nd ch from hook, in each ch to end, turn. Fasten off yarn A.

Row 2: Join yarn B, ch 3 (counts as 1 tr), 2 tr in same st, *ch 2, miss 2 sts, 1 dc in next st, ch 5, miss 3 sts, 1 dc in next st, ch 2, miss next 2 sts, 5 tr in next st; rep from * 1 time, ch 2, miss next 2 sts, 1 dc in next st, ch 5, miss next 3 sts, 1 dc in next st, ch 2, miss next 2 sts, 3 tr in last st, turn.

Row 3: Ch 4 (counts as 1 tr, ch 1), 1 tr in next st, ch 1, 1 tr in next st, *ch 2, 1 dc in ch-5 sp, ch 2, 1 tr in next str, [ch 1, 1 tr in next st] 4 times; rep from * 1 time, ch 2, 1 dc in next ch-5 sp, ch 2, [1 tr in next st, ch 1] 2 times, 1 tr in top of beg ch-3 from Row 2, turn.

Row 4: Ch 5 (counts as 1 tr, ch 2), 1 tr in next tr, ch 2, 1 tr in next tr, miss next 2 ch-2 sps, *1 tr in next tr, [ch 2, 1 tr in next tr] 4 times, miss next 2 ch-2 sps; rep from * 1 time, [1 tr in next tr, ch 2] 2 times, 1 tr in 3rd ch of beg ch-4 from Row 3, turn. Fasten off yarn B.

Row 5: Join yarn A, ch 3 (counts as 1 tr), 2 tr in next ch-2 sp, 1 tr in next st, [2 tr in next ch-2 sp] 2 times, *[1 tr in next st, 2 tr in next ch-2 sp] 3 times, 2 tr in next ch-2 sp; rep from * 1 time, 1 tr in next st, 1 tr in next ch-2 sp, 1 tr in 3rd ch of beg ch-5 from Row 4, turn. Fasten off yarn A.

Row 6: Join yarn B, ch 3 (counts as 1 tr), 2 tr in same st, *ch 2, miss 2 sts, 1 dc in next st, ch 5, miss 4 sts, 1 dc in next st, ch 2, miss next 2 sts, 5 tr in next st; rep from * 1 time, ch 2, miss next 2 sts, 1 dc in next st, ch 5, miss next 4 sts, 1 dc in next st, ch 2, miss next 2 sts, 3 tr in last st, turn.

Rep Rows 3 to 7 two times, and then Rows 3 to 6 one time (4 rep in total).

BORDER

Round 1: Join yarn A, ch 1, 1 dc in every st to corner, 3 dc in each corner st; rep from * 3 times, sl st in first dc to join. Fasten off yarn A.

Round 2: Ch 1, 1 dc in every dc to corner, 3 dc in centre dc of 3-sc corner group; rep from * 3 times, sl st in first dc to join.

Fasten off and darn in ends.

***
haight

Redolent of 1960s' San Francisco, this block is a hotchpotch arrangement of mini squares that allow endless scope for you to create your own psychedelic colour combinations. This is a fantastic square for using up all those teeny pieces of yarn, and it mixes well with all the other granny blocks.

TINY SQUARES

Foundation ring: Using first yarn, make magic ring.

Round 1: Ch 2 (counts as 1 htr), 2 htr in ring, [ch 2, 3 htr in ring] 3 times, ch 2, sl st in top of beg ch-2 to join. Fasten off.

Round 2: Join 2nd yarn in any ch-2 corner sp, ch 1, [2 dc, ch 1, 3 dc] in same ch-2 corner sp, ch 1, *[3 dc, ch 1, 3 dc] in next ch-2 corner sp, ch 1; rep from * 2 times, sl st in first ch to join. Fasten off.

Make 2 squares with yarn A for Round 1, yarn B for Round 2; make 2 squares with yarn C for Round 1, yarn B for Round 2; make 2 squares with yarn B for Round 1, yarn C for Round 2; make 2 squares with yarn B for Round 1, yarn A for Round 2; 8 squares in total.

A
B
C
D

LARGER SQUARES

Work as tiny square, then:

Round 3: Join 3rd yarn in any ch-1 corner sp, ch 2 (counts as 1 htr), (2 htr, ch 2, 3 htr) in same sp *ch 1, 3 htr in next ch-1 sp, ch 1, (3 htr, ch 2, 3 htr) in next corner ch-1 sp; rep from * 2 times, ch 1, 3 htr in next ch-1 sp, ch 1, sl st in top of beg ch-2 to join. Fasten off.

Round 4: Join 4th yarn in any corner ch-2 sp, ch 1, (2 dc, ch 1, 3 dc) in same sp, *ch 1, (3 dc in next ch-1 sp) 2 times**, (3 dc, ch 1, 3 dc) in next ch-2 corner sp; rep from * 2 times and from * to ** 1 time, sl st in top of beg ch-2 to join. Fasten off.

Make 1 square with yarn A for Round 1, yarn B for Round 2, yarn C for Round 3, yarn B for Round 4; make 1 square with yarn B for Round 1, yarn C for Round 2, yarn B for Round 3, yarn A for Round 4; 2 squares in total.

Arrange squares in pattern shown. Place two tiny squares WS tog, using yarn D, 1 dc in back lp of every st (including ch sts) along one seam. Join next 2 squares without breaking yarn by placing them WS tog and cont seam. Fasten off. Fold group of 4 squares horizontally across middle and join horizontal join with same method. Rep for other group of 4 tiny squares.

Now rep method to join composite tiny 4-square groups to larger squares into one large square. Do not fasten off.

BORDER

Using yarn D, ch 1, 1 dc in same st, *1 dc in every dc and every ch-sp to corner, 3 dc in corner ch-1 sp; rep from * 3 times, 1 dc in every dc to end, sl st in first dc to join.

Fasten off, darn in ends and block.

★★★

blue rose

This block is made up of many layers of petals, producing a raised motif and a dense square. You could choose to work each round of petals in a different colour to add even more depth.

A
B
C

Special stitches used:

Picot-3: Ch 3 (at point to add picot), sl st in first ch of ch-3, creating picot lp.

Make bobble (MB): Work 3 tr leaving last lp of each on hook, yoh, draw through all lps.

Foundation ring: Using yarn A, ch 5, sl st in first ch to form a ring.

Round 1: Ch 5 (counts as 1 tr, ch 2), [1 tr, ch 2] 7 times in ring, sl st in 3rd ch of beg ch-5 to join.

Round 2: Sl st in first ch-2 sp, *[1 dc, 1 htr, 1 tr, 1 dtr, picot-3, 1 tr, 1 htr, 1 dc] in ch-2 sp; rep from * 7 times, sl st in first sl st to join.

Round 3: *Ch 4, 1 dc between next 2 petals; rep from * 7 times, 1 dc in first ch of beg ch-4 to join. Tuck chains behind petals.

Round 4: Sl st in next ch-4 sp, *[1 dc, 1 htr, 2 tr, 1 dtr, picot-3, 2 tr, 1 htr, 1 dc] in ch-4 sp; rep from * 7 times, sl st in first sl st to join.

Round 5: *Ch 5, 1 dc between next 2 petals; rep from * 7 times, 1 dc in first ch of beg ch-5 to join. Tuck chains behind petals.

Round 6: Sl st in next ch-5 sp, *[1 dc, 1 htr, 3 tr, 1 dtr, picot-3, 3 tr, 1htr, 1 dc] in ch-5 sp; rep from * 7 times, sl st in first sl st to join.

Round 7: *Ch 6, 1 dc between next 2 petals; rep from * 7 times, 1 dc in first ch of beg ch-6 to join. Tuck chains behind petals.

Round 8: Sl st in next ch-6 sp, *[1 dc, 1 htr, 3 tr, 1 dtr, 3 tr, 1 htr, 1 dc] in ch-6 sp; rep from * 7 times, sl st in first sl st to join. Fasten off yarn A.

Round 9: Join yarn B in any dtr st in petal, ch 1, 1 dc in same dtr, *ch 3, 1 dtr in sp between next 2 petals (between dc sts), ch 3, [MB, ch 3, MB, ch 3, MB] in next dtr (forms corner), ch 3, 1 dtr in sp between next 2 petals, ch 3, 1 dc in next dtr; rep from * 3 times, sl st in first dc to join. Fasten off yarn B.

Round 10: Join yarn C in any corner bobble, ch 1, *[2 dc, ch 1, 2 dc] in bobble, 3 dc in next ch-3 sp, 1 dc in next bobble, 3 dc in next ch-3 sp, 1 dc in next dtr, 3 dc in next ch-3 sp, 1 dc in next dc, 3 dc in next ch-3 sp, 1 dc in next dtr, 3 dc in next ch-3 sp, 1 dc in next bobble, 3 dc in next ch-3 sp; rep from * 3 times, sl st in first ch to join.

Fasten off and darn in ends.

entwined

Crossed double treble stitches and interconnected rings make this elaborate block challenging but interesting to work. The centre is dense, so intersperse this block with other, thinner blocks to compensate when using in a composite piece.

Special stitch used:

Crossed double treble (crossed dtr): Insert hook behind dtr just worked and work in specified st, complete dtr st as normal.

FIRST RING

Foundation ring: Using yarn A, ch 14, sl st in first ch to form a ring.

Round 1: Ch 3 (counts as 1 tr), 35 tr in ring, sl st in top of beg ch-3 to join. Fasten off and darn in ends.

SECOND RING

Foundation ring: Using yarn B, ch 14, insert tail end of ch through centre of first ring, from back to front, sl st in first ch to form a ring. Complete as for first ring.

THIRD RING

Foundation ring: Using yarn C, ch 14, insert tail of ch through centre of 2nd ring, from back to front, sl st in first ch to join. Complete as for first ring.

FOURTH RING

Foundation ring: Using yarn D, ch 14, insert tail of ch from back to front through centre of 3rd ring, then from back to front through centre of first ring, in that order, sl st in first ch to join. Complete as for first ring.

Cut 4 lengths of a bright contrast yarn (or use st markers). Lay rings out flat, turning each so that ch-3 joins are all hidden under overlaps; thread one marker length in yarn sewing needle and place one st through outer point where two rings overlap (through 1 tr in each ring). Count along to ensure there are 14 tr between each marker, and rep for other 3 rings. This secures motif in place while adding border.

Round 1: Join yarn E in st to left of any marker, ch 1, 1 dc in every tr to end – 56 dc. Remove markers.

Round 2: Ch 2 (counts as 1 dc, ch 1), miss 1 dc, 1 dc in next dc, ch 1, miss 1 dc, 1 dc in next dc, ch 2, miss 2 dc, *[1 tr, ch 3, 1 tr] in next dc (forms corner), ch 2, miss 2 dc, [1 dc in next dc, ch 1, miss 1 dc] 4 times, 1 dc in next dc, miss 2 dc, ch 2; rep from * 2 times, [1 tr, ch 3, 1 tr] in next dc, ch 2, miss 2 dc, [1 dc in next dc, ch 1, miss 1 dc] 3 times, sl st in first ch of beg ch-2 to join. Fasten off.

Round 3: Join yarn F in any ch-3 corner sp, ch 1, *5 dc in corner sp, 1 dc in next tr, 2 dc in next ch-2 sp, [1 dc in next dc, 1 dc in next ch-1 sp] 4 times, 1 dc in next dc, 2 dc in next ch-2 sp, 1 dc in next tr; rep from * 3 times, sl st in first dc to join. Fasten off.

Round 4: Join yarn E in 3rd dc of any 5-dc corner group, ch 6 (counts as 1 tr, ch 3), 1 tr in same st, *ch 1, miss 3 dc, [1 dtr in next dc, ch 1, 1 crossed dtr 2 sts to right of last dtr worked, (working behind last dtr), ch 1] 2 times, miss 1 dc, 1 tr in next tr, ch 1, [miss 3 dc, 1 dtr in next dc, ch 1, 1 crossed dtr in st 2 sts to right of last dtr worked (working behind last dtr), ch 1] 2 times, miss 1 dc, **[1 tr, ch 3, 1 tr] in next sc; rep from * 2 times and from * to ** 1 time, sl st in 3rd ch of beg ch-6 to join.

Round 5: Ch 1, *5 dc in ch-3 sp, 1 dc in every st and every ch-1 sp (including between dtr and crossed dtr) to corner; rep from * 3 times, sl st in first dc to join.

Fasten off and darn in ends.

**

koi

Rows of fans create a fish scale-like texture that is stunning when worked in colours in close tones, as we have done here. Use a flat, shiny or matt yarn to show off the pattern. This block would be beautiful repeated over a pillow or for a stunning evening bag.

A
B
C
D

Foundation chain: Using yarn A, ch 33.

Row 1: 1 dc in 2nd ch from hook, *miss 2 ch, [3 sc, ch 1, 3 sc] in next ch, miss 2 ch, dc in next ch, ch 1, miss next ch, dc in next ch; rep from * 2 times, miss 2 ch, [3 tr, ch 1, 3 tr] in next ch, miss 2 ch, dc in last ch, turn.

Row 2: Ch 5 (counts as 1 htr, ch 3), *1 dc in next ch-1 sp (top of tr cluster), ch 3, [1 htr, ch 1, 1 htr] in next ch-1 sp between shells, ch 3; rep from * 2 times, dc in next ch-1 sp (top of tr cluster), ch 3, 1 htr in top of last st, turn.

Row 3: Ch 3 [counts as 1 tr], 2 tr in top of first htr from row below, *1 dc in next 3rd ch st, ch 1, 1 dc in first ch st of next group of ch sts, [3 tr, ch 1, 3 tr] in next ch-1 sp; rep from * 2 times, 1 dc in next 3rd ch st, ch 1, 1 dc in first ch st of the next group of ch sts, 3 tr in 3rd ch of ch-5 of row below, turn. Fasten off yarn A.

Row 4: Join yarn B, ch 4 (counts as 1 dc, ch 3), *[1 htr, ch 1, 1 htr] in next ch-1 sp, ch 3, 1 dc in next ch-1 sp (top of 3 tr cluster), ch 3; rep from * 2 times, [1 htr, ch 1, 1 htr] in next ch-1 sp, ch 3, 1 dc in top of ch-3 from row below (top of tr cluster), turn.

Row 5: Ch 1, *[3 tr, ch 1, 3 tr] in next ch-1 sp, 1 dc in next 3rd ch st, ch 1, 1 dc in first ch st of next group of ch sts; rep from * 2 times, [3 tr, ch 1, 3 tr] in next ch-1 sp, miss 2 ch, 1 dc in last ch st in row below, turn.

Row 6: Ch 5 (counts as 1 htr, ch 3), *1 dc in next ch-1 sp (top of tr cluster), ch 3, [1 htr, ch 1, 1 htr] in next ch-1 sp, ch 3; rep from * 2 times, 1 dc in next ch-1 sp (top of tr cluster), ch 3, 1 htr in top of last dc st, turn.

Row 7: Ch 3 (counts as 1 tr), 2 tr in top of htr from row below, *1 dc in next 3rd ch st, ch 1, 1 dc in first ch st of next group of ch sts, [3 tr, ch 1, 3 tr] in next ch-1 sp; rep from * 2 times, 1 dc in next 3rd ch st, ch 1, 1 dc in first ch st of next group of ch sts, 3 tr in 3rd ch of same group of ch sts. Fasten off yarn B.

Rows 8 to 11: Rep Rows 4 to 7, using yarn C.

Rows 12 to 15: Rep Rows 4 to 7, using yarn D.

Rows 16 to 19: Rep Rows 4 to 7, using yarn A.

Fasten off and darn in ends.

sea urchin

★★★

A pretty lace pattern that builds gradually to form a layered, intricate design. Keep the central area light to enhance the overall pattern. This block works best when made in a flat, matt yarn to show off its detail.

A
B
C
D
E

Special stitch used:

Double treble cluster (dtr cl): Make cl with 2 dtr (*see page 18*).

Foundation ring: Using A, ch 4, sl st in first ch to form ring.

Round 1: Ch 4, 1 dtr in ring, dtr cl in ring, ch 2, *dtr cl, ch 2; rep from * 6 times, sl st in first tr to join. Fasten off yarn A.

Round 2: Join yarn B in top of any dtr cl, ch 1, *1 dc in top of dtr cl, 3 dc in next ch-2 sp; rep from * 7 times, st in first dc to join. Fasten off yarn B.

Round 3: Join yarn C in any dc, ch 1, *1 dc in next dc, ch 2, miss 1 dc; rep from * 15 times, sl st in first dc to join.

Round 4: Sl st in next ch-2 sp, ch 1, *3 dc in same ch-2 sp, move to next ch-2 sp; rep from * 15 times, sl st in first st to join. Fasten off yarn C.

Round 5: Join yarn D in any dc, *ch 5, dc in same dc, [ch 3, miss 3 dc, dc in next dc] 3 times; rep from * 3 times, sl st in first ch of beg ch-5 to join.

Round 6: Sl st in next ch-5 sp, ch 3 (counts as 1 tr), [5 tr, ch 3, 6 tr] in next ch-5 sp, dc in next ch-3 sp, 7 tr in next ch-3 sp, dc in next ch-3 sp, *[6 tr, ch 3, 6 tr] in next ch-5 sp, dc in next ch-3 sp, 7 tr in next ch-3 sp, dc in next ch-3 sp; rep from * 2 times, sl st in top of beg ch-3 to join.

Round 7: Join yarn E in any corner, ch 1, *[1 dc, ch 3, 1 dc] in corner sp, [ch 4, 3 tr in next dc] 2 times, ch 4; rep from * 3 times, sl st in first st to join.

Round 8: Sl st in next corner sp, *5 dc in corner sp, [5 dc in next ch-4 sp, 1 dc in each of next 3 sts] 2 times, 5 dc in next ch-4 sp; rep from * 3 times, sl st in first st to join. Fasten off yarn E.

Round 9: Join yarn B in any middle st in corner, ch 5 (counts as 1 tr, ch 2), 1 tr in same corner sp, *1 tr in each of next 25 sts, [1 tr, ch 2, 1 tr] in next st; rep from * 2 times, 1 tr in each of next 25 sts, sl st in 3rd ch of beg ch-5 to join.

Round 10: Join yarn C in any corner sp, *[1 dc, ch 2, 1 dc] in corner sp, 1 dc in each of next 27 sts; rep from * 3 times, sl st in first st to join.

Fasten off and darn in ends.

**

bejewelled

A popcorn fiesta, this square has plenty of textural appeal and would mix well with flatter grannies and other bullion, puff or popcorn patterns. It works well for warmer blankets and throws, and children love the popcorn bobbles.

A
B
C
D
E
F

Special stitches used:

Beginning popcorn (beg pc): Ch 3, make popcorn with 5 tr (*see page 19*)

Popcorn (pc): Make popcorn with 6 tr.

Foundation ring: Using yarn A, make a magic ring.

Round 1: 8 dc in ring, sl st in first dc to join. Fasten off yarn A.

Round 2: Join yarn B in any dc, beg pc in same st, ch 2, pc in next st, *ch 2, pc in next st; rep from * 6 times, sl st in top of beg pc to join. Fasten off yarn B.

Round 3: Join yarn C in any ch-2 sp, ch 3 (counts as 1 tr), [2 tr, ch 2, 3 tr] in same sp (forms corner), 3 htr in next ch-2 sp, *[3 tr, ch 3, 3 tr] in next sp (forms corner), 3 htr in next ch-2 sp; rep from * 2 times, sl st in top of beg ch-3 to join. Fasten off yarn C.

Round 4: Join yarn D in any corner ch-3 sp, [beg pc, ch 3, pc] in same sp (forms corner), [ch 2, pc in next sp between 3 htr groups] 2 times, ch 2, *[pc, ch 3, pc] in same sp (forms corner), [ch 2, pc in next sp between 3 htr groups] 2 times, ch 2; rep from * 2 times, sl st in beg pc to join. Fasten off yarn D.

Round 5: Join yarn E in any ch-3 corner sp, ch 3 (counts as 1 tr), [2 tr, ch 3, 3 tr] in same sp (forms corner), 3 htr in each of next 3 ch-2 sps, *[3 tr, ch 3, 3 tr] in next ch-3 corner sp, 3 htr in each of next 3 ch-2 sps; rep from * 2 times, sl st in top of beg ch-3 to join. Fasten off yarn E.

Round 6: Join yarn F in any ch-3 corner sp, [beg pc, ch 3, pc] in same sp, ch 2, [pc, ch 2] in each of next 4 sps between 3 htr groups, *[pc, ch 3, pc] in next ch-3 corner sp, ch 2, [pc, ch 2] in each of next 4 sps between 3 htr groups; rep from * 2 times, sl st in beg pc to join. Fasten off yarn F.

Round 7: Join yarn C in any ch-3 corner sp, ch 3 (counts as 1 tr), [2 tr, ch 3, 3 tr] in same sp, ch 1, [3 htr, ch 1] in each of next 5 ch-2 sps, *[3 tr, ch 3, 3 tr] in next ch-3 corner sp, ch 1, [3 htr, ch 1] in each of next 5 ch-2 sps; rep from * 2 times, sl st in top of beg ch-3 to join, sl st in next corner ch-3 sp.

Round 8: Ch 3 (counts as 1 tr), [2 tr, ch 3, 3 dc] in same corner ch-3 sp, *1 tr in each of next 3 tr, 1 tr in next ch-1 sp, [miss next htr, 1 tr in each of next 2 htr, 1 tr in next ch-1 sp] 5 times, 1 tr in each of next 3 tr**, [3 tr, ch 3, 3 tr] in next ch-3 corner sp; rep from * 2 times and from * to ** 1 time, sl st in top of beg ch-3 to join.

Fasten off and darn in ends neatly.

**

snail shell

Working in a continuous spiral produces this snail-shell effect, best worked in two highly contrasting colours to show off the structure to advantage. Because this block also has a 'granny' edge, it mixes really well with many other blocks and looks stunning repeated over a throw.

A
B

Foundation ring: Using A, make a magic ring.

Round 1: Ch 1, [1 dc, 1 htr, 2 tr] in ring, do not fasten off yarn, join yarn B in ring, ch 1, [1 dc, 1 htr, 2 tr] in ring. Do not fasten off yarn. Pull ring tight.

Round 2: Cont with yarn B, 2 tr in next dc of yarn A, 2 tr in each of next 3 sts. Drop yarn B, but do not fasten off. Place m in lp of yarn B to show beg of rnd. Pick up lp of yarn A, 2 tr in next dc of yarn B, 2 tr in every tr to end of rnd (until you reach m again).

Round 3: Using yarn B, *2 tr in next tr, 1 tr in each of next 2 tr, move the m to final st of yarn B in this rnd; rep from * 8 times, pick up yarn A, **2 tr in next tr, 1 tr in each of next 2 tr; rep from ** 10 times, 2 tr in next tr, 1 tr in final tr of rnd.

Round 4: Using yarn B, *2 tr in next tr, 1 tr in each of next 3 tr; rep from * 10 times, 2 tr in next tr, 1 htr in next tr, 1 dc in last tr of rnd, using yarn A, *[2 tr, ch 2, 2 tr] in next tr, [miss 1 tr, ch 1, 2 tr in next tr] 6 times, miss 1 tr, ch 1; rep from * 4 times (last 2 tr group in st after final tr of yarn B).

Round 5: Sl st in next corner ch-2 sp, ch 3 (counts as 1 tr), [1 tr, ch 2, 2 tr] in corner sp, *[ch 1, 2 tr in next ch-1 sp] 7 times to next corner sp**, [2 tr, ch 2, 2 tr] in corner sp; rep from * 2 times and from * to ** 1 time, sl st in top of beg ch-3 to join.

Round 6: Join yarn B in any ch-2 corner sp, *[2 dc, ch 2, 2 dc] in corner sp, 1 dc in every tr to next corner sp; rep from * 3 times, sl st in first dc to join.

Fasten off and darn in ends.

**

can can

Bright frills adorn this linear block, which is reminiscent of the extravagant skirts of Parisian can-can dancers. A simple construction, this is easily adapted to include more or fewer rows of frills. Use bright colours to make the frills really pop.

A
B
C
D

Foundation chain: Using yarn A, ch 29.

Row 1: 1 dc in 2nd ch from hook, 1 dc in every ch to end, turn.

Row 2: Ch 1, 1 dc in every dc to end, turn.

Rows 3 to 6: Rep Row 2.

Row 7: Ch 1, 1 dc in first dc, remove hook and pull long lp of yarn A to temporarily secure st just worked (will be picked up again in Row 8), sl st yarn B to next dc along row, *ch 6, miss 3 dc, sl st in next dc; rep from * 5 times, turn, ch 1, *[2 dc, 3 htr, 2 dc] in next ch-6 lp, sl st in next sl st; rep from * 5 times. Fasten off yarn B.

Row 8: (RS facing) Pick up and tighten lp of yarn A dropped in Row 7, 1 dc in every dc to end, being careful to also work dc sts where sl sts of contrast yarn are worked to ensure row remains at 28 sts.

Rows 9 to 11: Rep Row 2.

Row 12: Rep row 7, using yarn C instead of yarn B.

Row 13: Rep Row 8.

Rows 14 to 17: Rep Row 2.

Row 18: Rep Row 7, using yarn D instead of yarn B.

Row 19: Rep Row 8.

Rows 20 to 23: Rep Row 2.

Row 24: Rep Row 12.

Row 25: Rep Row 8.

Rows 26 to 27: Rep Row 2.

Row 28: Rep Row 7.

Row 29: Rep Row 8.

Rows 30 to 33: Rep Row 2.

Fasten off and darn in ends neatly. Block work to shape.

★★★

marguerite

A lacy cluster flower that works up quickly, this delicate and pretty block would be perfect for summer use, in throws, picnic blankets, table linens or light shawls.

Special stitches used:

Beginning 3-quadruple-treble cluster (beg 3-quad tr cl): Ch 4, [yoh 4 times, insert hook in indicated st/sp, draw through a lp, yoh, draw through 2 lps 4 times] 2 times, yoh, draw through all lps on hook (see page 18).

3-quadruple-treble cluster (3-quad tr cl): [yoh 4 times, insert hook in indicated st/sp, draw through a lp, yoh, draw through 2 lps 4 times] 3 times, yoh, draw through all lps on hook.

Beginning 2-treble-crochet cluster (beg 2-tr cl): Ch 2, 1 tr leaving last lp on hook, draw through all lps.

2-treble-crochet cluster (2-tr cl): 2 tr, leaving last lp of each on hook, yoh, and draw through all lps.

Beginning 2-double-treble cluster (beg 2-dtr cl): ch 3, 1 dtr, leaving last lp on hook, yoh, draw through all lps on hook.

2-double-treble cluster (2-dtr cl): 2 dtr, leaving last lp of each on hook, yoh, draw through all lps on hook.

Foundation ring: Using yarn A ch 4, sl st in first ch to form ring.

Round 1: *1 dc in ring, ch 3; rep from * 7 times, sl st in first dc to join.

Round 2: Sl st in next ch-3 sp, beg 3-quad tr cl in ch-3 sp, ch 5, *3-quad tr cl in next ch-3 sp, ch 5; rep from * 6 times, sl st in top of beg 3-quad tr cl to join. Fasten off yarn A.

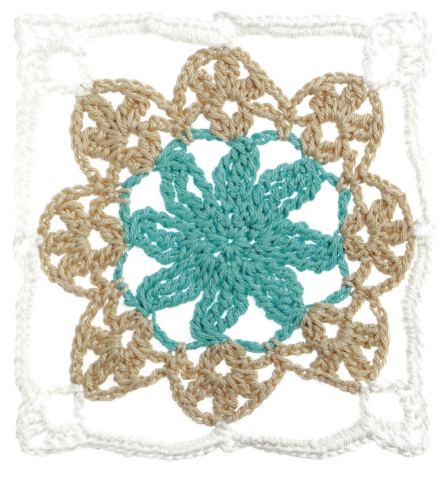

Round 3: Join yarn B in top of any quad tr cl, [beg 2-tr cl, ch 3, 2-tr cl] in top of quad tr cl from rnd below, ch 3, 1 dc in ch-5 sp, ch 3, *[2-tr cl, ch 3, 2-tr cl] in top of quad tr cl from rnd below, ch 3, 1 dc in ch-5 sp, ch 3; rep from * 6 times, sl st in top of beg 2-tr cl to join.

Round 4: Sl st in next ch-3 sp, [beg 2-dtr cl, ch 3, 2-dtr cl, ch 3, 2-dtr cl] in ch-3 sp, ch 3, 1 dc in dc st from rnd below, ch 3, *[2-dtr cl, ch 3] 3 times in ch-3 sp, 1 dc in dc st from rnd below, ch 3; rep from * 6 times, sl st in top of beg 2-dtr cl to join. Fasten off yarn B.

Round 5: Join C in top of any middle 2-dtr cl, *1 dc in middle 2-dtr cl, ch 10, [1 tr, ch 5 1 tr] in top of next middle 2-dtr cl, ch 10; rep from * 3 times, sl st in first dc to join.

Round 6: *14 dc in next ch-10 sp, [3 tr, ch 3, 3 tr] in next ch-5 sp, 14 dc in next ch-10 sp, ch 3; rep from * 3 times, sl st in first sc to join.

Fasten off and darn in ends.

teatime

***

A sister square to Van Gogh, this block uses the fascinating box diagonal stitch to create a series of steps that build into a square. If you want, you could change colour every row instead of every two rows as we have here. This dense block has tons of textural appeal and is fun to work.

A
B
C
D
E

Foundation row: Using yarn A, ch 6, turn, 1 tr in 4th ch from hook, 1 tr in each of last 2 tr of ch (5th and 6th from hook).

Row 1: Ch 6, turn, 1 tr in 4th ch from hook, 1 tr in each of last 2 tr of ch, flip work up towards you from bottom to access ch-3 sp from last row, sl st in ch-3 sp, ch 3, 3 tr in same sp.

Row 2: Ch 6, turn, 1 tr in 4th ch from hook, 1 tr in each of last 2 trs of ch, flip work up, sl st in ch-3 sp of next shell, ch 3, 3 tr in same sp, sl st in ch-3 sp of last shell in row, ch 3, 3 tr in same ch-3 sp. Fasten off yarn A.

Row 3: Join yarn B, ch 6, turn, 1 tr in 4th ch from hook, 1 tr in each of last 2 tr of ch, flip work up, *sl st in ch-3 sp of next shell, ch 3, 3 tr in same sp, rep from * 3 times.

Row 4: Work as Row 3 but rep from * 4 times instead of 3 times. Fasten off yarn B.

Row 5: Join yarn C, work as Row 3 but rep from * 5 times.

Row 6: Work as Row 3 but rep from * 6 times. Fasten off yarn C.

Row 7: Join yarn D, work as Row 3 but rep from * 7 times.

Row 8: Work as Row 3 but rep from * 8 times. Fasten off yarn D.

Row 9: Join yarn A, work as Row 3 but rep from * 9 times.

Row 10: Start decrease: ch 1, sl st in each of next 3 tr, *sl st in next ch-3 sp, ch 3, 3 tr in ch-3 sp; rep from * 9 times, sl st in last ch-3 sp. Fasten off yarn A.

Row 11: Join yarn B, work as Row 10 but rep from * 8 times, sl st in last ch-3 sp.

Row 12: Work as Row 10 but rep from * 7 times, sl st in last ch-3 sp. Fasten off yarn B.

Row 13: Join yarn C, work as Row 10 but rep from * 6 times, sl st in last ch-3 sp.

Row 14: Work as Row 10 but rep from * 5 times, sl st in last ch-3 sp. Fasten off yarn C.

Row 15: Join yarn D, work as for Row 10 but rep from * 4 times, sl st in last ch-3 sp.

Row 16: Work as Row 10 but rep from * 3 times, sl st in last ch-3 sp. Fasten off yarn D.

Row 17: Join yarn A, work as for Row 10 but rep from * 2 times, sl st in last ch-3 sp.

Row 18: Sl st in each of first 3 tr, sl st in next ch-3 sp, ch 3, 3 tr in same sp, sl st in last ch-3 sp.

Fasten off.

BORDER

Join yarn E in any corner sp, ch 1, *[1 dc, ch 1, 1 dc] in corner sp, 1 dc in every st to next corner; rep from * 3 times, sl st in first ch to end.

Fasten off and darn in ends.

*

aegean

Named for the gorgeous colours in the Greek sea, this block has rope-tie effects created through cleverly placed double crochet in a contrasting colour. The nautical theme makes it a lovely block to use in a bedspread or picnic afghan. Work fairly tightly to keep the block firm.

A
B
C
D
E

Foundation ring: Using yarn A, ch 10, sl st in first ch to form ring.

Round 1: Ch 3 (counts as 1 tr), 31 tr in ring, sl st in top of beg ch-3 to join. Fasten off yarn A.

Round 2: Join yarn B, ch 4, [miss 3 tr, 1 dc in next tr, ch 4] to end of rnd, sl st in base of first ch of beg ch-4 to join. Fasten off yarn B.

Round 3: Sl st yarn C in first ch-4 sp, ch 4 (counts as 1 dtr), 5 dtr in same ch-4 sp, [ch 1, 6 dtr] in next ch-4 sp, 7 times, ch 1, sl st in top of beg ch-4 to join. Fasten off yarn C.

Round 4: Join yarn A, [ch 7, 1 dc in ch-1 sp between group of sts] 8 times omitting last dc on last rep, sl st in first ch of beg ch-7 to join. Fasten off yarn A.

Round 5: Sl st yarn D in next ch-7 sp, ch 3 (counts as 1 tr), [5 tr, ch 3, 6 tr] in same sp (forms corner), *[ch 1, 6 htr, ch 1] in next ch-7 sp**, [6 tr, ch 3, 6 tr] in next ch-7 sp (forms corner); rep from * 2 times, then from * to ** 2 times, sl st in top of beg ch-3 to join. Fasten off yarn D.

Round 6: Join yarn A, *ch 6, [sl st, ch 3, sl st] in next corner sp (forms corner), ch 6, 1 dc in next ch-1 sp, ch 6**, 1 dc in next ch-1 sp; rep from * 2 times, then from * to ** 1 time, sl st in first ch of beg ch-6 to join. Fasten off yarn A.

Round 7: Sl st yarn E in next ch-6 sp, ch 3 (counts as 1 tr), 6 tr in same sp, *ch 1, [2 tr, ch 3, 2 tr] in next corner ch-sp, ch 1, 7 tr in next ch-6 sp, ch 1, 7 htr in next ch-6 sp, ch 1**, 7 tr in next ch-6 sp; rep from * 2 times, then from * to ** 1 time, sl st in top of beg ch-3 to join. Fasten off yarn E.

Round 8: Join yarn B, *ch 8, 1 dc in next ch-1 sp, ch 2, [sl st, ch 3, sl st] in next ch-3 sp (forms corner), ch 2, 1 dc in next ch-1 sp, ch 8, 1 dc in next ch-1 sp, ch 6**, 1 dc in next ch-1 sp; rep 2 times, then from * to ** 1 time, sl st in first ch of beg ch-8 to join. Fasten off yarn B.

Round 9: Sl st yarn A in next ch-8 sp, ch 3 (counts as 1 tr), 7 tr in same sp, *ch 1, 2 tr in next ch-2 sp, ch 1, [2 tr, ch 3, 2 tr] in next corner ch-3 sp, ch 1, 2 tr in next ch-2 sp, ch 1, 8 tr in next ch-8 sp, ch 1, 6 htr in next ch-6 sp, ch 1**, 8 tr in next ch-8 sp; rep from * 2 times, then from * to ** 1 time, sl st in top of beg ch-3 to join.

Fasten off and darn in ends neatly.

★★
floe

A bold stripy lace pattern, this block works up quickly and could easily be repeated to make a filigree window blind or special linens. Or perhaps a summer shawl or lightweight scarf: the possibilities are manifold.

Foundation row: Using yarn A, ch 34.

Row 1: 1 dc in 2nd ch from hook, *ch 5, miss next 3 ch, 1 dc in next ch; rep from * 7 times, turn.

Row 2: Ch 5 (counts as 1 tr, ch 2), 1 dc in next ch-5 sp, ch 5, 1 dc in next ch-5 sp, 4 tr in next dc, 1 dc in next ch-5 sp, *[ch 5, 1 dc in next ch-5 sp] 3 times, 4 tr in next dc, 1 dc in next ch-5 sp, ch 5, 1 dc in last ch-5 sp, ch 2, 1 tr in last dc. turn.

Row 3: Ch 1, 1 dc in first tr, ch 5, miss next ch-2 sp, 1 dc in next ch-5 sp, 4 tr in next dc, miss next 2 tr, 1 dc in sp before next tr sts, miss next 2 tr, 4 tr in next dc, 1 dc in next ch-5 sp, *[ch 5, 1 dc in next ch-5 sp] 2 times, 4 tr in next dc, miss next 2 tr, 1 dc in sp before next tr sts, miss next 2 tr, 4 tr in next dc, dc in next ch-5 sp, ch 5, miss last ch-2 sp, 1 dc in 3rd ch of ch-5 at beg of Row 2, turn.

Row 4: Ch 5 (counts as 1 tr, ch 2), 1 dc in next ch-5 sp, 4 tr in next dc, miss next 2 tr, 1 dc in sp before next tr st, ch 5, miss next 5 sts, 1 dc in sp before next tr st, miss next 2 tr, 4 tr in next dc, 1 dc in next ch-5 sp, ch 5, 1 dc in next ch-5 sp, 4 tr in next dc, miss next 2 tr, 1 dc in sp before next tr st, ch 5, miss next 5 sts, 1 dc in sp before next tr, miss next 2 tr, 4 tr in next dc, 1 dc in next ch-5 sp, ch 2, 1 tr in last dc, turn.

Row 5: Ch 1, 1 dc in first tr, 4 tr in next dc, miss next 2 tr, 1 dc in sp before next tr, ch 5, 1 dc in next ch-5 sp, ch 5, miss next 3 sts, 1 dc in sp before next tr st, miss next 2 tr, 4 tr in next dc, 1 dc in next ch-5 sp, 4 tr in next dc, miss next 2 tr, 1 dc in sp before next tr st, ch 5, 1 dc in next ch-5 sp, ch 5, miss next 3 sts, 1 dc in sp before next tr st, miss next 2 tr, 4 tr in next dc, 1 dc in 3rd of ch-5 at beg of Row 4, turn. Fasten off.

A
B
C
D

Row 6: Join yarn B, ch 3 (counts as 1 tr), 2 tr in first dc, miss next 2 tr, 1 dc in sp before next tr st, ch 5, 1 dc in next ch-5 sp, 4 tr in next dc, 1 dc in next ch-5 sp, ch 5, miss next 3 sts, 1 dc in sp before next tr, miss next 3 tr, 4 tr in next dc, miss next 2 tr, 1 dc in sp before next tr, ch 5, 1 dc in next ch-5 sp, 4 tr in next dc, 1 dc in next ch-5 sp, ch 5, miss next 3 sts, 1 dc in sp before next tr, miss next 2 tr, 3 tr in last dc, turn.

Row 7: Ch 1, 1 dc in first tr, ch 5, 1 dc in next ch-5 sp, 4 tr in next dc, miss next 2 tr, 1 dc in sp before next tr, miss next 2 tr, 4 tr in next dc, 1 dc in next ch-5 sp, ch 5, miss next 3 sts, 1 dc in sp before next tr, ch 5, 1 dc in next ch-5 sp, 4 tr in next dc, miss next 2 tr, 1 dc in sp before next tr, miss next 2 tr, 4 tr in next dc, 1 dc in next ch-5 sp, ch 5, miss next 2 tr, 1 dc in last tr, turn.

Rows 8 to 9: Rep Rows 4 to 5.

Rows 10 to 13: Change to yarn C, rep Rows 6 to 7, then Rows 4 to 5.

Rows 14 to 17: Change to yarn D, rep Rows 6 to 7, then Rows 4 to 5.

Rows 18 and 19: Change to yarn A, rep Rows 6 to 7.

Fasten off and darn in ends neatly.

229

*

curlicues

A
B

This block features simply constructed curls at regular intervals, forming a textural pattern that is designed to be playful. Wonderful for mixing with other texture or lace blocks, here we have used hand-painted yarn effectively to add extra appeal.

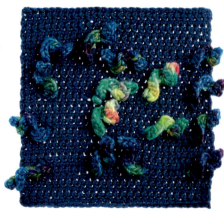

Special stitch used:

Make curlicue: Ch 6, 3 dc in 2nd ch from hook, 3 dc in each of next 4 ch, sl st in beginning st.

Foundation row: Using yarn A, ch 29.

Row 1: 1 dc in 2nd ch from hook, 1 dc in every ch to end, turn.

Row 2: Ch 1, 1 dc in every dc to end, turn.

Rows 3 to 8: Rep Row 2.

Row 9: Ch 1, 1 dc in each of next 3 dc, *change to yarn B, make curlicue, change to yarn A, 1 dc in each of next 6 dc; rep from * 2 times, change to yarn B, make curlicue, change to yarn A, 1 dc in each of next 3 dc, turn.

Row 10: Ch 1, 1 dc in every dc to end, working 1 dc across back post of first ch st of each curlicue instead of dc it stems from – 28 sts.

Rows 11 to 15: Rep Row 2.

Row 16: Ch 1, 1 dc in each of next 3 dc, change to yarn B, make curlicue, change to yarn A, 1 dc in each of next 6 dc, *change to yarn C, make curlicue, change to yarn A, 1 dc in each of next 6 dc; rep from * 1 time, change to yarn B, make curlicue, change to yarn A, 1 dc in each of last 3 dc, turn.

Row 17: Rep Row 8.

Rows 18 to 22: Rep Row 2.

Row 23: Rep Row 14.

Row 24: Rep Row 8.

Rows 26 to 29: Rep Row 2.

Row 30: Rep Row 7.

Row 31: Rep Row 8

Row 32: Rep Row 2.

Fasten off and darn in ends. To block, pin end of each curlicue in position you want it to fall, steam block and leave to dry.

230

★★★★

cromer

A
B
C
D

Inspired by the seaside resort of the same name, this bright and breezy square would be beautiful in a nautical-inspired blanket. Keep the seaside design going with Fleetwood, Sailboat and Starfish. Use a separate ball or length of yarn for each area of colour over the chart and remember to keep the yarn tails on the wrong side.

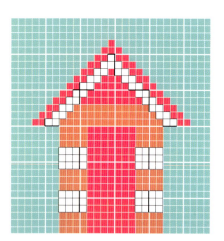

Foundation chain: Using yarn A, ch 30.

Row 1: 1 dc in 2nd ch from hook, 1 dc in every ch to end, turn.

Now work 30 rows of chart, changing colour where indicated and keeping yarn tails on WS instead.

Row 2 and every foll row: Ch 1, 1 dc in every dc to end, turn.

Fasten off and darn in ends neatly. Block work to size.

**
alpine

Small chain loops make the bobbles in this textural block. It works equally well made in a wool or flat cotton, so it's versatile in throws or pillows.

A

Foundation row: Ch 28.

Row 1: 1 dc in 2nd ch from hook, 1 dc in every ch to end, turn.

Row 2: Ch 1, 1 dc in every dc to end, turn.

Row 3: Ch 1, 1 dc in each of next 4 dc, ch 4, [1 dc in each of next 6 dc, ch 4] 3 times, 1 dc in each of next 5 dc, turn.

Row 4: Ch 1, *1 dc in each of next 4 dc, ch 4, 1 dc in each of next 2 dc, ch 4; rep from * 3 times, 1 dc in each of last 3 dc, turn.

Row 5: Ch 1, *1 dc in each of next 2 dc, ch 4, 1 dc in each of next 4 dc, ch 4; rep from * 3 times 1 dc in each of last 3 dc, turn.

Row 6: Ch 1, 1 dc in each of next 2 dc, ch 4, [1 dc in each of next 6 dc, ch 4] 4 times, 1 dc in last dc, turn.

Rows 7 to 10: Rep Row 2.

Row 11: Rep Row 3.

Row 12: Rep Row 4.

Row 13: Rep Row 5.

Row 14: Rep Row 6.

Row 15: Rep Row 5.

Row 16: Rep Row 4.

Row 17: Rep Row 3.

Rows 18 to 21: Rep Row 2.

Row 22: Rep Row 6.

Row 23: Rep Row 5.

Row 24: Rep Row 4.

Row 25: Rep Row 3.

Rows 26 to 27: Rep Row 2.

BORDER

Ch 4 (counts as 1 tr, ch 1) miss 1 dc, 1 tr in

next dc, *ch 1, miss 1 dc, 1 tr in next dc; rep from * to next corner, 3 dc in next corner sp, 1 dc in side post of every dc to next corner, ch 3 (counts as 1 tr), 1 tr in first ch, **ch 1, miss 1 ch, 1 tr in next ch; rep from ** to next corner, 3 dc in last dc, 1 dc around side post of every dc to last corner, 3 dc in last corner sp, sl st in 3rd ch of beg ch-3 to join.

Fasten off and darn in ends.

*
flores

A simple block with appliqued flowers on a basic ground, this is effective and would be lovely repeated with larger flower blocks in a little girl's blanket. Or use to make special table linens.

A
B
C

BACKGROUND

Foundation row: Using yarn C, ch 27.

Row 1: 1 dc in 2nd ch from hook, 1 dc in every ch to end, turn.

Rows 2 to 31: Ch 1, 1 dc in every dc to end, turn. Fasten off after Row 31.

FLOWERS

Foundation ring: Using yarn B, make a magic ring.

Round 1: Ch 1, 12 dc in ring, sl st in first chain. Pull ring tight, fasten off.

Round 2: Join yarn C in back lp of any dc, *ch 4, [sl st in back lp of next dc] 2 times; rep from * 5 times, sl st in first ch-4 sp.

Round 3: *[1 dc, 1 htr, 3 tr, 1 htr, 1 dc] in ch-4 sp, sl st in next ch-4 sp; rep from * 5 times to create 6 petals, sl st in first sl st to join.

Fasten off and darn in ends.

Make another flower the same, then two more using yarn C instead of B and yarn B instead of C.

Using a blunt darning needle and a length of yarn A, st the flowers on to the background.

**
cockleshell

The shells in this block stand up in pretty rows thanks to the ingenious use of double treble stitches at the rear to push them forwards. Great for use in a seaside-inspired throw or picnic blanket, this is fun to work and has lots of textural appeal.

A

B

Special stitch used:

Front-post double treble (FPdtr): Yoh 2 times, insert hook through front of st post from right to left, yoh, draw yarn through, [yoh, draw through 2 lps] 3 times (*see page 21*).

Foundation row: Using yarn A, ch 20.

Row 1: 1 dc in 2nd ch from hook, 1 dc in every ch to end, turn – 19 dc.

Row 2: Ch 1, 1 dc in first dc, *miss 2 dc, 7 tr in next dc, miss 2 dc, 1 dc in next dc; rep from * 2 times, turn. Join yarn B, do not fasten off yarn A.

Row 3: Using yarn B, ch 2, 1 dc in same sp, ch 2, *1 FPdtr in dc at base of shell from last row, ch 2, 1 dc in next dc**, ch 2; rep from * 1 time and from * to ** 1 time, 1 dc in last dc, turn.

Row 4: Ch 3, 2 tr in first dc, *1 dc in next dtr, 7 tr in next dc; rep from * 1 time, 3 tr in final dc, turn.

Row 5: Join yarn A, ch 2, 1 dc in same sp, ch 2, *1 dc in next dc, ch 2, 1 FPdtr in dc at base of shell from last row, ch 2; rep from * 1 time, 1 dc top of beg ch-3 from last row, turn.

Row 6: Ch 1, 1 dc in same sp, *7 tr in next dc, 1 dc in next dtr; rep from * 1 time, 7 tr in next dc, 1 dc in top of beg ch-2 from last row, turn.

Rows 7 to 10: Rep Rows 3 to 6

Rows 11 to 14: Rep Rows 3 to 6.

Row 15: Rep Row 3.

Row 16: Rep Row 4.

BORDER

Round 1: Join yarn A in any corner sp, *[1 dc, ch 1, 1 dc] in corner sp, 1 dc in every st to next corner sp, [1 dc, ch 1, 1 dc] in next corner sp, 19 dc worked evenly down side of square to next corner; rep from * 1 time, sl st in first corner sp.

Round 2: Ch 2 (counts as 1 htr), [ch 2, 1 htr] in same corner sp, 1 htr in every dc to next corner sp**, (1 htr, ch 1, 1 htr) in corner sp; rep from * 2 times and from * to ** 1 time, sl st in corner sp.

Round 3: Ch 2 (counts as 1 htr), [ch2, 1 htr] in corner sp, ch 1, [miss 1 htr, 1 htr in next htr, ch 1] to next corner sp**, [1 htr, ch 1, 1 htr] in corner sp; rep from * 2 times and from * to ** 1 time, sl st in corner sp. Fasten off yarn A.

Round 4: Join yarn B in any corner sp, ch 2 (counts as 1 htr), [1 htr, ch 2, 2 htr] in corner sp, *[ch 1, 1 htr in every ch-1 sp] to next corner**, [2 htr, ch 2, 2 htr] in corner ch-1 sp; rep from * 2 times and from * to ** 1 time, sl st in top of beg ch-2 to join.

Fasten off and darn in ends.

hoxton

★★

A modern minimalistic design with stacks of urban appeal, this filet pattern is worked with separate balls of yarn for each colour area. Remember to keep yarn tails on the wrong side when not in use.

A

B

Note: Before you begin, prepare 3 separate balls of yarn A and 2 of yarn B. Use separate ball of yarn for each colour section.

Foundation chain: Using yarn A, ch 33.

Row 1: 1 tr in 4th ch from hook, 1 tr in every ch to end, turn.

Row 2: Ch 3 (counts as 1 tr) 1 tr in each of next 2 tr, change to yarn B, [ch 1, miss 1 tr, 1 tr in next tr] 4 times, change to yarn A, ch 1, miss 1 tr, 1 tr in each of next 7 tr change to yarn B, [ch 1, miss 1 tr, 1 tr in

next tr] 4 times, change to yarn A, ch 1, miss 1 tr, 1 tr in each of last 3 tr, turn.

Rows 3 to 6: Rep Row 2. Fasten off yarn B after Row 6.

Row 7: Using yarn A, ch 3 (counts as 1 tr), 1 tr in every tr to end, turn.

Rows 8 to 9: Rep Row 7.

Rows 10 to 14: Rep Row 2, joining in yarn B as directed.

Row 15: Rep Row 7.

Fasten off and darn in ends.

---

starfish

★★

A playful twist on a four-patch block, this cute design would look lovely in a nautical-theme blanket, and children are sure to adore it. Team it with other seaside squares for fun on the ocean wave.

A

B

C

PATCHES

Foundation ring: Using yarn A, make a magic ring.

Round 1: Ch 1, 10 dc in ring, sl st in first dc to join.

Round 2: *Ch 4, sl st in 2nd ch from hook, 1 dc in next ch, 1 tr in last ch, miss 1 dc at base, sl st in next dc; rep from * 4 times, sl st in first sl st to join. Fasten off yarn A.

Round 3: Join yarn B to tip of any point, *ch 7, 1 dc in tip of the next point; rep from * 4 times, sl st in first ch to join.

Round 4: *7 dc in next ch-7 sp, 1 dc next dc; rep from * 4 times, sl st in first ch to join. Fasten off yarn B.

Round 5: Join yarn C in any dc, ch 3 (counts as 1 tr), [2 tr, ch 3, 3 tr] in same st (forms corner), 1 tr in each of next 9 dc, *[3 tr, ch 3, 3 tr] in next dc (forms corner), 1 tr in each of next 9 dc; rep from * 2 times, sl st in top of beg ch-3 to join. Fasten off yarn C.

Make another 3 patches in the same way.

Arrange patches so that each has one tip at top and two at bottom, place patches RS tog and using a length of yarn C and a blunt darning needle, stitch tog in front lps only (lps closest to you).

BORDER

Join yarn B in any corner, 3 dc in corner, 1 dc in every dc to next corner; rep from * 3 times, sl st in first dc to join.

Fasten off and darn in ends.

★★★

fair isle

A square influenced by the traditional knitting associated with the Scottish island of Fair Isle. A soft wool yarn is most suitable for this design. Colours are joined and fastened off at the beginning or end of rows as required, and stranded across the wrong side of the work.

A
B
C

Foundation chain: Using yarn A, ch 33.

Row 1: 1 tr in 4th ch from hook, 1 tr in every ch to end, turn.

Row 2: Ch 2, join yarn B, ch 1, (counts as 1 tr), *1 tr in next tr, change to yarn B, 1 tr in next tr, change to yarn A; rep from * to end, turn.

Row 3: Using yarn A, ch 3 (counts as 1 tr here and throughout), 1 tr in every tr to end, turn.

Row 4: Using yarn C, rep Row 3.

Row 5: Using yarns C and A respectively, rep Row 2.

Row 6: Rep Row 3.

Row 7: Rep Row 5.

Row 8: Rep Row 4.

Row 9: Rep Row 3.

Row 10: Using yarn A, ch 3, 1 tr in next tr, *change to yarn C, 1 tr in each of next 3 tr, change to yarn A, 1 tr in next tr; rep from * 6 times, 1 tr in last tr, turn.

Row 11: Using yarn A, ch 3, 1 tr in next tr, *change to yarn B, 1 tr in each of next 3 tr, change to yarn A, 1 tr in next tr; rep from * 6 times, 1 tr in last tr, turn.

Row 12: Rep Row 10.

Row 13: Rep Row 3.

Row 14: Rep Row 5.

Row 15: Rep Row 5.

Row 16: Using yarn B, rep Row 3.

Row 17: Using yarns B and C respectively, rep Row 5.

Row 18: Rep Row 4.

Row 19: Rep Row 3.

Fasten off and darn in ends neatly.

★★★

fleetwood

Designed with nostalgia, this picture block works wonderfully with Cromer, Sailboat and Flotilla as part of a nautical-themed warm blanket. Perfect for use in a child's room or a beach house, the little touches of embroidery bring this square to life.

A
B
C
D

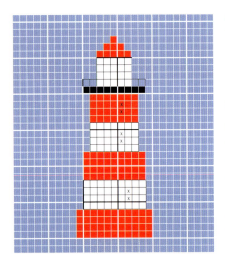

Note: Prepare two separate balls of yarn A before you start. Work colour chart using separate ball of yarn for each colour area and changing where indicated.

Foundation chain: Using yarn A, ch 30.

Row 1: 1 dc in 2nd ch from hook, 1 dc in every ch to end, turn.

Work rem 29 rows of chart, changing colour where necessary. Remember to keep yarn tails at WS of work.

Row 2 and every foll row: Ch 1, 1 dc in every dc to end, turn.

EMBROIDERY

Using a length of yarn D, stitch lighthouse balcony design as shown on chart and photograph: work straight stitches in a square pattern each of 8 dc in Row 23 (row above balcony base). Using another length of yarn D, stitch windows in at points shown on chart. Use straight stitch around dc sts, then cross stitch over each square.

Fasten off and darn in ends neatly. Block work to shape.

✷✷
danish square

An interesting twist on a granny-type block, this traditional Scandinavian square uses lattice patterning effectively with a taut, central square motif at its heart. A really good square for using many colours.

A
B
C
D

Foundation chain: Using yarn A, ch 10, sl st in first ch to form ring.

Round 1: Ch 1, 20 dc in ring, sl st in first dc to join.

Round 2: Ch 9, *miss 4 dc, 1 dc in next dc, ch 8; rep from * 2 times, sl st in first ch of ch-9 to join.

Round 3: Ch 1, 1 dc in same st [9 dc in next ch-8 sp, 1 dc in next sc] 3 times, 9 dc in next ch-8 sp, join with sl st in first dc. Fasten off yarn A.

Round 4: Join yarn B in 5th dc of any lp, *2 dc in next dc (forms corner), [1 dc in next dc] 9 times; rep from * 3 times, sl st in first st to join. Fasten off yarn B.

Round 5: Join yarn C, ch 1, *2 dc in next dc (forms corner), [1 dc in next dc] 10 times; rep from * 3 times, join with sl st in first st. Fasten off yarn C.

Round 6: Join yarn D in any corner, *1 tr, ch 1, 1 tr (forms corner), [ch 1, miss 1 st, 1 tr in next st] 5 times, ch 1; rep from * 3 times, sl st in first st to join.

Round 7: Sl st in next ch-1 sp, ch 1, *4 dc in same st (forms corner), [1 dc in next tr, 1 dc in ch-sp, 1 dc in next tr] 7 times; rep from * 3 times, sl st in first st to join. Fasten off yarn D.

Round 8: Join yarn B in any corner dc, *3 dc in each corner st and 1 dc in each dc; rep from * to end of round, sl st in first st to join. Fasten off yarn D.

Round 9: Join yarn A in centre st of any corner, ch 4 (counts as 1 tr), [ch 1, 1 tr], 3 times in same st, *[ch 1, miss 1 st, 1 tr, ch 1, miss 1 st] in corner ch-sp**, [ch 1, 1 tr] 4 times, ch 1 in same st (forms corner); rep from * 2 times, then from * to ** 1 time, sl st in first st to join – 8 tr along each side, four 4 tr corner groups.

Round 10: Sl st in corner st, ch 4 (counts as 1 tr), *[ch 1, 1 tr] 3 times in same corner sp (forms corner), ch 1, miss 1 st, [1 tr in the next dc, ch 1, miss 1 st, 1 tr in next tr]**; rep all along to corner, ch 1, [1 tr, ch 1] 4 times in same st (forms corner); rep from * to ** 2 times, sl st in first st to join – 11 tr along each side, four 4-tr corner groups. Fasten off yarn A.

Round 11: Join yarn B in any corner sp, ch 3 (counts as 1 tr), 2 tr in same sp, *1 tr in each st and each tr** and 5 tr in each corner sp, on final side rep from * to **, 1 tr in each st and 2 tr in last corner sp, sl st in first st to join. Fasten off yarn B.

Round 12: Join yarn C in corner sp, ch 1, 1 dc in same sp, *[1 dc, ch 1] in each st; rep from * to end of rnd, sl st in first dc to join.

Fasten off yarn C and darn in ends.

*

st tropez

A simple half-treble crochet block that turns frequently to offer a varied texture. Here we have used bright Mediterranean colours, but you could use any colour combination you want for this square, and it mixes easily with loads of other grannies.

A
B

Foundation ring: Using yarn A, ch 8, sl st in first ch to form ring.

Round 1: Ch 1, 24 tr in ring., sl st in first ch to join.

Round 2: Ch 1, 1 htr in first htr, *ch 1, miss 1 htr, 1 htr in next sp; rep from * 10 times, sl st in first htr to join. Fasten off yarn A.

Round 3: Join yarn B in any ch-1 sp, *[2 htr, ch 3, 2 htr] in corner ch-1 sp, [ch 1, 1 htr in next ch-1 sp] 2 times, ch 1; rep from * 3 times sl st in first htr to join, sl st to next ch-3 corner sp.

Round 4: Turn work to WS, ch 2 (counts as 1 htr), [1 htr, ch 3, 2 htr] in corner ch-3 sp, *[ch 1, 1 htr in next ch-1 sp] 3 times, ch 1**, [2 htr, ch 3, 2 htr] in corner ch-3 sp; rep from * 2 times and from * to ** 1 time, sl st in top of beg ch-2 to join. Fasten off yarn B.

Round 5: Turn work to RS, join yarn A in any ch-3 corner sp, ch 2 (counts as 1 htr), [1 htr, ch 3, 2 htr] in corner ch-3 sp, *[ch 1, 1 htr in next ch-1 sp] 4 times, ch 1**, [2 htr, ch 3, 2 htr] in next ch-3 sp; rep from * 2 times and from * to ** 1 time, sl st in top of beg ch-2 to join, sl st to next ch-3 corner sp.

Round 6: Turn work to WS, ch 2 (counts as 1 htr), [1 htr, ch 3, 2 htr] in ch-3 sp, *[ch 1, 1 htr in next ch-1 sp] 5 times, ch 1**, [2 htr, ch 3, 2 htr] in next ch-3 sp; rep from * 2 times and from * to ** 1 time, sl st in top of beg ch-2 to join. Fasten off yarn A.

Round 7: Turn work to RS, join yarn B in any ch-3 corner sp, ch 2 (counts as 1 htr) *[1 htr, ch 3, 2 htr] in ch-3 sp, *[ch 1, 1 htr in next ch-1 sp] 6 times, ch 1**; rep from * 2 times and from * to ** 1 time, sl st in top of beg ch-2 to join, sl st to next ch-3 corner sp.

Round 8: Turn work to WS, ch 2 (counts as 1 htr), [1 htr, ch 3, 2 htr] in ch-3 sp, *[ch 1, 1 htr in next ch-1 sp] 7 times, ch 1**; rep from * 2 times and from * to ** 1 time, sl st in top of beg ch-2 to join. Fasten off yarn B.

Round 9: Turn work to RS, join yarn A in any ch-3 corner sp, ch 2 (counts as 1 htr), [1 htr, ch 3, 2 htr] in ch-3 sp, *[ch 1, 1 htr in next ch-1 sp] 8 times, ch 1**; rep from * 2 times, and from * to ** 1 time, sl st in top of beg ch-2 to join, sl st to next ch-3 corner sp.

Round 10: Turn work to WS, ch 2 (counts as 1 htr), [1 htr, ch 3, 2 htr] in ch-3 sp, *[ch 1, 1 htr in next ch-1 sp] 9 times, ch 1**; rep from * 2 times and from * to ** 1 time, sl st in top of beg ch-2 to join.

Round 11: Turn work to RS, ch 2 (counts as 1 htr), [1 htr, ch 3, 2htr] in ch-3 sp, *[ch 1, 1 htr in next ch-1 sp 10 times, ch 1**; rep from * 2 times and from * to ** 1 time, sl st in top of beg ch-2 to join.

Fasten off and darn in ends.

filet diagonal

Another graphic, bold design worked in filet that is great for using in contemporary interior settings; repeated, this would make a fabulous table cover or runner, or perhaps as a modern window treatment such as a blind or café curtain.

Foundation chain: Using yarn A, ch 26.

Row 1: Ch 3 (counts as 1 tr, ch 1), miss 1 ch, 1 tr in each of next 7 ch, ch 1, miss 1 ch, 1 tr in each of next 9 ch, ch 1, miss 1 ch, 1 tr in each of next 5 ch, ch 1, miss 1 ch, 1 tr in last ch, turn.

Row 2: Ch 2 (counts as 1 tr), 2 tr, ch 1, miss 1 ch , 5 tr, ch 1, miss 1 st, 9 tr, ch 1, miss 1 st, 7 tr, turn.

Row 3: Ch 2 (counts as 1 tr), 4 tr, ch 1, miss 1 st, 9 tr, ch 1, miss 1 st, 5 tr, ch 1, miss 1 ch, 5 tr, turn.

Row 4: Ch 3 (counts as 1 tr, ch 1), miss 1 st, 5 tr, ch 1, miss 1 st, 5 tr, ch 1, miss 1 st, 9 tr, ch 1, miss 1 st, 3 tr, turn.

Row 5: Ch 3 (counts as 1 tr, ch 1), miss 1 st, 9 tr, ch 1, miss 1 st, 5 tr, ch 1, miss 1 st, 5 tr, ch 1, miss 1 st, 3 tr, turn.

Row 6: Ch 2 (counts as 1 tr), 4 tr, ch 1, miss 1 st, 5 tr, ch 1, miss 1 st, 5 tr, ch 1, miss 1 st, 9 tr, turn.

Row 7: Ch 2 (counts as 1 tr), 6 tr, ch 1, miss 1 st, 5 tr, ch 1, miss 1 st, 5 tr, ch 1, miss 1 st, 5 tr, ch 1, miss 1 st, 1 tr, turn.

Row 8: Ch 2 (counts as 1 tr), 2 tr, ch 1, miss 1 st, 5 tr, ch 1, miss 1 st, 5 tr, ch 1, miss 1 st, 5 tr, ch 1, miss 1 st, 5 tr, turn.

Row 9: Ch 2 (counts as 1 tr), 2 tr, ch 1, miss 1 st, 5 tr, ch 1, miss 1 st, 5 tr, ch 1, miss 1 st, 5 tr, ch 1, miss 1 st, 5 tr, turn.

Row 10: Ch 2 (counts as 1 tr), 6 tr, ch 1, miss 1 st, 5 tr, ch 1, miss 1 st, 5 tr, ch 1, miss 1 st, 5 tr, ch 1, miss 1 st, 1 tr, turn.

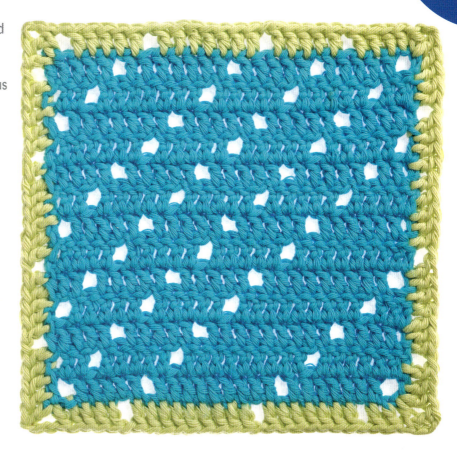

A
B

Row 11: Ch 2 (counts as 1 tr), 4 tr, ch 1, miss 1 st, 5 tr, ch 1, miss 1 st, 5 tr, ch 1, miss 1 st, 7 tr, ch 1, miss 1 st, 1 tr, turn.

Row 12: Ch 2 (counts as 1 tr), 2 tr, ch 1, miss 1 st, 7 tr, ch 1, miss 1 st, 5 tr, ch 1, miss 1 st, 5 tr, ch 1, miss 1 st, 3 tr, turn.

Row 13: Ch 3 (counts as 1 tr, ch 1), miss 1 st, 5 tr, ch 1, miss 1 st, 5 tr, ch 1, miss 1 st, 7 tr, ch 1, miss 1 st, 5 tr. Fasten off yarn A, do not turn.

BORDER

Using yarn B, insert hook in top right corner of work and work around square as foll:

Row 1: Top of square (1 st or sp in each st or sp as directed), ch 2 (counts as 1 tr), 4 tr, ch 1, miss 1 st, 5 tr, ch 1, miss 1 st, 7 tr, ch 1, miss 1 st, 5 tr, ch 1, miss 1 st, 1 tr in corner st.

Row 2: LH side of square (2 sts or sps for every row of work), ch 2 (counts as 1 tr) 2 tr, ch 1, miss 1 st, 5 tr, ch 1, miss 1 st, 7 tr, ch 1, miss 1 st, 5 tr, ch 1, miss 1 st, 5 tr.

Row 3: Bottom of square (1 st or sp in every st as directed) ch 3 in corner st, (counts as 1 tr, ch 1) miss 1 st, 4 tr, ch 1, miss 1 st, 9 tr, ch 1, miss 1 st, 7 tr, ch 1, miss 1 st, 3 tr.

Row 4: RH side of square (2 sts or sps for every row of work) ch 2 (counts as 1 tr) 3 tr, ch 1, miss 1 st, 7 tr, ch 1, miss 1 st, 9 tr, ch 1, miss 1 st, 4 tr, ch 3, sl st in beg st of round to join.

Fasten off and darn in ends neatly.

***

portobello

With its bohemian appeal this block is reminiscent of this trendy London neighbourhood. It is formed in the round but turned as if being made in rows, making it interesting to work.

A
B
C

Foundation chain: Using yarn A, ch 2.

Row 1: Ch 3 (counts as 1 tr) 1 tr in 4th and 5th ch sts from hook, fasten off, turn.

Row 2: Join yarn B, ch 3 (counts as 1 tr), 1 tr in each of next 2 tr, working down side, *ch 3, 1 tr around post of last tr worked, 1 tr in next st, 1 tr in next ch-sp, 1 tr in last st; rep from * along base, then working up side, ch 3, 1 tr around post of last tr worked, 1 tr in next st, [1 tr in next ch-sp] 2 times, 1 tr in next st, 1 tr in last st, fasten off, turn.

Row 3: Join yarn C, ch 3 (counts as 1 tr), 1 tr in each of next 2 tr, ch 1, miss 1 tr, 1 tr in each of next 3 tr, working down side, *ch 3, 1 tr around post of last tr worked, 1 tr in next st, 1 tr in next ch-sp, 1 tr in last st, ch 1, miss 1 ch, 1 tr in each of next 3 tr; rep from * along base, working up side, ch 3, 1 tr around post of last tr worked, 1 tr in base row, 1 tr in next st, 1 tr in next ch-1 sp, ch 1, miss 1 ch, 1 tr in each of next 5 sts, fasten off, turn.

Maintain the formula above – after ch-3 sps working 1 tr around post of last tr worked, then 1 tr in base row, 1 tr in next st, 1 tr in next ch-1 sp, for each foll row.

Row 4: Join yarn A, ch 3 (counts as 1 tr), 1 tr in each of next 2 tr, [ch 1, miss 1 ch, 1 tr in next tr] 3 times, 1 tr in each of next 2 tr, working down side, * ch 3, 4 tr, [ch 1, miss 1 ch, 1 tr in next tr] 3 times, 1 tr in each of next 2 tr; rep from along base, working up side, ch 3 , 4 tr, [ch 1, miss 1 ch, 1 tr in next tr] 3 times, 4 tr, fasten off, turn.

Row 5: Join yarn B, ch 3 (counts as 1 tr), 1 tr in each of next 2 tr, [ch 1, miss 1 ch, 1 tr in next tr] 5 times, 1 tr in each of next 2 tr, working down side, *ch 3, 4 tr, [ch 1, miss 1 ch, 1 tr in next tr] 5 times, 1 tr in each of next 2 tr; rep from * along base, working up side, ch 3, 4 tr, [ch 1, miss 1 ch, 1 tr in next tr] 5 times, 4 tr, fasten off, turn.

Row 6: Join yarn C, ch 3 (counts as 1 tr), 1 tr in each of next 2 tr, [ch 1, miss 1 ch, 1 tr in next tr] 7 times, 1 tr in each of next 2 tr, working down side, * ch 3, 4 tr, [ch 1, miss 1 ch, 1 tr in next tr] 7 times, 1 tr in each of next 2 tr; rep from * along base, working up side, ch 3. 4 tr, [ch 1, miss 1 ch, 1 tr in next tr] 7 times, 4 tr, fasten off, turn.

Row 7: Join yarn A, ch 3 (counts as 1 tr), 1 tr in each of next 2 tr, [ch 1, miss 1 ch, 1 tr in next tr] 9 times, 1 tr in each of next 2 tr, working down side, * ch 3, 4 tr, [ch 1, miss 1 ch, 1 tr in next tr] 9 times, 1 tr in each of next 2 tr; rep from * along base, working up side, ch 3, 4 tr, [ch 1, miss 1 ch, 1 tr in next tr] 9 times, 4 tr, fasten off, turn.

Row 8: Join yarn B, ch 3 (counts as 1 tr), 1 tr in each of next 2 tr, [ch 1, miss 1 ch, 1 tr in next tr] 11 times, 1 tr in each of next 2 tr, working down side, * ch 3, 4 tr, [ch 1, miss 1 ch, 1 tr in next tr] 11 times, 1 tr in each of next 2 tr; rep from * along base, working up side, ch 3, 4 tr, [ch 1, miss 1 ch, 1 tr in next tr] 11 times, 4 tr.

Fasten off and darn in ends.

***

hoops

An unusual construction method creates pretty little circular flaps that sit on top of the base fabric. The hoops are secure enough for use in a child's blanket; they are fun to play with and would look great worked in either bright or nursery colours.

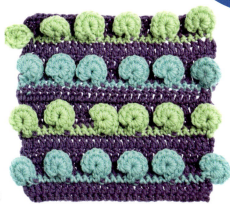

A
B
C

Special stitch used:

Make hoop: Ch 4, sl st in first ch to join, ch 2 (counts as 1 htr), 10 htr in ring, sl st in top of beg ch-2 to join hoop, turn square to WS, sl st in same base st ch-4 began from, turn to RS again. Turning work allows hoops to sit in same direction.

Note: When working Row 4, make sure you work a st in back of each hoop to allow for st hoop occupies, otherwise you will not retain 28 sts.

Foundation row: Using yarn A. ch 29.

Row 1: 1 dc in 2nd ch from hook, 1 dc in every ch to end, turn.

Row 2: Ch 3 (counts as 1 tr), 1 tr in every dc to end, turn. Fasten off yarn A.

Row 3: Join yarn B, 1 dc in first tr, *make hoop in next tr, 1 dc in each of next 4 tr; rep from * 4 times, make hoop in next tr, 1 dc in last dc. Fasten off yarn B.

Row 4: Join yarn A, ch 3 (counts as 1 tr), 1 tr in every dc along row including in back of hoops (push hoops to other side of work as you go along). Count sts at end of row to check you still have 28.

Rows 5 to 6: Rep Row 2.

Row 7: Rep Row 3, using yarn C.

Row 8: Rep Row 4.

Rows 9 to 10: Rep Row 2.

Row 11: Rep Row 3, using yarn B.

Row 12: Rep Row 4.

Rows 13 to 14: Rep Row 2.

Row 15: Rep Row 3, using yarn C.

Row 16: Rep Row 4.

Row 17: Ch 1, 1 dc in every tr to end.

Fasten off and darn in ends.

***

*

dobby

This square is named for the weaving that it resembles. A simple repeating fair isle pattern, which could be worked in many different colour combinations to create different effects. The yarns are joined and fastened off at the sides and carried across the wrong side of the block when not in use.

A
B
C

Foundation chain: Using yarn A, ch 33.

Row 1: (WS) 1 tr in 4th ch from hook, 1 tr in every ch to end, turn.

Row 2: (RS) Ch 2, join yarn B, ch 1 (counts as 1 tr), miss 1 tr, 1 tr in each of next 3 tr, *change to yarn A, 1 tr in next tr, change to yarn B, 1 tr in each of next 3 tr; rep from * 5 times, change to yarn A, 1 tr in last tr, turn.

Row 3: Using yarn A, ch 2, change to yarn B, ch 1 (counts as 1 tr), miss 1 tr, *change to yarn C, 1 tr in next tr, change to yarn B, 1 tr in next tr, change to yarn A, 1 tr in next tr, change to yarn B, 1 tr in next tr; rep from * 5 times, change to yarn C, 1 tr in next tr, change to yarn B, 1 tr in next tr, change to yarn A, 1 tr in last tr, turn.

Row 4: Rep Row 2.

Row 5: Using yarn A, ch 3, 1 tr in every tr to end, turn.

Rows 6 to 17: Rep Rows 2 to 5 three times.

Fasten off and darn in ends.

** bold filet blocks

A detailed diagonal filet pattern that alternates large and small blocks, this graphic design would look particularly effective used as part of a window treatment where the light would highlight the linear pattern perfectly.

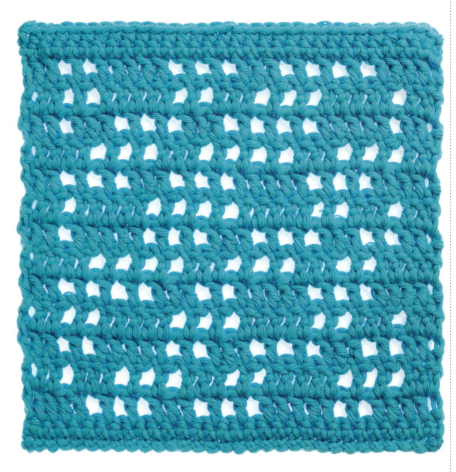

Foundation chain: Ch 31.

Row 1: 1 dc in 2nd ch from hook, 1 dc in every ch to end of row, turn.

Row 2: Ch 1, 1 dc in every dc to end of row, turn.

Row 3: Ch 2 (counts as 1 tr), 4 dc, ch 1, miss 1 st, 1 tr, ch 1, miss 1 st, 5 tr, [ch 1, miss 1 st, 1 tr] 2 times, ch 1, miss 1 st, 3 tr, [ch 1, miss 1 st, 1 tr] 2 times, ch 1, miss 1 st, 5 tr, turn.

Row 4: Ch 2 (counts as 1 tr), 2 tr, ch 1, miss 1 st, 3 tr, [ch 1, miss 1 st, 1 tr] 2 times, ch 1, miss 1 st, 3 tr, ch 1, miss 1 st, 1 tr, ch 1, miss 1 st, 5 tr, [ch 1, miss 1 st, 1 tr] 2 times, ch 1, miss 1 st, 3 tr, turn.

Row 5: Ch 2 (counts as 1 tr), 2 tr, ch 1, miss 1 st, 1 tr, ch 1, miss 1 st, 3 tr, [ch 1, miss 1 st, 1 tr] 2 times, ch 1, miss 1 st, 3 tr, ch 1, miss 1 st, 1 tr, ch 1, miss 1 st, 5 tr, ch 1, miss 1 st, 1 tr, ch 1, miss 1 st, 3 tr, turn.

Row 6: Ch 2 (counts as 1 tr), 2 tr, ch 1, miss 1 st, 1 tr, ch 1, miss 1 st, 5 tr, [ch 1, miss 1 st, 1 tr] 2 times, ch 1, miss 1 st, 5 tr, ch 1, miss 1 st, 1 tr, [ch 1, miss 1 st, 3 tr] 2 times, turn.

Row 7: Ch 2 (counts as 1 tr), 4 tr, [ch 1, miss 1 st, 1 tr] 2 times, ch 1, miss 1 st, 5 tr, ch 1, miss 1 st, 1 tr, ch 1, miss 1 st, 3 tr, [ch 1, miss 1 st, 1 tr] 3 times, ch 1, miss 1 st, 3 tr, turn.

Row 8: Ch 2 (counts as 1 tr), 4 tr, [ch 1, miss 1 st, 1 tr] 3 times, ch 1, miss 1 st, 3 tr, [ch 1, miss 1 st, 1 tr] 2 times, ch 1, miss 1 st, 3 tr, ch 1, miss 1 st, 1 tr, ch 1, miss 1 st, 5 tr, turn.

Row 9: Ch 2 (counts as 1 tr), 2 tr, ch 1, miss 1 st, 1 tr, ch 1, miss 1 st, 3 tr, [ch 1, miss 1 st, 1 tr] 2 times, ch 1, miss 1 st, 3 tr, [ch 1, miss 1 st, 1 tr] 2 times, ch 1, miss 1 st, 5 tr, ch 1, miss 1 st, 3 tr, turn.

Row 10: Ch 2 (counts as 1 tr), 2 tr, ch 1, miss 1 st, 5 tr, [ch 1, miss 1 st, 1 tr] 3 times, ch 1, miss 1 st, 5 tr, ch 1, miss 1 st, 1 tr, ch 1, miss 1 st, 3 tr, ch 1, miss 1 st, 3 tr, turn.

Row 11: Ch 2 (counts as 1 tr), 4 tr, [ch 1, miss 1 st, 1 tr] 2 times, ch 1, miss 1 st, 5 tr, [ch 1, miss 1 st, 1 tr] 2 times, ch 1, miss 1 st, 3 tr, [ch 1, miss 1 st, 1 tr] 2 times, ch 1, miss 1 st, 3 tr, turn.

Row 12: Ch 2 (counts as 1 tr), 4 tr, [ch 1, miss 1 st, 1 tr] 2 times, ch 1, miss 1 st, 3 tr, [ch 1, miss 1 st, 1 tr] 3 times, ch 1, miss 1 st, 3 tr, [ch 1, miss 1 st, 1 tr] 2 times, ch 1, miss 1 st, 3 tr, turn.

Row 13: Ch 2 (counts as 1 tr), 2 tr, ch 1, miss 1 st, 5 tr, [ch 1, miss 1 st, 1 tr] 3 times, ch 1, miss 1 st, 3 tr, [ch 1, miss 1 st, 1 tr] 2 times, ch 1, miss 1 st, 3 tr, ch 1, miss 1 st, 3 tr, turn.

Row 14: Ch 2 (counts as 1 tr), 2 tr, ch 1, miss 1 st, 1 tr, ch 1, miss 1 st, 5 tr, ch 1, miss 1 st, 1 tr, ch 1, miss 1 st, 3 tr, [ch 1, miss 1 st, 1 tr] 2 times, ch 1, miss 1 st, 5 tr, ch 1, miss 1 st, 3 tr, turn.

Row 15: Ch 2 (counts as 1 tr), 4 tr, [ch 1, miss 1 st, 1 tr] 3 times, ch 1, miss 1 st, 3 tr, [ch 1, miss 1 st, 1 tr] 2 times, ch 1, miss 1 st, 5 tr, ch 1, miss 1 st, 1 tr, ch 1, miss 1 st, 3 tr, turn.

Rows 16 to 17: Ch 1, 1 dc in every st to end.

Fasten off and darn in ends neatly.

★★★
agapanthus

Inspired by the extravagant African lilies, this block has a lacy structure combined with a loopy texture, making it tactile. It looks striking as part of a flower-garden piece, or for a lightweight blanket.

A
B
C

Special stitches used:

Picot-5 cluster (picot-5 cl): *Ch 5 (at point to add picot), sl st in first ch of 5-ch to form lp; rep from * 4 times in same sp to form cluster (*see page 18*).

Beginning 3-half-treble crochet cluster (beg 3-htr cl): Ch 2, make cluster with 2 htr in same st or sp (*see page 18*).

3-half-treble crochet cluster (3-htr cl): Make cluster with 3 htr in same st or sp.

Foundation ring: Using yarn A, make a magic ring.

Round 1: Ch 1, 16 dc in ring, sl st in first dc to join.

Round 2: Ch 4 (counts as 1 htr), *ch 5, miss 1 dc, 1 htr in next dc; rep from * 6 times, ch 5, miss 1 dc, sl st in top of beg ch-4 to join.

Round 3: Ch 1, 1 dc in same st, *5 dc in next ch-5 lp, 1 dc in next htr; rep from * 6 times, 5 dc in next ch-5 lp, sl st to first dc to join. Do not fasten off, leave yarn at back of work.

Round 4: Join yarn B with sl st, picot-5 cl in same st, sl st in back lp only of next 5 dc, sl st in next sc; rep from * 7 times, ending with sl st in first sl st to join. Do not fasten off; leave yarn at back of work.

Round 5: Pick up yarn A, ch 10 (counts as 1 tr, ch 7), *1 tr in back of next picot-5 cl (at base), ch 7; rep from * 6 times, sl st in 3rd ch of beg ch-10 to join.

Round 6: Ch 1, sl st in next ch-7 lp, 7 dc in same lp, *1 dc in next tr, 7 dc in next ch-7 lp; rep from * 6 times, sl st in first ch to join. Do not fasten off; leave yarn at back of work.

Round 7: Pick up yarn B, ch 1, picot-5 cl in same st, sl st in back lp only of next 7 dc, sl st in next dc; rep from * 7 times, ending with sl st in first sl st to join. Fasten off yarn B.

Round 8: Pick up yarn A, sl st in 2nd sl st of next ch-7 lp, ch 2 (counts as 1 htr), 1 htr in each of next 2 sl sts, *[3 tr, ch 2, 3 tr) in next sl st (forms corner), 1 htr in each of next 3 sl sts, ch 1, 1 dc in each of next 7 sl sts**, ch 1, 1 htr in each of next 3 sl sts; rep from * 2 times and from * to ** 1 time, ch 1, sl st in top of beg ch-2 to join. Fasten off yarn A.

Round 9: Join yarn C, ch 1, *1 dc in every st to corner ch-2 sp, [2 dc, ch 1, 2 dc) in corner ch-2 sp; rep from * 3 times, 1 dc in every st to end, sl st in first dc to join.

Round 10: Beg 3-htr cl, [miss 2 dc, ch 2, 3-htr cl in next dc] 2 times, *miss 2 dc, ch 2, [3-htr cl, ch 2, 3-htr cl] in next ch-1 corner sp, [miss 2 dc, ch 2, 3-htr cl in next dc] 8 times; rep from * 3 times, miss 2 dc, ch 2, [3-htr cl, ch 2, 3-htr cl] in next ch-1 corner sp, [miss 2 dc, ch 2, 3-htr cl in next dc] 5 times, miss 2 dc, ch 2, sl st in top of beg ch-2 to join. Fasten off yarn C.

Round 11: Join yarn B, ch 1, *1 dc in every 3-htr cl and 2 dc in every ch-2 sp to corner ch-2 sp, 3 dc in corner ch-2 sp; rep from * 3 times, 1 dc in every 3-htr cl and 2 dc in every ch-2 sp to end, sl st to first dc to join.

Fasten off and darn in ends.

**

hibiscus

A bold and ruffly bloom with a centre of bobbly stamens, this square is irresistible to handle and looks stunning as a highlight block in a composite piece. Team it with Maui and Aloha for extra tropical charm.

A
B
C

Special stitch used:

Make bobble (MB): Make bobble with 3 tr (*see page 19*).

Foundation ring: Using yarn A, ch 4, sl st in first ch to form ring.

Round 1: Ch 2 (counts as 1 htr), 11 htr in ring, sl st in front lp of top of beg ch-2 to join.

Round 2: *Ch 5, MB in 3rd ch from hook, ch 3, sl st in next 2 ch sts to base, sl st in front lp of top of same htr, sl st in front lp of each of next 2 htr, ch 4, MB in 3rd ch from hook, ch 3, sl st in next 2 ch sts to base, sl st in front lp of top of same htr, sl st in front lp of each of next 2 htr; rep from * 2 times, ending with sl st in first ch to join – 6 stamens made. Fasten off.

Round 3: Join yarn B to back lp of same st, ch 3 (counts as 1 tr), 2 tr in back lps of every htr from Round 1, 1 tr in same st as beg ch-3, sl st in top of beg ch-3 to join.

Round 4: Ch 2 (counts as 1 htr), *2 htr in next htr, 1 htr in next htr; rep from * all the way around, sl st in front lp of top of beg ch-2 to join.

Round 5: Working in front lps only, ch 2 (counts as 1 htr), [1 tr, 1 dtr] in same sp, [1 dtr, 1 tr, 1 htr] in next tr, *[1 htr, 1 tr, 1 dtr] in next tr, [1 dtr, 1 tr, 1 htr] in next tr; rep from * all the way around, sl st in first ch of beg ch-2 to join. Fasten off.

Round 6: Join yarn C in back lp of any htr from Round 4, ch 6 (counts as 1 dtr, ch 2), miss 1 htr, *1 ttr in back lp of next htr, ch 2, miss 1 htr, 1 quad tr in back lp of next htr, ch 2, miss 1 htr, 1 ttr in back lp of next htr, ch 2, miss 1 htr, 1 dtr in back lp of next htr, ch 4, miss 1 htr**, 1 dtr in back lp of next htr, ch 2, miss 1 htr; rep from * 2 times and from * to ** 1 time, sl st in 4th ch of beg ch-6 to join.

Round 7: Ch 1, 1 dc in same st, 4 dc in next ch-4 sp, *1 dc in next dtr, 2 dc in next ch-2 sp, 1 dc in next ttr, 2 dc in next ch-2 sp, [2 dc, ch 2, 2 dc] in next dtr dtr, 2 dc in next ch-2 sp, 1 dc in next ttr, 2 dc in next ch-2 sp, **1 dc in next ttr; rep from * 2 times, and from * to ** 1 time, sl st in first dc to join.

Round 8: Ch 2 (counts as 1 htr), ch 1, miss 1 st, *[1 htr in next dc, ch 1, miss 1 st] to corner, [2 htr, ch 3, 2 htr] in next corner ch-2 sp; rep from * 3 times, ch 1, miss 1 st, [1 htr in next st, ch 1, miss 1 st] to end, sl st in top of beg ch-2 to join.

Round 9: ch 1, *1 dc in each st and every ch-1 sp along to corner, [2 dc, ch 2, 2 dc] in next ch-3 corner sp; rep from * 3 times, 1 dc in each st and every ch-1 sp to end, sl st in first dc to join.

Fasten off and darn in ends.

★★★
raspberry cane

Adapted from an Edwardian pattern, this block has a neat diamond pattern of bobbles on a stripy double crochet ground. It would look equally effective worked in pastel colours, and was traditionally used in bedspreads.

Special stitch used:

Make bobble (MB): Make bobble with 5 dc, ch 1 to secure (*see page 19*). Pull tight on bobble for this pattern and carry yarn B along back of work between bobbles when not in use.

Foundation ring: Using yarn A, make a magic ring.

Round 1: Ch 2 (counts as 1 htr), 2 htr in ring, ch 2 [3 htr in ring, ch 2] 3 times, sl st in top of beg ch-2 to join.

Round 2: Ch 1, 1 dc in every htr to ch-2 corner sp, *[1 dc, ch 2, 1 dc] in ch-2 sp, 1 dc in every htr to next corner ch-2 sp; rep from * 2 times, [1 dc, ch 2, 1 dc] in ch-2 corner sp, 1 dc in every htr to end, sl st in first dc to join. Fasten off yarn A.

Round 3: Join yarn C in any corner ch-2 sp, *[1 dc, ch 2, 1 dc] in ch-2 sp, 1 dc in each of next 2 dc, MB using yarn B in next dc, change to yarn C, 1 dc in each of next 2 dc; rep from * 3 times, sl st in first dc to join.

Round 4: Ch 1, [1 dc, ch 2, 1 dc] in corner ch-2 sp, 1 dc in every st to corner ch-2 sp (take care to work in top of bobble rather than ch-1 to secure); rep from * 3 times, sl st in first dc to join. Fasten off yarn C.

Round 5: Join yarn A in any ch-2 corner sp, *[1 dc, ch 2, 1 dc] in ch-2 sp, 1 dc in each of next 3 dc, MB using yarn B in next dc, 1 dc in next dc using yarn A, MB in next

A
B
C

dc using yarn B, 1 dc in each of next 3 dc using yarn A; rep from * 3 times, sl st in first dc to join.

Round 6: Rep Round 4. Fasten off yarn A.

Round 7: Join yarn C in any ch-2 corner sp, *[1 dc, ch 2, 1 dc] in ch-2 sp, 1 dc in each of next 4 dc, [MB using yarn B in next dc, 1 dc using yarn A in next dc] 2 times, MB using yarn B in next dc, 1 dc in each of next 4 dc using yarn A; rep from * 3 times, sl st in first dc to join.

Round 8: Rep Round 4. Fasten off yarn C.

Round 9: Join yarn A in any ch-2 corner sp, *[1 dc, ch 2, 1 dc] in ch-2 sp, 1 dc in

each of next 8 dc, MB in next dc using yarn B, 1 dc using yarn A in next dc, MB using yarn B in next dc, 1 dc in each of next 8 dc; rep from * 3 times, sl st in first dc to join.

Round 10: Rep Round 4. Fasten off.

Round 11: Join yarn C in any ch-2 corner sp, *[1 dc, ch 2, 1 dc] in ch-2 sp, 1 dc in each of next 10 dc, MB in next dc using yarn B, using yarn A, 1 dc in each of next 10 dc; rep from * 3 times, sl st in first dc to join. Fasten off yarn B.

Rounds 12 to 13: As Round 4.

Fasten off and darn in ends.

248

**

sailboat

This bright and colourful block is ideal for a child's afghan or blanket, and is fun to work up in vibrant shades. Use a separate ball or length of yarn for each area of colour and remember to keep all your yarn tails at the back, then you will be shipshape.

A
B
C
D

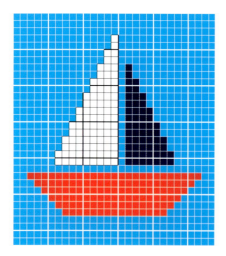

Note: When working this pattern, prepare 2 balls and 1 long length of turquoise before you begin. Work each separate area of colour using different ball of yarn, and length of turquoise between two sails, joining on last lp of each st of last area of colour. Keep all yarn ends at WS of work throughout or when you need to change colour, yarn may be on RS and inaccessible.

Foundation chain: Using yarn A, ch 30.

Row 1: (First row of chart) 1 dc in 2nd ch from hook and 1 dc in every ch to end, turn.

Work remaining 31 rows of chart, making sure you keep yarn ends on WS.

Rows 2 to 32: Ch 1, 1 dc in every dc to end, turn.

Fasten off and darn in ends neatly. Block work to shape.

249

***

cornflower

A frilly, dimensional flower block inspired by summer meadows, this is a large-scale design with an open work centre. It would look stunning in a throw, or as part of a flower-garden piece.

A
B
C
D

Special stitch used:

Picot-3: Ch 3 (at point to add picot), sl st in first of ch-3 to create picot lp.

Foundation ring: Using yarn A, ch 4, sl st in first ch to form ring.

Round 1: Ch 1, 16 tr in ring sl st in first tr to join.

Round 2: Ch 1, 1 dc in same st, *2 dc in next dc, 1 dc in next dc; rep from * to end, sl st in first dc to join – 24 dc.

Round 3: *Ch 8, sl st in 3rd ch from hook, ch 3, sl st in same ch again, sl st down remaining 4 ch to base of ring, sl st at base, sl st in front lp only of next 3 dc; rep from * 7 times, sl st in base of first ch-8 to join. Fasten off yarn A.

Round 4: Join yarn B in any RH ch-3 lp of any stamen, ch 1, 1 dc in same sp, *ch 2,

1 dc in next ch-3 lp of same stamen, ch 4, 1 dc in first ch-3 lp of next stamen; rep from * 7 times, ending last rep with sl st in first dc to join.

Round 5: Ch 1, 1 dc in same st, *2 dc in next ch-2 sp, 1 dc in next dc, 5 dc in next ch-5 lp**, 1 dc in next dc; rep from * 7 times and from * to ** 1 time, sl st in first dc to join. Fasten off yarn B.

Round 6: Join yarn C to front lp of any st, working in front lps only, ch 3 (counts as 1 tr), 1 tr in same st, *picot-3, 2 tr in next dc, picot-3, [2 tr in next dc] 2 times; rep from * to end, sl st in top of beg ch-3 to join. Fasten off yarn C.

Round 7: Join yarn D in back lp of any dc, 1 dc in same st, *ch 4, miss 3 dc, 1 dc in back lp of next dc; rep from * 15 times, sl st in first dc to join.

Round 8: Ch 3 (counts as 1 tr), [3 tr, 1 htr, ch 3, 1 htr, 3 tr] in next ch-4 sp (forms

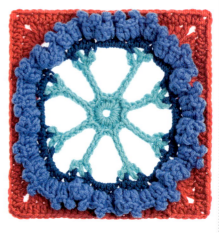

corner), 1 tr in next dc, 4 htr in next ch-4 sp, 1 htr in next dc, 4 dc in next ch-4 sp, 1 htr in next dc, 4 htr in next ch-4 sp, 1 tr in next dc; rep from * 3 times omitting last tr from last rep, sl st in top of beg ch-3 to join.

Round 9: Ch 2 (counts as 1 htr), 1 htr in every st to corner, [2 htr, ch 1, 2 htr] in corner ch-3 sp; rep from * 3 times, 1 htr in every st to end, sl st in top of beg ch-2 to join.

Fasten off and darn in ends.

**

glacial

This block uses front-post stitches of varying heights at intervals to create an interesting up-and-down texture around the edges. A cosy, warm square that would be good in any winter blanket or throw.

A
B
C
D

Special stitches used:

Front-post tr (FPtr): Bring hook to front, work in front vertical post of next st, inserting hook from right to left, draw yarn through and work st as usual (*see page 21*).

Front-post double treble (FPdtr): Yoh 2 times, insert hook through front of st post from right to left, yoh, draw yarn through, [yoh, draw through 2 loops] 3 times.

Front-post half-treble (FPhtr): Yoh, insert hook through front of st post from right to left, yoh, draw yarn through all 3 lps.

Foundation ring: Using yarn A, make a magic ring.

Round 1: Ch 6 (counts as 1 tr, ch 3), *1 tr in ring, ch 3; rep from * 2 times, sl st in 3rd ch of beg ch-6 to join.

Round 2: Ch 5 (counts as 1 tr, ch 2), *1 tr in next ch-3 sp ch 2, 3 tr in next tr, ch 2; rep from * 2 times, 1 tr in next ch-3 sp, ch 2, 2 tr in first tr (of Round 1), sl st in 3rd ch of beg ch-5 to join. Fasten off yarn A.

Round 3: Join yarn B in any single tr, ch 3 (counts as 1 tr), [1 tr, ch 3, 2 tr] in same tr (forms corner), ch 3, 1 FPtr in 2nd tr of next 3-tr cluster, ch 3, *[2 tr, ch 3, 2 tr] in next tr (forms corner), 1 FPtr in 2nd tr of the 3-tr cluster, ch 3; rep from * 2 times, sl st in top of beg ch-3 to join.

Round 4: Sl st in next ch-3 corner sp, ch 3 (counts as 1 tr), [1 tr, ch 3, 2 tr] in same sp (forms corner), 1 tr in each of next 2 tr, ch 3, 1 FPtr in next tr, ch 3, 1 tr in each of next 2 tr *[2 tr, ch 3, 2 tr] in next ch-3 sp (forms corner), 1 tr in each of next 2 tr, ch 3, 1 FPtr in next tr, ch 3, 1 tr in each of next 2 tr; rep from * 2 times, sl st in top of beg ch-3 to join. Fasten off yarn B.

Round 5: Join yarn C in any corner ch-3 sp, ch 4 (counts as 1 dtr), [1 dtr, ch 2, 2 dtr] in same sp (forms corner), 1 FPdtr in each of next 4 tr, 3 dtr in next ch-3 sp, 1 FPdtr in next FPtr, 3 dtr in next ch-3 sp, 1 FPdtr in each of next 4 tr, *[2 dtr, ch 2, 2 dtr] in next ch-3 corner sp, 1 FPdtr in each of next 4 tr, 3 dtr in next ch-3 sp, 1 FPdtr in next FPtr, 3 dtr in next ch-3 sp, 1 FPdtr in each of next 4 tr; rep from * 2 times, sl st in top of beg ch-4 to join. Fasten off yarn C.

Round 6: Join yarn D in any corner ch-2 sp, ch 4 (counts as 1 dtr), [1 dtr, ch 2, 2 dtr] in same sp (forms corner), 1 FPdtr in each of next 19 sts, *[2 tr, ch 2, 2 tr] in next ch-2 sp (forms corner), 1 FPdtr in each of next 19 sts; rep from * 2 times, sl st in top of beg ch-4 to join. Fasten off yarn D.

Round 7: Join yarn A in any corner ch-2 sp, ch 2 (counts as 1 htr), [1 htr, ch 2, 2 htr] in same sp (forms corner), 1 FPhtr in each of next 23 sts, *[2 htr, ch 2, 2 htr] in same sp (forms corner), 1 FPhtr in each of next 23 sts; rep from * 2 times, sl st in top of beg ch-2 to join.

Fasten off and darn in ends.

★★★
drawbridge

A
B
C

This intricately formed block is fascinating to work: it begins in linear mode, then is worked in filet in the round, before a separate frame section is made and inserted in the chain loops that hold it in place.

Foundation chain: Using yarn A, ch 7.

Row 1: 1 dc in 2nd ch from hook, 1 dc in every ch to end, turn.

Rows 2 to 6: Ch 1, 1 dc in every dc to end, turn. Fasten off at end of Row 6.

Round 7: Join yarn B, ch 3 (counts as 1 tr, *ch 1) miss 1 dc, 1 tr in next dc**; rep from * to last dc, [1 tr, ch 3, 1 tr] in last dc, work down side of square; rep from * to ** to next corner, [1 tr, ch 3, 1 tr] in next corner sp, working along base of square, rep from * to ** to next corner, [1 tr, ch 3, 1 tr] in next corner, working up side square rep from * to ** to end, ch 1, sl st in 2nd ch of beg ch-3.

Round 8: Ch 3 (counts as 1 tr), *ch 1, miss 1 tr, 1 tr in next tr**; rep from * to corner, [1 tr, ch 3, 1 tr] in 2nd ch of corner ch-3 sp, working down side of square rep from * to ** to next corner, [1 tr, ch 3, 1 tr] in 2nd ch of next corner ch-3 sp, working along base of square rep from * to ** to next corner, [1 tr, ch 3, 1 tr] in 2nd ch of next corner ch-3 sp, working up side square rep from * to ** to end, ch 1, sl st in 2nd ch of beg ch-3.

Round 9: Ch 14, sl st in same st, [1 dc in next ch-1 sp, 1 dc in next tr] 3 times, ch 14, sl st in same tr, *1 dc in next ch-1 sp, 1 dc in next tr, [2 dc, ch 14, 2 dc] in next ch-3 sp, 1 dc in next tr, 1 dc in next ch-1 sp**, 1 dc in next tr, ch 14, sl st in same tr, [1 dc in next ch-1 sp, 1 dc in next tr] 3 times, ch 14, sl st in same tr; rep from * 1 time and from * to ** 1 time, sl st in first dc to join. Fasten off yarn B.

Round 10: Using yarn A, 1 dc in tip of any ch-14 lp at corner of square, *ch 9, 1 dc in tip of next lp, ch 5, 1 dc in tip of next lp, ch 9, 1 dc in tip of next lp; rep from * to end, sl st in first dc to join. Fasten off yarn A.

Round 11: Using yarn A, rep Round 7. Fasten off yarn A.

Round 12: Ch 1, *1 dc in every tr and every ch-1 sp to corner, 3 dc in corner ch-3 sp; rep from * 3 times, sl st in first dc to join.

SEPARATE FRAME MOTIF

Foundation chain: Using yarn C, ch 80.

Round 1: 1 tr in 3rd ch from hook, 1 tr in each of next 18 ch, *ch 3, 1 tr in 2nd ch from hook, 1 tr base of last tr worked, 1 tr in each of next 18 ch; rep from * 2 times, thread piece through ch lps in larger piece, once in place, sl st final st in first ch and first tr to join.

Fasten off and darn in ends.

***

pebbles

A pleasingly textural block that uses tilted clusters to create a pebble-like effect; this is achieved by working around the side posts of stitches. This block is fun to work up and it's useful for mixing with other blocks in a composite piece. Used in repeat it would also make a cosy scarf or throw.

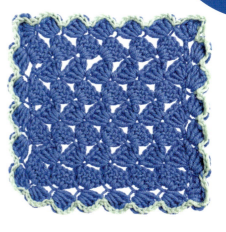

A

B

Special Stitch used:

Foundation chain: Using yarn A, ch 28.

Row 1: 4 tr in 4th ch from hook, miss 3 ch, *[1 dc, ch 2, 4 tr] in next ch, miss 3 ch; rep to last ch, 1 dc in last ch, turn.

Row 2: Ch 5, 4 tr in 4th ch from hook, *miss 4 tr, 1 dc between last miss tr and next ch-2 sp, ch 2, 4 tr in side of last dc worked; rep from * to last 4 tr, miss 4 tr, 1 dc in last ch, turn.

Rows 3 to 8: Rep Row 2. Do not fasten off.

BORDER

Ch 5, 4 tr in 4th ch from hook, 1 dc in base of next shell, ch 2, 4 tr in side of last dc worked, miss ch-5, 1 dc in side post of next shell, ch 2, 4 tr in side of last dc worked, 1 dc in ch-5 at beg of next row, ch 2, 4 tr in side post of last dc, 1 dc in base of next shell, ch 2, 4 tr in side of last dc, miss ch-5, 1 dc in base of next shell, ch 2, 4 tr in side of last dc, 1 dc in base of same shell, ch 2, 4 tr in side of last dc, *1 dc in base of next shell, ch 2, 4 tr in last dc; rep from * 4 times, 1 dc in last tr, ch 2, 4 tr in side of last dc, **1 dc in next ch-5, ch 2, 4 tr in side of last dc worked; rep from ** 4 times, sl st in first ch of next ch-5 to join.

Fasten off and darn in ends.

EDGING

Join yarn B in any tr, *ch 3, 1 dc in first tr of next cluster, ch 3, 1 tr in last tr of same cluster; rep to end, sl st in first dc to join.

Fasten off and darn in ends.

*

grid lines

A simple filet pattern, this block works up quickly and would be effective as a window treatment or table runner.

A

Foundation chain: Ch 30.

Row 1: 1 tr in 6th ch from hook, *ch 1, miss 1 ch, 1 tr in next ch; rep from * to end, turn.

Row 2: Ch 5 (counts as 1 tr, ch 2), miss 2 ch, [ch 1, 1 tr], *1 tr in next ch st (not ch-sp), ch 3, miss [1 tr, ch 1, 1 tr]; rep from * 4 times, 1 tr in next ch st, ch 2, miss [1 tr, ch 1], 1 tr in 3rd ch of turning ch, turn.

Row 3: Ch 4 (counts as 1 tr, ch 1), *miss 1 ch, 1 tr in next ch st, ch 1, miss 1 tr, 1 tr in next ch st; rep from * 5 times, ch 1, 1 tr in 3rd ch of turning ch, turn.

Rows 4, 6, 8, 10 and 12: Rep Row 2.

Rows 5, 7, 9, 11 and 13: Rep Row 3.

BORDER

Ch 3 (counts as 1 tr), 1 tr in each of next 25 tr and ch-1 sps to corner, [1 tr, ch 3, 1 tr] in corner sp, work 25 tr evenly along to next corner; rep from * 2 times, [1 tr, ch 3] in corner, sl st in top of beg ch-3 to join.

Fasten off and darn in ends.

254

*

mitre filet

A
B
C
D

A familiar pattern here updated with a filet twist, this block is a wonderful addition to a lightweight afghan or throw and works up quickly. Choose tonal colours or go for bold with bright contrasts; either way this is great fun to make and versatile to use.

Foundation chain: Using yarn A, ch 8.

Row 1: 1 tr in 6th ch from hook, ch 1, miss 1 ch, 1 tr in next ch, turn.

Row 2: Ch 4 (counts as 1 tr, ch 1), 1 tr in next tr, miss 1 ch, ch 1, 1 tr in last tr, turn. Fasten off yarn A.

Row 3: Using yarn B, ch 4 (counts as 1 tr, ch 1), [miss 1 ch, 1 tr in next tr] 2 times, (forms mitre point), ch 4 (counts as 1 tr, ch 1) 1 tr in last ch worked, *ch 1, miss 1 ch, 1 tr in base of next row; rep from * to end of row, turn.

Row 4: Ch 4 (counts as 1 tr, *ch 1) miss 1 ch, 1 tr in next tr; rep from * to mitre point; ch 4 (counts as 1 tr, ch 1) 1 tr in last ch worked, * ch 1, miss 1 ch, 1 tr in next tr; rep from * to end of row, turn. Fasten off yarn B.

Row 5: Using yarn C, rep Row 4. Fasten off yarn C.

Row 6: Using yarn A, rep Row 4. Fasten off yarn A.

Rows 7 to 8: Using yarn D, rep Row 4. Fasten off yarn D after Row 8.

Row 9: Using yarn B, rep Row 4. Fasten off yarn B.

Row 10: Using yarn C, rep Row 4. Fasten off yarn C.

Rows 11 to 12: Using yarn A, rep Row 4. Fasten off yarn A after Row 12.

Row 13: Using yarn B, rep Row 4.

Rows 14 to 15: Using yarn C, rep Row 4.

Fasten off after Row 15 and darn in ends.

255

*

chamonix

A
B
C

Adapted from a Victorian doily, this classic snowflake pattern combines simple stitches into a pretty block. Repeat blocks for festive table decorations, pillows or throws – this is light and versatile.

Special stitch used:

Picot-5: Ch 5 (at point to add picot), sl st in first ch of ch-5 to create picot lp. In this pattern, 3 picot-5 are combined to create a picot cluster.

Foundation ring: Using yarn A, make a magic ring.

Round 1: Ch 3 (counts as 1 tr), 23 tr in ring, sl st in top of beg ch-3 to join.

Round 2: [Ch 3, 1 dc in next tr] 24 times, sl st in first ch to join.

Round 3: Ch 3 (counts as 1 tr), 1 tr in same st, *ch 5, miss 1 ch-3 lp, 2 tr in next ch-3 lp; rep from * 10 times, ch 5, sl st in 3rd ch of beg ch-5 to join. Fasten off yarn A.

Round 4: Join yarn B in any 2nd tr, ch 1, 1 dc in same tr, ch 4, 1 tr in 3rd ch of next ch-5 lp, *3 picot-5 (working last sl st of each picot-5 in same sp), (1 picot cluster made), ch 4**, sl st in 2nd tr, ch 4, 1 tr in 3rd ch of next ch-5 lp; rep from * 10 times, and from * to ** 1 time, sl st in first dc to join. Fasten off yarn B.

Round 5: Join yarn C behind any picot cluster, at base of sl st where 3 picot-5s join, ch 1, *ch 6, 1 dc in back of base of next picot cluster; rep from * 10 times, ch 6, sl st in first ch-1 to join.

Round 6: Ch 1, *6 dc in next ch-6 lp, 1 dc in next dc, 6 dc in next ch-6 lp, 1 htr in next dc, [1 htr, 2 tr, ch 2, 2 tr, 1 htr] in next ch-6 lp (forms corner), 1 htr in next dc; rep from * 3 times, sl st in first cc to join.

Round 7: Ch 3 (counts as 1 htr, ch 1), *[miss 1 st, 1 htr in next dc, ch 1] 7 times, 1 htr in next st, [1 htr, 2 tr, ch 2, 2 tr, 1 htr] in next ch-6 sp, 1 htr in next st, ch 1, [miss 1 st, 1 htr in next st, ch 1] 2 times; rep from * 3 times, omitting last [1 htr, ch 1], sl st in 2nd ch of beg ch-3 to join.

Fasten off and darn in ends neatly.

ultramarine

A super-quick modern square with an unusual construction at the corners, this is reminiscent of the log-cabin pattern used in quilting. Lightweight and perfect for contemporary throws.

Foundation ring: Using yarn A, ch 8, sl st to first ch join in ring.

Round 1: Ch 5 (counts as 1 tr, ch 2), *1 tr in ring, ch 5, 1 tr in ring, ch 2; rep from * 2 times, ch 2, 1 tr in ring, ch 5, sl st to 3rd ch of beg ch-5 to join. Fasten off yarn A.

Round 2: Ch 3 (counts as 1 tr), 2 tr in next ch-2 sp, *1 tr in next tr, [3 tr, ch 5, 3 tr in next ch-5 corner sp]**, 1 tr in next tr, 2 tr in next ch-2 sp; rep from * 2 times, then from * to ** 1 time, sl st in top of beg ch-3 to join. Fasten off yarn B.

Round 3: Using yarn A, ch 4 (counts as 1 dtr), 1 dtr in each of next 3 tr, *ch 3, miss 3 tr, 3 dtr in corner sp, ch 4 (counts as 1 dtr), 3 dtr around post of last dtr made, 3 dtr in last part of corner sp in rnd below; ch 3, miss 3 tr**, 1 dtr in each of

next 4 tr along; rep from *2 times, then from * to ** 1 time, sl st to top of beg ch-4 to join. Fasten off yarn A.

Round 4: Using yarn B, ch 3 (counts as 1 tr), 1 tr in each of the next 3 tr, *ch 2, miss next ch-3 sp, 1 tr in each of the next 2 dtr, 1 tr in next ch-3 sp, 3 tr in next ch-4 sp of last rnd, ch 3 (counts as 1 tr), 2 tr around post of last tr made, 1 tr in last part of corner sp of rnd below, 1 tr in each of next 6 dtr, ch 2**, miss next ch-3 sp, 1 tr in each of next 4 dtr; rep from * 2 times, then from * to ** 1 time, sl st to top of beg ch-3 to join. Fasten off yarn B.

Round 5: Using yarn A, ch 4 (counts as 1 dtr), 1 dtr in each of next 3 tr, *ch 3, miss next ch-2 sp, 1 dtr in each of next 5 tr, 1 dtr in first part of corner sp of last rnd, 2 tr in ch-3 of last rnd, ch 4 (counts as 1 dtr) 3 dtr around post of last dtr made,

1 dtr in last part of corner sp of rnd below, 1 dtr in each of next 9 tr, ch 3, miss next ch-2 sp**, 1 dtr in each of next 4 tr along; rep from * 2 times, then from * to ** 1 times, sl st to top of beg ch-4 to join.

Fasten off and darn in ends neatly.

parlour lace

Adapted from a popular doily pattern, this familiar design uses regular increases as part of the floral shape. It is composed of basic stitches, so makes a great beginner square for use in lightweight throws. Repeat it in a series of shades and tones of the same hue to create a lovely blanket.

Foundation ring: Make a magic ring.

Round 1: Ch 5 (counts as 1 tr, ch 2), [1 tr in ring, ch 2] 7 times, sl st in 3rd ch of beg ch-5 to join.

Round 2: Ch 3 (counts as 1 tr), 1 tr in same st, *[1 tr, ch 2, 1 tr] in next ch-2 sp, 1 tr in next tr; rep from * 6 times, [1 tr, ch 2, 1 tr] in last ch-2 sp, sl st in top of beg ch-2 to join.

Round 3: Ch 3 (counts as 1 tr), 1 tr in same st, 1 tr in each of next 2 tr*, [1 tr, ch 2, 1 tr] in next ch-2 sp, 1 tr in each of next 3 sts; rep from * 6 times, [1 tr, ch 2] in next ch-2 sp, sl st in top of beg ch-3 to join.

Round 4: Ch 3 (counts as 1 tr), *1 tr in each of next 4 tr, ch 2, 1 dc in next ch-2 sp, ch 2, sl st in next tr, ch 3; rep from * 6 times, 1 tr in each of next 4 tr, ch 2,

1 dc in next ch-2 sp, ch 2, sl st in top of beg ch-3 to join.

Round 5: Ch 3 (counts as 1 tr), miss 1 tr, 1 tr in each of next 2 tr, *[ch 2, 1 dc in next ch-2 sp] 2 times, ch 2, sl st in next tr, ch 3, miss 1 tr, 1 tr in each of next 2 tr; rep from * 6 times, [ch 2, 1 dc in next ch-2 sp] 2 times, ch 2, sl st in top of beg ch-3 to join.

Round 6: Ch 1, 1 dc in same st, 1 dc in next st, *[ch 2, 1 dc in next ch-2 sp] 3 times, ch 2**, sl st in next st, 1 dc in each of next 2 sts; rep from * 6 times, and from * to ** 1 time, sl st in first sc to join.

Round 7: Ch 1, 1 dc in same dc, 1 dc in next ch-2 sp, *[2 dc in next ch-2 sp] 3 times, 1 dc in each of next 2 dc, 1 dc in next ch-2 sp, [1 htr, 1 tr] in next ch-2 sp,

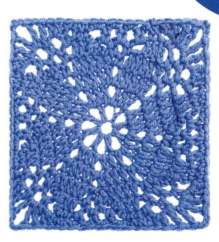

1 dtr in next dc, ch 1, [1 dtr, ch 3, 1 dtr] in next ch-2 sp (forms corner), ch 1, 1 dtr in next dc, [1 tr, 1 htr] in next ch-2 sp**, 1 dc in each of next 2 dc, 1 dc in next ch-2 sp; rep from * 2 times and from * to ** 1 time, sl st in first dc to join.

Fasten off and darn in ends. Block work.

*
winter daisy

A joyful large flower to brighten up the winter days, this block works up quickly and is a great beginner square. Repeat in varied or alternating colours for a bold bedcover; try alternating red and blue daisies for impact.

A
B
C

Special stitch used:

Double treble 3 stitches together (dtr3tog): Work 3 dtr over next 3 sts leaving last lp of each on hook, yoh, draw through all lps.

Foundation ring: Using yarn A, ch 4, sl st in first ch to form ring.

Round 1: Ch 3 (counts as 1 tr), 15 tr in ring, sl st in top of beg ch-3 to join.

Round 2: Ch 3 (counts as 1 tr), 1 tr in same st, 2 tr in every st to end, sl st in top of beg ch-3 to join – 32 tr.

Round 3: Ch 3 (counts as 1 tr), [2 tr in next tr, 1 tr in next tr] 15 times, 2 tr in last tr, sl st in top of beg ch-3 to join – 48 tr.

Round 4: Ch 3 (counts as 1 tr), [2 tr in next tr, 1 tr in next 2 tr] 15 times, 2 tr in next tr, 1 tr in last tr, sl st in top of beg ch-3 to join – 64 dc.

Round 5: Ch 1, 1 dc in each of next 4 tr, [2 dc in next tr, 1 dc in each of next 7 tr] 7 times, 2 dc in next tr, 1 dc in each of last 2 tr, sl st in first dc to join. Fasten off yarn A.

Round 6: Join yarn B to front lp of last st worked, *ch 3 (counts as 1 tr), working in front lps only for all this rnd, dtr3tog, ch 4, sl st in same st, ch 2, miss 2 tr, sl st in front lp of next tr; rep from * 11 times, sl st in first ch of beg ch-3 to join, fasten off – 12 petals made.

Round 7: Join yarn C behind top of any dtr3tog, 1 dc in same st, *ch 2, 2 tr in next ch-2 sp, ch 2, sl st behind top of next dtr3tog, ch 2, [1 tr, 1 dtr] in next ch-2 sp, ch 2, [1 tr, 1 dtr, ch 3, 1 dtr, 1 tr] behind next dtr3tog (forms corner), ch 2, [1 dtr, 1 tr] in next ch-2 sp, ch 2, sl st behind next dtr3tog; rep from * 3 times, ending with sl st in first sl st to join. Fasten off yarn B.

Round 8: Join yarn A in back lp of same st, *1 dc in back lps only of every st along side of square including ch sts (do not work in ch-2 lps), to 2nd ch of corner ch-3 sp, [2 dc, ch 1, 2 dc] in next ch st (forms corner), rep from * 3 times, 1 dc in back lps of every st to end, sl st in first dc to join.

Fasten off and darn in ends neatly.

alderney

Travelling front- and back-post stitches create a cable-like effect on this block, reminiscent of traditional fishermen's knitwear from the Channel Islands. Be sure to work the stitch at the top of the turning chains to remain with the right number of stitches throughout.

A
B

Special stitches used:

Front-post double treble (FPdtr): Yoh 2 times, insert hook through front of st post from right to left, yoh, draw yarn through, [yoh, draw through 2 loops] 3 times (*see page 21*).

Back-post double treble (BPdtr): Yoh 2 times, insert hook through back of st post from right to left, yod, draw yarn through, then [yoh, draw through 2 loops] 3 times.

Note: In this pattern, each post st is worked around post of corresponding st from last row, making continuous cable pattern.

Foundation chain: Using yarn A, ch 29.

Row 1: 1 htr in 3rd ch from hook, 1 htr in every ch to end, turn.

Row 2: Ch 2 (counts as 1 htr), 1 htr in each of next 12 htr, 1 BPhtr in each of next 2 htr, 1 htr in each of next 13 htr, turn.

Row 3: Ch 2 (counts as 1 htr), 1 htr in each of next 12 htr, miss 1 htr, 1 FPhtr in next BPhtr (over miss htr), 1 htr in each of next 2 sts, 1 FPdtr in next BPfftr, 1 htr in each of next 11 htr, turn.

Row 4: Ch 2 (counts as 1 htr), 1 htr in each of next 10 htr, miss 1 htr, 1 BPdtr in next FPdtr (over miss htr), 1 htr each of next 4 htr, 1 BPdtr in next FPdtr, 1 htr each of next 11 htr, turn.

Row 5: Ch 2 (counts as 1 htr), 1 htr in each of next 10 htr, miss 1 htr, 1 FPhtr in next BPhtr (over miss htr), 1 htr in each of next 6 htr, 1 FPhtr in next BPhtr, 1 htr in each of next 9 htr, turn.

Row 6: Ch 2 (counts as 1 htr), 1 htr in each of next 4 htr, ch 2, 1 htr in each of next 3 htr, miss 1 htr, 1 BPdtr in next FPhtr, 1 htr in each of next 6 htr, 1 BPdtr in next FPdtr, 1 htr in each of next 3 htr, ch 2, miss 2 htr, 1 htr in each of next 5 htr, turn.

Row 7: Ch 2 (counts as 1 htr), 1 htr in next htr, ch 2, miss 2 htr, 1 htr in next htr, 1 htr in next ch-1 sp, 1 htr in next htr, ch 2, miss 2 htr, 1 htr in each of next 2 htr, 1 FPhtr in next BPhtr, 1 htr in each of next 4 htr, 1 FPdtr in next BPdtr, 1 htr in next htr, ch 2, miss 1 htr, 1 htr in each of next 3 htr, ch 2, miss 2 htr, 1 htr in each of next 2 htr, turn.

Row 8: Ch 2 (counts as 1 htr), 1 htr in each of next 2 htr, 1 htr in next ch-1 sp, 1 htr in next htr, ch 2, miss 2 htr, 1 htr in each of next 5 htr, 1BPhtr in next FPhtr, 1 htr in each of next 2 htr, 1 BPdtr in next FPhtr, 1 htr in each of next 5 htr/ch-1 sps, ch 2, miss 2 htr, 1 htr in each of next 5 htr/ch-1 sps, turn.

Row 9: Ch 2 (counts as 1 htr), 1 htr in next htr, ch 2, miss 2 htr, 1 htr in each of next 3 htr, ch 2, miss 2 htr, 1 htr in each of next 4 htr, 1 FPdtr in each of next 2 BPdtr, 1 htr in each of next 3 htr, ch 2, miss 2 htr, 1 htr in each of next 3 htr, ch 2, miss 2 htr, 1 htr in each of next 3 htr, turn.

Row 10: Ch 2 (counts as 1 htr), 1 htr in each of next 4 htr, ch 2, miss 2 htr, 1 htr in each of next 6 htr, miss 1 st, 1 BPdtr in next st, working over the BPdtr: 1 BPdtr in miss st, 1 htr in each of next 6 htr, ch 2, miss 2 htr, 1 htr in each of next 5 htr, turn.

Row 11: Ch 2 (counts as 1 htr) 1 htr in next htr, ch 2, miss 2 htr, 1 htr in each of next 3 htr, ch 2, miss 2 htr, 1 htr in each of next 4 htr, 1 FPdtr in each of next 2 BPdtr, 1 htr in each of next 3 htr, ch 2, miss 2 htr, 1 htr in each of next 3 htr, ch 2, miss 2 htr, 1 htr in each of next 3 htr, fasten off, turn.

Row 12: Using yarn B, rep Row 10.

Row 13: Rep Row 9.

Row 14: Rep Row 8.

Row 15: Rep Row 7.

Row 16: Rep Row 6.

Row 17: Rep Row 5.

Row 18: Rep Row 4.

Row 19: Rep Row 3.

Row 20: Rep Row 2.

Fasten off and darn in ends.

260 ***
sparkle

An openwork star with an abundance of cluster formations. Great for practising working stitches together, this mixes well with other lacy blocks.

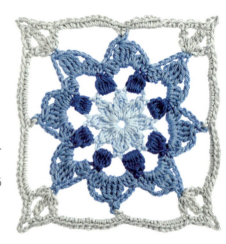

Special stitches used:

Beginning 4-double treble cluster (beg 4-dtr cl): Ch 4, make cluster with 3 dtr (see page 18).

4-double treble cluster (4-dtr cl): Make cluster with 4 dtr.

2-double treble cluster (2-dtr cl): Make cluster with 2 dtr.

Beginning 6-treble-crochet cluster (beg 6-tr cl): Ch 3, make cluster with 5 tr.

6-treble-crochet cluster (6-tr cl): Make cluster with 6 tr.

Beginning 3-treble crochet cluster (beg 3-tr cl): Ch 3, make cluster with 2 tr.

3-treble crochet cluster (3-tr cl): Make cluster with 3 tr.

Picot-3: Ch 3 (at point to add picot), sl st in first ch of ch-3 to create picot lp.

Foundation ring: Using yarn A, ch 4, sl st in first ch to form ring.

Round 1: *Beg 4-dtr cl in ring, ch 5, *4-dtr cl in ring, ch 5; rep from * 6 times, sl st in top of first cluster to join. Fasten off yarn A.

Round 2: Join yarn B in any ch-5 sp, beg 6-tr cl in same sp, ch 8, *6-tr cl in next ch-5 sp, ch 8; rep from * 6 times, sl st in top of beg 6-tr cl to join. Fasten off yarn B.

Round 3: Join yarn C in any ch-8 sp, [beg 3-tr cl, ch 4, dtr-4 cl, picot-3, ch 4, 3-tr cl] all in first ch-8 sp, 1 dc in top of tr cl from rnd below, *[3-tr cl, ch 4, 4-dtr cl, picot-3, ch 4, 3-tr cl] all in next ch-8 sp, 1 dc in top of tr cl from rnd below; rep from * 6 times, sl st in top of beg 6-tr cl to join. Fasten off.

Round 4: Join yarn D in any picot-3, *1 dc in picot-3, ch 10, [tr2tog, ch 3, 2-dtr cl, ch 3, tr2tog] in next picot-3, ch 10; rep from * 3 times, sl st in first dc to join.

Round 5: Ch 1, 12 dc in next ch-10 sp, 2 dc in next ch-3 sp, [1 dc, ch 3, 1 dc] in top of 2-dtr cl, 2 dc in next ch-3 sp, 12 dc in next ch-10 sp; rep from * 3 times, sl st in first dc to join.

Fasten off and darn in ends.

261 **
zebra

A gorgeous texture is created by working double treble stitches around the front vertical posts of rows below; this block is deliciously tactile and lends itself to being worked in a host of colour combinations. It's thick, so good for inclusion in winter blankets or bedspreads, or even for table mats.

Special stitch used:

Front-post double treble 2 stitches together (FPdtr2tog): work 2 dtr sts through front post of st leaving last lp of each on hook, yoh and pull through all lps (see page 21).

Foundation chain: Using yarn A, ch 28.

Row 1: 1 dc in 2nd ch from hook, 1 dc in every ch to end, turn.

Rows 2 to 4: Ch 1, 1 dc in every dc to end, turn. Fasten off yarn A.

Row 5: Change to new colour, ch 1, 1 dc in first dc, 1 FPdtr in st 2 rows below and 1 st to the left of current position, *miss 1 dc behind FPdtr just made, 1 dc in each of next 2 dc, 1 FPdtr2tog around vertical post of last FPdtr, miss 1 dc behind FPdtr just

made and finish FPdtr2tog around post of next st; rep from * 7 times, miss 1 dc behind FPdtr just made, 1 dc in each of next 2 dc, 1 FPdtr around vertical post of last FPdtr, miss 1 dc behind FPdtr just made, 1 dc in last dc, turn.

Rows 6 to 8: Rep Row 2.

Row 9: Using yarn A, rep Row 5.

Rows 10 to 12: Rep Row 2.

Row 13: Using yarn B, rep Row 5.

Rows 14 to 16: Rep Row 2.

Row 17: Rep Row 9.

Rows 18 to 20: Rep Row 2.

Row 21: Rep Row 13.

Rows 22 to 24: Rep Row 2.

Row 25: Rep Row 9.

Rows 26 to 28: Rep Row 2.

Row 29: Rep Row 13.

Rows 30 to 31: Rep Row 2.

Fasten off and darn in ends.

★★
gingham

Inspired by long summer days and chequered picnic cloths, this familiar pattern is easy to make using intarsia techniques (see page 17). Choose your favourite colour of gingham cloth to emulate, or create multiples in different colours to make a fantastic picnic blanket.

A
B
C

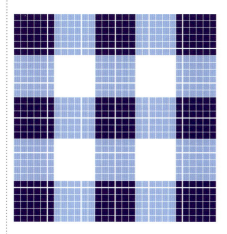

Note: When working this pattern prepare 3 small balls of navy, 3 of sky blue and 2 of cream before you begin. Work each separate area of colour using different ball of yarn, joining on last lp of each st of last area of colour. Keep all yarn ends at WS of the work throughout or when you need to change colour, yarn ends left on RS are inaccessible.

Foundation chain: Using A, ch 31.

Row 1: Work 1 dc in 2nd ch from hook and 1 dc in every ch to end, turn.

Rows 2 to 31: Work 30 rows of chart, beginning each row with ch 1, turning at end of each row. Make sure you keep yarns ends on WS.

Row 32: Using yarn A, ch 1, 1 dc in every dc to end.

Fasten off and darn in ends neatly. Block work to shape.

★★
zigzag

Another bobble block with a textured central panel, this can be used in any rotation, creating the possibility of making long rows in a composite piece. Repeat rows 4 to 28 for a continuous zigzag.

A

Special stitch used:

Make bobble (MB): Make bobble with 5 tr (see page 19).

Foundation chain: Ch 30.

Row 1: Work 1 dc in 2nd ch from hook, and in every ch to end, turn.

Row 2: Ch 1, 1 dc in every dc to end, turn.

Row 3 and every alternate row: Rep Row 2.

Row 4: Ch 1, 1 dc in each of next 7 dc, MB in next dc, [1 dc in each of next 3 dc, MB in next dc] 2 times, 1 dc in each of next 13 dc, turn.

Row 6: Ch 1, 1 dc in each of next 9 dc, MB in next dc, 1 dc in each of next 3 dc, MB in next dc] 2 times, 1 dc in each of next 11 dc, turn.

Row 8: Ch 1, work 1 dc in each of next 11 dc, MB in next dc, 1 dc in each of next 3 dc, MB in next dc] 2 times, 1 dc in each of next 9 dc, turn.

Row 10: Ch 1, work 1 dc in each of next 13 dc, MB in next dc, [1 dc in each of next 5 dc, MB in next dc] 2 times, 1 dc in each of next 7 dc, turn.

Row 12: Rep Row 8.

Row 14: Rep Row 6.

Row 16: Rep Row 4.

Row 18: Rep Row 6.

Row 20: Rep Row 8.

Row 22: Rep Row 10.

Row 24: Rep Row 8.

Row 26: Rep Row 6.

Row 28: Rep Row 4.

Rows 30 to 31: Rep Row 2.

Fasten off and darn in ends. Block to shape if necessary.

**

feathers

By changing colour as the pattern repeats, this block suggests a feather-like texture of layers. Changing colour more often would give an even more gradated effect – try bright parrot hues or rich peacock tones.

A
B

Foundation chain: Using yarn A, ch 28.

Row 1: 5 dtr in 8th ch from hook, miss 3 ch, 1 dtr in next ch, *miss 3 ch, 5 dtr in next ch, miss 3 ch, 1 dtr in next ch; rep from * to end of row, turn.

Row 2: Ch 4 (counts as 1 dtr), 2 dtr in next dtr, miss 2 dtr, 1 dtr in next dtr, * miss 2 dtr, 5 dtr in next dtr, miss 2 dtr, 1 dtr in next dtr; rep from * to last 3 sts, miss 2 dtr, 3 dtr in last ch, turn.

Row 3: Ch 4 (counts as 1 dtr), *miss 2 dtr, 5 dtr in next dtr, miss 2 dtr, 1 dtr in next dtr; rep from * to end of row (last dtr worked in top of beg ch-4 from last row), turn. Fasten off yarn A.

Rows 4 to 6: Join yarn B, rep Row 2, then Row 3, then Row 2. Fasten off yarn B.

Rows 7 to 9: Join yarn A, rep Row 3, then Row 2, then Row 3.

Fasten off and darn in ends neatly.

babylonian star

A striking design that lends itself to being repeated for a stunning throw, or a table runner. Choose contrasting colours for maximum impact, and use a flat yarn to maintain the clean lines of the star.

A
B

Special stitch used:

Front-post half-treble crochet (FPhtr): insert hook in front post of dtr just worked, then work 1 htr around the post (*see page 21*).

Foundation ring: Using yarn A, ch 6, sl st in first ch to form ring.

Round 1: Ch 6 (counts as 1 tr, ch 3), *1 tr, ch 3 in the ring; rep from * 6 times, sl st in 3rd ch of beg ch-6 to join.

Round 2: Sl st in next ch-3 sp, ch 4 (counts as 1 dtr), *1 dtr in next tr, 2 FPhtr in front post of dtr just worked, ch 1**, 1 dtr in next sp; rep from * 6 times, then from * to ** 1 time, sl st in top of beg ch-4 to join.

Round 3: *Ch 7, 1 dc in 3rd ch from hook, 1 htr in next ch, 1 tr in next ch, 1 htr in next ch, 1 htr in last ch, miss 4 sts, sl st in next htr from Round 2 to join; rep from * 7 times, sl st to first ch of the beg ch-7 to join. Fasten off yarn A.

Round 4: Join yarn B to tip of any point of star, 1 dc in same st, *ch 10, 1 dc in tip of next point of star; rep from * 7 times, sl st to first ch of beg ch-10 to join.

Round 5: 1 dc in same sp, *[6 dc, ch 3, 6 dc] in next ch-10 sp (forms corner), 1 dc in next dc, 10 dc in next ch-10 sp, 1 dc in next dc; rep from * 3 times, sl st to first dc to join.

Round 6: Ch 6, *1 dc in each of next 6 dc [1 dc, ch 3, 1 dc] in next corner sp, 1 dc in each of next 6 dc, 1 dc in next dc, 1 dc in each of next 10 dc, 1 dc in next dc; rep from * 3 times, sl st in first dc to join.

Round 7: Ch 3, 1 tr in each dc to corner ch-3 sp, [3 tr, ch 3, 3 tr] in next corner ch-3 sp, rep from * 3 times, sl st to top of beg ch-3 to join.

Round 8: Ch 1, 1 dc in same st, *1 dc in each tr to corner ch-3 sp, 4 dc in corner ch-3 sp, rep from * 3 times, sl st to first ch-1 join.

Fasten off and darn in ends neatly.

tutti frutti

**

A confection of colours, this granny is made of puff stitches and has a pleasing texture. It's easy and quick to work once you master puff stitch, and gives tremendous scope for different colour combinations to suit any interior design.

Special stitch used:

3-treble puff stitch (3-trpf): Make puff stitch with 3 tr, ch 1 to seal pf (*see page 19*).

Foundation ring: Using yarn A, ch 6, sl st in first ch to form ring.

Round 1: Ch 1, *3-trpf in ring; rep 7 times, sl st in top of first pf to join – 8 puff stitches. Fasten off.

Round 2: Join yarn B in next ch-1 sp, ch 1, *[3-trpf] 2 times in same sp; rep in each ch-1 sp all around, sl st in top of first pf to join. Fasten off.

Round 3. Join yarn C in next ch-1 sp, ch 1, *[3-trpf, ch 2, 3-trpf] in same sp (forms corner), 3-trpf in each of next 3 ch-1 sps; rep from * 3 times, sl st in top of first pf to join. Fasten off.

Round 4: Join yarn D in next ch-1 sp, ch 1, *[3-trpf, ch 2, 3-trpf] in same sp (forms corner), 3-trpf in each of next 4 ch-1 sps; rep from * 3 times, sl st in top of first pf to join. Fasten off.

Round 5: Join yarn E in next ch-1 sp, ch 1, *[3-trpf, ch 2, 3-trpf] in same sp (forms corner), 3-trpf in each of next 5 ch-1 sps; rep from * 3 times, sl st in top of first pf to join. Fasten off.

Round 6: Join yarn F in next ch-1 sp, ch 1, *[3-trpf, ch 2, 3-trpf] in same sp (forms corner), 3-trpf in each of next 6 ch-1 sps; rep from * 3 times, sl st in top of first pf to join. Fasten off.

Round 7: Join yarn G in next ch-1 sp, ch 1, *[3-trpf, ch 2, 3-trpf] in same sp (forms corner), 3-trpf in each of next 7 ch-1 sps; rep from * 3 times, sl st in top of first pf to join. Fasten off.

Round 8: Join yarn H in any ch-3 corner sp, ch 3 (counts as 1 tr), [1 tr, ch 3, 2 tr] in same sp (forms corner), *2 tr in every ch-1 sp along side of square to corner**, [2 tr, ch 3, 2 tr] in next ch-3 corner sp (forms corner); rep from * 2 times and from * to ** 1 time, sl st in top of beg ch-3 to join. Fasten off.

Round 9: Join yarn I in any ch-3 corner sp, ch 3 (counts as 1 tr), [1 tr, ch 3, 2 tr] in same sp (forms corner), *1 tr in every st to next corner**, [2 tr, ch 3, 2 tr] in next ch-3 corner sp (forms corner); rep from * 2 times and from * to ** 1 time, sl st in top of beg ch-3 to join.

Fasten off and darn in ends neatly.

A

B

C

D

E

F

G

H

I

**

amy

A series of crossed double trebles creates a pretty texture in this lacy block, which is satisfying to work up and mixes well with other grannies and textural blocks. This method of crossing double trebles keeps the stitches separate instead of connecting them in the centre.

A
B
C

Special stitch used:

Crossed double treble (crossed dtr):
Insert hook behind dtr just worked and work in specified st, complete tr st as normal.

Foundation ring: Using yarn A, ch 6, sl st in first ch to form ring.

Round 1: Ch 5 (counts as 1 dtr, ch 1), [1 dtr, ch 1] 11 times in ring, sl st in 4th ch of beg ch-5 to join. Fasten off yarn A.

Round 2: Join yarn B in any dtr st, ch 1, 1 dc in same st, *[1 dc in next ch-1 sp, 1 dc in next dtr] 2 times, [1 dc , ch 2, 1 dc] in next ch-1 sp, 1 dc in next dtr**; rep from * 2 times and from * to ** 1 time, sl st in first dc to join. Fasten off yarn B.

Round 3: Join yarn C in any ch-2 sp, ch 7 (counts as 1 dtr, ch 3) 1 dtr in same sp (forms corner), ch 1, miss 3 dc, ch 1, 1 dtr in next dc, ch 1, 1 crossed dtr in st 2 dc back along (to right), inserting hook behind dtr just worked; rep from * 1 time, ch 1, miss 1 dc**, [1 dtr, ch 3, 1 dtr] in next ch-2 sp (forms corner); rep from * 2 times, then from * to ** 1 time, sl st in 4th ch of beg ch-7 to join. Fasten off yarn C.

Round 4: Join yarn B in any corner ch-3 sp, ch 1, *[2 dc, ch 1, 2 dc] in same sp, [1 dc in next dtr, 1 dc in next ch-1 sp] 2 times, 1 dc in next dtr, [1 dc in next dtr, 1 dc in next ch-1 sp] 2 times, 1 dc in next dtr; rep from * 3 times, sl st in first dc to join.Fasten off yarn B.

Round 5: Join yarn A in any ch-1 corner sp, ch 7 (counts as 1 dtr, ch 3), 1 dtr in same sp, *ch 1, miss 3 dc, 1 dtr in next dc, ch 1, miss 1 dc, 1 crossed dtr in 2nd dc to right of last dtr; rep from * 3 times, ch 1**, miss 1 dc, [1 dtr, ch 3, 1 dtr] in next corner ch-1 sp; rep from * 2 times then from * to ** 1 time, sl st in 4th ch of beg ch-7 to join. Fasten off yarn A.

Round 6: Join yarn B in any corner ch-3 sp, ch 1, [2 dc, ch 1, 2 dc] in corner sp, [1 dc in next dtr, 1 dc in next ch-1 sp] 2 times, 1 dc in next dtr, [1 dc in next dtr, 1 dc in next ch-1 sp, 1 dc in next dtr] 3 times, 1 dc in next ch-1 sp, 1 dc in next dtr; rep from * 3 times, sl st in first dc to join. Fasten off yarn B.

Round 7: Join yarn C in any ch-1 corner sp, ch 7 (counts as 1 dtr, ch 3), 1 dtr in same sp, *ch 1, miss 3 dc, 1 dtr in next dc, ch 1, 1 crossed dtr in 2nd dc to right of last dtr worked, ch 1; rep from * to corner ch-1 sp**, [1 dtr, ch 3, 1 dtr] in ch-1 corner sp; rep from * 2 times and from * to ** 1 time, sl st in 4th ch of beg ch-7 to join.

Fasten off and darn in ends.

*

mountains

A simple motif with fun surface crochet, this block is warm and thick. Combine with other country-style blocks for a cosy cottage appeal.

A
B
C
D

Special stitch used:

Surface crochet: 1 sl st over vertical post of each st, creating a chain-stitch effect (*see page 22*).

Note: Use a hook two sizes down from regular hook for whatever yarn used when working surface crochet.

Foundation chain: Using yarn A, ch 22.

Row 1: 1 dc in 2nd ch from hook, 1 dc in every ch to end, turn – 21 dc.

Rows 2 to 21: Ch 1, 1 dc in every dc to end, turn.

SURFACE CROCHET

Using yarn B and smaller hook, join B by inserting hook in top RH corner of square, 2 dc in from edge and 4 rows down, 16 sl sts across, turn work 90 degrees, 15 sl sts down, turn work 90 degrees, 16 sl sts across, turn work 90 degrees, 15 sl sts back up to start, sl st to WS, fasten off.

Work 3 rows of crochet zigzags in yarns C and D: one row C, one row D, one row C. Insert hook 2 dc up from bottom RH corner of surface crochet box; sl st diagonally up and down to create zigzag patterns. Fasten off after each row.

BORDER

Round 1: Join yarn C in any corner sp, ch 2 (counts as 1 htr, [1 htr, ch 1, 2 htr] in corner sp, [miss 1 dc, 1 htr in next dc, ch 1] to next corner sp, *[2 htr, ch 1, 2 htr, ch 1] in corner sp, [miss 1 dc, 1 htr in next dc, ch 1] to next corner sp; rep from * 2 times, sl st in top of beg ch-2 to join.

Rounds 2 to 3: Sl st in next corner ch sp, ch 2 (counts as 1 htr) [1 htr, ch 1, 2 htr] in corner ch-1 sp, [1 htr, ch 1] in every ch-1 sp to next corner sp, *[2 htr, ch 2, 2 htr, ch 1] in corner sp, [1 htr, ch 1] in every ch-1 sp to next corner sp; rep from * 2 times, sl st in top of beg ch-2 to join. Fasten off yarn C.

Round 4: Join yarn B in any corner ch-1 sp, sl st surface crochet in every st around square.

Fasten off and darn in ends.

**

icicles

This wonderful block shows off the potential of spike stitch effectively as double crochets are worked into different rows below to produce a variegated spike pattern. Wonderful for mixing with other blocks in a geometric-themed blanket, this square is warm, cosy and dense.

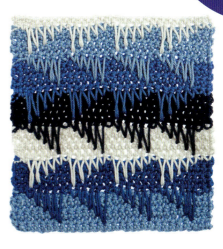

A
B
C
D
E

Special stitch used:

Spike stitch (spike): Insert hook in top of st below next st to be worked (in this pattern 2, 3, 4, 5 or 6 rows below), yoh, pull yarn through to height of rnd being worked, complete dc as normal (*see page 22*).

Foundation chain: Using yarn A, ch 28.

Row 1: 1 dc in 2nd ch from hook, 1 dc in every ch to end – 27 dc.

Row 2: Ch 1, 1 dc in every dc to end, turn.

Rows 3 to 6: Rep Row 2. Fasten off yarn A.

Row 7: Join yarn B, ch 1, 1 dc in first dc, *1 dc in next dc, 1 spike dc 2 rows below current row, 1 spike dc 3 rows below, 1 spike dc 4 rows below, 1 spike dc 5 rows below, 1 spike dc 6 rows below; rep from * 3 times, 1 dc in each of last 2 dc, turn.

Rows 8 to 12: Rep Row 2. Fasten off yarn B.

Row 13: Join yarn C, ch 1, 1 dc in first dc, *1 dc in next dc, 1 spike dc 6 rows below current row, 1 spike dc 5 rows below, 1 spike dc 4 rows below, 1 spike dc 3 rows below, 1 spike dc 2 rows below; rep from * 3 times, 1 dc in each of last 2 dc, turn.

Rows 14 to 18: Rep Row 2. Fasten off yarn C.

Row 19: Using yarn D, rep Row 7.

Rows 20 to 24: Rep Row 2. Fasten off yarn D.

Row 25: Using yarn E, rep Row 13.

Rows 26 to 30: Rep Row 2. Fasten off yarn E.

Row 31: Using yarn A, rep Row 7.

Rows 32 to 36: Rep Row 2. Fasten off yarn A.

Row 37: Using yarn C, rep Row 13.

Row 38: Rep Row 2.

Fasten off and darn in ends neatly.

★ ★ ★ ★

mola

This block has layers of back-post stitches that create ridges and give a stitched effect, like an appliquéd Mexican mola. Work this in contrasting colours to show off the ridges to best advantage.

A
B
C
D

Special stitches used:

Back-post treble crochet (BPtr): Yoh 2 times, insert hook through back of st post from right to left, yoh, draw lp through, [yoh, draw through 2 loops] 3 times.

Back-post double crochet (BPdc): Insert hook through back of st post from right to left, yoh, draw lp through, yoh, draw through 2 lps (*see page 21*).

Foundation ring: Using yarn A, ch 4, sl st in first ch to form ring.

Round 1: Ch 2 (counts as 1 htr), 15 htr in ring, sl st in top of beg ch-2 to join. Fasten off yarn A.

Round 2: Join yarn B, ch 3 (counts as 1 tr), 2 BPtr in each of next 15 htr, 1 BPtr in last htr – 32 sts. Fasten off yarn B.

Round 3: Join yarn C, ch 1, 1 dc in every st to end, sl st in first dc to join. Fasten off yarn C.

Round 4: Join yarn A, ch 3 (counts as 1 tr), 1 BPtr in same sc, *2 BPtr in next dc, 1 BPtr in next dc; rep from * to end, sl st in top of beg ch-3 to join. Fasten off yarn A.

Round 5: Join yarn D, ch 1, 1 BPdc in every st to end, sl st in first dc to join.

Round 6: Ch 3 (counts as 1 tr), *1 tr in each of next 3 tr, 2 tr in next tr; rep from * to end, sl st in top of beg ch-3 to join. Fasten off yarn D.

Round 7: Join yarn B, ch 1, 1 BPdc in every st to end, sl st in first dc to join.

Round 8: *Ch 9, miss 5 sts, 1 dc in each of next 10 dc; rep from * 3 times, sl st in first ch to join.

Round 9: Ch 3 (counts as 1 tr), *1 tr in each of next 4 ch sts (not ch-sp), [2 tr, ch 2, 2 tr] in next ch st, 1 tr in each of next 4 ch sts, 1 tr in each of next 10 dc; rep from * 3 times, omitting last 1 tr on last rep, sl st in top of beg ch-3 to join. Fasten off yarn B.

Round 10: Join yarn D, ch 1, *1 dc in every dc to corner ch-2 sp, [2 dc, ch 1, 2 dc] in ch-2 sp; rep from * 3 times, 1 dc in every dc to end, sl st in first dc to join. Fasten off yarn D.

Round 11: Join yarn C, ch 1, 1 BPdc in every st to corner ch-1 sp, 3 dc in ch-1 sp; rep from * 3 times, 1 BPdc in every st to end, sl st in first dc to join.

Fasten off and darn in ends neatly.

★★★
lifebuoy

This block uses front-post double treble stitches to create the lifebuoy's 'ropes' and would work well as part of a nautical-themed throw, a blanket for a child, or a picnic blanket. Or you could mix multiples with some plainer blocks for a summer pillow cover.

Special stitch used:

Front-post spike double treble (FPspike dtr): Yoh 2 times, bring hook to front of work; insert hook in front vertical post of st 3 rows below from right to left, yoh, draw up lp to same height as row you are working on, complete dtr as normal (*see pages 21 and 22*).

Foundation ring: Using yarn A, ch 4, sl st in first ch to form ring.

Round 1: Ch 1, 12 dc in ring, sl st in first ch to join. Fasten off yarn A.

Round 2: Join yarn B, ch 1, 1 dc in every dc to end, sl st in first dc to join.

Round 3: Ch 6 (counts as 1 tr, ch 3), *miss 1 dc, 1 tr in next dc, ch 3; rep from * to end, sl st in 3rd ch of beg ch-6 to join.

Round 4: Ch 1, 1 dc in same st, *4 dc in next ch-3 sp, 1 dc in next tr; rep from * to end, sl st in first dc to join. Fasten off yarn B.

Round 5: Join yarn C, ch 1, 2 dc in same st, *1 dc in each of next 2 dc, 2 dc in next dc; rep from * to end, ending with 1 dc in each of last 2 dc, sl st in first dc to join. Fasten off yarn C.

Round 6: Join yarn A, ch 2, 1 htr in every dc to end, sl st in top of beg ch-2 to join.

Round 7: Ch 2, 1 htr in same st, *1 htr in each of next 3 htr, 2 htr in next htr; rep from * to end, ending with 1 htr in each of last 3 htr, sl st in top of beg ch-2 to join.

Round 8: Ch 2, 1 htr in same st, *1 htr in each of next 4 htr, 2 htr in next htr; rep from * to end, ending with 1 htr in each of last 4 htr, sl st in top of beg ch-2 to join. Fasten off yarn A.

A
B
C
D

Round 9: Join yarn C, ch 1, 1 dc in each of next 2 htr, *1 FPspike dtr in dc directly below from Round 5 (last row of yarn C), 1 dc in each of next 2 htr, 1 FPspike dtr in dc immediately to left of dc last FPspike dtr was worked in, on Round 5, 1 dc in each of next 4 htr, miss 3 dc on Round 5, 1 FPspike dtr in next dc on Round 5, 1 dc in each of next 2 htr, 1 FPspike dtr in dc immediately to left of dc last FPspike dtr was worked in, 1 dc in each of next 3 htr, miss 3 dc on Round 5; rep from * to end, ending with 1 dc in last htr, sl st in first dc to join. Fasten off yarn C.

Round 10: Join yarn D, ch 3, 4 tr in same st (forms corner), *1 tr in next st, 1 htr in each of next 2 sts, 1 dc in each of next 8 sts, 1 htr in each of next 2 sts, 1 tr in next st, 5 tr in next st; rep from * to end, ending with 1 htr in each of last 2 sts, sl st in top of beg ch-2. Fasten off yarn D.

Round 11: Join yarn B, ch 3 (counts as 1 htr, ch 1), miss 1 st, 1 htr in next st, 5 htr in 3rd htr of 5-htr corner group, *[ch 1, miss 1 st, 1 htr in next st] to corner htr, 5 htr in corner htr; rep from * 2 times, [ch 1, miss 1 st, 1 htr in next st] to end, sl st in 2nd ch of beg ch-3 to join.

Round 12: Ch 3 (counts as 1 tr), *1 tr in every htr and every ch-1 sp to corner htr, 5 tr in corner htr; rep from * 3 times, 1 tr in every htr to end, sl st in top of beg ch-3 to join. Fasten off yarn B.

Round 13: Join yarn A, ch 1, *1 dc in every tr to corner, 3 dc in corner tr; rep from * 3 times, 1 dc in every tr to end, sl st in first dc to join.

Fasten off and darn in ends.

****
gifted

A
B
C

Designed to resemble a lavishly wrapped present, this block works multiple 'ribbon' loops into the same stitches to create a gift bow effect, then separate ribbon tails are worked before the plain square ground is worked to finish off. A showstopping centrepiece for a gift pillow, blanket or lap throw, this is sure to gain attention.

Foundation ring: Using yarn A, make a magic ring.

Round 1: Ch 3 (counts as 1 tr), 15 tr in ring, sl st in top of beg ch-3 to join. Fasten off yarn A.

Round 2: Join yarn B in front lp of top of beg ch-3, *ch 8, sl st in front lp of each of next 2 tr; rep from * 6 times, ch 8, sl st in front lp of last tr.

Round 3: Sl st in next ch-8 lp, *[2 dc, 4 htr, 2 dc] in ch-8 lp, sl st in first of next 2 sl sts**, sl st in next ch-8 lp; rep from * 6 times and from * to ** 1 time, sl st in first dc to join. Fasten off yarn B.

Round 4: Turn work to WS, join yarn A in back lp of any tr from Round 1, [ch 12, sl st in each of next 2 tr] 7 times, ch 12, sl st in last tr.

Round 5: Turn work to RS, sl st in next ch-12 lp, *[4 dc, 4 htr, 4 dc] in lp, sl st in next sl st, sl st in next ch-12 lp; rep from * 7 times, sl st in first dc to join.

RIBBONS

(WS) *Ch 1, 1 dc in same sp, 1 dc in each of next 3 sl sts at base of ribbon lp (1 st at RH base of lp, 2 sts within lp itself, 1 st at base of LH part of lp), turn, ch 1, 1 dc in each of next 2 dc, 2 dc in next dc, 1 dc in next dc, turn, [ch 1, 1 dc in every dc, turn] 5 times, ch 4 (counts as 1 dtr), 1 tr in same st, 1 dc in next st, sl st in next dc, 1 dc in next st, [1 tr, 1 dtr] in last st, fasten off.

Miss 1 ribbon lp; join yarn A, rep from * at base of next ribbon lp; rep from * 3 times.

Round 6: (WS) Join yarn C at RH base of any 'ribbon' just made, ch 1, 1 dc in same st, ch 4, 1 dc in same sp in next ribbon base; rep from * 3 times, ending with sl st in first dc to join.

Round 7: Ch 3 (counts as 1 tr), 5 tr in next ch-4 lp, *[1 tr, ch 2, 1 tr] in next dc; rep from * 2 times, [1 tr, ch 2, 1 tr] in last dc, sl st in top of beg ch-3 to join.

Round 8: Ch 3 (counts as 1 tr), 1 tr in each of next 7 tr, *[2 tr, ch 2, 2 tr] in next ch-2 sp (forms corner), 1 tr in each of next 8 tr; rep from * 2 times, [2 tr, ch 2, 2 tr] in next ch-2 sp, sl st in top of beg ch-3 to join.

Round 9: Ch 3 (counts as 1 tr), 1 tr in each of next 9 tr, *[2 tr, ch 2, 2 tr] in next ch-2 sp, 1 tr in each of next 12 tr; rep from * 2 times, [2 tr, ch 2, 2 tr] in next ch-2 sp, 1 tr in each of last 2 tr, sl st in top of beg ch-3 to join.

Round 10: Ch 3 (counts as 1 tr), 1 tr in each of next 11 tr, *[2 tr, ch 2, 2 tr] in next ch-2 sp, 1 tr in each of next 16 tr; rep from * 2 times, [2 tr, ch 2, 2 tr] in next ch-2 sp, 1 tr in each of last 4 tr, sl st in top of beg ch-3 to join.

Round 11: Ch 3 (counts as 1 tr), 1 tr in each of next 13 tr, *[2 tr, ch 2, 2 tr] in next ch-2 sp, 1 tr in each of next 20 tr; rep from * 2 times, [2 tr, ch 2, 2 tr] in next ch-2 sp, 1 tr in each of last 6 tr, sl st in top of beg ch-3 to join.

Round 12: Ch 1, 1 dc in every st to corner, [2 dc, ch 1, 2 dc] in corner ch-2 sp; rep from * 3 times, 1 dc in every st to end, sl st in first dc to join.

Fasten off and darn in ends.

***

annecy

A

With an antique French feel, this block was inspired by doily patterns and fine lace. It is light and delicate, lending itself to use in summer throws, scarves and shawls.

Foundation ring: Ch 4, join with sl st to form ring.

Round 1: Ch 1, 11 dc in ring, sl st in first dc to join.

Round 2: Ch 1, 1 dc in same sp, working in back lps only of each st, 2 dc in each st to end, sl st in first ch to join.

Round 3: Ch 3, *miss 1 dc, 1 dc in back lp of next dc, ch 2; rep from * to end, sl st in first ch of beg ch-3 to join.

Round 4: [1 dc, 1 tr, 2 dtr, 1 tr, 1 dc] in each ch-2 sp to end of rnd, sl st in first dc to join.

Round 5: Ch 7 (counts as 1 dtr, ch 3), 1 dtr in same dc, *ch 3, [1 dc in top of petal, working behind post of st, ch 3] 3 times, 1 dtr, ch 3, 1 dtr in dc between next 2 petals; rep from * to end, sl st in 4th ch of beg ch-7 to join.

Round 6: Ch 3 (counts as 1 tr), *[3 tr, ch 3, 3 tr] in corner ch-sp, 1 tr in next dtr, 2 tr in next ch-2 sp, [1 tr in next dc, 2 tr in next ch-2 sp] 3 times, 1 tr in next dtr; rep from * to end, sl st in top of beg ch-3 to join.

Round 7: Sl st into ch-3 corner sp, *ch 6, 1 tr in same corner sp, sl st in next tr st**, [ch 5, miss 2 tr sts, sl st in next tr st] 6 times to next corner; rep from * 3 times, and from * to ** 1 time, [ch 5, miss 2 tr sts, sl st in next tr st] 5 times, ch 2, miss 2 tr sts, 1 tr in next tr st.

Round 8: *Ch 3, [1 dc, ch 1, 1 dc] in 4th ch of ch-6 corner sp, [ch 3, 1 dc in 3rd ch of next ch-5 sp] 6 times; rep from * 4 times.

Round 9: Ch 1, 3 dc in next ch-3 sp, *ch 1, 5 dc in ch-1 corner sp, ch 1, [3 dc in next ch-3 sp] 7 times; rep from * 3 times, ch 1, 5 dc in ch-1 corner sp, ch 1, [3 dc in next ch-3 sp] 6 times, sl st in first dc to join.

Fasten off and darn in ends.

• •

*

bergen

A

B

A simple snowflake design that is fast to work up and would lend itself to a host of seasonal uses: tableware, blankets and throws, or festooned as bunting with the other snowflake designs in this book, Chamonix and Flurry.

Foundation ring: Using yarn A, ch 6, sl st in first ch to form ring.

Round 1: Ch 1, 16 dc in ring, sl st in first dc to join.

Round 2: *Ch 8, miss 1 dc, sl st in next dc; rep from * 7 times, fasten off.

Round 3: Join yarn A again in top of any ch-8 lp, 1 dc in same st, *ch 5, 1 dc in next ch-8 lp; rep from * 6 times, ch 5, sl st in first dc to join.

Round 4: Sl st in first ch-5 sp, *ch 2, [1 htr, 1 tr, ch 3, 1 tr, 1 htr] in ch-5 sp, ch 2, 1 dc in next dc; rep from * 7 times, omitting last dc on last rep, sl st in first dc to join.

Round 5: *Ch 5, [1 htr, 1 tr, ch 3, 1 tr, 1 htr] in ch-3 sp, ch 5, sl st in next dc; rep from * 7 times, fasten off.

Round 6: Join yarn B in any ch-3 sp, 1 dc in same st, *ch 8, 1 dc in next ch-3 sp, ch 14**, 1 dc in next dc; rep from * 2 times and from * to ** 1 time, sl st in first dc to join.

Round 7: Ch 2 (counts as 1 htr), *1 htr in each ch st (not the ch-sp), of ch-8 sp, 1 htr in next dc, 1 htr in each of next 5 ch sts, [1 htr, ch 3, 1 htr] in next ch st, 1 htr in each of next 5 ch sts, 1 htr in next dc; rep from * 3 times, omitting last htr from last rep, sl st in top of beg ch-2 to join.

Fasten off and darn in ends.

**

flamenco

A

B

A flamboyant popcorn fiesta, this block is fun to work and mixes well with a host of other squares: popcorns, grannies and circle-in-a-square types in particular. Make it in Spanish colours and team it with Sevilla, Granada, and Fiesta for a truly carnival-theme throw – *olé*!

Special stitches used:

Beginning 3-treble-crochet cluster (beg 3-tr cl): Ch 3, make cluster with 2 tr (*see page 18*).

3 treble-crochet-cluster (3-tr cl): Make cluster with 3 tr.

Surface crochet: 1 sl st over vertical post of each st, creating a chain-stitch effect (*see page 22*).

Beginning popcorn (beg pc): Ch 3, make popcorn with 4 tr (*see page 19*).

Popcorn (pc): Make popcorn with 5 tr.

Foundation ring: Using yarn A, make a magic ring.

Round 1: Beg 3-tr cl in ring, ch 3, *3-tr cl in ring; rep from * 4 times, sl st in top of beg ch-3 to join.

Round 2: Join yarn B in any ch-2 sp, ch 1, 3 dc in same sp, ch 1, [3 dc in next sp, ch 1] 5 times, sl st in first ch to join.

Round 3: Ch 3 (counts as 1 tr), 1 tr in each of next 2 dc, ch 3, miss 1 st, [1 tr in each of next 3 dc, ch 3, miss 1 st] 5 times, sl st in top of beg ch-3 to join. Fasten off yarn B.

Round 4: Join yarn A in any ch-2 sp, ch 1, 2 dc in same sp, 1 dc in each of next 3 tr, [3 dc in next sp, 1 dc in each of next 3 tr] 5 times, sl st in first ch to join.

Round 5: Ch 1, 1 dc in same sp, 2 dc in each of next 35 dc, sl st in first ch to join. Fasten off yarn A.

Round 6: Join yarn B, ch 4 (counts as 1 dtr), [1 dtr, ch 3, 3 dtr] in same st (forms corner), 1 dtr in each of next 17 dc, *[2 dtr, ch 3, 2 dtr] in next st (forms corner), 1 dtr in each of next 17 dc; rep from * 2 times, sl st in top of beg ch-4 to join. Fasten off yarn B.

Round 7: Join yarn A join in st to right of any corner sp, miss next dtr, surface crochet in front lp of next 20 dtr, *1 surface crochet over next corner sp, miss next dtr, surface crochet in front lp of next 20 dtr; rep from * 2 times, sl st in first surface crochet st at beg to join. Fasten off yarn A.

Round 8: Join yarn B in any ch-3 corner sp, [beg pc, ch 4, pc] in same sp (forms corner), ch 2, miss 2 dtr, 1 pc in back lp of next dtr, ch 2, miss 2 dtr, [1 hdc in back lp of next dtr, ch 2, miss 2 dtr] 4 times, 1 pc in back lp of next dtr, ch 2, *[pc, ch 4, pc] in next ch-3 corner sp (forms corner) ch 2, miss 2 dtr, 1 pc in back lp of next dtr, ch 2, miss 2 dtr, [1 htr in back lp of next dtr, ch 2, miss 2 dtr] 4 times, 1 pc in back lp of next dtr, ch 2; rep from * 2 times, sl st in top of beg pc to join.

Round 9: Sl st in next ch-4 sp, [beg pc, ch 4, pc] in same sp (forms corner), [ch 2, pc in next sp] 2 times, ch 2, [3 htr in next sp, miss 1 st, ch 1] 2 times, 3 htr in next sp, miss 1 st, [ch 2, pc in next sp] 2 times, ch 2, *[pc, ch 4, pc] in corner sp, [ch 2, pc in next sp] 2 times, ch 2, [3 htr in next sp, miss 1 st, ch 1] 2 times, 3 htr in next sp, miss 1 st, [ch 2, pc in next sp] 2 times, ch 2; rep from * 2 times, sl st in top of beg pc to join.

Round 10: Sl st in next ch-4 sp, ch 1 (counts as 1 dc), [3 dc, ch 2, 4 dc] in same sp (forms corner), 1 dc in each st, pc and sp to next corner, 2 dc in each ch-2 sp, *[4 dc, ch 2, 4 dc] in next corner sp, 1 dc in each st, pc and 1-ch sp to next corner, 2 dc in each ch-2 sp, sl st in first ch to join.

Fasten off and darn in ends.

✳✳

betty

A delightful fantasy flower that works up really quickly and adapts to a host of uses, from light throws and blankets to pretty tableware. Keep the colours bright for maximum impact. This flower is no shrinking violet.

Foundation ring: Using yarn A, make a magic ring.

Round 1: Ch 3 (counts as 1 tr), 15 tr in ring, sl st in top of beg ch-3 to join.

Round 2: *Ch 3, sl st in front lp only of next tr; rep from * to end, sl st in first sl st to join. Fasten off yarn A.

Round 3: Join yarn B in back lp of any tr from Round 1, 1 dc in same sp, *ch 11, 1 tr in 4th ch from hook, 1 tr in each of next 7 ch, miss 1 tr at base, sl st in back lp of next tr; rep from * 7 times, sl st in first dc to join. Fasten off yarn B.

Round 4: Join yarn C in any empty back lp from Round 1, *ch 11, 1 tr in 4th ch from hook, 1 tr in each of next 7 ch, miss 1 tr at base, sl st in back lp of next tr; rep from * 7 times, sl st in first dc to join. Fasten off yarn C.

Round 5: Join yarn B in top of any petal in ch-2 sp, *1 dc in same sp, ch 4, 1 dc in same place in next petal; rep from * 14 times, ch 4, sl st in first dc to join.

Round 6: Ch 1, 4 dc in next ch-4 sp, [1 dc, ch 1, 1 dc] in next dc, *4 htr in next ch-4 sp, [1 htr, ch 1, 1 htr] in next dc, [3 tr, ch 2, 3 tr] in next ch-4 sp, [1 htr, ch 1, 1 htr] in next dc, 4 htr in next dc**, [1 dc, ch 1, 1 dc] in next dc; rep from * 2 times and from * to ** 1 time, sl st in first dc to join.

Fasten off and darn in ends neatly.

✳✳

little crosses

A bold block of solid colour that lends itself to adapting to whatever colour combination you want, and mixes well with many other types of square. This one is easier to work than it looks.

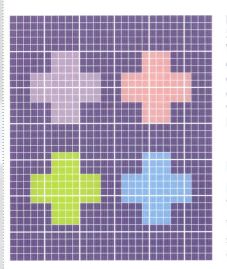

Note: When working this pattern prepare 3 separate balls of yarn A before you begin. Work each separate area of colour using a different ball of yarn, joining on last lp of each st of last area of colour. Keep all yarn ends at WS of work throughout otherwise when you need to change colour, yarn may be on RS and inaccessible.

Foundation chain: Using yarn A, ch 30.

Row 1: (First row of chart) 1 dc in 2nd ch from hook, 1 dc in every ch to end, turn.

Work remaining 33 rows of chart, making sure you keep yarn ends on WS, and changing colour where indicated.

Rows 2 to 34: Ch 1, 1 dc in every dc to end, turn.

Fasten off and darn in ends neatly. Block work to shape.

278

*

carnival

A simple structure but an interesting effect, this block is created entirely from double crochet stitches but with a three-colour alternating stripe that develops into a variegated pattern. A great beginner square, choose eye-popping colours for best effect.

A

B

C

Foundation chain: Using yarn A, ch 30.

Row 1: 1 dc in 2nd ch from hook, 1 dc in every ch to end, turn. Fasten off yarn A.

Row 2: Join yarn B, ch 1, 1 dc in every dc to end, turn. Fasten off yarn B.

Row 3: Join yarn C, ch 1, 1 dc in every dc to end, turn. Fasten off yarn C.

Row 4: Join yarn A, ch 1, 1 dc in every dc to end, turn. Fasten off yarn A.

Row 5 to 31: Rep Rows 2 to 4 in sequence 9 times.

Row 32: Rep Row 2.

Fasten off and darn in ends neatly.

279

**

polka

A simple construction belies the more complex appearance of this block. Its relative density makes it perfect for mixing with texture block, or more colourful grannies for a delightful cosy blanket

A

B

Foundation ring: Using yarn A, ch 6, sl st in first ch to form ring.

Round 1: Ch 1, 24 dc in ring, sl st in first ch-1 to join. Fasten off yarn A.

Round 2: Join yarn B in any dc, ch 1, 1 dc in same sp, *miss 1 dc, ch 1, 1 dc in next dc; rep from * 11 times, sl st in first ch to join. Fasten off yarn B.

Round 3: Join yarn A in any ch-1 sp, ch 1, 1 dc in same sp, *ch 2, 1 dc in next ch-1 sp, ch 1, 1 dc in next ch-1 sp; rep from * 4 times, ch 2, 1 dc in next ch-1 sp, ch 1, sl st in first dc to join. Fasten off yarn A.

Round 4: Join yarn B in any ch-2 sp, *ch 1, *[1 dc, ch 2, 1 dc, ch 1] in same corner sp, [1 dc, ch 1] in each of next 2 sps; rep from * 3 times, sl st in first ch to join. Fasten off yarn B.

Round 5: Join yarn A in any ch-2 corner sp, ch 1, *[2 dc, ch 2, 2 dc, ch 1] in corner sp, [1 dc, ch 1] in every ch-1 sp to next corner; rep from * 3 times, sl st in first ch to join. Fasten off yarn A.

Rounds 6, 8, 10, 12 and 14: Rep Round 5 using yarn B.

Rounds 7, 9, 11, 13 and 15: Rep Round 5 using yarn A.

Fasten off and darn in ends.

clematis

A simple block that uses easy fans of stitches to produce its doily-like pattern. This block could be given added pizazz by changing colours in the rounds, but it is useful when worked in a single colour for mixing with more elaborate blocks.

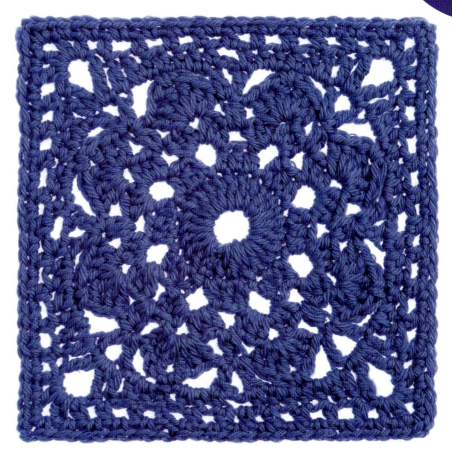

Special stitch used:

Half-treble crochet 2 stitches together (htr2tog): Work 2 htr, leaving last lp of each on hook, yoh and draw through all lps.

Foundation ring: Make a magic ring.

Round 1: Ch 2 (counts as 1 htr), 23 htr in ring, sl st in top of beg ch-2 to join.

Round 2: Ch 5 (counts as 1 htr, ch 3), 1 htr in each of next 3 htr, [ch 3, 1 htr in each of next 3 htr] 6 times, ch 3, 1 htr in each of last 2 htr, sl st in top of beg ch-2 to join.

Round 3: Ch 2 (counts as 1 htr), [2 htr, ch 3, 3 htr] in next ch-3 sp, *ch 1, [3 htr, ch 3, 3 htr] in next ch-3 sp; rep from * 7 times, ch 1, sl st in top of beg ch-2 to join.

Round 4: Sl st in next ch-3 sp, ch 3, (counts as 1 tr), [2 tr, ch 1, 3 tr] in same sp, *htr2tog in next ch-1 sp, [3 tr, ch 1, 3 tr] in next ch-3 sp; rep from * 6 times, htr2tog in next ch-1 sp, sl st in top of beg ch-3 to join.

Round 5: Sl st to next ch-1 sp, 1 dc in ch-1 sp, *ch 3, [1 tr, ch 2, 1 tr] in next htr2tog, ch 3, 1 dc in next ch-1 sp; rep from * 6 times, ch 3, [1 tr, ch 2, 1 tr] in next htr2tog, ch 3, sl st in first dc to join.

Round 6: Ch 3 (counts as 1 htr, ch 1), 2 htr in next ch-3 sp, *1 htr in next tr, ch 3, 1 htr in next tr, 2 htr in next ch-3 sp, 1 htr in next dc, [1 htr, 1 tr] in next ch-3 sp, 1 tr in next tr, [1 dtr, ch 3, 1 dtr] in next ch-2 sp, 1 tr in next tr, [1 tr, 1 htr] in next ch-3 sp**, 1 htr in next dc, 2 htr in next ch-3 sp; rep from * 2 times and from * to ** 1 time, sl st in 2nd ch of beg ch-3 to join.

Round 7: Ch 3 (counts as 1 htr, ch 1), miss 1 st, 1 htr in next htr, ch 1, 1 htr in next ch-3 sp, ch 1, [1 htr, miss 1 st, ch 1] to ch-3 corner sp, *[1 htr, ch 1, 1 htr, ch 2, 1 htr, ch 1, 1 htr] in corner ch-3 sp, [1 htr, miss 1 st, ch 1] to next corner, working [ch 1, 1 htr, ch 1] in centre ch-3 sp; rep from * 2 times and from * to ** 1 time, [ch 1, miss 1 st, 1 htr] to end, sl st in 2nd ch of beg ch-3 to join.

Round 8: Ch 1, *1 dc in next ch-1 sp, ch 1; rep from * to ch-2 corner sp, [1 dc, ch 1, 1 dc] in ch-2 corner sp; rep from * 3 times, [1 dc in next ch-1 sp, ch 1] to end, sl st in first dc to join.

Fasten off and darn in ends.

281

*

spinningfields

A two-colour square that is versatile and fairly quick to make, this was inspired by the cotton mills of the North-west of England. It's lightweight and mixes well with many other blocks.

A

B

Foundation ring: Using yarn A, ch 6, sl st in first ch to form ring.

Round 1: Ch 3, 15 tr in ring, sl st in top of begf ch-3 to join.

Round 2: Ch 5 (counts as 1 tr, ch 2), [1 tr in next tr, ch 2] 15 times, sl st in 3rd of beg ch-5 to join.

Round 3: Sl st in first ch-2 sp, ch 3, 1 tr in same sp, [ch 1, 2 tr in next sp] 15 times, ch 1, sl st in top of beg ch-3 to join.

Round 4: Sl st in next tr, sl st in next sp, 1 dc in same sp, *[ch 3, 1 dc in next sp] 3 times, ch 6, 1 dc in next sp; rep from * 3 times, omitting last 1 dc at end of last rep, sl st in first dc to join. Fasten off yarn A.

Round 5: Join yarn B in first 3-ch sp of any side, ch 3, 2 tr in same sp, *3 tr in each 3-ch sp to corner, [5 tr, ch 2, 5 tr] in corner ch-6 sp; rep from * 3 times, sl st in top of beg ch-3 to join.

Round 6: Ch 3 (counts as 1 tr), *1 tr in every tr to corner, [2 tr, ch 4, 2 tr] in corner sp; rep from * 2 times, 1 tr in every tr to end, sl st in top of beg ch-3 to join.

Rounds 7 to 8: Rep Round 6.

Fasten off and darn in ends.

282

**

wisteria

A simple twist on a familiar doily pattern, this block works up quickly and has a pretty picot edging. Useful for mixing with other circle-in-a-square blocks to create a bold blanket.

A

B

Special stitch used:

Picot-4: ch 4, sl st in same stitch first ch was worked in, to form lp.

Foundation ring: Using yarn A, ch 6, sl st in first ch to form ring.

Round 1: Ch 1, 16 dc in ring, sl st in first dc to join.

Round 2: Ch 4, 2 dtr in same sp, *ch 2, miss 1 dc, 3 dtr in next dc; rep from * 6 times, ch 2, sl st in top of beg ch-4 to join.

Round 3: Ch 4, 1 dtr in same sp, 1 dtr in next dtr, 2 dtr in next dtr, 1 dtr in last dtr of group, *ch 2, 1 dtr in next dtr, 3 dtr in next dtr, 1 dtr in last dtr of group; rep from * 6 times, ch 2, sl st in top of beg ch-4 to join.

Round 4: Ch 3, 1 tr in same sp, 1 tr in each of next 3 dtr, 2 tr in last dtr of group, *ch 2, 2 tr in first dtr, 1 tr in each of next 3 dtr, 2 tr in last dtr of group; rep from * 6 times, ch 2, sl st in top of beg ch-3 to join. Fasten off yarn A.

Round 5: Join yarn B in any ch-2 sp, ch 1, *[2 dc, ch 3, 2 dc] in corner sp, miss first tr, 1 dc in each of next 6 tr, 2 dc in next ch-2 sp, miss next tr, 1 dc in each of next 6 tr; rep from * 3 times, sl st in next corner sp.

Round 6: Ch 1, *[2 dc, ch 2, 2 dc] in corner sp, 1 dc in every dc to next corner; rep from * 3 times, sl st in first dc to join.

Round 7: Ch 1, *[2 dc, ch 2, 2 dc] in corner sp, 1 dc in every dc to next corner; rep from * 3 times, sl st in first dc to join.

Round 8: Ch 1, *[2 dc, ch 1, 2 dc] in corner sp, miss first dc, [1 picot-4 in next dc, sl st in each of next 2 dc] 8 times; rep from * 3 times, sl st in first sc to join.

Fasten off and darn in ends.

**

annelise

Another adapted doily pattern, this pretty block works up best if made in a flat, matt cotton yarn. Mix it with other lacy blocks for a lovely summer throw or blanket.

Special stitches used:

2-treble-crochet cluster (2-tr cl): Make cluster with 2 tr (*see page 18*).

2-double-treble crochet cluster (2-dtr cl): Make cluster with 2 dtr.

Foundation ring: Using yarn A, ch 5, sl st in first ch to form ring.

Round 1: Ch 3 (counts as tr), 15 tr in ring, sl st in top of beg ch-3 to join. Fasten off yarn A.

Round 2: Join yarn B in any tr, ch 4 (counts as 1 tr, ch 1), *1 tr in next st, ch 1; rep from * 14 times, sl st in 3rd ch of beg ch-4. Fasten off yarn B.

Round 3: Join yarn C in any ch-1 sp, *[1 dc, ch 1, 1 dc] in ch-1 sp; rep from * 15 times, sl st in first dc to join. Fasten off yarn C.

Round 4: Join yarn D in any ch-1 sp, 1 dc, *ch 5, 1 dc in next ch-1 sp; rep from * 14 times, ch 2, 1 tr in beg dc to join.

Round 5: *[1 tr, ch 1] 4 times in ch-5 sp, 1 tr in same ch-5 sp, 1 dc in next ch-5 sp; rep from * 7 times, sl st in first tr to join.

Round 6: Sl st in next ch-1 sp, [ch 3, 1 tr] in same ch-1 sp, *[ch 1, 2 tr in next ch-1 sp] 3 times, 2 tr in next ch-1 sp; rep from * 6 times, [ch 1, 2 tr in next ch-1 sp] 3 times, sl st in top of beg ch-3 to join. Fasten off yarn D.

Round 7: Join yarn E in next ch-1 sp, 1 dc in ch-1 sp, *[ch 5, 1 dc in next ch-1 sp] 2 times, ch 1, 1 dc in sp between next tr clusters, ch 1, 1 dc in next ch-1 sp; rep from * 6 times, [ch 5, 1 dc in next ch-1 sp] 2 times, ch 1, 1 sl st in sp between tr clusters, ch 1, sl st in first dc to join.

Round 8: *3 dc in next ch-5 sp, ch 2, 3 dc in next ch-5 sp, 1 dc in next st, [1 dc in next ch-1 sp, 1 dc in next st] 2 times, 2 dc in next ch-5 sp, ch 5, 3 dc in next ch 5 sp, 1 dc in next st, [1 dc in next ch-1 sp, 1 dc in next st] 2 times; rep from * 3 times, sl st in first st to join. Fasten off yarn E.

Round 9: Join yarn C in any ch-5 sp, [ch 3, 1 tr, ch 3, 2-dtr cl, ch 3, 2-tr cl] in ch-5 sp, *ch 4, miss next 5 sts, 2-tr cl in next st, ch 4, 2 dc in next ch-2 sp, ch 4, miss next 5 sts, 2-tr cl in next st, ch 4, [2-tr cl, ch 3, 2-dtr cl, ch 3, 2-tr cl] in next ch-5 sp; rep from * 2 times, ch 4, miss next 5 sts, 2-tr cl in next st, ch 4, 2 dc in next ch-2 sp, ch 4, miss next 5 sts, 2-tr cl in next st, ch 4, sl st in 3rd ch of beg ch-3 to join.

Round 10: Ch 1, *3 dc in next ch-3 sp, 2 dc in top of 2-dtr cl, 2 ch, 1 dc in same st (corner), 3 dc in next ch-3 sp, [1 dc in top of 2-tr cl, 4 dc in next ch-4 sp] 2 times, 1 dc in each of next 2 sts, [4 dc in next 4-ch sp, 1 dc in top of next 2-tr cl] 2 times; rep from * 3 times, sl st in first dc to join.

Fasten off and darn in ends.

*

granny's not square

A classic 'granny' with a pinwheel centre, this square could also be worked using different colours for each round. Great for mixing with other granny blocks.

Foundation ring: Ch 6, sl st in first ch to form ring.

Round 1: Ch 6 (counts as 1 tr, ch 3), [1 tr in ring, ch 3] 7 times, sl st in 3rd ch of beg ch-6 to join.

Round 2: Sl st in next ch-3 sp, ch 3 (counts as 1 tr), 3 tr in same sp, ch 2, [4 tr in next ch-3 sp, ch 2] 7 times, sl st in top of beg ch-3 to join.

Round 3: Ch 3 (counts as 1 tr), 5 tr in next ch-2 sp, ch 1, [6 tr in next ch-2 sp, ch 3, 6 tr in next ch-2 sp, ch 1] 3 times, 6 tr in next ch-2 sp, ch 3, sl st in top of beg ch-3 to join

Round 4: Ch 3 (counts as 1 tr), *ch 3, 1 dc between 3rd and 4th tr of next group, ch 3, 1 dc in next ch-1 sp, ch 3, 1 dc between 3rd and 4th tr of next group, ch 3, [2 tr, ch 3, 2 tr] in next ch-3 sp; rep from * 2 times, ch 3, 1 dc between 3rd and 4th tr of next group, ch 3, 1 dc in next ch-1 sp, ch 3, 1 dc between 3rd and 4th tr of next group, ch 3, [2 tr, ch 3, 1 tr] in last corner sp, sl st in top of beg ch-3 to join.

Round 5: Ch 3, 2 tr in next ch-sp, ch 1, *[3 tr in next ch-sp, ch 1]** 3 times, ch 1, 5 tr in next corner ch-sp, ch 2; rep from * to ** 4 times, ch 1, 5 tr in next corner ch-sp, ch 2; rep from * to ** 4 times, ch 1, 5 tr in next corner sp, ch 2; rep from * to ** 4 times, ch 1, 5 tr in corner sp, ch 2, sl st in top of beg ch-3 to join.

Round 6: Ch 4, *[3 tr in next ch-1 sp, ch 1]** 4 times, ch 2, 3 tr in 3rd tr of corner group of 5 tr; rep from * to ** 5 times, ch 2, 3 tr in 3rd tr of next corner group, ch 2; rep from * to ** 5 times, ch 2, 3 tr in 3rd tr of next corner group, ch 2; rep from * to ** 5 times, ch 2, 3 tr in 3rd tr of last corner group, ch 2, sl st in top of beg ch-3 to join.

Round 7: Ch 3, 2 tr in next ch-2 sp, [ch 1, 3 tr in next ch-1 sp] 4 times, ch 2, 3 tr in 2nd tr of corner group, ch 2, 3 tr in next ch-2 sp, [ch 1, 3 tr in next ch-1 sp] 5 times, ch 2, 3 tr in 2nd tr of corner group of 3 tr, ch 2, 3 tr in next ch-2 sp, [ch 1, 3 tr in next ch-1 sp] 5 times, ch 2, 3 tr in 2nd tr of corner group of 3 tr, ch 2, 3 tr in next ch-1 sp, [ch 1, 3 tr in next ch-1 sp] 5 times, ch 2, 3 tr in 2nd tr of corner group, ch 2, sl st in top of beg ch-3 to join.

Round 8: Ch 1, 1 dc in each st and ch-1 sp all the way around square, sl st in first dc to join.

Fasten off.

***
buddleia

This block features a pretty lace flower centre, which benefits from being worked in a contrasting colour to the background. Great for mixing with other medium-weight blocks, this square has a host of possibilities.

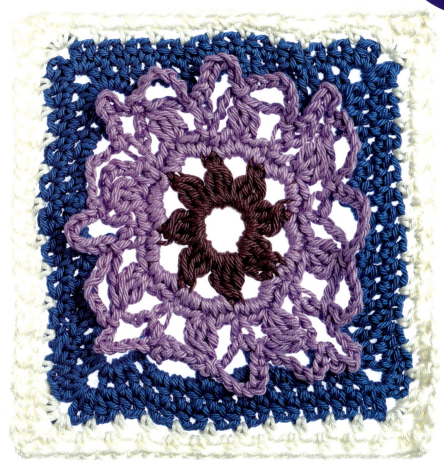

A
B
C
D

Special stitches used:

Puff stitch (pf): Make puff stitch with 3 htr joined together at top (see *page 19*).

Treble crochet 3 stitches together (tr3tog): Work 3 tr leaving last lp of each on hook, yoh, draw through all lps.

Crab stitch (crab st): Double crochet worked in reverse (see *page 22*).

Foundation ring: Using yarn A ch 10, sl st in first ch to form ring.

Round 1: Ch 1, *1 pf in ring, ch 3; rep from * 7 times, sl st in top of first pf to join.

Round 2: Join yarn B in any ch-3 sp, *5 dc in ch-3 sp, 1 dc in top of next pf; rep from * 7 times, sl st in first dc to join.

Round 3: Ch 1, 1 dc in same dc, *ch 4, miss 2 dc, tr3tog in next dc, ch 4, miss 2 dc, 1 dc in next dc; rep from * 7 times, sl st in first dc to join.

Round 4: *Ch 8, sl st in top of tr3tog, ch 8, sl st in next dc; rep from * 7 times, sl st in last dc of Round 3 to join.

Round 5: Turn to WS, join yarn C with sl st through sl st at top of any tr3tog from Round 4, *ch 5, sl st through sl st over dc from Round 4, ch 6, sl st through sl st at top of tr3tog from Round 4; rep from * 6 times, ch 5, sl st through sl st over dc from Round 4, ch 5, sl st in first sl st where yarn C was joined.

Round 6: Turn work to RS, ch 1, *[3 htr, ch 2, 3 htr] in ch-5 sp, 4 htr in each of next 3 ch-5 sps; rep from * 3 times, sl st in first ch to join, sl st to next corner sp.

Round 7: Ch 2 (counts as 1 htr), [1 htr, ch 2, 2 htr] in corner sp, *1 htr in every htr to next corner sp**, [2 htr, ch 2, 2 htr] in corner sp; rep from * 2 times and from * to ** 1 time, sl st in top of beg ch-2 to join.

Round 8: Join yarn D in any ch-2 corner sp, ch 2 (counts as 1 htr), [1 htr, ch 2, 2 htr] in corner sp, *[ch 1, miss 1 htr, 1 htr in next htr] to next corner sp**, [2 htr, ch 2, 2 htr] in corner sp; rep from * 2 times and from * to ** 1 time, sl st in top of beg ch-2 to join, sl st in next corner sp.

Round 9: Ch 2 (counts as 1 htr), [1 htr, ch 2, 2 htr] in corner sp, *[ch 1, 1 htr in every ch-1 sp] to next corner sp**, [2 htr, ch 2, 2 htr] in corner sp; rep from * 2 times and from * to ** 1 time, sl st in next corner space.

Round 10: Ch 1, 1 crab st (from left to right) in every st to end.

Fasten off and darn in ends.

***

tyrol

A host of tiny embroidery stitches supplement the stitch pattern in this block – it demonstrates how easy it can be to add more detail and turn a simple structure into a complex-looking square.

A
B

Foundation chain: Using yarn A, ch 30.

Row 1: 1 dc in 2nd ch from hook and 1 dc in every ch to end, turn.

Row 2: Ch 1, 1 dc in every dc to end, turn. Fasten off yarn A.

Row 3: Join yarn B, rep Row 2. Fasten off yarn B.

Row 4: Join yarn A, rep Row 2.

Rows 5 to 8: Rep Row 2.

Row 9: Ch 3 (counts as 1 htr, ch 1), *miss 1 dc, 1 htr in next dc, ch 1; rep from * to end, ending with 1 htr in last st, turn.

Rows 10 to 12: Rep Row 2. Fasten off.

Rows 13 to 22: Rep Rows 3 to 12.

Row 23: Rep Row 3.

Rows 24 to 25: Rep Row 2.

Fasten off and darn in ends.

EMBROIDERY TRIMS

1. Using a blunt darning needle and a length of yarn B, work a line of backstitch along each of following rows: 2, 8, 11, 18 and 21.

2. Using same needle and a length of yarn B, work a row of cross-stitch, with each stitch worked over 2 sts and 2 rows, along following pairs of rows: 5 and 6; 15 and 16.

Fasten off and darn all ends in neatly.

***

woodstock

A sister square to Haight, this block is a composite of small squares joined by double crochet. Make it in psychedelic colours or keep it 1970s-subdued; either way, this retro block mixes well with other grannies in many projects.

A
B
C
D
E

TINY SQUARES

Foundation ring: Using first yarn, make a magic ring.

Round 1: Ch 2 (counts as 1 htr), 2 htr in ring, [ch 2, 3 htr in ring] 3 times, ch 2, sl st in top of beg ch-2 to join. Fasten off first yarn.

Round 2: Join second yarn in any corner ch-2 sp, ch 1, [2 dc, ch 1, 3 dc] in same corner ch-2 sp, ch 1, *[3 dc, ch 1, 3 dc] in next corner ch-2 sp, ch 1; rep from * 2 times, sl st in first ch to join. Fasten off second yarn.

Make 12 tiny squares in total, 3 each:
3 x Row 1, yarn A; Row 2, yarn B.
3 x Row 1, yarn B; Row 2, yarn A.
3 x Row 1, yarn C; Row 2, yarn D.
3 x Row 1, yarn D; Row 2, yarn C.

LARGER SQUARE

Work as tiny square, using yarn A for Round 1, yarn B for Round 2, then:

Round 3: Join yarn C in any ch-1 corner sp, ch 2 (counts as 1 htr), [2 htr, ch 2, 3 htr] in same sp *ch 1, 3 htr in next ch-1 sp, ch 1, [3 htr, ch 2, 3 htr] in next corner ch-1 sp; rep from * 2 times, ch 1, 3 htr in next ch-1 sp, ch 1, sl st in top of beg ch-2 to join. Fasten off yarn C.

Round 4: Join yarn D in any corner ch-2 sp, ch 1, [2 dc, ch 1, 3 dc] in same sp, *ch 1, [3 dc in next ch-1 sp] 2 times**, [3 dc, ch 1, 3 dc] in next corner ch-2 sp; rep from * 2 times and from * to ** 1 time, sl st in top of beg ch-2 to join. Fasten off yarn D.

JOINING

Place two tiny squares WS tog and using a length of yarn E, work 1 dc in back lp of every st including ch sts, along one seam. Fasten off. Join next tiny square in same way, and rep for next one but do not fasten off yarn (corner reached). Join next square to last along next edge (to turn corner, fasten off). Cont in this way until you have made a frame of tiny squares, 4 x 4, join last square to first. Place larger square in centre of frame, WS tog, and attach to tiny squares in same way, working one long seam around larger square.

Fasten off and darn in ends.

nanaimo

With its wintery palette of subdued hues, this block has the look of the Pacific North-west, and would be great mixed in with other grannies or circle-in-a-square designs to create a fabulous afghan.

Special stitch used:

Picot-3: Ch 3 (at point to add picot), sl st in first ch of ch-3 to create picot lp.

Foundation ring: Using yarn A, ch 4, sl st in first ch to form ring.

Round 1: Ch 3 (counts as 1 tr), 11 tr in ring, sl st in top of beg ch-3 to join. Fasten off yarn A.

Round 2: Join yarn B between any 2 tr sts from rnd below, ch 3, 1 tr in same sp, *2 tr in next sp between two tr; rep from * 10 times, sl st in top of beg ch-3 to join. Fasten off yarn B.

Round 3: Join yarn C between any 2-tr clusters, ch 3, 2 tr in same sp, *3 tr in next sp between clusters; rep from * 10 times, ch 4, sl st in top of beg ch-3 to join. Fasten off yarn C.

Round 4: Join yarn D in any st, *1 tr in each st, 1 tr in sp between clusters; rep from * all the way around, sl st in top of beg ch-3 to join. Fasten off yarn D.

Round 5: Join yarn E in any st, ch 3, 1 tr in each of next 2 sts, *2 tr in next st, 1 tr in each of next 3 sts; rep from * 10 times, 2 tr in next st, sl st in top of beg ch-3 to join. Fasten off yarn E.

Round 6: Join yarn F in any st, ch 3, 2 tr in next st, 1 tr in next st, *ch 1, miss 1 tr, 1 tr in next st, 2 tr in next st, 1 tr in next st; rep from * 13 times, ch 1, sl st in top of beg ch-3 to join. Fasten off yarn F.

A
B
C
D
E
F
G

Round 7: Join yarn C in any ch-1 sp, ch 3, 1 tr in same sp, 1 tr in next st, ch 2, miss 2 sts, *1 tr in next st, 2 tr in ch-1 sp, 1 tr in next st, ch 2, miss 2 sts; rep from * 13 times, 1 tr in next st, sl st in top of beg ch-3 to join. Fasten off yarn C.

Round 8: Join yarn G in any ch-2 sp, *2 dc in ch-2 sp, 1 dc in each of next 4 sts; rep from * 14 times, sl st in first dc to join. Fasten off yarn G.

Round 9: Join yarn D in any dc, *1 dc in same st, ch 6, miss next 5 sts, 1 htr in next st, ch 6, miss next 4 sts, 1 tr in next st, ch 3, 1 tr in next st, *ch 6, miss next 4 sts, 1 htr in next st, ch 6, miss next 5 sts, 1 dc in next st, ch 6, miss next 4 sts, 1 htr in next st, ch 6, miss next 4 sts, 1 tr in next st, ch 3, 1 tr in next st; rep from * 1 time, sl st in first dc to join.

Round 10: Ch 1, *7 dc in each ch-6 sp, [2 dc, picot-3, 2 dc] in corner sp; rep from * 3 times, sl st in first dc to join. Fasten off yarn D.

Round 11: Join yarn A in any st, *1 dc in every st to corner picot-3, [1 dc, ch-3 picot, 1 dc] in each picot-3 corner; rep from * 3 times, sl st to in first dc to join. Fasten off yarn A.

Round 12: Join yarn B in any st, rep Round 11.

Fasten off and darn in ends.

*

vortex

This design uses double and treble crochet to create an off-centred pattern. This block would look really striking made in primary, Pop-art contrasts, such as black, red, yellow, white and cyan. Or keep it tonal, as we have done here; the optical effect remains strong.

A
B
C
D
E
F

Foundation ring: Using yarn A, make a magic ring.

Round 1: Ch 3, 1 tr, 1 dtr, 1 ttr, 1 dtr, [2 tr, 1 dtr, 1 ttr, 1 dtr] 3 times in ring, sl st in top of beg ch-3 to join. Pull tail to close.

Round 2: Ch 1, 1 dc in each of next 2 sts and *3 dc in next ttr (forms corner), 1 dc in each of next 4 sts; rep from * 2 times, 3 dc in last ttr, 1 dc in last 2 sts, sl st in first dc to join. Fasten off yarn A.

Round 3: Join yarn B. Ch 1, 1 dc in each of next 3 dc, [2 dc, 1 tr] in middle dc of 3-dc group (forms corner), 1 tr in each of next 6 dc, 3 tr in next dc (forms 2nd corner), 1 tr in each of next 6 dc, [1 tr, 2 dc] in next dc (forms 3rd corner), 1 dc in each of next 6 dc, 3 dc in next dc (forms 4th corner), 1 dc in each of last 3 dc, sl st in first sd to join. Fasten off yarn B.

Round 4: Join yarn C. Ch 1, 1 dc in each of next 4 dc, [2 dc, 1 tr] in next dc, 1 tr in each of next 8 tr, 3 tr in next tr, 1 tr in each of next 8 tr, [1 tr, 2 dc] in next dc, 1 dc in each of next 8 dc, 3 dc in next dc, 1 dc in each of last 4 dc, sl st in first dc to join. Fasten off yarn C.

Round 5: Join yarn D. Ch 1, 1 dc in each of next 5 dc, [2 dc, 3 tr] in next dc, 1 tr in each of next 10 tr, 5 tr in next tr, 1 tr in each of next 10 tr, [3 tr, 2 dc] in next dc, 1 dc in each of next 10 dc, 5 dc in next dc, 1 dc in each of last 5 dc, sl st in first dc to join. Fasten off yarn D.

Round 6: Join yarn E. Ch 1, 1 dc in each of next 7 dc, [2 dc, 1 tr] in next dc, 1 tr in each of next 14 tr, 3 tr in next tr, 1 tr in each of next 14 tr, [1 tr, 2 dc] in next dc, 1 dc in each of next 14 dc, 3 dc in next dc, 1 dc in each of last 7 dc; join with sl st to first sc. Fasten off yarn E.

Round 7: Join yarn F. Ch 1, 1 dc in each of next 8 dc, [2 dc, 3 tr] in next dc, 1 tr in each of next 16 tr, 5 tr in next tr, 1 tr in each of next 16 tr, [3 tr, 2 dc] in next dc, 1 dc in each of next 16 dc, 5 dc in next dc, 1 dc in each of last 8 dc, sl st in first dc to join. Fasten off yarn F.

Round 8: Join yarn B. Ch 1, 1 dc in each of next 10 dc, [2 dc, 3 tr] in next dc, 1 tr in each of next 20 tr, 5 tr in next tr, 1 tr in each of next 20 tr, [3 tr, 2 dc] in next dc, 1 dc in each of next 20 dc, 5 dc in next dc, 1 dc in each of last 10 dc, sl st in first dc to join. Fasten off yarn B.

Round 9: Join yarn C. Ch 1, 1 dc in each of next 12 dc, [2 dc, 3 tr] in next dc, 1 tr in each of next 24 tr, 5 tr in next tr, 1 tr in each of next 24 tr, [3 tr, 2 dc] in next dc, 1 dc in each of next 24 dc, 5 dc in next dc, 1 dc in each of last 12 dc, sl st in first dc to join.

Fasten off and darn in ends neatly.

primrose

**

Here is a dimensional, bell-shaped flower that uses clever variations in stitch heights to achieve the shaping. Team it with other spring flower blocks in this book for a delightful flower-garden blanket.

A
B
C
D
E

Foundation ring: Using yarn A ch 4 , sl st in first ch to form ring.

Round 1: Ch 1, 10 dc in ring, sl st in first ch to join. Fasten off yarn A.

Round 2: Join yarn B, ch 3 (counts as 1 tr), 1 tr in same st, 2 tr in each of next 9 sts, sl st in top of beg ch-3 to join. Fasten off yarn B.

Round 3: Join yarn C, *2 dc in next tr, 2 tr in next tr; rep from * 9 times, sl st in first dc to join.

Round 4: Ch 3 (counts as 1 tr), 1 tr in next st, 1 dc in each of next 2 sts, *1 tr in each of next 2 sts, 1 dc in each of next 2 sts; rep from * 8 times, sl st in top of beg ch-3 to join.

Round 5: Ch 3 (counts as 1 tr), 1 tr in same st, 1 dc in each of next 2 dc, *1 tr in each of next 2 tr, 1 dc in each of next 2 dc; rep from * 8 times, sl st in top of beg ch-3 to join. Fasten off yarn C.

Round 6: Turn work to WS, join yarn B in any dc from Round 2, *ch 5, miss 4 tr, sl st in next tr; rep from * 3 times, sl st in first ch to join.

Round 7: (WS) Sl st 1 time in beg of ch-5, ch 3 (counts as 1 tr), 9 tr in ch-5 sp, ch 2, *10 tr in next ch-5 sp, ch 2; rep from * 2 times, sl st in top of beg ch-3 to join. Fasten off yarn B, turn.

Round 8: On RS, join yarn D in any ch-2 corner sp, ch 4 (counts as 1 htr, ch 2), 1 htr in same sp (forms corner), miss next tr, 1 htr in each of next 9 sts, miss last tr, *[1 htr, ch 2, 1 htr] in the ch-2 sp (forms corner), miss next tr, 1 htr in each of next 9 sts, miss last tr; rep from * 2 times, sl st in 2nd ch of beg ch-4 to join.

Round 9: Sl st in next ch-2 sp, ch 4 (counts as 1 htr, ch 2), 1 htr in same sp (forms corner), miss next tr, 1 htr in each of next 10 sts, miss last tr, *[1 htr, ch 2, 1 htr] in next ch-2 sp (forms corner), miss next tr, 1 htr in each of next 10 sts, miss last tr; rep from * 2 times, sl st in 2nd ch of beg ch-4 to join.

Round 10: Sl st in next ch-2 sp, ch 4 (counts as 1 htr, ch 2), 1 htr in same sp (forms corner), miss next tr, 1 htr in each of next 11 sts, miss last tr, *[1 htr, ch 2, 1 htr] in next ch-2 sp (forms corner), miss next tr, 1 htr in each of next 11 sts, miss last tr; rep from * 2 times, sl st in 2nd ch of beg ch-4 to join. Fasten off yarn D.

Round 11: Join yarn E in any ch-2 sp, ch 6 (counts as 1 htr, ch 4), 1 htr in same sp (forms corner), miss next tr, 1 htr in each of next 12 sts, miss last tr, *[1 htr, ch 4, 1 htr] in next ch-2 sp (forms corner), miss next tr, 1 htr in each of next 12 sts, miss last tr; rep from * 2 times, sl st in 2nd ch of beg ch-6 to join.

Round 12: Sl st in next ch-4 sp, ch 6 (counts as 1 htr, ch 4), 1 htr in same sp (forms corner), miss next st, 1 htr in each of next 13 sts, miss last st, *[1 htr, ch 4, 1 htr] in next ch-2 sp (forms corner), miss next st, 1 htr in each of next 13 sts, miss last st; rep from * 2 times, sl st in 2nd ch of beg ch-6 to join.

Round 13: Sl st in next ch-4 sp, ch 8 (counts as 1 htr, ch 6), 1 htr in same sp (forms corner), miss next tr, 2 htr in next st, 1 htr in each of next 12 sts, 2 htr in next st, miss last st, *[1 htr, ch 6, 1 htr] in next ch-2 sp (forms corner), miss next st, 2 htr in next st, 1 htr in each of next 12 sts, 2 htr in next st, miss last st; rep from * 2 times, sl st in 2nd ch of beg ch-6 to join.

Round 14: Sl st in next ch-4 sp, ch 8 (counts as 1 htr, ch 6), 1 htr in same sp (forms corner), miss next tr, 2 htr in next st, 1 htr in each of next 15 sts, 2 htr in next st, miss last st, *[1 htr, ch 6, 1 htr] in next ch-2 sp (forms corner), miss next st, 2 htr in next st, 1 htr in each of next 15 sts, 2 htr in next st, miss last st; rep from * 2 times, sl st in 2nd ch of beg ch-6 to join. Fasten off yarn E.

Round 15: Join yarn D in any ch-6 sp, ch 1, 7 dc in same sp, 1 dc in every st to corner ch-6 sp, 8 dc in corner ch-6 sp, 1 dc in evert st to next corner ch-6 sp; rep from * 2 times, sl st in first ch to join.

Fasten off and darn in ends.

291
**

dolomite

Clever construction makes this classic chevron shape, here given a granny twist by using three-treble-crochet groups and chain spaces. Vary the colours and repeat the motif for a really jazzy bedspread or throw.

A
B
C

Special stitch used:

3-treble crochet cluster (3-tc cl):
Make cluster with 3 tr in same st or sp (*see page 18*).

Foundation chain: Using yarn A, ch 35 (counts as ch 32, 1 tr).

Row 1: Ch 1, 1 dc in 2nd ch from hook and in each ch to end, turn.

Row 2: Ch 3 (counts as 1 tr), miss 3 sts, [3 tr in next st, miss 2 sts] 2 times, [3 tr, ch 3, 3 tr] in next st, 3 tr in next st, miss next 2 sts, 3-tr cl in next st, miss next 3 sts, 3-tr cl in next st, miss next 2 sts, 3 tr in next st, miss next 2 sts, [3 tr, ch 3, 3 tr] in next st, [miss next 2 sts, 3 tr in next st] 2 times, 1 tr in last st.

Row 3: Ch 3 (counts as 1 tr) turn, [miss next 3 sts, 3 tr in sp before next tr] 2 times, miss next 3 sts, [3 tr, ch 3, 3 tr] in next ch-3 sp, miss next 3 sts, 3 tr in sp before next tr, miss next 3 sts, 3-tr cl in sp before next tr, miss next 2-tr clusters, 3-tr cl in sp before next tr, miss next 3 sts, 3 tr in sp before next tr, miss next 3 sts, [3 tr, ch 3, 3 tr] in next ch-3 sp, [miss next 3 sts, 3 tr in next sp before next tr] 2 times, miss next 3 sts, 1 tr in 3rd ch of beg ch-3 of row below. Fasten off yarn A.

Repeat Row 3 2 times using yarn B, 1 time using yarn C, 2 times using yarn A, 2 times using yarn B, 1 time using yarn C, and 2 times using yarn A.

Fasten off and darn in ends.

292
**

sherbet sky

A woven-effect texture is created here by the use of an unusual side puff stitch worked over the vertical posts of two-treble crochet stitches. This homespun square would be great in a winter afghan or blanket.

A
B

Special stitch used:

Side puff stitch (side pf): [Yoh, insert hook around post of last 2 tr] 3 times (7 lps on hook), [yoh and pull through 3 lps] 3 times (*see page 19*).

Foundation chain: Using yarn A, ch 28.

Row 1: 1 dc in 2nd ch from hook, 1 dc in every ch to end, turn – 27 sts.

Row 2: Ch 1, 1 dc in every dc to end, turn.

Row 3: Ch 2, 1 tr in first dc, *1 side pf over next 2 tr, 1 tr in next 2 sts; rep from * ending row with 1 tr in final dc, turn.

Row 4: Ch 1, 1 htr in first 3 tr, 1 htr in each of next 2 sts, miss 1 st, *1 htr in each of next 4 sts, miss 1 st; rep from * to last 2 sts, 1 htr in next st, 1 htr in top of beg ch-2, turn. Fasten off yarn A.

Row 5: Join yarn B, ch 2, *1 tr in each of next 2 htr, 1 side pf over next 2 tr; rep from * to end, ending row with 1 tr in final htr, turn. Fasten off yarn B.

Row 6: Join yarn A, ch 1, 1 htr in each of first 3 sts, miss 1 st, *1 htr in each of next 4 sts, miss 1 st; rep from * to end, ending row with 1 htr in each of last 3 sts, turn.

Row 7: Ch 2, 1 tr in first htr, *1 side pf over next 2 tr, 1 tr in each of next 2 sts; rep from * to end, ending row with 1 tr in final htr, turn.

Row 8: Ch 1, miss first tr, *1 htr in each of next 4 sts, miss 1 st, rep from * to end, ending row with 1 htr in top of beg ch-2, turn.

Rows 9 to 12: Rep Rows 5 to 8.

Rows 13 to 16: Rep Rows 5 to 8.

Row 17: Rep Row 2.

Fasten off and darn in ends.

★★★
sierra

A complex picture block in bold colours to suggest a cosy, fireside feel to a winter blanket, or substitute the sunset shades for sky blue, work the mountains in lighter greys and add a snowcap for a daytime scene.

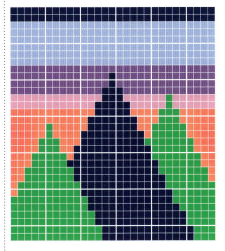

A
B
C
D
E
F

Note: When working this pattern prepare 2 small separate balls of yarn A, 4 of yarn C, 3 of yarn D and 2 of yarn E before you begin. Work each separate area of colour using a different ball of yarn, joining on last lp of each st of last area of colour. Keep all yarn ends at WS of work throughout otherwise when you need to change colour, yarn may be on RS and inaccessible.

Foundation chain: Using yarn A, ch 30.

Row 1: (First row of chart) 1 dc in 2nd ch from hook and 1 dc in every ch to end, changing colour as indicated, turn.

Work remaining 31 rows of chart, making sure you keep yarn ends on WS, and changing colour where indicated.

Rows 2 to 32 Ch 1, 1 dc in every dc to end, turn.

Fasten off and darn in ends neatly. Block work to shape.

★★★
pineapple

An old stitch pattern that produces highly raised bobbles on top of the fabric, this is incredibly tactile and once you grasp the method, lots of fun to work. This block would enhance any winter blanket whether for babies, children or adults.

A

Special stitch used:

Make pineapple (pn): Insert hook in next st to be worked, yoh, draw through, *yoh, insert hook in same place 2 rows below, yoh, draw through and pull through 2 lps; rep from * 5 times (6 tr with last lp of each unfinished, plus first yoh = 8 lps on hook), yoh, draw through all lps.

Foundation chain: Ch 28.

Row 1: 1 dc in 2nd ch from hook, 1 dc in each ch to end, turn.

Row 2: Ch 1, 1 dc in every dc to end, turn.

Row 3: Rep Row 2.

Row 4: Ch 1, 1 dc in each of next 3 dc, *pn in next dc, 1 dc in each of next 3 dc; rep from * 4 times, pn in next dc, 1 dc in each of last 3 dc, turn.

Rows 5 to 7: Rep Row 2.

Row 8: Ch 1, 1 dc in first dc, *pn in next dc, 1 dc in each of next 3 dc; rep from * 5 times, pn in next dc, 1 dc in last dc, turn.

Rows 9 to 11: Rep Row 2.

Row 12: Rep Row 4.

Rows 13 to 15: Rep Row 2.

Row 16: Rep Row 8.

Rows 17 to 19: Rep Row 2.

Row 20: Rep Row 4.

Rows 21 to 23: Rep Row 2.

Row 24: Rep Row 8.

Rows 25 to 27: Rep Row 2.

Row 28: Rep Row 4.

Rows 29 to 30: Rep Row 2.

Fasten off and darn in ends.

*

anemone

A big, bold central motif for a striking throw, warm blanket or afghan. This block makes up quickly and works really well used in multiples with varying bright middles and a dark background.

A
B

Foundation ring: Using yarn A, begin with magic ring method.

Round 1: Ch 3 (counts as 1 tr), 7 tr in ring, sl st in top of ch-3 to join – 8 sts.

Round 2: Ch 3 (counts as 1 tr) 1 tr in same st, *2 tr in next st; rep from * to end of rnd, sl st in top of ch-3 to join – 16 sts.

Round 3: Ch 3 (counts as 1 tr), *2 tr in next st, 1 tr in next st; rep from * to end of rnd ending with 2 tr, sl st in top of ch-3 to join – 24 sts.

Round 4: Rep Round 2 – 48 sts.

Round 5: Ch 1, 1 dc in same place, *[1 htr, 1 tr] in next st, 2 hdtr in next st, [1 tr, 1 htr] in next st, 1 dc in next st; rep from * 11 times, end with 1 htr for 12 petals, sl st in first dc to join. Fasten off yarn A.

Round 6: Sl st yarn B to middle st of first petal, ch 3 (counts as 1 tr), [2 tr, ch 3, 3 tr] in same st (first corner), *[ch 4, 1 dc in top of next petal] 3 times, ch 4**, 3 tr, ch 3, 3 dc; rep from * 3 times ending last rep at **, sl st in top of beg ch-3 to join.

Round 7: Sl st in first 2 tr of first corner, 1 sl st in ch-3 sp, ch 3, [2 tr, ch 3, 3 tr] in same sp (forms first corner), *[ch 2, 3 tr] in next ch-4 sp] 3 times, ch 2**, [3 tr, ch 3, 3 ch] in next corner ch-3 sp; rep from * 3 times ending last rep at **, sl st in beg ch-3 to join.

Round 8: Ch 1, 1 dc in same place, 1 dc in each dc, 5 dc in ch-3 sp, 1 dc in each of next 3 tr *[3 dc in ch-2 sp, 1 dc in next 3 tr] 3 times, 3 dc in ch-2 sp**, 1 tr in each tr, 5 dc in ch-3 sp, 1 dc in each of next 3 tr; rep from * 3 times ending at **, sl st in first dc to join.

Fasten off and darn in ends neatly.

*

concentric

This simple but eye-catching square works well in bright analogous shades of yarn, as we have done here, or try it with a hand-painted or space-dyed yarn to achieve a stunning spiral effect.

A
B
C
D
E

Foundation ring: Using yarn A, ch 5, sl st in first ch to form ring.

Round 1: Ch 3 (counts as 1 tr), 11 tr in ring, sl st in top of ch-3 to join – 12 sts.

Round 2: Ch 3 (counts as 1 tr), *2 tr in next st; rep from * to end of rnd, sl st in top of ch-3 to join – 24 sts. Fasten off yarn A.

Round 3: Join yarn B, ch 3 (counts as 1 tr), *2 tr in next st, 1 tr in next st: rep from * to end of rnd, sl st in top of ch-3 to join – 36 sts. Fasten off yarn B.

Round 4: Join yarn C, ch 3 (counts as 1 tr), 1 tr in same st, *1 tr in each of next 2 sts, 2 tr in next st; rep from * to end of rnd, sl st in top of ch-3 to join – 48 sts. Fasten off yarn C.

Round 5: Join yarn D, ch 3 (counts as 1 tr), 2 tr, ch 3, 3 tr in same st (forms first corner), *1 tr in next 11 tr, [3 tr, ch 3, 3 tr] in next st; rep from * to end of rnd, sl st in top of beg ch-3 to join. Fasten off yarn D.

Round 6: Join yarn E, ch 4 (counts as 1 tr, 1 ch), miss next st, [3 tr, ch 3, 3 tr] in ch-3 sp, *[ch 1, miss 1 st, 1 tr in next st] 8 times in total across, ch 1, [3 tr, ch 3, 3 tr]; rep from * 2 times omitting 8th rep, sl st in 3rd ch of beg ch-4 to join.

Round 7: Ch 3, (counts as 1 tr), 1 tr in ch-1 sp, 1 tr in next 3 tr, *5 tr in ch-3 sp, 1 tr in each tr and ch-1 sp across (23 sts); rep from * 3 times omitting last 5 tr, sl st in top of beg ch-3 to join.

Fasten off and darn in ends neatly.

**

flight

A wonderfully optical block that offers the quality of illusion through clever use of colour, this is actually created with straightforward methods. Show it off by teaming it with graphic blocks – this will avoid it becoming lost among more patterned squares.

A
B
C
D

Special stitches used:

Back-loop double crochet (BLdc): 1 dc in back loop only.

Front-loop treble crochet (FLtr): 1 tr in the front loop of st two rows below.

Foundation chain: Using yarn A, ch 29 (counts as ch 28, 1 turning ch).

Row 1: Miss 1 ch, 1 BLdc in each of next 28 ch, fasten off yarn A.

Row 2: Do not turn work, join yarn B in top of first st in last row, *1 BLdc in each of next 6 BLdc, 1 FLtr in next st; rep from * 3 times. Fasten off yarn B.

Row 3: Do not turn work, join yarn C in top of first st in last row, *1 FLtr in next st, 1 BLdc in each of next 6 sts; rep from * 3 times. Fasten off yarn C.

Row 4: Do not turn work, join yarn D in top of first st in last row, *1 BLdc in next st, 1 FLtr in next st, 1 BLdc in each of next 5 sts; rep from * 3 times. Fasten off yarn D.

Row 5: Do not turn work, join yarn A in top of first st in last row, *1 BLdc in each of next 2 sts, 1 FLtr in next st, 1 BLdc in each of next 4 sts; rep from * 3 times. Fasten off yarn A.

Row 6: Do not turn work, join yarn B in top of first st in last row, *1 BLdc in each of next 3 sts, 1 FLtr in next st, 1 BLdc in each of next 3 sts; rep from * 3 times. Fasten off yarn B.

Row 7: Do not turn work, join yarn C in top of first st in last row, *1 BLdc in each of next 4 sts, 1 FLtr in next st, 1 BLdc in each of next 2 sts; rep from * 3 times. Fasten off yarn C.

Row 8: Do not turn work, join yarn D in top of first st in last row, *1 BLdc in each of next 5 sts, 1 FLtr in next st, 1 BLdc in next st; rep from * 3 times. Fasten off yarn D.

Rows 9 to 24: Rep Rows 2 to 8, changing colours to join in appropriately. Work 24 rows in total. Fasten off.

BORDER

Round 1: Join yarn B in first st in last row, ch 1, *1 dc in each st to next corner, [1 dc, ch 2, 1 dc] in corner st, turn work and work on the next side, 1 dc in each row end to next corner, [1 dc, ch 2, 1 dc] in corner st; rep from * 2 times, sl st in first dc to join. Fasten off yarn B.

Round 2: Join yarn C in any corner ch-2 sp, 3 dc in corner sp, *1 dc in each st to next corner, 3 dc in corner ch-2 sp, turn work and work on next side, 1 dc in each st to next corner, 3 dc in next corner ch-2 sp; rep from * 2 times, sl st in first dc to join. Fasten off yarn C.

Round 3: Join yarn A in any centre dc of 3-dc group and rep Round 2, working 3 dc in centre st of 3-dc group at corner instead of in ch-2 sp.

Fasten off and darn in ends.

*

vasarely

Inspired by the artist of the same name, this bold square is simple to make and is at its best worked with dramatic colours. Used in multiples, it makes for a striking bedspread, pillow cover or afghan.

A
B
C

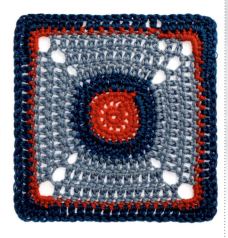

Foundation ring: Using yarn A, begin with magic ring method.

Round 1: Ch 2 (counts as 1 htr), 11 htr in ring, sl st in top of ch-2 to join – 12 sts.

Round 2: Ch 2 (counts as 1 htr), *2 htr in next st; rep from * to last st, 1 htr in last st, sl st in top of ch-2 to join – 24 sts. Fasten off yarn A.

Round 3: Join yarn B, ch 3 (counts as 1 tr), 1 tr in same st, *2 tr in next st, 1 tr in next st; rep from * to end of rnd, sl st in top of ch-3 to join – 36 sts. Fasten off yarn B.

Round 4: Join yarn C, ch 5 (counts as 1 tr, 2 ch), 1 tr in same st, *1 tr in each of next 8 tr**, [1 tr, ch 2, 1 tr] in next tr; rep from * to end of rnd ending at ** and omitting 8th tr, sl st in 3rd ch of beg ch-5 to join.

Round 5: Ch 3 (counts as 1 tr), [1 tr, ch 3, 1 tr] in next ch-2 sp, *1 tr in each of next 10 tr**, [1 tr, ch 3, 1 tr] in ch-2 sp; rep from * 3 times ending at ** and omitting 10th tr, sl st in top of beg ch-3 to join.

Round 6: Ch 3 (counts as 1 tr), 1 tr, [1 tr, ch 3, 1 tr] in ch-2 sp *1 tr in each of next 12 tr**, [1 tr, ch 3, 1 tr] in ch-3 sp; rep from * 3 times ending at ** and omitting last 2 tr, sl st in top of beg ch-3 to join. Fasten off yarn C.

Round 7: Join yarn A, ch 1, 1 dc in same st, 1 dc in next 2 tr, 7 dc in ch-3 sp, *1 dc in each of next 14 dc**, 7 dc in ch-3 sp; rep from * to end of rnd ending at ** and omitting last 3 dc, sl st in first sc to join. Fasten off yarn A.

Round 8: Join yarn B, ch 3, 1 tr in same st, 1 tr in each of next 3 dc, 1 tr in each of next 3 dc, 3 tr in next dc (middle of corner) 1 tr in each of next 3 dc, *1 tr in each dc to next corner**, 1 tr in each of next 3 dc, 3 tr in next dc (middle of corner); rep from * to end of rnd ending at ** at beg of rnd, sl st in first tr to join.

Fasten off and darn in ends neatly.

---

*

chelsea

This striking block has an optical pattern created by changing colour at strategic points in each round. Easy to master, this square would look bold repeated over a blanket or pillow, or mix it with plainer graphic or textural squares for a modern throw.

A
B
C
D

Foundation ring: Using yarn A, make a magic ring.

Round 1: Ch 3 (counts as 1 tr), 2 tr, [1 dtr, 3 tr] 3 times all in ring, 1 dtr, sl st in top of beg ch-3 to join. Fasten off.

Round 2: Join yarn B, ch 3 (counts as 1 tr), 1 tr in next tr, change to yarn C, *1 tr in next tr, 5 tr in next dtr, 1 tr in each of next 2 tr, ** change to yarn B, rep from * to **, change to yarn C, rep from * to **, change to yarn B, 1 tr in next tr, 5 tr in next dtr, sl st in top of beg ch-3 to join. Fasten off.

Round 3: Join yarn D, ch 3 (counts as 1 tr), 1 tr in each of next 4 tr, *5 tr in next tr, 1 tr in each of next 7 tr; rep from * 2 times, 5 tr in next tr, 1 tr in each of last 2 tr, sl st in top of beg ch-3 to join. Fasten off.

Round 4: Join yarn C, ch 3 (counts as 1 tr), 1 tr in next tr, change to yarn B, *1 tr in each of next 5 tr, 5 tr in next tr, 1 tr in each of next 6 tr**, change to yarn C; rep from * to **, change to yarn B, rep from * to **, change to yarn C, 1 tr in each of next 5 tr, 5 tr in next tr, 1 tr in each of last 4 tr, sl st in top of beg ch-3 to join. Fasten off.

Round 5: Join yarn A, ch 3 (counts as 1 tr), 1 tr in each of next 8 tr, *5 tr in next tr, 1 tr in each of next 15 tr; rep from * 2 times, 5 tr in next tr, 1 tr in each of next 6 tr, sl st in top of beg ch-3 to join.

Round 6: Join yarn B, ch 3 (counts as 1 tr), 1 tr in each next tr, change to yarn C, *1 tr in each of next 9 tr, 5 tr in next tr, 1 tr in each of next 10 tr, ** change to yarn B; rep from * to **, change to yarn C,

rep from * to **, change to yarn B, 1 tr in each of next 9 tr, 5 tr in next tr, 1 tr in each of last 8 rem, sl st in top of beg ch-3 to join.

Fasten off and darn in ends.

A traditional square that uses popcorn stitch to create a defined 'X' pattern. Simple to make and effective used in groups, when together, the squares form a diamond pattern. Great for bedspreads and throws, it's lightweight but warm.

A

Special stitches used:

Beginning popcorn (beg pc): Ch 3, make popcorn with 4 tr (*see page 19*).

Popcorn (pc): Make popcorn with 5 tr.

Foundation ring: Ch 8, sl st in first ch to form ring.

Round 1: Beg pc in ring, [ch 5, pc in ring] 3 times, ch 5, sl st in top of beg pc to join.

Round 2: Ch 3 (counts as 1 tr), *[2 tr, ch 2, pc, ch 2, 2 tr] in next ch-5 sp**, 1 tr in next pc; rep from * 2 times, then from * to ** 1 time, sl st in top of beg ch-3 to join.

Round 3: Ch 3 (counts as 1 tr), 1 tr in each of next 2 tr, *2 tr in next ch-2 sp, ch 2, pc in next pc, ch 2, 2 tr in next ch-2 sp**, 1 tr in each of next 5 tr; rep from * 2 times, then from * to ** 1 time, 1 tr in each of last 2 tr, sl st in top of beg ch-3 to join.

Round 4: Ch 3 (counts as 1 tr), 1 tr in each of next 4 tr, *2 tr in next ch-2 sp, ch 3, pc in next pc, ch 3, 2 tr in next ch-2 sp**, 1 tr in each of next 9 tr; rep from * 2 times, then from * to ** 1 time, 1 tr in each of last 4 tr, sl st in top of beg ch-3 to join.

Round 5: Ch 3 (counts as 1 tr), 1 tr in each of next 6 tr, *2 tr in next ch-3 sp, ch 3, pc in next pc, ch 3, 2 tr in next ch-3 sp**, 1 tr in each of next 13 tr; rep from * 2 times, then from * to ** 1 time, 1 tr in each of last 6 tr, sl st in top of beg ch-3 to join.

Round 6: Ch 3 (counts as 1 tr), 1 tr in each of next 8 tr, *2 tr in next ch-3 sp, ch 3, pc in next pc, ch 3, 2 tr in next ch-3 sp**, 1 tr in each of next 17 tr; rep from * 2 times, then from * to ** 1 time, 1 tr in each of last 8 tr, sl st in top of beg ch-3 to join.

Round 7: Ch 3 (counts as 1 tr), 1 tr in each of next 10 tr, *2 tr in next ch-3 sp, ch 3, pc in next pc, ch 3, 2 tr in next ch-3 sp**, 1 tr in each of next 21 tr; rep from * 2 times and from * to ** 1 time, 1 tr in each of last 10 tr, sl st in top of beg ch-3 to join.

Fasten off yarn and darn in ends neatly.

301 ✦✦
herringbone

A
B
C

A staggered zigzag pattern produces a solid, textural square that resembles woven fabric, but works up much more quickly than its woven equivalent would. We have used subtle tones here, but graphic black and white would be equally effective. Remember to keep yarn tails at the wrong side of the work when not in use.

Foundation chain: Using yarn A, ch 29.

Row 1: 1 dc in 2nd ch from hook, 1 dc in every ch to end, turn.

Work 26 rows of chart, joining in contrast yarns as indicated and carrying yarn not in use at back of work.

Rows 2 to 27: Ch 1, 1 dc in every dc to end, turn.

Row 28: Rep Row 2 using only yarn A.

Fasten off and darn in ends neatly. Block work to shape.

302 ✦
bull's-eye

A
B
C
D

A layered motif composed of chains and half-treble crochets, the many rounds give scope for using a plethora of colours, yet it works up quickly. Lightweight and lacy, this is a good block for using in summer throws.

Foundation ring: Using yarn A, ch 4, sl st in first ch to form ring.

Round 1: Ch 3 (counts as 1 htr, ch 1), [1 htr, ch 1] 7 times in ring, sl st in 2nd of beg ch-3 to join. Fasten off yarn A.

Round 2: Join yarn B in any htr st, ch 4 (counts as 1 htr, ch 2), [1 htr, ch 2] 7 times, sl st in 2nd ch of beg ch-4 to join. Fasten off yarn B.

Round 3: Join yarn C in any htr st, ch 2 (counts as 1 htr here and throughout), 1 htr in same st, [ch 2, 2 htr in next htr] 7 times, ch 2, sl st in top of beg ch-2 to join. Fasten off yarn C.

Round 4: Join yarn D, ch 2, 2 htr in next st, [ch 3, miss 1 htr, 3 htr in next htr] 7 times, ch 3, sl st in top of beg ch-2 to join. Fasten off yarn D.

Round 5: Join yarn B, ch 2, 1 htr in each of next 2 htr, [ch 4, 1 htr in each of next 3 htr] 7 times, ch 4, sl st in top of beg ch-2 to join. Fasten off yarn B.

Round 6: Join yarn C, ch 2, 1 htr in each of next 2 htr, [ch 6, 1 htr in each of next 3 htr] 7 times, ch 6, sl st in top of beg ch-2 to join. Fasten off yarn C.

Round 7: Join yarn D, ch 2, 1 htr in each of next 2 htr, [ch 8, 1 htr in each of next 3 htr] 7 times, ch 8, sl st in top of beg ch-2 to join. Fasten off yarn D.

Round 8: Join yarn B, ch 2, 1 htr in each of next 2 htr, [ch 9, 1 htr in each of next 3 htr] 7 times, ch 9, sl st in top of beg ch-2 to join. Fasten off yarn B.

Round 9: Join yarn D, ch 3 (counts as 1 tr), 1 tr in each of next 2 htr, *ch 9, 1 tr in each of next 3 htr, ch 4, [1 dtr, ch 2, 1 dtr, ch 3, 1 dtr, ch 2, 1 dtr] in next ch-9 sp, ch 4**, 1 tr in each of next 3 htr; rep from * 2 times and from * to ** 1 time, sl st in top of beg ch-3 to join.

Round 10: Ch 1, 1 dc in each of next 2 tr, *8 dc in next ch-9 sp, 1 dc in each of next 3 tr, 3 dc in next ch-4 sp, 1 dc in next dtr, 2 dc in next ch-2 sp, 1 dc in next dtr, [2 dc, ch 1, 2 dc] in next ch-3 sp, 1 dc in next dtr, 2 dc in next ch-2 sp, 1 dc in next dtr, 3 dc in next ch-4 sp **, 1 dc in each of next 3 tr; rep from * 2 times and from * to ** 1 time, sl st in first dc to join.

Fasten off and darn in ends.

****

berries & buds

Inspired by an early spring tree that bore both winter berries and buds of blossom at the same time, this square has little bud knops, petals and bobbles in sequence.

Special stitches used:

2-double treble cluster (2-dtr cl): Make cluster with 2 dtr (see page 18).

Picot-4: Ch 4 (at point to add picot), sl st in first ch of ch-4 to create picot loop.

3-double treble cluster (3-dtr cl): Make cluster with 3 dtr.

Make bobble (MB): Make bobble with 4 tr (see page 19).

Foundation ring: Using yarn A, ch 4, sl st in first ch to form ring.

Round 1: Ch 3 (counts as 1 tr), 2 tr in ring, ch 3, [3 tr in ring, ch 3] 3 times, sl st in top of beg ch-3 to join.

Round 2: Ch 1, *1 dc in same st, 1 dc in each of next 2 tr, *[2 dc, ch 1, 2 dc] in corner ch-3 sp, 1 dc in each of next 3 tr; rep from * 2 times, [2 dc, ch 1, 2 dc] in corner ch-3 sp, sl st in first dc to join. Fasten off yarn A.

Round 3: Join yarn B, sl st in FRONT lp of next st, *picot-4, sl st in front lp of next 3 sts, picot-4, sl st in front lp of each of next 5 sts; rep from * 3 times, omitting last 2 sl sts from last rep, sl st in first sl st to join. Fasten off yarn B.

Round 4: Join yarn C in BACK lp of ch-1 sp of any sc corner group from Round 2, ch 4 (counts as 1 dtr), [2-dtr cl, ch 3, 3-dtr cl] in same st, *ch 2, miss 2 dc, 3-dtr cl in back lp of next dc from Round 2, ch 3, miss 2 dc, 3-dtr cl in back lp of next dc from Round 2, ch 2, miss 2 dc**, [3-dtr cl, ch 3, 3-dtr cl] in back lp of next ch-1 sp (centre of corner group); rep from * 2 times and from * to ** 1 time, sl st in top of beg ch-4 to join. Fasten off yarn C.

Round 5: Join yarn A in ch-3 corner sp, ch 1, *[2 dc, ch 1, 2 dc] in ch-3 corner sp, 1 dc in top of next 3-dtr cl, 2 dc in next ch-2 sp, 1 dc in next 3-dtr cl, 3 dc in next ch-3 sp, 1 dc in next 3-dtr cl, 2 dc in next ch-2 sp; rep from * 3 times, sl st in first dc to join. Fasten off yarn A.

Round 6: Join yarn C in FRONT lp of any dc, sl st in same st, *picot-4, sl st in front lp of each of next 4 sts; rep from * to end, sl st in first dc to join. Fasten off yarn C.

Round 7: Join yarn D in BACK lp of ch-1 sp of dc corner group of Round 5, ch 1, *3 dc in same st, 1 dc in back lp of every st, and 1 dc behind each picot-4 to corner, 3 dc in ch-1 sp of next corner group; rep from * 3 times, sl st in first dc to join.

Round 8: Ch 1, *1 dc in every st to corner, 3 dc in 2nd dc of 3 dc corner group; rep from * 3 times sl st in first dc to join.

Round 9: Ch 1, *1 dc in next dc, [MB in next dc, 1 dc in next dc] 9 times, 1 dc in next dc, [1 dc, ch 1, 1 dc] in next dc; rep from * 3 times, sl st in first dc to join.

Round 10: Ch 1, dc in each st and in top of each bobble to corner, 3 dc in each ch-1 corner sp, all the way around, sl st in first dc to join. Fasten off.

Round 11: Join yarn A in any dc st, ch 1, *dc in each st to the middle dc st in each corner, 3 dc in each middle corner st; rep all the way around, sl st in first dc to join. Fasten off.

Fasten off and darn in ends neatly.

A
B
C
D

*
tartan

Simple areas of colour in double crochet make this a quick-to-work block that is then embellished with lines of surface crochet to make the tartan pattern.

Special stitch used:

Surface crochet: 1 sl st in the specified st, creating a chain-stitch effect (*see page 22*).

Foundation chain: Using yarn A, ch 31.

Row 1: 1 dc in 2nd ch from hook, 1 dc in each of next 14 ch, change to yarn B (do not cut yarn A), 1 dc in each of rem 15 dc, turn.

Row 2: With yarn B, 1 dc in each of next 15 dc, change to yarn A, 1 dc in each of rem 15 dc, turn.

Row 3: With yarn A, 1 dc in each of next 15 dc, change to yarn B, 1 dc in each of rem 15 dc, turn.

Rows 4, 6, 8, 10, 12, 14 and 16: Rep Row 2.

Rows 5, 7, 9, 11, 13 and 15: Rep Row 3. Fasten off yarns A and B.

Row 17: Using yarn C, 1 dc in each of next 15 dc, change to yarn D (do not cut yarn C), 1 dc in each of next 15 dc, turn.

Row 18: Using yarn D, 1 dc in each of next 15 dc, change to yarn C, 1 dc in each of next 15 dc, turn.

Rows 19, 21, 23, 25, 27, 29 and 31: Rep Row 17.

Rows 20, 22, 24, 26, 28, 30 and 32: Rep Row 18.

Fasten off and darn in ends.

SURFACE CROCHET

Using yarn E, hold yarn at back of work and insert hook from front to back, at base of block where yarns A and B meet. Draw lp of yarn E through, insert hook from front

to back again, one row further up join between A and B, and surface crochet in a straight line, at top cut and darn in end.

Work a vertical line either side of centre line, 2 sts further apart (3 lines). Rotate square 90 degrees and create a further 3 lines, positioned in same way, to make tartan cross.

Darn in all ends.

- -

**
french lavender

A traditional, small crochet pattern that uses puff stitch and picots to create a textured but light square. Four identical small squares are joined together here to create a larger 15-cm (6-inch) piece. Equally effective if turned diagonally, this square is beautifully lacy.

Special stitch used:

4-treble-crochet puff stitch (4-trpf): Make puff stitch with 4 tr, ch 1 to seal pf (*see page 19*).

Foundation ring: Ch 6, join with sl st to form ring.

Round 1: Ch 4 (counts as 1 tr, 1 ch), [1 tr in ring, 1 ch] 11 times, sl st in 3rd of beg 4-ch to join – 12 sps made.

Round 2: Sl st in next sp, ch 3, 4-trpf in same sp, *ch 2, 4-trpf in next sp, ch 3, 1 dtr in next tr, ch 3, 4-trpf in next sp, ch 2**, 4-trpf in next sp; rep from * 2 times and then from * to ** 1 time, sl st in top of first 4-trpf to join.

Round 3: Ch 1, 1 dc in same place, *ch 2, miss next ch-2 sp, 4 tr in next ch-3 sp, ch 2, 1 tr in next dtr, ch 3, insert hook down through top of last dtr and work sl st, ch 2, 4 tr in next ch-3 sp, ch 2, miss next ch-2 sp, 1 dc in next 4-trpf; rep from * 3 times omitting last dc at end of last rep, sl st in first dc to join. Fasten off.

Work 3 additional squares in same way. Join squares with RS tog, by stitching from corner picots and along side seams for 5 sts on each seam, leaving central 'V' shape open on each seam. See photo for guide.

Fasten off yarn and darn in ends neatly.

★★★
frame frill

A very striking block with a pronounced frill, this is easier than it looks to make, and is so much fun to use – it works well on bedspreads or flat areas where the frills can be seen to full advantage.

A
B
C

Foundation ring: Using yarn A, ch 4, join with sl st to form ring.

Round 1: Ch 3 (counts as 1 tr), 11 tr in ring, sl st in top of ch-3 to join.

Round 2: Ch 3 (counts as 1 tr), *[2 tr, 1 dtr] in next tr, [1 dtr, 2 tr] in next tr**, 1 tr in next tr; rep from * 2 times, then from * to ** 1 time, sl st in top of beg ch-3 to join.

Round 3: Ch 3, (counts as 1 tr), 1 tr in each of next 2 tr, *[2 tr, 1 dtr] in next tr, [1 dtr, 2 tr] in next tr**, 1 tr in each of next 5 tr; rep from * 2 times, then from * to ** 1 time, 1 tr in each of next 2 tr, sl st in top of beg ch-3 to join.

Round 4: Ch 1, 1 dc in same sp, 1 dc in each of next 4 tr, *2 dc in each of next 2 dtr**, 1 dc in each of next 9 tr; rep from * 2 times, then from * to ** 1 time, 1 dc in each of rem 4 tr, sl st in top of beg ch-3 to join.

Round 5: Ch 3, (counts as 1 tr), 1 tr in each of next 5 dc, *[2 tr, 1 dtr] in next dc, [1 dtr, 2 tr] in next dc**, 1 tr in each of next 11 dc; rep from * 2 times, then from * to ** 1 time, 1 tr in each of rem 5 dc, sl st in top of beg ch-3 to join.

Round 6: Ch 1, working all around square, 1 dc in each tr of prev rnd and 2 dc in each dtr at corners, sl st in first dc to join.

MAKE FRILL

Round 7: Working in front lps only of all sts in rnd, 2 dc in each dc around square.

Round 8: Still working on frill, 2 tr in every dc of frill around block. Fasten off yarn A.

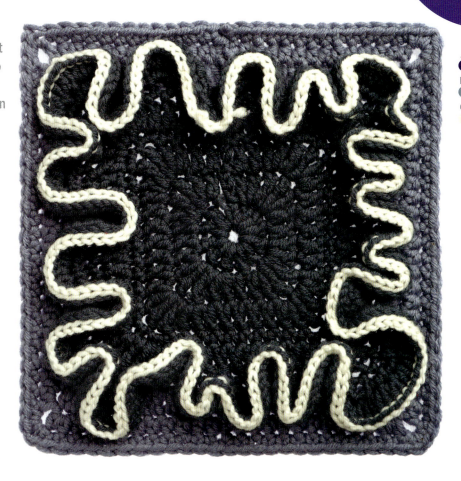

COMPLETE MAIN BLOCK

Round 9: Join yarn B at same point on main square that you began frill, working in back lps of sts from Round 5, ch 3 (counts as 1 tr), 1 tr in each of next 8 dc, *[2 tr, 1 dtr] in next dc, [1 dtr, 2 tr] in next dc**, 1 tr in each of next 17 dc; rep from * 2 times, then from * to ** 1 time, 1 tr in each of rem 8 dc, sl st in top of beg ch-3 to join.

Round 10: Ch 2 (counts as 1 htr), 1 htr in each tr around block, and [1 htr in dtr, ch 2, 1 htr in dtr] in each corner, sl st in top of beg ch-2 to join.

Round 11: Ch 1, 1 dc in every htr, and 3 dc in corner ch-2 sp around square, sl st in first dc to join. Fasten off yarn B.

FRILL TRIM

Using yarn C, and holding work so that outer edge of frill is facing, sl st in each tr of frill all around.

Fasten off yarn and darn in all ends neatly.

307

★ ★ ★

posy

A
B
C
D
E
F

With its pretty central ring of flowers, this square would work well in a lightweight throw or summer blanket. It is fun to make because the flowers are all attached one by one before the border is created.

Centre flower: Using yarn A, make a magic ring, *ch 3, 1 dtr, ch 3, sl st in ring; rep from * 7 times. Fasten off.

Flower 2: Using yarn B, make a magic ring, [ch 2, 1 tr in ring, ch 2, sl st in ring] 2 times, ch 2, sl st in dtr of any petal of Centre Flower, 1 tr, ch 2, sl st in ring, [ch 2, 1 tr, ch 2, sl st] in ring. Fasten off.

Flower 3: Using yarn C, make a magic ring, ch 2, 1 tr, ch 2, sl st in ring, ch 2, sl st in dtr of RH petal from Flower 2, [1 tr, ch 2, sl st] in ring, ch 2, sl st in next dtr of Centre Flower, [1 tr, ch 2, sl st] in ring, ch 2, [1 tr, ch 2, sl st] in ring. Fasten off.

Flower 4: Rep Flower 3 but using yarn D and joining to Flower 3 and Centre Flower.

Flower 5: Rep Flower 3 but using yarn E and joining to Flower 4 and Centre Flower.

Flower 6: Rep Flower 3 but using yarn B and joining to Flower 5 and Centre Flower.

Flower 7: Rep Flower 3 but using yarn C and joining to Flower 6 and Centre Flower.

Flower 8: Rep Flower 3 but using yarn D and joining to Flower 7 and Centre Flower.

Flower 9: Rep Flower 3 but using yarn E and joining 3 petals to Flower 8, Centre Flower and Flower 1.

BORDER

Round 1: Using yarn F, sl st in any ch-1 sp of any petal, *ch 10, sl st in next flower; rep from * 7 times, sl st in first ch-10 sp to join.

Round 2: *[6 tr, ch 2, 6 tr] in same ch-10 sp, 8 tr in next ch-10 sp; rep from * 3 times, sl st in first tr to join.

Round 3: Sl st in next ch-2 corner sp, *[2 tr, ch 2, 2 tr] in corner sp, 1 tr in every tr to next corner sp; rep from * 3 times, 1 tr in every tr to end, sl st in first tr to join.

Fasten off, darn in ends and and block if necessary.

308

★ ★ ★

mardi gras

A
B
C
D
E
F
G

Inspired by the beads and lights of carnival, this filet base is peppered with bobbles in contrasting colours. It's fun to work. Choose your own colourful lights or bead colours, and once you master the technique it's easy to add more bobbles if you want.

Special stitch used:

Make bobble (MB): Make bobble with 5 tr, using a length of contrast yarn as specified (*see page 19*).

Foundation chain: Using yarn A, ch 31.

Row 1: 1 tr in 4th ch from hook, 1 tr in each ch to end, turn.

Row 2: Ch 3 (counts as 1 tr), 1 tr in each of next 2 tr, [miss 1 st, ch 1, 1 tr in next tr] 12 times, 1 tr in each of last 2 sts, turn.

Row 3: Ch 3 (counts as 1 tr), 1 tr in each of next 2 tr, [miss 1 st, ch 1, 1 tr in next tr], ch 1, MB using yarn B in next tr, * ch 1, 1 tr in next tr, [miss 1 st, ch 1, 1 tr in next tr] 2 times, ch 1**, MB in next tr using yarn C; rep from * to ** 1 time, MB using

yarn D in next tr, ch 1, 1 tr in next tr, miss 1 st, 1 tr in each of next 3 tr, turn.

Rows 4 to 5: Rep Row 2.

Row 6: Rep Row 3 using yarns E, F and G instead of B, C and D.

Rows 7 to 8: Rep Row 2.

Row 9: Rep Row 3.

Rows 10 to 11: Rep Row 2.

Row 12: Rep Row 6.

Row 13: Rep Row 2.

Row 14: Ch 3 (counts as 1 tr), 1 tr in each tr and in each ch-1 sp to end.

Row 15: Ch 1, 1 dc in each st to end, at corner, rotate square 90 degrees and cont working up side of square, 1 dc in each

ch-1 sp and 1 dc in base of each row to bottom of square, work along bottom of square, 1 dc in every ch to next corner, then 1 dc in every ch-1 sp and in base of every row to end, sl st in first dc to join.

Fasten off and darn in all ends so that they do not show on either side of work.

wagon wheel

A bold and striking bloom design with surface crochet detail, which would work well combined with other graphic squares to create a contemporary throw. Or work this up in blue-tone colours as part of a nautical-themed afghan.

A
B
C
D
E
F

Special stitches used:

Spike stitch (spike st): Insert hook in top of stitch one rnd below next st to be worked, yoh, pull yarn through to height of rnd being worked, complete stitch as normal (*see page 22*).

Surface crochet: 1 sl st over vertical post of each st, creating a chain-stitch effect (*see page 22*).

Foundation ring: Using yarn A, ch 8, sl st in first ch to form ring.

Round 1: Ch 3 (counts as 1 tr), 31 tr in ring, sl st in top of beg ch-3 to join. Fasten off yarn A.

Round 2: Join yarn B in any tr, *ch 4, miss 3 tr, 1 dc in next tr; rep from * 7 times, sl st in first ch to join.

Round 3: Sl st in first ch-4 sp, ch 3 (counts as 1 tr), 5 tr in same sp, *ch 1, 6 tr in next ch-4 sp; rep from * 7 times, ch 1, sl st in top of beg ch-3 to join. Fasten off yarn B.

Round 4: Join yarn C in any ch-1 sp, *ch 6, 1 dc spike st in top of next dc from Round 2; rep from * 7 times, sl st in first ch st to join.

Round 5: Sl st in next ch-6 sp, ch 2 (counts as 1 htr), 5 htr in same ch-6 sp, *ch 1, 6 htr in next ch-6 sp; rep from * 7 times, sl st in top of beg ch-2 to join. Fasten off yarn C.

Round 6: Join yarn D in any ch-1 sp, ch 3 (counts as 1 tr), *1 tr in every htr and 2 tr in every ch-1 sp to end, sl st in top of beg ch-3 to join. Fasten off yarn D.

Round 7: Join yarn E around vertical post of any st from Round 6, surface crochet using sl st around post of every st from Round 6 to create circle, sl st in first sl st to join. Fasten off yarn E.

Round 8: Join yarn F in any tr from Round 6, 1 dc in same tr, *ch 8, miss 8 tr, 1 dc in next tr; rep from * 7 times, sl st in first dc to join.

Round 9: Sl st in next ch-8 sp, ch 2, [5 tr, ch 2, 6 tr] in same sp, *6 tr in next ch-8 sp, [6 tr, ch 2, 6 tr] in next ch-8 sp; rep from * 3 times, 6 tr in last ch-8 sp, sl st in top of beg ch-2 to join.

Round 10: Ch 1, 1 htr in every tr and [2 htr, ch 1, 2 htr] in every corner sp to end, sl st in first ch-1 to join.

Fasten off and darn in ends neatly.

310 ✳✳
morning star

A striking design that makes use of clusters to create its star-like shapes. Great for mixing with plainer blocks or other grannies.

Special stitches used:

2-treble crochet cluster (2-tr cl):
Make cluster with 2 tr in same st or sp (*see page 18*).

3-treble crochet cluster (3-tr cl):
Make cluster with 3 tr in same st or sp.

Foundation ring: Using yarn A, begin with magic ring method.

Round 1: Ch 3, 2-tr cl in ring, *ch 2, 3-tr cl in ring; rep from * 6 times, ch 2, sl st in top of first cluster to join. Fasten off yarn A.

Round 2: Join yarn B, ch 3, tr2tog in top of cluster, *ch 5, tr3tog in top of next cluster; rep from * 6 times, ch 5, sl st in top of first cluster to join. Fasten off yarn B.

Round 3: Join yarn C, ch 3 (counts as 1 tr), 1 tr in next st in top of cluster, *6 tr in ch-5 sp**, 2 tr in top of next cluster; rep from * 7 times ending at **, sl st in top of beg ch-3 to join. Fasten off yarn C.

Round 4: Join yarn B, ch 3 (counts as 1 tr), 1 tr, ch 2, 2 tr in same st, *1 tr in next 15 tr**, [2 tr, ch 2, 2 tr] in same st; rep from * 3 times ending at **, sl st in top of beg ch-3 to join. Fasten off yarn B.

Round 5: Sl st yarn D to first corner, ch 3, 1 tr, ch 3, 2 tr, *[1 tr in next tr, miss 1 tr, ch 1] 9 times, 1 tr in next st**, [2 tr, ch 3, 2 tr] in next corner; rep from * 3 times ending at **, sl st in top of beg ch-3 to join. Fasten off yarn D.

Round 6: Sl st yarn A to first corner, ch 3, 4 tr in ch-3 sp, *1 tr in each tr and ch-1 sp across side (23 sts), **5 tr in next corner; rep from * 3 times, ending at **, sl st in top of beg ch-3 to join.

Fasten off and darn in all ends neatly.

311 ✳✳
target

Inspired by the painter Jasper Johns, this square looks great on its own for a coaster, but would be spectacular in multiples for a bedspread. This pattern is best worked in a flat, smooth yarn with complementary colours for the target.

Foundation ring: Begin with magic ring method.

Round 1: With yarn A, ch 3 (counts as 1 tr), 15 tr in ring, sl st in top of beg ch-3 to join. Fasten off yarn A.

Round 2: Join yarn B, ch 3 (counts as 1 tr), 1 tr in same st, *2 tr in next tr; rep from * to end of rnd, sl st in top of beg ch-3 to join. Fasten off yarn B.

Round 3: Join yarn A, ch 3 (counts as 1 tr), 1 tr in next tr, 2 tr in next tr, *1 tr in each of next 2 tr, 2 tr in next tr; rep from * to end of rnd, sl st in top of beg ch-3 to join. Fasten off yarn A.

Round 4: Join yarn B, ch 3 (counts as 1 tr), 1 tr in same st, 1 tr in next tr, *2 tr in next tr, 1 tr in foll tr; rep from * to end of rnd ending with 1 tr, sl st in top of beg ch-3 to join. Fasten off yarn B.

Round 5: Join yarn C, ch 1, 1 dc in same st, ch 5, miss 3 tr, 1 dc in next tr, *[ch 2, miss 2 tr, 1 dc in next tr] 4 times**, ch 5, miss 3 tr, 1 dc in next tr; rep from * 2 times and from * to ** 1 time, sl st in first ch of beg ch-5 to join.

Round 6: Ch 3 (counts as 1 tr), 6 tr in next ch-5 sp, *ch 1, [3 tr in next ch-2 sp, ch 1], 4 times**, 7 tr in next ch-5 sp; rep from * 2 times and from * to ** 1 time, ch 1, sl st in top of beg ch-3 to join.

Round 7: Ch 4 (counts as 1 tr and ch 1), *miss 1 tr, 1 tr in next tr, ch 7, miss next 2 tr, 1 tr in next tr, miss 1 tr, ch 1, [1 tr in next ch-1 sp, ch 2] 4 times, 1 tr in next ch-1 sp; rep from * to end of rnd ending ch-2, sl st in 3rd ch of beg ch-4 to join.

Round 8: Ch 2 (counts as 1 dc), 2 dc in next ch-1 sp, *1 dc in next tr, 9 dc in next ch-7 sp, 1 dc in next tr, 2 dc in next ch-1 sp, [1 dc in next tr, 3 dc in next ch-2 sp] 3 times, 1 dc in next tr, 2 dc in next ch-1 sp; rep from * to end of rnd ending 2 dc in last ch-2 sp, sl st in top of beg ch-2 to join.

Fasten off and darn in all ends neatly.

A
B
C
D

A
B
C

**

rainy bobbles

Multicoloured bobbles in close tones worked on a dark background give the effect of raindrops in this simple square. Alternatively, you could choose bright colours and change the look completely.

A
B
C
D

Special stitch used:

Make bobble (MB): Make bobble with 5 tr (*see page 19*).

Notes: When working multicoloured bobbles, leave last 2 lps of dc before bobble unfinished, draw through with contrast colour of bobble. Hold main yarn A at front of work, facing you, while making bobble with contrast length. Leave 6 lps of bobble on hook, drop contrast yarn and draw through using main yarn A. Bobble made and colour changed neatly.

Before beginning, cut lengths of each contrast yarn approximately 61 cm (24 inches) long; you will need 8 lengths of each colour.

Foundation chain: Using A, ch 30 (counts as 29 ch, 1 tch).

Row 1: 1 dc in 2nd ch from hook, 1 dc in every ch to end of row, turn – 29 sts.

Row 2: Ch 1, 1 dc in every dc to end of row, turn.

Rows 3 to 5: Rep Row 2.

Row 6: Ch 1, 1 dc in each of next 18 dc, MB with yarn B in next dc, using yarn A, 1 dc in next 10 dc, turn.

Rows 7 to 9: Rep Row 2.

Row 10: Ch 1, 1 dc in each of next 10 dc, MB using yarn C in next dc, using yarn A, 1 dc in each of rem 18 dc, turn.

Row 11: Rep Row 2.

Row 12: Ch 1, 1 dc in each of next 2 dc, MB using yarn D in next dc, using yarn A, 1 dc in each of next 15 dc, MB using yarn D in next dc, using yarn A, 1 dc in next 10 dc, turn.

Rows 13 to 15: Rep Row 2.

Row 16: Ch 1, 1 dc in each of next 2 dc, MB using yarn B in next dc, using yarn A, 1 dc in each of next 7 dc, MB using yarn D in next dc, using yarn A, 1 dc in each of next 7 dc, MB using yarn C in next dc,

using yarn A, 1 dc in each of next 7 dc, MB using yarn B in next dc, using yarn A, 1 dc in each of rem 2 dc, turn.

Rows 17 to 19: Rep Row 2.

Row 20: Ch1, 1 dc in each of next 2 dc, MB using yarn C in next dc, using yarn A, 1 dc in each of next 7 dc, MB using yarn B in next dc, using yarn A, 1 dc in each of next 7 dc, MB using yarn D in next dc, using yarn A, 1 dc in each of next 7 dc, MB using yarn C in next dc, using yarn A, 1 dc in each of rem 2 dc, turn.

Rows 21 to 23: Rep Row 2.

Row 24: Ch 1, 1 dc in each of next 2 dc, MB using yarn D in next dc, using yarn A, 1 dc in each of next 7 dc, MB using yarn C in next dc, using yarn A, 1 dc in each of next 7 dc, MB using yarn B in next dc, using yarn A, 1 dc in each of next 7 dc, MB using yarn D in next dc, using yarn A, 1 dc in each of rem 2 dc, turn.

Rows 25 to 27: Rep Row 2.

Row 28: Ch 1, 1 dc in each of next 2 dc, MB using yarn B in next dc, using yarn A, 1 dc in each of next 7 dc, MB using yarn D

in next dc, using yarn A, 1 dc in each of next 7 dc, MB using yarn C in next dc, using yarn A, 1 dc in each of next 7 dc, MB using yarn B in next dc, using yarn A, 1 dc in each of rem 2 dc, turn.

Rows 29 to 31: Rep Row 2.

Row 32: Ch 1, 1 dc in each of next 2 dc, MB using yarn C in next dc, using yarn A, 1 dc in each of next 7 dc, MB using yarn B in next dc, using yarn A, 1 dc in each of next 7 dc, MB using yarn D in next dc, using yarn A, 1 dc in each of next 7 dc, MB using yarn B in next dc, using yarn C, 1 dc in each of rem 2 dc, turn.

Row 33: Rep Row 2.

Fasten off and darn in ends neatly.

*

denim corner

A play on the patchwork technique of mitred corners, this block works equally well repeated in the same rotation throughout a blanket or pillow, or rotated to create larger composite squares or crosses. See the Home Fires square for how this can work.

A
B
C
D

Foundation chain: Using yarn A, ch 2.

Row 1: 5 dc in 2nd ch from hook, turn.

Row 2: Ch 1, 1 dc in each of next 2 dc, [1 dc, ch 2, 1 dc] in next dc, 1 dc in each of next 2 dc, turn.

Row 3: Ch 1, 1 dc in each of next 3 dc, [1 dc, ch 2, 1 dc] in next ch-2 sp, 1 dc in each of next 3 dc, turn.

Row 4: Ch 1, 1 dc in each of next 4 dc, [1 dc, ch 2, 1 dc] in next ch-2 sp, 1 dc in each of next 4 dc, turn.

Row 5: Ch 1, 1 dc in same sp, 1 dc in each of next 4 dc, [1 dc, ch 2, 1 dc] in next ch-2 sp, 1 dc in each of next 5 dc. Fasten off yarn A, turn.

Row 6: Join yarn B, ch 1, 1 dc in each of next 6 dc, [1 dc, ch 2, 1 dc] in next ch-2 sp, 1 dc in each of next 6 dc, turn.

Row 7: Ch 1, 1 dc in same sp, 1 dc each of next 6 dc, [1 dc, ch 2, 1 dc] in next ch-2 sp, 1 dc in each of next 7 dc, turn.

Row 8: Ch 1, 1 dc in each of next 8 dc, [1 dc, ch 2, 1 dc] in next ch-2 sp, 1 dc in each of next 8 dc. Fasten off yarn B, turn.

Row 9: Join yarn C, ch 1, 1 dc in each of next 9 dc, [1 dc, ch 2, 1 dc] in next ch-2 sp, 1 dc in each of next 9 dc, turn.

Row 10: Ch 1, 1 htr in each of next 10 dc, [1 htr, ch 2, 1 htr] in next ch-2 sp, 1 htr in each of next 10 dc. Fasten off yarn C, turn.

Row 11: Join yarn D, ch 1, 1 htr in same sp, 1 htr in each of next 10 htr, [1 htr, ch 2, 1 htr] in next ch-2 sp, 1 htr in each of next 11 htr, turn.

Row 12: Ch 1, 1 htr in each of next 12 htr, [1 htr, ch 2, 1 htr] in next ch-2 sp, 1 htr in each of next 12 htr, turn.

Row 13: Join yarn B, ch 1, 1 htr in same sp, 1 htr in each of next 12 htr, [1 htr, ch 2, 1 htr] in next ch-2 sp, 1 htr in each of next 13 htr. Fasten off yarn D, turn.

Row 14: Join in yarn B, ch 1, 1 htr in each of next 14 htr, [1 htr, ch 2, 1 htr] in next ch-2 sp, 1 htr in each of next 14 htr, turn.

Row 15: Ch 1, 1 htr in each of next 15 htr, [1 htr, ch 2, 1 htr] in next ch-2 sp, 1 htr in each of next 15 htr. Fasten off yarn B, turn.

Row 16: Join yarn A, ch 1, 1 htr in same sp, 1 htr in each of next 15 htr, [1 htr, ch 2, 1 htr] in next ch-2 sp, 1 htr in each of next 16 htr, turn.

Row 17: Ch 1, 1 htr in same sp, 1 htr in each of next 16 htr, [1 htr, ch 2, 1 htr] in next ch-2 sp, 1 htr in each of next 17 htr, turn.

Row 18: Ch 1, 1 htr in same sp, 1 htr in each of next 17 htr, [1 htr, ch 2, 1 htr] in next ch-2 sp, 1 htr in each of next 18 htr. Fasten off yarn A, turn.

Row 19: Join yarn C, ch 1, 1 htr in each of next 19 htr, [1 htr, ch 2, 1 htr] in next ch-2 sp, 1 htr in each of next 19 htr, turn.

Row 20: Ch 1, 1 htr in each of next 20 htr, [1 htr, ch 2, 1 htr] in next ch-2 sp, 1 htr in each of next 20 htr. Fasten off yarn C, turn.

Row 21: Join yarn D, ch 1, 1 htr in same sp, 1 htr in each of next 20 htr, [1 htr, ch 2, 1 htr] in next ch-2 sp, 1 htr in each of next 21 htr.

Row 22: Ch 1, 1 htr in each of next 22 htr, [1 htr, ch 2, 1 htr] in next ch-2 sp, 1 htr in each of next 22 htr. Fasten off yarn D.

Fasten off and darn in all ends neatly.

granny's quads

Four individually worked patches are joined using the join-as-you-go method (see page 25) in the last round. If you are not confident at this, you can make four, then sew them together at the end. This block looks great mixed with full-sized grannies and the Nine Square granny in the yellow/green section.

A
B
C

SQUARE 1

Foundation ring: Using yarn A, ch 5, join with sl st to form ring.

Round 1: Ch 3, 2 tr in ring, ch 3, [3 tr in ring, ch 3] 3 times, sl st in top of beg ch-3 to join. Fasten off yarn A.

Round 2: Join yarn B to any ch-2 sp, ch 3, [2 tr, ch 2, 3 tr] in same sp, ch 1, *[3 tr, ch 3, 3 tr] in corner ch-sp; rep from * 2 times, ch 1, sl st in top of beg ch-3 to join. Fasten off yarn B.

Round 3: Join yarn C to any ch-3 corner sp, [ch 3, 2 tr, ch 2, 3 tr] in same corner sp *ch 1, 3 tr in next ch-1 sp, ch 1**, [3 tr, ch 2, 3 tr] in next corner ch-sp; rep from * 2 times, then from * to ** 1 time, sl st in top of beg ch-3 to join. Fasten off.

SQUARES 2, 3 and 4

Work as Square 1 for Rounds 1 and 2.

Round 3: Using the JAYGo method, join yarn C to any ch-3 corner sp, [ch 3, 2 tr, ch 2, 3 tr] in same sp, ch 1, *sl st to join to Square 1, 3 tr in next ch-1 sp, sl st to join to Square 1, [3 tr, ch 2, 3 tr] in next corner ch-3 sp; rep from * around square, join other squares at * in same way, where necessary, so they are all linked. Fasten off.

Round 4: Join yarn C in any corner ch-3 sp, ch 1, [2 dc, ch 2, 2 dc] in same corner sp, 1 dc in every tr and ch-sp around composite square and [2 dc, ch 2, 2 dc] in corner sps to the end, sl st in first dc to join.

Fasten off and darn in all ends neatly.

midnight snow

This large-scale snowflake design would be wonderful in a big cosy blanket, just the thing for snuggling up by the fire on a winter's eve.

A
B

Foundation ring: Using yarn A, begin with magic ring method.

Round 1: Ch 3 (counts as 1 tr), 15 tr in ring, sl st in top of ch-3 to join – 16 sts.

Round 2: Ch 5 (counts as 1 tr, ch 2), 1 tr in next st, *miss 1 tr, [1 tr, ch 2, 1 tr] in next st; rep from * to end of rnd, sl st in 3rd ch of beg ch-5 to join.

Round 3: Sl st in ch-2 sp, ch 3 (counts as 1 tr), [1 tr, ch 3, 2 tr] in same ch-1 sp, *[2 tr, ch 3, 2 tr] in next ch-2 sp; rep from * to end of rnd, sl st in top of beg ch-3 to join.

Round 4: Sl st in next st then in first ch-3 sp, ch 3 (counts as 1 tr), [2 tr, ch 3, 3 tr] in same ch-3 sp *[3 tr, ch 3, 3 tr] in next ch-3; rep from * to end of rnd, sl st in top of beg ch-3 to join.

Round 5: Sl st in next 2 sts then in first ch-3 sp, ch 3 (counts as 1 tr), [3 tr, ch 2, 4 tr] in same ch-3 sp, *[4 tr, ch 2, 4 tr] in next ch-3 sp; rep from * to end of rnd, sl st in top of beg ch-3 to join. Fasten off yarn A.

Round 6: With yarn B, ch 3 (counts as 1 tr), 1 tr in next 3 tr, *7 tr in ch-2 sp (first corner), 1 tr in next 6 tr, 1 dc in next 2 tr, 1 dc in ch-2 sp, 1 dc in next 2 tr, 1 tr in next 6 tr; rep from * 3 times, ending at 2nd tr of the last 6 tr, sl st in top of beg ch-3 to join.

Round 7: Ch 3 (counts as 1 tr), 1 tr in next 6 tr, *[1 tr, ch 3, 1 tr] in next st (first corner), 1 tr in next 9 tr, 1 htr in next 5 tr, 1 tr in next 9 tr; rep from * 3 times, ending at 2nd tr of the last 7 tr, sl st in top of beg ch-3 to join.

Fasten off and darn in ends.

*
albion

A
B
C

Worked in both linear and in-the-round techniques, this bright and breezy square combines shells and spaces to give a twist on the usual striped block. Perfect for cotton throws, bathroom mats or picnic blankets, it's a taste of summer.

Foundation chain: Using yarn A, ch 18.

Row 1: 1 dc in 2nd ch from hook, 1 dc in every ch to end, turn – 17 dc.

Row 2: Ch 1, 1 dc in first dc, * ch 3, miss 3 dc, 1 dc in next dc; rep from * 4 times, turn.

Row 3: Ch 1, 1 dc in first dc, * 5 tr in next ch-3 sp, 1 dc in next dc; rep from * 4 times, turn. Fasten off yarn A.

Row 4: Join yarn B, ch 3, 1 dc in first dc, miss 1 tr, 1 dc in each of 3 centre tr of shell, *ch 3, miss [1 tr, 1 dc and 1 tr], 1 dc in each of 3 centre tr of shell; rep from * 2 times, ch 2, 1 dc in last dc.

Row 5: Ch 3, 2 tr in next ch-2 sp, *miss 1 dc, 1 dc in next dc (centre dc of 3-dc group), miss 1 dc, 5 tr in next ch-3 sp, miss 1 dc, 1 dc in next dc, miss 1 dc; rep from * 2 times, 3 tr in last ch-3 sp. Fasten off yarn B.

Row 6: Join yarn A, ch 1, miss first tr, 1 dc in next tr, ch 3, *miss [1 tr, 1 dc, 1 tr], 1 dc in each of 3 centre tr of shell, ch 3; rep from * 2 times, miss [1 tr, 1 dc, 1 tr], 1 dc in last tr.

Row 7: Ch 1, 1 dc in first dc, *5 tr in next ch-3 sp, miss 1 dc, 1 dc in next dc (centre dc of 3-dc group); rep from * 3 times.

Rows 8 to 11: Rep Rows 4 to 7.

Row 12: Rep Row 4, using yarn A.

Row 13: Ch 1, miss first dc, 1 dc in next and every dc and 1 dc in every ch-3 sp to end – 17 dc.

BORDER

Round 1: Using yarn A, ch 2, 1 dc in every st around square, working 17 sts evenly per side and [1 dc, ch 2, 1 dc] in every corner, sl st in top of beg ch-2 to join. Fasten off yarn A.

Round 2: Join yarn C in any ch-2 corner sp, ch 2 (counts as 1 tr), [2 tr, ch 2, 3 tr] in same corner sp, *[ch 1, miss 3 dc, 3 tr in next dc] 4 times, ch 1, [3 tr, ch 2, 3 tr] in next corner sp; rep from *2 times, [ch 1, miss 3 dc, 3 tr in next dc] 4 times, sl st in top of beg ch-2 to join.

Round 3: Sl st in next corner ch-2 sp, *[ch 1, 1 htr, 1 tr, 1 htr, ch 2, 1 htr, 1 tr, 1 htr] in corner sp, ch 1, [1 htr, 2 tr, 1 htr in next ch-1 sp, ch 1] 5 times; rep from * 3 times.

Fasten off and darn in ends neatly.

pacific rim

Worked initially in linear form to create the central diagonal, this block is then completed in the round to make the opposing diagonal edge. Equally effective worked in starkly contrasting colours, it is a useful base to mix with more elaborate squares.

A
B
C
D

Foundation chain: Using yarn A, ch 2, 3 dc in 2nd ch from hook, turn.

Row 1: Ch 1, 2 dc in first dc, 1 dc in next dc and 2 dc in last dc, turn – 5 sts.

Row 2: Ch 1, 2 dc in first dc, 1 dc in each dc to last dc, 2 dc in last dc – 7 sts.

Rows 3 to 4: Rep Row 2.

Row 5: Ch 1, 1 dc in every dc to end, turn – 11 sts.

Rows 6 to 9: Rep Rows 2 to 5 – 17 sts.

Rows 10 to 13: Rep Rows 2 to 5 – 23 sts.

Rows 14 to 17: Rep Rows 2 to 5 – 29 sts.

Row 18: Join yarn B, rep Row 5.

Row 19: Ch 1, miss 1 dc, 1 dc in each dc to last 2 dc, miss 1 dc, 1 dc in last dc, turn – 27 sts.

Rows 20 to 21: Rep Row 19 – 23 sts.

Row 22: Rep Row 5.

Rows 23 to 27: Rep Rows 17 to 21 – 17 sts.

Rows 28 to 32: Rep Rows 17 to 21 – 11 sts.

Rows 33 to 37: Rep rows 17 to 21 – 5 sts.

Row 38: Ch 1, miss 1 dc, 1 dc in next 2 dc, miss next dc, 1 dc in last dc, turn – 3 sts.

Row 39: Ch 1, tr3tog.

BORDER

Working along edge of motif, and still using yarn B:

Round 1: Ch 1, 2 dc in same sp, 1 dc in every row sp to next corner, 2 dc in corner st at end of yarn B section of block. Fasten off yarn B and join yarn A, 2 dc in corner st at start of yarn A section of block, working along bottom edge of block, 1 dc in every st to next corner, [2 dc in next st] 2 times (forms corner), 1 dc in every row sp up side of block to next corner, 2 dc in corner at end of yarn A section of block. Fasten off yarn A, join yarn B, 2 dc in next st, 1 dc in every st along top edge of block to corner, 2 dc in last st, sl st in first ch-1 to join. Fasten off yarns A and B.

Round 2: Join yarn C to solid coloured corner of yarn A section of block, ch 1, 2 dc in same st, 1 dc in every st to next corner, [2 dc in next st] 2 times, 1 dc in every st to next corner, 2 dc in next st. Fasten off yarn C, join yarn D, 2 dc in next st, 1 dc in every st to next corner, [2 dc in next st] 2 times, 1 dc in every st to last corner, 2 dc in last st, sl st in first ch to join, turn.

Round 3: Ch 1, 2 dc in same st, 1 dc in every st to next corner, [2 dc in next st] 2 times, 1 dc in every st to next corner, 2 dc in next st. Fasten off yarn D, join yarn C, 2 dc in next st, 1 dc in every st to next corner, [2 dc in next st] 2 times, 1 dc in every st to last corner, 2 dc in last st, sl st in first ch to join, turn.

Round 4: Rep Round 2.

Fasten off and darn in ends. Block if necessary.

318

**

comma

Worked into a simple filet grid, these curly commas are simple to do once you master the positioning and turning the work.

FILET BASE

Foundation chain: Using yarn A, ch 30.

Row 1: 1 tr in 6th ch from hook, *ch 1, miss 1 ch, 1 tr in next ch; rep from * to end.

Row 2: Ch 4 (counts as 1 tr, ch 1), 1 tr in next tr, *ch 1, 1 tr in next tr; rep from * to

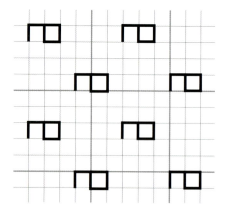

end, working last tr in top of ch-3 from last row.

Rows 3 to 12: Rep Row 2, 10 times (12 rows of 13 filet boxes). Fasten off.

BORDER

Starting in corner, ch 3 (counts as 1 htr, ch 1), 2 htr in same corner sp, *1 htr in each tr st and 1 htr each ch-1 sp across top of square to next corner, [2 htr, ch 1, 2 htr] in next corner sp, turn square 90 degrees, 1 htr in each tr st and 1 htr in side post of each tr st to next corner, [2 htr, ch 2, 2 htr] in corner sp; rep from * 1 time, 1 htr in first corner sp, sl st to top of beg ch-2 to join.

COMMAS

Begin at top LH comma: Turn work 90 degrees clockwise, join yarn A around vertical post of 3rd tr of Row 11 (counting in from left side). Ch 3 (counts as 1 tr), 2 tr

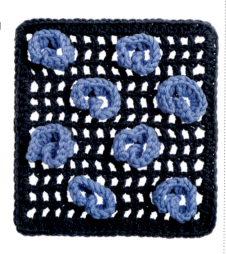

in same sp, turn work again, 3 tr in next ch-sp, turn work again, 3 tr around post of next tr, turn work again, [3 tr in next ch-3 sp] 2 times, turn work again, 3 tr around post of next tr. Fasten off. Rep for all commas, using chart as a guide.

Fasten off and darn in ends.

319

**

strata

In this square, different heights of stitches are used in the same row to create layers of colour. You could choose to create a sunset effect, or a thundery sky, by changing the colours you select.

Foundation chain: Using yarn A, ch 32.

Row 1: 1 dc in 2nd ch from hook, 1 dc in each of next 8 ch, 1 tr in each of next 10 ch, 1 dtr in each of next 11 ch, turn.

Row 2: Ch 4 (counts as 1 dtr), 1d tr in each of next 9 sts, 1 tr in each of next 10 sts, 1 dc in each of next 11 sts, turn.

Row 3: Change to yarn B, rep Row 2.

Row 4: Ch 1, 1 dc in each of next 9 sts, 1 tr in each of next 10 sts, 1 dtr in each of next 11 sts, turn.

Row 5: Rep Row 3.

Row 6: Change to yarn C, rep Row 2.

Row 7: Change to yarn A, rep Row 2.

Row 8: Change to yarn B, rep Row 2.

Row 9: Rep Row 4.

Row 10: Rep Row 3.

Row 11: Change to yarn A, rep Row 2.

Row 12: Rep Row 4, using yarn A.

Row 13: Rep Row 2.

Row 14: Change to yarn C, rep Row 2.

Row 15: Change to yarn B, rep Row 2.

Row 16: Rep Row 2, using yarn B.

Row 17: Ch1, 1 dc in every st to end.

Fasten off and darn in ends.

whitworth

**

A square worked in crossed treble crochet stitch with abstract blocks of colour, this is a contemporary take on solid areas of colour and would work well in a throw, blanket or scarf, either repeated or blended with other geometric blocks.

Special stitch used:

Crossed treble crochet (crossed tr): Insert hook in front of st just worked to access miss st, work tr as normal.

Foundation chain: Using yarn A, ch 32.

Row 1: 1 dc in 2nd ch from hook, 1 dc in every ch to end, turn.

Row 2: Ch 3 (counts as 1 tr), miss 2 sts, 1 tr in next st, 1 crossed tr in 2nd of miss sts, *[miss 1 st, 1 tr in next st, 1 crossed tr in miss st]; rep from * to last st, 1 tr in last st, turn.

Row 3: Rep Row 2.

Row 4: Ch 3 (counts as 1 tr), miss 2 sts, 1 tr in next st, 1 crossed tr in 2nd of miss st, *miss 1 st, 1 tr in next st, 1 crossed tr in miss st; rep from * 2 times, change to yarn B; rep from * 9 times, change to yarn A; rep from * 2 times, 1 tr in last st, turn.

Row 5: Ch 3 (counts as 1 tr), miss 2 sts, 1 tr in next tr, 1 crossed tr in 2nd of miss st, *miss 1 st, 1 tr in next tr, 1 crossed tr in miss st, change to yarn B; rep from * 9 times, change to yarn A; rep from * 4 times to end of row, 1 tr in last tr, turn.

Row 6: Rep Row 4.

Row 7: Rep Row 5.

Row 8: Rep Row 4.

Row 9: Ch 3 (counts as 1 tr), miss 2 sts, 1 tr in next tr, 1 crossed tr in 2nd of miss st, *miss 1 st, 1 tr in next tr, 1 crossed tr in miss st, change to yarn B; rep from * 9 times, change to yarn C; rep from * 2 times, change to yarn A; rep from * 2 times, 1 tr in last tr, turn.

Row 10: Ch 3 (counts as 1 tr), miss 2 sts, 1 tr in next tr, 1 crossed tr in 2nd of miss st, *miss 1 st, 1 tr in next st, 1 crossed tr in miss st, change to yarn C; rep from * 2 times, change to yarn B; rep from * 9 times, change to yarn A; rep from * 2 times, 1 tr in last tr, turn.

Row 11: Rep Row 9.

Row 12: Ch 3 (counts as 1 tr), miss 2 sts, 1 tr in next st, 1 crossed tr in 2nd of miss st, *miss 1 st, 1 tr in next tr, 1 crossed tr in miss st, change to yarn C; rep from * 2 times, change to yarn D; rep from * 4 times, change to yarn B; rep from * 5 times, change to yarn A; rep from * 2 times, 1 tr in last st, turn.

Row 13: Ch 3 (counts as 1 tr), miss 2 sts, 1 tr in next st, 1 crossed tr in 2nd of miss st, *miss 1 st, 1 tr in next tr, 1 crossed tr in miss st, change to yarn B; rep from * 5 times, change to yarn D; rep from * 4 times, change to yarn C; rep from * 2 times, change to yarn A; rep from * 2 times, 1 tr in last st, turn.

Row 14: Ch 3 (counts as 1 tr), miss 2 sts, 1 tr in next tr, 1 crossed tr in 2nd of miss st, *miss 1 st, 1 tr in next tr, 1 crossed tr in miss st, change to yarn C; rep from * 7 times, change to yarn A; rep from * 6 times, 1 tr in last tr, turn.

Row 15: Ch 3 (counts as 1 tr), miss 2 sts, 1 tr in next tr, 1 crossed tr in 2nd of miss st, *miss 1 st, 1 tr in next tr, 1 crossed tr in miss st; rep from * 4 times, change to yarn C; rep from * 7 times, change to yarn A; rep from * 2 times, 1 tr in next tr, turn.

Row 16: Rep Row 14.

Row 17: Rep Row 2.

Row 18: Ch 1, 1 dc in every st to end.

Fasten off and darn in ends.

A

B

C

D

★★★
daffodil

This friendly flower block has a dimensional centre, forming the familiar 'trumpet' shape. Perfect for inclusion in a spring-flower blanket or pillow, it has loads of textural appeal and will surely bring a smile to anyone's face.

A
B
C
D

Special stitches used:

2-half-treble-crochet cluster (2-htr cl): Make cluster with 2 htr (*see page 18*).

Picot-3: Ch 3 (at point to add picot), sl st in first ch of 3-ch, creating picot lp.

Double treble 3 stitches together (dtr3tog): Work 3 dtr over next 3 sts leaving last lp of each on hook, yoh, draw through all lps.

Foundation ring: Using yarn A, ch 4, sl st in first ch to form ring.

Round 1: Ch 2 (counts as 1 htr), 11 htr in ring, sl st in top of beg ch-2 to join.

Round 2: *Ch 3, 2-htr cl in 2nd ch from hook, ch 2, sl st in same ch as 2-htr cl, sl st in next ch, sl st in same htr in ring, sl st in front lp only of next htr; rep from * 5 times, sl st in first ch of beg ch-3 to join. Fasten off yarn A.

Round 3: Join yarn B in back lp of any htr from Round 1, ch 2 (counts as 1 htr), 1 htr in same st, 2 htr in every st to end, sl st in top of beg ch-2 to join.

Round 4: Working in front lps only, [2 htr, picot-3, 1 htr] in every st around to end. Fasten off yarn B.

Round 5: (RS) Bend trumpet and stamens forwards, join yarn B in any back lp, ch 4, (counts as 1 dtr), 1 dtr in same st, 1 dtr in each of next 2 sts, 2 dtr in next st, ch 3, *2 dtr in next st, 1 dtr in each of next 2 sts, 2 dtr in next st, ch 3; rep from * 4 times, sl st in top of beg ch-4.

Round 6: *Ch 4 (counts as 1 dtr), dtr3tog, dtr2tog, drawing last lp through ALL sts, ch 4, sl st in base of last dtr worked, 3 dc in next ch-3 sp, sl st in next dtr; rep from * 5 times, sl st in first ch of beg ch-4 to join. Fasten off yarn B.

Round 7: Join yarn C in top of any dtr3tog, ch 1, 1 dc in same st, *1 dc in each of next 2 sts (top of dtr2tog and ch 4), ch 3, 3 tr over next ch-3 and 3 dc lp, ch 3**, 1 dc in top of next dtr3tog; rep from * 4 times and from * to ** 1 time, sl st in first dc to join.

Round 8: Ch 1, 1 dc in every st and 3 dc in every ch-3 sp to end, sl st in first dc to join.

Round 9: *Ch 3 (counts as 1 tr), *1 tr in next st, 1 htr in each of next 3 sts, 1 dc in each of next 7 sts, 1 htr in each of next 3 sts, 1 tr in each of next 2 sts, [3 tr, ch 2, 3 tr] in next st (forms corner)**; 1 tr in next st; rep from * 2 times and from * to ** 1 time, sl st in top of beg ch-3 to join. Fasten off.

Round 10: Join yarn D in any ch-2 corner sp, *3 dc in corner sp, 1 dc in every st to next corner; rep from * 3 times, sl st in first dc to join.

Fasten off and darn in ends neatly.

★★★
ferris wheel

A play on the usual wheel structure, this block has bullion stitch to add texture and a side bullion stitch for extra interest. This is great to work up and is relatively quick: mix it with other wheel blocks for a country afghan, or with geometrics for a contemporary throw.

A

B

C

Special stitches used:

Side bullion: Yoh 10 times, insert hook around post of last tr, pull through lp, yoh and pull through all lps on hook.

Bullion stitch (bullion): Yoh 10 times, insert hook in st or sp to be worked, yoh, draw lp through to front, yoh, pull through all lps on hook, ch 1 to secure (*see page 20*).

Spike stitch (spike st): Insert hook in top of dc 2 rnds below, yoh, pull yarn through to height of rnd being worked, complete stitch as normal (*see page 22*).

Foundation ring: Using yarn A, ch 8, sl st in first ch to form ring.

Round 1: Ch 1, 16 dc in ring, sl st in first chain to join. Fasten off yarn A.

Round 2: Join yarn B in any dc, *ch 2, miss 1 dc, 1 dc in next dc; rep from * 7 times, sl st in first ch-2 sp.

Round 3: Ch 2, *1 tr in ch-2 sp, 1 side bullion around the post of last tr, ch 1; rep from * 7 times, sl st in top of beg ch-2 to join. Fasten off yarn B.

Round 4: Join yarn C in any ch-1 sp, *ch 5, 1 dc in next ch-1 sp; rep from * 7 times, sl st in first ch to join.

Round 5: Ch 1, *5 dc in ch-5 sp; rep from * 7 times, sl st in first ch to join. Fasten off yarn C.

Round 6: Join yarn A with a spike st in any dc from Round 4, *ch 6, 1 spike st in next dc from Round 4; rep from * 6 times, sl st in first st to join.

Round 7: Sl st in next ch-6 sp, [ch 1, *4 bullion, ch 1] in same ch-6 sp, sl st in next ch-6 sp; rep from * 7 times, sl st in first ch to join. Fasten off.

Round 8: Join yarn B in any ch-1 sp between sets of bullion sts, *ch 11 (counts as 1 tr, ch 8), 1 tr in next ch-1 sp between sets of bullion sts; rep from * 5 times, ch 8, sl st in top of beg ch-3 to join, sl st in next ch-8 sp.

Round 9: Ch 2, [4 tr, ch 2, 5 tr] in first ch-8 sp,*sl st in next ch-8 sp, 8 tr in ch-8 sp, sl st in next ch-8 sp, [5 tr, ch 2, 5 tr] in ch-8 sp; rep from * 2 times, sl st in last ch-8 sp, 8 tr in this sp, sl st in first ch to join.

Round 10: Sl st in next ch-2 corner sp, ch 1, *[2 htr, ch 2, htr] in ch-2 corner sp, 1 htr in every tr to next corner sp; rep from * 3 times, sl st in first ch to join.

Fasten off and darn in ends.

*

treasure box

A simple double-crochet construction provides a wonderful chance to go to town with vibrant optical colours in this great beginner block. Try to use single rows of popping highlights, to enhance the needlepoint-like appearance of this pattern.

A
B
C
D
E
F
G

Foundation ring: Using yarn A, ch 4, join with sl st to form ring.

Round 1: Ch1, 8 dc in ring, sl st in first dc to join – 8 sts.

Round 2: Join yarn B in any dc, ch 1, [1 dc, 1 htr, 1 dc] in same sp, *[1 dc in next dc, [1 dc, 1 htr, 1dc] in next sc; rep from * 3 times, 1 dc in last dc, sl st in beg ch-1 to join – 16 sts. Fasten off yarn B.

Round 3: Join yarn C in any htr, ch 1, [1 dc, 1 htr, 1 dc] in same sp, *1 dc in each of next 3 dc, [1 dc, 1 htr, 1 dc] in htr from last rnd; rep from * 3 times, 1 dc in each of last 3 dc, sl st in beg ch-1 to join – 24 sts. Fasten off yarn C.

Round 4: Join yarn D in any htr, ch 1, [1 dc, 1 htr, 1 dc] in same sp, *1 dc in each of next 5 dc, [1 dc, 1 htr, 1 dc] in htr from last rnd; rep from * 3 times, 1 dc in each of last 5 dc, sl st in beg ch-1 to join – 32 sts. Fasten off yarn D.

Round 5: Join yarn E in any htr, ch 1, [1 dc, 1 htr, 1 dc] in same sp, *1 dc in each of next 7 dc, [1 dc, 1 htr, 1 dc] in htr from last rnd; rep from * 3 times, 1 dc in each of last 7 dc, sl st in beg ch-1 to join – 40 sts. Fasten off yarn E.

Round 6: Join yarn F in any htr, ch 1, [1 dc, 1 htr, 1 dc] in same sp, *1 dc in each of next 9 dc, [1 dc, 1 htr, 1 dc] in htr from last rnd; rep from * 3 times, 1 dc in each of last 9 dc, sl st in beg ch-1 to join – 48 sts. Fasten off yarn F.

Round 7: Join yarn B in any htr, ch 1, [1 dc, 1 htr, 1 dc] in same sp, *1 dc in each of next 11 dc, [1 dc, 1 htr, 1 dc] in htr from last rnd; rep from * 3 times, 1 dc in each of last 11 dc, sl st in beg ch-1 to join – 56 sts. Fasten off yarn B.

Round 8: Join yarn D in any htr, ch 1, [1 dc, 1 htr, 1 dc] in same sp, *1 dc in each of next 13 dc, [1 dc, 1 htr, 1 dc] in htr from last rnd; rep from * 3 times, 1 dc in each of last 13 dc, sl st in beg ch-1 to join – 64 sts. Fasten off yarn D.

Round 9: Join yarn C in any htr, ch 1, [1 dc, 1 htr, 1 dc] in same sp, *1 dc in each of next 15 dc, [1 dc, 1 htr, 1 dc] in htr from last rnd; rep from * 3 times, 1 dc in each of last 15 dc, sl st in beg ch-1 to join – 72 sts. Fasten off yarn C.

Round 10: Join yarn A in any htr, ch 1, [1 dc, 1 htr, 1 dc] in same sp, *1 dc in each of next 17 dc, [1 dc, 1 htr, 1 dc] in htr from last rnd; rep from * 3 times, 1 dc in each of last 17 dc, sl st in beg ch-1 to join – 80 sts. Fasten off yarn A.

Round 11: Join yarn E in any htr, ch 1, [1 dc, 1 htr, 1 dc] in same sp, *1 dc in each of next 19 dc, [1 dc, 1 htr, 1 dc] in htr from last rnd; rep from * 3 times, 1 dc in each of last 19 dc, sl st in beg ch-1 to join – 88 sts. Fasten off yarn E.

Round 12: Join yarn D in any htr, ch 1, [1 dc, 1 htr, 1 dc] in same sp, *1 dc in each of next 21 dc, [1 dc, 1 htr, 1 dc] in htr from last rnd; rep from * 3 times, 1 dc in each of last 21 dc, sl st in beg ch-1 to join – 96 sts. Fasten off yarn D.

Round 13: Join yarn G in any htr, ch 1, [1 dc, 1 htr, 1 dc] in same sp, *1 dc in each of next 23 dc, [1 dc, 1 htr, 1 dc] in htr from last rnd; rep from * 3 times, 1 dc in each of last 23 dc, sl st in beg ch-1 to join – 104 sts.

Fasten off and darn in ends neatly.

off-centre granny

Worked initially in the round, then back and forth, this interesting twist on the classic lends itself to being used as a feature corner square in a bigger piece, or repeated patchwork-style to create a mid-weight afghan.

A
B
C
D
E
F

Foundation ring: Using yarn A, ch 4, join with sl st to form ring.

Round 1: Ch 3, 2 tr in ring, *ch 2, 3 tr in ring; rep from * 2 times, sl st in top of beg ch-3 to join.

Round 2: Sl st in next ch-2 sp, ch 3, 2 tr in same sp, ch 2, 3 tr in same corner sp, *[3 tr, ch 2, 3 tr] in next corner sp; rep from * 2 times, sl st in top of beg ch-3. Fasten off yarn A.

Row 3: Using yarn B, join in any ch-2 sp, ch 3, 2 tr in same sp, 3 tr in next sp, [3 tr, ch 2, 3 tr] in next corner sp, 3 tr in next sp between groups of tr, 3 tr in next corner sp, turn.

Row 4: Ch 3, [3 tr in next sp between groups of tr] 2 times, [3 tr, ch 2, 3 tr] in next corner sp, [3 tr in next sp between groups of tr] 2 times, 1 tr in ch-3 of last rnd, 1 htr in same sp, turn. Fasten off yarn B.

Row 5: Join yarn C in first sp, ch 3, 2 tr in same sp, [3 tr in next sp] 2 times, [3 tr, ch 2, 3 tr] in next corner sp, [3 tr in next sp] 2 times, 3 tr in last sp, turn.

Row 6: Ch 3, 3 tr in first sp, [3 tr in next sp] 2 times, [3 tr, ch 2, 3 tr] in next corner sp, [3 tr in next sp] 3 times, 1 tr in ch-3 of last rnd. Fasten off yarn C.

Row 7: Join yarn D in first sp, ch 3, 2 tr in same sp, [3 tr in next sp] 3 times, [3 tr, ch 2, 3 tr] in next corner sp, [3 tr in next sp] 3 times, 3 tr in last sp, turn.

Row 8: Ch 3, 3 tr in first sp, [3 tr in next sp] 3 times, [3 tr, ch 2, 3 tr] in next corner sp, [3 tr in next sp] 4 times, 1 tr in ch-3 of last rnd, turn. Fasten off yarn D.

Row 9: Join yarn E in first sp, ch 3, 2 tr in same sp, [3 tr in next sp] 4 times, [3 tr, ch 2, 3 tr] in next corner sp, [3 tr in next sp] 4 times, 3 tr in last sp, turn.

Row 10: Ch 3, 3 tr in first sp, [3 tr in next sp] 4 times, [3 tr, ch 2, 3 tr] in next corner sp, [3 tr in next sp] 5 times, 1 tr in ch-3 of last rnd. Fasten off yarn E.

Round 11: Join yarn F in first sp on side where other rnds have begun (RS up, off-centred square in bottom right), [ch 3, 2 tr, ch 2, 3 tr in same sp], *[3 tr in next sp] 5 times, [3 tr, ch 2, 3 tr in next corner sp; rep from * 2 times, sl st in 3rd ch of beg ch-3 to join.

Fasten off and darn in ends neatly.

*
emerald edge

A sweet crab-stitch edging finishes this block, and by working into the front loops only, two other crab stitch contrast ridges are created, adding textural detail to a simple granny. A pretty twist on a classic, this versatile block has oodles of possibilities.

A
B
C

Special stitch used:

Crab stitch (crab st): Double crochet worked in reverse (*see page 22*).

Foundation ring: Using yarn A, ch 4, sl st in first ch to form ring.

Round 1: Ch 2, 2 tr in ring, [ch 2, 3 tr in ring] 3 times, sl st in top of beg ch-2 to join. Fasten off yarn A.

Round 2: Join yarn B in any ch-2 corner sp, [ch 2, 2 tr, ch 2, 3 tr] in same corner sp, *[ch 1, 3 tr, ch 2, 3 tr] in next ch-2 corner sp; rep from * 2 times, ch 1, sl st in top of beg ch-2 to join. Fasten off yarn B.

Round 3: Join yarn C in any ch-2 corner sp, working in front lp only, and working from LEFT to RIGHT: work 1 crab st in each st around to beg, sl st in first crab st to join. Fasten off yarn C.

Round 4: Working in back lps of Round 2 and from right to left, join yarn A in first st of next ch-2 corner sp, ch 2, 2 tr in same lp, ch 2, 3 tr in next back lp of corner sp, *ch 1, 3 tr in centre back lp of next ch-1 sp from Round 2, ch 1, [3 tr, ch 2] in back lp of next ch-2 corner sp, 3 tr in next back lp of corner sp; rep from * 2 times, ch 1, 3 tr in centre back lp of next ch-1 sp from Round 2, sl st in top of beg ch-2 to join. Fasten off yarn A.

Round 5: Join yarn B in any ch-2 corner sp, [ch 2, 2 tr, ch 2, 3 tr] in same corner sp, *[ch 1, 3 tr in next ch-1 sp] 2 times, ch 1, [3 tr, ch 2, 3 tr] in next ch-2 corner sp, rep from * 2 times, [ch 1, 3 tr in next ch-1 sp] 2 times, ch 1, sl st in top of beg ch-2 to join. Fasten off yarn B.

Round 6: Rep Round 3.

Round 7: Working in back lps of Round 5, and from right to left, join yarn A in first st of next ch-2 corner sp, ch 2, 2 tr in same lp, ch 2, 3 tr in next back lp of corner sp, *[ch 1, 3 tr in centre back lp of next ch-1 sp from Round 5] 3 times, *3 tr, ch 2, in back lp of first st of next corner sp, 3 tr in next back lp; rep from * 2 times, [ch 1, 3 tr in centre back lp of next ch-1 sp from Round 5] 3 times, ch 1, sl st in top of beg ch-2 to join. Fasten off yarn A.

Round 8: Join yarn B in any ch-2 corner sp, [ch 2, 2 tr, ch 2, 3 tr] in same corner sp, *[ch 1, 3 tr in next ch-1 sp] 4 times, ch 1, [3 tr, ch 2, 3 tr] in next corner sp; rep from * 2 times, [ch 1, 3 tr in next ch-1 sp] 4 times, ch 1, sl st to top of beg ch-2 to join, sl st along to next corner sp.

Round 9: Ch 1, 1 dc in every st and every ch-1 sp around square, working [2 dc, ch 2, 2 dc] in every corner sp. Sl st to first dc to join. Fasten off yarn B.

Round 10: Join yarn C in any ch-2 corner sp, 1 crab st in every dc around square, working 2 crab sts in every ch-2 corner sp, sl st in first crab st to join.

Fasten off and darn in ends.

✱✱✱
blossom

A sister block to Bloom, this square features a four-layered flower with a detailed centre. It is ideal for use in pretty tableware, pillows or summer throws, and for use in a flower-garden afghan.

A
B
C
D
E

Special stitches used:

Picot-4: Ch 4 (at point to add picot), sl st in first ch of ch-4, creating picot loop.

Spike htr: Insert hook in top of htr 1 rnd below, yoh, pull yarn through to height of rnd being worked, complete htr as normal (see page 22).

Foundation ring: Using yarn A, make a magic ring, ch 1.

Round 1: [1 dc in ring, ch 4] 8 times, sl st in first ch to join. Fasten off yarn A.

Round 2: Join yarn B in ring between any two petals of Round 1, ch 4, [1 dc in ring between next two petals, ch 4] 7 times, sl st in first ch-4 sp.

Round 3: [1 dc, 1 htr, ch 1, 1 htr, 1 dc] in every ch-4 sp, sl st in first dc to join. Fasten off yarn B.

Round 4: Join yarn C using a sl st around post of any dc from Round 2, ch 5, [sl st around the post of next dc from Round 1, ch 5] 7 times, sl st in first ch-5 sp.

Round 5: Ch 3 (counts as 1 tr), [1 tr, ch 2, 2 tr] in same ch-5 sp, *sl st in next ch-5 sp, [2 tr, ch 2, 2 tr] in ch-5 sp; rep from * in every 5-ch space to end, sl st in first ch to join. Fasten off yarn C.

Round 6: Join yarn D around post of any sl st from Round 4, *ch 8, miss 1 post, sl st around next post; rep from * 3 times, ch 8, sl st in first ch-8 sp.

Round 7: *[1 dc, 1 tr, 3 tr, picot-4, 3 dtr, 1 tr, 1 dc] in ch-8 sp, sl st in next ch-8 sp, rep from * 3 times, ending with sl st in first ch-8 sp. Fasten off yarn D.

Round 8: Join yarn E around any miss post of Round 6, [ch 8, miss 1 post, sl st around next empty post] 3 times, ch 8, sl st in first ch-8 sp.

Round 9: *[1 dc, 1 tr, 3 dtr, picot-4, 3 dtr, 1 tr, 1 dc] in ch-8 sp, sl st in next ch-8 sp; rep from * 3 times, sl st in first dc to join. Fasten off yarn E.

Round 10: Join yarn A around post of any sl st from Round 8, [ch 10, sl st around next post of Round 7] 3 times, ch 10, sl st in first ch-10 sp.

Round 11: [Ch 1, 5 htr, ch 2, 5 htr in ch-10 sp] 4 times, sl st in first htr to join.

Round 12: Ch 2 (counts as 1 htr), 1 htr in every htr to corner, [2 htr, ch 2, 2 htr] in corner ch-2 sp; rep from * 3 times, 1 htr in every htr to end, sl st in top of beg ch-2 to join.

Round 13: Ch 2 (counts as 1 htr), 1 htr in each of next 6 htr, *[2 htr, ch 2, 2 htr] in corner ch-2 sp, 1 htr in each of next 7 htr, 1 spike htr in row 11**, 1 htr in each of next 7 htr; rep from * 2 times and from * to ** 1 time, sl st in top of beg ch-2 to join.

Round 14: *[Ch 1, miss 1 htr, 1 htr in next htr] in every htr to corner, [2 htr, ch 2, 2 htr] in corner ch-2 sp; rep from * 3 times, [ch 1, miss 1 htr, 1 htr in next htr] to end, sl st in first ch to join.

Round 15: *[Ch 1, 1 htr] in every ch-1 sp between htr to corner, [2 htr, ch 2, 2 htr] in corner ch-2 sp; rep from * 3 times, [ch 1, 1 htr] in every ch-1 sp between htr to end, sl st in first ch to join. Fasten off yarn A.

Round 16: Join yarn B in any ch-2 corner sp, ch 1, [1 htr, ch 1, 2 htr] in corner ch-2 sp, *1 htr in every htr and in every ch-1 sp to corner, [2 htr, ch 2, 2 htr] in corner ch-2 sp; rep from * 2 times, 1 htr in every ch-1 sp and every htr to end, sl st in first ch to join.

Fasten off and darn in ends.

✲✲

twinkle

A
B

Worked in contrasting yarn, this bobble star makes a boldly textural statement on this block: lovely for festive throws or pillows, you might even work the star in silver or gold for extra sparkle. The contrast yarn is carried at the back of the work, so remember to keep it there to avoid having to unravel rows if you are unable to access it later.

Special stitch used:

Make bobble (MB): Make bobble using 5 tr and ch-1 to secure (*see page 19*).

Note: Before you start, cut 4 long lengths of contrast yarn B, or wind small balls. Use one length for each spoke of the star.

Foundation chain: Using yarn A, ch 30.

Row 1: 1 dc in 2nd ch from hook and 1 dc in every ch to end, turn.

Row 2: Ch 1, 1 dc in every dc to end, turn.

Rows 3 to 5: Rep Row 2.

Row 6: Ch 1, 1 dc in each of next 14 dc, MB using yarn B in next dc, 1 dc using yarn A in each of next 14 dc, turn.

Row 7 and every alternate row: As Row 2.

Row 8: Ch 1, 1 dc in each of next 6 dc, MB using yarn B in next dc, [1 dc using yarn A in each of next 7 dc, MB using yarn B in next dc] 2 times, 1 dc using yarn A in each of next 6 dc, turn.

Row 10: Ch 1, 1 dc in each of next 8 dc, MB using yarn B in next dc, [1 dc using yarn A in each of next 5 dc, MB using yarn B in next dc] 2 times, 1 dc using yarn A in each of next 8 dc, turn.

Row 12: Ch 1, 1 dc in each of next 10 dc, MB using B in next dc, [1 dc using yarn A in each of next 3 dc, MB using yarn B in next dc] 2 times, 1 dc using yarn A in each of last 10 dc, turn.

Row 14: Ch 1, 1 dc in each of next 12 dc, MB using yarn B in next dc, [1 dc using yarn A in next dc, MB using yarn B in next dc] 2 times, 1 dc using yarn A in each of next 12 dc, turn.

Row 16: Ch 1, 1 dc in each of next 4 dc, MB using yarn B in next dc, [1 dc using yarn A in next dc, MB using yarn B in next dc] 10 times, 1 dc in each of last 4 dc, turn.

Row 18: Rep Row 14.

Row 20: Rep Row 12.

Row 22: Rep Row 10.

Row 24: Rep Row 8.

Row 26: Rep Row 6.

Rows 27 to 31: Rep Row 2.

Fasten off and darn in ends neatly. Block square to shape.

**

puffball

Two rounds of clusters make up the leafy pattern in this block, which works up relatively quickly. It is lovely mixed with other lace flower blocks, particularly when worked in a soft cotton yarn.

A
B
C

Special stitches used:

3-double-treble crochet cluster (3-dtr cl): Make cluster with 3 dtr in same st or sp.

2-double-treble crochet cluster (2-dtr cl): Make cluster with 2 dtr in same st or sp (*see page 18*).

2-triple-treble crochet cluster (2-ttr cl): Make cluster with 2 ttr in same st or sp.

Foundation ring: Using yarn A, ch 4, sl st in first ch to form ring.

Round 1: Ch 1, 8 dc in centre ring, sl st in first dc to join.

Round 2: Ch 5 (counts as 1 tr, ch 2), *1 tr in next dc, ch 2; rep from * 6 times, sl st in 3rd ch of beg ch-5 to join.

Round 3: Ch 1, 1 dc in same st, *3 dc in next ch-2 sp, 1 dc in next tr; rep from * 6 times, 3 dc in next ch-2 sp, sl st in first dc to join. Fasten off yarn A.

Round 4: Join yarn B in same st, ch 7 (counts as 1 htr, ch 5), miss 3 sts, *1 htr in next st, ch 5, miss next 3 sts; rep from * 6 times, sl st in 2nd ch of beg ch-7 to join.

Round 5: Ch 7 (counts as 1 dtr, ch 3), 3-dtr cl in same st, *[3-dtr cl, ch 3, 1 dtr, ch 3, 3-dtr cl] in next htr; rep from * 6 times, [3-dtr cl, ch 3] in beg st, sl st in 4th ch of beg ch-7 to join.

Round 6: Ch 9 (counts as 1 dtr, ch 5), 3-dtr cl in same st, ch 3, miss next 2 cl sts, *[3-dtr cl, ch 5, 1 dtr, ch 5, 3-dtr cl] in next dtr st, ch 3, miss next 2 cl sts; rep from * 6 times, [3-dtr cl, ch 5] in beg st, sl st in 4th ch of beg ch-9 to join. Fasten off yarn B.

Round 7: Join yarn C in any dtr st between 2 ch-5 sps, ch 1, *1 dc in dtr st, ch 8, [2-dtr cl, ch 2, 2-ttr cl, ch 2, 2-dtr cl] in next dtr st between 2 ch-5 sps, ch 8; rep from * 3 times, sl st in first dc to join.

Round 8: Ch 1, *1 dc in dc st, 10 dc in next ch-8 sp, 3 dc in next ch-2 sp, [1 dc, ch 2, 1 dc] in next ttr cl, 3 dc in next ch-2 sp, 10 dc in next ch-8 sp; rep from * 3 times, st in first dc to join. Fasten off yarn C.

Round 9: Join yarn A in any ch-2 corner sp, *[1 dc, 2 ch, 1 dc] in ch-2 sp, 1 dc in each st to next corner; rep from * 3 times, sl st in first dc to join.

Fasten off, darn in ends and block work.

★★★★
hydrangea

A wonderfully sumptuous, loopy flower forms the centre of this complex square that builds up in layers as you work. Make the most of this block's gorgeous texture by giving it centre stage in a flower-garden pillow or blanket; it is bound to gain admirers.

A
B
C
D

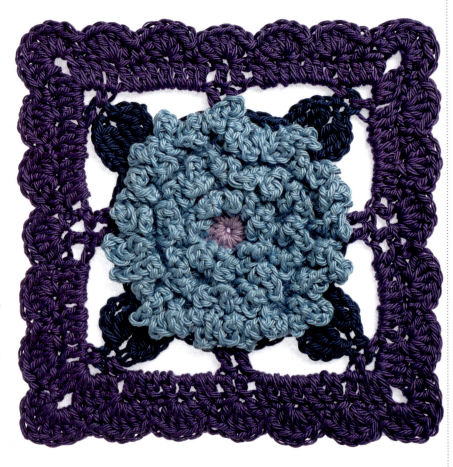

Special stitches used:

Front-loop double crochet (FLdc): Work in the front lp only of st (*see page 17*).

Front-post treble crochet (FPtr): bring hook to front, work in front vertical post of next st, inserting hook from right to left, draw yarn through and work st as usual (*see page 21*).

Back-loop treble crochet (BLtr): Work in the back lp only of st.

2-double-treble cluster (2-dtr cl): Make cluster with 2 dtr in same st or sp.

Picot-4: Ch 4 (at point to add picot), sl st in first ch of ch-4, creating picot lp.

Foundation ring: Using yarn A, begin with magic ring method.

Round 1: Ch 3, 15 tr in lp, sl st in top of beg ch-3 to join. Fasten off yarn A.

Round 2: Join yarn B, ch 1, 1 FPtr around vertical post of ch-3 of Round 1, ch 2, 1 FLdc in next tr, ch 2, *1 FPtr in next st, ch 2, 1 FLdc in next st, ch 2; rep from * to end of rnd, sl st in first FPtr to join. Fasten off yarn B.

Round 3: Join yarn B in any back lp of Round 1, ch 3 (counts as 1 tr), working in back of Round 1, 2 BLtr in each of next 3 tr, *1 BLtr in next tr, 2 BLtr in each of next 3 tr; rep from * 2 times, sl st in top of beg ch-3 to join.

Round 4: Ch 1, 1 FPtr around vertical post of ch-3 of Round 3, ch 3, 1 FLdc in next tr, ch 3, *1 FPtr in next st, ch 2, 1 FLdc in next st, ch 3; rep from * to end of rnd, sl st in first FPtr to join. Fasten off yarn B.

Round 5: Join yarn B in any back lp of Round 3, ch 3 (counts as 1 tr), working in back of Round 3, *[1 BLtr in next tr, 2 BLtr in next tr] 3 times**, 1 BLtr in next tr; rep from * to end ending last rep at **, sl st in top of beg ch-3 to join.

Round 6: Ch 1, 1 FPtr around vertical post of ch-3 of Round 5, ch 5, 1 FLdc in next tr, ch 5, *1 FPtr in next st, ch 5, 1 FLdc in next st, ch 5; rep from * to end of rnd, sl st in first FPtr to join. Fasten off yarn B.

Round 7: Join yarn C with sl st in any back lp of Round 5, *ch 4, 2 dtr cl in same st, picot-4, [2-dtr cl, ch 4] in next st (forms first leaf/corner), 1 BLdc in each of next 8 sts, sl st in next st; rep from * to end of rnd, sl st in first ch of beg ch-4 to join. Fasten off yarn C.

Round 8: Join yarn D with sl st in 4th dc along any side, ch 3, 1 tr in next dc, ch 6, *1 dc in picot-4, ch 3, 1 dc in same picot-4, ch 6, 1 tr in 4th dc along next side, 1 tr in next dc, ch 6; rep from * to end of round, sl st in top of beg ch-3 to join.

Round 9: Ch 3, 1 tr in next tr, 7 tr in next ch-6 lp, *1 tr in next dc [3 tr, ch 3, 3 tr] in next ch-3 sp, 1 tr in next dc, 7 tr in next ch-6 lp**, 1 tr in each of next 2 tr, 7 tr in next ch-6 lp; rep from * to end of rnd ending last rep at **, sl st in top of beg ch-3 to join. Fasten off.

Round 10: Rejoin yarn D with sl st in one of ch-3 corners, [ch 3 (counts as 1 tr), 6 tr] in same corner-sp, miss 1 tr, *[1 dc in next st, miss 1 tr, 5 tr in next st, miss 1 tr] 5 times across side of motif, miss 1 st, 1 dc in next st**, 7 tr in next ch-3 sp; rep from * to end of rnd ending last rep at **, sl st in top of beg ch-3 to join.

Fasten off and darn in ends neatly.

✱✱✱
waterlily

A classic crocodile-stitch flower motif that is worked in layers to create a 3D effect. Gorgeous as a centrepiece, or used in repeat to make a stunning pillow or throw.

Special stitches used:

Crocodile stitch (croc st): [5 tr, ch 2, 1 dc in side post of last tr made, 5 tr] in next ch-6 lp (*see page 20*).

Bubble stitch (bubble st): Working with WS facing, [1 dc, 1 dtr, 1 dc] in next sp.

Banded treble crochet (banded tr): Miss next st, 1 tr in each of next 2 sts, 1 htr around 2 tr just made.

Foundation ring: Using yarn A, ch 5, sl st in first ch to form ring.

Round 1: Ch 3 (counts as first tr), 15 tr in ring, sl st in top of beg ch-3 to join. Fasten off, cut yarn A and weave in ends.

Round 2: Join yarn B in top of any tr st from rnd below, ch 4 (counts as first tr, ch 1), *1 tr in next tr, ch 1; rep from * to end of rnd, sl st in top of beg ch-3 to join. Fasten off, cut yarn B and weave in ends.

Round 3: Turn and work with WS facing, join yarn C in any ch-1 sp, ch 1, 1 dc in same sp, ch 6, sl st in first ch st made (similar to picot st), bubble st in next ch-1 sp, *1 dc in next ch-1 sp, ch 6, sl st in first ch st made, bubble st in next ch-1 sp; rep from * to end of rnd, sl st in side of beg ch-1 to join.

Round 4: Ch 1, turn, with RS facing, *croc st in ch-6 lp, 1 dc in back lps of next bubble st; rep from * to end of rnd, sl st in beg ch to join. Fasten off, cut yarn C and weave in ends.

Round 5: Join yarn D in back lp of any bubble st (from Round 3), *ch 3, fold next petal forwards and, working behind petals, 1 dc in Round 3 st at centre of petal, ch 3, 1 dc in dc between next two petals (behind bubble st); rep from * to end of rnd, sl st in beg ch to join.

Round 6: Still working behind petals, ch 6, sl st in first ch st made, 3 dc in next ch-3 sp, 1 dc in next dc, 3 dc in next ch-3 sp, *1 dc in next dc, ch 6, sl st in first ch st made, 3 dc in next ch-3 sp, 1 dc in next dc, 3 dc in next ch-3 sp; rep from * to end of rnd, sl st in beg ch to join.

Round 7: Ch 1, *croc st in ch-6 lp, miss 3 dc, 1 dc in next dc, miss 3 dc; rep from * to end of rnd, sl st in beg ch-1 in next dc (to pin first petal in – keep petals folded up, so they don't get in the way). Fasten off, cut yarn D and weave in ends.

Round 8: Fold petals forwards and join yarn B with sl st in lps behind junction of any two petals, *ch 3, 1 tr in st at centre of next petal (forms corner sp), ch 3, 1 dc in st between next two petals, ch 3, 1 dc in st at centre of next petal, ch 3, 1 dc in st between next two petals; rep from * to end of rnd, sl st in beg ch to join.

Round 9: Ch 1, *[1 dc, 2 htr, 2 tr] in next ch-3 sp, ch 2, [2 tr, 2 htr, 1 dc] in next ch-3 sp (forms corner sp), 1 dc in dc, 3 dc in next ch-3 sp, miss next dc, 3 dc in next ch-3 sp, 1 dc in next dc; rep from * to end of rnd, sl st in beg ch to join.

Round 10: Sl st along to next corner ch-2 sp, ch 3 (counts as 1 tr), [1 tr, ch 2, 2 tr] in same sp, 1 tr in each of next 18 sts, *[2 tr, ch 2, 2 tr] in next corner sp, 1 tr in each of next 18 sts; rep from * to end of rnd, sl st in top of beg ch to join. Fasten off, cut yarn B and weave in ends.

Round 11: Join yarn A in any ch-2 corner sp, ch 3, [1 tr, ch 2, 2 tr] in same sp, ch 1, banded tr 7 times, *miss next tr, [2 tr, ch 2, 2 tr] in corner ch-2 sp, ch 1, banded tr 7 times; rep from * to end of rnd, sl st in top of beg ch to join. Fasten off, cut yarn A and weave in ends.

Round 12: Join yarn C in any ch-2 corner sp, ch 2, [1 htr, ch 2, 2 htr] in same sp, 1 htr in each of next 26 sts, *[2 htr, ch 2, 2 htr] in next corner sp, 1 htr in each of next 26 sts; rep from * to end of rnd, sl st in top of beg ch to join.

Round 13: Ch 1, 1 dc in same place, 1 dc in each tr and ch-1 sp of last rnd, 5 dc in each corner sp, sl st in beg sc to join.

Fasten off, cut yarn and weave in ends.

A ⊂⊃
B ⊂⊃
C ⊂⊃
D ⊂⊃

**

kyoto

A Japanese-inspired pattern, this block has unusual corner stitch arrangements and would complement any lightweight blanket. Best worked in cotton, this would make a stunning bedspread worked in repeat or mixed with Geisha.

A
B
C

Special stitches used:

Beginning 3-treble crochet cluster (beg 3-tr cl): Ch 3, make cluster with 2 tr in same st or sp (*see page 18*).

3-treble crochet cluster (3-tr cl): Make cluster with 3 tr in same st or sp.

Beginning 4-half-treble crochet cluster (beg 4-htr cl): Ch 2, make cluster with 3 htr over specified sts.

4-half-treble crochet cluster (4-htr cl): Make cluster with 4 htr over specified sts.

Foundation ring: Using yarn A, ch 4, sl st in first ch to form ring.

Round 1: *1 dc in ring, ch 3; rep from * 6 times, 1 dc in ring, ch 1, 1 htr in first dc to join.

Round 2: Beg 3-tr cl in same ch-3 sp, *ch 5, 3-tr cl in next ch-3 sp; rep from * 6 times, ch 5, sl st in top of beg 3-tr cl to join. Fasten off yarn A.

Round 3: Join yarn B in any ch-5 sp, ch 3 (counts as 1 tr), 4 tr in same ch-5 sp, 5 tr in next ch 5 sp, ch 3, *[5 tr in next ch-5 sp] 2 times, ch 3; rep from * 2 times, ch 3, sl st in top of beg ch-3 to join. Fasten off yarn B.

Round 4: Join yarn C in first tr after next ch-3 sp of Round 3, ch 3, 1 tr in same st, 1 tr in each of next 8 sts, 2 tr in next st, *ch 5, 2 tr in next st, 1 tr in next 8 sts, 2 tr in next st; rep from * 2 times, ch 5, sl st in top of beg ch-3 to join. Fasten off yarn C.

Round 5: Join yarn A in first tr after next ch-5 corner sp of Round 4, ch 3, 1 tr in each of next 11 sts, *ch 9, 1 tr in each of next 12 sts; rep from * 2 times, ch 9, sl st in 3rd ch of beg ch-3 to join. Fasten off yarn A.

Round 6: Join yarn B in first tr after next ch-9 corner sp of Round 5, beg 3-tr cl over next 3 sts, 1 tr in each of next 6 sts, 3-tr cl over next 3 sts, ch 5, *[3 tr, ch 3, 3 tr] in next ch-9 sp, ch 5 **, 3-tr cl over next 3 sts, 1 tr in each of next 6 sts, 3-tr cl over next 3 sts, 1 tr in each of next 6 sts, 3-tr cl over next 3 sts; rep from * 2 times and from * to ** 1 time, sl st in top of beg 3-tr cl to join. Fasten off yarn B.

Round 7: Join yarn C in top of any 3-tr cl after ch-5 sp, beg 4-htr cl over the next 4 sts, ch 3, 4-htr cl over next 4 sts, *ch 6, 1 htr in each of next 3 sts, ch 5, 1 htr in each of next 3 sts, ch 6, 4-htr cl over next 4 sts, ch 3, 4-htr cl over next 4 sts; rep from * 2 times, ch 6, 1 htr in each of next 3 sts, ch 5, 1 htr in each of next 3 sts, ch 6, sl st in top of beg 4-htr cl to join.

Round 8: *3 dc in next ch-3 sp, 7 dc in next ch-6 sp, 1 dc in each of next 3 sts, 5 dc in next ch-5 sp, 1 dc in each of next 3 sts, 7 dc in next ch-6 sp; rep from * 3 times, sl st in first dc to join.

Fasten off and darn in ends.

kaleidoscope

A variation on the usual granny design, this square uses half-treble crochets mixed with smaller and taller stitches. Careful use of colour will produce an optical effect: choose a cooler colour for the central rounds and warmer colours for the outer.

Foundation ring. Using yarn A, make a magic circle.

Round 1: ch 3 (counts as 1 tr), 2 tr in ring, [ch 3, 3 tr in ring] 3 times, ch 3, sl st in top of beg ch-3. Fasten off yarn A.

Round 2: Join yarn B in any ch-3 corner sp, ch 1, *[2 dc, ch 3, 2 dc] in same sp, ch 3; rep from * 3 times, sl st in top of beg ch-1 to join. Fasten off yarn B.

Round 3: Join yarn A in any ch-3 corner sp, ch 2 (counts as 1 htr), [2 htr, ch 3, 3 htr] in same sp (forms corner), *ch 1, 3 htr in next ch-3 sp, ch 1,** [3 htr, ch 3, 3 htr] in next sp; rep from * 2 times, then from * to ** 1 time, sl st in top of beg ch-2 to join. Fasten off yarn A.

Round 4: Join yarn B in any ch-3 corner sp, ch 1, *[2 dc, ch 3, 2 dc] in same sp, [ch 3, 2 dc in next ch-1 sp] 2 times; rep from * 3 times, sl st in top of beg ch-1 to join. Fasten off yarn B.

Round 5: Join yarn C in any ch-3 corner sp, ch 2 (counts as 1 htr), [2 htr, ch 3, 3 htr] in same sp, *[ch 1, 3 htr in next ch-3 sp] 3 times, ch 1, **[3 htr, ch 3, 3 htr] in next sp; rep from * 2 times, then from * to ** 1 time, sl st in top of beg ch-2 to join. Fasten off yarn C.

Round 6: Join yarn B in any ch-3 corner sp, ch 1, *[2 dc, ch 3, 2 dc] in same sp, [ch 2, 2 dc in next ch-1 sp] 4 times; rep from * 3 times, sl st in top of beg ch-1 to join. Fasten off yarn B.

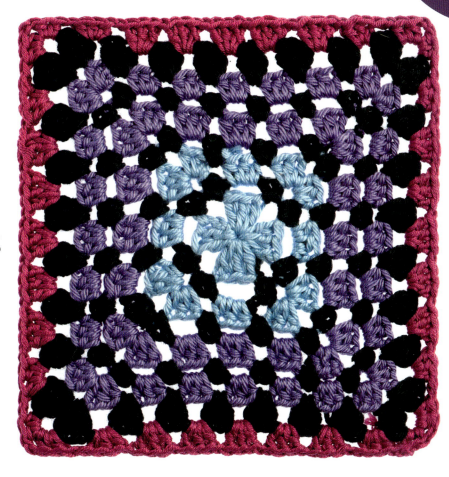

Round 7: Join yarn C in any ch-3 corner sp, ch 2 (counts as 1 htr), [2 htr, ch 3, 3 htr] in same sp, *3 htr in each of next 5 ch-2 sps, **[3 htr, ch 3, 3 htr] in next sp; rep from * 2 times, then from * to ** 1 time, sl st in top of beg ch-2 to join. Fasten off yarn C.

Round 8: Join yarn B in any ch-3 corner sp, ch 3 (counts as 1 tr), [2 tr, ch 3, 3 tr] in same sp, ch 1, [3 tr in sp between 3-htr groups, ch 1] 6 times, *[3 tr, ch 3, 3 tr] in next corner sp, ch 1, [3 tr in next sp between 3-htr groups, ch 1] 6 times; rep from * 2 times, sl st in top of beg ch-1 to join. Fasten off yarn B.

Round 9: Join yarn D in any ch-3 corner sp, ch 2 (counts as 1 htr), [1 htr, ch 2, 2 htr] in same sp, [ch 1, 3 htr in next ch-1 sp] 7 times, *[2 htr, ch 2, 2 htr] in next ch-3 sp, [ch 1, 3 htr in next ch-1 sp] 7 times; rep from * 2 times, sl st in top of beg ch-3 to join.

Fasten off and darn in ends.

A
B
C
D

333

** lisbon

This block has a Mediterranean feel with its lace and popcorns. Make it in Spanish colours for flouncy, sunny brightness or try it in dusty pastels for a faded, sun-bleached look. It is perfect for use in summer throws or picnic blankets.

A
B
C

Special stitches:

Beginning popcorn (beg pc): Ch 3, make popcorn with 4 tr (*see page 19*).

Popcorn (pc): Make popcorn with 5 tr.

Foundation ring: Using yarn A, ch 4, sl st in first ch to form ring.

Round 1: Ch 3 (counts as 1 tr), 19 tr in ring, sl st in top of beg ch-3 to join. Fasten off yarn A.

Round 2: Ch 5 (counts as 1 tr, ch 2), *1 tr in back lp of next st, ch 2; rep from * 18 times, sl st in 3rd ch of beg ch-5 to join. Fasten off yarn A.

Round 3: Join B in any ch-2 sp, beg pc, *ch 2, pc in next ch-2 sp; rep from * 18 times, sl st in top of beg pc to join. Fasten off yarn B.

Round 4: Join yarn C in any ch-2 sp, ch 4 (counts as 1 dtr), 2 dtr in same sp, *3 tr in next ch-2 sp, [3 htr in next ch-2 sp] 2 times, 3 tr in next ch-2 sp, [3 dtr, ch 3, 3 dtr] in next ch-2 sp; rep from * 2 times, 3 tr in next ch-2 sp, [3 htr in next ch-2 sp] 2 times, 3 tr in next ch-2 sp, 3 dtr in first ch-2 sp, ch 3, sl st to top of beg ch-4 to join.

Round 5: Ch 3 (counts as 1 tr), working in back lp only, 1 tr in each of next 5 sts, *ch 3, miss next 3 sts, 1 dc in next st, ch 3, miss next 2 sts, 1 tr in back lp of each of next 6 sts, [3 tr, ch 3, 3 tr] in next ch-3 corner sp, 1 tr in back lp of each of next 6 sts; rep from * 2 times, ch 3, miss next 3 sts, 1 dc in next st, ch 3, miss next 2 sts, 1 tr in back lp of each of next 6 sts, sl st in top of beg ch-3 to join.

Round 6: Ch 3 (counts as 1 tr), 1 tr in back lp of each of next 2 sts, *ch 5, 1 dc in next ch-3 sp, ch 5, 1 dc in next ch-3 sp, ch 5, miss next 3 sts, 1 tr in back lp of each of next 6 sts, [3 tr, ch 3, 3 tr] in ch-3 corner sp, 1 tr in back lp of each of next 6 sts; rep from * 2 times, [ch 5, 1 dc in next ch-3 sp] 2 times, ch 5, miss next 3 sts, 1 tr in back lp of each of next 6 sts, [3 tr, ch 3, 3 tr] in ch-3 corner sp, 1 tr in back lp of each of next 3 sts, sl st in top of beg ch-3 to join.

Round 7: Ch 1, 1 dc in each of next 2 sts, *5 dc in next ch-5 sp, 4 dc in next ch-5 sp, 5 dc in next ch-5 sp, 1 dc in each of next 9 sts, 3 dc in next ch-3 corner sp, 1 dc in each of next 9 sts; rep from * 2 times, 5 dc in next ch-5 sp, 4 dc in next ch-5 sp, 5 dc in next ch-5 sp, 1 dc in each of next 9 sts, 3 dc in next ch-3 corner sp, 1 dc in each of next 6 sts, sl st in first dc to join.

Round 8: Join yarn B in any 2nd dc of 3-dc group, ch 1, *[1 dc, ch 2, 1 dc] in same corner dc, 1 dc in every st to next corner; rep from * 3 times, sl st in first dc to join.

Fasten off and darn in ends.

pandora's box

A load of interesting stitches make this a fascinating block to work; a delicate lace is built up through chains, bullions and post-stitch clusters, which creates a pretty, lightweight square, great for summer throws, shawls or window panels.

Special stitch used:

Bullion stitch (bullion st): Yoh 7 times, insert hook in st or sp to be worked, yoh, draw loop through to front, yoh, pull through all loops on hook, ch 1 to secure (*see page 20*).

Foundation ring: Using yarn A, ch 4, sl st in first ch to form ring.

Round 1: *Ch 3 (counts as 1 tr), 2 tr in ring, 3 dc around vertical post of last tr made, sl st in ring; rep from * 3 times, sl st in ring to join. Fasten off yarn A.

Round 2: Join yarn B in any corner sp (between tr clusters) of Round 1, *ch 3 (counts as 1 tr), 2 tr in same sp, 3 dc around vertical post of last tr made, ch 4, sl st in next corner; rep from * 3 times, sl st in first ch of beg ch-3 to join. Fasten off yarn B.

Round 3: Join yarn C in top of any corner sp, *ch 3 (counts as 1 tr), 2 tr in same sp, 3 dc around vertical post of last tr made, ch 6, sl st in top of next corner; rep from * 3 times, sl st in first ch of beg ch-3 to join.

Round 4: Sl st along to next corner sp, ch 1, ch 3 (counts as 1 tr), [1 tr, ch 3, 2 tr] in same sp (forms corner) *ch 11 (counts as ch-8, 1 tr), sl st in next corner sp, ch 3, turn work to WS, sl st in 3rd ch of ch-11 just made, turn work back to RS, [ch 3, 2 tr] in same sp (forms corner); rep from * 2 times, ch 8, sl st in top of beg ch-3 to join. Fasten off yarn C.

Round 5: Join yarn B join in any corner, *ch 3 (counts as 1 tr), 2 tr in same sp, 3 dc around vertical post of last tr made, 1 dc in next sp between 2 tr sts, ch 10, 1 dc in next sp between 2 tr in next corner, sl st in next corner sp; rep from * 3 times, ending with sl st in first ch of beg ch-3 to join.

Round 6: Sl st in next corner sp, ch 3 (counts as 1 tr), 4 tr in same sp, miss 1 st, 1 dtr in next st, [ch 2, miss 2 ch, 1 bullion st in next ch] 3 times, ch 2, miss 2 ch, 1 dtr in next st, *5 tr in next corner sp, miss 2 sts, 1 dtr in next st, [ch 2, miss 2 ch, 1 bullion st in next ch] 3 times, ch 2, 1 dtr in next st; rep 2 times, sl st in top of beg ch-3 to join. Fasten off yarn B.

Round 7: Join yarn C in 3rd tr of 5-tr corner group from Round 6, ch 3 (counts as 1 tr), [1 tr, ch 3, 2 tr] in same sp (forms corner), 1 tr in each of next 2 sts, ch 2, miss next dtr, *[2 tr in next sp, ch 1] 3 times along side of square, miss next dtr, 1 tr in each of next 2 sts, *[2 tr, ch 3, 2 tr] in next st (forms corner), 1 tr in each of next 2 sts, ch 2, miss next dtr, [2 tr in the next sp, ch 1] 3 times along side of square, miss next dtr, ch 2, 1 tr in each of next 2 sts; rep from * 2 times, sl st in top of beg ch-3 to join. Fasten off yarn C.

Round 8: Join yarn D in any corner ch-3 sp, ch 2, [2 htr, ch 2, 3 htr] in same corner sp, *1 htr in each st, and 2 htr in each ch-1 sp along side of square to next corner**, [3 htr, ch 2, 3 htr] in next corner ch-3 sp; rep from * 2 times, and from * to ** 1 time, sl st in top of beg ch-2 to join.

Fasten off and darn in ends neatly.

**

isabelle

The traditional and somewhat retro 'almond pattern' is updated here by the use of contemporary colours and the addition of bobbles. A fun play on stripes mixes well with plainer blocks and grannies.

A
B
C
D

Special stitch used:

Make bobble (MB): Work a spike stitch (*see page 22*).

Spike stitch (spike dc): Make bobble with 5 tr (*see page 19*).

Note: Before starting cut lengths of yarn D about 35.5 cm (14 in) long; you will need 8 lengths.

Foundation chain: Using yarn A, ch 31 (counts as 30 sts, 1 tch).

Row 1: 1 dc in 2nd ch from hook, 1 dc in every ch to end, turn. Fasten off yarn A.

Row 2: Rep Row 1. Fasten off yarn A.

Row 3: Using yarn B, 1 dc in every st to end, turn. Fasten off yarn B.

Row 4: Join yarn C, ch 1, *[1 dc, 1 htr, 5 tr, 1 htr, 1 dc], miss 1 dc, ch 1; rep from * to end, sl st in tch, turn.

Row 5: Sl st, *1 dc in next dc, 1 htr in next htr, 1 tr in each of next 2 tr, using yarn D, MB, using yarn C, 1 tr in each of next 2 tr, 1 htr in next htr, 1 dc in next dc, ch 1]; rep from * to end, turn.

Row 6: Rep Row 3. Fasten off yarn C, join yarn B.

Row 7: Ch 1, *1 dc in each of next 9 sts, 1 spike dc in miss st from Row 3 (insert hook in sp left by miss st, 3 rows below, draw up lp to height of current row and continue with dc); rep from * 2 times, omitting last spike sc. Fasten off yarn B.

Rows 8 to 10: Rep Row 1. Fasten off yarn A, join yarn B.

Row 11: Rep Row 3. Fasten off yarn B. Join yarn C.

Row 12: Ch 3 (counts as 1 tr), 1 tr in each of next 2 sts, 1 htr, 1 dc, *[ch 1, miss 1 st, 1 dc, 1 htr, 5 tr, 1 htr, 1 dc]; rep from * 1 time, ch 1, miss 1 st, 1 dc, 1 htr, 1 tr in last 2 sts, turn.

Row 13: Ch 3 (counts as 1 tr), 1 tr in each of next 2 tr, 1 htr, 1 dc, *[ch 1, miss 1 st, 1 htr, 1 tr in each of next 2 tr, using yarn D, MB, using yarn C, 1 tr in each of next 2 tr, 1 htr, 1 dc, 1 ch, miss 1 st]; rep from * 1 time, 1 dc, 1 htr, 1 tr in each of last 2 tr, turn.

Row 14: Rep Row 11.

Row 15: Rep Row 6.

Rows 16 to 18: Rep Row 2. Fasten off yarn A, join in yarn B.

Row 19: Rep Row 3.

Row 20: Rep Row 4.

Row 21: Rep Row 5.

Row 22: Rep Row 4.

Row 23: Rep Row 6.

Rows 24 to 26: Rep Row 1.

Fasten off and darn in ends neatly.

*

sugared almonds

A simple textural pattern that produces a gentle undulation in the fabric. The reverse side of this block is equally pleasing, with a horizontal ridge at intervals – choose which side you like best. This is a relatively thick fabric, great for toasty warm afghans and throws.

A

B

Special stitch used:

Front-post treble crochet (FPtr): Bring hook to front, work in front vertical post of next st, inserting hook from right to left, draw yarn through and work st as usual (see page 21).

Foundation chain: Using A, ch 30.

Row 1: 1 tr in 2nd ch from hook, 1 tr in each ch to end, turn.

Row 2: Ch 2, 1 tr in each tr to end, turn. Fasten off yarn A.

Row 3: Join yarn B, ch 2, 1 FPtr in each tr to end, turn.

Row 4: Ch 2, 1 tr in each tr to end, turn.

Rows 5 to 19: Rep Rows 3 to 4, changing colour in foll sequence:

Rows 5 to 8: Use yarn A.

Rows 9 to 10: Use yarn B.

Rows 11 to 14: Use yarn A.

Rows 15 to 16: Use yarn B.

Rows 17 to 19: Use yarn A.

Fasten off and darn in all ends neatly.

*

candy cube

Another modern block, this one uses especially tall stitches and an interesting construction at the corners to create bold stripes. If your tension tends towards being loose, size down your hook or use thicker yarn to make the most of its open texture without losing structure.

A

B

C

D

E

Foundation ring: Using yarn A, make a magic ring, ch 3 (counts as 1 tr), 11 tr in ring, sl st in top of beg ch-3 to join. Fasten off yarn A and tighten magic ring well.

Round 2: Join yarn B, ch 4 (counts as 1 dtr), 1 dtr in each of next 3 tr, *[ch 5, 1 dtr] in same sp (forms corner), 1 dtr in each of next 3 tr; rep from * 2 times working final dtr in same st as first dtr, ch 5, sl st in top of beg ch-4 to join. Fasten off yarn B.

Round 3: Join yarn C, ch 4 (counts as 1 dtr), 1 dtr in each of next 3 dtr, 4 dtr in next ch-5 sp, ch 4, 3 dtr around vertical post of last dtr made, 3 dtr in same ch-5 sp, *1 dtr in each of next 4 dtr, 4 dtr in next ch-5 sp, ch 4, 3 dtr around vertical post of last dtr made, 3 dtr in same ch-5 sp; rep from * 2 times, sl st in top of beg ch-4 to join. Fasten off yarn C.

Round 4: Join yarn D, ch 5 (counts as 1 ttr), 1 ttr in each of next 7 sts, *3 ttr in next ch-4 sp, ch 5, 4 ttr around vertical post of last ttr made**, 1 ttr in each of next 14 sts; rep from * 2 times then from * to ** 1 time, 1 ttr in each of next 6 dtr, sl st in top of beg ch-5 to join. Fasten off yarn D.

Round 5: Join yarn E in any corner, *ch 2 (forms corner), 1 dc in each of next next 21 sts, 6 dc in next ch-5 sp ; rep from * 3 times, st st in top of beg ch-2 to join.

Round 6: Ch 2 (counts as 1 dc), *2 dc in next st (forms corner), 1 dc in each of next 25 sts; rep from * 3 times, sl st in top of beg ch-2 to join.

Fasten off and darn in ends.

338

** daisy doodle

A creative filigree flower that is fascinating to make, and that looks stunning used in multiples for throws or light afghans.

A
B
C

Foundation ring: Using yarn A, begin with magic ring method.

Round 1: Ch 1, 16 dc in ring, sl st in first dc to join.

Round 2: Ch 8 (counts as 1 tr, 5 ch), 1 tr in 6th ch from hook, *miss 1 dc, 1 tr in next dc, ch 5, 1 tr in top of last tr; rep from * to end of round, sl st in 3rd ch of beg ch-8 to join. Fasten off yarn A.

Round 3: Join yarn B, ch 9 (counts as 1 dtr, 5 ch), 1 tr in 6th ch from hook, *1 tr in next ch-5 sp, ch 5, 1 tr in top of last tr**, 1 dtr in next tr, ch 5, 1 tr in top of last dtr; rep from * to end of rnd ending last rep at **, sl st in 4th ch of beg ch-9 to join. Fasten off yarn B.

Round 4: Join yarn C, sl to first ch-5 sp, ch 3, 2 tr, ch 3, 3 tr (first corner), ch 2, *[1 dc in ch-5 sp, ch 2] 3 times, 3 tr, ch 3, 3 tr in next ch-5 sp, ch 2; rep from * 3 times ending with [1 dc in ch-5 sp, ch 2] 3 times, sl st in top of beg ch-3 to join.

Round 5: Sl st in first 2 tr of first corner, sl st in ch-3 sp, ch 3, 2 tr, ch 3, 3 tr (first corner) *ch 1, 1 tr in every st and every ch sp along side of motif (13 tr), ch 1, [3 tr, ch 3, 3 ch] in next corner ch-3 sp; rep from * 2 times, end with ch 1, 13 tr, ch 1, sl st in top of beg ch-3 to join. Fasten off yarn C.

Round 6: Join yarn B, sl to first ch-3 sp, ch 3, 6 tr in ch-3 sp (first corner) *1 tr in every tr and every ch-1 sp along side of motif (21 tr), 7 tr in next corner ch-3 sp; rep from * 2 times, end with 21 tr, sl st in beg ch-3 to join.

339

** dhurrie

Inspired by the hand-woven carpets of India and the East, this colourful, solid square uses the intarsia method of changing colour (see page 17). Here, toning shades of the same colour have been used in the horizontal stripes to achieve an interesting shadowed effect.

A
B
C
D

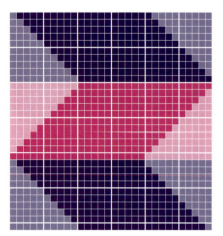

Notes: Beginning at bottom RH corner of chart, work 31 rows of chart in dc. When foll chart, read odd-numbered (RS) rows from right to left, and even-numbered (WS) rows from left to right. Use a separate ball of yarn for each area of colour, change colours where indicated. Keep all yarn ends at back (WS) of work.

Before you begin, prepare 2 small balls each of yarns A and C.

Foundation chain: Using one ball of yarn A, ch 31 (counts as 30 sts, 1 tch), turn.

Begin chart as follows:

Row 1: (RS) 1 dc in 2nd ch from hook and in each ch to end, turn – 30 sts.

Rows 2 to 31: Ch 1, 1 dc in every dc, turn.

Finishing row: Using yarn A, with RS facing, sl st through front lp of every dc along row to end.

Fasten off and darn in all ends neatly.

grapevine

A

A simple, stable mesh fabric block that is useful for mixing with solid textural blocks or with more patterned squares. It is good for more contemporary lightweight throws; you could add more rows to the border, or change its colour to vary the design.

Foundation chain: Ch 27, turn.

Row 1: 1 dc in 2nd ch from hook, 1 dc in each ch to end, turn.

Row 2: Ch 2, 1 tr in first dc, ch 2, *miss next 2 dc, tr2tog in next dc, ch 2; rep from * to end, ending tr2tog.

Rows 3 to 11: Ch 2, 1 tr in first st, ch 2, *tr2tog in tr2tog of last rnd, ch 2; rep from * to end, 2 tr in last tr2tog. Fasten off.

Row 12: Work a border of dc on three sides (4th side already has dc border as Round 1), join yarn in foundation rnd at corner, 3 dc in each tr2tog (working in vertical post of each st) and 1 dc in base of each st along vertical sides of block, 1 dc in every st along bottom of block, sl st in last dc to join.

Fasten off, darn ends in.

341

mallow

A
B
C

This block has a 3D quality and would look great in a blanket or afghan as a field of flowers, or put four together for a stylish pillow. Best worked in a flat, smooth yarn to accentuate the flower's dimensional qualities.

Foundation ring: Using yarn A, ch 5, sl st in first ch to form ring.

Round 1: Ch 4 (counts as 1 tr, ch 1), *1 tr in ring, ch 1; rep from * 6 times, sl st in 3rd ch of beg ch-4 to join.

Round 2: Ch 3 (counts as 1 tr), 1 tr in same st, ch 2, *2 tr in next tr; rep from * 6 times, sl st in top of beg ch-3 to join.

Round 3: *Ch 4 (counts as 1 dtr), 1 dtr in same st, [1 dtr, ch 4, sl st] in next tr, ch 2, sl st in next tr; rep from * 7 times, sl st in base of beg ch-4 to join. Fasten off yarn A.

Round 4: Join yarn B, sl st in top of first dtr, ch 2, 1 dc in same dtr, 1 dc in next dtr, *ch 5, 1 dc in each of next 2 dtr, ch 3, 1 dc in each of next 2 dtr; rep from * 3 times omitting last 2 dc and ending ch 3, sl st in first dc to join.

Round 5: Ch 3 (counts as 1 tr), 1 tr in next dc, *[4 tr, ch 3, 4 tr] in ch-5 sp, 1 tr in each of next 2 dc, 5 tr in ch-3 sp, 1 tr in next 2 dc; rep from * 3 times omitting last 2 tr, sl st in top of beg ch-3 to join.

Round 6: Ch 3 (counts as 1 tr), 1 tr in same sp, 1 tr in each of next 4 tr, *5 tr in ch-3 sp, 1 tr in each of next 17 tr; rep from * 3 times, ending with 1 tr in each of last 11 tr, sl st in first dc to join. Fasten off yarn B.

Round 7: Sl st yarn A to centre (3rd st) of corner 5-tr group, ch 3 (counts as 1 tr), 2 tr, ch 3, 3 tr in same st, *21 tr**, 5 tr in next tr; rep from * to end of rnd ending last rep at **, sl st in beg ch-3 to join. Fasten off yarn A.

Round 8: Join yarn C (work Round 8 over Round 2), sl st in ch-2 sp of Round 2, ch 3 (counts as 1 tr), 2 tr, ch 3, *3 tr in next ch-2 sp, ch 3; rep from * 6 times, sl st in top of beg ch-3 to join.

Fasten off and darn in ends.

269

★★★
flurry

This snowflake was developed from a vintage doily but has been given a modern touch by picking out the motif in a contrasting colour. Best worked in relatively thinner yarn to the hook ratio. Mix with other snow-theme squares for a festive throw, or give it centre stage in festive table linens.

A

B

Special stitch used:

Picot-5: Ch 5 (at point to add picot), sl st in first ch of ch-5, creating picot loop.

Note: Use small separate balls of each yarn for each colour area (6 of each), unless you want to carry yarn across when not in use.

Foundation ring: Using yarn A, ch 4, sl st in first ch to form ring.

Round 1: Ch 4 (counts as 1 dtr), * 23 dtr in ring, sl st in top of beg ch-4 to join.

Round 2: Ch 3 (counts as 1 tr), [1 tr, ch 2, 2 tr] in same st, join yarn B, ch 3, *miss 3 sts, with yarn A [2 tr, ch 2, 2 tr] in next st, with yarn B ch 3; rep from * 4 times, sl st in top of beg ch-3 to join.

Round 3: With yarn A, sl st in next ch-2 sp between 2 tr sts, [ch 3, 1 tr, ch 2, 2 tr] in ch-2 sp, with yarn B, ch 3, 1 tr in next ch-3 sp, ch 3, *with yarn A, [2 tr, ch 2, 2 tr] in next ch-2 sp, with yarn B, ch 3, 1 tr in next ch-3 sp, ch 3; rep from * 4 times, sl st in top of beg ch-3 to join.

Round 4: With yarn A, sl st in ch-2 sp between 2 tr sts, [ch 3, 1 tr, ch 2, 2 tr] in ch-2 sp, with yarn B, ch 3, [1 tr, ch 3, 1 tr] in next tr, ch 3, *with yarn A [2 tr, ch 2, 2 tr] in next ch-2 sp, with yarn B, ch 3, [1 tr, ch 3, 1 tr] in next tr; rep from * 4 times, sl st in top of beg ch-3 to join.

Round 5: With yarn A, sl st in ch-2 sp between 2 tr sts, [ch 3, 1 tr, ch 2, 2 tr] in ch-2 sp, with yarn B, ch 3, miss next ch-3 sp, [1 dtr, picot-5, 1 dtr, ch 5, 1 dtr, picot-5, 1 dtr] in next ch-3 sp, miss next ch-3 sp, ch 3, *with yarn A, [2 tr, ch 2, 2 tr] in next ch-2 sp, with yarn B, ch 3, miss next ch-3 sp, [1 dtr, picot-5, 1 dtr, ch 5, 1 dtr, picot-5, 1 dtr] in next ch-3 sp, miss next ch-3 sp, ch 3; rep from * 4 times, sl st in top of beg ch-3 to join. Fasten off yarn A.

Round 6: Join yarn B in any ch 2 sp between 2 tr sts, ch 3 (counts as 1 tr), 1 tr in same ch-2 sp, *ch 4, 1 dc in next ch-5 sp, ch 4, 2 tr in next ch-2 sp, ch 4, [2 ttr, ch 2, 2 dtr, ch 2, 2 tr] in next ch-5 sp, ch 5, 2 tr in next ch-2 sp, ch 5, [2 tr, ch 2, 2 dtr, ch 2, 2 ttr] in next ch-5 sp, ch 4, 2 tr in next ch-2 sp; rep from * 2 times omitting last 2 tr on last rep, sl st in top of beg ch-3 to join.

Round 7: Ch 1, *1 dc in each of next 2 sts, 4 dc in next ch-4 sp, 1 dc in next st, 4 dc in next ch-4 sp, 1 dc in each of next 2 sts, 4 dc in next ch-4 sp, 1 dc in each of next 2 sts, 3 dc in next ch-2 sp, 1 dc in each of next 2 sts, 2 dc in next ch-2 sp, 1 dc in each of next 2 sts, 5 dc in next ch-5 sp, 1 dc in each of next 2 sts, 5 dc in next ch-5 sp, 1 dc in each of next 2 sts, 2 dc in next ch-2 sp, 1 dc in each of next 2 sts, 3 dc in next ch-2 sp, 1 dc in each of next 2 sts, 4 dc in next ch-4 sp; rep from * 1 time, sl st in first dc to join. Fasten off yarn B.

Round 8: Join yarn A in any middle dc of any corner, *[1 dc, 2 ch, 1 dc] in middle corner st, 1 dc in each st to next corner, [1 dc, ch 2, 1 dc] in each middle corner st; rep from * 3 times, sl st in first dc to join.

Fasten off and darn in ends.

✶✶

cupcakes

Four delicious mini cupcakes in a baking tin, this fun square is relatively easy to work and allows scope for you to vary the toppings to your own tastes. Perfect for a child's pillow or blanket.

Special stitches used:

Make bobble (MB): Make bobble using 4 tr (see page 19).

Front-post double crochet (FPsc): See page 21 for how to work post stitches.

CUPCAKE 1: FLOWER CAKE

Foundation ring: Using yarn A, make a magic ring.

Round 1: Ch 1, 6 dc in ring, sl st in first dc to join.

Round 2: Ch 1, *[1 dc, 1 htr, 1 dc] in front lp of next dc; rep from * 5 times. Fasten off yarn A.

Round 3: Join yarn B in back lp of any dc from Round 1, ch 1, 1 dc in same sp, [1 dc in back lp of next dc, 2 dc in back lp of next dc] 5 times, 1 dc in back lp of last dc, sl st in first dc to join.

Round 4: Ch 2 (counts as 1 htr), [1 htr in next dc, 2 htr in next dc] 5 times, 1 htr in last dc, sl st in top of beg ch-2 to join. Fasten off yarn B.

Round 5: Join yarn C, ch 1, *1 FPdc in each of next 2 htr, ch 2; rep to end, sl st in first FPdc to join. Fasten off yarn C.

Round 6: Join yarn D in any htr of Round 4, *[ch 2, 1 htr, ch 2, 2 htr] in same st, 1 dc in each of next 6 htr; rep from * 3 times, sl st in top of beg ch-2 to join. Fasten off yarn D.

CUPCAKE 2: CHERRY

Foundation ring: Using yarn B, make a magic ring.

Round 1: Ch 1, 6 dc in ring, sl st in first dc to join.

Round 2: Ch 1, 2 dc in every dc to end, sl st in first dc to join.

Complete as for Cupcake 1 from Round 3 onwards.

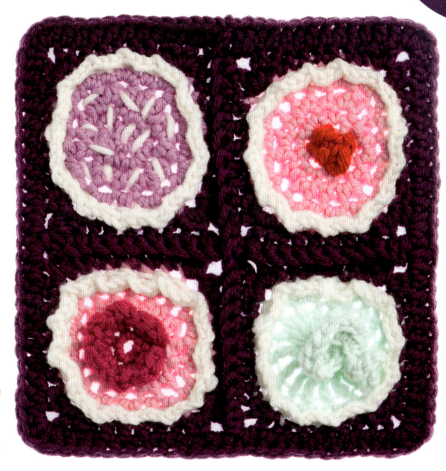

CUPCAKE 3: SPRINKLES

Complete as for Cupcake 2, using yarn E instead of B.

CUPCAKE 4: SWIRL

Using yarn F, ch 16, 3 dc in 2nd ch from hook, 3 dc in each of next 4 ch, 3 htr in each of next 3 ch, 3 tr in each of next 3 ch, 3 dtr in each of last 3 ch, curl the structure around so that it sits in a circle, sl st last ch to where it meets last rnd of sts (16 sts back), to secure.

Round 1: Ch 2, *2 htr in next st, 1 htr in next st; rep from * to end, sl st in top of beg ch-2 to join. Fasten off yarn F.

Round 2: Using yarn C, rep Round 4 of Cupcake 1.

Round 3: Join yarn D in any htr of Round 1, *[ch 2, 1 htr, ch 2, 2 htr] in same st, 1 dc in each of next 2 sts, 2 dc in next st, 1 dc in each of next 2 sts; rep from * to end, sl st in top of beg ch-2 to join. Fasten off yarn D.

TRIMS/FINISHING

Cupcake 1: Darn in ends.

Cupcake 2: Using yarn G, sl st in centre of cupcake, on RS, ch 3, MB, fasten off.

Cupcake 3: Using a length of yarn F, embroider sprinkles using straight stitch in a random pattern all over top of cupcake.

Cupcake 4: Stitch top of swirl down to secure.

JOINING

Place 2 squares WS tog, using yarn D, work 1 dc between each of pair of sts along whole join, add next pair of squares, continue to end, fasten off yarn, rotate 90 degrees and work other long join to join all 4 squares tog. Fasten off.

BORDER

Join yarn D, ch 2, *1 htr in every st and 2 htr in every ch-2 sp in centre corner of composite square, 3 htr in corner; rep from * to end, sl st in top of beg ch-2 to join.

Fasten off and darn in all ends.

* lewes

A simple, classic granny that dispenses with chain-1 spaces to create a slightly denser block than usual. Great for creating harmonious, rich colour combinations as there are many rounds to enjoy.

A
B
C
D
E
F

Foundation ring: Using yarn A, ch 4, sl st in first ch to form ring.

Round 1: Ch 3 (counts as 1 tr), 2 tr in ring, ch 2, *3 tr in ring, ch 2; rep from * 2 times, sl st in top of beg ch-3 to join. Fasten off yarn A.

Round 2: Join yarn B in any ch-2 corner sp, ch 3 (counts as 1 tr), [2 tr, ch 2, 3 tr] in same ch-2 corner sp, *[3 tr, ch 2, 3 tr] in next ch-2 corner sp; rep from * 2 times, sl st in top of beg ch-3 to join. Fasten off yarn B.

Round 3: Join yarn C in any ch-2 corner sp, ch 3 (counts as 1 tr), [2 tr, ch 2, 3 tr] in same ch-2 corner sp, *miss 3 sts, 3 tr in gap between tr cls, *[3 tr, ch 2, 3 tr] in next ch-2 corner sp; rep from * 2 times, miss 3 sts, 3 tr in gap between tr cls, sl st in top of beg ch-3 to join. Fasten off yarn C.

Round 4: Join yarn D in any ch-2 corner sp, ch 3 (counts as 1 tr), [2 tr, ch 2, 3 tr] in same ch-2 corner sp, *[miss 3 sts, 3 tr in gap between tr cls] 2 times, *[3 tr, ch 2, 3 tr] in next ch-2 corner sp; rep from * 2 times, [miss 3 sts, 3 tr in gap between tr cls] 2 times, sl st in top of beg ch-3 to join. Fasten off yarn D.

Round 5: Join yarn E in any ch-2 corner sp, ch 3 (counts as 1 tr), [2 tr, ch 2, 3 tr] in same ch-2 corner sp, *[miss 3 sts, 3 tr in gap between tr cls] 3 times, *[3 tr, ch 2, 3 tr] in next ch-2 corner sp; rep from * 2 times, [miss 3 sts, 3 tr in gap between tr cls] 3 times, sl st in top of beg ch-3 to join. Fasten off yarn E.

Round 6: Join F in any ch-2 corner sp, ch 3 (counts as 1 tr), [2 tr, ch 2, 3 tr] in same ch-2 corner sp, *[miss 3 sts, 3 tr in gap between tr cls] 4 times, *[3 tr, ch 2, 3 tr] in next ch-2 corner sp; rep from * 2 times, [miss 3 sts, 3 tr in gap between tr cls] 4 times, sl st in top of beg ch-3 to join. Fasten off yarn F.

Round 7: Join A in any ch-2 corner sp, ch 3 (counts as 1 tr), [2 tr, ch 2, 3 tr] in same ch-2 corner sp, *[miss 3 sts, 3 tr in gap between tr cls] 5 times, *[3 tr, ch 2, 3 tr] in next ch-2 corner sp; rep from * 2 times, [miss 3 sts, 3 tr in gap between tr cls] 5 times, sl st in top of beg ch-3 to join. Fasten off yarn A.

Round 8: Join B in any ch-2 corner sp, ch 3 (counts as 1 tr), [2 tr, ch 2, 3 tr] in same ch-2 corner sp, *[miss 3 sts, 3 tr in gap between tr cls] 6 times, *[3 tr, ch 2, 3 tr] in next ch-2 corner sp; rep from * 2 times, [miss 3 sts, 3 tr in gap between tr cls] 6 times, sl st in top of beg ch-3 to join.

Round 9: Ch 1, *1 dc in each st to corner, 3 dc sts in each corner sp; rep from * 3 times, sl st in first dc to join.

Fasten off and darn in ends.

* mulberry shell

An open and lacy square with a pretty shell centre, this block is perfect to combine with other lightweight lace blocks for a summer throw, or to make a stunning table runner.

A
B
C

Foundation ring: Using yarn A, make a magic ring.

Round 1: Ch 3 (counts as 1 tr), 7 tr in ring, sl st in top of beg ch-3 to join.

Round 2: Ch 5 (counts as 1 tr, ch 2), *1 tr in next tr, ch 2; rep from * 6 times, sl st in 3rd ch of beg ch-5 to join. Fasten off yarn A.

Round 3: Join yarn B, ch 3 in same st (counts as 1 tr), 3 tr in next ch-2 sp, *1 tr in next tr, 3 tr in next ch-2 sp; rep from * 6 times, sl st in top of beg ch-3 to join. Fasten off yarn B.

Round 4: Join yarn C, ch 1, 1 dc in same st, *ch 9, miss 3 tr, 1 dc in next tr; rep from * 6 times, ch 9, sl st in first dc to join. Fasten off yarn C.

Round 5: Join yarn A to centre st of next ch-9 lp, ch 1, 1 dc in same st, *ch 8, 1 dc in centre st of next ch-9 lp; rep from * 7 times, ending last rep with sl st in first dc to join.

Round 6: Ch 1 and sl st in same dc, *9 dtr in 4th ch of next ch-8 lp, 1 dc in next dc; rep from * 7 times, sl st in first dc to join. Fasten off yarn A.

Round 7: Join yarn B to centre dtr of any 9-dtr shell, ch 1, 1 dc in same st, *ch 11, 1 dc in 5th dtr next 9-dtr shell; rep from * 7 times, sl sl in first dc to join. Fasten off yarn B.

Round 8: Ch 3 (counts as 1 tr), [7 tr, ch 4, 8 tr] in same ch-11 sp (forms corner), *ch 1, [1 tr in next sp, ch 2] 4 times in next ch-11 sp, **[8 tr, ch 4, 8 tr] in next ch-11 sp (forms corner); rep from * 2 times, then from * to ** 1 time, sl st in top of beg ch-3 to join.

Fasten off and darn in ends neatly.

* nana square

A twist on the usual granny, this block is a great beginner square that combines basic stitches to striking effect and mixes well with other basic blocks. Use dramatic colours or create a bright centre as a focus point.

A
B
C
D

Foundation ring: Using yarn A, ch 4, sl st in first ch to join.

Round 1: Ch 3 (counts as 1 tr), 2 tr in ring, *ch 3, 3 tr in ring; rep from * 2 times, ch 3, sl st in top of beg ch-3 to join. Fasten off yarn A.

Round 2: Join yarn B in any ch-3 corner sp, ch 3 (counts as 1 tr), [2 tr, ch 3, 3 tr] in same sp (forms corner), [3 tr, ch 3, 3 tr] in next corner sp; rep 2 times, sl st in top of beg ch-3 to join. Fasten off yarn B.

Round 3: Join yarn C in any ch-3 corner sp, ch 3 (counts as 1 tr), [2 tr, ch 3, 3 tr] in same sp (forms corner), *3 tr in next sp between tr groups**, [3 tr, ch 3, 3 tr] in next corner sp; rep from * 2 times, then from * to ** 1 time, sl st in top of beg ch-3 to join. Fasten off yarn C.

Round 4: Join yarn D in any ch-3 corner sp, ch 3 (counts as 1 tr), [2 tr, ch 3, 3 tr] in same sp, 1 tr in each of next 9 sts, *[3 tr, ch 3, 3 tr] in next sp (forms corner), 1 tr in each of the next 9 sts; rep from * 2 times, sl st in top of beg ch-3 to join. Fasten off yarn D.

Round 5: Join yarn A in any ch-3 corner sp, ch 3 (counts as 1 tr), [2 tr, ch 3, 3 tr] in same sp, 1 tr in each of next 15 sts, *[3 tr, ch 3, 3 tr] in next sp (forms corner), 1 tr in each of the next 15 sts; rep from * 2 times, sl st in top of beg ch-3 to join. Fasten off yarn A.

Round 6: Join yarn B in any ch-3 corner sp, ch 3 (counts as 1 tr), [2 tr, ch 3, 3 tr] in same sp, 1 tr in each of the next 21 sts, *[3 tr, ch 3, 3 tr] in next sp (forms corner), 1 tr in each of the next 21 sts; rep from * 2 times, sl st in top of beg ch-3 to join. Fasten off yarn B.

Round 7: Join yarn D to any ch-3 corner sp, ch 3 (counts as 1 tr), [2 tr, ch 3, 3 tr] in same sp, 1 tr in each of the next 27 sts, *[3 tr, ch 3, 3 tr] in next sp (forms corner), 1 tr in each of the next 27 sts; rep from * 2 times, sl st in top of beg ch-3 to join.

Fasten off and darn in ends.

347

***

garland

Twelve pink and purple flowers adorn this block, each attached to the next as the work progresses. This square offers plenty of scope for creating your own colour combinations and it is easy to work to a larger size by simply increasing the number of flowers made.

A
B
C
D

FIRST FLOWER

Foundation ring: Using yarn A, ch 4, sl st in first ch to form ring.

Round 1: Ch 1, 12 dc in ring.

Round 2: *Ch 2, 2 tr in next dc, ch 2, sl st in same st, miss 1 dc; rep from * 5 times – one 6-petal flower made.

SECOND FLOWER

Foundation ring/Round 1: Using yarn B, work as first flower until Round 2.

Round 2: [Ch 2, 2 tr in next dc, ch 2, sl st] in same st, miss 1 dc, ch 2, 1 tr in next dc, sl st in petal of last flower, [1 tr, ch 2, sl st] in same st of 2nd flower, *[ch 2, 2 tr, ch 2,

sl st] in next dc on 2nd flower, miss 1 dc; rep from * 4 times – one 6-petal flower joined to another flower at one petal.

Make another 10 flowers in same way, joining 2, 3 or 4 petals to other flowers where necessary, as you work rnds. Make outer flowers then inner ones. Make a total of 4 flowers in each of 3 colours.

BORDER

Round 1: Join yarn D in corner petal of corner flower, *[1 dc, ch 2, 1 dc] in same st (forms corner), [ch 4, 1 dc in next petal of same flower, ch 8, 1 dc in petal of next flower] 2 times; rep from * 3 times, ch 4, sl st in first dc to join.

Round 2: Sl st in next ch-2 corner sp, *[2 dc, ch 1, 2 dc] in corner sp, [4 dc in ch-4 sp, 8 dc in ch-8 sp] 2 times, 4 dc in ch-4 sp, rep from * 3 times.

Fasten off and darn in all ends.

348

*

live wire

A filet variation, this lightweight mesh uses chains to create a wavy structure. Quick to work up, this block is great for light summer throws or curtain panels. You may find it useful to use two small balls of each colour and to carry the yarn up the side of the block to avoid loads of yarn tails to sew in.

A
B

Foundation chain: Using yarn A, ch 33.

Row 1: 1 tr in 5th ch from hook, *ch 1, miss 1 ch, 1 tr in next ch; rep from * to end, turn.

Row 2: Using yarn B, ch 5, 1 dc in next tr, *ch 5, miss 1 ch, 1 dc in next dc; rep from * to end of row, ending last rep with 1 dc, ch 5, 1 dc in last ch, turn.

Row 3: Using yarn A, insert hook in 3rd ch of last ch-5 lp, ch 3 (counts as 1 tr, ch 1), 1 tr in 3rd ch of next ch-5 lp,* ch 1, 1 tr in 3rd ch of next ch-5 lp; rep from * to end of row, turn.

Rows 4, 6, 8, 10, 12 and 14: Rep Row 2.

Rows 5, 7, 9, 11, 13 and 15: Rep Row 3.

Fasten off and darn in ends neatly.

✱✱
bloom

A layered flower makes up this sister block to Blossom; this is an easier flower to make, so is a good option for beginners wanting to improve their skills and to learn to work in multiple layers. Great for use in children's blankets because of its tactile appeal.

Foundation ring: Using yarn A, ch 6, sl st in first ch to form ring.

Round 1: Ch 1, 16 dc in ring, sl st in first dc to join.

Round 2: Ch 4 (counts as 1 htr, ch 2), miss next dc, *1 htr in next dc, ch 2, miss next dc; rep from * to end, sl st 2nd ch of beg ch-4 to join – 8 ch-3 sps.

Round 3: Sl st in first ch-2 sp, *[1 dc, 1 htr, 1 tr, 1 htr, 1 dc] in same ch-2 sp, sl st in next ch-2 sp; rep from * to end, sl st in first dc to join. Fasten off yarn A.

Round 4: (WS) Join yarn B around any post of any htr from Round 2, *ch 6, sl st around post of next htr from Round 2; rep from * to end, sl st in first ch to join.

Round 5: (RS) Sl st in first ch-6 sp, *[1 dc, 1 htr, 3 tr, 1 htr, 1 dc] in same ch-6 sp, sl st in next ch-6 sp; rep from * to end, sl st in first dc to join. Fasten off yarn B.

Round 6: (WS) Join yarn C with sl st around any post of Round 4 (behind post of Round 2), *ch 6, sl st around next post; rep from * 7 times, sl st in first ch-6 sp.

Round 7: (RS) *[1 dc, 4 tr, ch 3, 4 tr, 1 dc] in ch-6 sp, sl st in next ch-6 sp; rep from * 7 times, sl st in first dc to join. Fasten off yarn C.

A
B
C
D

Round 8: (WS) Join yarn D around any post of any htr from Round 6, ch 10, miss next htr post, *sl st around post of next htr from Round 6, ch 10; rep from * 2 times, sl st in first ch-10 sp – 4 ch-10 sps.

Round 9: Ch 3 (counts as 1 tr), [4 tr, ch 3, 5 tr] in same ch-10 sp, *[5 tr, ch 3, 5 tr] in next ch-10 sp; rep from * 6 times, sl st in top of ch-3 to join. Fasten off yarn D.

Round 10: Join yarn D in any ch-3 corner sp, ch 1, *[2 htr, ch 3, 2 htr] in corner sp, 1 htr in every tr to next corner sp; rep from * 3 times, 1 htr in every tr to end, sl st in first ch to join, sl st in next corner ch-3 sp.

Round 11: Ch 3 (counts as 1 tr), [1 tr, ch 3, 2 tr] in corner sp, *1 tr in every st to next corner sp, **[2 tr, ch 3, 2 tr] in next corner ch-3 sp; rep from * 2 times and from * to ** 1 time, sl st in top of beg ch-3 to join, sl st in next corner ch-3 sp.

Rounds 12 to 13: As Round 11.

Fasten off and darn in ends.

**

rosetta

A separate medallion is attached to a simple filet grid, offering the opportunity to play with placement to your own preference. Try a dark filet ground and a bright medallion, or go for pastel hues for a summery feel.

A
B
C
D

FILET GRID

Foundation chain: Using yarn A, ch 31.

Row 1: Ch 4 (counts as 1 tr,*ch 1) miss 1 ch,1 tr in next ch; rep from * to end, turn.

Rows 2 to 15: Rep Row 1, fasten off yarn A.

BORDER

Round 1: Join yarn B, ch 1, *1 dc in every st and every ch-1 sp to next corner, [1 dc, ch 1, 1 dc] in corner st, work 29 dc evenly along side of square to next corner, [1 dc, ch 1, 1 dc] in corner st; rep from * 1 time, sl st in first dc to join. Fasten off yarn B.

MEDALLION

Foundation ring: Using yarn A, ch 6, sl st in first ch to form ring.

Round 1: 9 dc in ring, sl st in first dc to join, fasten off yarn A.

Round 2: Using yarn C [1 dc in next dc, ch 1] to end, sl st in first dc to join, fasten off yarn C.

Round 3: Using yarn D, rep Round 2.

Round 4: Using yarn B, 1 dc in every dc and in every ch-1 sp to end, sl st in first dc to join, fasten off yarn B.

Round 5: Using yarn C, rep Round 4.

Round 6: Using yarn B, rep Round 2.

Round 7: Rep Round 6.

Round 8: Rep Round 4.

Round 9: Using yarn A, ch 6 (counts as 1 tr, *ch 3), miss 1 sts, 1 tr in next tr; rep from * to end, ending with ch 3, sl st in 3rd ch of beg ch-6 to join, fasten off yarn A.

Round 10: Using yarn D, insert hook in 2nd ch of ch-3 sp, ch 8 (counts as 1 tr, *ch 5) miss 3 sts, 1 tr in next tr; rep from * to end, finishing with ch 5, sl st in 3rd ch of beg ch-8 to join.

Fasten off and darn in ends. Using a length of yarn B and a blunt darning needle, attach medallion to filet grid with a series of short stitches, wherever you want.

**

tidal

The undulating wave pattern is created by increasing and decreasing stitches to distort the rows. This block is very straightforward to work up and would be lovely used in a window treatment in repeat, or for a pretty throw.

A
B
C

Foundation chain: Using yarn A, ch 32 (counts as ch 29, 1 tr).

Row 1: Miss 3 ch, *[2 tr in next st] 2 times, 1 tr in each of next 2 sts, tr2tog 2 times, 1 tr in each of next 2 sts; rep from * 2 times, [2 tr in next st] 2 times, 1 tr in each of next 2 sts, tr2tog 2 times, 1 tr in last st. Fasten off yarn A.

Row 2: Join yarn B, ch 3 (counts as 1 tr), turn, *tr2tog 2 times, 1 tr in each of next 2 sts, [2 tr in next st] 2 times, 1 tr in each of next 2 sts; rep from * 2 times, tr2tog 2 times, 1 tr in each of next 2 sts, [2 tr in next st] 2 times, 1 tr in last st. Fasten off yarn B.

Row 3: Join yarn C, ch 3 (counts as 1 tr), turn, *[2 tr in next st] 2 times, 1 tr in each of next 2 sts, tr2tog 2 times, 1 tr in each of next 2 sts; rep from * 2 times, [2 tr in next st] 2 times, 1 tr in each of next 2 sts, tr2tog 2 times, 1 tr in last st. Fasten off yarn C.

Row 4: Join yarn A, rep Row 2.

Row 5: Join yarn B, rep Row 3.

Row 6: Join yarn C, rep Row 2.

Row 7: Join yarn A, rep Row 3.

Row 8: Join yarn B, rep Row 2.

Row 9: Join yarn C, rep Row 3.

Rows 10 to 14: Repeat Rows 4 to 8.

Fasten off, darn in ends and block to shape if necessary.

★★

heartfelt

A funky twist on the traditional granny, this block has a warm, homespun feel and would look great in a classic afghan. The scalloped edges provide additional interest, creating fun possibilities for joining multiples.

A
B
C
D

Foundation ring: Using yarn A, begin with magic ring method.

Round 1: Ch 3, 2 dtr, 4 tr, ch 1, 1 dtr, ch 1, 4 tr, 2 dtr, ch 2, sl st in beg ch-3 to join.

Round 2: 3 dc around post of beg ch-3 of Round 1, 1 dc in each of next 6 sts, 1 dc in-ch 1 sp, [1 dc, 1 htr, 1 dc] in next dtr, 1 dc in ch-1 sp, 1 dc in each of next 6 sts, 3 dc around post of ch-2, sl st in first dc to join. Fasten off yarn A.

Round 3: Join yarn B, sl st in centre crook of heart, [ch 4, 2 dtr] in same st, ch 1, miss 2 sts, 3 tr in next st (top of heart curve), ch 3, 3 tr in next st, ch 1, miss 1 st, 3 tr in next st, ch 1, miss 1 st, 3 tr in next st, ch 3, 3 tr in next st, ch 1, miss 2 sts, 3 dc in next st (point of heart), ch 1, miss 2 sts, 3 tr in next st, ch 3, 3 tr in next st, ch 1, miss 1 st, 3 tr in next st, ch 1, miss 1 st, 3 tr in next

st, ch 3, 3 tr in next st, ch 1, sl st in top of beg ch-4 to join. Fasten off yarn B.

Round 4: Join yarn C, sl st in first ch-3 sp, [ch 3, 2 tr, 3 ch, 3 tr] in same ch-3 sp, *ch 1, 3 tr in ch-1 sp, 1 ch, 3 tr in next ch-1 sp, ch 1**, [3 tr, ch 3, 3 tr] in next ch-3 sp; rep from * to end of rnd ending last rep at **, sl st in top of beg ch-3 to join.

Round 5: Sl st in top of next tr and in ch-3 sp, [ch 3, 2 tr, 3 ch, 3 tr] in same ch-3 sp, *[ch 1, 3 tr in next ch-1 sp] 3 times, ch 1**, [3 tr, ch 3, 3 tr] in next ch-3 sp; rep from * to end of rnd ending last rep at **, sl st in top of beg ch-3 to join.

Round 6: Sl st in top of next tr and in ch-3 sp, [ch 3, 2 tr, 3 ch, 3 tr] in same ch-3 sp, *[ch 1, 3 tr in next ch-1 sp] 4 times, ch 1**, [3 tr, ch 3, 3 tr] in next ch-3 sp; rep from * to end of rnd ending last rep at **, sl st in top of beg ch-3 to join. Fasten off yarn C.

Round 7: Join yarn D, *sl st in top of 2nd tr of 3-tr cluster after next ch-3 sp**, [5 tr in next ch-1 sp, sl sl in top of next 3-tr cluster] 5 times, 7 tr in ch-3 sp, sl st in top of next 3-tr cluster; rep from * to end of rnd ending last rep at **, sl st in first sl st to join.

Fasten off and darn in ends neatly.

★★★

purple maze

A dimensional pattern worked into a filet base, this block has plenty of tactile appeal and is irresistible to children's fingers. Work it in a light colour on a darker ground for even more depth, and add the surface crochet trim to lead the eye around the structure.

A
B

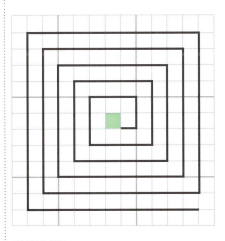

FILET BASE

Foundation chain: Using yarn A, ch 30.

Row 1: 1 tr in ch from hook, *ch 1, miss 1 ch, 1 tr in next ch; rep from * to end, turn.

Row 2: Ch 4 (counts as 1 tr, ch 1), 1 tr in next tr, *ch 1, miss 1 ch, 1 tr in next tr; rep from * to end, ending with last tr in 3rd ch of ch-4 of last row, turn.

Rows 3 to 13: Rep Row 2. Fasten off yarn A.

SPIRAL

Locate centre square on filet base (use chart as a guide, green square is starting point, count 7 squares in, 7 squares down). Join yarn A around vertical post of 8th tr of Row 7 (counting in from left side), ch 3 (counts as 1 tr), 2 tr in same sp, turn work 90 degrees clockwise, 3 tr in next ch-sp, turn work 90 degrees clockwise, 3 tr around post of next tr, turn work 90 degrees clockwise, [3 tr in next ch-3 sp] 2 times, turn work 90 degrees clockwise, 3 tr around post of next tr.

Cont in this way, following chart to place groups of 3 tr in each sp, turning work as indicated until you have created a spiral to last row and column of squares. Fasten off.

TRIM

Using yarn B, begin at centre and with RS facing, sl st along entire edge of spiral to end.

Fasten off and darn in ends.

354

**

elina

A square based on traditional Scandinavian knit designs. When changing colour, the yarn is joined or stranded on the wrong side of the work as required; keep all yarn tails on the wrong side of the work when not in use.

A
B

Foundation chain: Using yarn A, ch 30.

Row 1: (WS) 1 tr in 4th ch from hook, 1 tr in each ch to end, turn.

Row 2: (RS) Ch 2, join yarn B, ch 1 (counts as 1 tr), *1 tr in next tr, change to yarn B, 1 tr in next tr, change to yarn A; rep from * to end, turn.

Row 3: Using yarn A, ch 3 (counts as 1 tr), 1 tr in every tr to end, turn.

Row 4: Using yarn B, rep Row 3.

Row 5: Rep row 4.

Row 6: Ch 3 (counts as 1 tr), 1 tr in each of next 12 tr, change to yarn A, 1 tr in next tr, change to yarn B, 1 tr in each of next 13 tr, turn.

Row 7: Ch 3 (counts as 1 tr), miss 1 tr, 9 tr, change to yarn A, 1 tr, change to yarn B, 1 tr, change to yarn A, 3 tr, change to yarn B, 1 tr, change to yarn A, 1 tr, change to yarn B, 10 tr, turn.

Row 8: Rep Row 6.

Row 9: Ch 3 (counts as 1 tr), miss 1 tr, 1 tr in each of next 7 tr, change to yarn A, 1 tr in each of next 4 tr, change to yarn B, 1 tr in each of next 3 tr, change to yarn A, 1 tr in each of next 4 tr, change to yarn B, 1 tr in each of next 8 tr, turn.

Row 10: Rep Row 8.

Row 11: Rep Row 7.

Row 12: Rep Row 6.

Rows 13 to 14: Rep Row 4.

Row 15: Rep Row 3.

Row 16: Rep Row 2.

Row 17: Rep Row 3.

Fasten off and darn in ends neatly. Block work to shape.

355

**

box lace

This block has an interesting construction and produces a medium-weight fabric suitable for use in summer throws and blankets. Mix it up with other geometrics for a modern feel.

A
B

Foundation row: Using yarn A, ch 30.

Row 1: 1 dc in 9th ch from hook (forms 1 tr and ch-3 sp), turn, ch 1, 1 dc in last dc, 3 dc in ch-3 sp, [turn, ch 1, 1 dc in each of next 4 dc] 3 times, miss next 2 ch on foundation row, 1 tr in next ch, *ch 3, miss next 2 ch on foundation row, 1 dc in next ch, turn, ch 1, 1 dc in last dc, 3 dc in ch-3 sp, [turn, ch 1, 1 dc in each of next 4 dc] 3 times, miss next 2 ch on foundation row, 1 tr in next ch; rep from * to end, turn.

Row 2: Ch 6 (counts as 1d tr, ch 2), miss [1 tr, 3 dc], 1 dc in next dc, ch 2, 1 dtr in next tr, *ch 2, miss 3 dc, 1 dc in next dc, ch 2, 1 dtr in next tr; rep from * to end, ending with last dtr in top of ch of Row 1.

Row 3: Ch 6 (counts as 1 tr, ch 3), 1 dc in first dc, turn, ch 1, 1 dc in last dc, 3 dc in ch-3 sp, [turn, ch 1, 1 dc in each of next 4 dc] 3 times, 1 tr in next dtr, *ch 3, 1 dc in next dc, turn, ch 1, 1 dc in last dc, 3 dc in next ch-3 sp, [turn, ch 1, 1 dc in each of next 4 dc] 3 times, 1 tr in next dtr; rep from * to end, with last tr worked in 4th ch of beg ch-6 of last row, turn.

Row 4: Rep Row 2.

Row 5: Rep Row 3.

Row 6: Rep Row 2.

Row 7: Rep Row 3.

Row 8: Rep Row 2. Fasten off, turn.

BORDER

Join yarn B in any ch-2 sp after the corner, ch 1, 3 dc in same sp, [1 dc in next dc, 2 dc in next ch-sp, 1 dc in next st, 3 dc in next ch-sp] 3 times, 1 dc in next dc, 7 dc in next ch-sp (forms corner), [1 dc in next st, 2 dc in next ch-sp, 1 dc in next st, 3 dc in next ch-sp] 3 times, 1 dc in next st, 7 dc in corner sp, [1 dc in next st, 3 dc in next ch-sp, 1 dc in next dc, 2 dc in next ch-sp] 3 times, 1 dc in next st, 7 dc in corner sp, [1 dc in next st, 3 dc in next ch-sp, 1 dc in next st, 2 dc in next ch-sp] 3 times, 1 dc in last st, 3 dc in corner starting sp, sl st in first dc to join.

Fasten off and darn in ends. Block.

***

popcorn rosette

Popcorns of varying heights make the central ring of this block fun to work and create a lovely bobbly crown. Mix with other circle-in-a-square blocks, or other textural bobble or popcorn blocks for added tactile appeal.

A
B
C

Special stitches used:

5-half-treble crochet popcorn (5-htr pc): Make popcorn with 5 htr, ch 1 to secure.

7-double treble crochet popcorn (7-dtr pc): Make popcorn with 7 dtr sts, ch 1 to secure (*see page 19*).

6-half-treble crochet popcorn (6-htr pc): Make popcorn with 6 htr, ch 1 to secure.

Foundation ring: Using yarn A, make a magic ring.

Round 1: Ch 3 (counts as 1 tr), 23 tr in ring, sl st in top of beg ch-3 to join.

Round 2: Ch 6 (counts as 1 tr, ch 3), [miss 1 tr, 1 tr in next tr, ch 3] 11 times, sl st in 3rd ch of beg ch-6 to join. Fasten off yarn A.

Round 3: Join yarn B in any ch-3 sp, ch 2 (counts as 1 htr), 5-htr pc in same ch-3 sp, *7-dtr pc in next ch-3 sp, 6-htr pc in next ch-3 sp; rep from * 4 times, 7-dtr pc in last ch-3 sp, sl st in top of beg ch-2 to join. Fasten off yarn B.

Round 4: Join yarn A in back of any htr pc, ch 5 (counts as 1 tr, ch 2), *1 dc in back of next dtr pc, ch 2, 1 tr in back of next htr pc, ch 2; rep from * 4 times, 1 dc in back of last dtr pc, sl st in 3rd ch of beg ch-5 to join.

Round 5: Ch 5 (counts as 1 tr, ch 2), 1 tr in next ch-2 sp, ch 1, 1 tr in next dc, *ch 2, 1 tr in next ch-2 sp, ch 1, 1 tr in next tr, ch 2; rep from * to end, sl st in 3rd ch of beg ch-5 to join.

Round 6: Ch 3 (counts as 1 tr), *2 tr in next ch-2 sp, 1 tr in next tr, 1 tr in next ch-1 sp, 1 tr in next tr, 2 tr in next ch-2 sp, 1 tr in next tr, 1 tr in next ch-1 sp, 1 tr in next tr; rep from * to end, sl st in top of beg ch-3 to join. Fasten off yarn A.

Round 7: Join yarn B in any st, ch 1, 1 dc in same st, * ch 6, sl st in same tr, ch 5, miss 4 tr, 1 dc in next tr, ch 4, miss 4 tr, 1 dc in next tr, ch 5, miss 4 tr, 1 dc in next tr; rep from * 3 times, sl st in first dc to join. Fasten off yarn B.

Round 8: Join yarn C in any ch-6 lp, ch 3 (counts as 1 tr), [2 tr, ch 2, 3 tr] in same sp, *[1 tr, ch 2, 1 tr] in next ch-5 sp, ch 2, 1 dc in next dc, ch 1, 3 dc in next ch-4 sp, 1 dc in next dc, ch 2, [1 tr, ch 2, 1 tr] in next ch-5 sp**, [3 tr, ch 2, 3 tr] in next ch-6 sp; rep from * 2 times and from * to ** 1 time, sl st in top of beg ch-3 to join. Fasten off yarn C.

Round 9: Join yarn B in any ch-2 corner sp, ch 2 (counts as 1 htr), [1 htr, ch 1, 2 htr] in same ch-2 sp, *1 htr in each of next 3 tr, 2 dc in next ch-2 sp, ch 1, 2 htr in next ch-2 sp, ch 1 [1 htr, ch 1] in each of next 4 dc, 2 htr in next ch-2 sp, ch 1, 2 dc in next ch-2 sp, ch 1, 1 htr in each of next 3 tr**, [2 htr, ch 1, 2 htr] in next ch-2 sp; rep from * 2 times and from * to ** 1 time, sl st in top of beg ch-2 to join.

Fasten off and darn in ends.

*

merlot

This lace motif would work well in pastels or brights; it has many applications and mixes well with a variety of other lace blocks.

A
B
C

Foundation ring: Using yarn A, ch 4, sl st in first ch to form ring.

Round 1: Ch 8 dc in ring, sl st in first ch to join.

Round 2: Ch 4 (counts as 1 tr, ch 1), [1 tr in next dc, ch 1] 7 times, sl st in 3rd ch of beg ch-4 to join.

Round 3: Ch 3 (counts as 1 tr), 3 tr in next ch-1 sp, [1 tr in next tr, 3 tr in next ch-1 sp] 7 times, sl st in top of beg ch-3 to join. Fasten off yarn A.

Round 4: Join yarn B, ch 9 (counts as 1 dtr, ch 5) 1 dtr in same st, *miss 3 tr, [3 dtr, ch 5, 3 dtr] in next tr, miss 3 tr, [1 dtr, ch 5, 1 dtr] in next tr; rep from * 2 times, miss 3 ch, [3 dtr, ch 5, 3 dtr] in next tr, sl st in 4th ch of beg ch-9. Fasten off yarn B.

Round 5: Join yarn C in any ch-5 sp, *ch 9, 1 dc in next ch-5 lp; rep from * to end, ending with ch 9, sl st in first ch to join.

Round 6: Ch 4, (counts as 1 tr, *ch 1), miss 1 ch, 1 tr in next ch st; rep from * to end, sl st in 3rd ch of beg ch-4 to join.

Round 7: Ch 14 (counts as 1 dtr, ch 11), [miss 9 ch, 1 ttr in next st, ch 11, miss 9 ch, 1 dtr in next ch, ch 11] 3 times, miss 9 ch, 1 ttr in next st, ch 11, sl st in 3rd ch of beg ch-14 to join. Fasten off yarn C.

Round 8: Join yarn B, ch 1, 1 dc in same st, *11 dc in next ch-11 sp, [1 dc, ch 2, 1 dc] in next ttr, 11 dc in next ch-11 sp, 1 dc in next dtr; rep from * 3 times, omitting last dc on last rep, sl st in first dc to join.

Round 9: Ch 3 (counts as 1 tr), *1 tr in every dc to next corner [1 tr, ch 2, 1 tr] in corner ch-2 sp; rep from * 3 times, sl st in top of beg ch-3 to join.

Fasten off and darn in ends.

**

nantucket

A pretty square, this has a textural popcorn stitch border. A smooth cotton yarn emphasises the stitch formations. Suited to bedspreads, throws and cushions.

A

Special stitch used:

Popcorn (pc): Make popcorn with 5 tr (see page 19).

Foundation ring: Ch 4, sl st in first ch to form ring.

Round 1: Ch 5 (counts as 1 tr, ch 2), [3 tr in ring, ch 2] 3 times, 2 tr in ring, sl st in 3rd ch of beg ch-5 to join.

Round 2: Sl st in next sp, ch 7 (counts as 1 tr, ch 4), 2 tr in same sp, *1 tr in each tr along side of square to corner, [2 tr, ch 4, 2 tr] in ch-2 corner sp; rep from * 3 times, 1 tr in each tr along last side of square, 1 tr in same sp as beg ch-7, sl st in 3rd ch of beg ch-7 to join – 4 groups of 7 tr.

Round 3: Rep Row 2, making 4 groups of 11 tr.

Round 4: Sl st in next ch sp, ch 7 (counts as 1 tr, ch 4), 2 tr in same sp, *[1 tr, ch 1, miss 1 tr] 5 times, 1 tr in next tr, [2 tr, ch 4, 2 tr] in next ch-4 sp; rep from * 2 times, [1 trc, ch 1, miss 1 tr] 5 times, 1 tr in same sp as beg ch-7, sl st in 3rd ch of beg ch-7 to join.

Round 5: Sl st in next ch sp, ch 7 (counts as 1 tr, ch 4), 2 tr in same sp, *[1 tr, ch 1, miss 1 tr] 7 times, 1 tr in next tr, [2 tr, ch 4, 2 tr] in next ch-4 sp; rep from * 2 times, [1 trc, ch 1, miss 1 tr] 7 times, 1 tr in same sp as beg ch-7, sl st in 3rd ch of beg ch-7 to join.

Round 6: Sl st in next ch-sp, ch 7 (counts as 1 tr, ch 4), *1 tr in every tr and every ch-1 sp to next corner ch-4 sp**, [2 tr, ch 4, 2 tr] in corner ch-4 sp; rep from * 2 times and from * to ** 1 time, 1 tr in corner sp, sl st in 3rd ch of beg ch-7 to join.

Round 7: Sl st in next ch sp, 2 tr in same sp, *1 tr in next tr, pc in next tr, [1 tr in each of next 3 tr, pc in next tr] 4 times, 1 tr in next tr**, [2 tr, ch 4, 2 tr] in next ch sp; rep from * 2 times and from * to ** 1 time, 1 tr in same ch sp as beg ch-7, sl st in 3rd ch of beg ch-7 to join.

Round 8: Rep Row 2, making 4 groups of 27 tr.

Fasten off and darn in ends.

★★★
mary

Based on a traditional doily pattern, this block is bang up to date with a zingy colour combination. Beautiful used in lightweight throws or blankets.

Special stitches used:

Beginning 3-treble crochet cluster (beg 3-tr cl): Ch 3, make cluster with 2 tr (see page 18).

3-treble crochet cluster (3-tr cl): Make cluster with 3 tr.

3-triple-treble cluster (3-ttr cl): Make cluster with 3 ttr.

Picot-3: Ch 3 (at point to add picot), sl st in first ch of ch-3, creating picot loop.

Foundation ring: Using yarn A, ch 4, sl st in first ch to form ring.

Round 1: Ch 3 (counts as 1 tr), 23 tr in ring, sl st in top of beg ch-3 to join.

Round 2: Ch 14, 1 dc in 6th ch from hook, [ch 5, 1 dc in last dc] 2 times, ch 8, miss 1 tr st (from Round 1), 1 dc in next st; rep from * 11 times. Fasten off yarn A.

Round 3: Join yarn B in any middle ch-5 lp, 1 dc in ch-5 lp, *ch 8, 1 dc in next middle ch-5 lp; rep from * 10 times, ch 4, 1 dtr in first dc to join.

Round 4: *Ch 9, 1 dc in next ch-8 sp; rep from * 10 times, ch 9, sl st to first dc to join.

Round 5: [Beg 3-tr cl, ch 5, 3-tr cl] in same sc st, *ch 3, 1 dc in next ch-9 sp, ch 3, [3-tr cl, ch 5, 3-tr cl] in next dc st, ch 3, 1 dc in next ch-9 sp, ch 5, [3-ttr cl, ch 5, 3-ttr cl] in next dc st, ch 5, 1 dc in next ch-9 sp, ch 3, [3-tr cl, ch 5, 3-tr cl] in next dc st; rep from * 2 times, ch 3, 1 dc in next ch-9 sp, ch 3, [3-tr cl, ch 5, 3-tr cl] in next dc st, ch 3, 1 dc in next ch-9 sp, ch 5, [3-ttr cl, ch 5, 3-ttr cl] in next dc st, ch 5, 1 dc in next ch-9 sp, ch 3, sl st top of beg 3-tr cl to join.

Round 6: *Ch 10, 1 dc in ch-5 sp between 2 clusters, ch 10, [1 dc, picot-3, 1 dc] in ch-5 sp between next 2 clusters, ch 10,

1 dc in next ch-5 sp between 2 clusters; rep from * 3 times.

Round 7: Ch 1, 10 dc in each ch-10 sp, with [1 dc, picot-3, 1 dc] in each corner, sl st to first dc to join. Fasten off yarn B.

Round 8: Join yarn A in any picot-3 corner, 1 dc in each st around with [1 dc, picot-3, 1 dc] in each corner, sl st to first dc to join.

Fasten off and block work.

. . . .

★
city lights

This simple filet block has randomly filled squares that create the illusion of a tall city building at night. You could use midnight blues and greys accented with pale yellow and neon for a different look. This block is modern and edgy.

Note: This square is made by creating 15 filet squares per row. Create empty squares by working [ch 1, miss 1 ch, 1 tr in next tr]; create filled squares by replacing 'ch 1, miss 1 ch' with '1 tr in next st'.

Foundation chain: Using yarn A, ch 31.

Row 1: Ch 4 (counts as 1 tr, ch 1), miss 1 ch, 1 tr in next tr, ch 1, miss 1 ch, 1 tr in each of next 3 tr, [ch 1, miss 1 ch, 1 tr in next tr] 7 times, 1 tr in each of next 2 tr, [ch 1, miss 1 ch, 1 tr in next tr] 4 times, turn – 15 squares.

Rows 2, 4, 6, 8, 10, 12, 14, 16, 18 and 20: Ch 1, 1 dc in every tr and every ch-1 sp to end, turn. Fasten off.

Following stitch note above, work all squares as empty squares unless you are

directed otherwise on each row. Count in from right side towards right, in terms of square numbers.

Row 3: Using yarn B, fill squares 5, 7 and 15, turn at end of row.

Row 5: Using yarn C, fill squares 2, 6, 10 and 13, turn.

Row 7: Using yarn D, fill squares 1 and 15, turn.

Row 9: Using yarn B, fill squares, 3, 5, 9 and 15, turn.

Row 11: Using yarn E, fill squares 4 and 9, turn.

Row 13: Using yarn C, fill squares 6 and 11, turn.

Row 15: Using yarn B fill squares 1, 5, 7, 10 and 14, turn.

Row 17: Using yarn C, fill squares 1, 8, 10 and 12, turn.

Row 19: Using yarn E, fill squares 1, 3 and 12, turn.

Row 21: Using yarn D, fill squares 2, 9 and 13, turn. Fasten off.

Row 22: Join yarn A, rep Row 2.

Fasten off and darn in all ends.

*
sweet granny

A combination of simple, basic stitches produces a pretty square that is perfect for beginners. This block is ideal for mixing with other grannies, or solid all-double crochet squares. Use colours of a similar or toning hue, or graphic contrasts – such as navy and white – for maximum impact.

A
B
C
D
E
F

Foundation ring: Using yarn A, ch 4, sl st in first ch to form ring.

Round 1: Ch 3 (counts as 1 tr), 2 tr in ring, ch 2, [3 tr in ring, ch 2] 3 times, sl st in top of beg ch-3 to join. Fasten off yarn A.

Round 2: Join yarn B in any ch-2 sp, ch 3 (counts as 1 tr), [2 tr, ch 2, 3 tr] in same sp (forms corner), *[3 tr, ch 3, 3 tr] in next corner sp; rep from * 2 times, sl st in top of beg ch-3 to join. Fasten off yarn B.

Round 3: Join yarn C in any corner ch-2 sp, ch 3 (counts as 1 tr), [2 tr, ch 2, 3 tr] in same sp (forms corner), *3 tr in the next sp between tr groups, [3 tr, ch 3, 3 tr] in next sp (forms corner); rep from * 2 times, 3 tr in next sp between tr groups, sl st in top of beg ch-3 to join. Fasten off yarn C.

Round 4: Join yarn D in any corner ch-2 sp, ch 3 (counts as 1 tr), [2 tr, ch 2, 3 tr] in same sp (forms corner), *3 tr in the next 2 sps between tr groups, [3 tr, ch 3, 3 tr] in next ch-2 corner sp; rep from * 2 times, 3 tr in next 2 sps between tr groups, sl st in top of beg ch-3 to join. Fasten off yarn D.

Round 5: Join yarn E in any corner ch-2 sp, ch 3 (counts as 1 tr), [2 tr, ch 2, 3 tr] in same sp (forms corner), *3 tr in the next 3 sps between tr groups, [3 tr, ch 3, 3 tr] in next ch-2 corner sp; rep from * 2 times, 3 tr in next 3 sps between tr groups, sl st in top of beg ch-3 to join. Fasten off yarn E.

Round 6: Join yarn C in any corner ch-2 sp, ch 1, *[2 dc, ch 2, 2 dc] in same sp (forms corner), 1 dc in each of next 15 sts along side of square; rep from * 3 times, sl st in first dc to join.

Round 7: Ch 1, *[1 dc, ch 2, 1 dc] in same sp (forms corner), 1 dc in each of next 19 sts along side of square; rep from * 2 times, 1 dc in each of next 17 dc, sl st in first dc to join. Fasten off yarn C.

Round 8: Join yarn F in any corner ch-2 sp, *[1 dc, ch 2, 1 dc] in same sp (forms corner), 1 dc in each of next 21 dc; rep from * 3 times, sl st in first dc to join. Fasten off yarn F.

Round 9: Join yarn B in any corner ch-2 sp, *[1 dc, ch 2, 1 dc] in same sp (forms corner), 1 dc in each of next 23 dc; rep from * 3 times, sl st in first dc to join. Fasten off yarn B.

Round 10: Join yarn D in any corner ch-2 sp, *[1 dc, ch 2, 1 dc] in same sp (forms corner), 1 dc in each of next 25 dc; rep from * 3 times, sl st in first dc to join. Fasten off yarn D.

Round 11: Join yarn E in any corner ch-2 sp, [1 dc, ch 2, 1 dc] in same sp (forms corner), 1 dc in each of next 27 dc; rep from * 3 times, sl st in first dc to join. Fasten off yarn E.

Round 12: Join yarn C in any corner ch-2 sp, [1 dc, ch 2, 1 dc] in same sp (forms corner), 1 dc in each of next 29 dc; rep from * 3 times, sl st in first dc to join. Fasten off yarn C.

Round 13: Join yarn F in any corner ch-2 sp, [1 dc, ch 2, 1 dc] in same sp (forms corner), 1 dc in each of next 31 dc; rep from * 3 times, sl st in first dc to join.

Fasten off and darn in ends neatly.

classic granny square

*

Every crocheter's first square, this version changes colour through the design. You could choose to switch colour every round, or perhaps to alternate two colours; there are many permutations, all are highly satisfying to make and offer plenty of applications.

A
B
C

Foundation ring: Using yarn A, ch 6, join with sl st to form ring.

Round 1: Ch 3 (counts as 1 tr), 2 tr in ring, *ch 2, 3 tr in ring; rep from * 2 times, ch 2, sl st in top of ch-3 to join.

Round 2: Sl st in next ch-2 sp, ch 3, 2 tr in ch-2 sp, ch 2, 3 tr in same corner sp, ch 1, *[3 re in next ch-2 corner sp, ch 2, 3 tr in same sp, ch 1]; rep from * 2 times, sl st in top of ch-3 to join. Fasten off yarn A.

Round 3: Join yarn B in any ch-2 corner sp, ch 3, 2 tr in same corner sp, ch 2, 3 tr in same sp, ch 1, *[3 tr in ch-1 sp, ch 1, 3 tr in ch-2 corner sp, ch 2, 3 tr in same sp, ch 1]; rep from * 2 times, 3 tr in ch-1 sp, ch 1, sl st in top of ch-3 to join.

Round 4: Sl st in next ch-2 corner sp, ch 3, 2 tr in ch-2 corner sp, ch 2, 3 tr in same corner sp, ch 1, *[3 tr in ch-1 sp, ch 1, 3 tr in next ch-1 sp, ch 1, 3 tr in ch-2 corner sp, ch 2, 3 tr in same ch-2 corner sp, ch 1]; rep from * 2 times, [3 tr in ch-1 sp, ch 1] 2 times, sl st in top of ch-3 to join. Fasten off yarn B.

Round 5: Join yarn C in any ch-2 sp, ch 3, 2 tr in same corner sp, ch 2, 3 tr in same corner sp, ch 1, *[3 tr in ch-1 sp] 3 times, [3 tr in corner sp, ch 2, 3 tr in same corner sp]; rep from * 2 times, [3 tr in next ch-1 sp] 3 times, sl st in top of ch-3 to join.

Round 6: Sl st in next ch-2 corner sp, ch 3, 2 tr in ch-2 corner sp, ch 2, 3 tr in same ch-2 corner sp, ch 1, *[3 tr in ch-1 sp] 4 times, [3 tr in corner sp, ch 2, 3 tr in same corner sp]; rep from * 2 times, [3 tr

in next ch-1 sp] 4 times, sl st in top of ch-3 to join. Fasten off yarn C.

Round 7: Join yarn D in any ch-2 corner sp, ch 3, 2 tr in ch-2 corner sp, ch 2, 3 tr in same ch-2 corner sp, ch 1, *[3 tr in ch-1 sp] 5 times, [3 tr in corner sp, ch 2, 3 tr in same corner sp]; rep from * 2 times, [3 tr in next ch-1 sp] 5 times, sl st in top of ch-3 to join.

Fasten off and darn in all ends neatly.

***

desert aster

A bold flower with an interesting and intricate construction, this openwork block would be stunning in a table setting or as an edging for a blind. Or repeat for a wonderful summer wrap.

A
B
C
D

Special stitch used:

Back-post double crochet (BPdc): Insert hook around back post at very top of st in round below (*see page 21*).

Foundation ring: Using yarn A, ch 10, sl st in first ch to form ring.

Round 1: Ch 3 (counts as 1 tr), 23 tr in ring, sl st in top of beg ch-3 to join. Fasten off.

Round 2: Join yarn B, ch 4 (counts as 1 tr, ch 1), *miss 1 st, 1 tr in next st, ch 1, 1 tr in next st; rep from * 11 times, sl st in 3rd ch of beg ch-4 to join. Fasten off.

Round 3: Join yarn C, *ch 9, 1 dc in 2nd ch from hook, 1 htr in next ch, 1 tr in next ch, 1 hdtr in each of next 5 ch, sl st in next tr around; rep from * 11 times, sl st in base of next petal to join.

Round 4: Sl st in side of same petal, *1 dc in each st to top of petal, 3 dc in ch-1 at top, 1 dc in each st down other side of petal, sl st in side of next petal; rep from * 11 times, sl st in first dc to join. Fasten off.

Round 5: Join yarn A to top of any petal, *ch 12, 1 dc in top of next petal, [ch 7, 1 dc in top of next petal] 2 times; rep from * 3 times, sl st in first ch of beg ch-12 to join.

Round 6: Ch 3 in same st (counts as 1 tr), *[7 tr, ch 3, 7 tr] in same sp (forms corner), [1 tr in next tr, 7 tr in next ch-7 sp] 2 times**, 1 tr in next tr; rep from * 2 times, then from * to ** 1 time, sl st in top of beg ch-3 to join.

Round 7: Ch 1, 2 dc in same st, *1BPdc in each tr to corner, 4 dc in next corner ch-3 sp; rep from * 3 times, 1BPdc in each tr to beg of rnd, sl st in first dc to join.

Fasten off and darn in ends.

**

autumn leaves

A familiar granny layout but with a
defined textural twist, this block is
full of bullion stitches that give
a bobbly effect. It's fun to work and
is best made from a shiny cotton,
as we have done here, to show off
its rounded texture to full glory.

A
B
C

Special stitch used:

Bullion stitch (bullion): Yoh 9 times,
insert hook in st or sp to be worked, yoh,
draw loop through to front, yoh, pull
through all loops on hook, ch 1 to secure
(see *page 20*).

Foundation ring: Using yarn A, ch 4, sl st
in first ch to form ring.

Round 1: Ch 2 (counts as 1 tr), 1 bullion,
1 trc, ch 2, *1 tr, 1 bullion, 1 tr, ch 2; rep
from * 2 times, sl st in top of beg ch-2 to
join. Fasten off.

Round 2: Join yarn B in any ch-2 corner
sp, ch 2 (counts as 1 tr), [1 bullion, 1 tr,
ch 2, 1 tr, 1 bullion, 1 tr] in same corner
sp, *ch 1, [1 tr, 1 bullion, 1 tr, ch 2, 1 tr,
1 bullion, 1 dc] in next corner sp; rep from
* 2 times, ch 1, sl st in top of beg ch-2 to
join. Fasten off.

Round 3: Join yarn C in any ch-2 corner
sp, ch 2 (counts as 1 tr), [1 bullion, 1 tr,
ch 2, 1 tr, 1 bullion, 1 tr] in same corner
sp, *ch 1, [1 tr, 1 bullion, 1 tr] in next ch-1
sp, ch 1, [1 tr, 1 bullion, 1 tr, ch 2, 1 tr,
1 bullion, 1 tr] in next ch-2 corner sp; rep
from * 2 times, ch 1, [1 tr, 1 bullion, 1 tr] in
last ch-1 sp, ch 1, sl st in top of beg ch-2 to
join. Fasten off.

Round 4: Join yarn A in any ch-2 corner
sp, ch 2 (counts as 1 tr), [1 bullion, 1 tr,
ch 2, 1 tr, 1 bullion, 1 tr] in same corner
sp, *ch 1, [1 tr, 1 bullion, 1 tr] in each of
next 2 ch-1 sps, ch 1, [1 tr, 1 bullion,
1 tr, ch 2, 1 tr, 1 bullion, 1 tr] in next
corner ch-2 sp; rep from * 2 times, ch 1,
[1 tr, 1 bullion, 1 tr] in each of next
2 ch-1 sps, ch 1, sl st in top of beg ch-2
to join. Fasten off.

Round 5: Join yarn B in any ch-2 corner
sp, ch 2 (counts as 1 tr), [1 bullion, 1 tr,
ch 2, 1 tr, 1 bullion, 1 tr] in same corner

sp, *ch 1, [1 tr, 1 bullion, 1 tr] in each of
next 3 ch-1 sps, ch 1, [1 tr, 1 bullion,
1 tr, ch 2, 1 tr, 1 bullion, 1 tr] in next ch-2
corner sp; rep from * 2 times, ch 1, [1 tr,
1 bullion, 1 tr] in each of next 3 ch-1 sps,
ch 1, sl st in top of beg ch-2 to join.
Fasten off.

Round 6: Join yarn C in any ch-2 corner
sp, ch 1, *[2 dc, ch 2, 2 dc] in same corner
sp, [ch 2, 2 dc in next ch-1 sp] 4 times,
ch 2; rep from * 3 times, sl st in first ch
to join.

Fasten off and darn in ends.

**
vintage rose

A traditional Irish Rose motif worked in a vintage colour combination here, this block lends itself well to a host of applications: a cheery blanket for a child's room, pretty pillow covers or a flowery throw. Choose vivid colours for the roses, and a contrasting background for impact.

Foundation ring: Using yarn A, ch 5, sl st in first ch to form ring.

Round 1: Ch 1 (counts as 1 dc) 7 dc in ring, sl st in ch-1 to join.

Round 2: Ch 5 (counts as 1 tr, ch 2), [1 tr in next st, ch 2] 7 times, sl st in 3rd ch of beg ch-5 to join.

Round 3: *[Sl st, 1 dc, 1 htr, 1 tr, 1 htr, 1 dc, sl st] in next ch-2 sp; rep from * to end, sl st in first sl st to join. Fasten off yarn A.

Round 4: Turn work to WS, join yarn B in back of any tr from Round 3, *ch 4, join with sl st to back of tr in next petal; rep from * 7 times, sl st in first sl st to join.

Round 5: Turn work to RS, sl st in beg of next ch-4 sp, *[1 dc, 1 htr, 1 tr, 2 dtr, 1 tr, 1 htr, 1 dc] all in same ch-4 sp; rep from * in every ch-4 sp to end, sl st in first sl st to to join. Fasten off yarn B.

Round 6: Join yarn C in back lp of sl st of Round 4, *ch 6, sl st in back lp of sl st in next petal; rep from * 7 times, sl st in first sl st to join.

Round 7: Turn work to RS, sl st in beg of next ch-6 sp, *[1 sl st, 1 dc, 1 htr, 6 tr, 1 htr, 1 dc, 1 sl st] in ch-6 sp; rep from * all around motif, sl st in first sl st to join. Fasten off yarn C.

Round 8: Join yarn D between any two petals, ch 4 (counts as 1 dtr), 1 dtr in first sl st of next petal, miss 3 sts, 1 dc in each of next 4 sts, miss 3 sts, *1 dtr in each of next 2 sl sts between petals, miss 3 sts, 1 dc in each of next 4 sts; rep from * 6 times, sl st in top of beg ch-4 to join.

Round 9: Sl st in next sp between dtr and ch-4 from Round 8, ch 4 (counts as 1 dtr), [2 dtr, ch 2, 3 dtr] in same sp to form corner, *1 tr in each of next 2 sts, 1 dc in each of next 8 sts, 1 tr in next st**, [3 dtr, ch 2, 3 dtr] to form corner; rep from * 2 times, and from * to ** 1 time, sl st in top of beg ch-4 to join.

Round 10: Ch 1, 1 dc in same st, 1 dc in each of next 2 sts, *[2 dc, ch 2, 2 dc] in next ch-2 sp (forms corner)**, 1 dc in each of next 17 sts; rep from * 2 times, then from * to ** 1 time, 1 dc in each of last 14 sts, sl st to first dc to join.

Round 11: Ch 1, 1 dc in same st, 1 dc in each of next 4 sts, *[2 dc, ch 2, 2 dc] in same sp (forms corner)**, 1 dc in each of next 21 sts; rep from * 2 times then from * to ** 1 time, 1 dc in each of last 16 sts, sl st in first dc to join. Fasten off yarn D.

Round 12: Join yarn E at beg of any ch-2 sp, [1 tr, ch 3, 2 tr] in same sp (forms corner), 1 tr in each of next 25 sts, *[2 tr, 2 ch, 2 tr] in next corner sp, 1 tr in each of next 25 sts; rep 2 times, sl st in top of beg ch-3 to join. Fasten off yarn E.

Round 13: Join yarn B to any ch-2 sp, ch 1, [1 dc, ch 2, 2 dc] in same sp (forms corner), *1 dc in each of next 29 sts**, [2 dc, ch 2, 2 dc] in next corner sp; rep from * 2 times and from * to ** 1 time, sl st in first dc to join.

Fasten off and darn in ends.

A
B
C
D
E

index